Welcome to

Educational Research
with Research Navigator™

This text contains some special features designed to aid you in the research process and writing research papers. As you read this textbook, you will see special Research Navigator™ (RN) icons cueing you to visit the Research Navigator™ website to research important concepts of the text.

To gain access to Research Navigator™, go to **www.researchnavigator.com** and log in using the passcode you'll find on the inside front cover of your text.

Research Navigator™ includes three databases of dependable source material to get your research process started:

EBSCO's ContentSelect Academic Journal Database. EBSCO's ContentSelect Academic Journal Database contains scholarly, peer-reviewed journals. These published articles provide you with a specialized knowledge and information about your research topic. Academic journal articles adhere to strict scientific guidelines for methodology and theoretical grounding. The information obtained in these individual articles is more scientific than information you would find in a popular magazine, newspaper article, or on a Web page.

***The New York Times* Search by Subject Archive.** Newspapers are considered periodicals because they are issued in regular installments (e.g., daily, weekly, or monthly), and provide contemporary information. Information in periodicals—journals, magazines, and newspapers—may be useful, or even critical, for finding up-to-date material or information to support specific aspects of your topic. Research Navigator™ gives you access to a one-year, "search by subject" archive of articles from one of the world's leading newspapers—*The New York Times.*

"Best of the Web" Link Library. Link Library, the third database included on Research Navigator™, is a collection of Web links, organized by academic subject and key terms. Searching on your key terms will provide you a list of five to seven editorially reviewed Web sites that offer educationally relevant and reliable content. The Web links in Link Library are monitored and updated each week, reducing your incidence of finding "dead" links.

In addition, Research Navigator™ includes extensive online content detailing the steps in the research process including:

- Starting the Research Process
- Finding and Evaluating Sources
- Citing Sources
- Internet Research
- Using Your Library
- Starting to Write

For more information on how to use Research Navigator™ go to
http://www.ablongman.com/aboutrn.com.

Educational Research

Quantitative, Qualitative, and Mixed Approaches

BURKE JOHNSON

University of South Alabama

LARRY CHRISTENSEN

University of South Alabama

PEARSON

Boston ■ New York ■ San Francisco
Mexico City ■ Montreal ■ Toronto ■ London ■ Madrid ■ Munich ■ Paris
Hong Kong ■ Singapore ■ Tokyo ■ Cape Town ■ Sydney

Senior Editor: Arnis E. Burvikovs
Editorial Assistant: Christine Lyons
Senior Developmental Editor: Mary Kriener
Marketing Manager: Tara Whorf
Production Administrator: Michael Granger
Editorial-Production Service: Omegatype Typography, Inc.
Composition and Prepress Buyer: Linda Cox
Manufacturing Buyer: Andrew Turso
Cover Administrator: Kristina Mose-Libon
Interior Design: Denise Hoffman
Electronic Composition: Omegatype Typography, Inc.

For related titles and support materials, visit our online catalog at www.ablongman.com.

Between the time Website information is gathered and published, some sites may
have closed. Also, the transcription of URLs can result in typographical errors.
The publisher would appreciate notification where these errors occur so that
they may be corrected in subsequent editions.

Library of Congress Cataloging-in-Publication Data

Johnson, Burke.
  Educational research : quantitative, qualitative, and mixed approaches / Burke Johnson,
Larry Christensen. 2nd ed.
    p. cm
  Includes bibliographical references and index.
  ISBN 0-205-36126-9
  1. Education—Research. I. Christensen, Larry B., 1941- II. Title.

LB1028.J59 2004
370'.7'2–dc21

                                                                    2003052165

Printed in the United States of America

10 9 8 7 6 5 4 3 2   RRD-IN   08 07 06 05

BRIEF CONTENTS

CONTENTS

▨ P A R T   T W O   Planning the Research Study   54

3 Developing Research Questions and Proposal Preparation   54

PART THREE   Foundations of Research   122

5 Standardized Measurement and Assessment   122

8 Validity of Research Results   226

13 Historical Research   390

14 Mixed Method and Mixed Model Research   408

■ P A R T   F I V E   Analyzing the Data   432

15 Descriptive Statistics   432

16 Inferential Statistics   462

17 Data Analysis in Qualitative Research   498

PREFACE

Welcome to the second edition of *Educational Research: Quantitative, Qualitative, and Mixed Approaches*. This text was written for the introductory research methods course that is required in most colleges of education in the United States. We assume no prior knowledge of research methods on the part of our readers. Our book can be used as an undergraduate text or for more advanced graduate-level courses. Instructors should be able to cover the material in one semester.

PURPOSE

We had several purposes in writing this textbook. The first was a desire to write an introductory research methods book that was accurate and up-to-date. We come from interdisciplinary backgrounds and have attempted to incorporate our respective insights into this book. Dr. Johnson is an educational research methodologist and program evaluator, with additional graduate training in sociology; Dr. Christensen is a psychological research methodologist and author of a highly successful book entitled *Experimental Methodology*. We have kept up with the changes taking place in the field of research methods in our disciplines, and we incorporate the latest information in this textbook, including references that allow interested readers to further examine original sources.

Second, we have tried to write a research methods textbook that takes an evenhanded approach to the different types of educational research. Whereas many texts emphasize one method at the expense of others, we believe that all major approaches to research discussed in this text have merit when they are employed carefully and properly. We show the strengths and appropriateness of each method and demonstrate how the experts in each area conduct high-quality research and how they view their approach to research.

Third, we have tried to make our textbook highly readable and make learning about research fun. Believe it or not, learning about research methods can be exciting. We are excited about research methods, and we share our enthusiasm with you without losing the necessary rigor.

Finally, we have tried to enable readers to become critical consumers of research and potential users of research. We also suspect that most readers of this text will be called on at some point in their careers to summarize research literature, write a research proposal, develop a data collection instrument, or test an idea empirically. *Educational Research,* second edition, will help prepare you for these kinds of activities and will help you become adept at reading empirical articles.

NEW TO THE SECOND EDITION

We have made changes throughout the second edition to better reflect the latest trends in educational research. The following are of particular note:

- **A new chapter** introducing and comparing the three major methodological paradigms in educational research (Chapter 2: Quantitative, Qualitative, and Mixed Research) has been added.
- **A new chapter on mixed research** (Chapter 14) has been added to reflect the growing importance of this third major paradigm in educational research.
- **Every chapter now opens with a vignette** that gains students' attention and interest by providing them with a connection between current events and issues in the world of educational research.
- **Review questions** appear at the end of major sections within each chapter, allowing students to quiz themselves and review key concepts continually.
- **New end-of-chapter materials have been added,** including discussion questions, additional exercises, links to relevant websites, and suggested readings to provide students more opportunities to extend learning and to apply the lessons.
- **Content-specific search terms** appear in the margins throughout the text and exercises appear at the end of each chapter, prompting students to practice their research skills using the powerful online research tool, Research Navigator.
- **The latest changes to the APA publication manual** provide students with the most up-to-date information about how to prepare a research report (Chapter 18).
- **A special set of appendixes** contains abstracts of journal articles representing each of the research approaches discussed in *Educational Research,* second edition: a quantitative article, a qualitative article, and a mixed research article. The full-length articles can be accessed on the Companion Website for *Educational Research,* second edition, at www.ablongman.com/johnsonchristensen2e.

ORGANIZATION OF THE BOOK

We have organized *Educational Research,* second edition, to follow the major components or steps involved in the research process.

Part I. Introduction

In this section we introduce you to the field of educational research. We begin by defining science in an inclusive way and explaining the general research process, including the inductive and the deductive approaches to generating research knowledge. We also outline some general areas of research, such as basic research, applied research, action research, evaluation research, and orientational research. We then take a look at the three major research paradigms: (1) quantitative research, (2) qualitative research, and (3) mixed research.

Part II. Planning the Research Study

In this section we carefully explain how to come up with a research idea, conduct a review of the research literature, write research questions and hypotheses, and organize a research proposal. We also explore the importance of ethics in educational research and explain how to write an informed consent form.

Part III. Foundations of Research

In Part III we cover some concepts that researchers must master before conducting a research study. We begin with an introduction to measurement. Without reliable and valid measurement, nothing else really matters. Next we discuss the six major methods of data collection: tests, questionnaires, interviews, focus groups, observations, and secondary or existing data. We then discuss the procedures for selecting samples of people to participate in a research study. Finally, we discuss the importance of research validity or trustworthiness in quantitative and qualitative research, showing the primary threats to good research and providing specific techniques used to prevent mistakes.

Part IV. Selecting a Research Method

In Part IV we provide extensive discussion of the major methods of research and demonstrate how to match the appropriate research design with various research questions. We explain the following quantitative research methods—experimental research, quasi-experimental research and single-case research, and nonexperimental quantitative research; the following qualitative research methods—phenomenology, ethnography, case study, grounded theory, and historical research; and the following mixed research methods—mixed model research and mixed method research.

Part V. Analyzing the Data

In this section we provide two chapters on quantitative data analysis (descriptive and inferential statistics) and one chapter on how to analyze qualitative research data.

Part VI. Writing the Research Report

In this final part we explain how to prepare research manuscripts in a format that can be submitted to an education journal for publication. We explain how to use the guidelines from the 2001 edition of the *Publication Manual of the American Psychological Association,* the guidelines required by the vast majority of journals in education and psychology.

Appendixes: Examples of Research Articles

At the end of the book, we include abstracts of three research articles that were published in respected educational research journals. Each represents one of the three major types of research explored in *Educational Research,* second edition: quantitative research, qualitative research, and mixed research. Full-length copies of each article are provided on the book's Companion Website.

FEATURES OF THE TEXT

We have included several features in *Educational Research,* second edition, to make the task of learning about research easier. In addition to opening vignettes that connect current events with research, each chapter begins with a list of objectives to get students thinking about what they are going to be learning. Within the chapters themselves, several learning aids assist with reviewing key concepts. These include margin definitions of all the key terms, multiple examples of concepts from published research studies, review questions at the end of major sections, and suggested research terms that can be investigated further using the EBSCO research database called ContentSelect, accessible through the Research Navigator™ website. (Turn to pp. xxiii–xxvii for further details on Research Navigator™.) At the end of each chapter we provide a chapter summary, a list of the key terms used in the chapter, discussion questions, research exercises, Internet links, and recommended readings.

SUPPLEMENTS FOR INSTRUCTORS AND STUDENTS

Companion Website

A robust Companion Website (www.ablongman.com/johnsonchristensen2e) provides teachers and students with a vast array of materials to augment the text and classroom discussions. Materials include full lectures for each chapter, concept maps for each chapter, exercise sheets, bonus material, answers to all study questions, multiple-choice questions to use in practice quizzes, a glossary, overhead masters, three full-length research articles, and links to additional web materials.

Instructor's Manual

The Instructor's Manual, originally written by James Van Haneghan and updated by Burke Johnson, provides instructors with helpful suggestions for guiding and assessing student learning. The second edition reflects all updates to the second edition of the text and includes a new section for each chapter aimed at helping new instructors of educational research (showing what is most essential and how to get it across) as well as a discussion of how to approach each of the chapter learning objectives and supplemental teaching materials (e.g., additional discussion questions, exercise sheets).

Please note that we are putting 50 to 75 multiple choice test questions for each chapter along with answers online, rather than in the Instructor's Manual. Your Allyn and Bacon representative will tell you how to access these questions. To find the representative in your area, please go to www.ablongman.com/replocator.

NOTE TO STUDENTS

You are probably wondering how best to study for research methods. First and foremost, utilize the book's Companion Website, which has been developed to help you learn the material. In the book, we suggest you begin each chapter by reading the chapter objectives and the chapter summary at the end of the chapter. This will give you a brief overview of the material. Then look at the chapter concept map included on the book's Companion Website. Now you are ready to read the chapter. After finishing the chapter, read the chapter summary again, answer the study questions, and make sure you understand each concept shown in the concept map. Also read the lecture provided on the Companion Website, where we hit on most of the major points of each chapter. This will be quick reading after having read the chapter. As you prepare for tests, make sure that you know the definitions to all the key terms because the terms are the basic building blocks and language of research methods. Don't get lost in the details, however. Utilize the concept maps to see how the ideas are connected. Finally, as we point out several times in the text, one of the best ways to learn how to design and conduct an educational research study is to read high-quality, published research articles in your research area. We believe that if you do these things, you can become an expert researcher, as well as get an A in your class! You can also send questions to the book authors, and we will do our best to reply.

NOTE TO INSTRUCTORS

We have included three full-length journal articles on the Companion Website: one is a qualitative article, one is a quantitative article, and one is a mixed article. These articles were selected as examples of high-quality research. The abstracts of these articles and links to the web page are given in appendixes in the textbook. We highly recommend that your students read high-quality examples of published research. You will find many helpful teaching tips and materials in the Instructor's Manual and on the Companion Website (lectures, concept maps, overheads, bonus material that you may wish to cover). One useful in-class teaching strategy would be to make overheads of the concept maps and discuss these in class. We like concept maps because too often students get the detailed picture (the trees in the forest) or the big picture (the bird's eye view of the forest) but not both. The concept maps should help remedy this situation. Our goal is to provide you with the most up-to-date and useful book and set of supplements available in the field of education.

ACKNOWLEDGMENTS

First and foremost, Burke Johnson would like to thank his wife, Dr. Lisa A. Turner, for putting up with the late hours and for being the first reviewer of everything he wrote. We want to thank Nancy Forsyth of Allyn and Bacon for believing in our new ideas. We thank our Allyn and Bacon editors Sean Wakely (first edition), Arnis Burvikovs (second edition), and Paul Smith (both editions), senior development editor Mary Kriener, editorial assistant Christine Lyons, and the editorial-production staff of Omegatype Typography for all their help. We thank Professors Bill Gilley, University of South Alabama; Joe Newman, University of South Alabama; and Bikas Sinha, Indian Statistical Institute, Calcutta, India, for reviewing the chapters in their areas of expertise. Burke also wants to thank his students for their continued insightful thoughts on how to improve the book. We also thank the reviewers selected by Allyn and Bacon who provided invaluable input into the first edition: Amy Gillet, University of Wisconsin-Stout; Bryan Griffin, Georgia Southern University; Beverly A. Joyce, Dowling College; Robert W. Lissitz, University of Maryland at College Park; Doris L. Prater, University of Houston, Clear Lake; Joan Quilling, University of Missouri, Columbia; Thomas A. Romberg, University of Wisconsin; and Paul Westmeyer, The University of Texas at San Antonio. We thank the reviewers selected by Allyn and Bacon who provided invaluable input into the second edition: Kathy Green, University of Denver; Tony Onwuegbuzie, University of South Florida; Shaireen Rasheed, Long Island University; Vernelle Tyler, University of South Carolina–Aiken; and Daniel Weigel, Southern Oklahoma State University. Last, we extend our special thanks to Tony Onwuegbuzie, who with Burke Johnson wrote the newest chapter in our book (Chapter 14, Mixed Model and Mixed Method Research).

COMMENTS

We hope that you (students and instructors) will send your comments to us so that we can continually improve our textbook and our website. You can contact us at the following e-mail addresses: bjohnson@usouthal.edu (Burke Johnson) and lchriste@usouthal.edu (Larry Christensen).

USING RESEARCH NAVIGATOR™

This edition of *Educational Research* is designed to integrate the content of the book with the following resources of Research Navigator™, a collection of research databases, instruction, and contemporary publications available to you online at www.researchnavigator.com.

- **EBSCO's ContentSelect Academic Journal Database** organized by subject, with each subject containing leading academic journals for each discipline.
- *The New York Times,* one of the most highly regarded publications of today's news. View the full text of articles from the previous year.
- **Link Library** connects users to thousands of websites for discipline-specific key terms.
- **Research Review and Preparation.** A special section called "Understanding the Research Process" helps you work your way through the research process.

Connecting the Book with RN

As you read this book, you'll see special Research Navigator™ (RN) icons cueing you to visit the ContentSelect database on the Research Navigator™ website to expand on the concepts of the text and to further explore the work being done in the field of Educational Research. RN learning aids in the book include:

1. **Marginal keyword search terms.** Appearing in the margins of the text, these already tested terms will guide your search on topics relevant to the course content and will yield an abundance of sources from a variety of perspectives that will broaden your exposure to key topics. Begin by searching the ContentSelect database, and then check out the other databases as well.
2. **Applied research activities and projects.** At the end of each chapter, special RN exercises provide more practice using the ContentSelect database in Research Navigator™ and move you beyond the book to library and field research.

Research
Navigator.c✹m

class size

It's now time to enter Research Navigator™. Purchase of this book provides you free access to this exclusive pool of information and data. The following walk-through illustrates, step-by-step, the various ways this valuable resource can make your research process more interesting and successful.

Registration

In order to begin using Research Navigator™, you must first register using the personal access code found on the inside of the front cover of your book. Follow these easy steps:

1. Click "Register" under New Users on the left side of the home page screen.

2. Enter the access code exactly as it appears on the inside front cover of your book or on your access card. (Note: Access codes can only be used once to complete one registration. If you purchased a used text, the access code may not work.)

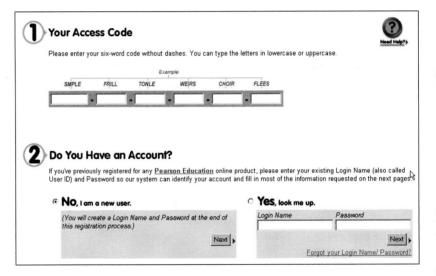

3. Follow the instructions on screen to complete your registration—you may click the Help button at any time if you are unsure how to respond.
4. Once you have successfully completed registration, write down the Login Name and Password you just created and keep it in a safe place. You will need to enter it each time you want to revisit Research Navigator™.
5. Once you register, you have access to all the resources in Research Navigator™ for six months. Each time you enter Research Navigator™, log in by simply going to the "Returning Users" section on the left side of the home page and type in your LoginID and Password.

Getting Started

You're now official! The options available to you on Research Navigator™ are plenty. From Research Navigator™'s home page, you have easy access to all of the site's main features, including a quick route to the three exclusive databases of source content. If you are new to the research process, you may want to start by browsing *Understanding the Research Process.*

This section of the site can be helpful even for those with some research experience but who might be interested in some helpful tips. Here you will find extensive help on all aspects of the research process including:

- Introduction to the Research Paper
- Gathering Data
- Searching the Internet
- Evaluating Sources
- Organizing Ideas
- Writing Notes
- Drafting the Paper
- Academic Citation Styles (i.e., MLA, APA, CMS)
- Blending Reference Material into Your Writing
- Practicing Academic Integrity
- Revising
- Proofreading
- Editing the Final Draft

Completing Research

The first step in completing a research assignment or research paper is to select a topic. Your instructor may assign you a topic, or you may find suggested topics in the margins or at the end of chapters throughout this book. Once you have selected and narrowed your research topic, you are now ready to *gather data.* Research Navigator™ simplifies your research efforts by giving you three distinct types of source material commonly used in research assignments: academic journals (ContentSelect), newspaper articles (*The New York Times*), and World Wide Web sites (Link Library).

1) EBSCO's ContentSelect

The first database you'll find on Research Navigator™ is ContentSelect, which contains the EBSCO Academic Journal and Abstract Database containing scholarly, peer-reviewed journals (such as *Journal of Education Policy* and *Assessment & Evaluation in Higher Education*). The information obtained in these individual articles is more scientific than information you would find in a popular magazine, in a newspaper article, or on a web page. Searching for articles in ContentSelect is easy!

Within the ContentSelect Research Database section, you will see a list of disciplines and a space to type keywords. You can search within a single discipline or multiple disciplines. Choose one or more subject databases, and then enter a keyword you wish to search. Click on "Go".

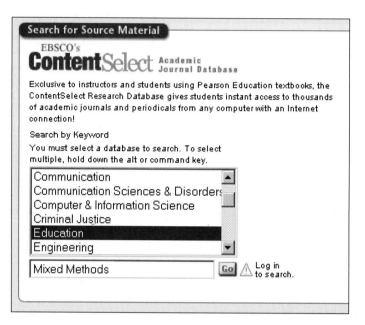

Now you'll see a list of articles that match your search. From this page you can examine either the full text or the abstract of each of the articles and determine which will best help with your research. Print out the articles or save them in your "Folder" for later reference.

2) *The New York Times*

Searching *The New York Times* gives you access to articles from one of the world's leading newspapers. The first step in using the search-by-subject archive is to indicate the subject area you wish to search. You have the option of searching one specific subject at a time by highlighting the subject area or searching all subjects by highlighting "All." Click on "Go" now for a complete listing of articles in your chosen subject area that have appeared in the New York Times over the last year, sorted by most recent article first. For a more focused search, type a word, or multiple words separated by commas, into the search box and click "Go" for a list of articles. Articles can be printed or saved for later use in your research assignment.

3)   "Best of the Web" Link Library

The third database of content included on Research Navigator™ is a collection of web links, organized by academic subject and key terms. To use this database, simply select a subject from the dropdown list and find the key term for the topic you are searching. Click on the key term and see a list of editorially reviewed websites that offer educationally relevant and credible content. The web links in Link Library are monitored and updated each week, reducing your incidence of finding "dead" links.

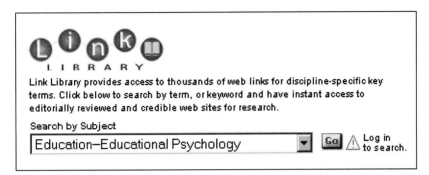

Using Your Library

While Research Navigator™ does contain a vast amount of information to assist you with your research, it does not try to replace the library. After you have selected your topic and gathered source material from the three databases of content, you may need to go to your school library to complete your research. Finding information at the library, however, can seem overwhelming. Research Navigator™ provides some assistance in this area as well. Research Navigator™ includes discipline-specific "library guides" for you to use as a roadmap. Each guide includes an overview of the discipline's major subject databases, on-line journals, and key associations and newsgroups. Print them out and take them with you to the library!

CAUTION! Please note that the Research Navigator™ site undergoes frequent changes as new and exciting options are added to assist with research endeavors. For the latest information on the options available to you on Research Navigator™, visit www.ablongman.com/aboutrn.com.

Educational Research

1

Introduction to Educational Research

LEARNING OBJECTIVES

To be able to

- Explain the importance of educational research.
- List at least five areas of educational research.
- Explain the difference between basic and applied research.
- Describe evaluation research, action research, and orientational research.
- Discuss the different sources of knowledge.
- Explain the scientific approach to knowledge generation.
- Explain how to determine the quality of a theory or explanation.
- List the five objectives of educational research and provide an example of each.

In June 2002, New York Governor George Pataki signed a state law giving Mayor Michael Bloomberg control of New York City's public school system. Most observers agree that this is a school system desperately in need of reform. The 1,100 schools within this system educate 1.1 million kids. However, using the word *educate* would seem to be somewhat of a misnomer because only about half of the city's public school students finish high school in four years. Only 40 percent of third through eighth grade students score at an acceptable level in reading, and only 34 percent do so in math. About 100 of the 1,100 schools are classified by the state as failing, and another 300 are almost as bad. Clearly, something needs to be done.

While campaigning for mayor, Michael Bloomberg had many ideas, one of which was to establish an unpaid Board of Education that functioned like a corporate board, providing fiscal oversight and expertise. This idea was approved by new legislation and was a radical departure from the old Board of Education, which was responsible for day-to-day management decisions, including even routine contracting and procurement decisions.

Bloomberg needs to do a lot more than just reconstitute the Board of Education because there is no single panacea for all of the problems facing the New York City school system. There is no shortage of ideas to assist Bloomberg in this process. Coles (2002) wrote an article in the *City Journal* giving his opinion as to what should be done. Coles stated that Bloomberg should choose a chancellor from outside the system so that he or she would not be constrained by existing relationships or vested interests. A uniform core curriculum should be established that focuses on basic skills, particularly in the elementary and middle schools. Social promotion should end. Finally, the best teachers should be rewarded, contends Coles, because fully 40 percent of the city's teachers failed the basic teacher certification test (Coles, 2002).

Given differing opinions about what should be done with a school system such as New York City's, which ideas do you think should be implemented? Which ones would provide the best return on capital expenditures and best help students? Obviously, there are many differing philosophies and many differing opinions. However, we contend that policymakers will benefit if they examine the findings of educational research studies comparing the outcomes resulting from implementing different ideas and approaches. This will help to eliminate personal bias and vested interests in particular approaches by providing strong evidence of what really works best. In short, research provides an effective and evidentiary way to help sort out and resolve differing ideas and opinions on educational issues. Perhaps our most important goal in writing this book is to convince you that it is important and helpful to add the examination and conduct of research to your list of ingredients to use when making decisions about education.

W elcome to the world of educational research! Research has been conducted in virtually every area in the field of education. In fact, the research techniques described in this book are used all over the world to help people in many fields to advance their knowledge and solve problems. The search for better and better answers to important questions will probably always continue. In this book, we will discuss the way in which research is conducted in an attempt to provide answers to important questions. We hope you will enjoy learning about research, and we hope it opens up new ways of thinking for you.

As you read this book, you will learn how to think about research, how to evaluate the quality of published research reports, and how to conduct research on your own. In a sense, you will also be learning a new language, because researchers use a specialized language or jargon. But remember, don't be afraid of new words. The words have definitions that represent ideas you can understand, and you have been learning new words all of your life. On the lighter side, perhaps you can use the new words to impress your friends. In sum, we welcome you to the world of research and hope that you will enjoy it. Because this is likely to be a required course for you, we will begin by discussing a few reasons for taking a course on educational research methods.

WHY STUDY EDUCATIONAL RESEARCH?

You might have asked, "Why do I have to take a class on educational research?" First of all, research can be more interesting than you might think. We hope that in time you will find the material and the ways of thinking both interesting and beneficial. Second, throughout this book, you will be learning critical thinking skills. Rather than assuming that what is written in a book or what someone says is "fact" or undeniable "truth," you can use the techniques that you will learn for evaluating arguments. In all cases, the question is one of evidence. As a start, we suggest that you take the word *proof* and eliminate it from your vocabulary this semester or quarter when you talk about research results. Proof exists in the realms of mathematics and deductive logic, but in science and research, the best we can do is to provide *evidence*. Sometimes the evidence is very convincing; at other times, it might not be. You must use your critical thinking skills to judge the available evidence on any given topic. These critical thinking skills will be helpful in your studies and professional work as long as you live. Learning about research methods should help to sharpen your critical thinking skills.

Another important reason to study research is to help you better understand discussions of research you hear and see in the media, such as television and radio, on the Internet, or at professional meetings. Examples of research in our society abound. For example, when you watch a television program, what comes in between those short segments of actual programming? Commercials! Do you ever wonder about those "research studies" that claim to "prove" that one laundry detergent is better than another? As you know, the purpose of commercials is to influence your buying behavior. Advertisers spend millions of dollars each year on marketing research to understand your thinking and behavior. If you watch a sporting event, you will likely see commercials for beer, cars, trucks, food, and tennis shoes. If you watch soap operas in the afternoon, you are likely to see very different commercials. The reason for this variation is that advertisers generally know who is watching what programs at what times. The actual commercials are developed to appeal to viewers' ways of thinking about what is fun, exciting, and important. And did you know that every major presidential candidate has a research consultant who tries to identify the most effective ways to get your vote and win the election? The point is that other people study you all the time, and in this book you will learn about the techniques they use. Understanding these techniques should help you to be more aware of their efforts.

You will learn here that not all research is created equal. That is, some research studies are more defensible than others. You will learn how to ask the right questions about research studies, and you will find out when to put confidence in a set of research findings. You will learn to ask questions such as these: Was the study an experiment or was it a nonexperimental research study? Were control groups included in the design? Did the researcher randomly assign participants to the different comparison groups? How did the researchers control for the influence of extraneous variables? How were the participants in the research selected? Did the researcher use techniques that help reduce the effects of human bias?

One day you might need to examine the research on a topic and make an informed judgment about what course of action to take or to recommend to someone else. Therefore, it is important that you understand how to review and evaluate research. Understanding research terminology, the characteristics of the different types of research, and how research can be designed to provide solid evidence will allow you to critically evaluate research results and make informed decisions based on research literatures. A **research literature** is the set of published research studies on a particular topic. A fundamental point to remember is that you should always place more confidence in a research finding when several different researchers in different places and settings have found the same result. You should never treat a single research study as the final word on any topic.

■ **Research literature** Set of published research studies on a particular topic

On a practical level, understanding research techniques might even help you in your career as a student and as a professional teacher, counselor, or coach. Perhaps one day you will be asked to write a proposal to obtain a grant or conduct a research study on your own. If you study the contents of this book, you will learn how to design and conduct a defensible study, and you will learn about the different sections in a research grant proposal. Furthermore, if you look at the bibliographies in the books you use in your other education courses, you will see that many of these references are research studies. After learning about research, you will be able to go back and evaluate the research studies on which your textbooks are based. In other words, you will not have to accept something as true just because someone said it was true. You might find that an article with what you believe to be a questionable finding is based on highly questionable research strategies.

1.1 Why should we study educational research?

R E V I E W

Q U E S T I O N

AREAS OF EDUCATIONAL RESEARCH

To give you a feel for educational research, let's look at some of the areas of research in education. In Table 1.1 you will find a list of the major divisions and the special interest areas in the American Educational Research Association (AERA). (The AERA website is at

▨ **T A B L E 1 . 1**   Divisions and Special Interest Groups in the American Educational Research Association. Note the special interest groups change slightly year to year.

Major Divisions in the AERA

Administration, Curriculum Studies	Measurement and Research Methodology
Counseling and Human Development	Postsecondary Education
Education in the Professions	School Evaluation and Program Development
History and Historiography	Social Context of Education
Learning and Instruction	Teaching and Teacher Education

Special Interest Groups in the AERA

Accelerated Schools	Organizational Theory
Action Research	Peace Education
Adolescence	Philosophical Studies of Education
Advanced Studies of National Databases	Politics of Education
American Indian/Alaskan Native Education	Professional Licensure and Certification
Artificial Intelligence and Education	Professors of Educational Research
Arts and Learning	Qualitative Research
Associates for Research on Private Education	Rasch Measurement
Basic Research in Reading and Literacy	Religion and Education
Bilingual Education Research	Research Focus on Black Education
Brain and Education	Research in Mathematics Education
Business Education and Information Systems Research	Research in Social Studies Education
Career Development	Research on Education of Asian and Pacific Americans
Classroom Management	Research on Education of Deaf Persons
Computer Applications in Education	Research on Evaluation
Constructivist Theory, Research, and Practice	Research on Giftedness and Talent
Critical Issues in Curriculum	Research on Learning and Instruction in Physical Education
Early Education and Child Development	Research Using NAEP Data
Economics Education	Research Utilization
Education and Student Development in the Cities	Restructuring Public Education
Education in Science and Technology	Rural Education
Educational Enterprises	School Effectiveness and School Improvement
Educational Statisticians	School-University Collaborative Research
Electronic Networking	Second Language Research
Faculty Evaluation and Development	Self-Study of Teacher Education Practices
Families as Educators	Semiotics in Education
Fiscal Issues, Policy, and Educational Finance	Society of Professors of Education
Futures Research and Strategic Planning	Sociology of Education
Instructional Supervision	Special Education Research
Instructional Technology	State and Regional Educational Research Associations
International Studies	Structural Equation Modeling
John Dewy Society	Study of Learning Environments
Language and Social Processes	Studying and Self-Directed Learning
Law and Education	Subject Knowledge and Conceptual Change
Leadership Development, Training, and Research	Survey Research in Education
Lesbian and Gay Studies	Teacher as Researcher
Literature	Teachers' Work and Teachers' Unions
Measurement Services	Teaching in Educational Administration
Media, Culture, and Curriculum	Textbooks, Textbook Publishing, and Schools
Middle Level Education	Training in Business and Industry
Military Education and Training	Vocabulary
Moral Development and Education	Vocational Education
Motivation in Education	Writing
Multiple Linear Regression	
Occupational Stress and Health	

http://aera.net.) The AERA is the largest and most prestigious research association in the field of education, and it has approximately 25,000 members. It is composed of university professors from all areas of education, governmental employees, teachers, and professionals from educational think tanks, consulting firms, and testing companies. Each year, approximately 11,000 of these members and many nonmembers attend a national conference sponsored by the AERA, where many attendees present the results of their latest research.

You can see in Table 1.1 that education is a broad field that includes many different research areas. Do you see any areas of research in Table 1.1 that seem especially interesting? If you are writing a research paper, you might pick one of these areas as your starting point. The areas of research listed in Table 1.1 are still fairly general, however. To see the specific areas and topics of current interest to educational researchers, go to the library and browse through the education journals.

EXAMPLES OF EDUCATIONAL RESEARCH

The majority of journal articles in education include an abstract on the front page of the article. An **abstract** is a brief summary of what is included in the article. We have reproduced the abstracts of several research articles here so that you can get a feel for what is done in an actual research study. Abstracts are helpful because they are short and include the main ideas of the research study. You can often decide whether you want to read a journal article by first reading its abstract. We recommend that you read some full-length research articles as soon as possible so that you will see some full examples of educational research. As you read the following abstracts, see whether you can determine (1) the purpose of the study, (2) how the researchers studied the phenomenon, and (3) what the major results were.

■ **Abstract**
Brief summary of what is in an article

I. The Development of a Goal to Become a Teacher, by Paul A. Schutz (University of Georgia), Kristen C. Croder (University of Georgia), and Victoria E. White (University of North Carolina at Greensboro), (2001), from *Journal of Educational Psychology,* Vol. 93(2), pp. 299–308.

The purpose of this project was to investigate how the goal of becoming a teacher emerges. The study used interviews to develop goal histories for 8 preservice teachers. There tended to be 4 sources of influence for their goal to become a teacher: (a) family influences, (b) teacher influences, (c) peer influences, and (d) teaching experiences. The categories developed from the interviews to describe the types of influences those sources provided were (a) suggesting that the person become a teacher, (b) encouraging the person to become a teacher, (c) modeling teacher behavior, (d) exposing the person to teaching experiences, and (e) discouraging the person from becoming a teacher. In addition, influences such as critical incidents, emotions, and social-historical factors, such as the status and pay of teachers, were prominent in the goal histories of the participants. Finally, the results of the study are discussed within the context of goals and self-directed behavior.

Research
Navigator.c☉m

class size

II. Getting Tough? The Impact of High School Graduation Exams by Brian A. Jacob at John F. Kennedy School of Government, Harvard University, (2001), from *Educational Evaluation and Policy Analysis,* Vol. 23(3), pp. 99–121.

The impact of high school graduation exams on student achievement and dropout rates is examined. Using data from the National Educational Longitudinal Survey (NELS), this analysis is able to control for prior student achievement and a variety of other student, school, and state characteristics. It was found that graduation tests have no significant impact on 12th-grade math or reading achievement. These results are robust with a variety of specification checks. Although graduation tests have no appreciable effect on the probability of dropping out for the average student, they increase the probability of dropping out among the lowest ability students. These results suggest that policymakers would be well advised to rethink current test policies.

III. Giving Voice to High School Students: Pressure and Boredom, Ya Know What I'm Saying? by Edwin Farreil, George Peguero, Rashed Lindsey, and Ronald White (1988), from *American Education Research Journal,* Vol. 25(4), pp. 489–502.

The concerns of students identified as at-risk of dropping out of school in an urban setting were studied using innovative ethnographic methods. Students from the subject population were hired to act as collaborators rather than informants and to collect taped dialogues between themselves and their peers. As collaborators, they also participated in the analysis of data and contributed to identifying the research questions of the inquiry. Data indicated that pressure and boredom were most often mentioned as negative factors in the lives of the students, with pressure emanating from social forces outside of school but contributing to boredom inside.

IV. Prediction of Reading Disabilities in Kindergarten and First Grade by Rollanda O'Connor (University of Pittsburgh) and Joseph Jenkins (University of Washington) (1999), from *Scientific Studies of Reading,* Vol. 3(2), pp. 159–198.

Attempts to better identify the at-risk children with reading disabilities to aid in early intervention before they encounter the years of reading failure usually associated with a formal diagnosis of reading disabilities. Tries to develop a small set of phonological, letter, and memory tasks that would reliably identify children likely to develop reading disabilities. (SC) We tested children in kindergarten and followed them through 1st grade. Segment phonemes and rapid letter naming qualified as primary discriminators of reading disability.

GENERAL KINDS OF RESEARCH

In this section we introduce you to some of the general kinds of research conducted by educational researchers (see Table 1.2). Although these general research types can overlap at times, they have different purposes and are intended for different audiences.

Basic and Applied Research

Research studies can be placed along a continuum with the words *basic research* at one end and the words *applied research* at the other end. The word *mixed* can be placed in the center to represent research that has characteristics of both basic and applied research. Basic research and applied research are typically conducted by researchers at universities. Basic research and applied research are also conducted by researchers working for think tanks,

■ **TABLE 1.2** Summary of General Kinds of Research

Kind of Research	Key Characteristics
Basic research	Focuses on generating fundamental knowledge
Applied research	Focuses on real-world questions and applications
Evaluation research	Focuses on determining the worth, merit, or quality of intervention programs
Action research	Focuses on solving local problems that practitioners face
Orientational research	Focuses on research that might help to reduce inequality

corporations, government agencies, and foundations. The primary outlet for basic and applied research is academic and professional research journals.

Basic research is aimed at generating fundamental knowledge and theoretical understanding about basic human and other natural processes. Research examining the effect of priming in memory is an example of basic research. Priming is "an enhancement of the processing of a stimulus as a function of prior exposure" (Anderson, 1995, p. 459). Assume that a researcher asks you to name a fruit and you say, "Pineapple." Then on the second trial, the researcher either asks you to name another type of fruit or asks you to name a type of dog. Which response do you think you could provide more quickly? It turns out that research participants could name another type of fruit faster than they could name a type of dog when they were asked to name a type of fruit first (Loftus, 1974, cited in Anderson, 1995). The naming of the fruit on the first trial primed the research participants' mental processing to name another fruit. It is believed that priming operates because the first exposure activates the complex of neurons in long-term memory, where the concept is being stored. Basic research is usually conducted by using the most rigorous research methods (e.g., experimental) under tightly controlled laboratory conditions. The primary audience includes the other researchers in the research area. The key purpose of basic research is to develop a solid foundation of reliable and fundamental knowledge and theory on which future research can be built.

■ **Basic research**
Research aimed at generating fundamental knowledge and theoretical understanding about basic human and other natural processes

At the other end of the continuum is applied research. **Applied research** is focused on answering real-world, practical questions to provide relatively immediate solutions. Topics for applied research are often driven by current problems in education and by policymakers' concerns. Applied research is often conducted in more natural settings (i.e., more realistic or real-world settings) than basic research. An applied research study might focus on the effects of retaining low-performing elementary school students in their present grade level or on the relative effectiveness of two approaches to counseling (e.g., behavior therapy versus cognitive therapy). In the former, the results would potentially have practical implications for education policy; in the latter, the results would potentially have implications for practicing counselors. The primary audiences for applied research are other applied researchers (who read the results in educational research journals) as well as policymakers, directors, and managers of programs who also read research journals. Applied research often leads to the development of interventions and programs aimed at improving societal conditions, which leads us to the next type of research.

■ **Applied research**
Research focused on answering practical questions to provide relatively immediate solutions

Research
Navigator.c⊛m

**evaluation
research**

■ **Evaluation**
Determining the
worth, merit, or quality
of an evaluation object

■ **Formative evaluation**
Evaluation focused on
improving the evalua-
tion object

■ **Summative
evaluation**
Evaluation focused on
determining the over-
all effectiveness and
usefulness of the eval-
uation object

Evaluation Research

When interventions and social or educational programs aimed at improving various conditions are implemented, evaluation research is often carried out to determine how well the
programs work in real-world settings and to show how they might be improved. Evaluation
research, or, more simply, **evaluation,** specifically involves determining the worth, merit,
or quality of an evaluation object such as an educational program. Evaluation requires evaluators to make value judgments about evaluation objects (e.g., Program XYZ is a good program, and it should be continued; Program ABC is a bad program, and it should be
discontinued). An evaluation object (also called the *evaluand*) is the thing being evaluated
(a program, a person, or a product) (Guba & Lincoln, 1981; Scriven, 1967; Worthen,
Sanders, & Fitzpatrick, 1997). An educational program might be an after-school program
for students with behavioral problems or a new curriculum at school. A person might be
your new school district superintendent. A product might be a new textbook or a new piece
of equipment a school is considering purchasing.

Evaluation traditionally is subdivided into two types according to the purpose of the
evaluation. When the primary purpose of an evaluation is to lead to judgments about how a
program can be improved, it is called a **formative evaluation.** Formative evaluation information helps program developers and support staff to design, implement, and improve their
program so that it works well. When the primary purpose of an evaluation is to lead to judgments about whether a program is effective and whether it should be continued, it is called a
summative evaluation. Summative evaluation information is important for policymakers
and others who commission programs when they make funding decisions and when they
have to make choices about which competing program will be supported and which will be
eliminated.

It is currently popular to divide evaluation into five areas or types (e.g., Rossi, Freeman, & Lipsey, 1999), each of which is based on a fundamental evaluation question:

1. Needs assessment (Is there a need for this type of program?)
2. Theory assessment (Is this program conceptualized in a way that it should work?)
3. Implementation assessment (Was this program implemented properly and according
   to the program plan?)
4. Impact assessment (Did this program have an impact on its intended targets?)
5. Efficiency assessment (Is this program cost effective?)

As you can see, evaluation can provide important information to educators. On the basis of
the evidence collected and the recommendations made, program evaluators provide an important voice in decision making about educational and other social programs.

Research
Navigator.c⊛m

action research

■ **Action research**
Applied research fo-
cused on solving prac-
titioners' local
problems

Action Research

Action research is focused on solving specific problems that local practitioners face in
their schools and communities (Lewin, 1946; Stringer, 1996). In action research practitioners in the local settings also have major roles in the design and conduct of the research
study. Action research follows the same research principles that are explained in depth in

this book. The key difference between action research and basic and applied research is that rather than being conducted by academic researchers, action research is more participatory and is conducted by teachers, administrators, counselors, coaches, and other educational professionals (sometimes in collaboration with university-based researchers) to answer questions that practitioners have about their immediate problems and to lead to actions that they can take to help solve their problems. Some examples are a principal studying teacher burnout at a local school, a group of teachers studying classroom discipline problems at their school, teachers and administrators studying the lack of parental involvement with their school's PTA, and a teacher studying a problem child in a particular classroom. To carry out an action research project, you would need to diagnose the specific problem you are facing, plan and carry out a research study (i.e., collect data to help answer your question), think about the new knowledge gained from your study, and implement recommendations that follow from the research findings to help solve the problem or improve the situation.

Action research is a never-ending process because most problems are not fully solved through a single research study. In fact, many school districts have departments that are specifically set up to conduct research about the schools. Also, many teachers and administrators now attempt to collect data about the problems they face and learn from their past attempts at problem solving. As you can see, action research is really a state of mind. It involves a commitment to lifelong individual and organizational learning and the belief that conducting research can lead to informed actions. Although action research is geared toward solving local problems, the results are sometimes presented at local, regional, or national conferences and can be published in newsletters and journals. If action research results are shared with the larger educational research community, the results can add to the general body of educational knowledge in addition to helping improve the specific local practices.

Orientational Research

The last general type of research, called **orientational research,** focuses on collecting information to help a researcher advance a specific ideological or political position that he or she believes will improve some part of our society (Patton, 2002). Orientational researchers are concerned about issues such as social discrimination and the inequitable distribution of power and wealth in society. Although all orientational researchers are concerned with reducing inequality of some form, there are several variants of orientational research. The most common areas of focus are class stratification (i.e., income and wealth inequality), gender inequality, racial and ethnic inequality, and sexual orientation inequality.

■ **Orientational research**
Research done for the purpose of advancing an ideological position

All researchers are ideological to some degree (e.g., in their selection of their research topics), but orientational researchers make their ideology and political agendas very explicit. Orientational research is sometimes called *critical theory research.* This is appropriate because these researchers often are critical of "mainstream research," which they believe supports the current power structure in society. If you are interested in orientational research, you might start by examining the following sources: Berge (2000), Dever (1997), Guerrero (1999), Lonborg and Phillips (1996), and Stanfield & Rutledge (1993).

Research
Navigator.c⊕m

critical theory

R E V I E W

Q U E S T I O N S

1.2 What are the definitions of the five general kinds of research?

1.3 Why is it important that both basic and applied research be done?

1.4 What is the difference between formative and summative evaluation?

1.5 What is the key question associated with each of the following forms of evaluation: needs assessment, theory assessment, implementation assessment, impact assessment, and efficiency assessment?

SOURCES OF KNOWLEDGE

**Research
Navigator.c⊛m**

epistemology

■ **Epistemology**
The study of how
knowledge is generated

Take a moment now to consider how you have learned about the world around you. Try to identify the source or sources of one of your particular beliefs. For example, consider your political party identification (i.e., Democrat, Republican, Independent, or something else). Political scientists have shown that college students' party identification can often be predicted by their parents' party identification. How does your party identification compare with your parents'? Obviously, there are many additional influences that affect party identification. Can you identify some of them?

We will examine the primary ways that people relate to the world and how and they generate knowledge. The study of how knowledge is generated is technically known as **epistemology.** We group the sources of knowledge into three areas: experiences, expert opinion, and reasoning. Perhaps you can think of some additional sources after you think about the ones we identify.

Experience

■ **Empiricism**
The idea that knowl-
edge comes from
experience

■ **Empirical statement**
A statement based on
observation, experi-
ment, or experience

Empiricism is the idea that knowledge comes from experience. We learn by observing, and when we observe, we rely on our sense perception. Each day of our lives, we look, feel, hear, smell, and taste so that we can understand our surroundings. According to the philosophical doctrine of empiricism, what we observe with our senses is said to be true. John Locke (1632–1704), a proponent of this idea, said that our mind at birth is a *tabula rasa,* a blank slate ready to be written on. Throughout our lives, our slate is filled up with knowledge based on our experiences. The statement "I know the car is blue because I saw it" is an example of an **empirical statement:** a statement based on observation, experiment, or experience. *Empirical* is a fancy word meaning "based on observation, experiment, or experience." The word *empirical* denotes that a statement is capable of being verified or disproved by observation, experiment, or experience. In the next paragraph, we try to trace some of the sources of experiences you might have had during your lifetime.

Throughout our lives, we participate in and learn about the world around us. We interact with people and generate our personal knowledge. In the beginning, we are born at a certain time, in a certain place, into a specific family that uses a specific language. When we are young, our family is the most important source of our knowledge, our attitudes, and our values. As we grow older, other people and social institutions around us influence us more and more, including our peers, our religion, our schools (and libraries), our economy, and the various media we are exposed to or seek out. We learn the customs, beliefs, and traditions of the people around us. We learn "how things are," and our personal knowledge continues to be constructed. Over time, many of our actions and beliefs become automatic and unquestioned.

Expert Opinion

In an information-rich society like the United States, another source of our knowledge is what experts say. We rely on experts or authorities because we don't have time to sift through all of the information needed to answer each and every question. Listening to experts can be informative; however, experts don't always agree. And don't forget that some experts are not experts on the topic about which they are quoted. Some purported "experts" speak far beyond their fields of expertise, and they might actually know no more than you or I do. For a humorous example, during the 1980s there was a television commercial that went something like this: "Hi. I'm not a doctor. I just play one on TV. And I recommend using Brand-X aspirin. It works." We always need to check the credentials of an expert, and we need to determine whether the expert has a vested interest in the particular statement being purported.

Reasoning

Rationalism is the philosophical idea that reason is the primary source of knowledge. The idea is most often associated with René Descartes (1596–1650) and Benedict de Spinoza (1632–1677). Reason involves thinking about something and developing an understanding of it through reasoning. In its extreme form, rationalism means that some truths are knowable independent of observation. In its less extreme form, rationalism simply refers to the use of reason in developing understandings about the world. Deductive reasoning and inductive reasoning are two important forms of reasoning.

■ **Rationalism**
The philosophical idea that reason is the primary source of knowledge

Deductive reasoning is the process of drawing a specific conclusion from a set of premises. In deductive reasoning, a conclusion will be true if a valid form of argument is used *and* the premises are true. One form of deductive reasoning is the syllogism. Here is an example:

■ **Deductive reasoning**
The process of drawing a specific conclusion from a set of premises

Major Premise:	All schoolteachers are mortal.
Minor Premise:	John is a schoolteacher.
Conclusion:	Therefore, John is mortal.

According to this deductive argument, John must be a mortal. Keep in mind, however, that reasoning like this depends on the validity of the premises. Just try replacing the word *mortal* with the word *Martians;* you then conclude that John is a Martian. In deductive reasoning, the conclusion will be false if any of the premises are false. In our Martian example, the conclusion is false because the major premise, "All schoolteachers are Martians," is false. Deductive reasoning can be very useful in helping us to understand things in our world, but we must always make sure that our premises are true, and we must use valid argument forms. We need to be careful about what we assume when we draw our conclusions.

■ **Inductive reasoning**
Reasoning from the particular to the general

Inductive reasoning involves reasoning "from particular instances of something to a general statement about them, from individuals to universals" (Angeles, 1992, p. 144). We engage in inductive reasoning frequently in our lives when we observe many specific instances of some phenomenon and draw conclusions about it. For example, you have certainly observed all of your life that the sun appears every morning (except on cloudy days). On the basis of your observations you probably feel comfortable in concluding that the sun will make its appearance again tomorrow (if it is not cloudy). In this case, you are indeed likely to be correct. But notice that when you use inductive reasoning, you are using a **probabilistic** form of reasoning. That is, you are stating what is likely to occur, not what necessarily will occur. Because of this, you are taking a risk (albeit a very small risk in this case) because induction involves making conclusions that go beyond the evidence in the premises. This is not necessarily a problem, but you should be aware that it could be one.

■ **Probabilistic**
Stating what is likely to occur, not necessarily what will occur

■ **Problem of induction**
Things that happened in the past might not happen in the future

The potential problem in inductive reasoning is known as the **problem of induction:** Although something might have happened many times in the past, it is still possible that it will not happen in the future. In short, *the future might not resemble the past.* Let's say that every cat you have ever seen had a tail. Using inductive reasoning, you might be led to conclude that all cats have tails. You can see the problem here because one day you might run across a Manx cat, which has no tail. The point is that inductive reasoning is useful in helping us to come up with generalizations about the world; however, we must remember that we have not proven our generalizations to be true. Our generalizations are only statements of probability.

REVIEW

QUESTIONS

1.6 What are the different sources of knowledge? Which ones are especially important for educational researchers?

1.7 What is the key difference between inductive reasoning and deductive reasoning?

THE SCIENTIFIC APPROACH TO KNOWLEDGE GENERATION

Although the word *science* has become a hot button or loaded word in some circles, the root of the word *science* is the Latin *scientia,* which simply means "knowledge." We define science in this book in a way that is inclusive of the different approaches to educational research. We define **science** as an approach for the generation of knowledge that places high regard for empirical data and follows certain norms and practices that develop over time because of their usefulness. Many of these norms and effective practices are explained in this book.

■ **Science**
An approach for the generation of knowledge

Science includes any systematic or carefully done actions that are carried out to answer research questions or meet other needs of a developing research domain (e.g., describing things, exploring, experimenting, explaining, predicting). Science often involves the application of a scientific method; however, as philosophers and historians of science have pointed out, science can also include other methods and activities that are carried out by researchers as they attempt to generate scientific knowledge. Science does not accept at face value taken-for-granted knowledge (i.e., things that we assume to be true); instead, it is used to uncover more accurate descriptions and explanations of people, groups, and the world around us. In this book, we will generally treat the term *science* (as just defined) and the term *research* as synonyms.

Dynamics of Science

Over time, science results in an accumulation of specific findings, theories, and other knowledge. As a result, science is said to be progressive. When researchers conduct new research studies, they try to build on and extend current research theories and results. Sir Isaac Newton expressed it well when he said, "We stand on the shoulders of giants." Newton's point was that researchers do not and cannot start completely from scratch, and Newton knew that he was no exception to this rule. In short, researchers usually build on past findings and understandings.

At the same time, science is dynamic and open to new ideas and theories that show promise. Different researchers approach research differently, and they often describe, explain, and interpret things in different though often complementary ways. New ideas emerge. As new ideas are generated and evidence is obtained, results are presented at conferences and are published in monographs, books, and journals so that other members of the research community can examine them. Before findings are published in journals, the studies are usually evaluated by a group of experts called *referees* to make sure there are no major flaws and that the procedures are defensible. Researchers are usually required to report exactly how they conducted their research so that other researchers can evaluate the procedures or even replicate the study. Once published, research findings are openly discussed and are critically evaluated by members of the research community. Overall, we can say that science is a never-ending process that includes rational thinking, the reliance on empirical observation, constant peer evaluation and critique, and—very important—active creativity and attempts at discovery.

Basic Assumptions of Science

Educational researchers must make a few general assumptions so that they can go about their daily business of doing research. Most practicing researchers do not think much about these philosophical assumptions as they carry out their daily research activities; nonetheless, it is helpful to examine some of these assumptions. The most common assumptions are summarized in Table 1.3.

First, at the most basic level, educational researchers assume that there is a world out there that can be studied. In education, this includes studying many phenomena that are internal to people (e.g., attitudes, values, beliefs, lived experiences) as well as many broader phenomena or institutions that are either connected to people or external to them (e.g., schools, cultures, and physical environments). Educational researchers study how the following factors relate to educational issues: psychological factors (e.g., characteristics of individuals and individual level phenomena), social psychological factors (e.g., examining

■ **TABLE 1.3**   Summary of Common Assumptions Made by Educational Researchers

1. There is a world out there that can be studied. This can include studying the inner worlds of individuals.
2. Some of the world is unique; some of it is regular or patterned or predictable; and much of it is dynamic and complex. (Note: These categories can sometimes overlap.)
3. The unique, the regular, and the complex in the world all can be examined and studied by researchers.
4. Researchers should try to follow certain agreed-on norms and practices.
5. It is possible to distinguish between more and less plausible claims and between good and poor research.
6. Science cannot provide answers to all questions.

how individuals interact and relate to one another and how groups and individuals affect one another), and sociological factors (e.g., examining how groups form and change, documenting the characteristics of groups, studying intergroup relations, and studying group level phenomena such as cultural, social, political, familial, and economic institutions).

Second, although these categories sometimes overlap, researchers assume that part of the world is unique, part of the world is regular or patterned or predictable, and much of the world is dynamic (i.e., changing) and complex (e.g., involving many pieces or factors). The majority of educational researchers are especially interested in the predictable part of the world because they want to generate findings that will apply to more than one person, group, kind of person, context, or situation. As you can imagine, it would be very difficult if we had to conduct research on every single individual! To see an example of regularity in the world, the next time you go to your research class, note the seats that you and a few people around you are sitting in. When your class meets again, see whether you and the others you observed sit in the same seats as during the previous meeting. You will probably notice that many of the people sit in the same seats. Why is this? This happens because humans are to some degree predictable. Understanding the predictable part of the world allows researchers to generalize and apply their findings beyond the people and places used in their particular studies.

Third, the unique, the regular, and the complex in the world can be examined and studied by researchers. In other words, "discoverability" exists in our world (i.e., it is possible to document the unique, discover the regularity in human behavior, and, in time, better understand many of the complexities of human behavior). This does not mean that the task of discovering the nature of educational phenomena is simple. For example, although significant progress has been made, we still do not know all of the causes of many learning disabilities. Research must continue, and over time, we hope to find more and more pieces to the puzzles we are trying to solve. One day we hope we will be able to solve many educational problems.

The fourth assumption is that researchers should follow certain agreed-on norms and practices. A few of these are the collection of empirical data, open discussion of findings, integrity, honesty, competence, systematic inquiry, neutrality and respect toward research participants, a healthy skepticism toward results and explanations, a sense of curiosity and openness to discovery, actively searching for negative evidence (e.g., instances that do not fit your emerging or current explanation of a phenomenon), carefully examining alternative explanations for your findings, and, above all, an adherence to the principle of evidence. One of this book's authors (Johnson) likes to tell his students that a researcher is a lot like the slogan on Missouri's license plates: "The Show Me State." If you have a claim to make, then "show me the evidence, please!" A good researcher tries to collect and assemble high-quality evidence and expects other researchers to do the same. Obviously, it is all but impossible for a researcher to fully follow all of the ideals listed here. Furthermore, because science is a human activity, it is also affected by social and power relationships among researchers and society (Kuhn, 1962; Lincoln & Guba, 2000). That's why it is so important that researchers strive to follow the norms we have listed.

The fifth assumption is that it is possible to distinguish between more and less plausible claims and between good and poor research. For example, through empirical research, we can choose between competing theories by determining which theory best fits the data. We can also judge the quality of a research study by examining the research strategies used and the evidence that is provided for each of the conclusions drawn by a researcher. We say that high-quality research is more *trustworthy* or more *valid* than low-quality research. We will explain throughout this textbook how to identify and carry out research that is trustworthy, valid, credible, and, therefore, defensible.

The sixth assumption made by researchers is that science cannot provide answers to all questions. For example, science cannot answer philosophical questions such as what the meaning of life is, what virtue is, or what beauty is. Science cannot settle issues of which position is morally correct (e.g., human cloning versus no human cloning; pro-choice versus pro-life in the abortion debate) or politically correct (e.g., Republican or Democrat) and cannot explain ideas such as the difference between good and evil in the world or the veracity of claims about the existence of life after death. As you can see, there are many areas that are important but simply lie outside the domain of science and empirical research.

Scientific Method(s)

Science is not a perfectly orderly process (Kuhn, 1962). It is a dynamic process that includes countless activities. However, several of the key features of science are (1) making empirical observations, (2) generating and testing **hypotheses** (predictions or educated guesses), (3) building and testing **theories** (explanations or explanatory systems), and (4) attempting to predict and influence the world to make it a better place to live (American Association for the Advancement of Science, 1990; Angeles, 1992). Although the conduct of research is clearly not a perfectly orderly process and is composed of many activities, it is still helpful to think about what we will call the *scientific methods*.

There are two major scientific methods that need to be distinguished: the deductive method and the inductive method. Although both of these methods involve empirical observation, the observation occurs at different points. The basic **deductive method** includes three steps. First, the researcher states a hypothesis, which is frequently based on existing theory (i.e., currently available scientific explanations). Second, the researcher collects data to be used to test the hypothesis empirically. Third, the researcher makes the decision to tentatively accept or reject the hypothesis on the basis of the data. The basic **inductive method** also includes three steps. First, the researcher starts by making observations. Second, the

■ **Hypothesis**
A prediction or educated guess

■ **Theory**
An explanation or an explanatory system

■ **Deductive method**
A top-down or confirmatory approach to research

■ **Inductive method**
A bottom-up or generative approach to research

researcher studies the observations and searches for a pattern (i.e., a statement of what is occurring). Third, the researcher makes a tentative conclusion about the pattern or how some aspect of the world operates; that is, the researcher makes a generalization.

The deductive method is a *top-down approach* because it starts with a theory or hypothesis. The steps move from the general to the particular (theory → hypothesis → data). The inductive approach is a *bottom-up approach* because it moves from the particular to the general: It starts with specific observations and then moves to a tentative generalization about how some aspect of the world operates. The deductive method is the traditional theory- or hypothesis-testing approach: It follows the "logic of justification." The inductive method is known as the theory or hypothesis generation approach: It follows the "logic of discovery." Again, the deductive scientific method is used to test hypotheses (or test theories), and the inductive scientific method is used to discover or generate new hypotheses and tentative theoretical explanations that can be tested at a later time.

Although we have talked about two separate scientific methods (the deductive method and the inductive method), it is important to understand that researchers use both of these methods in practice. As you can see in Figure 1.1, the use of the deductive and inductive methods follows a cyclical process. One researcher might start at the top of the research cycle (at theory), and another researcher might start at the bottom of the research cycle (at observation), but both researchers will usually go through the full cycle many, many times as they think about and carry out their research programs over time. In fact, **quantitative researchers** (i.e., traditional educational researchers who like "hard" quantitative data such as standardized tests) and **qualitative researchers** (i.e., educational researchers who like to explore educational issues using qualitative data such as open-ended interviews that provide data based on the participants' actual words and observations) both go through the full research cycle, but they prefer to *start* in different places: Quantitative researchers often start at the top of the circle, and qualitative researchers often start at the bottom of the circle.

Theory

The inductive and deductive scientific methods both involve the concept of theory (i.e., explanations). The inductive approach focuses on generating or building theory, and the deduc-

■ **Quantitative researcher**
A traditional researcher who focuses on testing hypotheses using quantitative data

■ **Qualitative researcher**
A researcher who focuses on exploration or theory generation using qualitative data

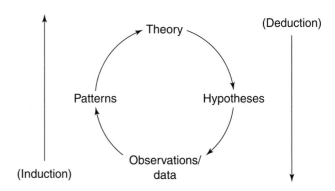

■ **FIGURE 1.1**
The research wheel

tive approach focuses on testing an existing theory. The term *theory* as used in this book most simply refers to an explanation or an explanatory system that discusses how a phenomenon operates and why it operates as it does. Theory often refers to a generalization or set of generalizations that are used systematically to explain some phenomenon. In other words, a well-developed theory explains how something operates in general (i.e., for many people), and it enables one to move beyond the findings of any single research study. Using a well-developed theory, you should be able to explain a phenomenon, make sense of it, and be able to make accurate predictions. When you need to judge the quality of a theory or explanation, you should try to answer the nine questions listed in Table 1.4. We now define and briefly elaborate on the *criterion of falsifiability* and the *rule of parsimony*.

One criterion used to judge theories is the **criterion of falsifiability** which was developed by Sir Karl Popper (1902–1994), who was one of the most famous philosophers of science of the twentieth century (Popper, 1985). The criterion of falsifiability is "the property of a statement or theory that it is capable of being refuted by experience" (Blackburn, 1994, p. 135). The key idea of the criterion of falsifiability is that if it is impossible ever to refute a statement or theory, then that statement or theory is not useful for science. If someone said, "I don't care what the actual results are, I'm going to conclude that my theory is supported," then that person would obviously not be doing the kind of research that could ever falsify a theory. The criterion of falsifiability also says that we should not just search out confirming evidence for our beliefs and explanations. Good researchers carefully examine any negative evidence that operates against their beliefs, research conclusions, and theoretical explanations.

Another criterion for evaluating theories is called the **rule of parsimony.** A theory is parsimonious when it is simple, concise, and succinct. If two competing theories explain and predict a phenomenon equally well, then the more parsimonious theory is to be preferred according to the rule of parsimony. In other words, simple theories are preferred over highly complex ones, other things being equal.

■ **Criterion of falsifiability**
The property that statements and theories should be refutable

■ **Rule of parsimony**
Preferring the most simple theory that works

▦ **TABLE 1.4**   How to Evaluate the Quality of a Theory or Explanation

1. Is it (i.e., the theory or explanation) logical and coherent?
2. Is it clear and parsimonious?
3. Does it fit the available data?
4. Does it provide testable claims?
5. Have theory-based predictions been tested and supported?
6. Has it survived numerous attempts by researchers to identify problems with it or to falsify it?
7. Does it work better than competing or rival theories or explanations?
8. Is it general enough to apply to more than one place, situation, or person?
9. Can practitioners use it to control or influence things in the world (e.g., a good theory of teaching helps teachers to positively influence student learning; a good theory of counseling helps counselors to positively influence their clients' mental health)?

Now let's look at a couple of theories so that you can see a little better what relatively well-developed theories look like. Several research studies have examined techniques for promoting attitude change. Dissonance theory was originally developed by Leon Festinger (1957) and has received some empirical support. According to dissonance theory, creating mental contradictions leads to dissonance, which leads to changes in attitudes. Dissonance is an uncomfortable state or form of mental anxiety that is created when an individual holds contradictory beliefs or behaves in ways that contradict his or her beliefs. Because dissonance creates discomfort, people are motivated to reduce it. Festinger points out that people often rationalize to reduce their dissonance. They might, for example, change a belief or an attitude, reinterpret the situation that caused the dissonance, or add new beliefs. This theory was used to explain the surprising research finding that the more money people are paid to argue for a position that they oppose, the less they will change their attitudes toward it (Linder, Cooper, & Jones, 1967). This result is counterintuitive according to everyday thinking, which might predict that greater pay would result in greater attitude change.

Another educational theory is called *expectation theory.* According to this theory, teachers' expectations about their students affect their behavior toward their students, which in turn affects their students' behavior. The theory is based on the self-fulfilling prophecy (Merton, 1948). Robert Rosenthal and Lenore Jacobson (1968) studied the effects of teachers' expectations and found that students whom teachers expected to perform well had higher increases in IQ than other students. These authors called this the *Pygmalion effect.* Rosenthal also found that "those children in whom intellectual growth was expected were described as having a significantly better chance of becoming successful in the future, as significantly more interesting, curious, and happy" (Rosenthal, 1991, p. 6). Students who had IQ increases but had not been expected to have increases by the teachers were not viewed more favorably by the teachers. These results suggest that teacher expectations can sometimes affect student performance. Note, however, that recent research has suggested that the power of expectations is not as great as had originally been concluded (Goldenberg, 1992). Nonetheless, the theory of expectations is a useful idea.

There are many other theories in education. A few are attribution theory, constructivism, labeling theory, Kohlberg's theory of moral development, operant conditioning, proximal development, rational emotive therapy, site-based management, situated learning, and social learning theory. If you want to find out more about any of these theories, just go to the library (or, using your computer, go to www.eric.ed.gov/) and conduct a search using ERIC or one of the other computerized search tools, which are discussed in Chapter 3. You can find nice descriptions of many educational and psychological theories at http://tip.psychology.org/theories.html.

Keep in mind as you read research articles that you will not always find the word *theory* in the article because there often will not be a well-developed or *explicit theory* available to the researcher, or the researcher might not have a fancy name for his or her theory. In this case, you can view the authors' explanations of their findings as their attempts to develop a theory. Remember that some theories are highly developed and others are very brief or not well developed. When we use the word *theory* in this book, you might replace the word *theory* with the word *explanation* until you get used to the idea that theory most simply means explanation.

The Principle of Evidence

Many beginning students believe that science and research are processes in which researchers constantly prove what is true. You might be surprised to learn that researchers rarely use the word *prove* when discussing their research findings. In fact, as we mentioned earlier, we recommend that you eliminate the word *prove* from your vocabulary when you are talking about research because most researchers hold knowledge to be ultimately tentative (Phillips & Burbules, 2000; Shadish, Cook, & Campbell, 2001). They recognize that things that are believed to be true today might change eventually and that some findings are later found to be only partially true or even patently false. What we obtain in research is scientific "evidence." It is essential that you understand this idea. An important educational methodologist, the late Fred Kerlinger (1986), made this point very clearly:

> The interpretation of research data culminates in conditional probabilistic statements of the "If p, then q" kind. We enrich such statements by qualifying them in some such way as: If p, then q, under conditions r, s, and t. . . . *Let us flatly assert that nothing can be "proved" scientifically. All one can do is to bring evidence to bear that such-and-such a proposition is true.* Proof is a deductive matter, and experimental methods of inquiry are not methods of proof. [emphasis added] (p. 145)

Here is the way the American Association for the Advancement of Science (1990) puts it:

> Science is a process for producing knowledge. The process depends on making careful observations of phenomena and on inventing theories for making sense out of those observations. Change in knowledge is inevitable because new observations may challenge prevailing theories. No matter how well one theory explains a set of observations, it is possible that another theory may fit just as well or better, or may fit a still wider range of observations. In science, the testing and improving and occasional discarding of theories, whether new or old, go on all the time. (p. 2)

As you learn more about research, keep these points in mind. It is also important to understand that you should never place too much weight on a single research study. **Replication** by other researchers, that is, research examining the same variables with different people and in different ways, should make you more confident about a research finding because the resulting evidence is much stronger. But even in the face of replication, strong evidence rather than proof is all that is obtained because we always leave open the possibility that future researchers will come up with new theories and findings.

Whenever you are tempted to use the word *prove,* stop and think and remind yourself about the fundamental nature of educational research. For now, whenever you want to use the word *proof,* just use the word *evidence* instead. Sometimes I (Johnson) like to tell my students that proof is what television commercials claim for their products' performance, but in research the best we can do is to obtain *evidence.* During a presidential election in the 1990s, a campaign manager kept a slogan posted in the campaign office that read "It's the economy, stupid!" to keep the staff focused on the economic performance of the current

■ **Replication**
Research examining the same variables with different people and in different ways

Research
Navigator.c⊛m

replication

administration as the primary campaign issue. In research our slogan goes like this: "It's about evidence, not proof!" We call this idea the **principle of evidence.**

1.8 Describe the two forms of the scientific method, and explain why both are important.

1.9 Explain why researchers do not use the word *proof* when they write up the results of their research in journal articles.

1.10 What criteria can you use to determine the quality of a theory or an explanation?

1.11 What does the principle of evidence state?

OBJECTIVES OF EDUCATIONAL RESEARCH

■ **Principle of evidence**
The philosophical idea that research provides evidence, not proof
■ **Exploration**
Attempting to generate ideas about phenomena

Discussions of science and empirical research often focus on the importance of explanation. However, there are several additional objectives that are also important if the field of educational research is to continue to operate effectively and progress. The first objective is **exploration,** or attempting to generate ideas about phenomena. Exploration is especially important in the early phases of research because researchers must generate ideas about phenomena before additional research can progress. To determine whether exploration was the objective of a research study, answer the following questions:

1. Were the researchers studying a phenomenon or some aspect of a phenomenon about which little was previously known?
2. Did the researchers choose to ignore previous research or explanations so that they could study a phenomenon without any preconceived notions?
3. Were the researchers trying to "discover" important factors or "generate" new ideas for further research?

If you answer yes to any of these questions, then the researchers were probably operating in the exploratory mode of research.

As is implied in the second and third questions, exploration does not always have to be done in the early phases of research. Sometimes researchers might want to enter the field without fixed or preconceived notions about what they are studying so that they can explore a phenomenon in a new way and so that they can avoid being biased or blinded by previous findings or theories. The article mentioned earlier in this chapter (in the section "Examples of Educational Research"), entitled "Giving Voice to High School Students" was exploratory because the researchers tried to uncover what at-risk students thought was important in their lives, why the students acted in the ways they did, and how the students viewed various formal and informal groups (e.g., teachers). The researchers tried to describe the at-risk adolescents' beliefs and circumstances to explain why they acted as they did. One finding was that some at-risk students formed subcultures that were in conflict with the teachers' culture; that is, the groups differed on criteria such as values, beliefs, and activities that were considered appropriate. These differences made it difficult for the teachers and the students to communicate, which resulted in student apathy and boredom in the classroom. For another example in which the objective was exploratory, you can reread the abstract of the article mentioned earlier (in the section "Examples of Educational Research") entitled "The Development of a Goal to Become a Teacher."

The key to exploration is the use of the inductive method of science. In particular, the researcher explores the specifics of something or some situation to develop tentative hypotheses or generalizations about it. Exploration is similar to basic descriptive activities in that it often includes description. However, attempts are also frequently made in exploratory research to generate preliminary explanations or theories about how and why a phenomenon operates as it does.

The second objective is **description,** or attempting to describe the characteristics of a phenomenon. To determine whether description was the main objective of a research study, answer the following questions:

■ **Description**
Attempting to describe the characteristics of a phenomenon

1. Were the researchers primarily describing a phenomenon?
2. Were the researchers documenting the characteristics of some phenomenon?

Description is one of the most basic activities in research. It might simply involve observing a phenomenon and recording what one sees. For example, a seasoned teacher might observe the behavior of a student teacher and take notes. At other times, description might rely on the use of quantitative measuring instruments such as standardized tests. For example, a researcher might want to measure the intangible construct called intelligence quotient, or IQ. To do this, the researcher must rely on some type of test that has been constructed specifically for this purpose. At other times, description might involve reporting attitudes and opinions about certain issues. For an example, see the September 1996 issue of *Phi Delta Kappan,* which reports national attitudes toward education each year. The study is conducted by the Gallup Organization and is commissioned by the education honor society Phi Delta Kappa. Two questions and their responses are shown in Table 1.5.

The third objective is **explanation,** or attempting to show how and why a phenomenon operates as it does. According to many writers, this is the key purpose of science. To determine whether explanation was the primary objective of a research study, answer the following questions:

■ **Explanation**
Attempting to show how and why a phenomenon operates as it does

1. Were the researchers trying to develop a theory about a phenomenon to explain how and why it operates as it does?
2. Were the researchers trying to explain how certain phenomena operate by identifying the factors that produce change in them? More specifically, were the researchers studying cause-and-effect relationships?

If the answer to either of these questions is yes, then the researchers' primary objective is probably explanation. The objective of the majority of educational research is explanation. An example of a research study focusing on explanation is a study entitled "Are Effects of Small Classes Cumulative?" by Nye, Hedges, and Konstantopoulos (2001). In that study, the researchers were interested in determining the effect of class size on student performance. They found that smaller classes in grades one through three resulted in improved reading and mathematics achievement scores and that the effect continues to occur over time. The study utilized a strong experimental design that provides relatively solid evidence about cause and

▨ **TABLE 1.5**   Items from Phi Delta Kappa/Gallup Poll (September 1996)

Question: Would you favor or oppose a requirement for high school graduation that all students in the local public schools perform some kind of community service?

	National Totals %	No Children in School %	Public School Parents %	Nonpublic School Parents %
Favor	66	66	67	75
Oppose	32	32	32	25
Don't know	2	2	1	*

Question: Just your impression, do you think that the national dropout rate of students in high school is higher today than it was twenty-five years ago, lower today, or about the same as it was twenty-five years ago?

	National Totals %	No Children in School %	Public School Parents %	Nonpublic School Parents %
Higher	64	62	66	73
Lower	15	15	15	8
About the same	18	19	17	16
Don't know	3	4	2	3

*Less than one-half of 1 percent.

effect. In a study like this, the cause (i.e., smaller class sizes) is used to explain the effect (i.e., improved achievement scores). For another example in which the objective was explanation, see the article mentioned earlier (in the section "Examples of Educational Research") entitled "Getting Tough? The Impact of High School Graduation Exams."

▪ **Prediction**
Attempting to predict or forecast a phenomenon

The fourth objective is **prediction,** or attempting to predict or forecast a phenomenon. To determine whether prediction was the primary objective of a research study, answer the following question: Did the researchers conduct the research so that they could predict or forecast some event in the future? A researcher is able to make a prediction when certain information that is known in advance can be used to determine what will happen at a later point in time. Sometimes predictions can also be made from research studies in which the primary focus is on explanation. That is, when researchers determine cause-and-effect operations (explanations), they can use this information to form predictions.

One research study in which the focus was on prediction was conducted by Fuertes, Sedlacek, and Liu (1994). These researchers conducted a ten-year research study and found that Asian American university students' academic performance and retention could be predicted by using the Scholastic Assessment Test (SAT) and another instrument called the Noncognitive Questionnaire. The strongest predictor of the students' GPAs was their SAT math scores. Other useful predictors (from the Noncognitive Questionnaire) were community service, realistic self-appraisal, academic self-concept, nontraditional knowledge, and handling racism. The strongest predictors of enrollment (i.e., retention) were self-concept, realistic self-appraisal, and SAT math score. For another example in which the objective was prediction, see the article mentioned earlier (in the section "Examples of Educational Research") entitled "Prediction of Reading Disabilities in Kindergarten and First Grade."

The fifth objective is called **influence,** or attempting to apply research to make certain outcomes occur. This objective is different from the previous ones because it refers to the application of research knowledge rather than the generation of research knowledge. It refers to the application of previous research to control various aspects of the world. Here you should ask the following question: Were the researchers applying research knowledge to make something useful happen in the world? The ultimate objective of most social, behavioral, and educational research is improvement of the world or social betterment. Therefore, influence is important. For teachers, influence involves things like helping students to learn more than they previously knew, helping children with special needs, and preventing negative outcomes such as dropping out of school or disruptive behavior in the classroom. For counselors, influence might involve helping clients to overcome psychological problems such as depression, personality disorders, and dysfunctional behaviors.

■ **Influence**
Attempting to apply research to make certain outcomes occur

As you work through this book and learn about the different methods of research, you will be learning more about these objectives. At this point, you should be able to examine a research article and determine what the researcher's objectives were. Don't be surprised if there appears to be more than one objective. That is not at all uncommon. You should also be aware that researchers often use the terms *descriptive research, exploratory research, explanatory research,* and *predictive research.* When they do this, they are simply describing the primary objective of the research.

1.12 What are the five main objectives of science? (Hint: The first letters form the acronym EDEPI.)

1.13 Why is each of the five main objectives of science important?

REVIEW

QUESTIONS

OVERVIEW OF BOOK

We have organized your textbook to follow the general steps involved in the research process. In Part I we introduce you to the kinds of educational research and the process and assumptions of research. In Part 2 we show how to come up with a research idea and how to plan a research study. In Part 3 we introduce some concepts required to design and conduct a good study. In Part 4 we discuss the major methods of research. In Part 5 we show how to analyze data resulting from a research study. In Part 6 we explain how to write a research manuscript.

To fully master the material you will need to take advantage of some of the application exercises provided in the book and on the companion website because this will give you some practice applying the material. As you start to review for exams, you can test your overall knowledge of the material by answering the multiple choice questions on the companion website (the answers are included) and by answering the study questions. You can also print the definitions of the terms given in the chapters. Don't look at the answers until you have stated your own answers, and then compare and identify your areas of strength and weakness. Use the concept maps on the companion website to keep things organized into the big picture.

We also strongly recommend that you read some examples of published research to see full-length examples of how research is done. Throughout the text we provide references to many articles that you can download and print. You can also find many full-length examples of research on the ContentSelect search index provided with this book. For example, you can start by printing the article "Bridging Research and Practice: A Cognitively Based Classroom Intervention for Teaching Experimentation Skills to School Children" by Toth. Although the article is a little long, it is interesting and it is based on data collected with children. You might want to browse it to get a feel for what research looks like.

Our practical conclusions for this chapter are clear: anyone can learn the material in this book if he or she works at it, and *you* can do it! We hope to show you that learning about research can actually be fun. Good luck, and don't forget to use the many learning tools that are available on the companion website to make your learning easier.

SUMMARY

It is important that educators and counselors be research literate because of the importance of research in education and our society. By learning about research you will be able to evaluate published research articles, and you will be able to conduct well-designed research studies on your own if the need ever arises in your professional career (e.g., perhaps one day your principal or manager will ask you to conduct a survey or to write a grant proposal). Educational researchers generate evidence about educational phenomena by collecting empirical data and using the inductive and deductive forms of the scientific method. The five general objectives of research are to explore, to describe, to explain, to predict, and to influence things in our world. When reading research articles, you should be able to determine the primary objective a researcher had when he or she conducted a research study. In the next chapter we will finish our introduction to educational research by describing the key features of the three major research paradigms: quantitative research, qualitative research, and mixed research.

KEY TERMS

abstract (p. 7)
action research (p. 10)
applied research (p. 9)
basic research (p. 9)
criterion of falsifiability (p. 19)
deductive method (p. 17)
deductive reasoning (p. 13)
description (p. 23)
empirical statement (p. 12)
empiricism (p. 12)
epistemology (p. 12)

evaluation (p. 10)
explanation (p. 23)
exploration (p. 22)
formative evaluation (p. 10)
hypothesis (p. 17)
inductive method (p. 17)
inductive reasoning (p. 14)
influence (p. 25)
orientation research (p. 11)
prediction (p. 24)
principle of evidence (p. 22)

probabilistic (p. 14)
problem of induction (p. 14)
qualitative researcher (p. 18)
quantitative researcher (p. 18)
rationalism (p. 13)
replication (p. 21)
research literature (p. 5)
rule of parsimony (p. 19)
science (p. 14)
summative evaluation (p. 10)
theory (p. 17)

DISCUSSION QUESTIONS

1. Which of the following do you think is the most important kind of research: basic, applied, evaluation, action, or orientational research? Why?
2. Why was it asserted in the chapter that one does not obtain final proof in educational research?
3. How does the presentation of two forms of the scientific method fit with your prior understanding of the scientific method or how researchers generate knowledge?
4. What is a research finding that you have heard (e.g., on the news or in another class) and wondered about?

RESEARCH EXERCISES

1. We have put a Research Methods Questionnaire on the book's companion website (www. ablongman.com/johnsonchristensen2e) under Chapter 1 bonus materials. Fill it out, and test your prior knowledge about research methods.
2. Try out ContentSelect (i.e., the search index that goes with this book). First go to the companion website, then click on Research Navigator and insert your password. Under ContentSelect, select all the databases (just click and cover them), and enter a search term or set of terms to find a research study that sounds interesting to you.
3. Take a moment to examine what is available on the web page that goes with this book. Here are some of the many features you will find: lectures, concept maps, answers to study questions, multiple-choice quizzes, application exercises, web resources, chapter supplements, and overheads. If you think of something else that will help you learn the material in your book, email us and let us know because we are always adding new features to our book's companion website. Our email addresses are bjohnson@usouthal.edu and lchriste@usouthal.edu.

RELEVANT INTERNET SITES

www.aera.net
Educational research.

www.eval.org
Program evaluation.

www.extension.umn.edu/people/fhoefer/educdsgn/ actresrc.htm
Action research.

www.pitt.edu/~pittcntr/Links/links.htm
Philosophy of science links.

RECOMMENDED READING

Arhar, J. M., Holly, M. L., & Dasten, W. C. (2001). *Action research for teachers: Traveling the yellow brick road.* Upper Saddle River, NJ: Merrill.

Kirkpatrick, D. L. (1998). *Evaluating training programs: The four levels.* San Francisco: Berrett-Koehler Publishers.

Kohli, W. R., & Burbules, N. C. (in press). *Feminism and educational research.* New York: Rowman & Littlefield.

Phillips, D.C., & Burbules, N. C. *Postpositivism and educational research.* New York: Rowman & Littlefield.

2

Quantitative, Qualitative, and Mixed Research

To be able to

- Describe the characteristics of quantitative research.
- List and explain the different types of variables used in quantitative research.
- Explain the difference between experimental and nonexperimental quantitative research.
- Explain the idea of a correlation coefficient.
- Describe the characteristics of qualitative research.
- List and explain the differences among the different types of qualitative research introduced in this chapter.
- Describe the characteristics of mixed research.
- List and explain the differences among the different types of mixed research introduced in this chapter.

This chapter is about the three major research paradigms in educational research. Each of these paradigms tends to bring a slightly different view or perspective on what we study. It seems appropriate to start this chapter with an age-old poem (written by the Persian poet/philosopher Rumi) that tells us that different perspectives can all have truth value and that when we put those perspectives together, we can come away with a fuller picture of what we are studying. We use the poem to support our view of the importance of using all three major research paradigms in educational research.

Elephant in the Dark*

Some Hindus have an elephant to show.
No one here has ever seen an elephant.
They bring it at night to a dark room.

One by one, we go in the dark and come out
saying how we experience the animal.

One of us happens to touch the trunk.
"A water-pipe kind of creature."

Another, the ear. "A very strong, always moving
back and forth, fan-animal."

Another, the leg. "I find it still,
like a column on a temple."

Another touches the curved back.
"A leathery throne."

Another, the cleverest, feels the tusk.
"A rounded sword made of porcelain."
He's proud of his description.

Each of us touches one place
and understands the whole in that way.

The palm and the fingers feeling in the dark are
how the senses explore the reality of the elephant.

If each of us held a candle there,
and if we went in together,
we could see it.

*From: Jelaluddin Rumi, *The Essential Rumi*. Trans. & Ed. by Coleman Barks. San Francisco, Castle Books. 1995. p. 252.

A **research paradigm** is a perspective based on a set of assumptions, concepts, values, and practices that are held by a community of researchers. More simply, it is an approach to thinking about and doing research. In this chapter we introduce you to the three major educational research paradigms or approaches: *quantitative research, qualitative research,* and

■ **Research paradigm**
A perspective based on a set of assumptions, concepts, and values that are held by a community of researchers

29

mixed research. Quantitative research was the generally accepted paradigm in educational research until the early 1980s, when the "paradigm wars" between advocates of quantitative and qualitative research reached a new peak (Guba, 1990; Tashakkori & Teddlie, 1998). During the 1980s, quantitative and qualitative research purists both argued that their approach was superior and that the other approach should not be used together because of differences in the worldviews or philosophies associated with the two approaches. This either-or position (i.e., one should use quantitative or qualitative research but not both) is called the **incompatibility thesis.**

Starting in the 1990s, many researchers rejected the incompatibility thesis and started advocating the pragmatic position that says that both quantitative and qualitative research are very important and often should be mixed in single research studies. According to **pragmatism,** what is important is not abstract philosophy but what works in practice. Although mixed research is still the "new kid on the block," the list of researchers advocating this approach is increasing rapidly.

The three research approaches can be viewed as falling on a research continuum with qualitative research on the left side, quantitative research on the right side, and mixed research in the center of the continuum. In other words, research may be relatively quantitative, relatively qualitative, or mixed. We start our discussion by comparing the characteristics and tenets of the three major research paradigms in their pure forms. Later in the chapter, we will introduce you to some ideas and terminology associated with each of the three research paradigms.

■ **Incompatibility thesis**
The proposition that one cannot mix quantitative and qualitative research

■ **Pragmatism**
Philosophical position that what works is what is important

**Research
Navigator.c⊕m**

pragmatism

CHARACTERISTICS OF THE THREE RESEARCH PARADIGMS

■ **Quantitative research**
Research that relies primarily on the collection of quantitative data

■ **Qualitative research**
Research that relies primarily on the collection of qualitative data

■ **Mixed research**
Research that involves the mixing of quantitative and qualitative methods or paradigm characteristics

Pure **quantitative research** relies on the collection of quantitative data (i.e., numerical data) and follows the other characteristics of the quantitative research paradigm shown in Table 2.1. Pure **qualitative research** relies on the collection of qualitative data (i.e., nonnumerical data such as words and pictures) and follows the other characteristics of the qualitative research paradigm shown in Table 2.1. **Mixed research** involves the mixing of quantitative and qualitative research methods, approaches, or paradigm characteristics. The exact mixture that is considered appropriate will depend on the research questions and the situational and practical issues facing a researcher. All three research approaches can provide insights as we attempt to solve the problems facing us in the field of education. Take a moment now to examine Table 2.1, and then read the following discussion of the key differences between the three research approaches.

First, the quantitative research approach focuses on the deductive component of the scientific method (discussed in Chapter 1) because the focus is generally on hypothesis testing and theory testing. Quantitative research is also sometimes said to be *confirmatory* because researchers test or attempt to confirm their hypotheses. On the other hand, qualitative research relies more on the inductive component of the scientific method and is used to come up with or generate new hypotheses and theories. Qualitative research is often exploratory; that is, it is often used when little is known about a certain topic or when an inductive approach is deemed more appropriate to learn more about a topic.

Most researchers probably take a mixed approach to the inductive-deductive distinction because at some point in the research process, most researchers will use both induction

■ TABLE 2.1   Emphases of Quantitative, Mixed, and Qualitative Research

	Quantitative Research	Mixed Research	Qualitative Research
Scientific method	Deductive or "top-down" The researcher tests hypotheses and theory with data	Deductive and inductive	Inductive or "bottom-up" The researcher generates new hypotheses and grounded theory from data collected during fieldwork
View of human behavior	Behavior is regular and predictable	Behavior is some-what predictable	Behavior is fluid, dynamic, situational, social, contextual, and personal
Most common research objectives	Description, explanation, and prediction	Multiple objectives	Description, exploration, and discovery
Focus	Narrow-angle lens, testing specific hypotheses	Multilens focus	Wide-angle and "deep-angle" lens, examining the breadth and depth of phenomena to learn more about them
Nature of observation	Attempt to study behavior under controlled conditions	Study behavior in more than one context or condition	Study behavior in natural environments Study the context in which behavior occurs
Nature of reality	Objective (different observers agree on what is observed)	Commonsense realism and prag-matic view of world (i.e., what works is what is "real" or true)	Subjective, personal, and socially constructed
Form of data collected	Collect quantitative data based on precise measurement using structured and validated data collection instruments (e.g., closed-ended items, rating scales, behavioral responses)	Multiple forms	Collect qualitative data (e.g., in-depth interviews, participant observation, field notes, and open-ended questions) The researcher is the primary data collection instrument
Nature of data	Variables	Mixture of variables, words, and images	Words, images, categories
Data analysis	Identify statistical relationships	Quantitative and qualitative	Search for patterns, themes, and holistic features
Results	Generalizable findings	Corroborated findings may generalize	Particularistic findings Representation of insider (i.e., "emic") viewpoint Present multiple perspectives
Form of final report	Statistical report (e.g., with correlations, comparisons of means, and reporting of statis-tical significance of findings)	Eclectic and pragmatic	Narrative report with contextual description and direct quotations from research participants

and deduction. As the research wheel in Chapter 1 showed (see Figure 1.1), scientific reasoning is a cyclical process of induction and deduction. In quantitative research, hypotheses are typically deduced from a theory or currently available explanations, and the predicted observable outcomes are deduced from the hypotheses. Data are then collected to determine whether the hypotheses, and as a result the theory or explanation, are supported. However, it is common for unanticipated outcomes to appear in quantitative research findings. When this happens, quantitative researchers commonly enter the inductive mode of generating new or revised hypotheses and explanations, which will be put to the test during a future research study. Likewise, in qualitative research, after inductive hypotheses and a tentative theory have been generated from initial observations, the observable consequences of these are often deduced and then tested through additional observations. In short, stating that quantitative researchers follow the deductive method and qualitative researchers follow the inductive method is really a matter of emphasis, not exclusion. Mixed researchers explicitly state that they use both induction and deduction.

Quantitative and qualitative research are also distinguished by different views of human behavior. It is generally assumed in quantitative research that behavior is highly predictable. The assumption of **determinism** was traditionally made, which means that all events have a cause (Salmon, 1984). For example, the process by which children learn to read is determined by one or more causes. Likewise, there are causes for adolescents dropping out of school. Because quantitative research has not identified any unerring laws of human behavior, most contemporary quantitative researchers search for **probabilistic causes** (Humphreys, 1989). A probabilistic statement might go like this: "Adolescents who become involved with drugs and alcohol are more likely to drop out of high school than are adolescents who do not become involved with drugs and alcohol." The point is that most quantitative researchers try to identify cause-and-effect relationships that enable them to make probabilistic predictions and generalizations. On the other hand, qualitative researchers often focus on the fluid and dynamic dimensions of behavior. Behavior is seen to be more situational and context bound than generalizable. Different groups are said to construct different realities or perspectives, and the focus is on how patterns of behavior vary from group to group and from situation to situation.

These views about human behavior are not set in stone, however. For example, when taking a mixed mode approach, quantitative researchers might study the influence of context and the dynamic processes of behavior (e.g., social psychologists examine individuals as they interact and change their behaviors in social situations). Quantitative research also focuses on how results vary according to the characteristics of the participants (e.g., see the discussion of *moderator variables* later in this chapter). Similarly, when taking a mixed mode approach, qualitative researchers often try to develop explanations of behavior (theories) that sometimes include causal language, and they attempt to make generalizations. In short, many researchers, including researchers who predominantly operate in either the quantitative or the qualitative mode, cross over into the mixed research mode.

Quantitative research often uses a narrow-angle lens in the sense that only one or a few factors are studied at the same time. Often, through experimental control, researchers attempt to hold constant the factors that are not being studied. This is often accomplished under laboratory conditions, in which an experimenter randomly assigns participants to groups, manipulates only one factor, and then examines the outcome. For example, a re-

■ **Determinism**
All events have causes

■ **Probabilistic causes**
Causes that usually produce an outcome

searcher might first randomly assign research volunteers to two groups. Random assignment helps to achieve experimental control because it makes the two groups similar. Then the researcher might expose one group to a new teaching method and use the traditional lecture method on the other group. The researcher examines which teaching approach results in the most learning and attributes the difference to the teaching method received. The researcher is able to make a causal attribution because the two groups were similar at the start of the experiment and the only factor they differed on was which teaching method they received.

On the other hand, qualitative research uses a wide- and deep-angle lens, examining behavior as it occurs naturalistically in all of its detail. Qualitative researchers do not want to intervene in the natural flow of behavior because they believe that this intervention would change the behavior. Qualitative researchers study behavior holistically. They try to look at many dimensions and layers of behavior, such as the types of people in a group, how they interact, what kinds of agreements or norms they have, and how these dimensions come together to describe the group. For example, perhaps a qualitative researcher wants to study the social climate and culture of a highly successful school. The researcher would probably spend a great deal of time studying the many aspects and dimensions of the school to come up with an analysis of how the school operates and why it is successful. Depending on the research questions, a researcher who was using the mixed approach might spend part of his or her time in each of the different focus modes (including wide-, narrow-, and deep-angle focus).

Quantitative researchers attempt to operate under the assumption of objectivity. They assume that there is an external reality "out there" to be observed and that rational observers who look at the same phenomenon in the world will basically agree on its existence and its characteristics. They also try to remain as value-free as they can, and they attempt to avoid human bias whenever possible. In a sense, quantitative researchers attempt to study the phenomena that are of interest to them "from a distance." For example, standardized questionnaires and other quantitative measuring tools are often used to measure carefully what is observed. In experiments, researchers frequently use a random process to assign participants to different groups to eliminate the possibility of human bias while constructing different groups for comparison. In judging results, statistical criteria are often used to form conclusions.

Qualitative researchers often contend that "reality is socially constructed" (e.g., Guba & Lincoln, 1989). An example of this viewpoint is the common belief that Eskimos see many types of snow, whereas the average American or European will probably only see a few types. The Eskimos' experiences might allow them to see distinctions that you do not see. In terms of the importance of remaining objective during the collection of data, many qualitative researchers would agree with the quantitative researchers, but at the same time they also want to "get close" to their objects of study through participant observation so that they can experience for themselves the subjective dimensions of the phenomena they study. In qualitative research, the researcher is the instrument of data collection. Rather than using a standardized instrument or measuring device, the qualitative researcher must collect the data, ask the questions, and make the interpretations about what is observed. In addition, the researcher must try to understand the people he or she is observing from their viewpoint. This is the concept of "empathetic understanding" (what the famous sociologist Max Weber, writing in the early twentieth century, called *verstehen*): understanding something from that person's viewpoint (Weber, 1968). This is similar to the familiar idea of putting yourself into someone else's shoes.

According to mixed method research, it is important to understand both the subjective and objective realities in the world. Although it is important not to influence or bias what you are observing, it is also important to get the insider's viewpoint. For example, if you were studying the culture of the snake-handling churches in the area where Alabama, Tennessee, and Georgia come together, it might be helpful to collect quantitative data by having the people fill out standardized instruments measuring their personality and demographic characteristics. It would also be helpful to collect qualitative data through in-depth personal interviews and observations of the members to gain a better understanding (from the insiders' perspectives) of the snake-handling culture. In short, the mixing of methods would add very useful and complementary information.

Quantitative research generally reduces measurement to numbers. In survey research, for example, attitudes are usually measured by using rating scales. The following five-point agreement scale is an example: (1) Strongly Disagree, (2) Disagree, (3) Neutral, (4) Agree, (5) Strongly Agree. The interviewer makes a statement, and the respondents reply with one of the five allowable response categories. After all respondents have been asked a question, the researcher typically calculates and reports an average for the group of respondents. Let us say, for example, that a researcher asks a group of teachers for their degree of agreement with the following statement: "Teachers need more training in the area of child psychopathology." The researcher might then calculate the average response for the whole group, which might be 4.15 based on a five-point scale. The researcher might also determine whether the ratings vary by years of teaching experience. Perhaps the average agreement for new teachers is 4.5 and the average for teachers with five or more years of experience is 3.9. As you might guess, quantitative data are usually analyzed by using statistical analysis programs on a computer.

On the other hand, qualitative researchers do not usually collect data in the form of numbers. Rather, they frequently conduct observations and in-depth interviews, and the data are usually in the form of words. For example, a qualitative researcher might conduct a focus group discussion with six or seven new teachers to discuss the adequacy of their undergraduate educational programs in preparing them to deal with real-world problems that they face in schools. The facilitator of the focus group would probably videotape the group and tape-record what was said. Later, the recording would be transcribed into words, which would then be analyzed by using the techniques of qualitative data analysis (see Chapter 17). Also, when a qualitative researcher enters the field and makes observations, the researcher will write down what he or she sees as well as relevant insights and thoughts. The data are again in the form of words. During qualitative data analysis, the researcher will try to identify categories that describe what happened as well as general themes appearing again and again in the data. The mixed research approach would use a variety of data collection and analysis approaches.

Finally, qualitative, mixed, and quantitative research reports tend to differ. Quantitative reports are commonly reported in journal articles ranging from five to fifteen pages. The reports will include many numbers and results of statistical significance testing (to be explained later). In contrast, qualitative research reports are generally longer, and they are written in narrative form, describing what was found and including interpretations to make sense out of it. Qualitative journal articles are frequently twenty to thirty pages long, and the results of qualitative research are often published in the form of books or monographs rather than journal articles. Mixed research might follow the quantitative style or the qualitative style or, more frequently, might use a mixture of the styles.

2.1 Describe the key features of quantitative and qualitative research.
2.2 Describe the key features of mixed method research.

R E V I E W

Q U E S T I O N S

QUANTITATIVE RESEARCH METHODS:
EXPERIMENTAL AND NONEXPERIMENTAL RESEARCH

You now know some of the characteristics of quantitative and qualitative research. Now we introduce some of the different methods of quantitative research. Before we do so, however, you need to know about variables because quantitative researchers usually describe the world by using variables, and they attempt to explain and predict aspects of the world by demonstrating the relationships among variables. You can see a summary of the types of variables in Table 2.2.

Research
Navigator.com

quantitative research

Variables

A **variable** is a condition or characteristic that can take on different values or categories. A much-studied educational variable is intelligence, which varies from low to high for different people. Age is another variable that varies from low to high (e.g., from 1 minute old to 130 years old or so). Another variable is gender, which is either male or female. To better understand the concept of a variable, it is helpful to compare it with a constant, its opposite. A **constant** is a single value or category of a variable. Here's the idea: The variable *gender* is a marker for two constants: male and female. The category (i.e., constant) *male* is a marker for only one thing; it is one of the two constants forming the variable called gender. Gender varies, but *male* does not vary. Therefore, *gender* is a variable, and *male* is a constant. In the case of the variable *age,* all of the ages make up the values (i.e., constants) of the variable, and each value (e.g., twelve years old or thirteen years old) is a constant. If you are still having a hard time with the distinction between a variable and a constant, think of it like this: A variable is like a set of things, and a constant is *one* of those things.

The variables that we just used, age and gender, are actually different types of variables. Age is an example of a quantitative variable, and gender is an example of a categorical variable. A **quantitative variable** is a variable that varies in degree or amount. It usually involves numbers. A **categorical variable** is a variable that varies in type or kind. It usually involves different groups. As described in the previous paragraph, age takes on numbers (e.g., number of years old), and gender takes on two types or kinds (male and female). Now consider the variable *annual income.* How does it vary? It varies in amount, ranging from no

■ **Variable**
A condition or characteristic that can take on different values or categories

■ **Constant**
A single value or category of a variable

■ **Quantitative variable**
A variable that varies in degree or amount
■ **Categorical variable**
A variable that varies in type or kind

■ **T A B L E 2 . 2** Common Types of Variables Classified by Level of Measurement and by Role of Variable

Variable Type	Key Characteristic	Example
Level of Measurement		
Categorical variable	A variable that is made up of different types or categories of a phenomenon	The variable *gender* is made up of the categories of male and female.
Quantitative variable	A variable that varies in degree or amount of a phenomenon	The variable *annual income* varies from zero income to a very high income level.
Role Taken by the Variable		
Independent variable (symbolized as IV)	A variable that is presumed to cause changes to occur in another variable, a causal variable	Amount of studying (IV) affects test grades (DV).
Dependent variable (symbolized as DV)	A variable that changes because of another variable, the effect or outcome variable	Amount of studying (IV) affects test grades (DV).
Mediating variable (It is also called an intervening variable)	A variable that comes in between other variables, helps to delineate the process through which variables affect one another	Amount of studying (IV) leads to input and organization of knowledge in long-term memory (mediating variable), which affects test grades (DV).
Moderator variable	A variable that delineates how a relationship of interest changes under different conditions or circumstances	Perhaps the relationship between studying (IV) and test grades (DV) changes according to the different levels of use of a drug such as Ritalin (moderator).

income at all to some very large amount of income. Therefore, income is a quantitative variable. If you think about how much money you made last year, you can determine your value on the variable *annual income*. Now think about the variable *religion*. How does this variable vary? It varies in kind or type. It can take on any of the categories standing for the different world religions (e.g., Christianity, Judaism, Islam). If you need a little more practice identifying quantitative and categorical variables, take a look at the examples in Table 2.3.

Yet another categorization scheme for variables is to speak of independent and dependent variables. An **independent variable** is a variable that is presumed to cause a change in another variable. Sometimes the independent variable is manipulated by the researcher (i.e., the researcher determines the value of the independent variable); at other times, the inde-

■ **Independent variable**
A variable that is presumed to cause a change in another variable

■ **TABLE 2.3**   Examples of Quantitative and Categorical Variables

Quantitative Variables	Categorical Variables
Height	Gender
Weight	Religion
Temperature	Ethnicity
Annual income	Method of therapy
Most aptitude tests	College major
Most achievement tests	Political party identification
School size	Type of school
Class size	Marital status of parents
Self-esteem level	Student retention (retained or not)
Grade point average	Type of teacher expectation
Teacher-pupil ratio	Native language
Time spent on homework	Teaching method
Age	Personality type
Anxiety level	Learning style
Job satisfaction score	Type of feedback
Number of behavioral outbursts	Computer use (or not)
Reading performance	Type of reading instruction
Spelling accuracy	Inclusion (or not)
Number of performance errors	Problem solving strategy used
Rate of cognitive processing	Memory strategy used
Dropout rate	Social class

pendent variable is studied by the researcher but is not directly manipulated (i.e., the researcher studies what happens when an independent variable changes naturally). The independent variable is an antecedent variable because it must come before another variable if it is to produce a change in it. A **dependent variable** is the variable that is presumed to be influenced by one or more independent variables. The dependent variable is the variable that is "dependent on" the independent (i.e., antecedent) variable(s). A **cause-and-effect relationship** between an independent variable and a dependent variable is present when changes in the independent variable tend to cause changes in the dependent variable. Sometimes researchers call the dependent variable an *outcome variable* or a *response variable* because it is used to measure the effect of one or more independent variables.

Here is a simple example of a cause-and-effect relationship. Think about the U.S. Surgeon General's warning printed on cigarette packages: "Smoking Causes Lung Cancer, Heart Disease, Emphysema, and May Complicate Pregnancy." Can you identify the independent and dependent variables in this relationship? It is smoking that is presumed to cause

Research
Navigator.c⊕m

causality

■ **Dependent variable**
   A variable that is presumed to be influenced by one or more independent variables

■ **Cause-and-effect relationship**
   Relationship in which one variable affects another variable

lung cancer and several other diseases. (You should be aware that extensive research beyond simply observing that smoking and lung cancer were associated was conducted to establish that the link between smoking and cancer was causal.) In this example, *smoking* is the independent variable (the values corresponding to the number of cigarettes smoked a day) and *presence of lung cancer* is the dependent variable (the values being *lung cancer present* and *lung cancer not present*).

For shorthand, we could use *IV* to stand for independent variable and *DV* to stand for dependent variable. We also sometimes use an arrow: IV → DV. The arrow (→) means "tends to cause changes in" or "affects." In words, this says that the researcher believes "changes in the independent variable tend to cause changes in the dependent variable." In the smoking example, we write Smoking → Onset of Lung Cancer.

- **Intervening variable**
  A variable that occurs between two other variables; it's a mediating variable

Another type of variable is an **intervening variable** (also commonly called a *mediating* or *mediator variable*). An intervening or mediating variable occurs between two other variables in a causal chain (Kenny, Kashy, & Bolger, 1998). In the case X → Y, we have only an independent variable and a dependent variable. In the case X → I → Y, we have an intervening variable (I) occurring between the two other variables. In the case of smoking, perhaps an intervening variable is the development of damaged lung cells. In other words, smoking tends to lead to the development of damaged lung cells, which tends to lead to lung cancer. It is helpful to identify intervening variables because these variables may help explain the process by which an independent variable leads to changes in a dependent variable.

Research
Navigator.c⊛m

mediating variable

moderator variable

As another example, let X stand for teaching approach (perhaps the levels of this variable are lecture method and cooperative group method), and let Y stand for test score on class exam (varying from 0 to 100 percent correct). Research may show that X → Y; that is, test scores depend on which teaching approach is used. In this case, an intervening variable might be student motivation (varying from low motivation to high motivation). Therefore, the full causal chain is X → I → Y, where X is teaching approach, I is student motivation, and Y is students' test scores; that is, teaching method → student motivation → student test scores.

- **Moderator variable**
  A variable that changes the relationship between other variables

The next type of variable is a moderator variable. A **moderator variable** is a variable that changes (i.e., moderates) the relationship between other variables. It's a variable that delineates how a relationship changes under different conditions or contexts or for different kinds of people. For example, you might analyze a set of research data and find that there is little or no difference between the performance scores of students who are taught by using the lecture approach and the students who are taught by using the cooperative learning approach. On further analysis, however, you might learn that cooperative learning works better for extraverted students and that lecture works better for introverted students. In this example, personality type is a moderator variable: The relationship between teaching approach and performance scores depends on the personality type of the student. One thing we commonly find in research on teaching is that what works well depends on the type of student. As you can see, it is helpful to know the important moderator variables so that you can adjust your teaching accordingly.

Experimental Research

The purpose of experimental research is to determine cause-and-effect relationships. The experimental research method enables us to identify causal relationships because it allows us to observe, under controlled conditions, the effects of systematically changing one or more variables. Specifically, in **experimental research,** the researcher manipulates the independent variable, actively intervening in the world, and then observes what happened. Thus, **manipulation,** an intervention studied by an experimenter, is the key defining characteristic of experimental research. The use of manipulation in studying cause-and-effect relationships is based on the activity theory of causation (Collingwood, 1940; Cook & Shadish, 1994). Active manipulation is not involved in any other type of research. Because of this (and because of experimental control), experimental research provides the strongest evidence of all the research methods about the existence of cause-and-effect relationships.

In a simple experiment, a researcher will systematically vary an independent variable and assess its effects on a dependent variable. For example, perhaps an educational researcher wants to determine the effect of a new teaching approach on reading achievement. The researcher could perform the new teaching approach with one group of participants and perform the traditional teaching approach with another group of participants. After the treatment, the experimenter would determine which group showed the greater amount of learning (reading achievement). If the group receiving the new teaching approach showed the greater gain, then the researcher would tentatively conclude that the new approach is better than the traditional approach.

Although the type of experiment just described is sometimes done, there is a potential problem with it. What if the two groups of students differed on variables such as vocabulary, reading ability, and/or age? More specifically, what if the students in the new teaching approach group happened to be older, had better vocabularies, and were better readers than the students in the traditional teaching approach group? Furthermore, suppose the students with better vocabularies, who were older, and who were better readers also tended to learn more quickly than other students. If this were the case, then it is likely that the students in the new teaching approach group would have learned faster regardless of the teaching approach. In this example, the variables *age, vocabulary,* and *reading ability* are called extraneous variables. **Extraneous variables** are variables other than the independent variable of interest (e.g., teaching approach) that may be related to the outcome. When extraneous variables are not controlled for or dealt with in some way, an outside reviewer of the research study may come up with competing explanations for the research findings. The reviewer might argue that the outcome is due to a particular extraneous variable rather than to the independent variable. These competing explanations for the relationship between an independent and a dependent variable are sometimes called *alternative explanations* or *rival hypotheses.* In our example, the researcher cannot know whether the students in the new teaching approach performed better because of the teaching approach or because they had better vocabularies, were older, or were better readers. All these factors are said to be *confounded;* that is, these factors are entangled with the independent variable, and the researcher can't state with any degree of confidence which is the most important factor. Sometimes we use the term **confounding variables** to refer to extraneous variables that were not controlled for by the researcher and could be the reason a particular result occurred.

Because the presence of extraneous variables makes the interpretation of research findings very difficult, the effective researcher attempts to control them whenever possible. The best way to control for extraneous variables in an experiment like the one above is to randomly assign research participants to the groups to be compared; that is, random assignment

■ **Experimental research**
Research in which the researcher manipulates the independent variable

■ **Manipulation**
An intervention studied by an experimenter

■ **Extraneous variable**
A variable that may compete with the independent variable in explaining the outcome

■ **Confounding variable**
A type of extraneous variable that was not controlled for and is the reason a particular "confounded" result is observed

is the most effective technique of experimental control. Random assignment helps to ensure that the people in the groups to be compared are similar before the intervention or manipulation. For example, if the researcher wants to randomly assign thirty people to two groups, then the researcher might put thirty slips of paper, each with one name on it, into a hat and randomly pull out fifteen pieces. The fifteen names that are pulled out will become one of the two groups, and the fifteen names remaining in the hat will become the other group. When this is done, the only differences between the groups will be due to chance. In other words, the people in the groups will be *similar* at the start of the experiment. After making the groups similar, the researcher administers the levels of the independent variable, making the groups different only on this variable. Perhaps teaching method is the independent variable, and the levels are cooperative learning and lecture. The administration of the independent variable, or manipulation, would involve exposing one group to cooperative learning and the other group to lecture. Then if the two groups become different after the manipulation, the researcher will know that the difference was due to the independent variable. In summary, (1) the experimenter uses random assignment to make the groups similar; (2) the experimenter does something different with the groups; and (3) if the groups then become different, the experimenter concludes that the difference was due to what the experimenter did (i.e., it was due to the independent variable). In later chapters, we will introduce you to additional methods that are used to control for extraneous variables when you are not able to use random assignment. For now, remember that random assignment to groups is the most effective way to make the groups similar and therefore control for extraneous variables.

Nonexperimental Research

- **Nonexperimental research**
Research in which random assignment to groups is not possible and there is no manipulation of an independent variable by the researcher

In **nonexperimental research,** random assignment to groups is not possible, and there is no manipulation of an independent variable by the researcher. As a result, evidence gathered in support of cause-and-effect relationships is severely limited. Nonetheless, when important questions need to be answered, research must still be conducted, even if an experiment cannot be done. It is important to remember this cardinal rule: Your research question should determine what you study, not your preference for a particular research method. Tashakkori and Teddlie (1998) emphasize the dominant role of the research question with the phrase "the dictatorship of the research question." For example, during the 1960s, extensive research linking cigarette smoking to lung cancer was conducted. Experimental research with humans was not possible because it would have been unethical. Therefore, in addition to experimental research with laboratory animals, medical researchers relied on nonexperimental research methods for their extensive research with humans.

- **Causal-comparative research**
A form of nonexperimental research in which the primary independent variable of interest is a categorical variable

One type of nonexperimental research is sometimes called *causal-comparative research.* Typically, in **causal-comparative research,** the researcher studies the relationship between one or more categorical independent variables and one or more quantitative dependent variables. In the most basic case, there is a single categorical independent variable and a single quantitative dependent variable. Because the independent variable is categorical in causal-comparative research (e.g., males versus females, parents versus nonparents, or public school teachers versus private school teachers), the different groups' average scores on a dependent variable are compared to determine whether a relationship is present between the independent and dependent variables. For example, if the independent variable is *student* *retention* (and the categories of the variable are *retained in the first grade* and *not retained in the first grade*) and the dependent variable is *level of achievement,* then the retained students' average achievement would be compared to the nonretained students' average achievement. (Which group do you think would have higher achievements on average: the retained or the nonretained students?)

Despite the presence of the word *causal* included in the term *causal-comparative research,* keep in mind that causal-comparative research is a nonexperimental research method, which means that there is no manipulation of an independent variable by a researcher. Furthermore, techniques of controlling for extraneous variables are more limited than in experimental research (in which random assignment may be possible). Because of the lack of manipulation and weaker techniques of controlling for extraneous variables, it is difficult to make statements about cause and effect. In short, do not be misled by the word *causal* in the name of this type of research, and remember that well-designed experimental research is virtually always better for determining cause and effect than is causal-comparative research or any other type of nonexperimental research.

An example of causal-comparative research is a study entitled "Gender Differences in Mathematics Achievement and Other Variables among University Students" (Rech, 1996). Rech compared the average performance levels of males with the average performance levels of females in intermediate algebra and college algebra courses at a large urban commuter university. In the intermediate algebra course, Rech found that females did slightly better than males. The average percentage correct for females was 75 percent, and the average percentage correct for males was 73.8 percent. In the college algebra course, the difference in female and male performance was even smaller (74.3 percent versus 73.9 percent). The data were collected from more than 2,300 research participants over six semesters.

It was mentioned earlier that the basic case of causal-comparative research involves a single categorical independent variable and a single quantitative dependent variable. To design a basic causal-comparative study as an exercise, look at Table 2.3 and find a categorical variable that can serve as your independent variable (i.e., one that you would not manipulate) and a quantitative variable that can be your dependent variable. As an example, we can select *retention* as the independent variable and *self-esteem* as a dependent variable. We hypothesize that student retention (retained versus nonretained) has an influence on self-esteem. More specifically, we predict that, on average, retained students will have lower self-esteem than nonretained students. We would have to go to a school and collect data if we actually wanted to conduct a research study to see whether there is any support for this hypothesis.

Another nonexperimental research method is called correlational research. As in causal-comparative research, there is no manipulation of an independent variable in correlational research. In **correlational research,** the researcher studies the relationship between one or more quantitative independent variables and one or more quantitative dependent variables; that is, in correlational research, the independent and dependent variables are quantitative. In this chapter, we will discuss the basic case in which the researcher has a quantitative independent variable and a quantitative dependent variable. To understand how to study the relationship between two variables when both variables are quantitative, you need a basic understanding of a correlation coefficient.

A **correlation coefficient** is an index that provides information about the strength and direction of the relationship between two variables. It provides information about how two

- **Correlational research**
  A form of nonexperimental research in which the primary independent variable of interest is a quantitative variable
- **Correlation coefficient**
  An index that indicates the strength and direction of the relationship between two variables

variables are associated. More specifically, a correlation coefficient is a number that can range from –1 to 1, with zero standing for no correlation at all. If the number is greater than zero, there is a positive correlation. If the number is less than zero, there is a negative correlation. If the number is equal to zero, then there is no correlation between the two variables being correlated. If the number is equal to +1.00 or equal to –1.00, the correlation is called perfect; that is, it is as strong as possible. Now we provide an explanation of these points.

■ **Positive correlation**
The situation when scores on two variables tend to move in the same direction

A **positive correlation** is present when scores on two variables tend to move in the same direction. For example, consider the variables high school GPA and SAT (the college entrance exam). How do you think scores on these two variables are related? A diagram of this relationship is shown in Figure 2.1(a). As you can see in Figure 2.1(a), the students who have high GPAs tend also to have high scores on the SAT, and students who have low GPAs tend to have low scores on the SAT. That's the relationship. We say that GPA and SAT are positively correlated because as SAT scores increase, GPAs also tend to increase (i.e., the variables move in the same direction). Because of this relationship, researchers can use SAT scores to help make predictions about GPAs. However, because the correlation is not perfect, the prediction is also far from perfect.

■ **Negative correlation**
The situation when scores on two variables tend to move in opposite directions

A **negative correlation** is present when the scores on two variables tend to move in opposite directions. For example, consider the variables amount of daily cholesterol consumption and life expectancy. How do you think these variables are related? Do you think the relationship meets the definition of a negative correlation? A diagram of this relationship is shown in Figure 2.1(b). You can see that as daily cholesterol consumption increases, life expectancy tends to decrease. That is, the variables move in opposite directions. As one variable goes up, the other tends to go down and vice versa. Therefore, researchers can use information about cholesterol consumption to help predict life expectancies. High values

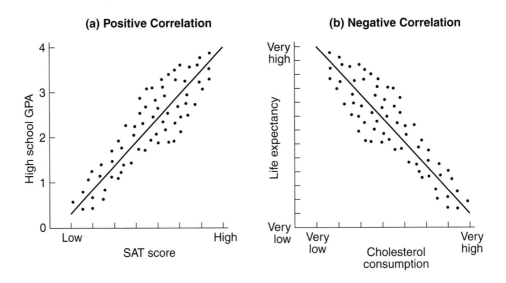

■ **FIGURE 2.1**   Examples of positive and negative correlation

on one variable are associated with low values on the other variable and vice versa. This is what we mean by a negative correlation.

At this point, you know the difference between a positive correlation (the variables move in the same direction) and a negative correlation (the variables move in opposite directions). There is, however, one more point about a correlation coefficient that you need to know. In addition to the direction of a correlation (positive or negative), we are interested in the strength of the correlation. By *strength,* we mean "How strong is the relationship?" Remember this point: Zero means no relationship at all, and +1.00 and −1.00 mean that the relationship is as strong as possible.

The higher the number, ignoring the sign if it is negative, the stronger is the relationship. For example, if you have a correlation of −.5, then ignore the negative sign and you have .5, which shows the strength of the correlation. Therefore, a correlation of −.5 and a correlation of +.5 have the same strength. The only difference between the two is the direction of the relationship (−.5 is a negative correlation, and +.5 is a positive correlation). When you are interested in its strength, it does not matter whether a correlation is positive or negative. The strength of a correlation operates like this: Zero stands for no correlation at all (i.e., it is the smallest possible strength), and +1.00 and −1.00 are as strong as a correlation can ever be. That is, +1.00 and −1.00 are equally strong; in research jargon, we say that both +1.00 and −1.00 are *perfect correlations.* The only difference between +1.00 and −1.00 is the direction of the relationship, not the strength. You can see some diagrams of correlations of different strengths and directions in Figure 2.2.

If you found the previous paragraph a little hard to take, here is a different way to determine how strong a correlation is. Simply check to see how far away the number is from zero. The farther the number is from zero, the stronger is the correlation. A correlation of .9 is stronger than a correlation of .2 because it is farther from zero. Likewise, a correlation of −.9 is stronger than a correlation of −.2 because it too is farther from zero. Now for a trick question. Which correlation do you believe is stronger: −.90 or +.80? The answer is −.90 because −.90 is farther from zero than +.80. (I think you've got it!)

This is only a brief introduction to the idea of a correlation coefficient. You will become more comfortable with the concept the more you use it, and we will be using the concept often in later chapters. For now, you should clearly understand that you can have positive and negative correlations or no correlation at all and that some correlations are stronger than other correlations. You have learned more already than you thought you would, haven't you?

In the most basic form of correlational research, the researcher examines the correlation between two quantitative variables. For example, perhaps an educational psychologist has a theory stating that global self-esteem (which is a relatively stable personality trait) should predict class performance. More specifically, the educational psychologist predicts that students entering a particular history class with high self-esteem will tend to do better than students entering the class with low self-esteem and vice versa. To test this hypothesis, the researcher could collect the relevant data and calculate the correlation between self-esteem and performance on the class examinations. We would expect a positive correlation (i.e., the higher the self-esteem, the higher is the performance on the history exam). In our hypothetical example, let's say that the correlation was +.5. That is a medium-size positive correlation, and it would support our hypothesis of a positive correlation.

(a) Perfect Correlations

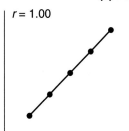

$r = 1.00$

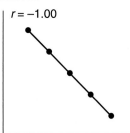

$r = -1.00$

(b) Large or Strong Correlations

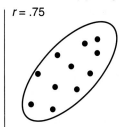

$r = .75$

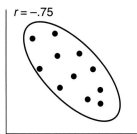

$r = -.75$

(c) Small or Weak Correlations

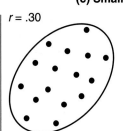

$r = .30$

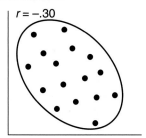

$r = -.30$

(d) No Correlation

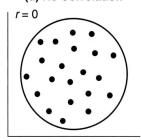

$r = 0$

FIGURE 2.2   Correlations of different strengths and directions

The researcher would be able to say virtually nothing about cause and effect based on the correlation of .5 in our example of self-esteem and class performance. About all that one can claim is that there is a relationship between self-esteem and class performance: The higher the self-esteem, the better is the class performance. This is the same problem that we experienced in the basic case of causal-comparative research, in which there is one independent variable and one dependent variable. In short, there are three main problems with the basic cases of correlational and causal-comparative research described in this chapter:

1. There is no manipulation of the independent variable by the researcher.
2. It is difficult to determine the temporal order of the variables (i.e., which variable occurs first).
3. There are usually too many other reasons why we might observe the relationship; that is, there are usually too many extraneous variables that are unexplained.

Remember this important point: You must not jump to a conclusion about cause and effect in a nonexperimental research study in which the researcher has examined only the relationship between two variables, such as examining a correlation coefficient in correlational research or comparing two group means in causal-comparative research. Simply finding a relationship between self-esteem and class performance (correlational research) or between gender and class performance (causal-comparative research) is not sufficient evidence for concluding that the relationship is causal. Therefore, you must not jump to that conclusion. We will discuss the issue of cause and effect more in later chapters. We will also show how you can obtain some evidence of cause and effect using nonexperimental research by improving on the basic cases discussed in this chapter. For now, make sure you remember that experimental research with random assignment is the single best method for determining cause-and-effect relationships and that nonexperimental research methods are much weaker.

2.3 What is the difference between a categorical variable and a quantitative variable? Think of an example of each.

2.4 Why is experimental research more effective than nonexperimental research when a researcher is interested in studying cause and effect?

2.5 What are the three main problems with the simple cases of causal-comparative and correlational research?

2.6 What are two variables that you believe are positively correlated?

2.7 What are two variables that you believe are negatively correlated?

REVIEW
QUESTIONS

QUALITATIVE RESEARCH METHODS

As you saw in Table 2.1, qualitative research is based on qualitative data and tends to follow the inductive mode of the scientific method. In this book, we will be discussing five types of qualitative research: phenomenology, ethnography, case study, grounded theory, and historical research. Chapters 12 and 13 provide detailed discussions of these five kinds of

Research
Navigator.com

qualitative
research

research. We only introduce you to the key ideas of each of these research methods now to foreshadow our later, in-depth discussions of these methods.

Phenomenology

- **Phenomenology**
  A form of qualitative research in which the researcher attempts to understand how one or more individuals experience a phenomenon

The first major type of qualitative research is **phenomenology.** When conducting a phenomenological research study, a researcher attempts to understand how one or more individuals experience a phenomenon. For example, you might conduct a phenomenological study of elementary school students who have lost a parent to better understand how schoolchildren experience bereavement. The key element of a phenomenological research study is that the researcher attempts to understand how people experience a phenomenon from the person's own perspectives. Your goal is to enter the inner world of each participant to understand his or her perspectives and experiences. Phenomenological researchers have studied many phenomena, such as what it is like to participate in a religious group that handles serpents as part of the worship service (Williamson & Pollio, 1999), the experience of grief (Bailley, Dunham, & Kral, 2000), the experience of learning to become a music teacher (Devries, 2000), the experience of living with alcoholism (Smith, 1998), the meaning of age for young and old adults (Adams-Price, Henley, & Hale, 1998), and elementary school children's experiences of stress (Omizo & Omizo, 1990).

Ethnography

- **Ethnography**
  A form of qualitative research focused on describing the culture of a group of people
- **Culture**
  The shared attitudes, values, norms, practices, patterns of interaction, perspectives, and language of a group of people
- **Holistic description**
  The description of how members of a group interact and how they come together to make up the group as a whole

Ethnography is one of the most popular approaches to qualitative research in education. The word **ethnography** literally means "writing about people." When ethnographers conduct research, they are interested in describing the **culture** of a group of people and learning what it is like to be a member of the group from the perspective of the members of that group. That is, they are interested in documenting things like the shared attitudes, values, norms, practices, patterns of interaction, perspectives, and language of a group of people. They may also be interested in the material things that the group members produce or use, such as clothing styles, ethnic foods, and architectural styles. Ethnographers try to use **holistic descriptions;** that is, they try to describe how the members of a group interact and how they come together to make up the group as a whole. In other words, the group is more than just the sum of its parts. Just a few of the many groups that ethnographers have studied recently are a group of panhandlers living on the streets of Washington, D.C. (Lankenau, 1999), men with mental retardation living in a group home (Croft, 1999), black and white sorority members (Berkowitz & Padavic, 1999), students in a U.S. history class (Keedy, Fleming, Wheat, & Gentry, 1998), sixth-grade students in science classes (Solot & Arluke, 1997), karaoke bar performers (Drew, 1997), Puerto Rican American parents with children in special education (Harry, 1992), and a group of Native American students who had dropped out of school (Deyhle, 1992). In all of these studies, the researchers were interested in describing some aspect of the culture of the people in the study.

Case Study Research

- **Case study research**
  A form of qualitative research that is focused on providing a detailed account of one or more cases

In **case study research,** the researcher provides a detailed account of one or more cases. Although case study research usually relies on qualitative data, multiple methods are also used. Case study research can be used to address exploratory, descriptive, and explanatory research questions (Stake, 1995; Yin, 1994). Unlike phenomenology, which focuses on individuals' experience of some phenomenon, or ethnography, which focuses on some aspect of culture, or grounded theory, which focuses on developing an explanatory theory, case study research is more varied. What all pure case studies do have in common, however, is a focus on each case as a whole unit (i.e., case study research is holistic) as it exists in its real-life context. For example, in "Building Learning Organizations in Engineering Cultures," Ford and Voyer (2000) examined how a specific organization changed over time into a learning organization. Although their focus was on a single case, other organizations might be able to learn from Ford and Voyer's experiences. In "The Journey through College of Seven Gifted Females: Influences on their Related Career Decisions," Dale (2000) examined in detail the personal, social, and academic experiences of seven people. After analyzing each case, Dale made cross-case comparisons, searching for similarities and differences.

Grounded Theory

Grounded theory research is a qualitative approach to generating and developing a theory from the data you collect in a research study. You will recall from Chapter 1 that a theory is an explanation of how and why something operates. We will explain the details of grounded theory in Chapter 12; for now, remember that grounded theory is an inductive approach for generating theories or explanations. One example of a grounded theory is found in "An Analysis of Factors that Contribute to Parent-School Conflict in Special Education" by Lake and Billingsley (2000). Lake and Billingsley wanted to explain why conflict takes place between the parents of children in special education programs and school officials. Lake and Billingsley conducted in-depth interviews (lasting an average of one hour) with parents, principals, special education program directors, and mediators. They identified several factors as contributing to the escalation of parent-school conflict. The primary or core factor was a discrepancy in views about the child's needs. The other factors were lack of knowledge (e.g., lack of problem solving knowledge), disagreements over service delivery, the presence of constraints (e.g., such as the lack of funds to deliver services), differences in how a child is valued, unilateral use of power, poor communication, and lack of trust. In addition to discussing what factors lead to conflict, the authors discussed how conflict can be reduced and how it can be prevented. As you can see, the authors generated a tentative explanation about conflict based on their data. To strengthen their explanation, they would need to further develop and test their theory with new empirical data.

- **Grounded theory research**
  A qualitative approach to generating and developing a theory from the data that the researcher collects

Historical Research

The last general type of research used by educational researchers and discussed in this chapter is **historical research,** or research about events in the past. Although in many ways historical research is mixed (e.g., quantitative data are often used), we place it under the heading of qualitative research because the data tend to be qualitative and the approach to the use of evidence and the forming of arguments is closer to qualitative research than to quantitative research. As you know, historical research is done so that researchers can better understand events that have already occurred.

Educational historians have been able to find historical data that lend themselves to data analysis and have studied how various educational phenomena operated in the past.

- **Historical research**
  Research about events in the past

For example, educational researchers document the history of education and important events that occurred in the past, study trends in education occurring over time, study the multiple factors that led to certain events in the past, and study how things operated in the past (e.g., different teaching practices and the different outcomes that resulted from those practices). They might also study the origin of current practices and document any changes over time. *Historiography* is the word historians sometimes use to mean "research methods." As you will learn in Chapter 13, historiography involves the posing of questions, the collection of authentic source materials, the analysis and interpretation of those materials, and the composition of the results into a final report. Historical research, like the other methods of research, has an important place in education.

REVIEW QUESTION

2.8 What are the different types of qualitative research, and what is the defining feature of each of these?

Research Navigator.c⊕m

mixed method
multimethod
research

MIXED RESEARCH METHODS

As we discussed earlier, *mixed research* involves the mixing of quantitative and qualitative research methods, approaches, or paradigm characteristics. Because we have a full chapter on mixed research in this book (Chapter 14), we will only briefly discuss the two major types of mixed research to lay the foundation for the later discussion. The two major types are mixed method research and mixed model research (Tashakkori & Teddlie, 1998).

Mixed Method Research

■ **Mixed method research**
Research in which the researcher uses the qualitative research paradigm for one phase of a research study and the quantitative research paradigm for a different phase of the study

In **mixed method research,** the researcher uses the qualitative research paradigm for one phase of a research study and the quantitative research paradigm for another phase of the study. In other words, a qualitative research study and a quantitative research study are conducted either concurrently (conducting both at roughly the same time) or sequentially (conducting one first and the other second) to address a research topic. For example, let's say that you are interested in studying the phenomenon of living with dyslexia for high school students. You might decide to first conduct a qualitative study (phase one) by conducting open-ended or unstructured interviews with 10 or 20 high school students who have dyslexia so that you can hear from these students in their own words what it is like to live with dyslexia. On the basis of the data from this phase of your overall study and from your reading of the current research literature, you next develop a closed-ended and more structured questionnaire so that you can in a quantitative study (phase two) ask another group of high school students with dyslexia how descriptive the characteristics (identified in phase one) are of them. You select a larger sample of students with dyslexia from several high schools, and you have these students fill out your questionnaire. You then analyze your data and write up your findings from the qualitative and quantitative parts of your research study. By doing this, in effect, you conduct a qualitative study (phase one) and follow it with a quantitative study (phase two). Both of these phases are important for your broader study.

Mixed Model Research

The second major type of mixed research is mixed model research. In **mixed model research,** the researcher uses both qualitative and quantitative research within a stage or across two of the stages in the research process. In a simplified three-stage model of the research process, you first determine the research objective, then collect the data, and finally analyze and interpret the data. Here are the steps again:

1. *Research objective.* Typical objectives of qualitative research are exploration and description; typical objectives of quantitative research are explanation, prediction, and description.
2. *Type of data.* Quantitative research relies heavily on standardized, numerical data; qualitative research relies heavily on words and images.
3. *Type of analysis and interpretation.* Quantitative research involves statistical analysis; qualitative research relies on the searching for themes and patterns in narrative data.

> ■ **Mixed model research**
> Research in which the researcher uses both qualitative and quantitative research within a stage or across two of the stages in the research process

You could mix within the research objective stage—for example, by designing a study to answer a research question that suggests both exploration and hypothesis testing (e.g., "What are the important factors that predict student attrition?"). This kind of movement back and forth between exploring and testing of working hypotheses is common in field-work. You could mix models within the type of data stage by using a questionnaire that includes closed-ended questions and open-ended questions. You could mix within the type of analysis stage by examining narrative data both qualitatively (searching for major themes) and quantitatively (counting the number of times key words occur). You can also mix across the three stages—for example, by collecting narrative data but analyzing those data using quantitative techniques.

Here is an example of a mixed model research study. In the dyslexia study just discussed, you might decide to collect only qualitative data based on open-ended or unstructured interviews with the high school students. Then, although you first analyze the qualitative research data using qualitative analysis techniques (e.g., reading the interview transcripts and looking for common themes or patterns in the data), you also decide to convert some of the data into variables and statistically analyze these data using quantitative analysis techniques. In other words, you have mixed the quantitative and qualitative research paradigms or models in a single study without conducting separate studies as was the case in mixed method research. In the example just given, the researcher mixed the models or paradigms across the data collection and analysis stages (qualitative data were followed by quantitative analysis) as well as within data analysis (by analyzing the data using both qualitative and quantitative techniques). For now, the key point is that using the mixed method means that you conduct separate studies within a broader research study, and using mixed models means that you mix the approaches within or across the stages of a study.

The Advantages of Mixed Research

We view the use of multiple perspectives, theories, and research methods as a strength in educational research. In fact, we view the quantitative and qualitative research approaches and the specific quantitative and qualitative research methods as complementary. When

■ **Fundamental principle of mixed research**
Advises researchers to mix research methods or procedures in a way that the resulting mixture or combination has complementary strengths and nonoverlapping weaknesses

mixing research or when you read and evaluate research that involved mixing, be sure to consider the **fundamental principle of mixed research,** which says that it is wise to collect multiple sets of data using different research methods in such a way that the resulting mixture or combination has complementary strengths and nonoverlapping weaknesses (Brewer & Hunter, 1989; Johnson & Turner, 2002; Webb, Campbell, Schwartz, Sechrest, & Grove, 1981). This helps to improve the quality of research because the different research methods have different strengths and different weaknesses.

By combining two (or more) research methods with different strengths and weaknesses in a research study, you can make it less likely that you will make a mistake. Lincoln and Guba (1985) explain this idea using the metaphor of fish nets. Perhaps a fisherman has several fishing nets, each with one or more holes. To come up with one good net, the fisherman decides to overlap the different fishing nets, forming one overall net. All the nets have holes in them; however, when the nets are put together, there will probably no longer be a hole in the overall net. In the case of research methods, an experimental research study might demonstrate causality well, but it might be limited in realism because of the confines of the research laboratory. On the other hand, an ethnographic research study might not demonstrate causality especially well, but it can be done in the field, which enables a researcher to observe behavior as it naturally takes place and therefore increases realism. When both methods are used, causality is strong, and realism is no longer a big problem. Although it is often not practical to use more than one research method or strategy in a single research study, you should be aware of the potential benefit of using multiple methods and strategies. Furthermore, even if a researcher does not use multiple methods in a single research study, the relevant set of published research studies will usually include research based on several different research methods. The research literature is therefore mixed method. As a result, the mixed method (or mixed fishing net) advantage will be gained in the overall area of research.

R E V I E W **QUESTION**	**2.9** What are the different types of mixed research, and what is the defining feature of each of these types of research?

OUR RESEARCH TYPOLOGY

The forms of research that we have covered in this chapter are shown in Figure 2.3. We will discuss each of these types of research in later chapters. It is important to understand that all of the major types of research that we discuss in this textbook have value. It is not uncommon for an educational researcher to use several different types of research at different times. A researcher should always select the appropriate research method on the basis of a consideration of the research question(s) of interest, the objective(s) of the research, time and cost constraints, available populations, the possibility (or not) of the manipulation of an independent variable, and the availability of data. Sometimes a researcher will use more than one research approach within a single study. However, even if researchers never used

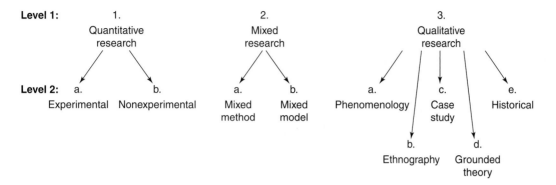

FIGURE 2.3 Research typology (Later chapters will add a third level to this typology.)

more than one method in a single study, published research literature would still tend to include articles based on different approaches and methods because of the diversity of the researchers working in the area.

When a research finding has been demonstrated by using more than one type of research, one can place more confidence in it. We say that a finding has been *corroborated* if the same result is found by using different types of research. Conversely, if different data sources or types of research result in conflicting information, then additional research will be needed to explore the nature of the phenomenon more completely and to determine the source of conflict. That is, if different types of research result in different findings, then the researcher should study the phenomenon in more depth to determine the exact reason for the conflicting findings. The world is a complex and ever-changing place. As we study it, it is helpful to be equipped with the best methods and approaches currently available. You will probably find that some methods and approaches we discuss will fit your style or personality better than others. However, we hope that you will keep an open mind as you learn about all of the kinds of research. All the research methods can be useful if used properly.

2.10 What are the three research paradigms in education and what are the major types of research in each of these paradigms? (Hint: We showed the answer in Figure 2.3.)

SUMMARY

The three major research traditions in educational research are qualitative research, quantitative research, and mixed research. All three of these traditions are important and have value. Qualitative research tends to use the inductive form of the scientific method to generate hypotheses and develop theory about phenomena in the world. It is discovery oriented and is conducted in naturalistic settings. Quantitative research is typically done under more tightly controlled conditions and tends to use the deductive form of the scientific method, focusing on hypothesis testing and theory testing. Mixed research involves mixing qualitative and quantitative research in various ways. It is based on the philosophy of pragmatism (i.e., what works is what is important). Eight research types or methods were introduced in this chapter. These include two types of quantitative research (experimental and nonexperimental research), two types of mixed research (mixed method and mixed model research), and five types of qualitative research (phenomenology, ethnography, case study, grounded theory, and historical). We will elaborate on each part of our research typology (i.e., our classification of the different types of research) in later chapters.

KEY TERMS

case study research (p. 46)
categorical variable (p. 35)
causal-comparative research (p. 40)
cause-and-effect relationship (p. 37)
confounding variable (p. 39)
constant (p. 35)
correlational research (p. 41)
correlation coefficient (p. 41)
culture (p. 46)
dependent variable (p. 37)
determinism (p. 32)
ethnography (p. 46)
experimental research (p. 39)

extraneous variable (p. 39)
fundamental principle of mixed research (p. 50)
grounded theory research (p. 47)
historical research (p. 47)
holistic description (p. 46)
incompatibility thesis (p. 30)
independent variable (p. 36)
intervening variable (p. 38)
manipulation (p. 39)
mediating variable (p. 38)
mixed method research (p. 48)
mixed model research (p. 49)

mixed research (p. 30)
moderator variable (p. 38)
negative correlation (p. 42)
nonexperimental research (p. 40)
phenomenology (p. 46)
positive correlation (p. 42)
pragmatism (p. 30)
probabilistic causes (p. 32)
qualitative research (p. 30)
quantitative research (p. 30)
quantitative variable (p. 35)
research paradigm (p. 29)
variable (p. 35)

DISCUSSION QUESTIONS

1. Which of the three research paradigms do you like the most? Why?
2. If you find a statistical relationship between two variables (e.g., income and education, or gender and grades, or time spent studying and grades) in a nonexperimental research study, should you confidently conclude that one variable is the cause of the other variable?
3. What is an example of a positive correlation? What is an example of a negative correlation?
4. Following are several research questions. For each, list the research method that you believe would be most appropriate to use in answering the question.
   a. How do individuals experience the phenomenon of being one of only a few minority students in a predominantly homogeneous high school?
   b. What is the effect of a new teaching technique on elementary school students' arithmetic performance?

   c. Does cognitive therapy or behavioral therapy work better for treating childhood depression?
   d. What is the culture of the band at a high school in your local community?
   e. What is the relationship between the GRE and student performance in graduate school?
   f. Do males and females have different performance levels in high school English classes?
   g. Does the student-to-teacher ratio have an effect on elementary students' level of performance in the classroom?
   h. What was it like being a middle school student in 1921 in the four-room school (where primary through high school were taught) in Great Bridge, Virginia (which is located in the city of Chesapeake)?
   i. Was John Dewey an effective school teacher?
   j. Do students perform better on an academic test when they are exposed to a cooperative learning style or a lecture style of teaching?

1. The abstract and the link to a full-length example of quantitative research is provided in Appendix A, a full-length example of qualitative research is linked in Appendix B, and a full-length example of mixed research is linked in Appendix C. Print out these articles and browse them so that you can see some examples of educational research published in academic journals. What do you consider as the key features of each of these articles? How are they different?

2. Using ContentSelect, locate a qualitative research article or a quantitative research article or a mixed research study. (Remember, to get to ContentSelect, go to the book web page and then select Research Navigator.) Explain why you classified the article you found as a qualitative, a quantitative, or a mixed research study.

3. Read the quantitative research study linked in Appendix A, and write a two-page (typed, double-spaced) summary of the article. Organize your paper into the following three sections: (1) purpose (What was the research study about? What did the researchers hope to learn?), (2) method (How did the researchers carry out their research study? What did they actually do?), and (3) results (What were the key findings of the research study?). Don't worry about the technical jargon in the research article. Just try to get the main ideas.

4. Read the qualitative research study linked in Appendix B, and write a two-page summary of the article. Organize your paper into the three sections described in Exercise 3 (purpose, method, and results).

5. Read the mixed research study linked in Appendix C, and write a two-page summary of the article. Organize your paper into the three sections described in Exercise 3 (purpose, method, and results).

RELEVANT INTERNET SITES

www.ablongman.com/
Quantitative research book materials and links. Go to Larry Christensen's *Experimental Methodology* textbook web page (under the Website Gallery section).

http://ebook.stat.ucla.edu/textbook/ and
http://glass.ed.asu.edu/stats/lesson4/
Correlation coefficients.

www.nova.edu/ssss/QR/web.html
Qualitative research links.

RECOMMENDED READING

Christensen, L. B. (2003). *Experimental methodology* (9th ed.). Boston: Allyn and Bacon.

Patton, M. Q. (2002). *Qualitative research and evaluation methods* (3rd ed.). Thousand Oaks, CA: Sage.

Pedhazur, E. J., & Schmelkin, L. P. (1991). *Measurement, design, and analysis: An integrated approach.* Hillsdale, NJ: Lawrence Erlbaum Associates.

Tashakkori, A., & Teddlie, C. (Eds.) (2003). *Handbook of mixed methods in the social and behavioral sciences.* Thousand Oaks, CA: Sage.

3

Developing Research Questions and Proposal Preparation

LEARNING OBJECTIVES

To be able to

- Identify research problems.
- Explain why it is necessary to conduct a literature search.
- Conduct a literature search.
- Explain the difference in the problem statement in a qualitative and quantitative study.
- Explain the reason for stating the purpose of a research study and the research questions.
- Explain the difference between purpose statements and research questions in qualitative and quantitative studies.
- Explain the purpose and necessity of stating your research questions and hypotheses.
- Specify the components that must be included in written preparation of a research plan.
- Specify the content of each major component of a research plan.

One of the stereotypes that many people seem to harbor privately but few openly express is that poor students who attend the nation's worst public schools are a lost cause, regardless of how much money you throw at them or the innovative attempts that are made to teach them because they are inherently unteachable. This myth, however, is being exposed for exactly what it is in about two dozen schools statewide (*Atlanta Journal and Constitution,* 2002). Bethune Elementary School in Vine City, Georgia, is one of the schools that has achieved success, in spite of its location in one of Atlanta's most depressed intown neighborhoods. About 86 percent of the fourth-graders scored at or above the state average in math and reading tests in 2001.

Bethune has clearly defied the odds against poverty and has proved that children from poverty-stricken inner-city areas can perform well academically. The test scores vividly verify that Bethune has accomplished something that has eluded numerous other schools across the country. An educational researcher, however, would want to go beyond applauding the success of these schools and learn why Bethune and other such schools were successful when most schools in depressed inner-city areas are not. An educational researcher would look at the overall program instituted at Bethune and search for the primary reason for the success of the program. It might be that all components are needed. However, it is also possible that one of the components, such as soliciting the help and cooperation of the parents, was more important than the additional discipline, encouragement, and accountability implemented by the school staff. It is important to identify the most vital components of a successful program such as the one at Bethune because this is the primary way to transport the success that was achieved to other programs.

This example illustrates how a real-life event can lead to a good research study, and it might suggest that research problems and questions are easy to generate. This is often true for the veteran researcher. However, beginning researchers frequently have difficulty identifying a research question that they can investigate. In this chapter, we will try to minimize this difficulty by discussing the origin of most research questions and the way these research questions are converted to ones that can be investigated.

Up to this point in the text, we have discussed the basic characteristics of research and the different models, quantitative, qualitative and mixed models, used in the research process. However, the research process begins when you have a problem in need of a solution, because a research study is conducted in an attempt to solve a problem.

Identifying a research problem should be relatively simple in the field of education because of the numerous problems that need to be solved and because of the exposure and experience we have all had in this arena. All of us have participated in the educational system, first as students and then perhaps as teachers or instructors. In one or both of these capacities, you have probably observed and discussed a host of problems with our current educational system and been exposed to the implementation of new techniques and methods of instruction. For example, you might think that certain instructional strategies such as computer-assisted instruction, team teaching, or cooperative learning enhance learning, or you might have questioned the value of activities such as field trips and extracurricular programs or some new approach to teaching biology, chemistry, or physics.

From a research perspective, each of these issues represents a potential legitimate research problem. All you have to do is adjust your thinking a bit. For example, an article in the local newspaper (Fournier, 2002) quoted President Bush as stating, "We've spent billions of dollars with lousy results. Now it's time to spend billions of dollars and get good results." The President obviously believes that the additional academic testing and spending for literacy will result in an improvement in the education received by the youth of America. Let's assume, however, that you disagree because you don't think that general programs such as broadened academic testing will improve academic instruction. You believe that the money could be spent more effectively by reducing class size. You might even have gotten into arguments with your colleagues about the value of such alternatives and found that you could not change their opinions. Such an argument or disagreement is legitimate subject matter for a research study. All you have to do is convert the argument into a research question and ask, for example, "What benefits are derived from increasing academic testing?" or "What benefit is derived from reducing class size, and will this benefit be greater than doing more academic testing?"

Once you have converted the disagreement into a researchable question, you have taken the first step in developing a research study. Researchable questions are numerous in education. To identify them, all you have to do is develop an inquisitive attitude and ask questions.

SOURCES OF RESEARCH IDEAS

Where do ideas for research studies originate? Where should you look for a researchable idea? In all fields, research ideas can grow out of existing theories and prior research. In education, we are fortunate in that we have our own experiences and the experiences of others to draw from. Typically, research ideas originate from one of four sources: everyday life, practical issues, past research, or theory.

Everyday Life

Research
Navigator.c⊕m

strategies of
instruction

One of the most fruitful sources of ideas for beginning researchers is their own experience as educators. In the course of conducting your job as an educator, you continuously have to make decisions about such things as the best method of teaching students, how to maintain discipline in the classroom, how best to use technology in the classroom, and how to motivate a bright but underachieving student. You might observe that some students aggressively pursue their studies, whereas others procrastinate and do anything but study. Some students might be very aggressive and constantly disrupt the classroom, while others are model students. Experiences such as these can be turned into research problems. For example, you could ask why some strategies of instruction work better with some students than with others or why some students use one method of study and others use another and whether there is any relationship between the method of study and the grades achieved.

You could even get research ideas from reading your local newspaper. For example, in the course of reading the local paper, Christensen encountered an article (Jones, 1997) discussing the effect of the mayors of several large cities having taken over the operation of the school system in their city. The Illinois legislature handed Mayor Richard Daley total control of Chicago's 400,000-student system in 1995. One of the innovations that Mayor Daley has pushed in Chicago is military-style schools (Johnson, 2002). This approach has captured the attention of school leaders around the nation. California opened a public military high school in 2002, and Prince George's County in Maryland had plans to open one. You could ask a question such as "Are these military-style schools more effective than traditional schools?" The initial data are encouraging. Attendance at the Chicago academy is running at 95 percent, a figure that is unheard of in most urban schools. However, there has been some concern over the loss of autonomy and independence that might be needed to effectively run a school system, so there is a need to evaluate the overall effectiveness of these schools.

Practical Issues

Many research ideas can arise from practical issues that require a solution. Educators are constantly faced with such problems as the instruction of our youth, disruptive behavior in the classroom, selection of textbooks, cheating, prejudice, and providing instruction for the culturally diverse, as well as issues such as salaries and burnout. One controversial issue that generated considerable discussion was the decision in the 1990s of the school board in Oakland, California, to teach ebonics (a term derived from the words *ebony* and *phonics* that refers to the African American speech pattern) as a second language. This decision was based on the apparently favorable results found by several teachers who taught English using a contrastive analysis technique, in which the teacher used books written in both ebonics and standard English to point out differences in syntax. This decision by the Oakland school board created a swell of rhetoric, particularly because it suggested that schools might use the ebonics issue to seek federal funds earmarked for bilingual programs. Most of the reaction, including that from the black community, was negative and nonsupportive. A decision was also made that federal funds could not be used to support the instruction of ebonics. Reactions and decisions were made with very little research data, although the limited data that were available were supportive (Leland & Joseph, 1997). Clearly, this is a practical issue that deserves investigation and one that easily lends itself to the formulation of a research question such as "Is learning standard English enhanced among African American students if they are taught by using the contrastive analysis technique involving ebonics and standard English?"

Research
Navigator.c⊕m

ebonics

Past Research

The research literature of previously conducted studies represents an excellent source of research ideas and might represent the source that produces the most research ideas. This might sound like a contradiction because a research study is designed to answer a research question or questions. One of the interesting features of research is that it tends to generate more questions than it answers. Although each well-designed study does provide an advancement in knowledge, phenomena are multidetermined. Any study can investigate only a limited number of variables, and the investigation of the variables that are selected can lead to hypotheses about the effects of other variables.

To illustrate the way in which past research leads to subsequent research ideas, consider the study conducted by Imich (1994), who investigated the issue of students being excluded or expelled from school in Great Britain. Prior research had indicated that student exclusions from school were increasing. Because of this increase, student exclusions from school became an issue of national concern in Great Britain in the early 1990s. However, the prior studies that had been conducted did not separate students who were temporarily expelled from those who were permanently expelled. Therefore, no information existed that would identify whether the increase in exclusions was owing to students being temporarily or permanently expelled. In an attempt to obtain a clearer picture of the nature of school exclusions, Imich (1994) first identified three types of exclusions: fixed-term (exclusion for a fixed period of time), indefinite (exclusion for an unspecified time period), and permanent, as specified under the 1986 Education Act. On the basis of an analysis of data obtained from a population of approximately 225,000 students over a three-year period, he found that permanent exclusions rose about 50 percent, fixed-term exclusions almost doubled, and indefinite exclusions tripled. Imich (1994) also found that the rate of exclusion of students from school depended on the area in which the student lived and the school attended. However, the rate of exclusion was not related to the level of social disadvantage within a school, the size of the school, or the academic performance of the students in the school.

The Imich (1994) study did provide a clearer picture of the rate of exclusion of students from schools in Great Britain, but the study generated more questions than it answered. The study demonstrated that exclusions of all types were rising, the indefinite exclusions rising most rapidly. However, the pattern of exclusions varied considerably between areas and schools, and no clear picture emerged to explain these differences. Further studies are needed to identify the causes of this variability.

This example demonstrates how one study can provide the stimulus for further research. Research is an ongoing and continuous process. Table 3.1 lists a variety of ways in which past research can provide research ideas. These suggestions are frequently quite valid and represent good sources of research ideas. Mining such suggestions is a relatively easy way to come up with a good research topic.

Theory

■ **Theory**
An explanation or explanatory system that discusses how a phenomenon operates and why it operates as it does

Theory, as defined in Chapter 1, is an explanation or explanatory system that discusses how a phenomenon operates and why it operates as it does. Theory serves the purpose of making sense out of current knowledge by integrating and summarizing this knowledge. This is referred to as the *goal function* of theory. Theory also guides research by making predictions. This is the *tool function* of theory. It is the tool function that is of interest to us. A good theory goes beyond the goal function of summarizing and integrating what is currently known to suggest new relationships and make new predictions. It is in this manner that theories guide research. The suggested relationships and new predictions have to be tested or subjected to a research study to verify their authenticity. The suggested relationships and new predictions represent the research ideas for investigation.

Weiner's (1974) attributional theory of success and failure is an example of a theory that suggests a way of thinking about and explaining test anxiety. Attribution theory has therefore been used to stimulate a number of research studies investigating test anxiety. From this theory, Bandalos, Yates, and Thorndike-Christ (1995) hypothesized and validated

Research
Navigator.c⊕m

attribution

■ TABLE 3.1   Ways in Which Prior Studies Can Provide Ideas for New Studies

Method	Rationale
Replication	You might decide that you want to repeat a study to see whether you can replicate the results because you think the author's results have significant educational importance and you want to verify them.
Test the external validity of a study	You might have read a laboratory-based study that has suggestions for important issues such as reading, control of aggression, or improving instruction. You want to find out whether the laboratory methods tested would work equally well in the classroom.
Improve a study's internal validity	In reading a study, you might realize that the study did not control one or more important variables and the lack of control of these variables led to an ambiguous interpretation of the results. For example, Gladue and Delaney (1990) thought that the Pennebaker et al. (1979) study that found that girls in bars got prettier at closing time did not answer the question of whether it was time or alcohol consumption that contributed to the perceptions of attractiveness.
Reconcile conflicting results	In reading the literature on a topic, you might find conflicting results. These conflicting results can lead to a study trying to resolve the conflict. This conflict might be due to different ways in which the studies were conducted, the use of different measurement instruments, or the use of different participant populations. When studies conflict, you need to look for any differences in the studies because these differences might represent the cause of the apparent conflict.
Suggestions for future research	One of the easiest ways to get ideas from past research is to look for the author's suggestions for future research. Often, particularly in review articles, the author(s) of the article will make suggestions for the future direction of the research. These suggestions are frequently quite valid and represent good sources of research ideas.
Theses and dissertations	Theses and dissertations often have a section devoted to future research that will identify subsequent studies that need to be completed.

the prediction that test anxiety was related to the type of attribution a student made for his or her good or bad grade on a test. Individuals who attributed failure on a test to a lack of effort on their part reported lower levels of test anxiety than did those who cited a lack of ability or some external cause such as the difficulty of the test. Similarly, students who attributed successful performance on a test to some external factor such as the test being easy or to luck reported higher levels of test anxiety.

These four sources of research ideas—everyday life, practical issues, past research, and theory—represent the primary sources of research ideas. The important issue, however, is not the identification of sources of research ideas but the generation of researchable ideas from these sources. Generation of research ideas represents the initial stage of a research project, and development of these research ideas requires the development of a questioning and inquisitive way of thinking.

Identifying a research idea does not mean that this will be the exact focus of your research study, because the idea you have come up with might have already been investigated. The generation of a research idea really identifies the topic area that you intend to investigate. For example, assume you believe that teachers do a more effective job and the students learn more when they have a class size of eighteen than when they have a class size of twenty-eight. You want to verify this belief in an empirical research study. However, this is a topic that others have probably thought of and investigated, so there is probably a considerable amount of past research on this issue. What you have done is to identify a **research topic,** or a broad subject matter area that you want to investigate. The research topic that you have identified is class size and its effect on academic performance. Identification of the research topic is the beginning of a sequential process that starts with the identification of the research topic and ends with the research question and research hypothesis, as illustrated in Figure 3.1.

■ **Research topic**
The broad subject matter area to be investigated

■ **FIGURE 3.1**
Flowchart of the development of a research idea

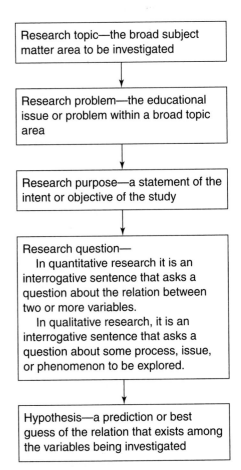

IDEAS THAT CAN'T BE RESEARCHED EMPIRICALLY

Not all ideas that might be developed are appropriate for an educational research study. Some ideas are very important, are debated vigorously, and consume inordinate amounts of time and energy but are not appropriate for an empirical research study. These ideas typically involve issues of value, morality, and religion. Consider, for example, the issue of school prayer, which has been debated for years, has polarized segments of the U.S. population, and has even been debated in the courts, ultimately resulting in the ruling that prayer should not be a regular part of public school activities. This ruling was based on the legal opinion of members of the judicial system and did not arise as a result of an empirical research study because the issue of school prayer is a value and moral issue. As such, it implies notions of what is right and wrong or proper or improper. Empirical research cannot provide answers to such questions, although it can provide information on opinions, attitudes, and behaviors of individuals. The key point is that empirical research cannot resolve the issue of which value position is the *morally best* or correct one.

3.1 What sources of research ideas have been identified in this chapter?

3.2 How would you get a research idea from each of these sources?

3.3 How do research ideas and questions differ from ideas and questions that cannot be empirically researched?

REVIEW

QUESTIONS

REVIEW OF THE LITERATURE

After you have identified a research idea, many investigators believe that your next step should be to conduct a literature review to familiarize yourself with the available information on the topic selected. However, the use of the literature review varies depending on whether one is conducting a qualitative or a quantitative study. We will therefore discuss the purpose of the literature review separately for quantitative and qualitative research studies.

Literature Review for Quantitative Research Studies

In quantitative research, the literature review is done before the actual conducting of the study. For example, assume that you want to conduct research on the effect of students' self-concept on academic achievement. Before beginning to design this research project, you should first become familiar with the available information on the individual topics of self-concept and academic achievement.

The general purpose of the literature review is to gain an understanding of the current state of knowledge about your selected research topic. Specifically, a review of the literature:

1. Will tell you whether the problem you have identified has already been researched. If it has, you should either revise the problem in light of the results of other studies or look for another problem unless you think there is a need to replicate the study.

2. Might give you ideas as to how to proceed and design the study so that you can obtain an answer to your research question(s).
3. Can point out methodological problems specific to the research question(s) you are studying. Are special groups or special pieces of equipment needed to conduct the research? If so, the literature can give clues as to where to find the equipment or how to identify the particular groups of participants needed.
4. Can identify appropriate data collection instruments.

Gaining familiarity with the literature will also help you after you have collected your data and analyzed your results. One of the last stages of a research project is to prepare a research report in which you communicate the results of the study to others. In doing so, you not only have to describe the study and the results you found, but also have to explain or interpret the results of your study. In trying to make sense of data collected from a study, it is often valuable to be aware of the literature, because it can frequently provide clues as to why the effects occurred. If you are familiar with the literature, you can also discuss your results in terms of whether they support or contradict prior studies. If your study is at odds with other studies, you can speculate as to why this difference occurs, and this speculation then forms the basis for another study to attempt to resolve the contradictory findings.

Literature Review for Qualitative Research Studies

The literature review in qualitative research can be used in a number of ways. It can be used to explain the theoretical underpinnings of the research study, to assist in formulation of the research question and selection of the study population, or to stimulate new insights and concepts throughout the study. Qualitative researchers often integrate the literature review throughout their study, working back and forth between the literature and the completion of the research study (LeCompte, Preissle, & Tesch, 1993). Still, there are two schools of thought about the use of literature reviews in qualitative research, and they often depend on the type of study being conducted. One school of thought believes that it is important to conduct a thorough literature review on your research topic before collecting data. In an ethnographic study, for example, you would probably conduct a more thorough literature review at the beginning of the study and use the literature in a manner similar to that of a quantitative study.

The second school of thought seems to believe that "ignorance is bliss" (Shank, 2002). This school of thought believes that the researcher must set aside any preconceived notions and use an inductive approach in which additional research questions, hypotheses and theory emerge from the data collected. From this perspective, you should familiarize yourself with the literature only enough to make sure that the study you are planning to conduct has not been done. Only after you have collected much of your data, or at the completion of data collection, do you conduct a more thorough literature review to try to integrate what you have found with the prevailing literature.

For example, if you were to conduct a grounded theory (Glaser, 1978) study (a qualitative research approach that we discuss in depth later), a comprehensive review of the literature before data collection might not be recommended. Researchers using the grounded theory approach attempt to develop a set of constructs, relationships, and theory uncontaminated by knowledge of prior research or theory. It is assumed that a fresh and uncontaminated perspective on the data collected and a novel set of constructs, relationships, and theories could not be developed if the researcher's perspective were contaminated with a prior knowledge of the relationships, constructs, and theories that had been discovered and elaborated on by other researchers. This does not mean that the literature does not have a place in the grounded theory approach. Glaser (1978) recommends that the literature be reviewed after the theory is sufficiently grounded and developed so that the prior literature can be related to it and, in this way, show additional support for the developed theory or show how the developed theory and the literature conflict. In this way, ideas for further investigation will be developed.

Although Glaser (1978) recommended not reviewing the literature until the theory was sufficiently grounded and developed, this approach is not recommended by others. The current position among qualitative researchers seems to be that a literature review can be of value, although it should not constrain and stifle the discovery of new constructs, relationships, and theory. Strauss and Corbin (1990) specify several different ways in which a literature review conducted before data collection can be of value:

1. The literature review can be used to stimulate theoretical sensitivity of concepts and relationships that prior literature has repeatedly identified and that therefore appear to be meaningful and significant. Because of their apparent significance, you might want to bring these concepts into the situation you are studying to identify the role they might play. For example, if the concept of isolation is repeatedly identified in the literature as being significantly related to creative achievement and you are studying creative achievement in underprivileged children, you might want to look for evidence of how isolation relates to creative achievement in your study.

2. The literature can stimulate questions. In conducting a grounded theory study, you will be collecting data by asking the research participants a variety of questions and/or observing them. The literature can assist you in deriving an initial list of pertinent questions to ask or behaviors that you might want to observe.

3. Finally, the literature can provide some information about the situations and populations that you need to study so that you can uncover phenomena that are important to the development of your theory. For example, in a study of creativity, the literature might indicate that you should look at individuals who are experiencing various emotional states because this might represent an important variable in the development of your theory of creativity.

Sources of Information

The two primary sources for tracking down information relevant to any research topic are books and journals, although information can also be found in technical reports and academic theses and dissertations.

Books Books are a good place to start your literature search because they will provide a general overview of the research topic and a summary of the literature published up to the time the book was written. Most books focus on a specific topic, such as team teaching or Head Start. If you have selected a research topic that focuses on one of these issues, then a book written about that topic will give you a good overview of the subject matter, as well as a bibliography of other works that might be of use to you. Remember, however, that the literature that is cited in books is generally several years old, so books do not provide the most current information. Even books that have just been published do not contain the most recent information because there is a delay between the time when the book was written and the time when it is available for consumers to buy.

In addition to books on a single topic, there are reference books that provide integrative reviews and summaries of studies on a number of specific educational topics. Specialized encyclopedias and dictionaries provide background information, frequently used words or concepts, names of the important people who have had major influence, dates, legal cases of consequence, and usually a bibliography of other sources that are considered important. For example, the *Encyclopedia of Educational Research* provides a review of the research literature on several hundred topics in education. Check your library's reference collection for a copy of this encyclopedia to see whether your research topic is included. If it is, you might be able to obtain valuable information for your research project. Some of the books that provide a review of education-related literature are listed in Table 3.2. Use your library's catalog or ask at the reference desk for help finding reference books, as well as books you can check out and take home. Once you identify a call number area for your topic, you should spend some time browsing for other relevant items in this area.

Although books provide a good introduction and overview of the issues of importance in your chosen research area, they do not provide a comprehensive review of all the research conducted on any specific topic. Any book author has to be selective and present only a small portion of the literature. To be sure that you have not read a biased orientation, you should select and examine several books on your chosen research topic.

Journals   After you have examined several books and have become familiar with your research topic, your next step is to identify relevant articles contained in any of the numerous journals that publish educational research. Most of the current information about a research topic is usually found in educational journals. If you already have some familiarity with your chosen research topic, you might forgo examining books and go directly to educational journals.

There are numerous journals that publish educational research. It would be impossible to go through each journal looking for relevant information. This is where periodical indexes, abstract journals, and citation indexes become valuable. The indexes that are of most value and importance to educational researchers are the ***Current Index to Journals in Education*** **(CIJE)** and ***Resources in Education*** **(RIE),** which are produced by the **Educational Resources Information Center (ERIC).** CIJE provides an index and a short annotation of about 600,000 published articles from over 1,000 education-related journals spanning the period from 1966 to the present. RIE provides abstracts from sources other than journal articles, such as instructional materials, speeches, information analyses, statistical data, and research, feasibility, and evaluation reports.

In the past, literature reviews were conducted by manually searching through indexes such as these to identify relevant journal articles and research reports. However, this approach has become unwieldy and very impractical, given the vast amount of information and number of journal articles and research reports in existence. At the present time, the

- *Current Index to Journals in Education (CIJE)*
  An annotated index of articles from educational journals
- *Resources in Education (RIE)*
  An index of abstracts of research reports
- **Educational Resources Information Center (ERIC)**
  A database containing information from CIJE and RIE

▓ **T A B L E 3 . 2**   Books that Contain Reviews of Education-Related Literature

Book	Content
Encyclopedia of Educational Research	Brief summary of the research on several hundred topics in education
The International Encyclopedia of Educational Evaluation	Contains discussions on the basic concepts in all areas of educational evaluation including evaluation studies, curriculum evaluation, measurement theory and application, tests, and educational policy and planning
The International Encyclopedia of Education: Research and Studies	Provides a scholarly and professional discussion of educational problems, practices, and institutions around the world
International Encyclopedia of Higher Education	A ten-volume series that provides a discussion of contemporary topics in higher education
Encyclopedia of Higher Education	Contains articles and essays that attempt to integrate the current international knowledge about higher education
Handbook of Research on Teaching	Contains articles by specialists who list, summarize, and critically discuss the research on selected topics in the field of education
Encyclopedia of Special Education	Provides information on the special needs, characteristics, and problems in the education of exceptional children
Handbook of Reading Research	Provides a summary of research related to the teaching and learning of reading
Handbook of Research on Curriculum	A summary of research on topics and issues related to curriculum development
Handbook of Research on Educational Administration	A summary of research on issues related to educational administration
Handbook of Research on Mathematics Teaching and Learning	A summary of research on topics related to the teaching and learning of mathematics
Handbook of Research on Social Studies Teaching and Learning	A summary of research on topics related to the teaching and learning of social studies
Handbook of Research on the Teaching of English	A summary of research on topics related to the teaching and learning of English
Handbook of Research on the Education of Young Children	A summary of research on development and education of young children
Handbook of Research on School Supervision	A summary of research on topics related to school supervision
Handbook of Research on Multicultural Education	A summary of the research relating to multicultural education since the field emerged in the 1960s and 1970s
Handbook of Research on Music Teaching and Learning	A summary of research on topics related to the teaching and learning of music
Handbook of Research on Teaching	A summary of research on five major areas of teaching ranging from classroom dynamics to the various grade levels and subject areas

available volumes of CIJE and RIE contain over a million entries, and this number is growing at a rate of over 30,000 a year.

Computer Databases With advances in computer technology, and particularly the Internet, it has become possible to electronically store and access large data sets such as the entries published in CIJE and RIE. In an effort to expedite and improve the accuracy of literature searches, a number of comprehensive computerized information storage and retrieval systems, such as OVID, SilverPlatter, FirstSearch, and EBSCO, have been developed. Information retrieval systems like these have access to many databases, and each database is generally specific to a given field. For example, the information that is of primary interest to educational researchers is found in the ERIC database, which includes all the entries for CIJE and RIE. Educational researchers may also be interested in other databases such as those listed in Table 3.3. If a study deals with a psychological or sociological as well as an educational issue, you would want to use PsycINFO or SocioFile to search the Psychological Abstracts or Sociological Abstracts databases. There are times when you might want to search several databases. However, the ERIC database is the one most widely used in education and the one that contains the most relevant research related to the field of education.

Most universities give students access to many databases through use of an Internet connection in a dorm room, computer lab, or office. Check your library's home page or ask your reference librarian to tell you which of the education, psychology, and sociology databases your library subscribes to. The information stored in these databases cannot be found by using typical Internet search engines that search only the public part of the Internet. These electronic tools are paid for through the library and are usually restricted by login and password to the students, faculty, and staff of your university. Reference librarians often de-

TABLE 3.3 Databases Incorporating Educational Publications

Database	Subject Coverage	Internet Address
ERIC	Education	www.eric.ed.gov or connect through your library
PsycINFO	Psychology, mental health, biomedicine	Connect through your university library
Social Sciences Index	Social science, politics, economics, psychology, humanities	Connect through your university library
MEDLINE	Medicine, biomedicine, health care	www.ncbi.nlm.nih.gov/pubmed
SocioFile	Sociology and related disciplines	Connect through your university library
UMI Dissertation Abstracts International	Dissertation research	www.lib.umi.com

velop guides and web page aids that will help you to use these databases. In addition, they often have class sessions that are specifically designed to teach you efficient search strategy and database search techniques. Become familiar with your library's home page and the numerous information sources that are available to you through the library.

3.4 What is the purpose of conducting a review of the literature in a quantitative study?	**R E V I E W**
3.5 What is the purpose of conducting a review of the literature in a qualitative study?	**Q U E S T I O N S**
3.6 What are the information sources you would use in conducting a literature review and what is the advantage of each source?	
3.7 Why is ERIC such a valuable resource for educational researchers?	

CONDUCTING THE LITERATURE SEARCH

Most literature searches are conducted by making use of the Internet. The **Internet** is a "network of networks" consisting of millions of computers and tens of millions of users all over the world, all of which are interconnected to promote communication. All colleges and universities provide access to the Internet.

■ **Internet**
A "network of networks" consisting of millions of computers and tens of millions of users all over the world, all of which are interconnected to promote communication

Using Databases

There are several ways to use the Internet to assist in your literature review. The most effective use of the Internet is to gain access to the databases to which your library subscribes. The one database that will definitely be available to you is the ERIC database because this is a federally funded, nationwide information network that is designed to give you access to educational literature. Because ERIC is federally funded, it is available to anyone and can be accessed either through an information retrieval system to which your college or university subscribes or through the public Internet. Accessing ERIC through the public Internet will give you access to the literature contained in its database and enable you to identify relevant literature. However, if you use the Internet to access ERIC through a retrieval system to which your college or university subscribes, you will have the added advantage of getting access to a full text version of some of the literature. Therefore, we suggest that you access ERIC through your library so that you can make full use of the resources provided by your university library.

Because ERIC is such an important database for educational researchers, we want to provide some detailed instruction on its use. Table 3.4 identifies the steps to follow in conducting a literature search using the ERIC database. If you follow these steps, you should be able to identify many articles pertaining to your research topic.

Personal Communication

Many groups, organizations, and corporations have developed web pages that they make available over the Internet. These include conferences, debates, journals, and lists of

■ **TABLE 3.4**   Steps in Searching the ERIC Database

To illustrate the steps involved in searching the ERIC database, let's assume that you want to search the literature on the phenomenon of being raped while on a date.

Step 1.   Connect to the ERIC web site either through your library home page or using the Internet address in Table 3.3, the one we will use. Using this address, open the ERIC home page. You want to search the ERIC database, so you would click on the *Search ERIC Database* link in the upper left-hand corner of the ERIC home page. This will bring you to a web page with several different links, one of which is "How do I search the ERIC database." This will be instructive for the novice because it will go through the procedure for doing a search of the ERIC database.

Step 2.   Identify descriptors or search terms. These are terms or descriptors that will direct your search. Because you are interested in the topic of being raped while on a date, the terms you would logically use as your descriptors or search terms are *date* and *rape.* However, there might be other descriptors that would also be valuable to use. If you want help in identifying additional descriptors, click on the *ERIC Thesaurus* link, and you will be able to find other important descriptors.

Step 3.   Link to the search page of ERIC by clicking on the *selected fields* link. Enter your search terms in the boxes on the left. To the right is a box that says *Keyword.* Another box contains the word "and." This means that only articles with both search descriptors in the abstract of the article will be located. If you check the *Journal articles* box, you will limit the search to only this type of articles. There are other ways to delimit the search that you can use as you become more familiar with doing an ERIC search.

Step 4.   Click the *Submit* button, which will bring up a screen that allows you to review your search request. After reviewing this information, you would click the *Submit* button again if the information is accurate. This will bring up another screen that provides a list of journal articles about date rape.

Step 5.   Examine the titles of each of the articles located to identify those that seem relevant to your research topic. To get an abstract of a relevant article, click on the number to the left of the author listing. This will bring up a web page showing the abstract of the article. You can read this abstract to further determine whether the article is one you wish to get and possibly use. This is the procedure you should use when reviewing all the articles located by your search.

references, as well as the results of research studies. Educational researchers have formed computer networks that enable them to carry on electronic discussions and inform each other of upcoming events as well as results of their research projects. One general email list, sponsored by the American Educational Research Association, is the Educational Research

List (ERL-L). This general email list contains a discussion of general educational issues and can be accessed at www.aera.net/resources/listarch.htm. Links to a number of more specialized discussion lists, covering topics ranging from curriculum studies to postsecondary education, can be found at www.aero.net/listarch.htm Accessing one or more of these links can provide valuable information about your research topic.

Using the Public Internet

In addition to searching subscription databases such as ERIC or PsycINFO, you should also consider making use of the public Internet. Remember that databases such as PsycINFO are proprietary databases, and some, such as PsycINFO, charge a fee to access them. You should access them through your library because the library has already paid the fee to permit your access. Others, such as ERIC, are funded by the federal government and dedicated to making the database accessible to everyone. However, a vast amount of information is available on the public Internet in addition to these databases. To access the information on the public Internet, you can make use of any of a number of general search tools, such as those listed in Table 3.5.

From Table 3.5, you can see that there are at least three ways to search the public Internet: subject directories, search engines, and meta-search engines. Which one should you use? This is a good question because the information that you get will differ depending on the search service you use. Also, some of these services are labeled *directories* and others *search engines,* which means that the databases they develop to search are created in different ways. However, most of the services offer both search engine and directory information, though they predominantly feature one type of result over another.

Research Navigator.c⊛m

search engine

The databases that are searched by the search services listed in Table 3.5 consist of web pages and not necessarily scholarly products such as books and journal articles. So the information that you will receive will differ greatly from that received from a search of ERIC or PsycINFO. Additional information about these search services can be obtained from the following two Internet sites:

1. Search Engine Showdown: www.notess.com. This site provides information on subject directories, search engines, and metasearch engines, including reviews, tips for conducting an Internet search, and statistics on the various search engines.
2. Search Engine Watch: www.searchenginewatch.com. This site list provides a comprehensive list of search tools as well as a brief description of each, search tips, and ratings of the major search engines.

Directories Directories group web pages by topics or categories. For example, Yahoo! uses directories to categorize web pages. If you go to Yahoo!, you will see many of the general categories used, such as Arts and Humanities, Business and Economy, and Education. Under each general category are a number of additional choices. For example, if you click on the "Education" link, you will bring up a web page with many other choices ranging from "Adult and Continuing Education" to "Teaching." You can then use one of these links to get information on a more specific area in the general category of "Education." The advantage of directories is that the web pages are reviewed and categorized by humans, giving

■ **TABLE 3.5**   Internet Search Tools

Type of Search	Internet Address
Subject Directory	
Argus Clearinghouse	www.clearinghouse.net
Education Internet Guide	www.library.usyd.edu.au/Guides/
Britannica Internet Guide	www.britannica.com
Librarians' Index	www.lii.org
Open Directory	www.dmoz.org
WWW Virtual Library	www.vlib.org
Yahoo!	www.yahoo.com
Search Engines	
Alta Vista	www.altavista.com
Fast Search	www.alltheweb.com
Ask Jeeves	www.askjeeves.com
Google	www.google.com
HotBot	www.hotbot.com
Lycos	www.lycos.com
Northern Light	www.northernlight.com
Meta-Search Engines	
Dogpile	www.dogpile.com
Metacrawler	www.metacrawler.com
ProFusion	www.profusion.com
Search.com	www.search.com
SavvySearch	www.savvysearch.com
Vivisimo	www.ixquick.com

more assurance that the web pages that are identified will yield information related to your topic of interest.

Search Engines   Search engines develop a large database of web pages by using software called spiders or webcrawlers that search the public Internet, capturing information from each web page they visit. The database of each search engine is therefore dependent on the web pages it has visited and the information it has captured. A search using one of these search engines will provide web pages with terms or words that are identical to or close to your search terms. For example, a search of information on the term *home schooling* using the AltaVista search engine provides twenty pages of links to web pages with information ranging from curriculum aids to a magazine on home schooling. You must search through these web pages to identify relevant information.

In spite of the vast amount of information provided by these search engines, Lawrence and Giles (1999) have concluded that fewer than 20 percent of the available web pages appear in the databases of even the largest search sites. Also, there is often little overlap between the databases used by each search engine, so several search engines should be used for a more comprehensive search. If you are going to use the public Internet in your search, we suggest that you use Google because if offers the largest collection of web pages of any crawler-based search engine.

Meta-Search Engines A meta-search engine, such as Dogpile, submits your search to several search engine databases at the same time. The results are then blended together into one page. Use of meta-search engines would seem to be the best approach, as there is so little overlap between the databases searched by each search engine. Although meta-search engines are commendable, they have some significant limitations. Most retrieve only the top ten to fifty web pages from each search engine, so the total number of web pages retrieved might be considerably less than would be found by doing a search using only one search engine such as Google.

The public Internet is a vast resource that can provide a wealth of information about almost any topic. Its tremendous advantage is that it is accessible twenty-four hours a day and can be accessed from the comfort of your own home, apartment, office, or dorm room. However, there are some significant disadvantages to using the public Internet for conducting a literature search. Conducting a literature search is very time consuming because much of the information on the Internet is disorganized. A search will give you links to web pages with any information related to the key words you use for your search. This means that you must sift through a lot of material to try to capture the information you desire. However, the biggest disadvantage of the public Internet is the potential lack of credibility or accuracy of the information received. Anyone can put up a web page with any kind of information. This means that you must judge each website to determine whether the information contained is reliable and accurate. Table 3.6 provides some guidelines to use in evaluating the accuracy of information obtained from the Internet.

Research
Navigator.com

**Internet
credibility**

The Internet is potentially a valuable resource with access to a wealth of information. The challenge is learning how to mine the Internet and effectively use its vast array of information. As you spend more and more time navigating the Internet, you will become increasingly proficient in locating information and maximizing the tremendous resources that are at your fingertips.

3.8 What is the difference between directories, search engines, and meta-search engines?

3.9 What are the advantages and disadvantages of using the public Internet in conducting a literature search?

3.10 How would you evaluate the validity of information obtained over the Internet?

REVIEW

QUESTIONS

■ **T A B L E   3 . 6**   Evaluating Internet Resources

One of the main problems with the public Internet is determining the validity of the information obtained because anyone can establish a website and produce a web page. To help you differentiate good from bad information, ask yourself the following questions:

1. What is the source of the information?
   a. An address ending with .edu is from an institution of higher education. This information is probably accurate, particularly if it is part of the official information put out by the institution. Information produced by a faculty member or student could contain varying degrees of bias.
   b. An address ending with .gov is from some branch of the federal government. This information will probably be accurate.
   c. An address ending with .org is from a nonprofit organization. The accuracy of this information will depend on the organization. You can rely on information from organizations such as the American Educational Research Association. But other organizations might have a specific agenda and provide biased information. You need to look at the mission of the organization to assess the accuracy of the information.
   d. An address ending with .com is from a commercial vendor or a private individual. The accuracy of at least some of the information from a commercial vendor should always be suspect because a profit motive typically drives the information provided. The intentions of private individuals can vary, so the information on their pages should be handled with care also.
   e. An address ending with .net is from anyone that can afford to pay for the space on a server. Information from this source is the most suspect because it can come from anyone.
2. What is the purpose of the web page? Is it a public service, sales, educational, editorial, etc. web page? The purpose of the web page may suggest the type of bias that may exist in the information presented.
3. Does the information display or present information that is traceable to factual information presented in some bibliographic or internal reference? Information that does would appear to be accurate.
4. Is there some acknowledgement of the limitations of the information particularly if the information is a report of some data or study? Such acknowledgements suggest accuracy.
5. Does the web page state when it was last revised? This will give some information about its currency.
6. Is the information appropriate for your purpose? In other words, is the information scholarly, trade, or popular information? For a research study, you would want scholarly information.

FEASIBILITY OF THE STUDY

After you have completed your literature review, you are ready to synthesize this wealth of material and not only identify the research problems within the topic area you have se-lected, but also formulate the specific research questions and research hypotheses to be investigated. As you develop your research questions and hypotheses, you must make a decision as to whether the study you want to conduct is feasible. Every research study that is conducted varies with respect to the amount of time required to gather the data, type of research participants needed, expense, expertise of the researcher, and ethical sensitivity. Studies that either are too time consuming, require skills that you might not have, or are too expensive should not be initiated.

For example, if you wanted to investigate the efficacy of a new instructional program for teaching reading to children with attention deficit hyperactive disorder (ADHD), you would have to have access to a population of children with ADHD and ensure that each child in the study had met the diagnosis of ADHD. Then you would have to obtain the cooperation of the children's parents, the children themselves, the school system, and the teacher or teachers. Even if you had this cooperation, the study would take time because you would be investigating a reading instruction program. Therefore, you would have to be prepared to spend six months to a year in data collection. Finally, conducting such a study would entail some expense in providing the diagnosis of ADHD and obtaining the instructional materials and the assessment instruments. Overall, this would seem to be an ambitious study that would be out of reach of most students.

STATEMENT OF THE RESEARCH PROBLEM

After you have completed the literature review and have read and digested the literature, you should have a good idea of the problems in your topic area that need a solution. These problems represent research problems. Note that there is a difference between a research topic area and a research problem. A research topic is the broad area in which you are interested, such as *distance education, mainstreaming,* or *self-esteem.* A **research problem** is an education issue or problem within the broad topic area. For example, within the topic area of *distance learning,* there might be issues or problems of a lack of student interest, or accuracy of assessment of performance. However, the way in which the research problem is specified will differ somewhat depending on whether you are conducting a quantitative or a qualitative study.

■ **Research problem**
An education issue or problem within a broad topic area

Stating a Quantitative Research Problem

In stating a quantitative research problem, the emphasis is on the need to explain, predict, or describe some outcome or event. Look at this first paragraph of a quantitative study conducted by DeLaPaz (2001):

> Difficulties with written language production have been well documented among students with learning disabilities (LD). Those students typically lack important knowledge of the writing process and demonstrate limited abilities to generate plans, organize text, or engage in substantive revision (Englert & Raphael, 1998; McCutchen, 1998; Thomas, Englert, & Gregg, 1987). Problems with mechanics, including spelling, capitalization, and punctuation, further interfere with composing. Consequently, the writing of students with LD is less polished, expansive, coherent, and effective than that of their peers (Englert & Raphael; Graham,

1990; Graham & Harris, 1989; Montague, Graves, & Leavelle, 1991; Newcomer & Barenbaum, 1991; Wong, Wong, & Blenkinsop, 1989). (p. 37)

DeLaPaz introduced the general topic area in the first sentence as being "difficulties with written language production." She then identified the population in which this was a problem: students with learning disabilities. She continued by identifying the problems these students have, such as their limited ability to generate plans, organize text, and revise material. All of these are legitimate research problems because they represent educational issues that need a solution. Quantitative studies could be conducted to attempt to explain why the problems exist as well as how to ameliorate them.

Stating a Qualitative Research Problem

In a qualitative study, the research problem will focus on exploring some process, event, or phenomenon as illustrated in Otieno's (2001) introduction of her qualitative study of the educational experiences of seven African women:

> According to the late Dr. Kwegyir Aggrey of Ghana, educate a man and you have educated an individual, educate a woman and you have educated a nation. More than half of the population of Africa is made up of women. While this statement is true, female education in Africa has not developed at the same pace as that of males. There are many recent studies that examine problems African women encounter while attempting to pursue higher education (Yeboah, 1997, 2000; Namuddu, 1992; Lindasy, 1980; Bappa, 1985; and Eshwani, 1983). Most African countries have identified education as a key element in economic development. The linkage between female education and development in general cannot be overemphasized. Moreover, research has found that female education is highly correlated with better use of family planning, low fertility rates, and low infant mortality (Yehoah, 1997, 2000). The recognition by educators in the international community of the fact that female education is essential to national and global development is perhaps one reason why the education of women and girls is now a popular topic for many researchers. Returns on education are significant both for the individual and for society. Education is a particularly powerful achievement for women as it opens up the potential for wider participation in the economy. This increased awareness has raised questions as to what problems the female population face, what factors hold them back, and how these factors can be overcome to enable the majority of women to obtain higher education. It is through full inclusion in the process of obtaining higher education that women can participate fully in the process of the continent's development. (p. 3)

In this example, Otieno opens with a statement about the value of education, particularly for women. This is the general topic area of the study. She then points out the primary research problem: African women are less likely to receive an education than men are. She continues by pointing out that when women receive an education, many positive effects occur for both the individual and society. This emphasizes the importance of studying this research problem. Otieno then notes that the awareness of the positive effects that result from an educated female population has raised questions regarding the problems these individuals face in getting a higher education. What holds them back from attaining a higher education, and how can these difficulties be overcome? This leads her to state that women can participate in the continent's development only by exploring the complete process by which women obtain a higher education. This represented Otieno's statement of her research problem. She then proceeded to conduct a study exploring this process.

STATEMENT OF THE PURPOSE OF THE STUDY

The statement of the **purpose of a research study** is a statement of the researcher's intent or objective of the study. This is a statement that logically follows from the identification of one or more research problems. This statement needs to be made because making it ensures that you have a good grasp of the specific problem you wish to investigate. A specific statement of the purpose of the study will also enable you to communicate your research project to others. Providing a specification of the study purpose at the outset also has the advantage of guiding the research process by, for example, indicating how and by what methods the data will be collected. However, the nature of this statement will differ somewhat depending on whether you are conducting a qualitative or quantitative study.

- **Purpose of a research study**
  A statement of the researcher's intent or objective of the study

Statement of Purpose in a Quantitative Study

The purpose statement in a quantitative study is a declarative statement that identifies the type of relationship being investigated between a set of variables. This relationship could be causal or descriptive. For example, if you wanted to investigate the causal connection that might exist between a treatment for learning disability and the effect of that treatment on spelling ability, your purpose statement could be stated as follows:

> The purpose of this study is to investigate the effect that treatment for a learning disability has on the spelling proficiency of children with a learning disability.

However, if the intent of your study was to describe the relationship between spelling proficiency and the extent of a person's learning disability, your purpose statement could be stated as follows:

> The purpose of this study is to describe the degree of relationship that exists between spelling proficiency and the extent of a person's learning disability.

Both of these statements of purpose have identified the intent of the study and the variables being investigated. The difference is that one study is attempting to determine whether learning disability is causally related to academic achievement, whereas the other is attempting to describe the relationship that exists between these two variables. These two illustrate the basic and essential characteristics that should exist in a statement of purpose. Both identify the variables being investigated and the intent of the study or the way in which these variables will be investigated. Although this illustrates the desired form of a statement of purpose, the actual statement of purpose in research articles frequently differs from the ideal. For example, Burnam and Kafai's (2001) statement of the purpose of their research study was as follows:

> The purpose of this study is to investigate the moral reasoning of children within the unique domain of computer and Internet use. (p. 114)

This statement of purpose identifies the variables being investigated in the study, moral reasoning and the computer and Internet, but it does not mention what is being investigated with regard to these two variables. The study could be describing the level of moral reasoning of children who use the computer and Internet, or it could be attempting to determine whether there is a difference between the moral reasoning of children who do and do not use the computer and Internet. There is no way to tell exactly what the researchers are attempting to do in studying these two variables.

A better statement of purpose would have been something like the following:

> The purpose of this study is to determine if the level of moral reasoning of children who are frequent computer and Internet users is different from that of children who seldom use the computer and Internet.

This statement of purpose identifies the exact type of relationship that is being investigated and the variables that are being investigated. This degree of specificity is desired to ensure that an accurate statement of purpose is being communicated.

Statement of Purpose in a Qualitative Study

The statement of purpose in a qualitative study should be a statement that the intent of the study is to explore or understand some phenomenon experienced by certain individuals at a specific research site. This means that a qualitative study's statement of purpose should do the following:

1. Convey a sense of an emerging design by stating that the purpose of the study is to describe, understand, develop, or discover something
2. State and define the central idea that you want to describe, understand, or discover
3. State the method by which you plan to collect and analyze the data by specifying whether you are conducting an ethnographic study, grounded theory study, case study, or phenomenological study
4. State the unit of analysis and/or the research site, such as fourth-grade students participating in a specific program

For example, Drew (1986) stated the following purpose of her study:

> The focus of the present study was to explore distressing and nurturing encounters of patients with caregivers and to ascertain the meanings that are engendered by such encounters. The study was conducted on one of the surgical units and the obstetrical/gynecological unit of a 374-bed community hospital. (p. 40)

This purpose statement contains several of the essential ingredients characterizing a qualitative study. It conveys the sense of an emerging design and defines the central idea by stating that the researcher intends to "explore distressing and nurturing encounters." It also states that the research site will be a specific unit in a community hospital. Although this statement of purpose does not explicitly state the method used to collect and analyze the data, it does contain most of the elements of a statement of purpose for a qualitative study. This example also demonstrates that not every statement of purpose will contain all the fundamental characteristics of a good, qualitative purpose statement. However, good purpose statements will contain most of these characteristics.

STATEMENT OF RESEARCH QUESTIONS

A research question is a statement of the specific question(s) to which the researcher seeks an answer. It is therefore an extension of the statement of the purpose of the study in that it specifies exactly the questions that the researcher will attempt to answer. Although research questions are found in both quantitative and qualitative studies, they differ somewhat in their structure. Quantitative research questions state exactly the relationship being investigated between the target variables. Qualitative research questions are not as specific. Instead, qualitative research questions are more likely to ask a general question about a process or about exploring a particular phenomenon.

Statement of a Quantitative Research Question

A **quantitative research question** is an interrogative sentence that asks a question about the relationship that exists between two or more variables. Common forms are descriptive, predictive, and causal research questions, as illustrated in Table 3.7. Regardless of the type of research question, you should make sure that you formulate it in very specific terms because a research question that is stated in very specific terms ensures that you have a good understanding of the variables you are investigating. It also aids in the design and conduct of your research study. To drive these points home, consider the difficulties you would encounter if you asked the question "What is the effect of participation in extracurricular activities on academic performance?" This is a good research question in that it asks an important question. However, it is worded so vaguely that it is difficult to pinpoint what is being investigated. What type of extracurricular activity and what type of academic performance? There are many different types of extracurricular activity, and it would be inappropriate to assume that all types would have similar effects. Similarly, academic performance could refer to overall average performance or to performance in specific subject areas.

Now contrast this question with the following question:

> What effect does playing football have on students' overall grade point average during the football season?

This question specifies exactly the variables that are to be investigated: the extracurricular activity of playing football and academic performance as measured by overall grade point average.

■ **Quantitative research question**
An interrogative sentence that asks a question about the relationship that exists between two or more variables

▓ **TABLE 3.7**   Writing Quantitative Research Questions

Descriptive Questions

Descriptive research questions seek answers to "How much?," "How often?," or "What changes over time or over different situations?" type of questions. The script for a descriptive research question would be as follows:

- (Descriptive question) Do(es) (participants) (variable being studied) at (research site)?
- This script could lead to the following descriptive question:
- How frequently do kindergarten children engage in aggressive acts on the playground?

Descriptive questions can seek to identify the degree of relationship that exists between two or more variables. The script for a descriptive relationship question would be as follows:

- What is the relationship between (variable 1) and (variable 2) for (participants)?
- This script could lead to the following relationship questions:
- What is the relationship between amount of time studied and the grades students make?

Predictive Questions

Predictive questions are questions that seek to determine whether one or more variables can be used to predict some future outcome. The script for a predictive question would be as follows:

- Does (predictor variable) predict (outcome variable) in (setting)?
- This script could lead to the following predictive question:
- Does parental educational level predict students' propensity to drop out of high school?

Causal Questions

Causal questions are questions that compare different variations of some phenomenon to identify the cause of something. These questions often involve the manipulation of an independent variable and the comparison of the outcome of this manipulation. The script for causal questions would be as follows:

- Does variation (or change) in the (independent variable) produce changes (e.g., increase, decrease) in (a dependent variable)?
- This script could lead to the following causal question:
- Does variation in amount of homework assigned produce a change in students' test performance?

As you should be able to see from this example, making a specific statement of the research question helps ensure that you understand the problem you are investigating. It also helps you to make decisions about factors such as who the research participants will be and what materials or measures you will need to conduct the study. A vaguely stated research question gives no such assistance. To drive this point home, go back and reread the two research questions stated above and ask yourself, "What research participants should I use?" and "What outcome measures should I use?"

You might be asking yourself, "How specific should I be in formulating the research questions?" Remember that the purpose of formulating a specific research question is to ensure that you have a good grasp of the variables being investigated and to assist you in designing and completing your research study. If the formulation of your research questions is specific enough to serve these purposes, you have probably been specific enough. If these purposes have not been met, you need to rethink your research question and increase the specificity.

Statement of a Qualitative Research Question

A **qualitative research question** is an interrogative sentence that asks a question about some process, issue, or phenomenon that is to be explored. It is a general, open-ended, and overarching question that you would like to answer. From this overarching research question you can frequently narrow the purpose of a study into more specific questions. It can be helpful to state the general purpose of the study and then state a number of subquestions that break the overall research question into the components that will be investigated. For example, Bodycott, Walker, and Kin (2001) investigated the beliefs that preservice teachers held about their principals. Their statement of purpose was as follows:

> The purpose of this study was to explore how the social context of schools and schooling influenced preservice teachers' personal constructs of the principal. (p. 15)

The research question that follows from this purpose statement is:

> How does the social context of a school influence preservice teachers' beliefs about the principal?

The overall research question, as you can see, is very similar to the statement of purpose and tends to restate the purpose statement in question form. Because the overarching research question is, to a great extent, a restatement of the purpose of the study, many researchers omit it, although it can provide a focus to the statement of the purpose of the study. However, a number of subquestions or more specific questions are typically asked, because these questions break the central research question into the specific topics or processes that are explored in the study. For example, Bodycott et al. (2001) asked the following two subquestions in the form of "aims" of the research:

1. "The first aim of the study was to determine preservice teachers' beliefs about principals."
2. "The second aim was to identify what or who influenced these beliefs." (p. 16)

These two questions provide a specific focus to the study and help to ensure that the researcher knows exactly what is being investigated in the study. It also aids in the design and conduct of the study because in a qualitative study, the more specific subquestions will serve as a guide to the type of questions asked of participants. For example, look at the general research question posed in the Bodycott et al. (2001) study cited above. This general research question provides little direction in formulating interview questions that might be

■ **Qualitative research question**

An interrogative sentence that asks a question about some process, issue, or phenomenon to be explored

asked of preservice teachers. However, the statement of the two "aims" of the research would direct the development of interview questions such as the following:

What is the role of the principal of a school?
What kind of relationship should exist between a teacher and the principal?
Who talks to you about the principal?
Who do you think has the most accurate information about the principal?

FORMULATING HYPOTHESES

In quantitative research, after you have identified a research problem that you want to investigate and you have stated your research purpose and your research question(s), you are ready to formulate your hypothesis. The **hypothesis** represents the formal statement of the researcher's prediction of the relationship that exists among the variables under investigation. It logically follows the statement of the research question, because you could not formulate the hypothesis without having first stated, either explicitly or implicitly, the research question. For example, the research question that Butler and Neuman (1995) formulated was as follows:

■ **Hypothesis**
The formal statement of the researcher's prediction of the relationship that exists among the variables under investigation

Will the perceptions and actual help-seeking behaviors of children differ in task (an instructional set that told the children that they would learn to solve puzzles) versus ego-involving (an instructional set that told the children that kids who solve the puzzles are very smart) settings?

From this research question, they hypothesized or predicted the following:

Children in ego-involving settings will be less likely to request help than children in task-involving settings.

Note that this hypothesis took the two variables stated in Butler and Neumann's research question—help-seeking behaviors (the dependent variable) and type of setting (the independent variable)—and made a prediction about how help-seeking behaviors would differ depending on the type of setting the children were in. You can use the following script for stating a hypothesis:

(group 1 participants, independent variable) will (differ in some way—increase, decrease, improve, etc.) (dependent variable) than (group 2 participants, independent variable).

The hypothesis for the Butler and Newman study used this script in the following way:

Group 1, independent variable = children in ego-involving settings
Differ = be less likely to request
Dependent variable = help
Group 2, independent variable = children in task-involving settings

Another example using this script might be as follows:

> Learning-disabled children receiving individualized instruction will show greater gains in academic achievement than learning disabled children receiving group instruction.

This progression from the statement of the research question to the hypothesis should seem logical because the hypothesis merely represents a statement of the predicted relation between the variables stated in the research question. In reading the journal articles that you identify in your literature review, you will probably have difficulty finding a statement of the research question in every study because many authors do not make such an explicit statement. Experienced researchers often have such familiarity with their field that they consider the research question to be self-evident. Their predicted solutions to these problems or their hypotheses are not apparent, however, so they should always be stated.

The stated hypothesis typically emerges from the literature review or from theory. As we stated earlier, one of the functions of theory is to guide research. One of the ways in which a theory accomplishes this function is to make a prediction of the relationship between variables. Similarly, the research literature that you have read might suggest the relationship that should exist between the variables being investigated. However, hypotheses can also come from reasoning based on casual observation of events. For example, you might have noticed that some children get very nervous when they take a test and that these children seem to be the ones who get the poorest grades. From this observation, you might formulate a research question that asks, "How does test anxiety affect performance on a test?" Your hypothesis might be that performance will decrease as test anxiety increases.

Regardless of the source of the hypothesis, it must meet one criterion: A hypothesis must be capable of being either refuted or confirmed. A hypothesis that fails to meet this criterion, or is nontestable, removes the question from the realm of empirical research. This is why moral, ethical, and religious questions and the hypotheses that follow from them are outside the realm of empirical research. One can neither confirm nor refute hypotheses that focus on such issues because it is not possible to collect data that will resolve the issues. For example, it is not possible to collect data that would support or refute a hypothesis stating that students get a better science education if they are taught both evolutionary and Christian perspectives on the origin of humans.

The importance of hypotheses exists primarily in quantitative studies because their goal and purpose differs from those of qualitative research studies. Quantitative research has the goal of identifying the relationships that exist between sets of variables, whereas qualitative research attempts to discover, explore, or describe a given setting, event, or situation. Therefore, hypothesis formulation is appropriate at the outset of a quantitative research study. In this type of study, we not only specify the variables being investigated, but also make a prediction about the relationship that exists between these variables. We then conduct the study to determine whether the relation that we predict among these variables actually exists. In a qualitative study, we often do not have such knowledge of the variables. The study is generally conducted to describe or discover the significant variables. This discovery is accomplished by asking very general questions that permit a lot of latitude in participants' responses. From the participants' responses, additional research questions and even hypotheses might emerge. However, in many studies, the qualitative researcher only poses research questions, some of which might emerge as the study is conducted, rather than formulating hypotheses.

<table>
<tr><td rowspan="2">**R E V I E W**

Q U E S T I O N S</td><td>**3.11** What factors should you consider in determining whether it is possible for you to conduct a study?</td></tr>
<tr><td>**3.12** How do research problems in qualitative and quantitative research differ?</td></tr>
<tr><td></td><td>**3.13** How does the statement of the purpose of a study differ in qualitative and quantitative research?</td></tr>
<tr><td></td><td>**3.14** How do research questions differ in qualitative and quantitative research, and what is their purpose?</td></tr>
<tr><td></td><td>**3.15** Why should research questions in quantitative research be very specific?</td></tr>
<tr><td></td><td>**3.16** What is a hypothesis, and what is the one criterion that it must meet?</td></tr>
<tr><td></td><td>**3.17** Why are hypotheses typically not formulated in qualitative research, and what is typically used instead?</td></tr>
</table>

Research
Navigator.c⊛m

research proposal

■ **Research proposal**
A written document
that summarizes the
prior literature, identi-
fies the research topic
area and the research
questions to be an-
swered, and specifies
the procedure that will
be followed in obtain-
ing an answer to these
research questions

———— THE RESEARCH PROPOSAL

The next step in the research process is to prepare a written research proposal. Preparing a research proposal forces you to spell out the rationale for your research study and to specify each step in detail. The process helps you to identify issues that you had not thought of but need to plan for to complete your study. Students working on their thesis or dissertation research are required to prepare a written research proposal.

   The **research proposal** is a written document that summarizes the prior literature, identifies the research topic area and the research questions to be answered, and specifies the procedure that will be followed in obtaining an answer to these research questions. The research proposal is the formal description of the procedure to be used in the study. You will submit a research proposal to your thesis or dissertation committee for critique, and the committee members will read the proposal critically and provide suggestions for its improvement. At some point in your career, you might even be asked to prepare a grant proposal. The preparation of a grant proposal will have the same requirements as a thesis or dissertation proposal. This is therefore a skill that any researcher must master. Most research proposals contain the following elements:

Title Page
Abstract
Introduction
    1. A statement of the research topic
    2. A statement of the research problem(s) and a summary of prior literature
    3. The purpose of the study
    4. The research questions(s)
    5. The hypotheses of the study if a quantitative study is being conducted

Method
    1. Research participants
    2. Apparatus and/or instruments
    3. Procedure
Data analysis
References

Additional headings can be included if they provide clearer communication of the research study and its results. For example, some research plans include a separate design section if the design of the study is complicated. This design section either precedes the method section or is a separate section within the method section and provides details of the design used in the study. A thesis or dissertation often includes a separate section entitled "Literature Review" and another section entitled "Hypotheses." Whether such additional sections are to be included is a function of the type of study being conducted, the requirements of your graduate program, and the approach that will most effectively present your research plan.

Introduction

The introduction to any research study is broad at the beginning and narrow at the end. It should begin with a very general introduction to the research topic and then start to narrow the focus by discussing the results of prior studies that bear on the problem you are investigating. This discussion should identify research problems that remain unanswered within the broad topic area you have chosen to provide a rationale for your chosen study. The literature review should lead directly into a statement of the purpose of your study and in this way show the continuity between what you are investigating and prior research. After stating the purpose of the study, you should state the study research questions. If you are conducting a quantitative study, you should state your research hypothesis.

Method

The purpose of the method section is to specify exactly how you plan to conduct the study. In this section, you must be sufficiently exact that someone else can read your method section and conduct exactly the same study that you are going to conduct. If another researcher can read the method section and replicate the study that you are going to conduct, you have adequately described this section. Although this section might vary depending on whether you are conducting a quantitative or a qualitative study, it generally consists of a description of the research participants, any apparatus or instruments that are to be used in data collection, and the design and procedure to be followed in collecting the data.

Research Participants In this section, you should specify exactly who the research participants will be, how many will participate in the study, their characteristics (e.g., age, gender), and how they are going to be selected for inclusion in your study. Any other information relating to the research participants should also be included in this section. For example, you should mention whether you are going to give the research participants an inducement to participate or where the participants are located if you are conducting a qualitative study. A description of the research participants might be as follows:

> The research participants will be 140 randomly selected children from those attending grades two and six in three Midwestern schools serving a primarily middle-class neighborhood. There will be an equal number of male and female children from each grade. Each child will be given a free ticket to one of the local theaters when he or she completes the research study.

Apparatus and/or Instruments   In this section, you describe the instruments (such as intelligence tests, achievement tests, a measure of self-concept or attitude) and any materials (such as booklets or training manuals) or apparatus (such as a computer or biofeedback equipment) that you plan to use to collect your data. This description should include information about the validity and reliability of the instruments as well as where they can be obtained. The apparatus should be described in sufficient detail to enable someone else to obtain comparable equipment. Following the description of the apparatus and/or instruments, you should explain why each item is being used. For example, this section might read as follows:

> The Information and Block Design subtests of the Wechsler Preschool and Primary Scale of Intelligence-Revised (WPPSI-R) (Wechsler, 1989) will be used to estimate the research participants' general level of intellectual functioning. The Information subtest . . . [Briefly explain what it is and what type of response is required of the child.] The Block Design subtest . . . [Briefly explain what it is and what type of response is required of the child.] Test-retest reliability of the Information subtest ranges from .74 to .84 and .79 to .86 for the Block Design subtest.

Procedure   In the procedure section, you describe not only the design of the study, but also how you are going to implement it. You must describe how you are going to execute the study from the moment you meet the first research participant to the moment when you terminate contact. You must present a step-by-step account of what both you and the research participant will do. This should include any instructions or conditions to be presented to the participants and the responses that are required of them, as well as any control techniques used, such as random assignment to groups. One criterion that you can use to determine whether you have adequately described the procedure section is to ask someone else to read it and then have that person explain to you how the study will be conducted. If your reader can read your procedure section and conduct the study you designed, you have adequately communicated the procedure you will use to collect the data. Look at Manthei and Gilmore's (1996) description of the procedure used in their study investigating teacher stress:

> The Stress in Teaching Questionnaire was administered to all eight schools five times; at the end of term 1 and near the end of term 3 in years 1987 and 1988; and at the end of term 3 of 1990 (the end of the first year of the implementation of the Tomorrow's Schools administrative reforms). In each instance, the purpose of the questionnaire was explained to the whole staff. Teachers either completed them during a scheduled staff meeting or indi-

vidually over the next few days. Completed questionnaires were either handed directly to one of the researchers or were collected by a designated staff member and posted directly to a researcher. (p. 6)

In the procedure section, these researchers identified the type of questionnaire that was administered, which identifies the type of information they received, and they specified when the questionnaire was administered. The procedure also specified how the questionnaires were handled after completion by the participants. From this description you should be able to collect data in the same manner as Manthei and Gilmore did. Although this represents a rather simple procedure section and one that was probably easy to write, it illustrates the detail that must be included and the characteristics of the section.

Data Analysis

After you have provided a description of how you are going to collect the data for your study, you need to specify how you are going to analyze your data. In most instances, the nature of the data analysis will evolve directly from the study design. As you develop your study design, you should ask yourself, "How am I going to analyze the data collected to test the hypotheses I have formulated?" This is necessary to ensure that the data you collect can be analyzed appropriately. It also provides a check on the design of your study, because if you cannot identify a way of analyzing the data that are collected so that they provide information about the study hypotheses, you must redesign the study.

The appropriate method of analyzing your data depends on whether you are conducting a qualitative or quantitative study and the specific components of each type of study. For example, if you were conducting a quantitative study in which the research participants were randomly assigned to one of three groups and each group of participants received a different method of instruction, you would probably use a one-way analysis-of-variance statistical test. Therefore, to specify the appropriate test for analyzing your data, you must have some knowledge of statistics. Only when you know something about both statistics and research methodology can you design a quantitative study from beginning to end.

Qualitative data analysis is much more eclectic, and there is no single "right" way of analyzing the data because of the nature of the qualitative data collected. The data that are collected from a qualitative study come from observations, interviews, documents, and audiovisual materials such as photographs, videotapes, and films. Data analysis requires the reduction and interpretation of the voluminous amount of information collected. Analysis of this volume of data requires reduction to certain patterns, categories, or themes, which are then interpreted by using some schema. In general, qualitative data analysis requires coding and searching for relationships and patterns until a holistic picture can emerge.

CONSUMER USE OF THE LITERATURE

In this book, we attempt to give you detailed information on how to conduct a research study in the field of education. However, the reality of the situation is that most of you will not be engaged in a lifetime of research and might never conduct a formal study. Even if you do not become an educational researcher, courses such as this one are valuable because they make you a better consumer of research. After taking this course, you will have the basic information you need to evaluate a research study to determine whether the conclusions are valid and whether it was conducted correctly. Tables 3.8 and 3.9 provide a checklist of elements to consider in evaluating quantitative and qualitative research studies.

To be an effective consumer of research, you should not and must not consider the results of any one study to be conclusive. You need to look across studies to see whether the findings are repeatedly confirmed or replicated. For example, assume that you read a study demonstrating that computer-assisted instruction resulted in better performance than did instruction that did not have the aid of computers. Does this mean that you can definitely conclude that computer-assisted instruction is the superior mode of instruction? Of course not! One study does not produce a conclusive finding on which you can rely. For a study to be reliable, the results must be replicated by other researchers on other populations in other locations because the phenomena that educational researchers investigate are too complex to be explained by a single study, and the ability to control the research environment, the research participant sample, and the procedures used vary considerably from study to study. Therefore, many studies will be conducted on a given phenomenon, and each study will be conducted in a slightly different way on a slightly different participant sample. The results will vary slightly from study to study, and you must somehow integrate them.

The technique that is used for summarizing the results of multiple quantitative studies of a given phenomenon is called meta-analysis. **Meta-analysis** is a term introduced by Glass (1976) to describe a quantitative approach that is used to integrate and describe the results of a large number of studies. Meta-analysis gets around the problem of making subjective judgments and preferences in summarizing the research literature because it involves the use of a variety of quantitative techniques to analyze the results of studies conducted on a given topic. Therefore, when you are conducting your literature review and trying to reach some conclusion about a given phenomenon, pay particular attention to literature summaries that have made use of meta-analysis because the results of these summaries are more accurate in the conclusions reached.

■ **Meta-analysis**
A quantitative technique that is used to integrate and describe the results of a large number of studies

To illustrate the use of meta-analysis, let us look at the meta-analysis conducted by Forness and Kavale (1996) on studies that investigated the efficacy of a social skills training program for children with learning disabilities. Fifty-three studies were identified from abstract and citation archives, reference lists from prior literature reviews, and bibliographies of research reports. Forness and Kavale applied standard meta-analytic statistical procedures to the results of these fifty-three studies to provide an overall integration and description of the findings of these studies. This analysis revealed that the social skills training programs that were applied to children with learning deficits had a very small but positive effect. This is the primary conclusion that you should retain from the currently available literature. If you looked at individual studies, you might find some that indicated that social skills training programs were totally ineffective and others that indicated that they were very effective. Without the benefit of a meta-analysis, you might be influenced more by one or several of these studies and reach an inappropriate conclusion. Meta-analysis eliminates this type of bias and provides an overall synopsis of the available literature.

◼ **T A B L E 3 . 8**   Checklist for Evaluating a Quantitative Study

The following checklist can be used to help in evaluating the quality of a quantitative research study although some of the questions apply only to experimental studies. If you are evaluating a nonexperimental study, you should disregard questions that focus on experimental studies.

Introduction

1. Is the research topic area clearly stated in the first paragraph?
2. Is (are) the research problem(s) clearly stated?
3. Does the literature review accurately convey the past research?
4. Does the literature review suggest and lead to the statement of the research purpose and/or research question(s)?
5. Is the purpose of the research clearly stated?
6. Is each research hypothesis clearly stated, and does it clearly state the expected relationship between the independent and dependent variables?
7. Is the theory from which the hypotheses came clearly explained?

Method

8. Are the demographics of the participants accurately described, and are they appropriate to this study?
9. Was an appropriate method of sampling used, given the purpose of the study?
10. Were enough participants included in the study to test the hypotheses?
11. Are the research instruments that were used reliable and valid for the participants used in the study?
12. For experimental research, do the manipulations of the independent variable represent the constructs (e.g., failure, poverty, self-esteem) being investigated or does the study have construct validity?
13. Do the measurements of the dependent variable represent the phenomenon (e.g., learning, aggression, stress) of interest?
14. For experimental research, were the participants randomly assigned to conditions?
15. Are there elements in the procedure that might have biased the results?
16. Did the researchers take appropriate actions to control for biases?
17. Were the participants treated ethically?

Results

18. Are appropriate statistical tests and calculations of effect sizes used to analyze the data?
19. Are the results presented clearly?
20. Is any part of the data being ignored, such as some participants being dropped?
21. Can the results be generalized to the populations and settings the researcher desires?

Discussion

22. Do the researchers clearly explain the results of the study?
23. Have the findings of the study been discussed in relation to the theoretical framework with which they began?
24. Have alternative explanations for the study results been examined?
25. Do the results conflict with prior research? If they do, has an explanation been provided for the conflicting data?
26. Have any limitations of the study been discussed?
27. Are future directions for research suggested?

■ **TABLE 3.9**   Checklist for Evaluating a Qualitative Study

The following checklist can be used to help in evaluating the quality of a qualitative research study.

Introduction

1. Is the research topic specified at the outset of the article?
2. Is (have) the research problem(s) (been) clearly identified?
3. Is there a sufficient review of the relevant research literature?
4. Is the purpose of the research clearly stated?
5. Are specific research questions identified and stated clearly?

Method

6. Have the characteristics of the participants, the research site, and the context been accurately described?
7. Are the participants appropriate for the purpose of the study?
8. Is the number of participants large enough?
9. Were adequate data collected to address the research question?
10. Were triangulation and other validity-enhancing strategies used to help produce trustworthy evidence?
11. Were the participants treated ethically?

Results

12. Are the findings presented clearly?
13. Are any potentially important data ignored by the researcher(s)?
14. Is sufficient evidence provided to convince you of the trustworthiness of the findings?

Discussion

15. Are the results discussed in relation to other research in this area?
16. Are the limitations of the study discussed?
17. Have the researchers examined alternative explanations for their findings?
18. Have suggestions for future research been provided?

SUMMARY

The first step in conducting a research study is identifying a research topic and then identifying a research problem in need of a solution. Although the beginning researcher might have difficulty in identifying a research problem, the field of education has numerous problems that are in need of solutions. To identify a research problem, you need to develop an inquisitive attitude and ask questions. Once you develop this mental set, then problem identification is relatively easy.

Educational research problems arise from a number of traditional sources, such as theories, practical issues, and past research. Additionally, in education, we have our own experience to draw on, because educational research is concerned with the field of education, and we have all had experience with this field. However, many problems dealing with moral, ethical, and religious issues cannot be subjected to empirical research even though they are frequently significant issues that must be dealt with in education.

Once a research problem has been identified, you must conduct a literature search. A review of the literature will reveal the current state of knowledge about your selected topic and suggest ways in which you can investigate the problem as well as point out related methodological issues. However, if you are conducting a qualitative research study rather than a quantitative study, you might want to just familiarize yourself with the literature to make sure that the study you want to conduct has not been done. This approach assumes that the researcher can take a fresh and uncontaminated perspective on the data collected and, it is hoped, develop a novel set of constructs, relationships, and theories if he or she has not conducted a thorough literature search.

In conducting the literature review, you should probably begin with books written on the topic and actual research reports in journals. In reviewing the past research on a topic, the most efficient means is to make use of one of the various information retrieval systems, particularly one that has access to the ERIC database, because this database contains the information that is of primary interest to educational researchers. The Internet can also assist in your literature review because many groups, organizations, and corporations have developed websites with considerable information that can be accessed through the public Internet. Additionally, there are conferences, debates, and journals as well as the results of research studies that are accessible through the Internet. The biggest disadvantage of using the public Internet is determining the reliability and validity of the information because much of the information can be biased, reflecting the motivation of the organization, company, or person providing the information.

After you have conducted the literature review, you must determine whether the study you want to conduct is feasible. This means that you must make an assessment of the amount of time, research participant population, expertise, and expense requirement, as well as the ethical sensitivity of the study. If this assessment indicates that a study will be feasible to conduct, then you must identify the research problem or problems that need to be explained, described, or predicted in quantitative studies and explored in qualitative studies. After stating the research problems in the topic area, you should state the purpose of the study. In a qualitative study, the purpose statement should express the language and methodology of a qualitative paradigm. If you were conducting a quantitative study, you would formulate your purpose statement in a way that identifies the intent of the study. A statement of the research question should follow the purpose statement, although it frequently does not. In qualitative studies, the purpose statement is more frequently followed by a statement of aims or a series of subquestions that specify the components of the study that will be investigated.

In quantitative studies, the research question is a statement asking whether a relationship exists between two or more variables. This relationship must be capable of being empirically tested. The statement must also be specific enough to assist you in making decisions about such factors as participants, apparatus, and the general design of the research study. The research question is then followed by a hypothesis, typically derived from past research, that makes a prediction about the relationship that exists between the variables being investigated. If the hypothesis is confirmed, the results not only answer the question asked, but also provide additional support to the literature that suggests the hypotheses. There is one criterion that any hypothesis must meet: It must be stated so that it is capable of being either refuted or confirmed. Remember also that hypotheses are used most frequently and are most important in quantitative research. Hypotheses frequently are not formulated in qualitative studies. Instead, qualitative studies focus on posing questions, some of which emerge as the study progresses.

KEY TERMS

Current Index to Journals in Education (CIJE) (p. 64)
Educational Resources Information Center (ERIC) (p. 64)
hypothesis (p. 80)

Internet (p. 67)
meta-analysis (p. 86)
purpose of a research study (p. 75)
qualitative research question (p. 79)
quantitative research question (p. 77)

research problem (p. 73)
research topic (p. 60)
Resources in Education (RIE) (p. 64)
theory (p. 58)

STUDY TIP   Visit the companion website for educational research at www.ablongman.com/johnsonchristensen2e for study questions and multiple-choice questions to find out how well you have mastered the material in this chapter. Also look at the other activities we have included to promote your mastery of the material in this chapter.

DISCUSSION QUESTIONS

1. In this chapter, we have listed several sources of research ideas.
   a. Which of these sources would produce the most ideas for research studies in education?
   b. If you had to produce an idea for a research study, which source would you use and why would you use this source?
2. What is the best use of a literature review? Is it best to use it to assist in specifying the research question and hypothesis and designing the study as is

done in quantitative studies, or should the literature review be used only after much of the data have been collected to integrate the study findings with prior research as some qualitative researchers recommend?
3. We constantly hear and read about the results of studies from television, radio, and newspaper reports. When you read the results of studies from these sources, what questions should you ask, and how should you evaluate the research reported?

RESEARCH EXERCISES

1. Develop a quantitative research question by answering the following:
   a. My topic area is _____.
   b. The research problems within this topic area are _____.
   c. The purpose of my study is _____.
   d. My research question is _____.
   e. My hypothesis is _____.
2. For the quantitative research question you identified in Exercise 1, make use of Research Navigator, and conduct a mini literature review by finding three research studies related to your research question and answering the following questions for each study.
   a. Title
   b. Author
   c. Journal with volume and page number
   d. Abstract

4

Research Ethics

LEARNING OBJECTIVES

To be able to

- Explain why it is necessary to consider ethical issues when designing and conducting research.
- State the guidelines that must be followed in conducting research with humans.
- Explain the procedures that must be followed to obtain approval to conduct a study.
- Specify the issues involved in conducting research with minors.

On April 26, 2002, Robert Steinhaeuser, a nineteen-year-old man dressed all in black, entered his former high school carrying a pump-action shotgun and a handgun and began mowing down teachers in classrooms and corridors. Fourteen teachers and administrators, two female students, and a police officer were killed before hundreds of police commandos surrounded the four-story building and charged inside. Mr. Steinhaeuser retreated to a classroom, barricaded himself inside, and then fatally shot himself as the police closed in (Biehl, 2002).

Students described Steinhaeuser as an intelligent person who was not aggressive but was often late for classes and had difficulties with teachers. However, Mr. Steinhaeuser had been expelled for poor grades that prevented him from taking university entrance exams. He apparently was angry over this, and this seemed to be the impetus for the shootings.

Teenage violence and mass murders, as illustrated in the case of Robert Steinhaeuser, are not isolated events. All we have to do is think back a few years to the April 1999 shootings at Columbine High School in Littleton, Colorado. Such violent expressions of anger always promote the questions "Why?" and "How could this have happened in our school?" These are questions that researchers are also asking and seeking to provide answers for. However, conducting research on such questions generates a variety of ethical concerns. One of the most serious is the harmful effect it could have on the participants.

Identifying the teenagers with pent-up anger might also lead others, such as the teachers in the school system, to view and react to these participants differently because they might now view these students as a threat. In the course of conducting the study, the researcher might identify a teenager who has severe anger and a tendency to vent the anger in aggressive ways. The researcher has a responsibility to protect the research participant as well as the potential target of the anger. This would mean that the participant's anger and his or her potential for engaging in violent behavior would become public. Although this would be appropriate behavior for the researcher, the privacy of the teenager would have been violated.

As you can see, a variety of ethical issues surround the investigation of certain types of behavior and phenomena of interest to educational researchers. This means that there is a need for a set of ethical guidelines for researchers to follow in conducting educational research. In this chapter, we will discuss the issues surrounding the ethics of educational research.

If you look at the journals in which educational researchers publish, you will see that these individuals are interested in a wide range of topics, such as learning strategies, factors affecting achievement, prediction of performance, types of instruction, and teacher effectiveness, all in an effort to acquire knowledge that will enhance the educational process. In pursuing these interests educational researchers make use of many different types of research approaches, such as interviews, surveys, ethnographic research, and experiments. In other words, to acquire knowledge about the educational process, educational researchers make use of the techniques that we are presenting in this book. In using these techniques, researchers ask questions, observe behavior, and manipulate various stimuli such as different teaching techniques in order to obtain information that will ultimately improve the educational process.

If you just think about the potential good that can come out of an educational research study, it makes a lot of sense to interview or survey students and teachers or ask them to participate in an experiment. However, we live in a society in which we have the right to privacy and the right to expect freedom from surveillance of our behavior without our consent. We also have the right to know whether our behavior is being manipulated and, if so, why.

Unfortunately, these basic rights can easily be violated when a research study is conducted. The possibility of such violation creates a problem for researchers because the public constantly demands to see improvements in the educational system. Whenever SAT scores decline or when results are publicized indicating that "Johnny can't read," the educational system is attacked, and demands are made for improving instruction. Improvements in education are a result, however, of well-designed and well-conducted research studies. In conducting these research studies, it is sometimes necessary to infringe on people's right to privacy and ask personal questions or observe their behavior because this is the only way in which researchers can collect the information needed for improving the educational system as a whole. Additionally, for the educator who is trained in research techniques, a decision *not* to conduct research is a matter of ethical concern.

Consideration of research ethics constitutes an integral part of the development and implementation of any research study. It would be very difficult, for example, to conduct a study investigating various strategies of teaching children with attention deficit hyperactive disorder (ADHD) without violating the children's right to privacy because it would be necessary first to identify and label certain children as having ADHD. This would be only one of the many ethical concerns to be considered in conducting such a study.

Such issues certainly create an ethical dilemma for the researcher, who must decide whether to conduct the research and violate certain rights of individuals for the purpose of gaining knowledge that could help others or to sacrifice such a gain in knowledge for the purpose of preserving human rights. As you can see, consideration of the ethics of any research study is necessary to assist the researcher in preventing abuses that could occur and in delineating the responsibilities of the investigator. This is why issues such as maintaining participants' anonymity and obtaining their informed consent before conducting the study are so important.

Research
Navigator.c⊛m

research ethics

■ **Ethics**
The principles and guidelines that help us to uphold the things we value
■ **Deontological approach**
An ethical approach that says ethical issues must be judged on the basis of some universal code

▬▬▬ WHAT ARE RESEARCH ETHICS?

Ethics is the principles and guidelines that help us to uphold the things we value. When most people think of ethics, they first think of moralistic sermons and endless philosophical debates. Whenever ethical issues are discussed, it is typical for individuals to differ about what does and what does not constitute ethical behavior. Most of the disagreements seem to arise because of the different approaches people take in attempting to resolve an ethical issue.

There are three basic approaches—deontology, ethical skepticism, and utilitarianism—that people tend to adopt when considering ethical issues in research. These approaches differ in terms of the criteria used to make decisions about what is right and wrong (Schlenker & Forsyth, 1977). The **deontological approach** takes the position that ethical issues must be judged on the basis of some universal code. Certain actions are inherently unethical and should never be performed regardless of the circumstances. For example, Baumrind (1985) used the deontological approach to argue that the use of deception in research is morally wrong and should not be used under any circumstances because it involves lying to research participants and precludes obtaining their informed consent.

A person using **ethical skepticism** would argue that concrete and inviolate moral codes such as those used by the deontologist cannot be formulated. Such a skeptic would not deny that ethical principles are important but would claim that ethical rules are arbitrary and relative to one's culture and time. According to this approach, an ethical decision must be a matter of the individual's conscience, and the researcher should do what he or she thinks is right and refrain from doing what he or she thinks is wrong. Research ethics are therefore a matter of the individual's conscience.

The third approach to assessing ethical issues is that of **utilitarianism.** This position maintains that judgments regarding the ethics of a particular research study depend on the consequences of that study for both the individual research participant and the larger benefit that may arise from the study results. In this position, ethical decisions are based on weighing the potential benefits that might accrue from a research study against the potential costs, as illustrated in Figure 4.1. If the benefits are sufficiently large relative to the costs, then the decision is that the study is ethically acceptable. This is the primary approach used by the federal government, most professional organizations, and institutional review boards in reaching difficult ethical decisions about studies that place research participants at risk but also have the potential for yielding important knowledge and significant benefit to humans. This approach says that research ethics should be a set of principles to assist the researcher in deciding which goals are important in reconciling conflicting values (Diener & Crandall, 1978). The utilitarian approach seems to be the primary approach that permits a

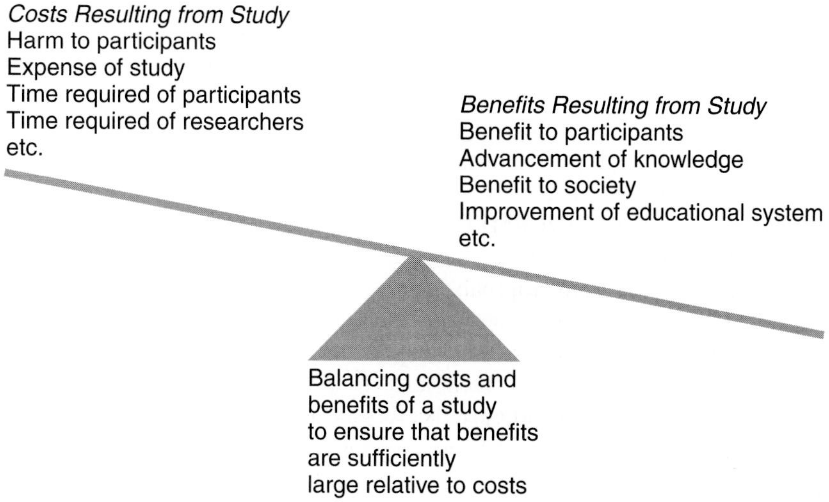

■ **Ethical skepticism**
An ethical approach that says concrete and inviolate moral codes cannot be formulated
■ **Utilitarianism**
An ethical approach that says judgments of the ethics of a study depend on the consequences the study has for the research participants and the benefits that may arise from the study

Costs Resulting from Study
Harm to participants
Expense of study
Time required of participants
Time required of researchers
etc.

Benefits Resulting from Study
Benefit to participants
Advancement of knowledge
Benefit to society
Improvement of educational system
etc.

Balancing costs and
benefits of a study
to ensure that benefits
are sufficiently
large relative to costs

■ **FIGURE 4.1**   Utilitarian approach to judging the ethical acceptability of a research study

rational and logical basis for debating ethical issues that arise in the conduct of research and the only approach that permits reaching a decision as to whether to conduct the research or to forgo the research because the potential benefit does not outweigh the potential cost. Regardless of the approach one takes, research ethics should not be a set of moralistic dictates imposed on the research community. Rather, they should be a set of principles that will assist researchers in deciding how to conduct an ethical study.

▬▬▬▬ ETHICAL CONCERNS

■ **Research ethics**
A set of principles to guide and assist researchers in conducting ethical studies

If **research ethics** are a guiding set of principles that are to assist researchers in conducting ethical studies, it is important to identify the ethical issues that are of importance to researchers. Diener and Crandall (1978) have identified three areas of ethical concern for social and behavioral scientists: (1) the relationship between society and science, (2) professional issues, and (3) the treatment of research participants.

Relationship between Society and Science

The ethical issue concerning the relationship between society and science revolves around the extent to which societal concerns and cultural values should direct the course of research. The society in which we live tends to dictate to a great extent the issues and research areas that are considered important and should be investigated. For example, the common cold is a condition that afflicts everyone at some point. However, little time is spent investigating ways to eliminate this affliction, probably because a cold is typically a temporary discomfort that is not life threatening. There are many other issues that have more far-reaching implications, such as the education of our children. Society considers such problems much more important, and it encourages research in areas that are considered important.

One of the ways in which these priorities are communicated to researchers is through the numerous funding agencies that exist within our society. The largest funding agency is the federal government. The federal government spends millions of dollars every year on both basic and applied research. However, it also sets priorities for how the money is to be spent. To increase the probability of obtaining a portion of these research funds, investigators often orient their research proposals toward these priorities, which means that the federal government at least partially dictates the type of research that is conducted. Every year these funding agencies announce "Requests for Proposals" in specific areas. For example, the Office of Educational Research and Development of the U.S. Department of Education recently issued a request for research proposals focused on field-initiated studies. These are studies that apply current knowledge to the field of education. This request for proposals was very broad and was looking for research proposals that range from those focusing on improving student achievement in core content areas to those that would promote excellence and equity in the education of children at risk for educational failure.

Professional Issues

■ **Fraudulent activity**
Fabrication or alteration of results

The primary professional ethical issue is that of **fraudulent activity** by scientists. Researchers are trained to ask questions, to be skeptical, and to use the scientific method in

■ EXHIBIT 4.1   A Case of Fraudulent Research

Steven E. Breuning received his doctorate from the Illinois Institute of Technology in 1977. Several years later, he obtained a position at the Coldwater Regional Center in Michigan. At Coldwater, Breuning was invited to collaborate on an NIMH-funded study of the use of neuroleptics on institutionalized people who were mentally retarded. In January 1981, he was appointed director of the John Merck program at Pittsburgh's Western Psychiatric Institute and Clinic, where he continued to report on the results of the Coldwater research and even obtained his own NIMH grant to study the effects of stimulant medication on retarded subjects. During this time, Breuning gained considerable prominence and was considered one of the field's leading researchers. In 1983, however, questions were raised about the validity of Breuning's work. The individual who had initially taken Breuning on as an investigator started questioning a paper in which Breuning reported results that had an impossibly high reliability. This prompted a further review of Breuning's published work, and contacts were made with personnel at Coldwater, where the research had supposedly been conducted. Coldwater's director of psychology had never heard of the study and was not aware that Breuning had conducted any research while at Coldwater. NIMH was informed of the allegations in December 1983. Following a three-year investigation, an NIMH team concluded that Breuning "knowingly, willfully, and repeatedly engaged in misleading and deceptive practices in reporting his research." He reportedly had not carried out the research that was described, and only a few of the experimental participants had ever been studied. It was concluded that Breuning had engaged in serious scientific misconduct (Holden, 1987).

seeking knowledge. This search for truth is completely antithetical to engaging in any form of deception. The most serious professional crime any researcher can commit is to cheat or present fraudulent results to the research community, such as that illustrated in Exhibit 4.1. Although there is an unwritten rule that scientists present uncontaminated results, there seems to be a disturbing increase in the tendency of some scientists to forge or falsify data, manipulate results to support a theory, or selectively report data (Woolf, 1988).

Research Navigator.com

research fraud

There seem to be both personal and nonpersonal factors that contribute to scientific misconduct (Knight, 1984). Nonpersonal factors include such things as the pressure to publish and the competition for research funding. Most research is conducted at research institutions, most of which are universities. These institutions evaluate researchers on the basis of the grants they receive and the articles they publish. Receiving a promotion or even keeping one's position might be contingent on the number of articles published and grants obtained. This pressure is frequently reported by researchers who engage in fraudulent activities. Other nonpersonal factors include inadequate supervision of trainees, inadequate procedures for keeping records or retaining data, and the diffusion of responsibility for jointly authored studies.

Personal factors focus on the psychological makeup of the individual. Fraudulent activity is attributed to the researcher's reaction to the extreme stress resulting from participation in a highly competitive academic research environment. Although there might be personal and nonpersonal factors contributing to a person's tendency to engage in fraudulent activity, there is never any justification for engaging in such behavior. The cost of fraudulent activity is enormous, both to the profession and to the researcher. Not only is the whole research enterprise discredited, but the professional career of the individual is destroyed.

Although fraudulent activity is obviously the most serious form of scientific misconduct, there are several other issues of a less serious nature that are beginning to receive attention (Hilgartner, 1990; Grisso et al., 1991). The two issues of concern with respect to research publication are partial publication and duplicate publication. **Partial publication** refers to collecting data for one study and then publishing several articles based on this one large set of data rather than publishing all the findings and data in one article. This piecemeal publication is generally considered to be undesirable (APA, 1994) unless it facilitates scientific communication.

■ **Partial publication**
Publishing several articles from the data collected in one large study

Although partial publication is discouraged, there are times when it is appropriate. In large-scale studies, researchers frequently collect a massive amount of data to use as the basis for seeking answers to several research questions. In reporting these large-scale studies, it is entirely appropriate to use the database and publish several articles. However, each published article would focus on a different research question or set of interrelated questions. The problem of partial publication is confined to situations in which part of the data pertaining to one research question is published in one article and another part of the data relevant to that same question is published in another article. In such a situation, all the data pertaining to the same research question should be published in one article.

Duplicate publication refers to publishing the same data and results in more than one journal or in other publications. According to William Russell, Executive Director of AERA, duplicate publication is explicitly forbidden by some organizations, such as the Educational Research Association, and is generally discouraged (personal communication). However, different outlets such as research journals and books and articles for the popular press reach different audiences and serve different purposes. The ethical issue that must be considered is whether presenting the data to these different audiences represents an ethical violation or effective communication of scientific data.

■ **Duplicate publication**
Publishing the same data and results in more than one journal or in other publications

In addition to partial and duplicate publication, there are ethical issues surrounding the use and archiving of videotaped data, and research with vulnerable populations such as children. These are being discussed in organizations such as the American Psychological Association.

Treatment of Research Participants

Treatment of research participants is the most important and fundamental issue that researchers must confront. The conduct of research with humans has the potential for creating a great deal of physical and psychological harm. The grossly inhumane medical experiments conducted by Nazi scientists during World War II immediately come to mind. For example, individuals were immersed in ice water to determine how long it would take them to freeze to death. Bones were broken and rebroken to see how many times they could be broken before healing was not possible. These experiments were conducted by individuals living in what is thought to have been a demented society, and we seem to think that such studies could not be performed in our culture. Before the 1960s, comments about the ethics of research were virtually nonexistent. In the mid-1960s, ethical issues became a dominant concern as it increasingly became clear that research did not invariably operate to benefit others and experiments were not always conducted in a manner that ensured the safety of participants. The most dramatic examples of unethical research have been conducted in the

■ **EXHIBIT 4.2   The Tuskegee Experiment**

In July 1972, the Associated Press released a story that revealed that the U.S. Public Health Service (PHS) had for forty years been conducting a study of the effects of untreated syphilis on black men in Macon County, Alabama. The study consisted of conducting a variety of medical tests (including an examination) on 399 black men who were in the late stages of the disease and on 200 controls. Physicians employed by the PHS administered a variety of blood tests and routine autopsies to learn more about the serious complications that resulted from the final stages of the disease.

This was a study aimed strictly at compiling data on the effects of the disease and not on the treatment of syphilis. No drugs or alternative therapies were tested or ever used. The participants were never told the purpose of the study or what they were or were not being treated for. The PHS nurse moni-

toring the participants informed the local physicians of the individuals who were taking part in the study and that they were not to be treated for syphilis. Participants who were offered treatment by other physicians were advised that they would be dropped from the study if they took the treatment.

The participants were not aware of the purpose of the study or the danger it posed to them, and no attempt was ever made to explain the situation to them. In fact, participants were enticed with a variety of inducements, physical examination, free rides to and from the clinic, hot meals, free treatment for other ailments, and a $50 burial stipend and were followed to ensure that they did not receive treatment from other physicians. This study violated almost every standard of ethics for research with humans, from informed consent to physical harm of the participants.

medical field, the Tuskegee experiment (Jones, 1981) described in Exhibit 4.2 representing the most blatant example of a violation of human rights.

In December 1996, the *Cleveland Plain Dealer* reported on the results of its investigation of internal Food and Drug Administration records. This analysis revealed that some research is still conducted on unknowing people and that in other cases, the participants are not fully informed of the risks of their participation.

The Tuskegee experiment was clearly unethical and inflicted extensive harm and psychological pain on the research participants. Educational research does not appear to have the potential for inflicting a similar degree of physical or psychological harm to its research participants. It would be easy to become complacent and conclude that consideration of ethical issues is something that other fields have to contend with and that educational research is spared. Reaching such a conclusion is wrong because ethical issues are part and parcel of educational research. However, the ethical issues that educational researchers must face are often not as dramatic or blatant as those that frequently exist in medical research. Consequently, the educational researcher frequently must be *more* rather than less attuned to the ethical issues that surround his or her research.

To illustrate the subtle ethical issues that can exist in a study that an educational researcher might conduct, consider the survey study conducted by Phillips (1994). Phillips was interested in studying adolescents' attitudes and behaviors related to HIV/AIDS prevention. Specifically, she was interested in collecting data that would provide insight into adolescents' thoughts about using condoms during sexual intercourse and how their thinking influenced their decision to either use or not use the condoms. Collecting the data involved surveying sexually related attitudes and behavior. This research did not inject, expose, medicate, touch, deceive, or assign the participants to treatment or control groups, nor did it require them to reveal their identity. Therefore, although it did investigate "sensitive" behavior, it did not, at least on the surface, seem to represent a study that had the potential for violating the participants' rights.

Fortunately, Phillips met with various groups before conducting her study, and these meetings revealed a number of ethical concerns that led her to alter her instrument and her procedures. For example, she met with a student peer group and a combined parent-teacher group to discuss the objectives of the research and the content of the questionnaire. In addition to asking questions about sexual attitudes and behavior, the questionnaire was initially constructed to inquire about the adolescents' drug use. In the combined parent-teacher group discussion, teachers and parents joked about how they would be glad to find out about the drug users because they had some children that were suspected of using drugs. Although Phillips had told the schools that she would provide them with aggregate data only for each school, there was still the potential that a teacher, after learning that her school had, say, ten drug users, would assume that she or he had guessed right and treat the suspected student differently. To avoid such a possibility, Phillips removed all questions regarding illicit drug use except one on alcohol and cigarette smoking. The same concern did not exist for sexual activity because many teachers seemed to assume that this was a widespread activity, which minimized the possibility for singling out a specific student.

Another subtle ethical issue Phillips had to contend with was the issue of privacy. Because the survey instrument focused on sexual behavior, students who had not experienced sexual intercourse would find many of the questions not applicable. These students would therefore skip most of the questions and finish more rapidly than their sexually active classmates. This more rapid completion could convey their sexual inexperience to their classmates. To avoid such a possibility, Phillips constructed a second set of questions for the sexually inactive student that were designed to take about as long to complete as the sections for the sexually active student. This seemed to solve this problem. However, listening to students talk about completing surveys revealed that they would listen to or watch when their friends turned the page to branching questions to discern how they had answered the question. This is a sophisticated attempt to pry into another student's answers. To get around this privacy issue, Phillips reorganized the questionnaire to ensure that all branching questions were at the bottom of the page and that all students would have to turn a page.

Although the survey study that Phillips conducted did not place the participants in any physical danger, there was the potential for some emotional harm. Some of the students volunteered that they had been raped and/or were incest victims. This was information that was not requested in the survey, but it would have been unethical to disregard it because the questionnaire created an environment in which these unpleasant events were recalled. Some of the questions on the sexual survey could also threaten the well-being of the adolescents. For example, a question asking the adolescents to identify their sexual preference could result in the student having to confront lesbian or homosexual tendencies, which could cause some emotional distress or discomfort. To deal with these issues, Phillips gave each student her office phone number and told them that they could call her with any questions. During the administration of the questionnaire, students could ask questions in private, and any other questions they might have would be answered after completion of the questionnaire.

Additionally, each student was given a pamphlet, published by the American Red Cross, that included telephone numbers for counseling referral services.

These are some of the more subtle ethical issues Phillips had to contend with in conducting her study. You might think that such ethical concerns are limited primarily to sensitive research such as the issue of sexuality investigated by Phillips. However, similar issues can arise in many other types of studies. For example, educational researchers conducting qualitative research may make extensive use of interviews. In the course of these interviews, the research participants can, and often do, reveal sensitive information that is not part of the goal of the study. Research participants often view the researchers as "experts" and frequently feel comfortable conveying confidential and sensitive information. For example, students might reveal that they are being abused, that they are having difficulty with a teacher, or that they are abusing drugs. When this information is revealed, the researcher must be prepared to address such issues rather than dismiss them as outside the confines of the purpose of the study. It is these types of ethical issues that can creep into a study, and the researcher must anticipate them and have a plan to conduct a study that is ethically sound. As you can see, there are ethical issues surrounding virtually any study, and the investigator must consider the ethics of research before it is conducted.

REVIEW

QUESTIONS

4.1 What is the definition of *ethics,* and how does this definition relate to research?

4.2 How do the three approaches that are used in considering ethical issues in research differ?

4.3 How do societal concerns relate to research ethics?

4.4 What are the professional issues involved in research ethics, and what is the appropriate ethical behavior related to each of these issues?

4.5 Why is treatment of the research participant an ethical issue to be considered in educational research when the potential for physical and psychological harm is minimal?

ETHICAL GUIDELINES FOR RESEARCH WITH HUMANS

We hope that we have convinced you of the necessity of considering the ethics of your research study before actually collecting any data. Even so, a novice researcher might not be sophisticated enough to know what types of issues to consider even if he or she is motivated to make the study as ethical as possible and provide as much protection for participants as possible. To assist the researcher in conducting an ethically sound study, a number of organizations such as the American Educational Research Association, American Psychological Association, the Society for Research in Child Development, and the American Counseling Association have prepared a set of ethical guidelines that can be used by a researcher to assist in the conduct of the most ethically acceptable study. The American Educational Research Association (AERA, 1992) has developed a set of standards designed specifically to guide the work of researchers in education. This set of standards seems to be most appropriate for the educational researcher and can be accessed by logging onto www.aeta.net/about/policy/ethics.htm.

Research
Navigator.com

ethical guidelines

These guidelines state that it is the investigator's responsibility to ensure that the study he or she is planning is ethically acceptable and that research participants are treated ethically by everyone involved in the study. Assurance of the ethical acceptability of the study means that

1. You have to get the informed consent of the participant.
2. Any deception must be justified by the study's scientific, educational, or applied value.
3. The research participants must know that they are free to withdraw from the study at any time without prejudice.
4. The research participants are protected from physical and mental discomfort, harm, and danger that may arise from the research procedures.
5. The confidentiality or anonymity of the participants and the data must be protected.

Let's look at each of these very important points in some detail.

Informed Consent

■ **Informed consent**
Agreeing to participate in a study after being informed of its purpose, procedures, risks, benefits, alternative procedures, and limits of confidentiality

Research
Navigator.c⊛m

informed consent

Federal regulations as well as the guidelines established by the AERA state that research participants must give **informed consent** before they can participate in a study. Consent must also be given before a researcher can use individuals' existing records for research purposes. The Buckley Amendment, or the Family Education Rights and Privacy Act of 1974, protects the privacy of the records maintained by agencies such as a school system. This privacy act states that records maintained by an agency for one purpose cannot be released for another purpose without the consent of the individual. Records such as student grades that are collected and maintained for the purpose of recording student performance cannot be released to a researcher for research purposes without the student's consent or parent's consent for minors.

Before a participant can participate in a research study, the researcher must give the prospective participant a description of all the features of the study that might reasonably influence his or her willingness to participate. If you are planning to conduct a survey of sexual attitudes, you must inform the prospective participants of the nature of the survey and the type of questions to which they might have to respond, because some of the participants might not want to answer explicit sex-related questions. Similarly, if you are conducting a study pertaining to academic achievement and you are going to ask the students about their grades in other classes, you have to inform the students of this fact. In other words, you must look at the tasks you are going to ask your research participants to complete and ask yourself whether this task could hurt, embarrass, or in some other way create a reaction in the participants that could make them not want to participate in the study. Table 4.1 specifies the information that should be included in a consent form.

Exhibit 4.3 provides an example of an informed consent form. It is only when you have given the participant this information and he or she still volunteers to participate in the study that you have obtained informed consent.

Although the general guideline is that informed consent must be obtained before a person can participate in a research study, it is also recognized that there are some types of research that cannot be conducted if the research participants are fully informed of all aspects

■ **TABLE 4.1**   Information to Include in a Consent Form

Purpose of the research along with a description of the procedures to be followed and the length of time it will take the participant to complete the study

A description of any physical or psychological risks or discomforts the participant may encounter

A description of any benefits the participant or others may expect from the research

A description of any alternative procedure or treatment that might be advantageous to the participant

A statement of the extent to which the results will be kept confidential

Names of people the participant may contact with questions about the study or the research participant's rights

A statement indicating that participation is voluntary and the participant can withdraw and refuse to participate at any time with no penalty

A statement of the amount and schedule of payment if participants are to be paid for participation

The information should be written at an eighth-grade reading level; in cases targeting specific populations, a sixth-grade reading level might be appropriate

For additional tips on preparation of the consent form, go to http://ohrp.osophs.dhhs.gov/humansubjects/guidance/ictips.htm.

of the research because this might invalidate the study. Resnick and Schwartz (1973) provided an excellent demonstration of this fact. They used a verbal conditioning task in which the experimenter merely says "good" or "okay" whenever the participant constructed a sentence beginning with either the pronoun "I" or "we." The experimenter's saying "good" or "okay" after sentences beginning with the "I" or "we" pronoun served as a reinforcer that encouraged the participant to increase the likelihood of selecting one of these two pronouns. In this study, Resnick and Schwartz varied the amount of information they gave the participants. They gave the "uninformed" group a rationale for the study and told them of the type of task they were to complete. The "informed" group was informed totally about the nature of the study. They were told that it was a verbal conditioning study and that the experimenter would say "good" or "okay" whenever they selected an "I" or "we" pronoun in an attempt to increase their frequency of using these pronouns. Figure 4.2 shows that the uninformed group demonstrated verbal conditioning, whereas the informed group did not. The uninformed group appeared enthusiastic and arrived at their scheduled time. The informed participants were uncooperative and "often haughty, insisting that they had only one time slot to spare which we could take or leave" (Resnick & Schwartz, 1973, p. 13).

From this study, you can see clearly that informing participants of all aspects of the research can, in some studies, totally alter the results. Federal as well as AERA guidelines

■ **EXHIBIT 4.3   Consent Form**

Informed Consent

Title: Predictors of speech rate in normally fluent people

Principal Investigator: Sally Smith

Department: Education

Telephone Number: 111-123-4567

You are invited to participate in a research study investigating the things that affect how fast normal people of different ages speak. If you volunteer to participate in this research study, we will test the clarity of your hearing, language, and speech.

The research will involve asking you to talk about different things such as telling what you see on picture cards, saying words and sounds as fast as you can, and repeating words and sentences. You will be asked to name animals, colors, letters, and numbers as fast as you can and to read a paragraph. If you get tired before the tests are finished, you can rest and finish the study later. Your speech will be recorded so we can study that later.

The study will take between one and one-and-one-half hours.

You may not get any benefit from participating in the study, but the tests we give you may help us understand how different things affect how fast people speak.

If you volunteer to participate in this study, you should always remember that you may withdraw and stop participating in the study at any time you wish. You will not be penalized in any way if you withdraw and stop participating in the study.

There are no risks from participating in this study other than perhaps you may get tired of doing the tests.

All information that you provide to us will be kept strictly confidential. At no time will we give any information to anyone outside the research staff. The recordings of your speech will be erased when the research is finished. The results of this study may be presented at professional meetings or published in a professional journal, but your name and any other identifying information will not be revealed.

If you have any questions about this study or if you have any questions regarding your rights as a research participant, you may call the Institutional Review Board of the university at 111-123-5678. You may also contact Dr. Sally Smith at 123-4567.

Agreement to Participate in Research

I have read, or have had read to me, the above study and have had an opportunity to ask questions, which have been answered to my satisfaction. I agree voluntarily to participate in the study as described.

_____

Participant's Name

_____   _____

Date   Signature of Consenting Party

_____   _____

Date   Signature of Investigator

_____   _____

Date   Signature of Witness

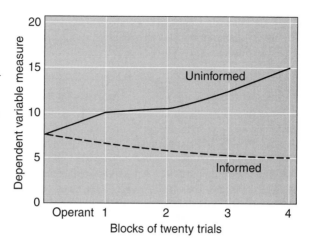

FIGURE 4.2 Verbal conditioning data obtained by Resnick and Schwartz

(Adapted from L. Christensen, *Experimental Methodology,* p. 162. Copyright © 1997 by Allyn and Bacon. Used by permission of the publisher.)

recognize the necessity of sometimes forgoing the requirement of informed consent. Whenever a judgment is made that informed consent would alter the outcome of a study or that the study could not be conducted if informed consent were required, the investigator incurs an added ethical obligation to ensure that the benefits of the research outweigh the risks. However, federal guidelines state that a waiver of the requirement of informed consent can be obtained only if the following four conditions have been satisfied:

1. The research presents minimal risk to the participants.
2. The waiver will not affect the rights and welfare of the participants.
3. The research could not be practically carried out without the waiver.
4. The participants will be provided with additional information after participation.

Remember that it is the Institutional Review Board that must make the final determination of whether these conditions have been met.

Informed Consent and Minors as Research Participants

The principle of informed consent refers to the fact that a person, once given the pertinent information, is competent and legally free of the desire of others to make a decision as to whether to participate in a given research study. Minors, however, are presumed to be incompetent to make decisions and cannot give consent. Consent has to be obtained from parents (or the minor's legal guardian) after they have been informed of all features of the study that could affect their willingness to allow their child to participate (see Exhibit 4.4). Once consent has been obtained from the minor's parent or guardian, **assent** must be obtained from the minor. This means that the minor has to agree to participate in the research after being informed of all the features that could affect his or her willingness to participate.

Federal regulations state that the assent of the minor should be obtained when he or she is capable of providing assent. However, the age at which a person is capable of providing

■ **Assent**
Agreeing to participate after being informed of all the features of the study that could affect the participant's willingness to participate

■ **EXHIBIT 4.4**   **Example of a Parental Consent to Participate in Research for Use with Minors**

Dear Parent or Legal Guardian:

I am doing research about children's ideas about effort. I would like to know whether ideas about effort are related to how children study and remember in learning and testing situations. I am asking for your permission to let your child be in this research.

There will be two 30-minute sessions alone with your child or in small groups. The sessions will be held in a room at your child's school during school hours. The time will be selected by your child's teacher. The first session will include two questionnaires. The Students' Perception of Control Questionnaire will be given to small groups. The questionnaire has sixty questions about why things happen in school. It measures the students' beliefs about whether they can make good grades if they try. The second questionnaire is a measure of self-esteem. It measures how a child feels about himself or herself in different situations such as at school and with friends.

In the second session, your child will be asked to put together a difficult puzzle. Each child will be shown the solution to the puzzle and then will be asked to study and remember some pictures. Some children will be told that the memory task is a test to see how well they remember, and others will be told it is a chance to learn how to remember better. Finally, children will be asked to rate how well they did, how they feel about what they just did, and whether they would like to do something like this again.

I would also like to look at your child's intelligence and achievement test scores. I am asking permission to use your child's records. Any personal information about you or your child will be confidential. The results from this research may be presented at a professional meeting or published in a professional journal, but your child's name and other identifying information will not be revealed.

You are under no obligation for your child to participate in this project. If you give your consent, you are free to change your mind and remove your child at any time without negative consequences. Also, your child is free to refuse to participate at any time without negative consequences.

If you are willing for your child to participate, and your child wants to participate, please sign below and return this form to school with your child. If you have any questions, please contact me at 765-4321.

Sincerely,

Jane Doe, Ph.D.
Assistant Professor

I give my permission for my child to be tested on the memory task described in this letter, and to complete the questionnaires concerning beliefs about effort and self-esteem. I grant the County Public School System permission to release to Dr. Jane Doe or her assistant my child's test scores and/or access to my child's files.

_____   _____
        Child's Name   Birthdate

_____   _____
  Signature of Parent/Legal Guardian   Date

assent can differ among children. To provide assent, the child must be able to understand what is being asked, to realize that permission is being sought, and to make choices that are free from outside constraints. This depends on the cognitive capabilities of the child. Unfortunately, the cognitive capabilities of children develop at different rates, making it difficult to state an age at which a child is capable of providing assent. Individuals over the age of nine generally have sufficient cognitive ability to make a decision concerning participation in research, and individuals over the age of fourteen seem to make the same decisions as adults (Leikin, 1993). This should not be taken to mean that assent should definitely be obtained from individuals over age fourteen, possibly from individuals over age nine, and not from individuals age nine or younger. Rather, most individuals (e.g., Leikin, 1993) and the ethical guidelines provided by the Society for Research in Child Development (1993) state that assent should be obtained from all children. This is the guideline that we also recommend. Not only is it more ethically acceptable to obtain the assent of minors, but it may also enhance the validity of the study. Insisting that minors participate when they clearly state that they do not want to can alter their behavioral responses and represent a confounding influence on the data collected.

Passive versus Active Consent

Our discussion of consent has, up to this point, focused on active consent. **Active consent** involves consenting to participate in a research study by signing a consent form. However, educational researchers conduct many studies using minors as the research participants. This means that consent has to be obtained from the minors' parents or legal guardians. The typical way in which consent is obtained is to provide the parent or legal guardian with a consent form by some means such as mailing the consent form or sending it home with the minor. Ideally, the parent would read the consent form, either give or refuse consent, and return the consent form to the researcher. However, studies (e.g., Ellickson, 1989) have revealed that only 50 to 60 percent of parents return the consent forms even when follow-up efforts are made. One interpretation of the failure to return the consent forms is that the parents are denying consent. However, there are a number of other reasons why parents do not return the consent forms. They might not have received the consent form, they might have forgotten to sign and return the consent form, or they might not have taken enough time to read and consider the request. The existence of any or all of these possibilities would reduce the sample size and possibly bias the results.

To increase the participation in research studies, Ellickson (1989) recommended the use of passive consent. **Passive consent** is a process whereby consent is given by not returning the consent form. Parents or legal guardians return the consent form only if they do *not* want their child to participate in the research. Some investigators have promoted passive consent as a legitimate means of securing parental consent. Ethical concerns have been raised when passive consent procedures are used, however, because these studies might include children whose parents actually oppose their participation in the research but did not return the consent form or maybe did not receive it. However, studies (e.g., Ellickson and Hawes, 1989; Severson and Ary, 1983) have revealed that active and passive consent procedures yield comparable rates of participation when the active consent procedures included extensive follow-up techniques. This suggests that nonresponse to passive consent represents latent consent and that it might

■ **Active consent**
A process whereby consent is provided by signing a consent form

■ **Passive consent**
A process whereby consent is given by not returning the consent form

Research
Navigator.c✺m

passive consent

be an appropriate means of obtaining consent. Exhibit 4.5 provides an example of a passive consent form.

Although there is a place for passive consent and some cogent arguments for its use in certain situations, we recommend that you use active consent whenever possible. This is the best form of consent. Passive consent should be considered only when the integrity of the study would be seriously compromised by requiring active consent. For additional information regarding passive consent, you should visit the following web site: www.uiuc.edu/unit/vcres/irb/passive.htm.

■ **EXHIBIT 4.5**   **Example of a Passive Consent Form**

Dear Parent or Legal Guardian:

I am a faculty member in the Education Department at Excel University. I am interested in finding the best method of teaching mathematical concepts. To identify the best method, I am planning a study that will compare two different methods of teaching mathematical concepts. Both teaching methods are acceptable and standard methods of teaching these concepts, but we do not know which is the more effective method. My research will identify the more effective method.

To identify the more effective method, during the next six weeks I will be presenting material in two different ways to separate classes. To test the effectiveness of each method, I will measure students' performance by giving them a standard math test.

Your child's responses will remain confidential and will be seen only by myself and my research assistant.

No reports about this study will contain your child's name. I will not release any information about your child without your permission.

Participation in this study is completely voluntary. All students in the class will take the test. If you do **not** wish your child to be in this study, please fill out the form at the bottom of this letter and return it to me. Also, please tell your child to hand in a blank test sheet when the class is given the mathematics test so that your child will not be included in this study.

I will also ask the children to participate and tell them to hand in a blank test sheet if they do not want to be included in the study. Your child may choose to stop and not participate at any time.

If you have any questions about the study, please contact professor John Doe, Excel University, Department of Education, Good Place, Al. 12345, phone 251-246-8102. You may also contact me at [provide address and phone number].

Thank you,

Tom Thumb

Return this portion only if you do not want your child to participate in the study described above.

I do not wish for my child _____ to be in the research study on the teaching of math concepts being conducted in his/her classroom.

_____   _____
            Parent's Signature   Date

Additional Consent

There are many educational research studies that are conducted within the confines of a school system. These studies require the cooperation of a number of individuals such as the teacher, principal, and superintendent. These individuals must give their approval to the study, which means that informed consent must also be received from them. This is a very important step in the conduct of a successful study, and the researcher must not underemphasize the importance of this cooperation. All questions posed by these individuals must be answered, and their right to choose to participate or to discontinue participation at any time should be respected.

4.6 What must a researcher do to ensure that his or her study is ethical?

4.7 What kinds of information does a consent form have to include?

4.8 Under what conditions can an investigator get a waiver of the requirement of informed consent?

4.9 What is the difference between consent from a minor's legal guardian and assent from the minor, and why are both important?

4.10 What is the difference between active and passive consent, and what are the advantages and disadvantages of each?

R E V I E W

Q U E S T I O N S

Deception

Under the principle of informed consent, research participants are supposed to receive information about the purpose and nature of the study in which they are being asked to participate so that they can evaluate the procedures to be followed and make an informed judgment as to whether they want to participate. Sometimes, however, providing full disclosure of the nature and purpose of the study will alter the outcome and invalidate the study, as we illustrated earlier in discussing the Resnick and Schwartz study. In such instances, it is necessary to mislead or withhold information from the research participants. In other words, it is necessary to engage in **deception** to conduct a valid study.

Research
Navigator.com

deception in research

■ **Deception**
Misleading or withholding information from the research participant

Although the AERA ethical guidelines discourage the use of deception, these guidelines do recognize that some research studies cannot be conducted without its use. For example, Butler and Neuman (1995) investigated some of the variables that influenced help-seeking behaviors among children. In conducting this study, the experimenters did not inform the children that they were studying the variables that influence whether they would seek help. Rather, the children were invited to try out some materials that consisted of completing several puzzles. They were not given any information suggesting that the variable of interest was help seeking but were given instructions as to how to seek help if they were so inclined. Obviously, in this study, it was necessary to make use of deception in the form of withholding information because if the true purpose of the study had been revealed, it could have altered the outcome and invalidated the results.

The form of deception used by Butler and Neuman consisted of withholding information. Withholding information represents one of the milder forms of deception. However, even use of this mild form of deception violates the principle of informed consent and therefore is of ethical concern. This is why the AERA ethical guidelines explicitly state that deception is discouraged unless it is necessary for the integrity of the study.

If deception is used, the reasons for the deception should be explained to the participants in the debriefing session held after the study has been completed. **Debriefing** refers to an interview conducted with each research participant after the participant has completed the study. In this interview, the experimenter and research participant talk about the study. It is an opportunity for each research participant to comment freely about any part of the study and express any concerns that he or she had about the study. Phillips (1994), for example, realized that her survey of adolescents' attitudes and behavior related to HIV/AIDS prevention was bound to raise questions not only about the survey but also about other related issues. Consistent with Phillips' expectations, the student research participants asked numerous questions regarding HIV/AIDS specifically and sexuality more generally.

Debriefing is also an opportunity for the researcher to reveal aspects of the study that were not disclosed at the outset. Holmes (1976a, 1976b) has pointed out that debriefing should meet the two goals of dehoaxing and desensitizing. **Dehoaxing** refers to informing the participants about any deception that was used in the study. Not only can any deception used be revealed, but the reasons for its use can also be explained. **Desensitizing** refers to helping the participants, during the debriefing interview, deal with and eliminate any stress or other undesirable feeling that the study created, as might exist if you are studying cheating behavior or failure. Desensitizing might be accomplished by suggesting that any undesirable behavior or feeling was the result of some situational variable rather than some characteristic of the participant. Another tactic used by experimenters is to point out that the participant's behavior or feeling was normal and expected.

The important question is whether a debriefing session is effective in desensitizing or dehoaxing the participants. In Holmes's (1976a, 1976b) review of the literature relating to these two techniques, he concluded that they were generally effective. However, this means only that effective debriefing is possible. These results hold only if debriefing is carried out properly. A sloppy or improperly prepared debriefing session can have a very different effect. Therefore, it is necessary not only to include a debriefing session after each study, but also to ensure that the debriefing session is appropriately conducted.

Freedom to Withdraw

The AERA ethical standards explicitly state that research "participants have the right to withdraw from a study at any time, unless otherwise constrained by their official capacity or roles" (p. 24). This principle seems very straightforward and easily accomplished. Merely inform the participant that he or she is free to withdraw from the study at any time. From the researcher's perspective, such a statement would seem to be sufficient to comply with the "freedom to withdraw" principle. However, from the participant's perspective, such a statement might not be sufficient because he or she might feel coercive pressure to participate. Such pressure could arise if a teacher requests students to participate or if a principal or superintendent asks teachers to participate in a study. Students might feel coercive pressure if they think that their grades might be affected if they don't participate, or teachers might believe that their jobs are in jeopardy if they refuse participation. In such instances, the participant is not completely free to withdraw, and the researcher must make a special effort to

---

■ Debriefing
A poststudy interview in which all aspects of the study are revealed, any reasons for deception are explained, and any questions the participant has about the study are answered

■ Dehoaxing
Informing study participants about any deception that was used and the reasons for its use

■ Desensitizing
Helping study participants deal with and eliminate any stress or other undesirable feelings that the study might have created

ensure that the research participants are convinced that refusing to participate or withdrawing from the study will have no adverse effect on them.

Special consideration should be given to minors and their freedom to dissent. Minors are generally viewed as not having the ability to provide informed consent to participate or to decline participation. This is why consent is sought from the minor's legal parent or guardian. However, the minor can provide assent or dissent as to whether he or she wants to participate. The ethical issue that must be considered here is whether parents or guardians can overrule the dissent of their children. The *Ethical Standards for Research with Children* published by the Society for Research in Child Development (1993) states that the child's freedom to choose not to participate should be respected. As a general rule, dissent from participation should always be honored unless the study provides a substantial benefit to the child that he or she could not get elsewhere.

Although it seems most appropriate to respect the right of a child to dissent, there is obviously an age at which it does not seem reasonable to seek assent or dissent. The most obvious situation involves infants. Here it is important for the researcher to be sensitive to any indicators of discomfort in the infant. With older children, the situation is more difficult, because they have varying cognitive capabilities. There is some evidence (see Pence, 1980) to suggest that researchers should honor the dissent of children down to the age of seven. However, if children below that age seem disturbed about or uncomfortable with participation, the researcher should seriously consider excusing the child from the study and in such a way as to ensure that no adverse effects are incurred.

Protection from Mental and Physical Harm

The most important and fundamental issue confronting the researcher is the treatment of the research participants. Earlier, we provided examples of unethical medical studies that inflicted both physical and mental harm on the participants. Fortunately, studies conducted by educational researchers seldom if ever run the risk of inflicting such severe mental and physical harm on participants. In fact, educational research has historically engaged in research that imposes either minimal or no risk to the participants and has enjoyed a special status with respect to formal ethical oversight. A large portion of this research has been singled out for exempt status in the Code of Federal Regulations for the Protection of Human Subjects (OPRR Reports, 1991). Paragraph 46.101(b)(1) of this code states that "Research conducted in established or commonly accepted educational settings involving normal educational practices such as (i) research on regular and special educational instructional strategies, or (ii) research on the effectiveness of or the comparison among instructional techniques, curricula, or classroom management methods" (p. 5) are exempt from oversight.

The problem with this statement lies in its ambiguity. It is worded so vaguely as to leave considerable room for competing interpretations as to what represents "commonly accepted educational settings involving normal educational practices." Additionally, educational research is not a static entity but one that is constantly changing. One of the more notable changes is the increased use of qualitative research methods.

Qualitative research, as Howe and Dougherty (1993) have pointed out, has two features, intimacy and open-endedness, that muddy the ethical waters and might exclude it from the special exempt status reserved for many educational research studies. Qualitative research is an ongoing and evolving process, with the data collection process proceeding more like a friendship between the participant and the researcher. Interviewing, for example, requires one-to-one contact and removes the participant from his or her normal activities. Video and audio taping create permanent records that can pose a threat to confidentiality and anonymity. It is these activities as well as the ambiguity of the wording identifying "exempt" that indicate a need for some type of ethical oversight of educational research. The ethical oversight provided by virtually any institution that conducts research is the **Institutional Review Board (IRB).**

■ **Institutional Review Board (IRB)**
The institutional review committee that assesses the ethical acceptability of research proposals

■ **Anonymity**
Keeping the identity of the participant from everyone, including the researcher

■ **Confidentiality**
Not revealing the identity of the participant to anyone other than the researcher and his or her staff

Confidentiality and Anonymity

AERA ethical guidelines state that research participants have the right to remain anonymous and the confidentiality of both the participants and the data must be protected. Confidentiality and anonymity are two of the ways in which researchers protect participants. **Anonymity** means that the identity of the participants is not known to the researcher. Anonymity could be achieved in a survey on the frequency with which high school students cheated on examinations if this survey did not ask the students for any information that could be used to identify them, for example, and the survey administered was conducted in large groups of, say, 100 students. **Confidentiality** means that the participant's identity, although known to the research group, is not revealed to anyone other than the researcher and his or her staff. Confidentiality would be maintained, for example, if you were conducting a study on children with learning disabilities. Although the research staff would know which children were in the study and, therefore had a learning disability, this information would not be revealed to anyone outside the research staff. Confidentiality and anonymity are important to avoid connecting the participant with any information that would be embarrassing or harmful. Because it is impossible to know how people might interpret responses or what responses might have adverse consequences for the participant, maintaining the participant's anonymity is recommended. When anonymity cannot be maintained, confidentiality of the participant's responses and identity is essential.

R E V I E W

QUESTIONS

4.11 What is deception, and when is it used in a research study?

4.12 What are the ethical obligations of a researcher who makes use of deception?

4.13 Why can participants still feel pressured to participate in a study even after the researcher has stated that they can withdraw or decline to participate?

4.14 What are the issues relating to freedom to withdraw with respect to minors?

4.15 Why do educational researchers have to be concerned with protecting participants from mental and physical harm in their studies?

4.16 What is the difference between confidentiality and anonymity?

INSTITUTIONAL REVIEW BOARD

The legal requirement of having all human research reviewed by the IRB dates back to 1966. At that time, there was a concern for the way in which medical research was designed and conducted. As a result of this concern, the Surgeon General initiated an institutional review requirement at the Department of Health, Education, and Welfare (DHEW). This policy was extended to all investigations funded by the Public Health Service that involved human participants, including those in the social and behavioral sciences. By 1973, the DHEW regulations governing human research required a review by an IRB for all research receiving Public Health Service funds. This meant that virtually all institutions of higher education had to establish an IRB and file an assurance policy with the Office for Protection from Research Risks of the Department of Health and Human Services. This assurance policy articulates the responsibilities and purview of the IRB within that institution. Although the Public Health Service mandated only that federally funded projects be reviewed by the IRB, most institutions extended the scope of the IRB to include all research involving human participants, even those falling into the exempt category. Once this institutional assurance policy is approved, it becomes a legal document with which the institution and researchers must comply. If your institution has such an assurance policy, you as an educational researcher must submit a proposal to the IRB to determine whether your study is exempt from ethical oversight. In this proposal, you should state whether you believe that it falls into the exempt category. A member of the IRB makes the decision as to whether the study is exempt and therefore can proceed as proposed or must be reviewed by the full IRB. In short, this means that **exempt studies** refers to being exempt from certain requirements and full committee review, not exempt from IRB oversight altogether.

■ **Exempt studies**
Studies involving no risk to participants and not requiring full IRB review

In reviewing the research proposals, members of the IRB are required to make judgments regarding the ethical appropriateness of the proposed research by ensuring that research protocols are explained to the research participants and that the risks of harm are reasonable in relation to the hoped-for benefits. To make this judgment, the IRB members must have sufficient information about the specifics of the research protocol. This means that the investigator must submit a research protocol that the IRB can review. Table 4.2 identifies the information that must be included in this protocol. A sample protocol excluding the consent form appears in Exhibit 4.6.

■ **TABLE 4.2**   Information to Be Included in a Research Protocol

Information about the purpose and rationale of the research

Information about the research participants to be used in the study

The location of the research

The tasks or variables and procedures to be used

Whether the procedures are experimental

The research design used to answer the research question

The potential benefits to the research participants or general knowledge acquired from the study

Any risks or hazards from participation in the research

Precautions taken to reduce the risks and hazards

A description of how confidentiality will be ensured

A consent form for participation

■ EXHIBIT 4.6 Example of a Research Protocol Submitted to the IRB

Title of Protocol: The Relationship of Attributional Beliefs, Self-Esteem, and Ego Involvement to Performance on Cognitive Tasks in Students with Mental Retardation.

Primary Investigator: Jane A. Donner, Department of Psychology, University of the Southeast, 460-6321.

Co-Investigator: Carolyn L. Pickering, Graduate Student, Department of Psychology, University of the Southeast, 460-6321.

Relevant Background and Purpose Recent research suggests that the way in which a cognitive task is presented influences performance on the task. Nicholls (1985) suggested that ego involvement would often result in diminished task performance. He describes ego involvement as a task orientation in which the goal is to either demonstrate one's ability relative to others or avoid demonstrating a lack of ability. This ego orientation is in contrast to task involvement, where the goal is simply to learn or improve a skill. In support of the Nicholls position, Graham and Golan (1991) found that ego-involving instructions resulted in poorer recall in a memory task than task-orienting instructions. Apparently, the focus on performance detracted from the necessary information processing.

The present investigation is designed to determine potential individual differences in the ego-involvement effect. It is possible that some persons are more at risk for the debilitating effects of ego-involving instructions than others. It is predicted that students with mental retardation who have low self-esteem and negative attributional beliefs will be influenced negatively by ego-involving instructions.

Participant Population Forty students with mental retardation will be recruited from special education classrooms at approximately three elementary schools in the Mobile County Public School System. Students will be recruited from the intermediate classes (fourth–sixth grades). The students' participation will be voluntary and they will have parental consent.

Materials and Procedure

Overview The research will be conducted at the students' school and will include two sessions, each approximately a half-hour long. In the first session, students will first complete attributional and self-esteem questionnaires, which will be read aloud to them, in small groups of about three. Students will be read pretraining exercises and provided guidance in answering the questions to be sure they understand how to answer the actual questionnaires.

In the next session, students will be tested individually. They will first work on a geometric puzzle task which they will not have time to finish. The examiner will then show them how to finish the puzzle. Next, half the subjects will receive a categorization memory task with ego-orienting instructions and the other half will receive the same task with task-orienting instructions.

Questionnaires The attributional questionnaire (attached) is designed to assess the students' beliefs about the importance of different casual factors (e.g., effort, ability, luck, and powerful others) in academic performance. The self-esteem questionnaire (attached) is designed to measure global self-worth and self-esteem in four domains.

Experimental Tasks The geometric puzzle task will use a difficult block design task from an intelligence test for children. One pattern on a card, which is not included in the intelligence test, will be shown to children for them to copy with their blocks, and they will be given 60 seconds to work on the design. It is not expected that the children will be able to finish the puzzle, and the examiner will then show the students how to finish the puzzle.

The categorization memory task will be used to assess students' performance. Each child will be presented with sixteen pictures classifiable according to categories (e.g., clothes, vehicles, animals) with four items in each category. Relatively typical items (e.g., car, truck, boat, motorcycle) are used as stimuli. Children will first be given 60 seconds to arrange the pictures in any way that will help them remember. If a student does not touch the items, he or she will be reminded that he or she can arrange them in any way he or she would like. After 60 seconds, students will be given an additional 60 seconds to study their arrangement of the items, after which they will recall the items in any order. Students will be given three trials of the task. This task will yield three measures: (a) clustering (ARC) at organization (Roenker, Thompson, & Brown, 1971), (b) ARC at recall, and (c) recall accuracy. ARC scores indicate the amount of clustering relative to chance. An ARC score of 1 reflects perfect clustering, whereas an ARC score of 0 reflects the degree of clustering that would be expected by chance.

Instructional Formats The categorization memory task will be presented in two instructional formats (adapted from Graham and Golan, 1991). Students will be randomly assigned to receive either the task-involvement format or the ego-involvement format. The instructions for the task-involvement format are as follows:

> You will probably make mistakes on this memory task at first, but you will probably get better as you go on. If you think about the task and try to see it as something you can learn from, you will have more fun doing it.

The instructions for the ego-involvement format are as follows:

> You are either good at this memory task compared to others or you are not. How well you do in this task will tell me something about your memory ability in this kind of activity.

After being read the instructions, the students will begin the task. At the end of the session, students will be asked to rate from 1 to 5 how well they think they did, how much fun they thought the task was, whether they would like to do the memory task again in the future, and whether they felt certain emotions (such as happy, sad, proud, and ashamed) during the task. Following this questionnaire, students will be told that since they performed so well on the tasks, they will receive a prize, such as a sticker or piece of candy.

Design and Methodology Following approval by the appropriate school personnel, the attached con-

sent form will be distributed by the classroom teacher. Students who return the consent form signed by their parent or guardian are then invited to participate in the research. Parental consent will also be requested to obtain students' IQ scores from their school files. These scores will be used to determine whether students' scores are within the range specified by the American Association of Mental Retardation and to obtain a group mean for the students. The data will be analyzed through multiple regression with attributions, self-esteem, and instructional format as predictors of performance.

Potential Benefit The present literature on ego- and task-involvement indicates that ego instructions can negatively affect performance. It is important to determine the individual differences in this phenomenon. It is possible that children with mental retardation and with low self-esteem and with negative attributional beliefs may be especially at risk for the debilitating effects of ego-involving instructions. If this is the case, one could reduce these individual differences in performance and support optimal learning by presenting tasks primarily in a task-involvement format.

Risks The risks are minimal. It is possible that students will be discouraged by not having time to complete the puzzle and by not remembering all of the pictures. However, at the end of the session, we will make it clear to each student that the tasks were designed to be difficult for everyone. In addition, all students will be told at the end of the session that they did very well on the task.

Confidentiality All personal information will remain confidential. All data will be stored securely in a locked laboratory on campus. Only the principal investigator and her assistants will have access to these data.

Signatures:

_____

Department Chairperson

_____

Primary Investigator

Used by permission of the author.

Once the research protocol has been submitted, the IRB administrators must determine whether the protocol should be reviewed by the full board. There are seven different categories of review. The three most frequently used are exempt studies, studies that receive expedited review, and studies that receive review by the full board. Exempt studies are those that appear to involve no risk to the participants and do not require review by the full IRB. However, studies involving fetal participants and prisoners are never exempt unless the study involves observing these participants in the absence of any type of intervention. Also, studies with children involving survey or interview procedures or observation of public behavior by the researchers are never exempt.

If the IRB staff reviews a protocol and places it in the exempt category, the protocol is typically returned to the investigator within a few days, and the investigator is free to begin his or her research project. Remember that it is the IRB staff, not the researcher, that must make the decision as to whether the protocol is exempt. In making this decision, the IRB staff makes use of the exempt categories that are set forth in the OPRR Reports (1991) and listed in Table 4.3. These exempt categories reveal that a large portion of educational research is exempt. Even if a study does fall into one of the exempt categories and receives approval from the IRB, that does not mean that there are no other ethical issues to be considered. Phillips (1994) submitted her survey of adolescents' attitudes and behaviors related to HIV/AIDS prevention to the IRB and received approval pending only minor changes in the vocabulary of the consent form. Phillips requested a full board review of her research protocol even though the study was an anonymous survey of adolescents' attitudes. Even with IRB approval, Phillips identified a number of ethical concerns ranging from privacy issues to potential harm to the participants. This example illustrates that the investigator must remain attuned to the ethics of his or her research and not become complacent just because IRB approval has been received.

If you do submit a study that is exempt, you should not assume that this exempts you from the necessity of obtaining informed consent. The IRB might waive the requirement of informed consent under two conditions. If the consent document is the only record that could link the participant to the research and the primary harm arising from the research is a breach of confidentiality, informed consent might be waived. Also, if the research presents no more than minimal risk to participants and consent procedures are typically not required outside of the research context, informed consent might be waived. All other studies must obtain informed consent. Remember that it is the IRB that must provide the waiver of informed consent.

■ **Expedited review**
A process by which a study is rapidly reviewed by fewer members than constitute the full IRB board

Some studies qualify for expedited review. **Expedited review** is a process whereby a study is rapidly reviewed by fewer members than constitute the full IRB board. Studies that receive expedited review are typically those involving no more than minimal risk, such as the following:

1. Research involving data, documents, records, or specimens that have been collected or will be collected solely for nonresearch purposes
2. Research involving the collection of data from voice, video, digital, or image recordings made for research purposes
3. Research on individual or group characteristics or behavior or research employing survey, interview, oral history, focus groups, program evaluation, human factors evaluation, or quality assurance methodologies when they present no more than minimal risk to participants

■ **Full board review**
Review by all members of the IRB

All other studies receive **full board review,** or review by all members of the IRB.

▓ **TABLE 4.3** Exempt Categories

1. Research conducted in established or commonly accepted educational settings, involving normal educational practices, such as (a) research on regular and special education instructional strategies or (b) research on the effectiveness of or the comparison among instructional techniques, curricula, or classroom management methods.
2. Research involving the use of educational tests (cognitive, diagnostic, aptitude, achievement), survey procedures, interview procedures, or observation of public behavior, unless:
   a. information obtained is recorded in such a manner that the participants can be identified, directly or through identifiers linked to the participants; and
   b. any disclosure of the participants' responses outside the research could reasonably place the participants at risk of criminal or civil liability or be damaging to the participants' financial standing, employability, or reputation.
3. Research involving the use of educational tests (cognitive, diagnostic, aptitude, achievement), survey procedures, interview procedures, or observation of public behavior that is not exempt under 2 above if
   a. the participants are elected or appointed public officials or candidates for public office, or
   b. federal statute(s) require(s) without exception that the confidentiality of the personally identifiable information will be maintained throughout the research and thereafter.
4. Research involving the collection or study of existing data, documents, records, pathological specimens, or diagnostic specimens if these sources are publicly available or if the information is recorded by the investigator in such a manner that participants cannot be identified, directly or through identifiers linked to the participants.
5. Research and demonstration projects that are conducted by or subject to the approval of department or agency heads and that are designed to study, evaluate, or otherwise examine:
   a. public benefit or service programs,
   b. procedures for obtaining benefits or services under those programs,
   c. possible changes in or alternatives to those programs or procedures, or
   d. possible changes in methods or levels of payment for benefits or services under those programs

From OPRR Reports, (1991). *Code of Federal Regulations 45* (Part 46, p. 5). Washington, DC: U.S. Government Printing Office.

4.17 What is the purpose of the IRB?

4.18 What kinds of information should be contained in a research protocol submitted to the IRB?

4.19 What are exempt studies, and what type of studies meet the exempt criterion?

4.20 What is expedited review, and what type of studies would receive expedited review?

REVIEW
QUESTIONS

SUMMARY

In conducting educational research, it is necessary to ask questions and observe the behavior of students, teachers, and administrators. In doing so, researchers must be careful not to impinge on the well-recognized rights of these individuals to privacy and freedom from surveillance without consent. Research ethics are necessary to assist researchers in conducting ethically sound studies by providing a set of principles that will assist in conducting an ethical study.

There are three areas of ethical concern for the educational researcher:

1. *The relationship between society and science.* The society in which we live influences the research issues that are important and that need to be investigated. The most influential agency is the federal government because this agency not only provides most of the funds for research but also identifies priority areas.

2. *Professional issues.* The primary professional issue of ethical importance is fraudulent activity by scientists. In recent years, there has been an increase in the presentation of fraudulent results. This increase seems to be due primarily to the pressure to obtain grants and publish articles because these activities are frequently tied to promotions, raises, and tenure, although psychological makeup and other nonpersonal factors might contribute. Other, less serious professional issues include partial and duplicate publication, the use and archiving of videotaped data, and the conduct of research with vulnerable populations such as minors.

3. *Treatment of research participants.* Treatment of the research participants is the most fundamental ethical issue. Although most educational research does not run the risk of physical harm, there are subtle ethical issues that must be addressed relating to the potential for emotional harm, deception, and protecting the privacy of research participants.

The AERA has developed a set of ethical guidelines, specifically directed toward the educational researcher, which need to be followed when conducting a research study. Some of the important points included in these guidelines are the following:

1. *The necessity of obtaining informed consent.* This means that a person can participate in a research study only when he or she has agreed to participate and has been given all information that would influence his or her willingness to participate. Providing full disclosure of the nature or purpose of the research will alter the outcome and invalidate the results of some studies. In these cases, deception may be used, but the investigator must justify the use of the deception. If deception is used, it must be revealed during a debriefing session and any negative effects occurring from it must be eliminated.

2. *Assent and dissent with minors.* Minors cannot provide informed consent, but when they are capable of providing assent, it must be obtained.

3. *Passive versus active consent.* Although active consent is preferable and ensures that the participant has understood the demands and risks of the study, passive consent is sometimes used in educational research to increase participation and minimize bias. However, passive consent makes the assumption that nonresponse represents informed consent, which might or might not be the case.

4. *Deception.* Sometimes it is necessary to mislead or withhold information from the research participants. When this is necessary, the researcher must, at the conclusion of the study, explain that deception was used, explain the reason for the deception, and make sure that the deception did not cause any undue stress or other undesirable feelings. If such feelings were incurred, the researcher must incorporate procedures to eliminate the undesirable stress or feelings.

5. *Freedom to withdraw.* The research participants must be told that they are free to withdraw from the research study at any time without penalty. As a general rule, the dissent of a minor should also be respected even if the guardian or parent has provided informed consent. Children below the age of being able to provide consent or infants should be excused from the research study if they seem to be disturbed by or uncomfortable with the procedures.

6. *Confidentiality and anonymity.* Ideally, the research participant's identity is not known to the researcher (anonymity). In cases in which it is not possible to maintain anonymity, the identity of the participant and his or her responses must not be revealed to anyone other than the research staff (confidentiality).

In all cases, it is necessary to present a research proposal to the IRB for approval even if the guidelines presented by the AERA have been followed and the proposal seems to fall into the exempt category. Most institutional assurance policies state that *all* research involving humans is to be reviewed by the IRB, which means that it is the IRB that makes the decision as to whether a study falls into the exempt category.

KEY TERMS

active consent (p. 107)
anonymity (p. 112)
assent (p. 105)
confidentiality (p. 112)
debriefing (p. 110)
deception (p. 109)
dehoaxing (p. 110)
deontological approach (p. 94)

desensitizing (p. 110)
duplicate publication (p. 98)
ethical skepticism (p. 95)
ethics (p. 94)
exempt studies (p. 113)
expedited review (p. 116)
fraudulent activity (p. 96)
full board review (p. 116)

informed consent (p. 102)
Institutional Review Board
     (IRB) (p. 112)
partial publication (p. 98)
passive consent (p. 107)
research ethics (p. 96)
utilitarianism (p. 95)

STUDY TIP Visit the companion web site for education research at www.ablongman.com/johnsonchristensen2e for study questions and multiple-choice questions to find out how well you have mastered the material in this chapter. Also look at the other activities we have included to promote your mastery of the material in this chapter.

DISCUSSION QUESTIONS

1. One research area that has demonstrated an increase in recent years is research conducted over the Internet. Researchers have conducted surveys and even experiments over the Internet. Is it ethical to conduct such research? In discussing this topic, consider the ethical issues that must be considered in conducting any research study, such as risks and benefits, privacy, and informed consent. After you have discussed this issue, go to www.aaas.org/spp/dspp/sfrl/projects/intres/main.htm. Click on "report," and read their discussion of ethics and research on the Internet.

2. Go to www.indiana.edu/~poynter/index.html, and click on the *Teaching Research Ethics* link. From this link click on *Moral Reasoning in Scientific*

Research: Cases for Teaching and Assessment. Read the sample case, and then discuss whether Jessica Banks should photocopy the notebooks relating to her dissertation research.

3. Most of the research educational researchers conduct falls into the exempt category. This means that requiring IRB review of educational research studies represents an intrusion and a hurdle that accomplishes nothing. Therefore, IRB review of educational studies should be eliminated. Defend or refute this view.

4. Should passive consent be allowed, or does it violate ethical standards, meaning that active consent should always be obtained prior to participation in a research study?

RESEARCH EXERCISES

Using Research Navigator, find a published article on a topic area that interests you. Then get the published article and complete the following exercises.

1. Using the published article you selected, construct a research protocol that might have been submitted to the IRB by completing the following:

    Title of Protocol
    Primary Investigator
    Co-Investigator
    Relevant Background and Purpose
    Participant Population
    Materials and Procedure
    Design and Methodology
    Potential Benefit
    Risks
    Confidentiality

2. Using the published article you selected, construct an informed consent form that might be used in conjunction with this research study. Include the following:

    a. Statement of Invitation to Participate
    b. Statement of What the Study Will Ask the Participant to Do or Have Done to Him/Her
    c. Statement of the Benefits Derived from Participating in the Study
    d. Statement of the Risks Encountered from Participating in the Study
    e. Statement of How Confidentiality Will Be Maintained
    f. Identification of Person(s) Who Can Be Contacted If Questions Arise Regarding the Study

RELEVANT INTERNET SITES

http://onlineethics.org/index.html/
The home page of the online ethics center.

http://ori.dhhs.gov/
The Office of Research Integrity of the Department of Health and Human Services.

http://venus.soci.niu.edu/~jthomas/ethics/ethics.html
A site that contains articles on the ethics of research in cyberspace.

RECOMMENDED READING

Sales, B. D., & Folkman, S. (2002). *Ethics in research with human participants.* Washington, DC: American Psychological Association.

Committee on Government Operations. (1990). *Are scientific misconduct and conflicts of interest hazardous to our health?* Washington, DC: U.S. Government Printing Office.

5

Standardized Measurement and Assessment

LEARNING OBJECTIVES

To be able to

- Explain the meaning of measurement.
- Explain the different scales of measurement, including the type of information communicated by each one.
- Articulate the twelve assumptions underlying testing and assessment.
- Explain the meaning of reliability.
- Explain the differences among each of the methods for computing reliability.
- Explain the meaning of validity and validity evidence.
- Explain the different methods of collecting validity evidence.
- Identify the different types of standardized tests and the sources of information on these tests.
- Locate tests used to measure the constructs of interest to you.

In the 1990s, the National Center for Education Statistics published a government report entitled "Adult Literacy in America." This report stated that 47 percent of American adults scored in the two lowest levels of the 1992 National Adult Literacy Survey and that 21 percent scored at the lowest of the five literacy levels. The implications of this survey were astounding because it suggested that many Americans could not perform even the simplest tasks such as understanding a simple news article or calculating the cost of a movie ticket. The headlines of newspapers across the country stated that 50 percent of Americans were functionally illiterate. Politicians were alarmed and advocated increased testing and immediate school reform.

In February 2002, the *Chronicle of Higher Education* (Baron, 2002) reported that a new analysis of the 1992 survey data shows that less than 5 percent of the adult population is functionally illiterate. How can it be that a reanalysis of the same data dropped the illiteracy rate from 50 percent to less than 5 percent? Did the nation suddenly become more literate? Certainly, such a change cannot occur easily! In this case, the statisticians of the original report admitted that they misread the data. They had originally used a single standard to evaluate the test results but later realized that literacy data should be viewed from multiple perspectives. Additionally, the more current 5 percent figure includes people with linguistic or physical problems that could have affected their performance. Of those scoring at the lowest proficiency level, 25 percent were immigrants, and many others were school dropouts, people older than 65, people who had significant physical or mental impairments, or people who had vision problems. Such problems would obviously impact the response to the survey.

As you can see from the reanalysis of the original survey data and the characteristics of the participants who scored in the lowest quartile of the survey, "literacy" is a complex issue, and it is difficult to assess. To make a statement about the literacy of the American people, we must not only collect data from which we can make inferences about literacy, but also collect data that will provide us with strong evidence that the inferences we make are defensible. Assessing literacy is not a simple matter of sorting people into those who "can read" and those who "can't read."

As educators or educational researchers, we are constantly faced with the question of how to measure the variables that are important to us. We want to measure various educational abilities and achievement levels such as mathematical performance. We also want to measure constructs such as depression, stress, and self-esteem and be able to diagnose various problems such as learning disorders. In making these measurements, we collect data and then make inferences or assessments based on the data in a way very similar to the "literacy survey." In this chapter, we will discuss many of the issues that must be considered to ensure that the inferences we make on the basis of our measurements are accurate, useful, and defensible.

Let's start with a conversation between a researcher and a new research methods student. The student asks, "Why do we need to learn about measurement in an educational research book?" The professor replies, "Hmm . . . Have you heard of GIGO? In case you haven't, GIGO refers to the principle of garbage-in garbage-out. It is a cardinal rule in research that poor measurement results in GIGO. Without good measurement, you don't really have anything. Please remember that important point!"

Think for a moment about what you have learned about conducting an educational research study. All research studies begin with research questions. After the research questions are formulated, you have to develop a way of providing an answer to each research question by collecting information, or data, that will give you the answer you are looking for. Whenever you collect data, you are measuring or assessing something, and if your measurement is poor, your research will necessarily be poor.

In your own experience, you have probably had exposure to the measurement of many different types of variables. Students are frequently given some type of achievement test, some of which are constructed by teachers and others by measurement professionals. Tests are often used to diagnose learning and/or behavior problems, intelligence, aptitude, and/or interests. More recently, students in some areas of the country are being evaluated at the end of their high school education to determine whether they have acquired the minimal knowledge and skills that are expected of a high school graduate. Measurement therefore is something that exists in many areas, and educational research is one of them.

Measuring variables of interest to educational researchers is often a rather difficult task. Educational researchers investigate variables such as memory, dyslexia, motivation, self-efficacy, and educational achievement. When we measure these variables, we frequently express them as numbers. However, converting variables such as these to numbers or dimensions is difficult, and considerable time and energy are often devoted to this process. Because of this difficulty, we briefly discuss the nature of measurement and the various scales of measurement.

DEFINING MEASUREMENT

■ **Measurement**
Assigning symbols or numbers to something according to a specific set of rules

Research
Navigator.c⊛m

measurement

Measurement refers to the act of measuring. When we measure something, we identify the dimensions, quantity, capacity, or degree of something. The measurement process operates by assigning symbols or numbers to objects, events, people, characteristics, and so forth according to a specific set of rules. Actually, this is something we do all the time. For example, whenever you determine how tall a person is or how much he or she weighs, you are engaged in measurement because you are assigning numbers according to a given set of rules. If you are measuring height in inches, the rule you are using is that you are assigning the number 1 to a length that is exactly one inch on a standard ruler. Height in inches is determined by counting the number of these one-inch lengths it takes to span the height of the person whom you are measuring. If you are measuring or evaluating people's gender, you use the rule of assigning the symbol of female to individuals that have female characteristics and the symbol of male to individuals that have male characteristics. The result of any measurement is that you have a guideline for representing the dimensions or magnitude of something, such as the height or gender of a person. Stating that a person is 68 inches tall communicates the exact height of that person, just as the symbol of female communicates the gender dimension of that person.

Educational researchers might be interested in variables such as aggression, shyness, depression, dyslexia, gender, and intelligence. To conduct a study investigating these variables, a procedure or technique is needed to represent the dimensions of categorical variables (such as gender and college major) and the magnitude of quantitative variables (such as income and IQ). The number that is derived from an intelligence test represents an index of the magnitude of intellect. The number of times a child hits another has been used as an index of the magnitude of aggression. The biological makeup of a child is often used as an index of gender.

5.1 What is measurement?

REVIEW

QUESTION

SCALES OF MEASUREMENT

Measurement can be categorized in terms of the type of information communicated by the symbols or numbers that are assigned. We now introduce you to a popular four-level classification scheme. This four-level scheme provides more information than the two-level (i.e., categorical versus quantitative variables) system used in earlier chapters. The earlier scheme also works fine, and there is nothing wrong with it. Sometimes, however, researchers prefer to make the finer gradations that are provided by the four level system.

The four-level system, originally developed by Stevens (1946, 1951), includes four levels or scales of measurement: nominal, ordinal, interval, and ratio. As Table 5.1 illustrates, each of these conveys different kinds of information. To help you remember the order of the four levels, note that the first letters of the four scales spell the French word for black:

TABLE 5.1
Scale of Measurement

Scale	Characteristics
Nominal	Ability to categorize, label, classify, name, or identify
Ordinal	Rank order objects or individuals from first to last or best to worst
Interval	Ability to rank order objects or individuals; has equal intervals or distances between adjacent numbers
Ratio	Ability to rank order objects or individuals; has equal intervals between adjacent numbers and has an absolute zero point that permits forming ratio statements

noir. (You didn't know you were going to learn French in your research methods course, did you?) It is important to know the level of measurement being employed because it suggests the type of statistical manipulations of the data that are appropriate and identifies the type of information being communicated.[1]

Nominal Scale

■ **Nominal scale**
A scale of measurement that uses symbols, such as words or numbers, to label, classify, or identify people or objects

Nominal scales are the simplest form of measurement. A **nominal scale** of measurement uses symbols, such as words or numbers, to label, classify, or identify people or objects. In Chapter 2, we called variables that are measured at this level *categorical variables.* Therefore, you are already familiar with this type of measurement. A few examples of nominal scales or nominal variables are gender, school type, race, political party, state, college major, teaching method, counseling method, and personality type. The symbols that you attach to the levels of a nominal variable do little more than serve as markers. For the variable *school type,* you might use 1 for public school and 2 for private school, or you might use the full words (i.e., *public* and *private*) as your markers. For the variable *political party identification,* you might choose the markers 1 for Republican, 2 for Democrat, and 3 for other. The symbols that are used to mark the nominal variable categories are used exclusively for identification purposes. If you use numbers as your markers, they cannot be added, subtracted, ranked, or averaged. However, you can count the frequency within each category, and you can relate a nominal variable to other variables.

The nominal scale is important because many observations made by educational researchers take place at this level. For example, educational researchers frequently create an independent variable by categorizing people by some characteristic such as gender or the presence or absence of a disorder such as ADHD, and then they compare the performance of the people placed in the different categories. Wang and Staver (1997), for example, compared the performance of male and female children in China on science achievement. In analyzing the data collected in this study, they could have labeled females 1 and males 2 or kept the word symbols *female* and *male.* In this study, Wang and Staver also analyzed the science achievement data by province as well as gender, as illustrated in Table 5.2.

▦ **T A B L E 5 . 2**   Science Achievement of Male and Female Students in Five Provinces in China

Province	Mean		Standard Deviation	
	Female	Male	Female	Male
Gansu	15.405	17.657	4.556	4.296
Guangxi	15.264	17.195	4.318	4.291
Hubci	15.701	18.160	4.276	4.099
Inner Mongolia	15.460	17.772	4.525	4.305
Jiangshu	15.306	17.834	4.253	3.944

Source: Based on data presented by Wang and Staver (1997).

Ordinal Scale

The **ordinal scale** of measurement is a rank-order scale. This scale of measurement is frequently used to determine which students will be accepted into graduate programs. Most graduate programs receive many more applicants than they can accept; therefore, applicants are frequently rank ordered from the one with the most outstanding credentials to the one with the least outstanding credentials, and a specified number of students with the highest ranks are selected for admission. In another situation, students might be rank ordered in terms of their need for remedial instruction. In both examples, the key characteristic is that individuals are compared with others in terms of some ability or performance and assigned a rank, with 1 perhaps being assigned to the person with the most ability or the person who performs best, 2 to the next best, and so forth.

> ■ **Ordinal scale**
> A rank-order scale of measurement

From this example, you can see that an ordinal scale of measurement allows you to make ordinal judgments; that is, it allows you to determine which person is higher or lower than another person on a variable of interest. However, it does not give you any indication as to how much higher one person is than another. If you ranked ten students in terms of their need for remedial instruction, as illustrated in Table 5.3, you would know that the person receiving a rank of 1 is the person who needs remedial instruction the most (i.e., he or she has the highest or greatest need based on our measurement). However, you would not know how much more the person who was ranked first needed remedial instruction than the person who was ranked second. That is because an ordinal scale of measurement says nothing about *how much* greater one ranking is than another. All you can do with ordinal-level data is rank individuals on some characteristic according to their position on that characteristic.

Interval Scale

The **interval scale** of measurement has the rank-order feature of ordinal scales, but it also includes the additional characteristic of equal distances, or equal intervals, between adjacent numbers on the scale. In other words, the difference between any two adjacent numbers on the scale is equal to the difference between any two other adjacent numbers.

> ■ **Interval scale**
> A scale of measurement that has equal intervals of distances between adjacent numbers

Two examples of interval scales are the Celsius temperature scale (illustrated in Figure 5.1) and the Fahrenheit temperature scale, because all points on these scales are equally distant from one another. A difference in temperature between 0 and 20 degrees Fahrenheit is the same as the difference between 40 and 60 degrees Fahrenheit. However, you must

■ **TABLE 5.3**
Ranking of Students
on Need for Remedial Instruction

Student	Ranking	Student	Ranking
Tommy	1	William	6
Jerry	2	Joyce	7
Sally	3	Bob	8
Suzie	4	Pam	9
Nancy	5	Ben	10

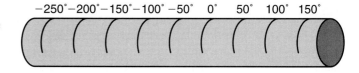

■ **FIGURE 5.1**
A Celsius temperature
scale

remember that the zero point on an interval scale is arbitrary. The zero point on the Celsius scale refers to the point at which water freezes at sea level, not a complete absence of heat, which is what a true zero point would designate. Actually, the absence of heat is approximately –273 degrees Celsius, not the zero point on this temperature scale.

This absence of an absolute zero point restricts the type of information that is conveyed by interval-level measurements. Specifically, it means that you cannot make "ratio statements." For example, it seems logical to say that 20 degrees Celsius is *twice* as warm as 10 degrees Celsius because the difference between 0 and 20 degrees is twice as great as the difference between 0 and 10 degrees, or 20/10 = 2. However, you cannot make this ratio statement because interval scales do not have absolute zero points. To illustrate this point further, consider the two temperatures 40 and 80 degrees Fahrenheit. If ratio statements could be made, 80 degrees Fahrenheit should be twice as warm as 40 degrees Fahrenheit. If this relationship is true, it should exist regardless of whether we are talking about temperature measured according to the Fahrenheit scale or the Celsius scale. However, 40 degrees Fahrenheit converts to approximately 5.4 degrees Celsius, and 80 degrees Fahrenheit converts to approximately 26.7 degrees Celsius. This is the paradox of an interval scale, which is a function of the absence of an absolute zero point.

Once an interval level of measurement has been reached, it is possible to engage in arithmetic operations such as computing an average and getting a meaningful result. Many of the scores (e.g., IQ, personality, attitude, aptitude, educational level, reading achievement) that we use in educational research are taken to be at the interval level of measurement. However, for most of the characteristics we investigate, remember that zero does not mean an absence of that characteristic. If a person got a science achievement score of zero, that would not necessarily mean that there was a complete absence of achievement in science, just as an IQ score of zero would not necessarily mean an absence of intelligence.

Ratio Scale

■ **Ratio scale**
A scale of measurement that has a true zero point as well as the characteristics of the nominal (labeling), ordinal (rank ordering), and interval scales (equal distances)

The fourth level of measurement, the ratio scale, represents the highest level of quantitative measurement. The **ratio scale** of measurement has all the properties of the nominal (presence of a characteristic), ordinal (rank order), and interval scales (equal distances between points) plus it has a *true zero point*. The number zero represents an absence of the characteristic being measured. On the Kelvin temperature scale, zero refers to the absence of heat (and you thought zero degrees Fahrenheit was cold!). Most physical measurements are done at the ratio level (e.g., height, weight, age, distance, area). Something weighing zero pounds means that it is weightless. (If your weight is zero, you are in big trouble!) Similarly, if your annual income was zero dollars last year, you did not earn any money at all. Because the ratio scale of measurement has the characteristics of rank order, equal intervals, and a true or absolute zero point, all mathematical operations can meaningfully be performed.

In education, ratio-level measurement is occasionally used. For example, if you are interested in the number of test items a student got correct or the amount of time taken to complete an assignment, you have ratio-level measurement. However, most of the characteristics that we measure in education are not at this level because educational researchers frequently deal with attributes such as educational attainment, learning disorders, personality, attitudes, opinions, and learning strategies. Such attributes and characteristics do not have the characteristics of a ratio scale of measurement. Therefore, ratio-level measurement, desirable as it is, is not the level of measurement that is used in most educational research studies.

For more information on the four measurement scales, we recommend this link: www.creative.net.au/mirrors/neural/measurement.html.

5.2 What are the four different levels or scales of measurement, and what are the essential characteristics of each one?

REVIEW

QUESTION

ASSUMPTIONS UNDERLYING TESTING AND ASSESSMENT

As they go about the process of conducting their research studies, education researchers engage in a variety of procedures in an attempt to obtain measures of characteristics that are often considered subjective and difficult to assess, such as personality or teacher morale. Measuring these characteristics involves both testing and assessment. The distinction between testing and assessment is often somewhat ambiguous and has been slow in developing and becoming integrated into everyday parlance. However, there is a difference in spite of this overlap, and this difference needs to be made clear. For our purposes, we will follow the lead of Cohen, Swerdlik, and Philips (1996) and define **testing** as "the process of measuring . . . variables by means of devices or procedures designed to obtain a sample of behavior" and **assessment** as "the gathering and integration of . . . data for the purpose of making . . . an educational evaluation, accomplished through the use of tools such as tests, interviews, case studies, behavioral observation, and specially designed apparatus and measurement procedures" (p. 6).

- **Testing**
  Measurement of educational variables
- **Assessment**
  Gathering and integrating data to make educational evaluations

When assessing characteristics of interest, educational researchers use a variety of tools ranging from educational and psychological tests to interviews and behavioral observations. Educational researchers and psychometricians (i.e., professionals who specialize in test development) may devise a new assessment tool, use an existing tool, or adapt an existing tool previously used to measure a characteristic. Innovative tools are often devised to assess people with disabilities. Wilson, Thompson, and Wylie (1982), for example, devised a dental plate that could be activated by the tongue for individuals who lack the capacity for speech or control of their hands or limbs. This dental plate made it possible for these individuals to provide five different types of responses by depressing the tongue on different areas of the plate.

Now we are going to list some assumptions that are commonly made by psychometricians and other educational researchers who develop and use standardized tests. Here are the twelve assumptions that are basic to the enterprise of testing and assessment, as identified by Cohen et al. (1996).

1. *Psychological traits and states exist.* According to this assumption, psychological traits and states such as anxiety, motivation, shyness, and aggressiveness exist in the sense that they provide labels for real phenomena that many people consider important and worth measuring. **Traits** are "any distinguishable, relatively enduring way in which one individual varies from another" (Guilford, 1959, p. 6). **States** refer to distinguishable ways in which individuals vary, but they differ from traits in that they are less enduring (Chaplin, John, & Goldberg, 1988), or are more transient characteristics. The psychological trait of anxiety, for example, indicates an enduring or constant level of anxiety that persists both over time and across situations. The psychological state of anxiety indicates a more temporary condition, such as might exist if you were walking in the woods and saw a snake on the path in front of you.

2. *Psychological traits and states can be quantified and measured.* This assumption states that it is often possible to assign numbers to psychological traits and states and that if the test is well developed and administered properly, these numbers will be representative of the properties of the states and traits being measured. The numerical test score that is obtained to represent a state or trait is presumed to represent the nature or strength of the state or trait being measured. This means that the higher the test score, the higher the test taker is presumed to be on the targeted trait or state.

3. *Various approaches to measuring aspects of the same thing can be useful.* The same trait, state, interest, ability, or aptitude can be measured by using a number of different measurement techniques and tests. Tests vary on a number of dimensions, such as the extent to which they are linked to theory; the extent to which the stimulus materials are verbal or nonverbal; whether they were derived on an empirical or a rational basis; how the test items are presented; and the way in which they are administered, scored, and interpreted. These differences do not imply that there is confusion in the field in terms of how some characteristic should be measured. Rather, it indicates that there are many different and complementary ways of measuring the characteristics of interest to educational researchers.

4. *Assessment can provide answers to some of life's most momentous questions.* Educational researchers are asked to provide answers to questions ranging from the most effective way to teach to determining which children should be targeted for special educational attention. These are not trivial questions, and users of assessment tools need to know when the measurement tools they use can help them to answer their research questions.

5. *Assessment can pinpoint phenomena that require further attention or study.* The idea here is that assessment tools are frequently used for making diagnoses similar to the way a physician uses medical tests to diagnose problems. When a doctor assesses a patient, the doctor makes a diagnosis. Diagnostic tests in education might be used to determine where a student is having academic difficulty or whether a student is at risk for a future problem. Educational researchers frequently conduct studies on special populations such as children with learning disabilities or children with ADHD. To study these populations, the children with these disorders must be identified, and this identification is made using some

---

■ **Traits**
Distinguishable, relatively enduring ways in which one individual differs from another

■ **States**
Distinguishable but less enduring ways in which individuals vary

type of assessment tool. Once identified, the researcher can engage in a research study of people with special characteristics.

6. *Various sources of data enrich and are part of the assessment process.* Decision making about an individual should not be made on a single test score but from a variety of different sources. Overreliance on a single test can lead to an uninformed decision. For example, to diagnose ADHD, you need information from psychological tests measuring this disorder as well as information from teachers, parents, a physician, and a school psychologist.

7. *Various sources of error are always part of the assessment process.* It is a maxim that there is no such thing as perfect measurement. Some error is always present. **Error** is defined as the difference between the person's true score and the observed score. In the assessment process, error occurs because the scores obtained in any assessment are influenced by many variables in addition to the trait or characteristic being assessed. For example, if you are trying to assess students' intelligence by giving them an intelligence test, the IQ score obtained on the test will be a result of these persons' actual intellectual level plus a variety of other factors, such as how tired they are when they take the test, whether they are physically sick, or whether they are experiencing some interpersonal difficulty such as going through a divorce. These other variables will partially determine the score obtained from the assessment and introduce error into the assessment. The greater the amount of error, the more inaccurate the assessment.

■ **Error**
The difference between a person's true score and the observed score

8. *Tests and other measurement techniques have strengths and weaknesses.* It probably seems like common sense to state that every assessment technique has its own strengths and weaknesses. The important issue is a recognition of the fact not that these strengths and weaknesses exist but that the user of the assessment should make every attempt to recognize and understand these strengths and weaknesses so that he or she can appropriately interpret the results of the assessment.

9. *Test-related behavior predicts non-test-related behavior.* Every test or assessment requires test takers to do something while they take the test. These test behaviors might range from blackening grids with a number 2 pencil (for example, for the purpose of measuring sensation seeking as a personality trait) to more performance type measures such as key pressing or perhaps even bungee jumping (as a measure of sensation seeking). According to this assumption, these vastly different approaches to measurement can provide valid data when they are carried out systematically, and these data can be used to predict other behaviors. For example, paper-and-pencil achievement tests are given to children on the assumption that their performance on the test will say something about their level of achievement in mathematics, reading, or comprehension. The mechanics of measurement can vary widely and still provide good measurement of educational, psychological, and other types of variables.

10. *Present-day behavior sampling predicts future behavior.* Perhaps the most important reason for giving tests is to predict future behavior. According to this assumption, behavior emitted in the here-and-now (or even in the past for case history type data) can be used to predict future behavior. For example, the GRE is used to measure aptitude and predict performance in graduate school. The Beck Depression Inventory is used to measure depression and predict whether a serious problem will occur for the test taker (e.g., hurting oneself). An IQ test score can be used to predict a person's future level of ability and perhaps how well he or she might do in school or in some other intellectually stimulating task.

11. *Testing and assessment can be conducted in a fair and unbiased manner.* Today all major test publishers attempt to develop tests that, when used according to the procedures outlined in the test manuals, are fair and unbiased. If a test is intended to be widely applicable, the test maker must carefully construct the test items and test the items with different types of people. Fairness and biasing problems can arise when a test is administered to people whose background and experience are different from those for whom the test was intended. In such cases, the test or assessment probably will be unfair and biased, which emphasizes that any assessment device can be used inappropriately. This is why the person administering the assessment device must be aware of its strengths and weaknesses so that it can be applied appropriately and valid assessments can be made. For more information on fairness in testing, we recommend that you examine the four chapters on fairness in testing in the book *Standards for Educational and Psychological Testing* (AERA, APA, & NCME, 1999).

12. *Testing and assessment benefit society.* Many critical decisions are made on the basis of tests and assessments. Minimal teacher competency in some states is established on the basis of tests. Tests are used to determine whether a person has a learning disability, to assess teacher morale, and to evaluate the mental competency of a person. Without the existence of testing and assessment, the world would be much more unpredictable.

REVIEW
QUESTION

5.3 What are the twelve assumptions underlying testing and measurement?

IDENTIFYING A GOOD TEST OR ASSESSMENT PROCEDURE

When we conduct a research study, we want to select measuring instruments that give us the best and most accurate measure of the variables we are investigating. If we are conducting a study investigating the usefulness of a reading program in teaching reading to children with dyslexia, we want a good assessment of dyslexia to ensure that the children who are included in our study are truly dyslexic. We also want a good measure of reading so that we can document any change in reading achievement of the children with dyslexia as a result of having participated in the reading program. When selecting and using a measurement instrument (e.g., a test), we must always consider the issues of reliability and validity.

Overview of Reliability and Validity

Reliability and validity are the two most important psychometric properties to consider in using a test or assessment procedure. *Reliability* refers to the consistency or stability of the test scores, and *validity* refers to the accuracy of the inferences or interpretations you make from the test scores. For example, let's say that you just got home from your local department store, where you bought a new set of scales used for weighing yourself. The scales have a LCD readout that displays a number that indicates pounds. Assume that you weight 125 pounds. You step on your new scales, and the readout says 130 pounds. You think this seems a little high, so you weigh yourself again, and this time the readout says 161. You think, "Wow! What's going on here?" You weigh yourself again, and this time the readout says 113. What is the problem with these scales? The problem is that the scores are not consistent: The scores provided by your new scales are not reliable. Because the scores are not reliable, the issue of validity is irrelevant, and you need to return your new scales to the store.

Now assume that you have a different kind of problem with your new LCD scales. Again assume that you weigh 125 pounds. You step on the scales for the first time, and the readout says 135. You know that's high, so you weigh yourself again, and the readout says 136. You weigh yourself five more times, and the readouts are 134, 135, 134, 135, 135. This time your scales are reliable because you get approximately the same score each time. What is the problem with your new scales in this case? The problem is that there is a **systematic error** that occurs every time you use the scales. Your scales are systematically high by about 10 pounds, so if you use them to infer your weight, you will be systematically wrong! In this example, the weights were reliable, but your inferences about your weight were not valid because the scales gave you the wrong weight. Just as in the first case, you need to return your new scales to the store.

■ **Systematic error**
An error that is present every time an instrument is used

In the third case, your new scales are going to work as promised. Again assume that you weigh 125 pounds. You step on the scales, and the readout says 125. You weigh yourself five more times, and the readouts are 124, 125, 125, 126, 125. In this case, the scores are reliable (the scores are consistent), and you are also able to make a valid inference about your weight. This is the case of reliability *and* validity. You can keep your new scales because they work properly. If you think about it, you will see that *reliability is a necessary but not sufficient condition for validity,* which simply means that if you want validity, you must have reliability (Nunnally & Bernstein, 1994). Stated another way, reliability is no guarantee of validity. When judging the performance of a test and your interpretations based on that test, remember that reliability and validity are both important properties. You need both. Keep this point in mind as you read about how to obtain evidence of reliability and validity for testing and other measurements.

5.4 What is the difference between reliability and validity? Which is more important?

REVIEW

QUESTION

Reliability

In psychological and educational testing, **reliability** refers to the consistency or stability of a set of test scores. If a test or assessment procedure provides reliable scores, the scores will be similar on every occasion. For example, if the scores from a test of intelligence are reliable,

■ **Reliability**
The consistency or stability of test scores

■ **TABLE 5.4**
Summary of Methods for
Computing Reliability

Type of Reliability	Number of Testing Sessions	Number of Test Forms	Statistical Procedure
Test-retest	2	1	Correlation coefficient
Equivalent-forms	1 or 2	2	Correlation coefficient
Internal consistency	1	1	Kuder-Richardson, coefficient alpha, or correlation coefficient
Inter-scorer	1	1	Correlation coefficient

the same, or just about the same, IQ scores will be obtained every time it is administered to a particular group of people.

The reliability of scores from a measure must be determined empirically. You can see a summary of the different ways of assessing reliability in Table 5.4. Each way provides a slightly different index of reliability. Researchers should select the method that provides the kind of information they need; often, several different ways of computing reliability are used to demonstrate the different ways in which the scores are reliable to provide corroborating evidence of reliability (e.g., test-retest and internal consistency reliability information is often reported in high-quality journal articles).

Reliability is often calculated by using some type of correlation coefficient. If you are a little rusty on the concept of correlation, you need to take a moment *right now* and reread the five pages in Chapter 2 on correlation coefficients (see pages 41–45). When we calculate a correlation coefficient as our measure of reliability, we call it a **reliability coefficient.** A reliability coefficient of zero stands for no reliability at all. (If you get a negative correlation, treat it as meaning no reliability and that your test is faulty.) A reliability coefficient of +1.00 stands for perfect reliability. Researchers want reliability coefficients to be strong and positive (i.e., as close to +1.00 as possible) because this indicates high reliability. Now let's look at the different forms of reliability.

■ **Reliability coefficient**
A correlation coefficient that is used as an index of reliability

REVIEW

QUESTION

5.5 What are the definitions of reliability and reliability coefficient?

Test-Retest Reliability **Test-retest reliability** refers to the consistency or stability of test scores over time. For example, if you were to assess the reliability of the scores from an intelligence test using the test-retest method, you would give the test to a group of, say, 100 individuals on one occasion, wait a period of time, and then give the same intelligence test to the same 100 individuals again. Then you would correlate the scores on the first testing occasion with the scores on the second testing occasion. If the individuals who received high IQ scores on the first testing occasion received high IQ scores on the second testing occasion and the individuals who received low IQ scores on the first testing occasion also received low IQ scores on the second testing occasion, the correlation between the scores on the two testing occasions would be high, indicating that the test scores were reliable. If these individuals received very different scores on the two testing occasions, the correlation between the two sets of scores would be low, indicating that the test scores were unreliable.

■ **Test-retest reliability**
A measure of the consistency of scores over time

Table 5.5 shows two sets of scores, one set that is reliable and another set that is unreliable, perhaps from an intelligence test that you are currently developing. For the reliable intelligence test, the scores from the first and second testing period are about the same, which means that the test is providing about the same measure of intelligence on both testing occasions. The actual correlation (i.e., the reliability coefficient) is equal to .96, suggesting that the test-retest reliability is quite high. For the unreliable intelligence test, the scores and the rank order of the scores from the first and second testing periods are quite different. The actual correlation (i.e., the reliability coefficient) in this case is .23, which is extremely low for a reliability coefficient. As you can see, the assessment of intelligence would be very different in these two cases. In the first case, the scores were consistent over time; in the second case, the scores were not consistent.

One of the problems with assessing test-retest reliability is knowing how much time should elapse between the two testing occasions. If the time interval is too short, the scores obtained from the two testing occasions might be partially due to individuals remembering how

■ **TABLE 5.5**
Illustration of Reliable and Unreliable Intelligence Tests Using the Test-Retest Reliability Procedure

Reliable Test		Unreliable Test	
First Testing	Second Testing	First Testing	Second Testing
110	112	110	95
123	120	123	103
115	116	115	147
109	113	109	100
99	95	99	120
103	102	103	110
131	128	131	125
128	130	128	142
119	114	119	111
121	124	105	135

they responded when they took the test the first time. In this case, the reliability of the test is artificially inflated. On the other hand, if the time interval is too long, the response to the test might be due to changes in the individuals. As time passes, people change. They might, for example, learn new things, forget some things, or acquire new skills. Unfortunately, there does not seem to be an ideal time interval in which to administer a test that works in all cases. It is safe to say that less than a week is usually too short a time interval for most tests. The best time interval to use depends on the kind of test involved, the participants taking the test, and the specific circumstances surrounding the test that may affect participants' performance. Generally, as the length of time increases, the correlation between the scores obtained on each testing decreases. Because the time interval can have an effect on test-retest reliability, this information should always be provided in addition to the actual reliability coefficient.

Equivalent Forms Reliability Have you ever taken an exam in which some people got one form of the test and other people got a different form of the test? If so, you have experienced the use of alternative forms. In constructing alternative forms, the instructor attempts to make them equivalent in all respects. If you have ever wondered whether alternative forms are really equivalent, you have wondered about equivalent-forms reliability. **Equivalent-forms reliability** refers to the consistency of a group of individuals' scores on two equivalent forms of a test designed to measure the same characteristic. Equivalent forms means that two tests are constructed so that they are identical in every way except for the specific items asked on the test. This means that they have the same number of items, the items are of the same difficulty level, the items measure the same construct, and the test is administered, scored, and interpreted in the same way.

■ **Equivalent-forms reliability**
The consistency of a group of individuals' scores on two equivalent forms of a test measuring the same thing

Once the two equivalent tests have been constructed, they are administered concurrently to a group of individuals, or the second test is administered shortly after the first test. Either way, each person takes both tests and has scores on both tests. The two sets of scores (participants' scores on each form) are then correlated. This correlation coefficient shows the consistency of the test scores obtained from the two forms of the test. We want this reliability coefficient to be very high and positive; that is, the individuals who do well on the first form of the test should also do well on the second form, and the individuals who perform poorly on the first form of the test should perform poorly on the second form.

Although the equivalent-forms-reliability method is an excellent way of assessing reliability, the success of this method depends on the ability to construct two equivalent forms of the same test. It is difficult to construct two equivalent tests that measure the same construct because the two tests cannot include the same items. To the extent to which they are not equivalent, measurement error is introduced, which lowers the reliability of the test. In addition, the participants have to take essentially the same test twice in a short period of time. Sometimes this is difficult. Just think about the reaction you might have if you were told that you had to take the GRE twice in the same day. Because of these problems, particularly the necessity of having to construct two equivalent forms, researchers seldom use this method of assessing reliability.

■ **Internal consistency**
The consistency with which the items on a test measure a single construct

■ **Homogeneous test**
A unidimensional test in which all the items measure a single construct

Internal Consistency Reliability **Internal consistency** refers to how consistently the items on a test measure a single construct or concept. The test-retest and equivalent-forms methods of assessing reliability are general methods that can be used with just about any test. Many tests, however, are supposed to be homogeneous. A test is **homogeneous** or unidimensional when the items measure a single construct or a single dimension such as reading comprehension or spelling ability. This is in contrast to a test that is heterogeneous or multi-dimensional, which occurs when the test measures more than one construct or dimension. For example, contrast a test that is constructed to measure academic performance of sixth-grade students with a test designed to measure just the reading comprehension of sixth-grade students. A test of academic performance would be more heterogeneous in content than a test of reading comprehension because academic performance involves many skills, one of which is reading comprehension.

Homogeneous tests have more inter-item consistency (i.e., internal consistency) than do heterogeneous tests of equal length because the items focus on one construct and there-fore sample a relatively narrow content area. Test homogeneity is generally desirable be-cause it allows straightforward test score interpretation. If your test is multidimensional, then you should always check the internal consistency of each component of the test. For example, if your IQ test includes a reading component, a reasoning component, a mathe-matics component, and a creativity component, then you would need to check each of these components for internal consistency.

Internal consistency measures are convenient and are very popular with researchers because they require one group of individuals to take the test one time. You do not have to wait for a period of time to elapse after administering the test before you can give it again (as in test-retest reliability), and you do not have to construct two equivalent forms of a test (as in equivalent forms reliability). We will discuss two indexes of internal consistency: split-half reliability and coefficient alpha. Coefficient alpha is by far more popular with re-searchers, and you will commonly see it reported in journal articles.

Split-half reliability, as the name implies, involves splitting a test into two equivalent halves and then assessing the consistency of the scores across the two halves of the test. In par-ticular, you divide the test into halves and correlate the scores from the two halves. This method of computing reliability can be used when it is impractical or undesirable to assess reliability by using the test-retest or equivalent-forms methods because of factors such as time or expense.

■ **Split-half reliability**
A measure of the con-sistency of the scores obtained from two equivalent halves of the same test

Inherent in this method is the necessity of dividing a test into two halves. There are several ways of accomplishing this. The first procedure is to divide the test in the middle. This procedure is not recommended because factors such as different levels of fatigue influ-encing the first versus the second half of the test, different amounts of test anxiety, and dif-ferences in item difficulty as a function of placement in the test could spuriously raise or lower the reliability coefficient. A more acceptable way to split a test is to use the odd-numbered items for one half of the test and the even-numbered items for the other half of the test. Randomly assigning the items to one or the other half of the test is also acceptable. A fourth way is to divide the test by content so that each half contains an equal number of items that are equivalent in content and difficulty. In general, you want each half to be equal to the other in format, style, content, and other aspects. Once you have created the two halves, reliability of the scores is determined using the following steps:

1. Score each half of the test for every person to whom it was administered.
2. Compute the correlation between scores on the two halves of the test.
3. Adjust the computed correlation coefficient using the **Spearman-Brown formula** (The formula is provided and explained on the book's companion website for inter-ested readers).

■ **Spearman-Brown formula**
A statistical formula used for correcting the split-half reliability co-efficient

The adjusted correlation is the split-half estimate of reliability. A low correlation indicates that the test was unreliable and contained considerable measurement error; a high correlation indicates that the test was reliable. Nunnally and Bernstein (1994) point out that before computers were commonly available, the split-half procedure was the most popular way used to estimate reliability. One of the problems of using the split-half procedure is that different results can be obtained from the different ways of subdividing the test. The next technique (coefficient alpha) is generally a better measure of internal consistency reliability.

The second approach to measuring internal consistency is known as **coefficient alpha.** Lee Cronbach (1951) developed coefficient alpha from an earlier internal consistency formula developed by G. Frederic Kuder and M. W. Richardson (1937). (Note: One of the well-known Kuder and Richardson formulas is included on the book's companion website.) Coefficient alpha provides a reliability estimate that can be thought of as the average of all possible split-half correlations, corrected by the Spearman-Brown formula. Another way of saying this is that coefficient alpha tells you the degree to which the items are interrelated.

A popular rule of thumb is that the size of coefficient alpha should generally be, at a minimum, greater than or equal to .70 for research purposes and somewhat greater than that value (e.g., ≥.90) for clinical testing purposes (i.e., for assessing single individuals). This rule should be taken with a grain of salt, however, because the actual size that is considered adequate depends on the context and many other considerations, some of which we address below (also see Nunnaly & Bernstein, 1994).

A strength of coefficient alpha is its versatility. It can be used for test items that allow for a range of responses. For example, on a five-point agreement scale (strongly agree, agree, neutral, disagree, strongly disagree), respondents can select from a range of five answers. Coefficient alpha can also be used for dichotomous items. On a dichotomous item, either two choices are provided (e.g., true or false) or the item is scored as having only two answers (e.g., multiple-choice questions are scored as either right or wrong).

Now we will examine a version of the formula for coefficient alpha that is instructive because it can be used to demonstrate two important points about coefficient alpha.[2] (We have included the traditional computational formula for coefficient alpha on the book's companion website for interested readers.)

■ **Coefficient alpha**
A formula that provides an estimate of the reliability of a homogeneous test or an estimate of the reliability of each dimension in a multidimensional test

Research
Navigator.c⊛m

coefficient alpha

$$r_\alpha = \frac{k\bar{r}}{1 + k\bar{r} - \bar{r}}$$

where
   r_α is coefficient alpha
   k is the number of items
   $\bar{r}$ is the average inter-item correlation (i.e., the average correlation between the items)

Note that k is the number of items on your test or subscale, and $\bar{r}$ is the average of all of the correlations between the items (i.e., every item is correlated with every other item and the average of these is taken). You would not want to use this formula to compute coefficient alpha by hand because it would be cumbersome. For example, if there were 10 items on your test, you would have to get 45 correlations between the 10 items and then average them to obtain $\bar{r}$.[3] If your test had 20 items, you would have to get 190 correlations! Today, researchers almost always use computer packages to calculate coefficient alpha for them.

Now let's look at the formula and make those two important points we promised you. First, the formula shows that coefficient alpha depends on the correlation among the items on the test. In particular, the stronger the correlations among the items (symbolized by the $\bar{r}$ in the formula), the larger coefficient alpha will be. Because coefficient alpha measures internal consistency, one would expect the items to be correlated with one another. The second point, however, is sometimes overlooked. This is the point that coefficient alpha depends on the number of items in your test (symbolized by k in the formula). In particular, the more items you include in your test or subscale, the larger the coefficient alpha will be. This means that it is possible to get a large coefficient alpha even when the items are not very homogeneous or internally consistent when many items are included on the test (John & Benet-Martinez, 2000).

Therefore, be sure to consider the number of items when interpreting coefficient alpha as a measure of internal consistency, and don't just assume that because coefficient alpha is large, the items are strongly related. Today, because of the availability of personal computers and because it requires only one test taken at a single time, coefficient alpha seems to be the preferred statistic for obtaining an estimate of internal consistency reliability (Keith & Reynolds, 1990). Remember, however, to be careful when interpreting coefficient alpha.

Interscorer Reliability There are many instances in which an evaluation of a research participant's performance is made by someone such as an instructor, a teacher, or some other professional. For example, we have all taken essay examinations. We always hope that the teacher is a consistent evaluator and that the score we receive is the same regardless of who is doing the evaluation. However, the score we receive on such an examination is partially a function of our performance and partially a function of the person doing the scoring. This fact was vividly demonstrated many years ago when Starch and Elliott (1912) revealed that the grade given to one student's English composition ranged from a low of 50 percent to a high of 98 percent depending on the teacher or volunteer who graded the paper. Because of the wide variability that can occur in the scoring of performance, it is important to determine the consistency of such an evaluation. Evaluation of the degree of agreement that exists between two or more scorers, judges, or raters is referred to as **interscorer reliability,** although it is also sometimes referred to as judge reliability, interrater reliability, and observer reliability.

■ **Interscorer reliability**
The degree of agreement or consistency between two or more scorers, judges, or raters

The simplest way to determine the degree of consistency between two scorers in the scoring of a test or some other performance measure is to have each scorer independently evaluate the test or performance measure and then compute a correlation coefficient between the scores provided by the different scorers. For example, assume that you had each student in a class read a passage and had two scorers score the reading ability of each of these students. The scores provided by each scorer on the students' reading ability are then correlated, and the correlation between these scorers represents the interscorer reliability.

Frequently, the agreement between two or more scorers is not very good unless some degree of training and practice precedes the scoring. Fortunately, with training, the degree of agreement can improve. The important issue is that training is often required and that a measure of the reliability of an evaluation of performance by scorers is necessary.

REVIEW

QUESTIONS

5.6 What are the different ways of assessing reliability?

5.7 Under what conditions should each of the different ways of assessing reliability be used?

Validity

When we select a test or some other assessment procedure for use in a research study, we naturally want to select the one that will give us the information we want. If we want to measure a child's IQ, we obviously want some assessment that will provide us with a score that we can use to make a judgment about that particular child's intellectual level. This is the issue of **validity,** which is defined as the appropriateness of the interpretations, inferences, and actions that we make based on test scores (AERA, APA, & NCME, 1999; Messick, 1989).[4] Validity is not a property of an assessment instrument that applies in all cases, and it is therefore inappropriate to state that a given test is always valid or always invalid, because this implies that validity is only a property of the test. What is important in validity is that we make sure that our test is measuring what we intend it to measure for the particular people in a particular context and that the interpretations we make on the basis of the test scores are correct.

■ **Validity**
The accuracy of the inferences, interpretations, or actions made on the basis of test scores

To make an assessment, we must get one or more scores from each individual or case. The assessment procedure can be a psychological or educational test, a behavioral observation, a performance rating, data such as the number of school dropouts, or any of many other assessment procedures. Each of these procedures produces one or more scores, and we make inferences from these scores. For example, the number of school dropouts occurring in an academic year might be used to make inferences about the quality of education delivered or the extent to which the families of the students value education. If the assessment procedure were a measure of intelligence, the score obtained from this test would be used to infer the person's intellectual level. On the basis of this interpretation of a person's intellectual level, we might also take some specific action such as placing the child in a special program for gifted children.

When we make inferences or when we take some action on the basis of scores, we want our inferences to be accurate, and we want our actions to be appropriate. Whether the inferences and the actions are appropriate and accurate is an empirical question. To validate the inferences that we make requires collecting validity evidence. **Validity evidence** specifically refers to the empirical evidence and theoretical rationales that support the interpretations and actions that we take on the basis of the score or scores we get from an assessment procedure. For example, if we give a student an intelligence test and that student gets a score of 130, we would infer from that score that the student is bright and can master almost any academic skill attempted. To validate this inference, we would have to collect evidence indicating that a person obtaining a score of 130 on this test is a very bright person who can master subjects ranging from chemistry to philosophy.

■ **Validity evidence**
Empirical evidence and theoretical rationales that support the inferences or interpretations made from test scores

■ **Validation**
The process of gathering evidence that supports inferences made on the basis of test scores

Validation, therefore, is the inquiry process of gathering validity evidence that supports our score interpretations or inferences. It involves looking at our interpretations or inferences for their soundness and relevance. Cronbach (1991) puts it like this: "A test may be excellent in other respects, but if it is wrongly interpreted it is worthless in that time and place" (p. 150). There are many different types of validity evidence that can be collected, and in general, the best rule is to collect multiple sources of evidence. As we discuss how to collect validity evidence, remember that our discussion applies to any kind of measurement or assessment procedure and not just tests. Our discussion applies to the measurement of virtually anything that a researcher plans on empirically studying.

In recent years, our thinking about validity issues has moved from a discussion of types of validity (i.e., content validity, criterion validity, and construct validity) to a focus on obtaining evidence for a unitary validity.[5] The latest thinking is clearly outlined in the following quote from the authoritative *Standards for Educational and Psychological Testing* (1999):[6,7]

> These sources of evidence [content, criterion, and construct] may illuminate different aspects of validity, but they do not represent distinct types of validity. Validity is a unitary concept. It is the degree to which all the accumulated evidence supports the intended interpretation of test scores for the proposed purpose. (p. 11)

Validity evidence can come from many different sources such as those summarized in Table 5.6. Keep in mind that complete validation is never fully attained. Validation is very similar to theory development (you state your expectations or hypotheses, you collect data,

TABLE 5.6   Summary of Methods for Obtaining Validity Evidence

Type of Evidence	Procedures
Evidence based on content	Study the construct to measure, examine the test content, and make a decision whether the test content adequately represents the construct. This is usually done by experts.
Evidence based on internal structure	First, determine how many dimensions or constructs the test measures using the technique called *factor analysis.*
	Second, examine the *homogeneity* of the items (for the whole test and for each of the subscales if the test measures more than one dimension). You can do this by calculating the *item-to-total correlation* (for a test measuring only one dimension) and by calculating *coefficient alpha* for the test and for each subscale for a test measuring more than one dimension.
Evidence based on relations to other variables	Relate the test scores to a known criterion by collecting *concurrent* and/or *predictive* evidence.
	Correlate the test scores with measures of the same construct and measures of different constructs to obtain *convergent* and *discriminant* evidence.
	Determine whether groups differ on the test in the way that would be expected (e.g., for a liberalism scale, determine whether Republican Party members differ from Democratic Party members).

you examine the results, and you refine the theory; then you go through this cycle again and again over time). Validation therefore should be viewed as a never-ending process (Messick, 1995). At the same time, the more validity evidence you have, the more confidence you can place in your interpretations. So let's see how educational researchers obtain evidence of the validity.

REVIEW

QUESTIONS

5.8 What are the definitions of validity and validation?

5.9 What is meant by the unified view of validity?

■ **Content-related evidence**
Validity evidence based on a judgment of the degree to which the items, tasks, or questions on a test adequately represent the construct domain of interest

Evidence Based on Content When you use **content-related evidence,** you make a judgment of the degree to which the evidence suggests that the items, tasks, or questions on your test adequately represent the domain of interest (e.g., educational achievement, teacher morale, shyness, or any other area of interest to an educational researcher). This representation is based on item content, but it is also based on the formatting, wording, administration, and scoring of the test.

Basically, content validation follows three steps: First, you must understand the construct that the test is supposed to measure (i.e., make sure that you understand how the construct is defined and understand the content domain the items should represent); second, you need to examine the content on the specific test; third, you make a decision as to whether the content on the test adequately represents the content domain. If the answer is yes to step 3, you have some evidence that you are measuring the construct you hope to be measuring. When making your decision, try to answer these three questions:

1. Do the items appear to represent the thing you are trying to measure?
2. Does the set of items underrepresent the construct's content (i.e., have you excluded any important content areas or topics)?
3. Do any of the items represent something other than what you are trying to measure (i.e., have you included any irrelevant items)?

As you can see, the process of content validation is basically a rational or deductive approach for judging the test content. You define the content you want to represent, and then you determine whether the items represent the content adequately.

To illustrate the process of content validation, let's assume that you are investigating the efficacy of a new instructional method for helping students acquire knowledge of educational statistics. To conduct this study, you obviously need some measures of statistical knowledge. Statistical knowledge is typically measured by administering a statistics achievement test and using the test scores to infer students' mastery of statistics. If the test questions, items, and tasks are formatted appropriately, are administered appropriately, and adequately represent the domain of information covered during the statistics instructional period, then you will have good content-related evidence of validity. If the instruction covered the theory, rationale, and computational procedure of Pearson product moment correlation, *t*-tests, and analysis of variance, then the items, questions, and tasks on the statistics test should also cover this material. The proportion of material covered in the statistics test should match the proportion of material covered during the instructional period. If 20 percent of the instruction time was spent covering correlation, 30 percent of the time was spent on *t*-tests, and 50 percent of the time was spent on analysis of variance, then obviously, 20 percent of the test questions and tasks should be devoted to correlation, 30 percent to *t*-tests, and 50 percent to analysis of variance. If you came in to take the test and all of the items were on analysis of variance, the test would not be very valid because it would underrepresent the content domain. Likewise, if the test had items from the areas listed plus the additional area of regression analysis, then the test would not be very valid because it would include measurement of an irrelevant content area (one that had not been covered and was not supposed to be on the test). In both cases, you would be displeased. You would also be displeased if the items were poorly written.

Content validation is usually carried out by experts. Individuals who are experts in the area covered by the test review the test to determine whether it adequately represents the construct. In accomplishing this task, the experts will generally review the content domain, such as the material covered during the instruction in statistics and the general procedure used in developing the test. This might include a review of the course syllabus, the text, the objectives, and the notes used by the instructor. From this review, experts make a judgment about how well the items, questions, and tasks included on the test sample the content. In the case of the new method of instruction in statistics, the experts would review the syllabi, text, objectives, and notes used by the instructor and then look at the test questions, formatting, administration, and tasks. They would make a judgment as to whether the test should work for the students and whether it adequately represents the material covered during the course instruction. Then the experts would make a judgment of the degree to which the content-related evidence supports the validity of the test.

Evidence Based on Internal Structure   Some tests are designed to measure a general construct, but other tests are designed to measure several components or dimensions of a construct. The Rosenberg Self-Esteem Scale is a 10-item scale designed to measure the construct of global self-esteem. (A copy of this test is shown in Figure 6.1 in Chapter 6.) All ten items on this test are intended to measure the same thing. You could check the internal structure of this self-esteem scale in several ways. Your goal in obtaining internal structure evidence for this self-esteem scale would be to make sure that the items do measure a single underlying construct (i.e., make sure it is unidimensional). In contrast, the Harter Self-Perception Profile for Children provides a measure of global self-esteem, but it also provides measures of five dimensions of self-esteem (i.e., scholastic competence, social acceptance, athletic competence, physical appearance, and behavioral conduct). So in the case of the Harter scale, when examining the internal structure, you would make sure that the different sets of items did indeed measure the separate dimensions.

A very useful technique for examining the internal structure of tests is called factor analysis. **Factor analysis** is a statistical procedure that analyzes the relationships among items to determine whether a test is *unidimensional* (i.e., all of the items measure a single

■ **Factor analysis**
A statistical procedure that analyzes correlations among test items and tells you the number of factors present. It tells you whether the test is unidimensional or multidimensional

construct) or *multidimensional* (i.e., different sets of items tap different constructs or different components of a broader construct). You would run a factor analysis using a statistical software program (such as SPSS), you would look at the results, and then you could see if your test items appear to measure one dimension or more than one dimension.

An example will make this idea clear. Let's say that you did a factor analysis on the ten items that make up the Rosenberg Self-Esteem Scale. Past research has shown that the Rosenberg Self-Esteem Scale is unidimensional, so your factor analysis should confirm that the items are indeed measuring a single dimension or "factor." Now let's add 10 new items to the original 10, and let these new items come from a test that measures "introversion." When you run a factor analysis on these 20 items, what do you think you will get? The results should show that your 20 items measure *two* dimensions (a self-esteem dimension and an introversion dimension).

As another example, assume that you just did a factor analysis on the Harter scale we mentioned above. How many dimensions should this factor analysis show are present? We bet you said five (i.e., scholastic competence, social acceptance, athletic competence, physical appearance, and behavioral conduct). That's really all you need to know about factor analysis here. The technical details of factor analysis are beyond the scope of this text, but the basic idea is simply that a factor analysis tells you how many dimensions or factors your test items represent.

When examining the internal structure of a test, you can also obtain a measure of test **homogeneity** (i.e., the degree to which the different items measure the same construct or trait). One index of homogeneity is obtained by correlating the scores on each test item with the scores on the total test (i.e., the item-to-total correlation). For example, if you want to obtain evidence of the homogeneity of a test of student morale, you could give the test to a group of students and then correlate the scores on each test item with the total test scores. If all the items were correlated with the total test scores, you would have evidence that the test was internally consistent and that it measured the construct of student morale. If a particular item correlated poorly with the total test score, it should be eliminated or revised because the low correlation indicates that it did not measure the same thing as the total test.

A second index of homogeneity has already been discussed: coefficient alpha. You can tell your computer to calculate coefficient alpha for the test (or for each of the dimensions of the test if it is multidimensional as the Harter test was). If the alpha is low (e.g., <.70) for the test, then some items might be measuring different constructs or some items might be bad. When coefficient alpha is low, you should examine the items that are contributing to your low coefficient alpha and consider eliminating or revising them.[8]

Evidence Based on Relations to Other Variables   Another form of validity evidence is obtained by relating your test scores to a relevant criterion. The first form of evidence focuses on the usefulness of a test in predicting how people taking the test will perform on some criterion of interest. A **criterion** is the standard or benchmark that you want to predict accurately on the basis of the scores from your test. That is, useful validity evidence comes when the researcher has evidence of the extent to which the scores from a test can be used to infer or predict the examinees' performance on some other criterion activity or variable. This general form of evidence is called **criterion-related evidence** because you attempt to gain valid-

■ **Homogeneity**
In test validity, refers to how well the different items in a test measure the same construct or trait

■ **Criterion**
The standard or benchmark that you want to predict accurately on the basis of the test scores

■ **Criterion-related evidence**
Validity evidence based on the extent to which scores from a test can be used to predict or infer performance on some criterion such as a test or future performance

ity evidence by examining the relationship that exists between your focal test and the scores from a well-established criterion variable. For example, perhaps you have designed a test to give to middle school students to predict whether they will drop out of high school. You have selected a good criterion when your audience accepts it as important and when you have examined it for its relevance, completeness, and freedom from bias. After identifying a good criterion, you measure your participants on your focal test and on the criterion measure, you correlate the two sets of scores, and then you see whether you get a high correlation.

When you calculate correlation coefficients for the study of validity, you should call them **validity coefficients.** For example, if you are developing a test to predict student performance in advanced high school mathematics, you want a positive and high correlation (i.e., validity coefficient) between students' scores on the test and their mathematics performance scores. Specifically, the students who get low scores on the aptitude test should get low scores in the advanced high school mathematics class, and the students who get high scores on the aptitude test should get high scores in the advanced math class.

Criterion-related evidence is divided into concurrent evidence and predictive evidence. You obtain **concurrent evidence** by administering the focal test and the criterion test at approximately the same point in time (i.e., concurrently) and then correlating the two sets of scores. If the two sets of scores are highly correlated, you have concurrent evidence. Concurrent validity studies are popular because they can be completed relatively quickly. In concurrent studies, you select a criterion that you can obtain right away. For example, perhaps you develop a new, shorter version of the SAT. You hypothesize that your test will, like the SAT, predict college grade point average. Rather than waiting four years, however, you might administer your new test to high school students and see whether it is correlated with their high school grade point average. Although you ultimately want to predict college GPA, you use high school GPA as a substitute or proxy variable because it is easy to obtain right now.

You obtain **predictive evidence** of validity by measuring your participants at one point in time on your test and then, at a future time, measuring them on the criterion measure. This obviously takes more time and effort than concurrent evidence, but it can provide superior evidence that your test does what you want it to do. Let's say that you are still validating the high school test for predicting college GPA. You would give the test to high school seniors and then wait four years to obtain their college GPA. Then you would correlate their scores on the test with their college GPA. If the correlation is high, you have good evidence that the test does what it is supposed to do: It accurately predicts students' performance in college. The only difference between concurrent and predictive evidence is that with concurrent validation, the focal test and the criterion measure are given at about the same time, but with predictive validation, a time period must intervene between the focal test measurement and the criterion test measurement. In both of these, you have a very practical goal: You want to determine the usefulness of the test in predicting performance on a criterion variable.

Validity evidence based on relations to other variables can also be obtained by collecting what is called convergent and discriminant evidence. The ideas of convergent and discriminant evidence come from a landmark work by Campbell and Fiske (1959). These kinds of evidence are used to demonstrate what your test measures and what it does not measure. **Convergent evidence** is based on the relationship between the focal test scores and other independent measures of the same construct. You get the participants to take both tests, and

■ **Validity coefficient**
A correlation coefficient that is computed to provide validity evidence, such as the correlation between test scores and criterion scores

■ **Concurrent evidence**
Validity evidence based on the relationship between test scores and criterion scores obtained at the same time

■ **Predictive evidence**
Validity evidence based on the relationship between test scores collected at one point in time and criterion scores obtained at a later time

Research
Navigator.c⊕m

predictive validity

■ **Convergent evidence**
Validity evidence based on the relationship between the focal test scores and independent measures of the same construct

you correlate the two sets of scores. If the two measures are based on different modes of data collection (e.g., one is a paper-and-pencil test, and the other is based on observation or performance), that is fine because independent measures of the same thing should provide measures that are highly correlated. For example, you might collect evidence in support of the Rosenberg Self-Esteem Scale (which is based on a self-report measure) by showing that another self-esteem test based on peer ratings and one based on teacher observations are highly correlated with the Rosenberg Scale. This kind of evidence would be important because it would show that your test is related to other measures of the same construct (as you would expect) and that your focal test measurement (in this case, the Rosenberg Scale based on a self-report questionnaire) is not just an artifact of the method of measurement you have used (e.g., if you get similar results using different measurement methods such as peer ratings and observations).

■ **Discriminant evidence**
Evidence that the scores on your focal test are *not* highly related to the scores from other tests that are designed to measure theoretically different constructs

Discriminant evidence exists when test scores on your focal test are *not* highly related to scores from other tests that are designed to measure theoretically different constructs. This is important because it is also important to demonstrate what your test does *not* measure. In the words of Lee Cronbach (1991), "This principle of divergence of indicators keeps a science from becoming overloaded with many names for the same thing" (p. 182). For example, let's think about the Rosenberg Self-Esteem Scale again. First, the correlation between self-esteem and authoritarianism should be small or zero because these two constructs are not expected (for theoretical reasons) to be related. If you get a small or zero correlation, you will have some discriminant evidence that the Rosenberg scale measures something different from the construct of authoritarianism. Second, this discriminant correlation should be much smaller than the convergent validity correlations (i.e., the correlations between measures of the same construct). For example, you would expect the Rosenberg Self-Esteem Scale test to correlate more strongly with other measures of self-esteem than with measures of different constructs such as authoritarianism, attitude toward contraception, and need for recognition. Basically, the goal is to show that your scale is correlated with what it should be correlated (convergent evidence) and that it is not correlated with different or theoretically unrelated constructs.

■ **Known groups evidence**
Evidence that groups that are known to differ on the construct do differ on the test in the hypothesized direction

The last type of validity evidence we will discuss is called **known groups evidence.** The idea here is to relate scores from the test you are studying with a grouping variable on which you would expect the members to differ. You would examine groups that are known to differ on your focal construct and see whether they differ in the hypothesized direction on the test you are using. For example, if you are developing a test measuring depression, you could administer your test to a group of participants who have been diagnosed with clinical depression and a group of participants who have not been diagnosed with clinical depression. The depressed participants should score higher on your depression test than the "normal" participants. For another example, you would expect members of the Democratic Party to score higher on a liberalism scale than members of the Republican Party.

Using Reliability and Validity Information

There is another important issue that must be considered. To legitimately use reliability and validity information, the participants on which this information was collected must be similar to the participants on which you are conducting your study. For example, if you are conducting a study investigating the academic achievement of fifth- and sixth-grade students with IQs below the normal range, the reliability and validity information provided with the academic achievement test that you select for this study must be based on norms from fifth- and sixth-grade students of below-normal intelligence. If the reliability and validity coefficients provided were derived from fifth- and sixth-grade students with normal or higher IQs, these coefficients would give little information about the reliability and validity of the scores of fifth- and sixth-grade students with below-normal intelligence. Therefore, before you make use of any assessment procedure, you must look at the characteristics of the **norming group,** which is the group of people on which the reliability and validity coefficients are computed. These coefficients are typically reported in the test manual that comes with the standardized test. If the characteristics of the participants in your study match the characteristics of the participants in the reliability and validity studies, you can use these coefficients to assess the quality of the assessment procedure. If they do not, you have no direct information by which to assess the quality of the assessment procedure. You can still get scores from using the assessment procedures. However, you will not know what they mean, so you essentially will be collecting data that you cannot interpret.

■ **Norming group**
The specific group for which the test publisher or researcher provides evidence for test validity and reliability

It is important to understand that it is *not* wise to rely solely on previously reported reliability and validity information, especially when the characteristics of your participants do not closely match the characteristics of the norming group. When feasible, you should attempt to collect additional empirical reliability and/or validity evidence demonstrating how well your selected test operates with your research participants or students. For example, reliability information, such as coefficient alpha and test-retest reliability, are often reported in high-quality journals (such as the *Journal of Educational Psychology*). Validity information, such as convergent and discriminant evidence, is often reported when researchers need to justify the use of their measures. The point is that when reading an empirical research report, you should be sure to look for any direct evidence that the researchers provide about reliability and validity and then upgrade your evaluation of the measurement component of the research to the degree that the authors provide evidence of reliability and validity. You will find this information in either the Method section or the Results section of an article.

Research
Navigator.c**om

construct validation

5.10 What are the characteristics of the different ways of obtaining validity evidence?

R E V I E W

Q U E S T I O N

EDUCATIONAL AND PSYCHOLOGICAL TESTS

Whenever an educational researcher conducts a study, measurements must be taken on a number of variables. For example, if you are conducting an experimental study investigating the effect of exposure to a Head Start program on later academic achievement of disadvantaged children, you have to have some way of identifying children who are disadvantaged and some measure of academic achievement. One way of doing this is to administer a test that is designed to measure the extent to which a child is disadvantaged and a test that is designed to measure a child's level of academic achievement. Fortunately, educational and psychological tests have been developed to measure most situations, characteristics, and types of performance, and educational researchers make extensive use of these tests in their research projects. Although there are too many tests to mention in this textbook, we identify the primary areas in which tests have been developed, and we mention some of the more popular tests in each of these areas.

Intelligence Tests

Intelligence tests have probably received the most attention and are the ones people are most familiar with because most of us have completed one at some time in our life. Intelligence, however, is an interesting construct because of the difficulty in coming up with an agreed-on definition. For example, what does intelligence mean to you? If you have difficulty answering this question, you are not alone. Sternberg, Conway, Ketron, and Bernstein (1981) asked 476 people, including students, commuters, and supermarket shoppers, to identify behaviors they considered intelligent and unintelligent. Behaviors that were most often associated with intelligence included "reasons logically and well," "reads widely," "displays common sense," "keeps an open mind," and "reads with high comprehension." Unintelligent behaviors most frequently included "does not tolerate diversity of views," "does not display curiosity," and "behaves with insufficient consideration of others." Do these examples fit your conception of intelligent and unintelligent behaviors? If they do not, don't be alarmed, because even the experts cannot agree on a definition.

■ **Intelligence**
The ability to think abstractly and to learn readily from experience

One general definition is that **intelligence** is the ability to think abstractly and to learn readily from experience (Flynn, 1987). However, this is a general definition and not one that is universally accepted. Neisser (1979) has even concluded that intelligence, because of its nature, cannot be explicitly defined because for certain constructs, a single prototype does not exist. This is certainly true of intelligence. However, just because a universally accepted definition of intelligence does not exist does not mean that the concept does not exist, that it lacks utility, or that it cannot be measured. Indeed, it is a multifaceted construct, and many tests have been developed to measure intelligence. A summary of some of the tests of intelligence that have been developed and used in educational research as well as other settings is provided on the book's companion website.

Personality Tests

■ **Personality**
The relatively permanent patterns that characterize and can be used to classify individuals

Personality is a construct that, like intelligence, has been defined in many different ways. A generally agreed-on definition is Mischel's (1999) statement that **personality** refers to "the distinctive patterns (including thoughts as well as feelings, emotions, and actions) that characterize each individual enduringly." Feist (1990) defines personality as "a global concept referring to all those relatively permanent traits, dispositions, or characteristics within the individual, which give some degree of consistency to that person's behavior." It is clear that personality is a multifaceted construct; as a result, many tests have been developed to measure different facets of personality (such as emotional, motivational, interpersonal, and attitudinal characteristics of individuals).

Many personality tests are of the **self-report** variety (sometimes called *self-report inventories*), in which the test taker is asked to respond, either on a pencil-and-paper form or on a computer, to a series of questions about his or her motives and feelings. These self-reports provide a window into the test taker's behavioral tendencies, feelings, and motives, which are in turn summarized with a specific label. Some of these labels are clinical labels, such as neuroticism; others are trait labels, such as dominance or sociability. Still other labels refer to attitudes, interests, or the values a person holds. The numerous summary labels that are used to portray and measure a person's "personality" and the numerous self-report inventories that have been developed to measure these further reflect the fact that personality is a multifaceted construct.

■ **Self-report**
A test-taking method in which the participants check or rate the degree to which various characteristics are descriptive of themselves

Although self-report measures of personality can be a valuable source of information, they are always subject to contamination. In some instances, to attain his or her goals, a person might be motivated to "fake good"; in other instances, he or she might be motivated to "fake bad." For example, assume that you want your child to attend an elite private school that will not take children with negative attitudes on the assumption that they might be prone to violent behavior. If you are asked to report on your child's behavioral tendencies and attitudes, you might not tell the truth ("fake good") to enhance the probability of your child's being admitted into the school. Additionally, different individuals have different response styles that can influence the impression communicated by the responses to the personality test. For example, some people have a tendency to answer "yes" or "true" rather than "no" or "false" to short-answer items. Others may not have the insight into their own behavior or thinking to answer a question in a way that will accurately communicate information about them. These limitations of self-report inventories always have to be considered when using them to collect information.

In addition to self-reports, personality dimensions are sometimes measured using **performance measures.** The idea here is that the researcher provides the examinee with a task to perform, and then the researcher makes an inference about the examinee's personality characteristics on the basis of his or her task performance. These kinds of testing situations are often designed to simulate everyday-life or work situations. It is usually important to keep the precise nature or purpose of the performance testing disguised to help minimize faking or other types of reactive behaviors. An advantage of performance measures is that the researcher can directly observe the test taker's behavior rather than relying only on self-report measures.

■ **Performance measures**
A test-taking method in which the participants perform some real-life behavior that is observed by the researcher

The last technique for tapping into personality is the use of **projective measures.** The major feature of projective measures or techniques is that the test taker has to make a response to a relatively unstructured task using test stimuli that are usually vague or ambiguous. For example, the test taker might be asked to tell what he or she sees in a blot of ink on a piece of paper or to make up a story from a card that shows an ambiguous picture of several people who are in a specific environment, such as what appears to be a surgical room. The underlying assumption is that the way in which the test taker structures and interprets the ambiguous test stimuli will reflect fundamental aspects of his or her personality or psychological functioning

■ **Projective measures**
A test-taking method in which the participants provide responses to ambiguous stimuli

and in this way reveal his or her needs, anxieties, and conflicts. However, many projective techniques are inadequately standardized with respect to administration and scoring, which means that reliability and validity information might be hard to obtain.

Educational Assessment Tests

One of the things many people associate with education is testing because it seems to be an inherent part of the educational process. The type of testing that many people think of is some type of performance or knowledge testing, because one of the most common ways of identifying whether a person has mastered a set of material is to measure whether he or she can answer questions about the material or measure his or her performance on activities that are indicative of mastery. However, many other types of tests are administered in public and private schools: intelligence tests, personality tests, tests of physical and sensory abilities, diagnostic tests, learning styles tests, and so forth. In this section, we look at the general categories of educational assessment tests and mention some of the tests that fall into each of these categories.

Preschool Assessment Tests

Many of the tests that are used with preschool children are referred to as *screening tests* rather than intelligence tests or academic achievement tests primarily because the predictive validity of many of the preschool tests is weak. During the preschool years, many factors other than children's cognitive capacity influence their later development and ability. A child's health, the characteristics of the family environment, and temperament differences all influence the child's development. Therefore, testing at a young age typically fails to yield sufficient information about later performance in the classroom. When tests are used as screening tests, they are used to identify children who are "at risk" and in need of further evaluation. The term *at risk,* however, is not clearly defined. For example, it could refer to a child who is in danger of not being ready for the first grade, or it might describe a level of functioning that is not within normal limits. It might even refer to a child who has difficulties that might not have been identified were it not for routine screening. Preschool assessment tests do have a place. However, they must be used with caution and not be overinterpreted.

Preschool tests include tests such as the Early Screening Profile (Lasee & Smith, 1991) and the Miller Assessment for Preschoolers (Schouten & Kirkpatrick, 1993). The Early Screening Profile focuses on developmental functioning of children from age two to just under age seven and includes cognitive/language, motor, and self-help/social subtests. The Miller Assessment for Preschoolers focuses on the detection of developmental problems of children age two years nine months to five years eight months by making use of verbal, coordination, and nonverbal foundations subtests. These are just two of many tests that assess the various behaviors and cognitive skills of young children.

■ **Achievement tests**
Tests that are designed to measure the degree of learning that has taken place after a person has been exposed to a specific learning experience

Achievement Tests

Achievement tests are designed to measure the degree of learning that has taken place after a person has been exposed to a specific learning experience. This learning experience can be virtually anything. In the context of education, the learning experience that is most frequently encountered is classroom learning experience. After a teacher has covered a certain amount of material in a course such as American history, he or she wants to measure how much of this material the students have learned. The typical way of doing this is to give a test covering the material. This test is an achievement test because it is designed to measure the degree to which the students have learned the material covered. Teacher-constructed tests such as the history test just mentioned are legitimate achievement tests, but they are not the only variety. Other achievement tests are the more standardized tests, such as the Metropolitan Achievement Test, which have been produced by a test publisher (e.g., Psychological Corporation) and contain normative data (data indicating how certain groups of individuals, such as sixth-grade white females, perform on the test). These tests might be given at the end of a school year so that the performance of the students who took the achievement test can be compared to the normative group. The comparison with the normative group is often used to measure accomplishment or achievement in various academic areas, such as biology, English, mathematics, and reading comprehension. These standardized achievement tests can be used for a variety of purposes ranging from gauging the quality of instruction of a teacher, a school district, or even a state to screening for academic difficulties to identify areas in which remediation is needed.

The primary difference between teacher-constructed achievement tests and standardized achievement tests is their psychometric soundness. For rather obvious reasons, reliability and validity studies are seldom if ever done on teacher-constructed tests. Teachers do not have the luxury of having the time to collect validity and reliability data. They must cover a given segment of material and then construct a test that seems to sample the content area and represent a reasonable measure of achievement. Reliability and validity data can be collected on standardized achievement tests because these tests can go through a typical developmental process that permits the collection of such data.

Achievement tests can vary from measuring general achievement to measuring achievement in a specific subject area. Measures of general achievement cover a number of academic areas and are typically referred to as *achievement batteries* because they consist of a number of subtests. Each subtest typically focuses on a different academic area or skill. Measures of achievement in specific subject areas are tests that are designed to gauge achievement in specific areas such as reading, arithmetic, and science. We provide a list of both general and specific standardized achievement tests on the book's companion website.

Aptitude Tests

Aptitude Tests **Aptitude tests** focus on information acquired through the informal learning that goes on in life as opposed to the formal learning that exists in the educational system. Each individual's particular mental and physical abilities allow him or her to acquire different amounts of information through everyday life experiences as well as through formal learning experiences such as course work in school. Aptitude tests attempt to tap the information people acquire under the uncontrolled and undefined conditions of life. This is in contrast to achievement tests, which attempt to measure specific information that is acquired in a formal and relatively structured environment, such as a French or computer programming class. Aptitude test performance therefore reflects the cumulative influence of all of our daily living experiences. There is an overlap and a sometimes blurry distinction between achievement and aptitude tests. If you remember that achievement tests are more limited in scope and reflect the learning that takes place in definable conditions, such as a

■ **Aptitude tests**
Tests that focus on information acquired through the informal learning that goes on in life

specific class designed to teach a specific subject matter, and aptitude tests reflect the learning that takes place in all life's uncontrolled conditions, you should be able to maintain the distinction between the two.

Another distinction that is often made between achievement and aptitude tests is that aptitude tests are typically used to make predictions, whereas achievement tests are used to measure accomplishment. This does not mean that achievement tests are never used to make predictions, because they can be and sometimes are. For example, achievement test performance in a first-semester foreign language course might be considered predictive of achievement in subsequent foreign language courses. However, future predictions are most frequently made from aptitude tests.

Aptitude tests are used to make predictions about many things, ranging from readiness for school and aptitude for college-level work to aptitude for work in a given profession such as law or medicine. For example, the Metropolitan Readiness Tests are several group-administered tests that assess the development of reading and mathematics skills in kindergarten and first grade. The Scholastic Aptitude Test is a group-administered test that is divided into verbal and mathematics sections. It is used in the college selection process and for advising high school students as to what might be their best course of action. Other aptitude tests consist of the Graduate Record Examination, used as a criterion for admission to many graduate schools; the Medical College Admission Test, which is required of students applying to medical school; and the Law School Admission Test, which is required of students applying to law school.

■ **Diagnostic tests**
Tests that are designed to identify where a student is having difficulty with an academic skill

Diagnostic Tests In the field of education, **diagnostic tests** are designed to identify where a student is having difficulty with an academic skill. For example, a diagnostic mathematics test consists of subtests measuring the different types of knowledge and skills needed in mathematics. Poor performance on one or more subtests identifies the nature of the difficulty the student is having with mathematics, and attention can be directed to these areas to ameliorate the difficulty. These tests are generally administered to students who are suspected of having difficulty with a specific subject area because of poor performance either in the classroom or on an achievement test. For example, the Woodcock Reading Mastery Test is an individually administered test that is designed to measure skills inherent in reading. Its five subtests consist of letter identification, word identification, word attack, word comprehension, and passage comprehension. The KeyMath Revised test is an individually administered test for assessing difficulties with mathematical concepts, operations, and applications.

It is important to recognize that diagnostic tests are useful only in identifying where a student is having a problem with an academic skill. They do not give any information as to why the difficulty exists. The difficulties could stem from physical, psychological, or situational difficulties or some combination of these. Educators, psychologists, and physicians must provide the answers to the question of why.

SOURCES OF INFORMATION ABOUT TESTS

We have focused on things such as the types of tests that have been constructed and the characteristics that a test or any other type of assessment measure must have to be considered a "good" test or assessment measure. Throughout the twentieth century, educators, psychologists, and sociologists have been constructing tests to measure just about any construct you might be interested in. This means that if you are planning a research study investigating a construct such as teacher morale, you do not have to worry about developing a measure of this construct because one probably exists. However, you have to know where to find such a measure. Fortunately, there are a number of reference sources that provide information about both published and unpublished tests. Many of these resources are available on-line (so you can even find tests while you sit at home at your computer). Table 5.7 lists some useful reference books for locating tests, and Table 5.8 lists some convenient Internet sites that you can use to find the test you want to use. Remember that if a test is already available to measure the construct of interest to you, then it is usually a good idea to use it rather than constructing a new test.

TABLE 5.7   Sources of Information about Tests and Test Reviews

Source	Description
Dictionary of Behavioral Assessment Techniques (Hersen & Bellack, 1988)	Presents a description, purpose, development, psychometric characteristics, clinical use, and future directions of behavioral assessment techniques.
Test Critiques (Keyser & Sweetland, 1984–1994)	A series of ten volumes which provide a description, practical application, use, psychometric characteristics, and reviewer's critique of over 700 tests.
ETS Test Collection, Princeton, NJ, 08541	A collection of published and unpublished educational tests and measurement devices. A brief annotation including the scope, target audience, and availability of each test is provided.
Handbook of Individual Differences, Learning, and Instruction (Jonassen & Grabowski, 1993)	Includes descriptions and related research on tests in seven areas: learning and instruction, mapping mental abilities, cognitive controls, information gathering, learning styles, personality and learning, and prior knowledge.
Handbook of Research Design and Social Measurement (Miller, 1991)	A source book presenting many sociological and psychological tests as well as a discussion of the steps involved in conducting a social science research study.
Tests: A Comprehensive Reference for Assessment in Psychology, Education, and Business (Maddox, 1997)	Includes descriptions (not reviews) of over 2000 assessment instruments.
Measures of Personality and Social Psychological Attitudes (Robinson, Shaver, & Wrightsman, 1991)	Reviews measures of personality and attitudes, including not only a brief description of each scale and its psychometric properties but also a brief presentation of its liabilities.

■ **TABLE 5.8**   Internet Sources Helpful in Locating Tests and Other Measurement Instruments

Source	URL	Description
Measurement Excellence Initiative	www.measurementexperts. org/index.asp	Click on the "find an instrument" link, and you will find links to over thirty testing and measurement sites.
Online Evaluation Resource Library	http://oerl.sri.com/ instruments/instruments.html	This library is funded by the National Science Foundation. It includes model instruments that users are encouraged to use or adapt to their needs.
ERIC/AE Test Locator	http://ericae.net/ testcol.htm#ETSTF	This is an excellent source based on a collaborative effort of ERIC, ETS, Buros, Region III Comprehensive Center, and Pro-Ed test publishers.
ETS Test File	http://ericae.net/ testcol.htm#ETSTF	This link takes you to the Educational Testing Service database containing descriptions of over 10,000 tests and research instruments.
Test Review Locator	http://ericae.net/ testcol.htm#trev	This link allows you to search for test review citations for measures included in the Buros and Pro-Ed directories.
Buros/ERIC Test Publisher Directory	http://ericae.net/ testcol.htm#Testpub	This link lets you search for the names and addresses of over 900 commercial test publishers.
Buros Institute of Mental Measurements	www.unl.edu/buros	This takes you directly to the Buros Institute of Mental Measurements and it has lots of useful links for you to use.
Educational Testing Service	www.ets.org/testcoll/	This takes you directly to the Educational Testing Service TestLink site. This database has 20,000 tests and related measurement devices.
Center for Equity and Excellence in Education Test Database	http://ericae.net/eac/	This link gives you access to over 200 tests that have been used with Limited English Proficient students.
The Evaluation Center	www.wmich.edu/ evalctr/ess.html	This is the link for the Evaluation Center. Click on *Web Resource Links* and then click on *Assessment, Measurement, and Instruments.* Also check this link from this site http://141.218.173.232:120/xchange/ for more testing instruments.

Probably the most important source of information about published tests is the **Mental Measurements Yearbook** (MMY) and **Tests in Print** (TIP), both of which are published by the Buros Institute of Mental Measurements at the Department of Educational Psychology of the University of Nebraska–Lincoln. If you are attempting to locate and learn about a test, you should consider consulting TIP first because it is a comprehensive volume that describes every test currently published as well as references to these tests. You can directly access MMY and TIP by going to your library or by simply going to this web site: http://ericae.net/testcol.htm#ETSTF. Although the MMY and TIP are probably the most comprehensive resources for information on published tests, additional tests and reviews can also be found in a number of other sources, such as those shown in Tables 5.7 and 5.8.

Information about tests can also be obtained from catalogs distributed by test publishers and from the published literature. Publishers' catalogs describing tests are easy to obtain by merely calling the publisher. They are limited, however, in that they typically contain only a brief description of each test without the detailed critical review that would exist in a publication such as the MMY. Remember that publishers are in the business of selling tests and a critical review will be omitted. There are also a number of specialized journals in which researchers routinely publish test validation studies. Some popular measurement journals include *Educational and Psychological Measurement, Applied Psychological Measurement, Applied Measurement in Education,* and the *Journal of Educational Measurement.* We highly recommend that you go to your library and browse through these and related journals so that you see lots of examples of how validation and other measurement research is conducted.

- **Mental Measurements Yearbook**
  One of the primary sources of information about published tests
- **Tests in Print**
  A primary source of information about published tests

5.11 What are the purposes and key characteristics of the major types of tests discussed in your textbook?

5.12 What is a good example of each of the major types of tests that are discussed in this chapter?

REVIEW
QUESTIONS

SUMMARY

Measurement refers to the act of assigning symbols or numbers to objects, events, people, and characteristics according to a specific set of rules. There are four different scales of measurement, which communicate different kinds of information. The nominal scale is a "name" scale that typically uses symbols to label, classify, or identify people or objects. The ordinal scale rank orders the people, objects, or characteristics being studied. The interval scale has the additional characteristic of equal distances between adjacent numbers. The ratio scale has the additional property of having a true zero point.

The two major characteristics of tests and assessments that must always be considered in using tests or other measures are reliability and validity. Reliability refers to the consistency or stability of the scores from a test. Reliability of a test or assessment procedure can be determined in several ways. Test-retest reliability refers to the consistency of scores over time. Equivalent forms reliability refers to the consistency of scores on two equivalent forms of a test. Internal consistency refers to the homogeneity of the items on a test, and split-half correlations and coefficient alpha provide internal consistency reliability estimates. Interscorer reliability refers to the consistency of scores provided by two or more people scoring the same performance.

Validity refers to the appropriateness of the interpretations and actions we make on the basis of the scores we get from a test or assessment procedure. Validity evidence can be collected in many ways. Validity evidence is based on the content of the test (Does the content adequately represent the construct?), the internal structure of the test (Does the test measure the number of dimensions it is purported to measure?), and the relationship between the test and other variables (Is the test related to other measures of the construct? Is it unrelated to different constructs? Can it be used to predict future performance on important criteria? Do groups that are known to differ on the construct get different scores on the test in the hypothesized direction?).

Reliability and validity evidence can be used to select the test or assessment procedure that will provide interpretable scores. Being able to use this information is necessary because education researchers have developed many tests and assessment procedures. The education researcher can consult a number of resource books and Internet sites to identify intelligence tests, personality tests, and different educational assessment tests that can be used for his or her research study. Reliability and validity evidence should always be used in making the selection of the test or assessment procedure. In addition, researchers should collect reliability and validity evidence with the people in their studies to provide further evidence that the testing instruments worked for their unique research participants.

KEY TERMS

achievement tests (p. 150)
aptitude tests (p. 151)
assessment (p. 129)
coefficient alpha (p. 138)
concurrent evidence (p. 145)
content-related evidence (p. 142)
convergent evidence (p. 145)
criterion (p. 144)
criterion-related evidence (p. 144)
diagnostic tests (p. 152)
discriminant evidence (p. 146)
equivalent-forms reliability (p. 136)
error (p. 131)
factor analysis (p. 143)
homogeneity (p. 144)
homogeneous test (p. 136)

intelligence (p. 148)
internal consistency (p. 136)
interscorer reliability (p. 139)
interval scale (p. 127)
known groups evidence (p. 146)
measurement (p. 124)
Mental Measurements
    Yearbook (p. 155)
nominal scale (p. 126)
norming group (p. 147)
ordinal scale (p. 127)
performance measures (p. 149)
personality (p. 148)
predictive evidence (p. 145)
projective measures (p. 149)
ratio scale (p. 128)

reliability (p. 133)
reliability coefficient (p. 134)
self-report (p. 149)
Spearman-Brown formula (p. 137)
split-half reliability (p. 137)
states (p. 130)
systematic error (p. 133)
testing (p. 129)
test-retest reliability (p. 135)
Tests in Print (p. 155)
traits (p. 130)
validation (p. 140)
validity (p. 140)
validity coefficient (p. 145)
validity evidence (p. 140)

DISCUSSION QUESTIONS

1. Assume that you have just finished developing a new test that you believe measures graduate education aptitude (you call it the GEA). How would you validate this instrument? (Ultimately, you hope that your university will use this new test rather than the test it currently requires of all applicants.)

2. What are some variables at each of the following levels of measurement: nominal, ordinal, interval, and ratio?

3. Your new bathroom scales provide the same weight each time you step on them. The problem is that the reported weight is wrong. What is the problem with your new scales?

4. Can a measurement procedure be reliable but not valid? Can it be valid but not reliable? Explain your answers.

5. What is your definition of measurement validity? How well does it match the definition provided in the chapter?

RESEARCH EXERCISES

1. To illustrate the type of research one would conduct in the field of testing and measurement, select one of the following articles (all of which are available in ContentSelect, the database that came with your book). As you read your article, answer the following questions:
   a. What was measured?
   b. Were there any subscales? If so, what were they?
   c. How were the scales or measures constructed and scored?
   d. How were they validated?
   e. How was reliability assessed?
   f. Did the researchers follow the principles of test validation presented in this chapter? Be sure to explain your answers.

Select one of these articles and download it from ContentSelect so you can review it:

Burney, D. M., & Kromery, J. (2001). Initial development and score validation of the Adolescent Anger Rating Scale. *Educational and Psychological Measurement, 61*(3), 446–460.

Copenhaver, M. M., & Eisler, R. M. (2000). The development and validation of the Attitude Toward Father Scale. *Behavior Modification, 24*(5), 740–750.

Kember, D., & Leung, Y. P. (2000). Development of a questionnaire to measure the level of reflective thinking. *Assessment and Evaluation in Higher Education, 25*(4), 381–395.

Shore, T. H., Tashchian, A., & Adams, J. S. (2000). Development and validation of a scale measuring attitudes toward smoking. *The Journal of Social Psychology, 140*(5), 615–623.

2. Select the quantitative or the mixed research article from an appendix in this book. Then answer the following questions:
   a. What variables did the researcher study?
   b. How was each of these variables measured?
   c. Did the researcher present any evidence of reliability? What was the evidence?
   d. Did the researcher present any evidence of validity? What was the evidence?
   e. What is your evaluation of the measures used in the article?

3. If you are planning to propose or conduct a research study, fill out the following Problem Sheet.

Research Problem Sheet

(If an item is not applicable to your study, write N/A)
1. The variables in my research study are as follows. _____
2. Listed next, for each variable, are the variable types or functions (independent variable, dependent variable, intervening variable, moderator variable, control variable). _____
3. I plan on using an already existing instrument to measure the following variables (provide the name of the instrument and sample questions or items for each of these variables). _____
4. I plan on writing the new items to measure the following variables (provide sample questions or items for each variable). _____
5. Listed next is the level of measurement (nominal, ordinal, interval, ratio) for each of my variables. _____
6. Listed next, for each variable, is the reliability and validity evidence that is currently available and/or that I plan on obtaining during the conduct of my research. _____

RELEVANT INTERNET SITES

http://www.ncme.org/
National Council on Measurement in Education.

www.hbem.com/library/glossary.htm
Glossary of measurements terms.

http://ericae.net/edo/ed315430.htm
Another glossary of measurement terms.

www.creative.net.au/mirrors/neural/measurement.html
Frequently asked questions about measurement.

http://ericae.net/seltips.txt
How to evaluate a test.

RECOMMENDED READING

American Educational Research Association, American Psychological Association, & National Council on Measurement in Education. (1999). *Standards for educational and psychological testing.* Washington, DC: AERA.

Cronbach, L. J., & Meehl, P. E. (1955). Construct validity in psychological tests. *Psychological Bulletin, 52,* 281–302.

John, O. P., & Benet-Martinez, V. (2000). Measurement: Reliability, construct validation, and scale construction. In H. T. Reis & C. M. Judd (Eds.), *Handbook of research methods in social and personality psychology* (pp. 339–369). Cambridge, England: Cambridge University.

ENDNOTES

1. Although Steven's system is commonly used in selecting statistical procedures, there are some limitations to this usage. These limitations are discussed by Velleman and Wilkinson (1993).
2. This version of coefficient alpha assumes that the items are standardized to have the same variance.
3. The number of inter-item correlations that would be calculated and then averaged to get the average inter-item

correlation (i.e., $\bar{r}$) is equal to $[p(p-1)]/2$, where p is the number of items in your test or subscale. For example, your test or subscale has ten items on it, the number of inter-item correlations is $[10(10-1)]/2 = 90/2 = 45$. Therefore, to get $\bar{r}$, you would have to take the average of the forty-five inter-item correlations.

4. According to the *Standards for Educational and Psychological Testing* (AERA, APA, & NCME, 1999), "Validity refers to the degree to which evidence and theory support the interpretations of test scores entailed by proposed uses of tests." In the words of Samuel Messick (1989), the determination of validity is "an evaluative judgment of the degree to which empirical and theoretical rationales support the adequacy and appropriateness of interpretations and actions on the basis of test scores or other modes of assessment."

5. The current view is that construct validation is the unifying concept for validity evidence. We no longer say *construct validation* because the word *construct* would be redundant. A construct is the theoretical variable that you want to represent. It's what you want to measure. The idea of a construct is used broadly and refers to abstract variables such as self-efficacy, intelligence, or self-esteem as well as very concrete variables such as age, height, weight, and gender.

6. This book was written by a committee of experts approved by the following national associations: the American Educational Research Association, the American Psychological Association, and the National Council on Measurement in Education.

7. To study the evolution of thinking about validity, you can start by examining the following sources in chronological order: American Psychological Association, 1954; Cronbach and Meehl (1955); Campbell and Fiske (1959); AERA, APA, & NCME (Standards for educational and psychological testing) (1985); Messick, 1989; and AERA, APA, & NCME (Standards for educational and psychological testing) (1999).

8. The exception to this rule is when you have what are called *formative measures* (Bollen & Lennox, 1991; Pedhazur & Schmelkin, 1991). Formative measures determine the distinct aspects of a construct (rather than reflecting the construct) and they need *not* be correlated with one another. Therefore, the use of coefficient alpha and item-to-total correlations are generally inappropriate.

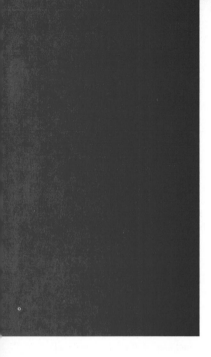

6

Methods of Data Collection

LEARNING OBJECTIVES

To be able to

- List the six methods of data collection.
- Explain the difference between method of data collection and research method.
- Define the fundamental principle of mixed research.
- Define and explain the characteristics of each of the six methods of data collection.
- Explain each of the fifteen principles of questionnaire construction.
- Know when open-ended questions and closed-ended questions are used.
- Explain the concept of standardization.
- Explain the key characteristics of the four different types of interviews.
- Describe the four roles the researcher can take in qualitative interviewing.
- Give multiple examples of response categories used for completely anchored rating scales.
- List at least five commonly used probes.
- Explain how the fundamental principle of mixed research can be applied to methods of data collection.

September 11, 2001, is a day we will all remember. Our feelings of security and invulnerability to the attacks of terrorists were shattered. Before this time, terrorists' attacks were largely something that happened to people in other countries. As President Bush has stated, the terrorists' goal is to frighten us, not just kill, maim, and destroy. Indeed, the terrorists have made progress in this regard.

Flying is a case in point. Gallup polls taken before September 11th indicated that 44 percent of the public felt fearful when flying. After September 11th, traffic fell 20 percent. This didn't necessarily mean that people were traveling less; many people drove some of those unflown miles. Driving all of these additional miles would translate into 800 more highway deaths, or three times the number of people that were killed on the four hijacked planes. Myers (2001) notes that data from the National Safety Council revealed that in the last half of the 1990s, people were 37 times more likely to die in a vehicle crash than in a crash of a commercial plane. Crashing and dying while flying on a commercial flight were less likely than getting heads every time on twenty-two flips of a coin. The terrorists' attacks on September 11th were tragic and created a tremendous amount of grief for everyone involved, especially those who lost loved ones. Yet fear, particularly of flying, will result in more rather than fewer deaths. Reports such as the National Safety Council's provide a lot of numerical information. Other reports include other types of information and data.

Collection of data is necessary to obtain information that will provide answers to important questions. In the above example, data were collected and converted to percentages to document the fact that flying is less dangerous than driving. Educational researchers also have to collect data to provide answers to their research questions. In this chapter, we will review the six most common forms of data collection used by educational researchers. With your understanding of these forms of data collection, you will be armed with knowledge of the procedures needed to collect data that will provide an answer to your own research questions.

In Chapter 5, we introduced you to the concept of measurement. We also discussed the different kinds of tests that are used for collecting data in educational research. If an already constructed test is available for the topics of interest to you, you should strongly consider using that test because reliability and validity information will usually be available. However, an already developed data-collection instrument may not be available for your particular research needs. In this case, you must construct a new test or another type of data collection instrument such as a questionnaire or an interview protocol, and this takes a lot of time and effort if you plan to do it properly.

The purpose of this chapter is to help you understand the different ways to collect research data and to show you how to construct a data-collection instrument when one is not already available. You will learn how to answer these three questions:

What data-collection method or methods will allow me to obtain the information I need to answer my research questions?

How can I construct a data-collection instrument when the need arises?

What are the strengths and weaknesses of the different methods of data collections?

The following list shows the most common methods of data collection that are used by educational researchers:

1. Tests
2. Questionnaires
3. Interviews
4. Focus groups
5. Observation
6. Secondary data

Using the methods of data collection discussed in this chapter, researchers can have their participants fill out an instrument or perform a behavior designed to measure their ability or degree of skill (tests); researchers can have research participants fill out self-report instruments (questionnaires); researchers can talk to participants in person or over the telephone (interviews); researchers can discuss issues with multiple research participants at the same time in a small-group setting (focus groups); researchers can examine how research participants act in natural and structured environments (observation); and researchers can use data that came from an earlier time for a different purpose than the current research problem at hand (secondary data).

In a typical research study, researchers begin by identifying the important research problems and research questions that they want to address. Then they select the most appropriate **research method** or methods (experimental research, qualitative research, correlational research, causal-comparative research, etc.) that will help them to decide on a research design and a research strategy that will allow them to answer their research questions. Researchers next decide how they are going to collect their empirical research data. That is, they decide what **methods of data collection** (tests, questionnaires, interviews, focus groups, observations) they are going to use to physically obtain research data from their research participants.

As you read this chapter, keep in mind the **fundamental principle of mixed research.** According to this principle, mixing methods is an excellent way to conduct high-quality research. It states that you should mix methods in a way that provides complementary strengths and nonoverlapping weaknesses. For example, you might collect standardized test data and then collect qualitative interview data to provide a fuller picture of a group of teachers' aptitude for teaching reading. As another example, a researcher might find a statistical relationship between parental social class and the likelihood of children joining the middle school band (e.g., perhaps higher social class is related to band membership). A researcher might mix into this study some focus groups with the parents and children from different social classes to explore the reasons and thinking that produce the quantitative relationship.

Mixing methods is like putting together several flawed fishing nets, each of which has a hole, a torn part, or a weak point, to construct a "new," stronger net that works well despite the problem with each individual net. We highly recommend that you print out the six tables on the book's companion website that list the strengths and weaknesses of the six major methods of data collection. You will find these tables under bonus materials for this chapter. Using these tables and the material in this chapter, you will be able to decide how to mix and match the methods in your own research study in a way that follows the fundamental principle of mixed research.

■ **Research method**
Overall research design and strategy

■ **Method of data collection**
Technique for physically obtaining data to be analyzed in a research study

■ **Fundamental principle of mixed research**
Researchers should mix methods to provide complementary strengths and nonoverlapping weaknesses

Although our focus in this chapter is on methods of data collection, the principle of mixed research also applies to the mixing of other research ingredients such as research methods (e.g., experiments, ethnographies), sampling methods, measurement methods, and analysis methods. The key point is that educational research is about providing solid evidence for your conclusions, and evidence is often greater when you employ a logical mixing strategy.

Remember that in this chapter we are concerned with how research data are collected from research participants, not with the different research methods. You will learn more about the different research methods in Chapters 9–14. Now we will explain the different methods of data collection.

6.1 What is a method of data collection?

6.2 What are the six main methods of data collection? (Hint: The first letters make the rather awkward acronym SQIFOS.)

REVIEW
QUESTIONS

TESTS

Tests are commonly used in quantitative research to measure attitudes, personality, self-perceptions, aptitude, and performance of research participants. Perhaps the most common type of test is the standardized test, which is developed by psychometricians and usually includes psychometric information on reliability, validity, and reference group norms. In fact, the previous chapter was about standardized tests, so you already know a lot about this form of tests (e.g., their characteristics, the different types, and where to find already developed tests). Furthermore, we emphasize again that if a relevant test is already available that measures the variables of interest to you, then you should seriously consider using that test.

Although many tests are available for use (e.g., standardized tests of intelligence and personality, achievement, preschool, aptitude, and diagnostic tests), experimental researchers often need to generate their own tests to measure very specific constructs that are operationalized in quite unique ways. An experimental researcher might design a test procedure to measure a cognitive or memory process or to measure participants' response time to a mental activity. For example, a researcher studying particular types of mathematics story problems might develop a test that deals specifically with those particular problem types. The point is that when a researcher is looking at the manipulation of instructional content or context, tests usually need to be tailored to the content or task. Note that even though such "experimenter constructed" tests are not normed for specific populations, the researcher is obliged to do his or her best to find ways to affirm the reliability and validity of the assessments.

Because you have already read a full chapter on tests, we will not elaborate any more on tests in this chapter. Do keep in mind, however, that as with all methods of data collection, you may want to *mix* tests with other methods when you conduct a research study. For an example of mixing, you might take a look at a study by Mantzicopoulos and Knutson (2000). These researchers used school records, parent interviews, teacher questionnaires, and standardized tests of achievement to determine the relationship of school and family mobility to children's academic achievement.

QUESTIONNAIRES

■ **Questionnaire**
A self-report data-collection instrument filled out by research participants

Research Navigator.c⦿m

questionnaire construction

A **questionnaire** is a self-report data-collection instrument that each research participant fills out as part of a research study. Researchers use questionnaires so that they can obtain information about the thoughts, feelings, attitudes, beliefs, values, perceptions, personality, and behavioral intentions of research participants. In other words, researchers attempt to measure many different kinds of characteristics using questionnaires.

We view the term *questionnaire* broadly, meaning that questionnaires are not restricted to a single research method. Questionnaires can be used to collect data with multiple research methods (experimental, qualitative, correlational, etc.). Furthermore, the content and organization of a questionnaire will correspond to the researcher's research objectives. The key point is that the questionnaire is a versatile tool available to you and other educational researchers.

Questionnaires typically include multiple questions and statements. For example, a researcher might ask a question about the present (Do you support the use of corporal punishment in elementary schools?), the past (Have you ever used corporal punishment with one of your students?), or the future (Do you think that you will use corporal punishment sometime in the future?). See Table 6.1 for more examples. Questionnaires can also include statements that participants consider and respond to. For example, when filling out the Rosenberg Self-Esteem Scale in Figure 6.1, research participants must indicate their degree of agreement or disagreement with ten statements measuring their attitudes toward themselves.

■ **T A B L E   6 . 1**   Type of Question Matrix, with Examples

Question Focus	Time Dimension		
	Past (Retrospective)	Present (Current)	Future (Prospective)
Behavior	When you were a teenager, did you use any illicit drug?	Do you currently watch educational television?	Do you plan on moving to a new residence within the next calendar year?
Experiences	What was it like taking a class from your favorite teacher?	What is it like being interviewed about your childhood?	What do you think shopping for a new car will be like ten years from now?
Attitudes, opinions, beliefs, and values	When you were a child, did you like school or church more?	Do you support school vouchers?	Do you think you will change political parties in the future?
Knowledge	Did you know the definition of tabula rasa when you first started college?	What is the definition of tabula rasa?	Do you think you will learn the definition of tabula rasa sometime in the future?
Background and demographic	How old were you when you entered the first grade?	How old are you?	What state do you plan on living in when you retire?

■ **FIGURE 6.1** The Rosenberg Self-Esteem Scale

Circle one response for each of the following ten items.

	Strongly Agree	*Agree*	*Disagree*	*Strongly Disagree*
1. I feel that I am a person of worth, at least on an equal basis with others.	1	2	3	4
2. I feel that I have a number of good qualities.	1	2	3	4
*3. All in all, I am inclined to feel that I am a failure.	1	2	3	4
4. I am able to do things as well as most other people.	1	2	3	4
*5. I feel I do not have much to be proud of.	1	2	3	4
6. I take a positive attitude toward myself.	1	2	3	4
7. On the whole, I am satisfied with myself.	1	2	3	4
*8. I wish I could have more respect for myself.	1	2	3	4
*9. I certainly feel useless at times.	1	2	3	4
*10. At times I think I am no good at all.	1	2	3	4

*Items marked with an asterisk have reversed wording. The numbers on items with reversed wording should be reversed before summing the responses for the ten items. For example, on item 3, "strongly agree" becomes 4, "agree" becomes 3, "disagree" becomes 2, and "strongly disagree" becomes 1.

Source: Morris Rosenberg's "Self-Esteem Scale" from pp. 325–327 of *Society and Adolescent Self-Image* © 1989 by Morris Rosenberg, Wesleyan University Press.

How to Construct a Questionnaire

The most important principles of questionnaire construction are shown in Table 6.2. Take a moment to examine this list of fourteen principles so that you will have an overview of what is important to consider when constructing a questionnaire. We explain each of these principles in more detail.

Principle 1. Make sure the questionnaire items match your research objectives. This cardinal principle should be obvious. You must always determine why you intend to conduct your research study before you can write a questionnaire. If you plan on conducting an

■ **TABLE 6.2**   Principles of Questionnaire Construction

Principle 1	Make sure the questionnaire items match your research objectives.
Principle 2	Understand your research participants.
Principle 3	Use natural and familiar language.
Principle 4	Write items that are clear, precise, and relatively short.
Principle 5	Do not use "leading" or "loaded" questions.
Principle 6	Avoid double-barreled questions.
Principle 7	Avoid double negatives.
Principle 8	Determine whether an open-ended or a closed-ended question is needed.
Principle 9	Use mutually exclusive and exhaustive response categories for closed-ended questions.
Principle 10	Consider the different types of response categories available for closed-ended questionnaire items.
Principle 11	Use multiple items to measure abstract constructs.
Principle 12	Consider using multiple methods when measuring abstract constructs.
Principle 13	Use caution if you reverse the wording in some of the items to prevent response sets in multi-item scales.
Principle 14	Develop a questionnaire that is easy for the participant to use.
Principle 15	Always pilot test your questionnaire.

exploratory research study (i.e., you want to collect some preliminary information about a research problem), your questionnaire will usually not need to be as detailed as when you plan on conducting a confirmatory research study (i.e., when you intend on collecting data that will enable you to test research hypotheses). In both cases, you should carefully review the existing research literature as well as any related instruments that have already been used for your research objectives before deciding to construct your own questionnaire.

Principle 2. Understand your research participants. A key to effective questionnaire construction is understanding your research participants. Remember that they, not you, are the ones who will be filling out the questionnaire. A useful strategy when writing a questionnaire is to try to develop an empathetic understanding, or an ability to "think like" your potential research participants. If you can effectively consider how your research participants will interpret and react to each item on your questionnaire, then it is very likely to provide useful information.

Principle 3. Use natural and familiar language. You should use language that is understandable to the types of people that are going to fill out your questionnaire. Try to avoid the use of jargon or technical terms. Consider the age of your participants, their educational level, and any relevant cultural characteristics of your participants when deciding on the kind of language you need to use. Remember that it is very possible that not everyone uses the same everyday language as you. If you are reading this book, you are probably a college graduate and you are also working on a graduate degree. Using natural and familiar language makes it easier for participants to fill out a questionnaire and helps participants to feel more relaxed and less threatened by the task of filling it out.

Principle 4. Write items that are clear, precise, and relatively short. Each item on your questionnaire should be understandable to you (the researcher) and to the participant (the person filling out the questionnaire). Because each item is measuring something, it is important for it to be clear and precise. The GIGO principle is relevant here: "garbage in, garbage out." If the participants are not clear about what is being asked of them, their responses will result in data that cannot or should not be used in a research study. Your goal is for each research participant to interpret the meaning of each item in the questionnaire in exactly the same way. You should also avoid technical terms; if you must use a technical term, remember to define it for the participants. Finally, try to keep most items relatively short because long items can be confusing and stressful for research participants.

Principle 5. Do not use "leading" or "loaded" questions. A leading or loaded question biases the response the participant gives to the question. A **loaded question** is one that contains emotionally charged words (words that create a positive or negative reaction). For example, the emotionally charged word *liberal* was often avoided by politicians during the 1980s, even by liberals, because the word created a negative reaction in some people regardless of the content of the statement. Some other examples of loaded words are *politician, communist, welfare, drug czar, soccer mom, pro-life, pro-choice, gay, drug abuser,* and *juvenile.* A **leading question** is one that is phrased in such a way that it suggests a certain answer. Here is an example of a leading question:

■ **Loaded question**
A question containing emotionally charged words

■ **Leading question**
A question that suggests a certain answer

Don't you agree that teachers should earn more money than they currently earn?

☐ Yes, they should earn more.
☐ No, they should not earn more.
☐ Don't know/no opinion.

The phrase "Don't you agree" leads the participant here. A more neutral wording of this question would be as follows:

Do you believe teacher salaries are a little lower than they should be, a little higher than they should be, or about right?

☐ Teacher salaries are a little lower than they should be.
☐ Teacher salaries are a little higher than they should be.
☐ Teacher salaries are about right.
☐ Don't know/no opinion.

Always remember that your goal is to write questionnaire items that help participants feel free to provide their natural and honest answers. You want to obtain responses that are undistorted by the particular question wording.

■ **Double-barreled question**
A question that combines two or more issues or attitude objects

Principle 6. Avoid double-barreled questions. A **double-barreled question** combines two or more issues or attitude objects in a single item. Here is an example: Do you think that teachers should have more contact with parents and school administrators? As you can see, this single question asks about two different issues. The question is really asking, Do you think that teachers should have more contact with parents? *and* Do you think that teachers should have more contact with school administrators? Each of these two issues may elicit a different attitude, and combining them into one question makes it unclear which attitude or opinion is being measured. Therefore, it is a good rule to avoid double-barreled questions. As a general rule, if the word *and* appears in a question or statement, you should check to see whether it is double-barreled.

Principle 7. Avoid double negatives. When participants are asked for their agreement with a statement, double negatives can easily occur. For example,

Do you agree or disagree with the following statement?
      Teachers should not be required to supervise their students during library time.

■ **Double negative**
A sentence construction that includes two negatives

If you disagree with the statement, you must construct a **double negative** (a sentence construction that includes two negatives). If you disagree, you are saying that you do *not* think that teachers should *not* supervise students during library time (Converse & Presser, 1986). In other words, you probably believe that teachers should supervise students during library time.
      Here is another example of a double negative:

Teachers should not be able to do the following things:

Spank children

☐ Yes
☐ No

Expel children from school

☐ Yes
☐ No

If you use a negative item, you should consider underlining the negative word or words to catch the participant's attention.

■ **Open-ended question**
A question that allows participants to respond in their own words
■ **Closed-ended question**
A question that forces participants to choose a response

Principle 8. Determine whether an open-ended or a closed-ended question is needed. An **open-ended question** enables participants to respond in any way that they please. Open-ended questions provide primarily qualitative data. In contrast, a **closed-ended question** requires participants to choose from a limited number of responses predetermined by the researcher. Closed-ended questions provide primarily quantitative data.
      To determine someone's marital status, you could use the question, What is your current marital status? and leave sufficient space for participants to write in their answers. In this case, the question is called an open-ended question because the participants must pro-

vide answers in their own words. On the other hand, you could use a closed-ended question to determine someone's marital status. Here is an example of a closed-ended question:

What is your marital status? (Check one box.)

☐ Single
☐ Married
☐ Divorced
☐ Separated
☐ Widowed

You will notice that the **item stem** (the words forming the question or statement) is the same in our open-ended and closed-ended question examples (both ask, What is your marital status?). The key difference between an open-ended question and a closed-ended question is in the way the participants are allowed to respond. In open-ended questions, participants must come up with their own answers; in closed-ended questions, participants must select from the predetermined categories provided by the researcher.

Open-ended questions are usually used in exploratory research (i.e., when the researcher knows little about the topic), and closed-ended questions are usually used in confirmatory research (i.e., when the researcher plans to test specific hypotheses). Open-ended questions are valuable when the researcher needs to know what people are thinking and when the dimensions of a variable are not well defined. Because the participants respond by writing their answers in their own words, open-ended questions can provide rich information. For example, the following open-ended question would provide some interesting information: What do you think teachers can do to keep students from using illicit drugs? It can be difficult, however, to analyze the data obtained from open-ended questions. Closed-ended questions should be used when the dimensions of a variable are already known. Closed-ended questions expose all participants to the same response categories and allow more quantitative statistical analysis.

Principle 9. Use mutually exclusive and exhaustive response categories for closed-ended questions. Categories are **mutually exclusive** when they do not overlap. For example, the following categories for a question about the participant's age are *not* mutually exclusive:

10 or less
10 to 20
20 to 30
30 to 40
40 to 50
50 to 60
60 to 70
70 to 80
80 or greater

Do you see the problem with these response categories? The problem is that they overlap. For example, a person who is 20 years old could be placed into two categories. In fact, persons aged 10, 20, 30, 40, 50, 60, 70, and 80 can all be placed into more than one category. In

■ **Item stem**
The set of words forming a question or statement

■ **Mutually exclusive**
Response categories that don't overlap

short, the response categories are not mutually exclusive. In a moment, we will show you how to fix this problem.

■ **Exhaustive**
Response categories that include all possible responses

A set of response categories is **exhaustive** when there is a category available for all legitimate responses. For example, what is the problem with the following categories from a question asking you for your current age?

    1 to 4
    5 to 9
    10 to 14

The problem is that these three categories are not exhaustive because there is no category available for anyone over the age of fourteen or anyone less than one year old. A set of categories is not exhaustive unless there is a category available for all potential responses.

Putting the ideas of mutually exclusive and exhaustive categories together, you can see that the following set of response categories is mutually exclusive and exhaustive:

Which of the following categories includes your current age? (Check one box.)
☐ Less than 18
☐ 18 to 29
☐ 30 to 39
☐ 40 to 49
☐ 50 to 59
☐ 60 to 69
☐ 70 to 79
☐ 80 or older

The principle of mutually exclusive categories applies because none of the categories overlap. The principle of exhaustive categories applies because there is a category available for all possible ages. Whenever you write a standard closed-ended question (a question with an item stem and a set of predetermined response categories), remember to make sure that your response categories are mutually exclusive and exhaustive.

Principle 10. Consider the different types of response categories available for closed-ended questionnaire items. In this section we introduce several popular types of closed-ended response categories by explaining the ideas of rating scales, rankings, semantic differentials, and checklists.

Rating Scales Researchers often obtain data from research participants by providing them with questions or statements (the item stem) and rating scales (the response choices) with instructions to make judgments about each item stem using the rating scale that is provided.

■ **Rating scale**
A continuum of response choices

A **rating scale** is a continuum of response choices that participants are told to use in indicating their responses. Rating scales produce numerical (quantitative) data rather than qualitative data (nominal-level data). Rating scales have been used by researchers for quite a long time. In an early review of the history of rating scales, Guilford (1936) provides examples from as early as 1805 and many other examples shortly after 1900. Some important early developers of rating scales are Sir Francis Galton (1822–1911), Karl Pearson (1857–1936), and, somewhat later, Rensis Likert (1903–1981).

A **numerical rating scale** consists of a set of numbers and "anchored" endpoints. When you **anchor** a point on a rating scale, you label the point with a written descriptor. Here is an example of an item stem and a numerical rating scale with anchored endpoints:

- **Numerical rating scale**
  A rating scale with anchored endpoints
- **Anchor**
  A written descriptor for a point on a rating scale

How would you rate the overall job performance of your school principal?

1	2	3	4	5	6	7
Very Low						Very High

As you can see, the first endpoint ("1") is anchored with the words "Very Low." The other endpoint ("7") is anchored with the words "Very High." This is a seven-point rating scale because there is a total of seven points on the scale.

A similar type of rating scale is called a fully anchored rating scale. A **fully anchored rating scale** has all points anchored with descriptors. Here is an example of an item stem followed by a fully anchored rating scale:

- **Fully anchored rating scale**
  All points are anchored on the rating scale

My principal is an effective leader.

1	2	3	4	5
Strongly Agree	Agree	Neutral	Disagree	Strongly Disagree

This scale is a five-point rating scale because there are five points on the scale. Some researchers prefer to exclude the numbers and provide just the descriptors in a fully anchored rating scale. This scale is sometimes called an "agreement" rating scale because the participants report on their agreement or disagreement with the statement provided by the researcher in the item stem.

You might be wondering how many points a rating scale should have. Research suggests that you should use somewhere from four points to eleven points on a rating scale (e.g., McKelvie, 1978; Nunally, 1978). Rating scales with fewer than four points are not as reliable as rating scales with more points. On the other hand, rating scales with more than eleven points can be confusing because most participants have limited abilities to make fine discriminations when there are a great number of scale points. Exhibit 6.1 includes four-point and five-point rating scales because these are very popular with educational researchers and have been shown to work quite well.

You might also wonder whether you should include a center or middle category in your rating scale. Research suggests that omitting the middle alternative ("neutral," "about the same," "average," "no difference," etc.) does not appreciably affect the overall pattern of results (Converse & Presser, 1986, pp. 36–37; Schuman & Presser, 1981, Chap. 6). As a result, some researchers choose to include a middle alternative, and others choose not to include it. You can see in Figure 6.1 that Rosenberg used four-point rating scales (i.e., he omitted the middle alternative) in his Self-Esteem Scale. Some researchers, such as Rosenberg, prefer to omit the middle alternative because it forces research participants to lean one way or the other.

■ E X H I B I T 6 . 1   **Examples of Response Categories for Rating Scales**

Agreement

(1) Strongly Agree   (2) Agree   (3) Disagree   (4) Strongly Disagree

(1) Strongly Agree   (2) Agree   (3) Neutral   (4) Disagree   (5) Strongly Disagree

Amount

(1) Too Much   (2) About the Right Amount   (3) Too Little

(1) Too Many   (2) About the Right Amount   (3) Not Enough

Approval

(1) Strongly Approve   (2) Approve   (3) Disapprove   (4) Strongly Disapprove

(1) Strongly Approve   (2) Approve   (3) Neutral   (4) Disapprove   (5) Strongly Disapprove

Belief

(1) Definitely True   (2) Probably True   (3) Probably False   (4) Definitely False

Comparison

(1) Much Better   (2) Better   (3) About the Same   (4) Worse   (5) Much Worse

(1) Much More   (2) Somewhat More   (3) About the Same   (4) Somewhat Less   (5) Much Less

Effectiveness

(1) Very Effective   (2) Somewhat Effective   (3) Not Very Effective   (4) Not at All Effective

Evaluation

(1) Excellent   (2) Good   (3) Fair   (4) Poor

(1) Very Good   (2) Good   (3) Fair   (4) Poor   (5) Very Poor

(1) Very Good   (2) Somewhat Good   (3) Somewhat Bad   (4) Very Bad

Frequency

(1) Always   (2) Frequently   (3) Sometimes   (4) Never

(1) Regularly   (2) Fairly Often   (3) Seldom   (4) Never

(1) Very Often   (2) Fairly Often   (3) Sometimes   (4) Hardly Ever   (5) Never

Importance

(1) Very Important   (2) Fairly Important   (3) Not Very Important   (4) Not at All Important

Knowledge

(1) Very Familiar   (2) Somewhat Familiar   (3) Not Very Familiar   (4) Not at All Familiar

Probability

(1) A Lot More Likely   (2) Somewhat More Likely   (3) No Difference   (4) Somewhat Less Likely
(5) A Lot Less Likely

Satisfaction

(1) Very Satisfied   (2) Satisfied   (3) Not Very Satisfied   (4) Not at All Satisfied

Take a moment now to examine Exhibit 6.1, and you will see some other rating scales that researchers and practitioners commonly use. Note that the ordering of the categories does not appear to affect response patterns (Barnette, 1999; Weng & Cheng, 2000). For example, both of these patterns are workable: (1) strongly agree, agree, disagree, strongly disagree and (2) strongly disagree, disagree, agree, strongly agree. As you can see in looking at Exhibit 6.1, you can ask participants for many different kinds of ratings. For example, you might ask participants about agreement, approval, importance, satisfaction, or frequency.

Rankings Sometimes you might want your research participants to rank order their responses. A **ranking** indicates the importance or priority assigned by a participant to an attitudinal object. Rankings can be used with open-ended and closed-ended questions. For example, you might first ask an open-ended question such as, In your opinion, who are the three top teachers in your school? Then you could follow up this question with a ranking item such as, Please rank order the teachers you just mentioned. Rankings can also be used with closed-ended items. For example, you might use the following closed-ended item:

■ **Ranking**
The ordering of responses in ascending or descending order

> Please rank the importance of the following qualities in a school principal. (Fill in your rank order in the spaces provided using the numbers 1 through 5.)
> _____ A principal that is sincere.
> _____ A principal that gets resources for the school.
> _____ A principal that is an advocate for teacher needs.
> _____ A principal that is a strong disciplinarian.
> _____ A principal that is a good motivator.

As you can see, this is a closed-ended item because predetermined response categories are provided. As a general rule, you should not ask participants to rank more than three to five responses or response categories because ranking can be a difficult task for participants.

Semantic Differential The **semantic differential** is a scaling technique that is used to measure the meaning that participants give to various attitudinal objects or concepts (Osgood, Suci, & Tannenbaum, 1957). The participants are asked to rate each object or concept provided in the item stem on a series of seven-point, bipolar rating scales. The scales are "bipolar" because they have contrasting adjectives anchoring the endpoints. The contrasting adjectives are often antonyms. Some attitudinal objects you may wish to have your research participants rate are principal, teacher, student, disabled, and gifted. You can see an example of a semantic differential in Exhibit 6.2.

■ **Semantic differential**
A scaling technique in which participants rate a series of objects or concepts

Semantic differentials are useful when you want to "profile" or describe the multiple characteristics associated with attitudinal objects. In Exhibit 6.2, you are asked to rate your school principal on twenty different bipolar rating scales. If you used this semantic differential with all the teachers in a school, you could average all the responses and profile the teachers' view of the principal. You might find that different groups produce different profiles. For example, males and females may view the principal differently. If you need to develop a semantic differential, it is helpful to look at a book of antonyms for contrasting word pairs. You can also find some useful lists of commonly used semantic differential word pairs in Isaac and Michael (1995) and in Jenkins, Russell, and Suci (1958).

■ **EXHIBIT 6.2   Example of Semantic Differential Scaling Technique**

Please rate your school principal on each of the following descriptive scales. Place a checkmark on the space between each pair of words that best indicates how you feel.

Your School Principal

Sociable	____	____	____	____	____	____	____	Unsociable
Kind	____	____	____	____	____	____	____	Cruel
Successful	____	____	____	____	____	____	____	Unsuccessful
Wise	____	____	____	____	____	____	____	Foolish
Severe	____	____	____	____	____	____	____	Lenient
Masculine	____	____	____	____	____	____	____	Feminine
Active	____	____	____	____	____	____	____	Passive
Excitable	____	____	____	____	____	____	____	Calm
Fast	____	____	____	____	____	____	____	Slow
Predictable	____	____	____	____	____	____	____	Unpredictable
Clear	____	____	____	____	____	____	____	Confusing
Authoritarian	____	____	____	____	____	____	____	Democratic
Flexible	____	____	____	____	____	____	____	Rigid
Happy	____	____	____	____	____	____	____	Sad
Work	____	____	____	____	____	____	____	Fun

■ **Checklist**
A list of response categories that respondents check if appropriate

Checklists   Researchers sometimes provide a list of response categories (a **checklist**) and ask the research participants to check the responses that apply to them. Multiple responses may be allowed. Here is an example of a checklist:

Where do you get your information about the most recent advances in teaching? (Please check all categories that apply to you.)

____ Other teachers

____ Professors

____ Principal

____ Parents

____ Superintendent

____ Academic journals

____ Professional journals

____ Magazines

____ Television

____ Other. Please list: _____

Principle 11. Use multiple items to measure abstract constructs. The use of multiple items to measure a construct is done to increase the reliability and validity of the measure. One common procedure for the measurement of abstract constructs is called a summated rating scale. A **summated rating scale** (also called a **Likert scale**) is different from the numerical rating scales and the fully anchored rating scales that we discussed earlier. Rather than being composed of a single item stem and one rating scale, a summated rating scale is composed of multiple items that are designed to measure the same idea or the same construct. The ratings on the multiple items are then summed for each research participant, providing a single score for each person.

The summated rating scale was developed by Rensis Likert (pronounced LICK-ert), who published the results of his dissertation in an article in 1932 (Likert, 1932). Since this time, summated rating scales have been extensively used by researchers. The key advantages of multiple-item rating scales compared to single-item rating scales are that multiple-item scales provide more reliable (i.e., more consistent or stable) scores and that they produce more variability, which helps the researcher to make finer distinctions among the respondents. If you want to measure a complex construct (such as self-esteem, self-efficacy, locus of control, or temperament), the use of a multiple-item scale is pretty much a necessity.

The Rosenberg Self-Esteem Scale shown in Figure 6.1 is a good example of a summated rating scale. It consists of ten items designed to measure self-esteem. The lowest possible total score on the full scale for a person is ten, and the highest possible total score for a person is forty. Most participants will score somewhere in between these two extremes (i.e., between the minimum and the maximum scores).

Principle 12. Consider using multiple methods for measuring abstract constructs. This principle follows from the longstanding maxim in social research that our measurements are partially an artifact of our method of measurement. In fact, if you use one method of measurement for all of your variables, it is possible that your variables are correlated simply because you used the same measurement procedure (Cronbach & Meehl, 1955). The relationship between variables that you thought you were interpreting could be nothing but a measurement problem or artifact! To avoid this problem, it is recommend that researchers use multiple methods of measurement. The major methods of measurement (or data collection) are questionnaires, interviews, focus groups, observations, tests, and secondary data. Furthermore, within each of these types are myriad additional possibilities. For example, an interview can be done face to face, over the Internet, or on the telephone. Within each of these, you might use a summated rating scale as well as open-ended items.

The use of multiple measurement methods is so important today that more and more researchers are using "measurement models" based on two or even three measurement methods or procedures. The resulting data are often analyzed by using advanced statistical software such as LISREL or EQS. The point is that the more methods a researcher uses to measure the relevant concepts or constructs, the more confidence you can place in the researcher's ability to tap into the essential characteristics of the concept being measured.

Principle 13. Use extreme caution if you reverse the wording in some of the items to help prevent response sets in multi-item scales. When participants rate multiple items using the same or similar rating scale, an "acquiescence response set" may occur. A **response set** is the tendency for a research participant to respond to a series of items in a specific direction regardless of their content. One type of response set is called the **acquiescence response set,** which is the tendency to say yes rather than no or to agree rather than to disagree

■ **Summated rating scale**
A multi-item scale that has the responses for each person summed into a single score

■ **Likert scale**
A summated rating scale

■ **Response set**
The tendency to respond in a specific direction regardless of content

■ **Acquiescence response set**
The tendency to either agree or to disagree

■ **Social desirability response set**
The tendency to provide answers that are socially desirable

on a whole series of items. Another response set, called the **social desirability response set,** is the tendency to provide answers that are socially desirable. One technique used to help prevent response sets (especially the acquiescence response set) is to reverse the wording in some of the items. This technique is intended to encourage participants to read each item on the questionnaire more carefully. An example of reversed wording is shown in Figure 6.1. You can see that items 3, 5, 8, 9, and 10 of the Rosenberg Self-Esteem Scale are "reversed" (i.e., agreement indicates *low* self-esteem). Although reversing the wording in selected items is still practiced and done with good intentions, there is evidence that this practice can reduce the reliability and validity of multi-item scales (Barnette, 2000; Bensen & Hocevar, 1985; Deemer & Minke, 1999; Weems & Onwuegbuzie, 2001; Wright & Masters, 1982). Therefore, we recommend caution and careful consideration of the tradeoffs involved in using this technique.

Principle 14. Develop a questionnaire that is easy for the participant to use. The ordering, or sequencing, of questionnaire items is one consideration. For example, Roberson and Sundstrom (1990) found that placing the important questions first and demographic questions (age, gender, etc.) last in an employee attitude survey resulted in the highest return rate. It is usually a good idea to begin a questionnaire with positive or nonthreatening items to obtain some commitment from the participant to fill out the questionnaire. Demographic questions should generally go last in a section, with a lead-in such as "To finish this questionnaire, we have a few questions about you." The questionnaire should also not be overly long for the types of people in your target population. Otherwise, they might not fill out the questionnaire properly, or they might refuse to complete the entire questionnaire.

■ **Contingency question**
An item that directs participants to different followup questions depending on their response

It is also a good idea to limit the number of contingency questions used in a questionnaire because participants might become confused or agitated. A **contingency question** (also called a filter question) is an item that directs participants to different followup questions depending on their response. It allows the researcher to "filter out" participants from questions that these participants cannot or should not attempt to answer. Here is an example of an item operating as a contingency question:

Question 1: What is your gender?
    Male   → (IF MALE, GO TO QUESTION 5)
    Female → (IF FEMALE, GO TO QUESTION 2)

■ **Web surveys**
Participants read and complete a survey form that is developed for and located on the web

The use of contingency questions might not be a problem for **web surveys** (i.e., those in which participants go to a website to complete a questionnaire), because in web surveys, the skip patterns associated with contingency questions can be programmed to take place automatically.

You should also include clear instructions throughout your questionnaire, and do not put too many items on a page. If a questionnaire has several different topical sections, you need to provide transitional or "lead-in" statements to orient the participants to each new topic. Other tips are to give your questionnaire a title (e.g., "School Culture Questionnaire"), provide an open-ended question at the end of your questionnaire to give the participant a place to add any comments or additional insights (e.g., "Is there anything else that you would like to add?"), provide clear instructions (e.g., "please check one of the following categories"), and thank the participant for filling out your questionnaire (you can just put a "Thank You for Completing this Questionnaire" at the bottom of the last page). Finally, always try to make your questionnaire look professional because participants are then more likely to fill it out. Remember that the appearance and quality of your questionnaire also reflect on you and your organization.

Principle 15. Always pilot test your questionnaire. It is a cardinal rule in research that you must "try out," or **pilot test,** your questionnaire to find out whether it operates properly. You should conduct your pilot test with a minimum of five to ten people. You may want to start with colleagues or friends, asking them to fill out the questionnaire. Then you will need to pilot test the questionnaire with several individuals similar to those who will be in your research study.

■ **Pilot test**
A preliminary test of your questionnaire

One useful technique to use during your pilot test is called the **think-aloud technique** which requires participants to verbalize their thoughts and perceptions while they engage in an activity. When this technique is used as part of a pilot test, you ask the participants to verbalize their thoughts and perceptions about the questionnaire while they are filling it out. You must record or carefully write down exactly what they say. It is also helpful to make audiotape or videotape recordings of the pilot test sessions for later review. The think-aloud technique is especially helpful for determining whether participants are interpreting the items the way you intended.

■ **Think-aloud technique**
Has participants verbalize their thoughts and perceptions while engaged in an activity

You will want to use the think-aloud technique with some of the participants in your pilot test, but you should have some others in the pilot test fill out the questionnaire under circumstances that are as similar as possible to those of the actual research study. When you conduct a pilot test, you need to think about several issues. For example, be sure to check how long it takes participants to complete the questionnaire under circumstances similar to those of the actual research study. This will help you know whether the questionnaire is too long. You will always be able to think of some additional items that you would like to add, so writing overlong questionnaires is something you must be careful to avoid.

Using the think-aloud technique, you can listen to how the participants think about the instructions and the items in your questionnaire. Try to determine whether any of the questionnaire items are confusing or threatening. Ask your participants to tell you when they reach an item that is difficult to understand, and then ask them to paraphrase what they believe the problem item is intended to measure. Determine whether your participants understand the items in a consistent way. Be sure to also check the veracity of the responses of your participants (i.e., whether their answers are true and accurate). These strategies will help you to determine whether the items actually measure what they are intended to measure. When the participants are filling out the questionnaire, check to see whether they skip to the correct place if you have filter questions in your questionnaire.

After the participants finish filling out the questionnaire, you can discuss the questionnaire with them individually or in group sessions. Explain the purpose of your questionnaire to them, and ask them whether they believe anything important was left out, whether the instructions were clear, whether there were any items that stood out for any reason, and probe for an explanation. If the questionnaire has an experimental manipulation embedded in it, be sure to check to see that the manipulation is working as intended. For example, if a statement or a vignette is supposed to increase empathy toward minority groups, ask your participants whether they understood it and whether they felt empathetic afterwards. After completing your pilot test, revise your questionnaire and then pilot test it again. Remember that you do not want to use a questionnaire in a research study until all of the kinks have been worked out.

We have included two questionnaires under Bonus Materials on the book's companion website that demonstrates some of the principles of questionnaire construction just discussed. For additional information on questionnaire construction, we recommend the free thirty-page booklet entitled *SPSS Survey Tips*. You can download it at this address: www.spss.com/uk/SurveyTipsnew.pdf.

REVIEW

QUESTIONS

6.3 What principles should you follow when constructing a questionnaire?

6.4 Think of an example of a leading or loaded question.

6.5 What is an item stem?

6.6 If you are conducting an exploratory research study, are you more likely to use closed-ended questions or open-ended questions?

6.7 How many points should a rating scale have?

6.8 When should you use a contingency question?

6.9 Explain how to pilot test a questionnaire or an interview protocol.

INTERVIEWS

- **Interview**
  A data-collection method in which interviewer asks interviewee questions
- **Interviewer**
  The person asking the questions
- **Interviewee**
  The person being asked questions
- **In-person interview**
  An interview conducted face-to-face
- **Telephone interview**
  An interview conducted over the phone
- **Probes**
  Prompts to obtain response clarity or additional information

You learned in the last section that you can collect data from research participants by having them fill out a questionnaire. Another way to collect data is to interview research participants. An **interview** is a data-collection method in which an **interviewer** (the researcher or someone working for the researcher) asks questions of an **interviewee** (the research participant). That is, the interviewer collects the data from the interviewee, who provides the data. Interviews that are done face-to-face are called **in-person interviews,** interviews conducted over the telephone are called **telephone interviews.** A strength of interviews is that a researcher can freely use **probes** (prompts used to obtain response clarity or additional information). Some commonly used probes are given in Table 6.3.

An interview is an interpersonal encounter. It is important that you (the interviewer) establish rapport with the person you are interviewing (the interviewee). The interview should be friendly. At the same time, you must be impartial to whatever the interviewee says to you. If you react positively or negatively to the content of the interviewee's statements, you may bias the responses. It is also important that the interviewee trusts you because without trust you are likely to obtain biased research data.

Some techniques for establishing trust and rapport are to explain who the sponsoring organization is, to explain why you are conducting the research, and to point out to the participant that his or her responses are either anonymous (no name or identification will be attached to the respondent's data) or confidential (the respondent's name or identification will be attached to the respondent's data, but the researcher will never divulge the respondent's name to anyone). You want each potential participant to understand that your research is important and that his or her participation is important for the integrity of your study. We have included in Table 6.4 a list of tips that you should find helpful if you ever need to conduct an interview.

TABLE 6.3　Commonly Used Probes and Abbreviations

Standard Interviewer's Probe	Abbreviation Used on Interview Protocol
Repeat question.	(RQ)
Anything else?	(AE or Else?)
Any other reason?	(AO?)
Any others?	(Other?)
How do you mean?	(How mean?)
Could you tell me more about your thinking on that?	(Tell more)
Would you tell me what you have in mind?	(What in mind?)
What do you mean?	(What mean?)
Why do you feel that way?	(Why?)
Which would be closer to the way you feel?	(Which closer?)

Source: From University of Michigan Survey Research Center, (1976). *Interviewer's manual* (rev. ed.). Ann Arbor, MI: University of Michigan Survey Research Center.

TABLE 6.4　Tips for Conducting an Effective Interview

1. Make sure all interviewers are well trained.
2. Do background homework on the interviewees so that you will know a little about the people you will be interviewing.
3. Establish rapport and trust with your interviewee.
4. Be empathetic *and* remain neutral toward the content of what the interviewee says.
5. Use gentle nonverbal head nods and verbal "Um-hms" to show your interest in what the interviewee says.
6. Be reflexive (i.e., monitor yourself).
7. Make sure the interviewee is doing most of the talking, not you.
8. Be sensitive to gender, age, and cultural differences between you and the interviewee.
9. Make sure the interviewee understands exactly what you are asking.
10. Provide sufficient time for the interviewee to answer each question.
11. Maintain control of the interview and keep the interview focused.
12. Utilize probes and follow-up questions to gain clarity and depth of responses.
13. Maintain a respect for the interviewee's valuable time.
14. Typically, you should tape record the interview session.
15. After an interview is completed, check your notes and recordings for quality and completeness.

In Table 6.5, you can see four types of interviews (Patton, 1987, 1990). They are called the closed quantitative interview, the standardized open-ended interview, the interview guide approach, and the informal conversational interview. These four types can be further subdivided into quantitative interviews (which include the closed quantitative interview) and qualitative interviews (which include the standardized open-ended interview, the interview guide approach to interviewing, and the informal conversational interview). We first discuss quantitative interviews.

Quantitative Interviews

■ **Interview protocol**
Data-collection instrument used in an interview

When carrying out quantitative interviews, you must carefully read the words as they are provided in the interview protocol. The **interview protocol** is the data-collection instrument that includes the items, the response categories, the instructions, and so forth. The interview protocol in a quantitative interview is basically a script written by the researcher and read by the interviewer to the interviewees. The interviewer also records the interviewee's responses on the interview protocol. The interview protocol is usually written on paper for in-person interviews and shown on a computer screen for telephone interviews.

■ **Standardization**
Presenting the same stimulus to all participants

The goal of the quantitative interview is to standardize what is presented to the interviewees. **Standardization** has been achieved when what is said to all interviewees is the same or as similar as possible. Researchers want to expose each participant to the same stimulus so that the results will be comparable. Not surprisingly, quantitative interviews result in mostly quantitative data that are later analyzed using quantitative statistical procedures. The reason we say "mostly" is because quantitative interview protocols will often include a few open-ended items. If an open-ended question is asked in a quantitative interview, however, it is asked in exactly the same way for each participant in the study.

In Exhibit 6.3, you can see a section taken from an interview protocol. The exhibit includes five closed-ended items (items 25–30) from the 1998 Phi Delta Kappa/Gallup Education Poll. Note that DK stands for "don't know." Question 27 asks the participants to make their ratings using a four-point rating scale. The instruction provided at the end of question 27 tells the interviewer to go to item 28 *if* the respondent has one or more children in a public, parochial, or private school. *Otherwise,* the interviewer is instructed to go directly to item 30 (skipping items 28 and 29). (The participants are asked early in the interview whether they have one or more children in a public, parochial, or private school.) As you can see, this instruction operates just like a filter question.

The interview protocol used in the quantitative interview looks very similar to a questionnaire. In fact, many researchers call their interview protocol a questionnaire (e.g., Babbie, 1998; Converse and Presser, 1986; Frankfort-Nachmias and Nachmias, 1992). Although the data-collection instruments are similar in interviews and questionnaires, there is a key difference in how the instruments are used. When conducting an interview, an *interviewer* reads the questions or statements exactly as written on the interview protocol and he or she records the interviewee's answers in the spaces that are provided. When using a questionnaire, the *research participant* reads and records his or her own answers in the spaces provided on the questionnaire.

The 15 principles of questionnaire construction discussed earlier also apply to the construction of interview protocols. You might want to examine the list of principles shown in

▨ TABLE 6.5   Patton's Classification of Types of Interviews

Type of Interview	Characteristics	Strengths	Weaknesses
Informal conversational interview	Questions emerge from the immediate context and are asked in the natural course of things; there is no predetermination of question topics or wording.	Increases the salience and relevance of questions; interviews are built on and emerge from observations; the interview can be matched to individuals and circumstances.	Different information collected from different people with different questions. Less systematic and comprehensive if certain questions do not arise "naturally." Data organization and analysis can be quite difficult.
Interview guide approach	Topics and issues to be covered are specified in advance, in outline form; interviewer decides sequence and wording of questions in the course of the interview.	The outline increases the comprehensiveness of the data and makes data collection somewhat systematic for each respondent. Logical gaps in data can be anticipated and closed. Interviews remain fairly conversational and situational.	Important and salient topics may be inadvertently omitted. Interviewer flexibility in sequencing and wording questions can result in substantially different responses from different perspectives, thus reducing the comparability of responses.
Standardized open-ended interview	The exact wording and sequence of questions are determined in advance. All interviewees are asked the same basic questions in the same order. Questions are worded in a *completely* open-ended format.	Respondents answer the same questions, thus increasing comparability of responses; data are complete for each person on the topics addressed in the interview. Reduces interviewer effects and bias when several interviewers are used. Permits evaluation users to see and review the instrumentation used in the evaluation. Facilitates organization and analysis of the data.	Less flexibility in relating the interview to particular individuals and circumstances; standardized wording of questions may constrain and limit naturalness and relevance of questions and answers.
Closed quantitative interview	Questions and response categories are determined in advance. Responses are fixed; respondent chooses from among these fixed responses.	Data analysis is simple; responses can be directly compared and easily aggregated; many questions can be asked in a short time.	Respondents must fit their experiences and feelings into the researcher's categories; may be perceived as impersonal, irrelevant, and mechanistic. Can distort what respondents really mean or experience by so completely limiting their response choices.

Source: Adapted from M. Q. Patton, *How to Use Qualitative Methods in Evaluation,* pp. 116–117, copyright © 1987 by Sage Publications, Inc. Used by permission of Sage Publications, Inc.

■ **EXHIBIT 6.3**   **Example of a Section of a Telephone Interview Protocol (Questions 25–30 Are from the Phi Delta Kappa/Gallup Poll Education Poll, 1998)**

25. There is always a lot of discussion about the best way to finance the public schools. Which do you think is the best way to finance the public schools—by means of local property taxes, by state taxes, or by taxes from the federal government in Washington, D.C.?
    1. Local property taxes   4. (DK)
    2. State taxes   5. (Refused)
    3. Federal taxes   _____

26. In your opinion, is the quality of the public schools related to the amount of money spent on students in those schools, or not?
    1. Yes   3. (DK)
    2. No   4. (Refused)   _____

27. How serious a problem would you say each of the following is in the public schools in your community? Would you say *(read and rotate A-G)* (is/are) a very serious problem, fairly serious, not very serious, or not at all serious?
    1. Very serious   A. Discipline   _____
    2. Fairly serious   B. Drugs   _____
    3. Not very serious   C. Alcohol   _____
    4. Not at all serious   D. Smoking   _____
    5. (DK)   E. Fighting   _____
    6. (Refused)   F. Gangs   _____
                             G. Teenage pregnancy   _____

    (If code "1" in S4 or S5, continue; otherwise, skip to #30)
28. Thinking about your oldest child when he or she is at school, do you fear for his or her physical safety?
    1. Yes   3. (DK)
    2. No   4. (Refused)   _____

29. When your oldest child is outside at play in your own neighborhood, do you fear for his or her physical safety?
    1. Yes   3. (DK)
    2. No   4. (Refused)   _____

30. In your opinion, should children with learning problems be put in the same classrooms with other students, or should they be put in special classes of their own?
    1. Yes, same classrooms   3. (DK)
    2. No, should be put in   4. (Refused)
       special classes   _____

Used with permission of Phi Delta Kappa.

Table 6.2 again to convince yourself that the principles apply to interview protocols. When writing an interview protocol, the key point to remember is that the interviewer will read what you write and the research participant will hear what the interviewer reads. You will therefore need to make sure that your interview protocol operates properly for that purpose. You must also make sure that your interviewers are well trained in interviewing techniques and the proper use of an interview protocol.

Qualitative Interviews

Qualitative interviews consist of open-ended questions and provide qualitative data. Qualitative interviews are also called depth interviews because they can be used to obtain in-depth information about a participant's thoughts, beliefs, knowledge, reasoning, motivations, and feelings about a topic. Qualitative interviewing allows a researcher to enter into the inner world of another person and to gain an understanding of that person's perspective (Patton, 1987). The interviewer must establish trust and rapport, making it easy for the interviewee to provide information about his or her inner world.

> ■ **Qualitative interview**
> An interview providing qualitative data

The interviewer should listen carefully and be the repository of detailed information. The interviewer should also be armed with probes or prompts to use when greater clarity or depth is needed from the person being interviewed. For example, the interviewer should freely use the probes shown in Table 6.3. The interviewer can also ask followup questions that may naturally emerge during the qualitative interview. A qualitative interview will typically last anywhere from thirty minutes to more than one hour.

Not surprisingly, qualitative interviews are very popular with qualitative researchers. It is not uncommon, however, for quantitative researchers also to conduct some qualitative interviews as part of their overall research study. The three different types of qualitative interviews are shown in Table 6.5. They are the informal conversational interview, the interview guide approach, and the standardized open-ended interview. The key characteristics of these three types of qualitative interviews are also given in Table 6.5.

The **informal conversational interview** is the most spontaneous and loosely structured of the three types of qualitative interviews. The interviewer discusses the topics of interest and follows all leads that emerge during the discussion. Because there is no interview protocol in the informal conversational interview, it is a good idea to tape record the interview so that no important information will be lost. Many times this will not be possible, however, if the interview occurs at an unexpected or unscheduled time. You should always take some field notes during the interview and/or immediately after conducting the informal conversational interview.

> ■ **Informal conversational interview**
> Spontaneous, loosely structured interview

In the next approach to qualitative interviewing, the **interview guide approach,** the interviewer enters the interview session with a plan to explore specific topics and to ask specific open-ended questions of the interviewee. These topics and questions are provided on an interview protocol written by the researcher before the interview session. The interviewer, however, does not have to follow these topics and questions during the interview in any particular order. The interviewer can also change the wording of any questions listed in the interview protocol. In short, the interview session is still a relatively unstructured interaction between the interviewer and the interviewee. At the same time, because of the interview protocol, the interviewer will cover the same general topics and questions with all of

> ■ **Interview guide approach**
> Specific topics and/or open-ended questions are asked in any order

the interviewees. The interviewer must try to keep the interview on track, bringing the respondent back when he or she goes off on a topic that is not relevant to the research purpose.

Cross and Stewart (1995) used the interview guide approach in their study of what it is like to be a gifted student attending a rural high school. They were interested in studying gifted students attending rural high schools because gifted students attending urban schools had been examined in previous research. Here is Cross and Stewart's discussion of the qualitative interviewing process that they used in their research study:

> To obtain highly elaborated descriptions, the researchers asked subjects to situate their experiences in specific settings. The process attempted to get subjects to regress to the actual experience so that pure descriptions would emerge. The interviews consisted of a beginning question, which asked subjects:
>
> - When you think of your experience of being a student in your high school, what stands out in your mind?
>
> Followup questions included:
>
> - Can you think of a particular situation and describe it to me?
>
> After the subject described the situation, the researcher would follow up with prompts like:
>
> - Tell me more about that; or
> - What were you aware of at that time?
>
> When subjects exhausted their depictions, the researcher asked:
>
> - Can you think of another time when that happened?
>
> At this point, the aforementioned process would repeat. The researcher attended to the ideas conveyed by the subjects and tried not to lead the interviews in any direction. The interviews ranged in length from 40 to 90 minutes. All interviews were recorded on cassette tape and later transcribed. (p. 275)

■ **Standardized open-ended interview**
A set of open-ended questions are asked in a specific order and exactly as worded

In the third approach to qualitative interviewing, the **standardized open-ended interview,** the interviewer enters the interview session with a standardized interview protocol similar to the interview protocol used in quantitative interviewing. The key difference is that the interview protocol in the quantitative interview includes primarily closed-ended items, but the interview protocol in the standardized open-ended interview includes primarily open-ended items. The standardized open-ended interview is more structured than the interview guide approach to qualitative interviewing because the interviewer does not vary from the interview protocol in the former but can vary from the interview protocol in the latter. In the standardized open-ended interview, the questions are all written out, and the interviewer reads the questions exactly as written and in the same order to all interviewees.

REVIEW

QUESTION

6.10 What is the difference between a quantitative and a qualitative interview?

━━━ FOCUS GROUPS

A **focus group** is a type of group interview in which a moderator (working for the researcher) leads a discussion with a small group of individuals (e.g., students, teachers, teenagers) to examine, in detail, how the group members think and feel about a topic. It is called a "focus" group because the moderator keeps the individuals in the group focused on the topic being discussed. The moderator generates group discussion through the use of open-ended questions, and he or she acts as a facilitator of group process. Focus groups are used to collect qualitative data that are in the words of the group participants. The origin of focus groups is usually attributed to sociologist Robert K. Merton. He and his Columbia University students published the earliest works on focus groups (Merton, Fisk, & Kendall, 1956; Merton & Kendall, 1946).

Focus groups can be used for multiple purposes. Here are some of the many uses of focus groups identified by Stewart and Shamdasani (1998):

1. Obtaining general background information about a topic of interest.
2. Generating research hypotheses that can be submitted to further research and testing using more quantitative approaches.
3. Stimulating new ideas and creative concepts.
4. Diagnosing the potential for problems with a new program, service, or product.
5. Generating impressions of products, programs, services, institutions, or other objects of interest.
6. Learning how respondents talk about the phenomenon of interest (which may, in turn, facilitate the design of questionnaires, survey instruments, or other research tools that might be employed in more quantitative research).
7. Interpreting previously obtained quantitative results. (pp. 506–507)

A focus group is composed of six to twelve participants who are purposively selected because they can provide the kind of information of interest to the researcher. A focus group is usually homogeneous (composed of similar kinds of people) because the use of a homogeneous group promotes discussion. Homogeneous groups are less likely than heterogeneous groups to result in the formation of cliques and coalitions. The conduct of two to four focus groups as part of a single research study is quite common because it is unwise to rely too heavily on the information provided by a single focus group. Although each focus group is usually homogeneous, the set of focus groups used by the researcher may include some heterogeneity depending on the purpose of the research.

The **group moderator** (the person leading the focus group discussion) must have good interpersonal skills and he or she must know how to facilitate group discussion. He or she needs to get everyone involved in discussing the researcher's questions and not allow one or two people to dominate the discussion. If conflicts or power struggles occur, the moderator must skillfully bring the group back to the task. The moderator must know when to probe or ask for more information and know when the discussion about a particular topic has been exhausted. It is not uncommon for the moderator to have an assistant who observes the group process, provides information to the moderator when needed, and takes notes during the session. Some useful moderator roles (or metaphors) are the seeker of wisdom,

■ **Focus group**
A moderator leads a discussion with a small group of people

Research
Navigator.com

focus groups

■ **Group moderator**
The person leading the focus group discussion

the enlightened novice, the expert consultant, the challenger, the referee, the writer, the team member, the therapist, and the serial interviewer (Krueger, 1998).

The focus group moderator needs to cover all the open-ended questions included in the focus group interview protocol. The interview protocol is basically an interview guide. It typically consists of a sheet of paper with approximately ten open-ended questions typed on it. The more general questions are often placed early and the more specific questions are placed later in the interview protocol. The moderator may have anywhere from one to three hours to complete the group session. The moderator does not have to take many notes during the session because focus groups are almost always recorded (using audio- and/or videotapes) so that the data can be analyzed at a later time.

Focus groups are especially useful as a complement to other methods of data collection. They are very useful for providing in-depth information in a relatively short period of time. In addition, the results are usually easy to understand. Researchers must, however, be very careful in making generalizations from focus groups because the sample size typically is too small and because the participants are usually not randomly selected from any known population. If you need more information about focus groups, examine *The Focus Group Kit* (Morgan & Krueger, 1998).

REVIEW QUESTION

6.11 Why would a researcher want to conduct a focus group?

OBSERVATION

■ **Observation**
Watching the behavioral patterns of people

Research Navigator.c⊕m

observational research

The next method of data collection involves something that you do most of your waking hours: observe things. Researchers are also observers of things in the world. In research, **observation** is defined as the watching of behavioral patterns of people in certain situations to obtain information about the phenomenon of interest. The observer should attempt to be unobtrusive so as not to affect what is being observed. Observation is an important way of collecting information about people because people do not always do what they say they do. It is a maxim in the social and behavioral sciences that attitudes and behavior are not always congruent.

A classic study done by a social scientist named Richard LaPiere (1934) demonstrated many years ago that attitudes and behaviors are not always congruent. LaPiere traveled over 10,000 miles in the United States over a two-year period (1930–1931) with a Chinese couple. LaPiere usually had the Chinese male secure the lodging and restaurant accommodations so that he could observe behavior toward the Chinese. LaPiere reported that he and his friends were denied service only once. LaPiere later sent a questionnaire to the same establishments asking whether a Chinese person would be accepted as a guest. Fully 92 percent reported that they would *not* accept Chinese customers. This reported attitude was clearly at odds with the behavior that was observed by LaPiere.

Because of the potential incongruence between attitudes and behavior, it is helpful when researchers collect observational data in addition to self-report data (e.g., tests, questionnaires, interviews, and focus groups). An advantage of observation over self-report methods is the researcher's ability to record actual behavior rather than obtain reports of preferences or intended behavior. Observation is not without weaknesses, however, some of which are that it generally takes more time than self-report approaches, it usually costs more money than self-report approaches, it may not be possible to determine exactly why people behave as they do (i.e., to determine their inner states) through the use of observations, and people may act differently when they know they are being observed.

Observational data are collected in two different types of environments. **Laboratory observation** is carried out in settings that are set up by the researcher and inside the confines of a research lab. An example would be a researcher observing the behavior of children through a one-way window in the researcher's laboratory. A one-way window is a mirror on one side and a window through which the researcher can observe, on the other. **Naturalistic observation** is carried out in the real world. To make a naturalistic observation, you must go to wherever the behavior naturally occurs. LaPiere made naturalistic observations because he observed the behavior of hotel and restaurant proprietors in natural settings. Observing the behavior of children in their classrooms is another example of naturalistic observation. We now contrast how quantitative and qualitative researchers collect observational data.

- **Laboratory observation**
  Observation done in lab or other setting set up by the researcher

- **Naturalistic observation**
  Observation done in real-world settings

Quantitative Observation

Quantitative (or structured) **observation** involves the standardization of all observational procedures in order to obtain reliable research data. Quantitative observation frequently involves the standardization of each of the following: who is observed (what kinds of people are to be studied, such as teachers or students), what is observed (what variables are to be observed by the researcher, such as time on task or out of seat behavior), when the observations are to take place (during the morning hour, during break time), where the observations are to be carried out (in the laboratory, in the classroom, in the lunchroom, in the library, on the playground), and how the observations are to be done (this involves the extensive training of observers so that they use the same procedures and so that high inter-rater reliability can be obtained). Quantitative observation usually results in quantitative data such as counts or frequencies and percentages.

- **Quantitative observation**
  Standardized observation

Different events may be of interest in quantitative observation (Weick, 1968). First, the researcher may observe nonverbal behavior (body movements, facial expressions, posture, eye contact, etc.). Second, the researcher may observe spatial behavior (the distance between different people and the distance between people and objects). Third, the researcher may observe extralinguistic behavior (characteristics of speech such as rate, tone, and volume). Fourth, the researcher may choose to observe linguistic behavior (what people say and what they write).

Quantitative observation might also involve observational sampling techniques. One technique is called **time-interval sampling,** which involves checking for events during time intervals specified in advance of the actual data collection. An example of time-interval sampling is a researcher observing student behavior for the first ten minutes of

- **Time-interval sampling**
  Checking for events during specific time intervals

■ **Event sampling**
Observing only after specific events have occurred

every hour. Another technique is called **event sampling,** which involves making observations only after a specific event has occurred. An example of event sampling is observing the behavior of students in a classroom after the teacher sends a student to the principal's office. For more information on quantitative observation sampling, see Bakeman (2000), Dane (1990), and Suen and Ary (1989).

Researchers conducting quantitative observation usually use checklists or other types of data-collection instruments, such as a laptop computer to record the research data or a videotape recorder for later coding. The content of the data-collection instrument will depend on the research problem and objectives of interest to the researcher. Data-collection instruments in quantitative observation are usually more specific and detailed than those used in qualitative observation. Usually, data-collection instruments are closed-ended in quantitative observation and open-ended in qualitative observation because quantitative observation tends to be used for confirmatory purposes (i.e., to test hypotheses), and qualitative observation tends to be used for exploratory purposes (i.e., to generate new information).

Qualitative Observation

■ **Qualitative observation**
Observing all potentially relevant phenomena

Qualitative observation involves observing all relevant phenomena and taking extensive field notes without specifying in advance exactly what is to be observed. In other words, qualitative observation is usually done for exploratory purposes. Qualitative observation is usually done in natural settings. In fact, the terms *qualitative observation* and *naturalistic observation* are frequently treated as synonyms in the research literature. Not surprisingly, qualitative observation is usually carried out by qualitative researchers.

Whenever you conduct qualitative observations, you must remember exactly what you have observed. In fact, the researcher is said to be the data-collection instrument because it is the researcher who must decide what is important and what data are to be recorded. If you are wondering what to observe when you conduct a qualitative observation, you can consider the Guidelines for Directing Observation provided in Exhibit 6.4. Most importantly, you need to look for anything and everything to observe that may be relevant to your research questions.

■ **Field notes**
Notes taken by observer

Researchers record what they believe is important in their **field notes** (notes taken by the observer during and after making observations). It's a good idea to correct and edit any notes you write down during an observation as soon as possible after they are taken because that is when your memory is best. If you wait too long, you might forget important details and not be able to make sense of your handwritten, scribbled, field notes. In addition to taking field notes during your observations, consider audiotaping and videotaping the important scenes.

Research
Navigator.com

participant observation

The form of interaction or type of role taken by the researcher during the conduct of a qualitative observation (called "fieldwork") varies along the following continuum (Gold, 1958):

Complete	Participant-	Observer-	Complete
Participant	as-Observer	as-Participant	Observer

Although one role may be primary, the researcher may play all four roles at different times and in different situations during the conduct of a single qualitative research study. This is especially true when the researcher is in the field for an extended period of time.

■ EXHIBIT 6.4   Guidelines for Directing Qualitative Observation

1. *Who* is in the group or scene? How many people are there, and what are their kinds, identities, and relevant characteristics? How is membership in the group or scene acquired?
2. *What* is happening here? What are the people in the group or scene doing and saying to one another?
   A. What behaviors are repetitive, and which occur irregularly? In what events, activities, or routines are participants engaged? What resources are used in these activities, and how are they allocated? How are activities organized, labeled, explained, and justified? What differing social contexts can be identified?
   B. How do the people in the group behave toward one another? What is the nature of this participation and interaction? How are the people connected or related to one another? What statuses and roles are evident in this interaction? Who makes what decisions for whom? How do the people organize themselves for interactions?
   C. What is the content of participants' conversations? What subjects are common, and which are rare? What stories, anecdotes, and homilies do they exchange? What verbal and nonverbal languages do they use for communication? What beliefs do the content of their conversations demonstrate? What formats do the conversations follow? What processes do they reflect? Who talks and who listens?
3. *Where* is the group or scene located? What physical settings and environments form their contexts? What natural resources are evident, and what technologies are created or used? How does the group allocate and use space and physical objects? What is consumed, and what is produced? What sights, sounds, smells, tastes, and textures are found in the contexts that the group uses?
4. *When* does the group meet and interact? How often are these meetings, and how lengthy are they? How does the group conceptualize, use, and distribute time? How do participants view the past, present, and future?
5. *How* are the identified elements connected or interrelated, either from the participants' point of view or from the researcher's perspective? How is stability maintained? How does change originate, and how is it managed? How are the identified elements organized? What rules, norms, or mores govern this social organization? How is power conceptualized and distributed? How is this group related to other groups, organizations, or institutions?
6. *Why* does the group operate as it does? What meanings do participants attribute to what they do? What is the group's history? What goals are articulated in the group? What symbols, traditions, values, and world views can be found in the group?

From M. D. LeCompte, J. Preissle, and R. Tesch, *Ethnography and Qualitative Design in Educational Research,* p. 294, copyright © 1993 by Academic Press. Reprinted by permission of Academic Press and the authors.

The **complete participant** takes on the role of an insider, essentially becoming a member of the group being studied and spending a great deal of time with the group. For example, you might spend a year teaching at a "model school" that you want to learn about. During the year, you would take extensive field notes, documenting what you observe and what you experience. Because the complete participant does not inform the group members that they are in a research study, many researchers question the use of this approach on ethical grounds. It is a cardinal rule in research ethics that research participants should know that they are involved in a research study, that they have the right *not* to participate, and that they are free to withdraw at any time during a research study if they do choose not to participate. You should

■ **Complete participant**
Researcher becomes member of group being studied and does not tell members they are being studied

therefore be very careful about doing "undercover" research except in legally open and accessible places such as a mall, a playground, or a sporting event.

■ **Participant-as-observer**
Researcher spends extended time with the group as an insider and tells members they are being studied

The **participant-as-observer** attempts to take on the role of an insider (a participant), similar to the complete participant. The participant-as-observer also spends a good deal of time in the field participating and observing. The participant-as-observer, however, explains to the people in the group being studied that he or she is a researcher and not a bonafide group member. The previous example of someone spending a year in a model school would be a participant-as-observer if the researcher informed the people in the school that he or she was conducting research and then participated in the school functions. An advantage of this approach is that, for ethical reasons, the researcher can request permission to collect and record data as needed. In addition, the researcher can obtain feedback about the researcher's observations and tentative conclusions from the people in the research study. A weakness is that the participants might not behave naturally because they are aware that they are being observed. Fortunately, this problem usually disappears as the people begin to trust the researcher and as they adjust to his or her presence.

■ **Observer-as-participant**
Researcher spends limited amount of time observing group members and tells members they are being studied

The **observer-as-participant** takes on the role of observer much more than the role of participant. The participants are fully aware that they are part of a research study. The observer-as-participant does not spend very much time in the field. Rather, the observer-as-participant has more limited and briefer interactions with the participants. For example, the researcher might negotiate entry to one faculty meeting, to one PTA meeting, and one or two classes as part of a research study. The researcher might also conduct several planned one-visit interviews with research participants. Compared to the complete participant and participant-as-observer roles, a disadvantage of the observer-as-participant role is that it is more difficult to obtain an insider's view. On the other hand, it is easier to maintain objectivity and neutrality.

■ **Complete observer**
Researcher observes as an outsider and does not tell the people they are being observed

■ **Reactivity**
Changes that occur in people because they know they are being observed

The **complete observer** fully takes on the role of outside observer. He or she does not inform the people in the group being studied that they are being observed. The people usually will not know that they are being observed. For example, the complete observer might view people through a one-way window or might sit in the back of the room at an open meeting. The advantage of this approach is that there is minimal **reactivity** (changes in the behavior of people because they know they are being observed). On the other hand, you can take the role of complete observer only in open settings because of ethical concerns.

Perhaps the most useful styles of observation are the participant-as-observer and the observer-as-participant. These are generally preferred because they allow voluntary consent by research participants. In addition, they allow the researcher to take on a mix of the insider's role and the outsider's role. The complete participant always runs the risk of losing his or her objectivity, and the complete observer always runs the risk of not understanding the insider perspective. Not surprisingly, the participant-as-observer and observer-as-participant styles of observation are the most commonly used by researchers.

■ **Frontstage behavior**
What people want or allow us to see

■ **Backstage behavior**
What people say and do only with their closest friends

If you are going to enter the field and carry out qualitative observation, you should carry with you the general research question, a desire to learn, and an open mind. Good social skills are a must (Shaffir & Stebbins, 1991). Trust and rapport with the group being studied are essential if valid data are going to be obtained. Keep in mind, however, Goffman's warning (1959) that much social behavior observed is **frontstage behavior** (what people want or allow us to see) rather than **backstage behavior** (what people say and do with their closest friends, when "acting" is at a minimum). After getting in the field, the researcher must learn the ropes, maintain relations with the people being studied, and, at the end of the study, leave and keep in touch (Shaffir & Stebbins, 1991). We provide a few more practical tips for conducting fieldwork in Table 6.6.

6.12 What are the main differences between quantitative and qualitative observations?

6.13 What are the four main roles that a researcher can take during qualitative observation?

6.14 What is the difference between frontstage behavior and backstage behavior?

REVIEW

QUESTIONS

■ **TABLE 6.6**   Tips for Conducting Fieldwork and Qualitative Observation

1. Make sure all observers are well trained, are good note takers, and know how to fit into diverse situations.

2. Do background homework on the people and cultural settings to be observed.

3. Be sensitive to gender, age, and cultural differences between you and the people being observed.

4. Establish rapport and trust, starting with gatekeepers and informants.

5. Don't promise anything to anyone in the setting that you cannot or should not deliver.

6. Be reflexive (i.e., monitor yourself).

7. Be unobtrusive (i.e., try to fit in and don't stand out).

8. Remain alert at all times, and pay attention to anything that may be important.

9. Find an effective way to record what is being observed (i.e., taking field notes or using audio-visual recorders).

10. Try to corroborate anything important that you see, hear, or learn about.

11. Conduct opportunistic interviews while you are in the field when possible.

12. Be empathetic, but also remain neutral to the content of what people say to you.

13. Make observations in multiple and disparate settings.

14. Include descriptive detail in your field notes. Get direct quotes when possible. Include your own insights and interpretations when they arise, but keep them separate from the description and verbatims (i.e., quotes).

15. Observe and record characteristics of the setting and context, interpersonal interactions, significant behaviors, verbal and nonverbal communication, formal and informal interactions, what does *not* happen, power and status hierarchy in the group, and anything else that seems important to you at the time.

16. Spend sufficient time in the field to collect useful data and to allow corroboration of your findings.

17. When you leave the field, immediately write up your field notes so that you don't forget what you have seen, heard, and experienced.

SECONDARY DATA (EXISTING DATA)

Secondary data
Existing data originally collected or left behind at an earlier time by a different person for a different purpose

The last major method of data collection involves the collection of secondary data for use in a research study. **Secondary data** (also called "existing data" or "already available data") are data that were collected, recorded, or left behind at an earlier time, usually by a different person from the current researcher and often for an entirely different purpose than the current research purpose at hand. In other words, the researcher uses what is already there. The researcher must, however, find these data or artifacts so as to use them in his or her research study. Secondary data may be used with other data for corroboration, or they may be the primary data to be used in a research study. There are several common types of secondary data that the researcher can go find such as personal documents, official documents, physical data, and archived research data.

Personal documents
Anything written, photographed, or recorded for private purposes

Official documents
Anything written, photographed, or recorded by an organization

Documents are one major type of secondary data. **Personal documents** include anything that is written, photographed, or otherwise recorded for private purposes. Some examples of personal documents are letters, diaries, correspondence, family videos, and pictures. **Official documents** are written, photographed, or recorded by some type of public or private organization. Some examples are newspapers, educational journals and magazines, curriculum guides, annual reports, minutes of school board meetings, student records, student work, books, yearbooks, published articles, speeches, personnel files, and videos of things like news programs and advertisements. Documents are frequently used by qualitative researchers and by historical researchers.

Physical data
Any material thing created or left by humans that might provide information about a phenomenon of interest to a researcher

Physical data include any physical traces left by people as they take part in various activities. Some examples of physical data that have been used by social scientists are wear in floor tiles in museums, wear on library books, soil from shoes and clothing, radio dial settings, fingerprints, suits of armor, and contents of people's trash (Webb et al., 2000). Physical data can also include instances of material culture (e.g., clothes, buildings, books, billboards, art).

Archived research data
Data originally used for research purposes and then stored

Archived research data are data that were originally used for research purposes and then stored for possible later use. Archived research data may be in print form but are usually stored in a computer-usable form (floppy disks or CD-ROM). Some examples of archived research data are census data and social science research data stored and kept by researchers or research-related organizations such as the U.S. Census Bureau (www.census.gov/), the Institute for Survey Research at the University of Michigan (www.isr.umich.edu/), the National Opinion Research Center in Chicago (www.norc.uchicago.edu/), and the Gallup Organization (www.gallup.com/). Archived research data are usually quantitative. We expect that qualitative research data will increasingly be archived for later access and reanalysis.

The largest repository of archived social science data is kept by the Interuniversity Consortium for Political and Social Research (ICPSR) (www.icpsr.umich.edu). Based in Ann Arbor, Michigan, the ICPSR is a consortium that includes the membership of over 500 colleges and universities in the United States and across the world. The ICPSR currently houses over 20,000 computer-readable data files, and faculty at member institutions (such as your local university) can obtain the data sets at very modest costs. Typically, the data were part of a research study by an academic researcher. Many studies were grant funded. After a researcher has finished with the data, he or she provides a copy to the ICPSR, which makes it available to member institutions or anyone else who has a legitimate reason to use it. If you want to see some of the many data files that are available, visit the ICPSR web site or go to your library and browse through the *ICPSR Guide to Resources and Services,* a book that includes descriptions of hundreds of research data files.

6.15 What are some examples of secondary, or existing, data?

SUMMARY

A method of data collection is the procedure that a researcher uses to physically obtain research data from research participants. The method of data collection that is used in a research study is discussed in the method section of a research report. There are six major methods of data collection. Researchers can have their participants fill out an instrument or perform a behavior designed to measure their ability or degree of a skill (tests); researchers can have research participants fill out self-report instruments (questionnaires); researchers can talk to participants in person or over the telephone (interviews); researchers can discuss issues with multiple research participants at the same time in a small-group setting (focus groups); researchers can examine how research participants act in natural and structured environments (observation); and researchers can use data that came from an earlier time for a different purpose than the current research problem at hand (secondary data). Tests, questionnaires, interviews, observation, and secondary data can be used to collect both quantitative and qualitative research data. Focus groups are used to collect qualitative data. The researcher must pay particular attention to the construction of the data collection instrument that is used to collect the research data. Finally, the methods of data collection discussed in this chapter can be mixed by using the fundamental principle of mixed research to strengthen the evidence provided by a research study.

KEY TERMS

acquiescence response set (p. 175)
anchor (p. 171)
archived research data (p. 192)
backstage behavior (p. 190)
checklist (p. 174)
closed-ended question (p. 168)
complete observer (p. 190)
complete participant (p. 189)
contingency question (p. 176)
double-barreled question (p. 168)
double negative (p. 168)
event sampling (p. 188)

exhaustive (p. 170)
field notes (p. 188)
focus group (p. 185)
frontstage behavior (p. 190)
fully anchored rating scale (p. 171)
fundamental principle of mixed
    research (p. 162)
group moderator (p. 185)
informal conversational
    interview (p. 183)
in-person interview (p. 178)
interview (p. 178)

interviewee (p. 178)
interviewer (p. 178)
interview guide approach (p. 183)
interview protocol (p. 180)
item stem (p. 169)
laboratory observation (p. 187)
leading question (p. 167)
Likert scale (p. 175)
loaded question (p. 167)
method of data collection (p. 162)
mutually exclusive (p. 169)
naturalistic observation (p. 187)

DISCUSSION QUESTIONS

1. We talked about six major methods of data collection in this chapter. Can you think of any other method of data collection not mentioned in the chapter? What is it? Does it fit into one of the six major methods or does it deserve a new category?

2. Which of the six major methods of data collection do you think is most commonly used by educational researchers? Why?

3. Which of the six methods of data collection would you feel most comfortable using? Why?

4. What is the point of the fundamental principle of mixed research? Think of an example of its use to share with your classmates.

5. Should one use a single item to measure an abstract concept such as self-esteem, intelligence, or teaching self-efficacy? If not, how should one measure such concepts?

RESEARCH EXERCISES

1. Fill out the Rosenberg Self-Esteem Scale shown in Figure 6.1. Then sum your responses to the ten items to obtain your overall score (i.e., your summated score). Be sure that you "reverse score" items 3, 5, 8, 9, and 10 (i.e., a 4 becomes a 1, a 3 becomes a 2, a 2 becomes a 3, and a 1 becomes a 4) before you add up your item scores to obtain your overall score. After doing this, you will know how to score a summated scale.

2. Pick a topic and construct a fifteen-item questionnaire. Collect data from five of your classmates. Have them evaluate your data-collection instrument on the basis of what they have learned in this chapter. Revise your questionnaire.

3. Go to ContentSelect and search using the term *questionnaire*. List five questionnaires that you found. What was the purpose of each of these?

RELEVANT INTERNET SITES

www.amstat.org/sections/srms/whatsurvey.html
Free brochures explaining survey research, including data collection and questionnaire construction.

www.spss.com/uk/SurveyTipsnew.pdf
Free guide on questionnaire and interview protocol construction.

www.ehr.nsf.gov/EHR/REC/pubs/NSF97–153/ start.htm
Free handbook on mixed methods data collection.

survey.sesrc.wsu.edu/dillman/
Survey research materials and papers at Don A. Dillman's website.

RECOMMENDED READING

Babbie, E. (2001). *Survey research methods* (9th ed.). Belmont, CA: Wadsworth.

Dillman, D. A. (2000). *Mail and internet surveys: The tailored design method.* New York: Wiley.

Johnson, B., & Turner, L. A. (2003). Data collection strategies in mixed methods research. In A. Tashakkori & C. Taddlie (Eds.), *Handbook of mixed methods research.* Thousand Oaks, CA: Sage.

Krueger, R. A., & Casey, M. A. (2000). *Focus groups: A practical guide for applied research* (3rd ed.). Thousand Oaks, CA: Sage.

Wolcott, H. F. (2001). *The art of fieldwork.* Walnut Creek, CA: Altamira.

7

Sampling

LEARNING OBJECTIVES

To be able to

- Explain the difference between a sample and a census.
- Define the key terms used in sampling (representative sample, generalize, element, statistic, parameter, and so forth).
- Compare and contrast the different random sampling techniques.
- Know which sampling techniques are equal probability selection methods.
- Draw a simple random sample.
- Draw a systematic sample.
- Explain the difference between proportional and disproportional stratified sampling.
- Explain the characteristics of one-stage and two-stage cluster sampling.
- List and explain the characteristics of the different nonrandom sampling techniques.
- Explain the difference between random selection and random assignment.
- List the factors that you should consider when determining the appropriate sample size to be selected when using random sampling.
- Discuss sampling in qualitative research and compare and contrast the different sampling techniques used in qualitative research.

The concept of sampling has important applications in daily life. For example, most farm products that are grown in the United States are subject to inspection by the Federal-State Inspection Service. Because it is not possible for each apple, each ham, or each peanut to be inspected individually, the Inspection Service selects samples of each farm commodity for inspection. Analyses of these samples are used to infer the characteristics of large quantities of various farm products. Inspections of farm products by these government officials serve the purpose of protecting the general public by ensuring that the products in grocery stores are safe for public consumption.

Let's look at the example of peanuts more closely. Thousands of tons of peanuts are grown in the United States annually. As with other farm products, peanuts are subject to analysis by the Inspection Service before they can be put on the market. The inspectors need to know the percentages of specified components in each load of peanuts such as whole peanut kernels, half-kernels, shriveled kernels, hulls, foreign material (e.g., hay, sand, and pebbles), and the percentage of moisture in the peanuts.

A typical truckload of peanuts brought to market by a U.S. farmer ranges in size from approximately 2,000 to 6,000 pounds. The Inspection Service inspectors draw a sample of peanuts from each load with the use of a special tool called a peanut auger, a hollow, stainless-steel cylinder approximately four inches in diameter and seven feet long. The inspector pushes the auger into the peanuts from the top surface to the very bottom of the load. This procedure allows the auger to take a sample of peanuts from every level in the load. The inspector performs this procedure for each of several positions randomly selected by a computer that graphs the top surface of the load of peanuts. Theoretically, each peanut (and other components of the load) has an equal chance of being included in the sample. This produces samples that are representative of the loads of peanuts. In this chapter, we will discuss several sampling methods that produce representative samples as well as several other commonly used approaches.

In this chapter, we examine the idea of sampling. **Sampling** is the process of drawing a sample from a population. When we sample, we study the characteristics of a subset (called the sample) selected from a larger group (called the population) to understand the characteristics of the larger group (the population). After researchers determine the characteristics of the sample, they **generalize** from the sample to the population; that is, researchers make statements about the population based on their study of the sample. A sample is usually much smaller in size than a population; hence, sampling can save time and money.

Random sampling is frequently used in **survey research,** which is a form of nonexperimental research in which questionnaires or interviews are used to gather information, and the goal is to understand the characteristics of a population. A well-known example of survey research is any of the many studies done to determine national voter attitudes and opinions about political candidates or various issues of national interest (education, family, crime, foreign affairs, and so on). The random sampling techniques discussed in this chapter are also used in most other types of quantitative research. Later in the chapter, we devote an entire section to the special sampling techniques that are used in *qualitative* research. For now, however, our focus is on sampling in quantitative research.

- **Sampling**
  The process of drawing a sample from a population
- **Generalize**
  Make statements about a population based on sample data
- **Survey research**
  A term applied to nonexperimental research based on questionnaires or interviews

Research
Navigator.com

survey research

197

■ **Census**
A study of the whole population rather than a sample

If you study *every individual* in a population, you are actually conducting a census and not a survey. In a **census,** the whole population is studied, not just a sample, or subset, of the population. A well-known example of a census is the United States Decennial Census conducted by the Census Bureau every ten years. The purpose of this census is to determine the demographic characteristics (age, gender, race, income level), educational characteristics (educational attainment, school enrollment), family characteristics (number of children, age at marriage, family structure), and work characteristics (e.g., type of job, occupational prestige of job, number of hours worked per week) of *all* individual citizens of the United States. That's over 280,000,000 people! As you can probably imagine, a census is quite expensive and very difficult to conduct.

When we conduct research using sampling techniques, we do not study every individual in the population of interest. Instead, we study a sample of the population. The use of random sampling saves time and money compared to a census, and such resources are nearly always limited. Using the random sampling techniques discussed in this chapter, characteristics of the United States population can be estimated within a small margin of error (plus or minus a few percentage points) using only 1,000 to 1,500 individuals. Conducting a census for large populations is generally too difficult and too expensive. On the other hand, if a population is very small (e.g., all twenty-five teachers at a single elementary school), including all of the individuals in your research study is your best bet. The real power of random sampling comes when you are studying large populations.

In this chapter, we discuss random (also called probability) sampling techniques and nonrandom (also called nonprobability) sampling techniques. Random sampling techniques are based on the theory of probability and usually produce "good" samples. A good sample is one that is representative of the population it came from. That is, *a representative sample resembles the population that it came from on all characteristics* (the proportions of males and females, teachers and nonteachers, young and old people, Democrats and Republicans, and so forth) *except size. A representative sample is like the population except that it is smaller.* Although a random sample is rarely perfectly representative, random samples are almost always more representative than nonrandom samples. Nonrandom samples are said to be **biased samples** because they are almost always systematically different from the population on certain characteristics. In contrast, random samples are said to be unbiased samples because they tend to be representative of the populations from which they come.

As you read the rest of this chapter, remember that the main purpose of sampling in quantitative research is to enable the researcher to generalize to a population. In short, obtaining a sample is a means to an end. We focus here on helping you understand the concept of sampling in quantitative research, know about the most important sampling methods, and understand how to draw samples. We conclude the chapter with a discussion of sampling methods used in qualitative research. For more information on sampling in qualitative research, see LeCompte and Preissle (1993) and Patton (1987, 2002).

■ **Representative sample**
A sample that resembles the population

■ **Biased sample**
A sample that is systematically different from the population

REVIEW

QUESTIONS

7.1 What type of sampling produces representative samples?

7.2 What is a representative sample, and when is it important to obtain a representative sample?

TERMINOLOGY USED IN SAMPLING

To understand sampling better, it is helpful to know some specialized terms. A **sample** is a set of elements taken from a larger population according to certain rules. An **element** is the basic unit selected from the population. "Individuals" are the most common element sampled; however, other types of elements are possible, such as "groups" (e.g., schools, classrooms, clinics) or "objects" (e.g., textbooks, school records, television commercials, calculators produced on a production line). A sample is always smaller than a population, and it is often much smaller. In sampling, the letter N stands for the population size (the total number of people or elements in a population), and n stands for the sample size (the number of people or elements in a sample). For example, if we selected a sample of 500 people from a population of 150,000, then n would be 500 and N would be 150,000. Sampling rules tell you how to select a sample. The methods of sampling discussed in this chapter follow different rules for selection.

A **population** (sometimes called a target population) is the set of all elements. It is the large group to which a researcher wants to generalize his or her sample results. It is the total group that you are interested in learning more about. A few possible populations are the citizens of the United States, all the students attending public and private schools in Los Angeles, all middle school teachers in the city of Atlanta, and all counselors working at a mental health center in Ann Arbor, Michigan.

A **statistic** is a numerical characteristic of a sample. For example, on the basis of the people included in a sample, a researcher might calculate the average reading performance, the correlation between two variables (e.g., test grades and study time), or the percentage of students receiving A grades. A **parameter** is a numerical characteristic of a total population. For example, it could be an average, a correlation, or a percentage that is based on the complete population rather than on a sample. We rarely know the values of the population parameters of interest. Therefore, we collect sample data so that we can estimate the probable values of the population parameters. A sample statistic will rarely be exactly the same as the population parameter, but most of the time it will not be very far off (assuming that the sample is a random sample of adequate size). The actual difference between a sample statistic value (let's say you calculated an average for the sample) and the population parameter (the actual average in the population) is called **sampling error.** Sampling error will fluctuate randomly over repeated sampling when a random sampling method is used. That is, a sample statistic (e.g., an average or a percentage) will sometimes be a little larger than a population parameter and it will sometimes be a little smaller. However, it will *not* be consistently too large or too small. That is, it will not be biased.

When we draw a sample, we typically begin by locating or constructing a **sampling frame,** which is a list of all the elements in the population. For example, if we are interested in drawing a sample of college students from Ohio State University, then the sampling frame is the list of all students attending Ohio State University. The researcher draws the sample from the sampling frame using one of the sampling methods discussed later. After the sample is selected, the members of the sample are contacted and asked if they will participate in the research study.

Typically, some of the people in a sample will refuse to participate in the research study. You can determine the percentage that actually participates by calculating the response rate. The **response rate** is the percentage of people in a sample that participates in

Sample
A set of elements taken from a larger population

Element
The basic unit that is selected from the population

N
The population size

n
The sample size

Population
The large group to which a researcher wants to generalize the sample results

Statistic
A numerical characteristic of a sample

Parameter
A numerical characteristic of a population

Sampling error
The difference between the value of a sample statistic and a population parameter

Sampling frame
A list of all the elements in a population

Response rate
The percentage of people in a sample that participate in a research study

the research study. The response rate will usually be less than 100 percent. If you select, for example, a sample size of 200 people and only 183 of the 200 individuals participate, then the response rate is 91.5 percent ($183/200 \times 100$). The formula for the response rate is

$$\text{Response rate} = \frac{\text{Number of people in the sample who participate in the research}}{\text{Total number of people in the sample}} \times 100$$

If you want a sample to be representative of a population, then it is essential that the response rate be as high as possible. Response rates around 70 percent and higher are generally considered acceptable. However, the sample might still be *biased* (not representative of the population) even when the response rate is high because the kinds of people who drop out of the sample may be different from the kinds of people who remain in the sample. Researchers should discuss the issues of sample selection procedures, response rates, and sample integrity when they write up their reports. Generally, you should not trust research reports in which this is not done.

REVIEW

QUESTIONS

7.3 What is the difference between a statistic and a parameter?

7.4 What is a sampling frame?

RANDOM SAMPLING TECHNIQUES

Simple Random Sampling

A simple random sample is what researchers are usually referring to when they say they have a random sample or a probability sample. Simple random sampling is the most basic form of random sampling. It is the cornerstone of sampling theory. In fact, all the other random sampling methods use simple random sampling at some point during the sampling process. A simple random sample is formally defined as a sample drawn by a procedure in which every possible sample of a given size (e.g., size 100) has an equal chance of being selected from the population. More simply, a **simple random sample** is a sample drawn by a procedure in which every member of the population has an equal chance of being selected for the study. When every member has an equal chance of being selected, the sampling method is called an **equal probability selection method** (EPSEM).

One way to visualize the drawing of a simple random sample is to think about the "hat model." Here is how it works. First, go to a good hat store and buy a big top hat. Next, make one slip of paper for each individual in the population, and place all of the slips in the hat. Make sure you use standard sized slips of paper so that they will all be the same shape, size, and weight. If there are 1,000 people in the population of interest, you will need 1,000 slips of paper. Now, let's say you want to obtain a simple random sample of 100 people. To make

- **Simple random sample**
  A sample drawn by a procedure in which every member of the population has an equal chance of being selected

- **Equal probability selection method**
  Any sampling method where each member of the population has an equal chance of being selected

sure all the pieces of paper are thoroughly mixed in the hat, cover the top of the hat and shake it up vigorously. Next, select one slip of paper from the hat. After selecting the slip of paper, shake the hat up again to be sure the remaining slips are well mixed, and then select another slip of paper. After you have selected all 100 names, you will have a simple random sample size of 100 ($n = 100$) from a population size of 1,000 ($N = 1,000$). After you finish selecting the sample, you can look at the names to see who is included in the sample. These are the 100 people you will study.[1]

Drawing a Simple Random Sample Now let's get a little more practical and see how researchers actually draw random samples. Although the hat model was a convenient metaphor for thinking about simple random sampling, it is rarely used in practice. A more common approach is to use a **table of random numbers,** which is a list of numbers that fall in a random order. This means no number will appear more often than any other number in the long run. All numbers have an equal chance of appearing. Furthermore, there will be no systematic pattern in the table. If you ever think you see a pattern in a table or that some number occurs more frequently than it should, you need only look farther in the table. The apparent pattern will disappear.

■ **Table of random numbers**
A list of numbers that fall in a random order

　　An excerpt of a table of random numbers is given in Figure 7.1. The numbers in Figure 7.1 were generated by a computer using a random number generator (a computer program). If you need a larger set of random numbers, most computers will do this, or you can go to the library and check out a book of random numbers (e.g., Kendall & Smith, 1954). A book of random numbers includes nothing but random numbers. (Talk about dry reading!) Before drawing a simple random sample, you should keep in mind that when a sample is not large enough, random sampling might not work very well. Basically, the more numbers you select, the better the process operates. Random selection cannot work magic, but if you use it properly, it has been shown repeatedly, both mathematically and empirically, that it works. In a later section, we will talk more about how large samples should be.

■ **FIGURE 7.1**   Table of random numbers

Line/Column	1	2	3	4	5	6	7	8	9	10
1	10480	15011	01536	02011	81647	91646	69179	14194	62590	36207
2	22368	46573	25595	85393	30995	89198	27982	53402	93965	34095
3	24130	48360	22527	97265	76393	64809	15179	24830	49340	32081
4	42167	93093	06243	61680	07856	16376	39440	53537	71341	57004
5	37570	39975	81837	16656	06121	91782	60468	81305	49684	60672
6	77921	06907	11008	42751	27756	53498	18602	70659	90655	15053
7	99562	72905	56420	69994	98872	31016	71194	18738	44013	48840
8	96301	91977	05463	07972	18876	20922	94595	56869	69014	60045
9	89579	14342	63661	10281	17453	18103	57740	84378	25331	12565
10	85475	36857	53342	53988	53060	59533	38867	62300	08158	17983

To use a table of random numbers, all of the elements in the sampling frame must have a number attached to them. Remember, a sampling frame is just a list of all the people (elements) in a population. If you are sampling from a list of your students or your clients, then you need to give each person a unique number. These numbers serve as an index. An example of a sampling frame is shown in Figure 7.2. This is a list of people in a small population with their associated identification numbers. The information on gender (a categorical variable) and age (a quantitative variable) are provided in the sampling frame because we want to be able to calculate the average age and the percent male and female later. This way we can see how well the sample that we draw compares with the actual population shown in Figure 7.2. Usually, you would have to collect this kind of information (data) before you would know how good the sample is. That is, a sampling frame usually contains only the names and the identification numbers.

Now let's draw a sample of size ten from this population of size 60 in Figure 7.2. First we need to select ten numbers from the table of random numbers. But how is this done? The

FIGURE 7.2   A sampling frame with information on gender and age included[a]

Number	Name	Age	Number	Name	Age	Number	Name	Age
01	Johnny Adams (M)	64	21**	Scott House (M)	21	41	Beth Sanders (F)	63
02*	Fred Alexander (M)	18	22	Jan Hoffman (F)	60	42*	Lena Schmitt (F)	33
03**	Kathy Anderson (F)	57	23	Robert Johnson (M)	43	43	Cindy Scott (F)	31
04	Larry Barnes (M)	30	24	John Jones (M)	18	44	Sam Shepherd (M)	20
05	Hasem Basaleh (M)	38	25	John Locke (M)	52	45**	Max Smart (M)	47
06*	Tom Baxter (M)	31	26	Carlton Lawless (M)	35	46	Rhonda Smith (F)	23
07*	Barry Biddlecomb (M)	52	27*,**	Pam Mackey (F)	35	47	Kin Sullivan (F)	29
08	Don Campbell (M)	42	28	Ronald May (M)	20	48	Jimmy Thompson (M)	42
09**	Martha Carr (F)	21	29	Mike McNuty (M)	64	49	Susan Tyler (F)	23
10*	Eugene Davis (M)	21	30*	John Mills (M)	19	50	Lisa Turner (F)	57
11	Marion Dunn (F)	55	31	Doug Morgan (M)	33	51**	Velma Vandenberg (F)	43
12	James East (M)	44	32	Jean Neal (F)	33	52	Richard Viatle (M)	20
13	Greg Ellis (M)	50	33**	Anh Nguyan (M)	40	53*	Larry Watson (M)	26
14	Alex Evans (M)	65	34	David Payne (M)	57	54	Melvin White (M)	29
15**	Donna Faircloth (F)	27	35	Susan Poole (F)	28	55	Mark Wiggens (M)	46
16*	Barbara Flowers (F)	37	36	Brenda Prine (F)	38	56	Leon Wilson (M)	31
17	Kirk Garner (M)	37	37	Andrea Quinn (F)	30	57**	Andrew Young (M)	39
18*	Marie Gaylord (F)	46	38	Mohamed Rashid (M)	64	58	Hun Yu (F)	51
19	William Gilder (M)	30	39**	Anneke Reeves (F)	32	59	Alex Zellars (M)	42
20	Mark Harris (M)	63	40	Charlie Rogers (M)	46	60	Ellen Zimmer (F)	46

[a]Data on variables such as age and gender are usually not included in a sampling frame. Data are obtained after they are collected from the sample respondents. To do a couple of calculations, data on age and gender are provided in the columns and parentheses.

*Elements selected in simple random sampling example discussed in the text.

**Elements selected in systematic sampling example discussed in the text.

answer is that you can do it in many different ways as long as you are consistent. You can start anywhere in the table of random numbers, and then you can go in any direction (up, down, across, forward, or backward) as long as you keep going in that direction. It is important that you select a different starting point every time you use a table of random numbers so that you don't end up with the same numbers every time. If you decide to start at the top and move down in the table until you hit the bottom of the list, then go to the top of the next column and continue moving down. Generally speaking, moving either down or across is the easiest. The key is that once you pick a direction, you must stick with it. There are only two digits in 60 (i.e., N), so we will need to find two-digit numbers in the table.

Let's pick our starting point at the top of column 4 and move downward using the first two digits listed. Look at Figure 7.1 as you read this paragraph. The first two-digit random number is 02. Do you see it at the top of column 4? Because 2 is a "valid" number (it is between 1 and 60), it is included in the sample. The second number is 85. It is outside the range (1–60), so just ignore it and move down to the next two-digit number. The next two numbers are 97 and 61. They are also out of range. The next number, 16, is a usable number. We now have selected two numbers. Look at the table and find the next usable number. If you said 42, you are right. The next three usable numbers after that are 7, 10, and 53. Because you are now at the bottom of column 4 and still need more numbers, go to the top of column 5 and continue. The first number, 81, is not usable; however, the second number, 30, is. After 30, the next number in the usable range of 1–60 is 7. However, do not use this number because person 7 is already in the sample. Remember, you should always use sampling without replacement. Keep moving. The final three usable numbers are 6, 27, and 18. The sample is therefore composed of persons 2, 16, 42, 7, 10, 53, 30, 6, 27, and 18.

The final step is to see who these people are so you can go and see whether they will participate in your research study. As you can see in Figure 7.2, the sample is composed of Fred Alexander (element 2), Barbara Flowers (element 16), Lena Schmitt (element 42), Barry Biddlecomb (element 7), Eugene Davis (element 10), Larry Watson (element 53), John Mills (element 30), Tom Baxter (element 6), Pam Mackey (element 27), and Marie Gaylord (element 18). This is your sample of size 10. Single asterisks are placed by these names in Figure 7.2.

After collecting data (e.g., age) from the individuals in the sample, you would conduct a statistical analysis. Let's do a very simple calculation. The age was given for each individual. (Generally data would have been collected on many additional variables or characteristics besides age.) Now calculate the average age for the individuals in the sample. Just add the ages for the ten people and divide that number by 10. That is, $(18 + 31 + 52 + 21 + 37 + 46 + 35 + 19 + 33 + 26)/10 = 31.8$. The average age of the individuals in the sample is 31.8, and this is our estimate of the average age of all of the individuals in the population.

In this case, we know that the population average is 38.95 or about 39 years old. To get 38.95, just add up the ages for all 60 people in the population and divide that number by 60. The sample value of 31.8 was off by approximately 7 years. Don't be alarmed if this seems like a big sampling error; a sample size of 10 is actually quite small. The difference between the sample average and the population average occurred because of chance. That is how random sampling works. If you were to select another sample of size 10, the average age in the sample would probably also be different from the population average. Try it. Draw another sample of size 10 from the sampling frame, and make sure you can draw a simple random sample on your own. Basically, sampling error follows a normal, bell-shaped curve. The vast majority of the time, the sample mean will be relatively near the population mean, but it is possible for it to be far from the population mean.

We conclude this section with an excerpt from an actual journal article that relied on simple random sampling (Lance, 1996):

> Participants were selected from the 1992 Membership Directory of the Association on Higher Education and Disability (AHEAD), a professional organization for service providers to students with disabilities at institutions of higher education. Entries in the directory were assigned numbers, excluding those members who were students, were specialists in only one type of disability, did not reside in the United States, or were not affiliated with an institution of higher education. A statistical computer program was used to select a random sample of 250 of the members deemed eligible for participation in the study. . . . The final sample included 190 members from 47 states and the District of Columbia. (p. 280)

As you can see, the Membership Directory of the AHEAD was the researcher's sampling frame. Also, the researcher used a computer program to generate the random numbers rather than taking the numbers from a table of random numbers.

Systematic Sampling

- **Systematic sample**
  A sample obtained by determining the sampling interval, selecting a random starting point between 1 and k, and then selecting every kth element
- **Sampling interval**
  The population size divided by the desired sample size
- **k**
  The size of the sampling interval
- **Starting point**
  A randomly selected number between 1 and k

Systematic sampling is an adaptation of simple random sampling.[2] It uses a shortcut for selecting the elements to be included in the sample. A **systematic sample** is defined as a sample that is obtained by determining the **sampling interval** (i.e., the population size divided by the desired sample size, N/n, which is symbolized by k), selecting at random a **starting point** (a number between 1 and k, including 1 and k), and then selecting every kth element in the sampling frame. Systematic sampling is generally easier than simple random sampling when you are selecting from lists (e.g., lists of names, lists of schools).

Let's hypothetically say that there are 50 teachers in your middle school and we have a list of these 50 middle school teachers, with the teachers numbered from 1 through 50. You have decided that you want to select 5 teachers to be on a PTA committee. We can select a systematic sample from our list of 50 teachers by following the three steps given in the definition of systematic sampling. First, determine the sampling interval (symbolized by the letter k). To obtain k, you need the population size and the desired sample size. Then just divide the population size by the desired sample size. In this case, the population size is 50, and we want a sample of size 5. If you divide 50 by 5, you will see that k is equal to 10 (i.e., $50/5 = 10$).[3]

Second, randomly select one number between 1 and k (including 1 and k). You should use a table of random numbers for this step because we want the sample to be a random sample. In our example, we want to randomly select a number between 1 and 10 because k equals 10. Therefore, go to the table of random numbers (Figure 7.1) and select a random number between 1 and 10. To do this, you need to pick a place in a table of random numbers to begin sampling for a number in the range of 1 to 10 and then select the first usable number (i.e., the first number in the 1–10 range). If you start at the top of column 2 in Figure 7.1

and move down the column examining two-digit numbers, you will see that the first five numbers are not usable (15, 46, 48, 93, and 39). The next number, however, is 6, which is usable. Therefore, the teacher with the ID number 6 will be the first person selected to be in our sample. The number 6 also has a special name in our systematic sampling; it is called the starting point.

Third, after you have determined k (the sampling interval) and the starting point, you can select the rest of the systematic sample. In our example, we randomly selected the number 6, which is our starting point. This is also the first person to be included in the sample. We now need 4 more people so that we will have a sample of size 5. To get the rest of the elements in our sample, we need to select every kth element starting at the starting point. In this example, our starting point is 6 and $k = 10$; therefore, the second person to be included in the sample is person 16 because we started at 6 and we added 10 (i.e., $6 + 10 = 16$). To get the third person, we start with the second person's number (i.e., 16) and add k (i.e., 10). Therefore, the third person is person 26 ($16 + 10 = 26$). We continue adding k to get the other two people in the sample. The other two people in the sample will be person 36 ($26 + 10 = 36$) and person 46 ($36 + 10 = 46$). Summarizing, we started with 6 and continued adding 10 until we obtained our desired sample of size 5 ($6, 6 + 10 = 16, 16 + 10 = 26, 26 + 10 = 36$, and $36 + 10 = 46$). The systematic random sample is composed of persons 6, 16, 26, 36, and 46. That is 5 people.

Now let's select a systematic sample from the sampling frame given in Figure 7.2. Earlier, we selected a simple random sample from this sampling frame. Specifically, we selected a simple random sample of size 10 from the population of size 60 shown in Figure 7.2. The 10 people chosen in the simple random sample are marked with single asterisks in Figure 7.2. Now we will select a systematic sample of size 10 from this same population, and we will calculate the average age so that we can compare it with the average age in the simple random sample (31.9) and with the average age in the population (38.95).

What do we do first? Remember, there are three steps, and in the first step, we must find k. In this case, k is $60/10 = 6$. Now we select a random number between 1 and 6 (with 1 and 6 also being possible selections). To do this, go to the table of random numbers in Figure 7.1. This time let's start at column 10 and move downward, examining only one-digit numbers (since 1 through 6 are all one-digit numbers). As it turns out, the first number is 3, so we need not go farther. Three is our starting point. What are the remaining 9 numbers in our sample? Just keep adding 6, and you will see that they are 9, 15, 21, 27, 33, 39, 45, 51, and 57. The sample is therefore composed of persons 3, 9, 15, 21, 27, 33, 39, 45, 51, and 57. Specifically, it is composed of Kathy Anderson, Martha Carr, Donna Faircloth, Scott House, Pam Mackey, Anh Nguyan, Anneke Reeves, Max Smart, Velma Vandenberg, and Andrew Young. These 10 people are marked in Figure 7.2 with double asterisks. Now calculate the average age for the 10 individuals in this systematic sample. It is $57 + 21 + 27 + 21 + 35 + 40 + 32 + 47 + 43 + 39$ divided by 10. That's 362 divided by 10, which is 36.2. Because the population value is 38.95, 36.2 is a pretty good estimate, especially with such a small sample size ($n = 10$).

In this case, the average age in our systematic sample (36.2) is a better estimate of the population average (i.e., it is closer to 38.95) than the average age in the simple random sample selected (31.8). This will not, however, always be the case. Sometimes simple random sampling will work better and sometimes systematic sampling will work better. Basically, if a list (a sampling frame) is randomly ordered, then the results of a simple random sampling and systematic sampling will tend to be very similar (Tryfos, 1996). If lists are ordered according to the levels of a categorical variable (e.g., females are listed and then males are listed) or according to the values of a quantitative variable (e.g., the list is ordered in ascending or descending order on age), then systematic sampling will tend to perform a little better than simple random sampling (Kalton, 1983; Scheaffer, Mendenhall, & Ott, 1996).[4] By "better," we mean it will tend to be a little more representative of the population, given a certain sample size. Systematic sampling produces representative samples in general because it is an equal probability selection method; that is, each individual in the population has an equal chance of being included in the sample (Kalton, 1983).

If the list is ordered in such a way that there are cycles in the data that coincide with the sampling interval (k), then systematic sampling can fail dramatically. You must watch out for this potentially serious problem. Look at the sampling frame given in Figure 7.3. The principal and assistant principals at 10 schools making up a hypothetical local school district are listed. Each school is assumed to have one principal and one assistant principal (i.e., there are 10 assistant principals and 10 principals). Let's say that we want to select a systematic sample of 5 of these 20 school administrators. Because the population size is 20 ($N = 20$), and we want a sample size of 5 ($n = 5$), the sampling interval k is 20/5, which is 4. Therefore we will select every fourth person (i.e., element) after randomly selecting a starting point between 1 and 4. Let the randomly selected starting point be 2; that is, assume that you went to the table of random numbers and selected the number 2. As a result, element 2 is included in the sample. Now select every fourth element after 2 until you have 5 elements. That would be 6, 10, 14, and 18. The sample is composed of elements 2, 6, 10, 14, and 18.

FIGURE 7.3
A periodic or cyclical sampling frame. Elements marked by an asterisk are in the example discussed in the text.

Element 1	Principal 1
*Element 2	Assistant Principal 1
Element 3	Principal 2
Element 4	Assistant Principal 2
Element 5	Principal 3
*Element 6	Assistant Principal 3
Element 7	Principal 4
Element 8	Assistant Principal 4
Element 9	Principal 5
*Element 10	Assistant Principal 5
Element 11	Principal 6
Element 12	Assistant Principal 6
Element 13	Principal 7
*Element 14	Assistant Principal 7
Element 15	Principal 8
Element 16	Assistant Principal 8
Element 17	Principal 9
*Element 18	Assistant Principal 9
Element 19	Principal 10
Element 20	Assistant Principal 10

But look at what happened this time. We included only assistant principals in the sample. All of the principals were excluded! This is obviously a major problem because our selected sample is not at all representative of the population; it is a biased sample that includes only assistant principals and no principals. The sampling frame in this case is said to have a cyclical pattern; it is sometimes said to be "periodic." The cyclical pattern in the sampling frame is obvious because each assistant principal is directly preceded and followed by a principal. In this case, the **periodicity** (the presence of a cyclical pattern in a sampling frame) has caused a major problem. What should we learn from the bad experience we just had? Basically, always examine your sampling frame carefully. If you believe that there is a cyclical pattern in the list, then do not use systematic sampling.

- **Periodicity**
  The presence of a cyclical pattern in the sampling frame

Stratified Random Sampling

Stratified sampling is a technique in which a population is divided into mutually exclusive groups (called strata) and then a simple random sample or a systematic sample is selected from each group (each stratum). For example, we could divide a population into males and females and take a random sample of males and a random sample of females. The variable that we divide the population on is called the **stratification variable.** In the case of males and females, the stratification variable is gender. If you are wondering why this approach is called stratified sampling, it is probably because the strata can be viewed metaphorically as being similar to the discrete levels or layers below our earth's surface. The word was probably borrowed from the field of geology.

- **Stratified sampling**
  Dividing the population into mutually exclusive groups and then selecting a random sample from each group
- **Stratification variable**
  The variable on which the population is divided

Proportional Stratified Sampling The most commonly used form of stratified sampling is called **proportional stratified sampling.** If the stratification variable is gender, then the proportions of males and females in the sample are made to be the same as the proportions of males and females in the population. For example, if the population is composed of 70 percent females and 30 percent males, then 70 percent of the people in the sample will be randomly selected from the female subpopulation (i.e., all females in the total population) and 30 percent of the people in the sample will be randomly selected from the male subpopulation (i.e., all males in the total population). That is why it is called "proportional" stratified sampling. The proportions in the sample are made to be the same as the proportions in the total population on certain characteristics. (We tell you how to do this shortly.)

- **Proportional stratified sampling**
  Type of stratified sampling in which the sample proportions are made to be the same as the population proportions on the stratification variable

Proportional stratified sampling tends to be a little more efficient (it requires fewer people) than simple random sampling (Kalton, 1983, p. 21). When you draw a proportional stratified sample, the proportions in the sample on the stratification variable will be perfectly or almost perfectly representative of the proportions on that same stratification variable in the population. For example, if the stratification variable is gender, then the proportions of males and females in the sample will be the same as the proportions in the population. Other possible stratification variables can be used (e.g., grade level, intelligence, education, type of school attended), and you can use more than one stratification variable at the same time if you want (e.g., gender, education). A stratified random sample will also be representative of the population on the other variables that are not included as stratification variables because random samples are selected from each population group (i.e., from each subpopulation) or stratum. Proportional stratified sampling is an equal probability selection method, which means that every individual in the population has an equal chance of being included in the sample. That's why proportional stratified sampling produces representative samples.

As an example, suppose that you are interested in selecting a sample of students in grades one through three in an elementary school. We will use grade level as our stratification variable (rather than gender). The levels of the stratification variable are grade one, grade two, and grade three. Because we are using proportional stratified sampling, we want to make sure that the percentages of students in grades one through three in the sample are the same as the percentages in grades one through three in the school, while making sure that our sample is random in every other respect. As you can see, you have to know the percentages of students in grades one through three in the school *before drawing your sample* so that you can select the right number of students from each grade to be in your sample. Therefore, proportional stratified sampling requires that you know certain information before drawing a sample. If you have the required information, you can randomly select the right numbers of people so that your sample will be proportional to the population on the stratification variable and random in every other way. In our current example, assume that you know beforehand that 30 percent of the students in grades one through three are in the first grade, 35 percent are in the second grade, and 35 percent are in the third grade. This type of information might be available on the principal's computer files. If you know this information, you can then use proportional stratified sampling to make sure that you obtain the correct percentages of students in grades one through three in your sample.

Now let's use a more specific example. Suppose we want to select a sample of 100 students from a high school composed of 1,000 students. To select a stratified sample, you know that you must have information about the stratification variable(s) before selecting the sample. For this example, assume that information obtained before selecting the sample tells us that 53 percent of the students in the high school are female and 47 percent are male. That means there are 530 females and 470 males in the high school (530 + 470 = 1,000). Next, we need to develop separate lists of the females and males so that we can take a random sample from each list. One list will include all the female students, and the other list will include all the male students. Together, these two subpopulations (all females and all males) make up the total population of 1,000 students.

Again, there are 530 females and 470 males in the high school, and we want a sample of size 100. How many females and how many males do you think we need to select if we want the percentages of females and males in our sample to be the same as the percentages in the high school? If you said 53 females and 47 males, you are correct. If we randomly select 53 females and 47 males, then the percentages of females (53 percent) and males (47 percent) in the sample will be the same as the percentages of females (53 percent) and males (47 percent) in the high school. In addition, our sample will be a random sample in every other respect. That is how proportional stratified sampling improves on the simple random sampling method. The sample will be exactly (or almost exactly, depending on rounding) representative of the population on gender composition, and since we are taking random samples from each group, we are still generating a random sample, which means that the sample will also be approximately representative of the population in every other respect. Proportional stratified random sampling is therefore very similar to simple random sampling, except it is usually a little better.

How many females and how many males would you select from our hypothetical high school of 530 females and 470 males *if you wanted a sample of size 500,* rather than a sample of size 100 as demonstrated in the previous example? The answer is 265 females and 235 males. To determine the number of females you need, just take 53 percent of 500, which is 265. To see how many males you need, take 47 percent of 500, which is 235. As you can see, 265 plus 235 is 500, which is your desired sample size. This is how you get a proportional stratified sample. You make sure that the proportions (or percentages) in your sample are the same as the proportions (or percentages) in the population, and you use random sampling within the groups.

If you are still not confident about selecting a stratified sample, we have provided one more example on the book's companion website under Bonus Material for this chapter.

Up to this point, we have shown that once you determine the number of people to select in each stratum (group), you can take a simple random sample of the appropriate size from each group. There is, however, a way to select a proportional stratified sample without having to worry about the number of people to select from each group (strata). Here's what you do. First, make sure that your list (your sampling frame) is ordered by group (strata). If gender is your stratification variable, for example, then order the list by gender; that is, list all of the females first, and then list all of the males second. Second, simply take a *systematic sample* from the list. Kalton (1983) shows that systematic sampling from ordered lists is the way to proceed rather than determining the sample sizes and taking simple random samples. We agree that this is certainly easier in practice, and we also recommend this procedure in general because when a list is ordered by a stratification variable, it is unlikely that the problem of periodicity (a cyclical pattern in the list) will be present.

The sampling frame in Figure 7.4 is ordered by administrative status, with the 10 principals listed first and the 10 assistant principals listed second. In other words, the sampling frame is stratified by administrative status. Let's take a *systematic sample* of size 10 from the 20 school administrators listed in the sampling frame in Figure 7.4. Because there are 10 principals and 10 assistant principals, a proportional stratified sample would include 5 principals and 5 assistant principals. Because the population size is 20 and we want 10 people in our sample, $k = 2$ ($20/10 = 2$). (Remember: k is the sampling interval, which is the population size, 20, divided by the desired sample size, 10.) Since k is 2, we next randomly select a number from 1 to 2. Assume that we randomly selected the number 2. Therefore, the 10 people in the sample will be persons 2, 4, 6, 8, 10, 12, 14, 16, 18, and 20. The sampled elements are marked by asterisks in Figure 7.4. That includes five principals and five assistant principals. We have a proportional stratified sample with 10 people.[5]

Disproportional Stratified Sampling   So far, we have focused on proportional stratified sampling. Sometimes, however, you might need to select a **disproportional stratified sample.** That is, you might want to select a larger percentage of certain groups of people than you would obtain if you used proportional stratified sampling. For example, you might want 50 percent of your sample to be African Americans and 50 percent to be European Americans. Because only 12 percent of the general population in the United States is African American and because European Americans are a much larger percent than 50, you would definitely not get a 50/50 split using proportional stratified sampling. Therefore, you would oversample African Americans and undersample European Americans if you decided to obtain a

■ **Disproportional stratified sampling** A type of stratified sampling in which the sample proportions are made to be different from the population proportions on the stratification variable

▧ **FIGURE 7.4**

A sampling frame set up for proportional stratified sampling using systematic sampling[a]

Element 1	Principal 1
Element 2*	Principal 2
Element 3	Principal 3
Element 4*	Principal 4
Element 5	Principal 5
Element 6*	Principal 6
Element 7	Principal 7
Element 8*	Principal 8
Element 9	Principal 9
Element 10*	Principal 10
Element 11	Assistant Principal 1
Element 12*	Assistant Principal 2
Element 13	Assistant Principal 3
Element 14*	Assistant Principal 4
Element 15	Assistant Principal 5
Element 16*	Assistant Principal 6
Element 17	Assistant Principal 7
Element 18*	Assistant Principal 8
Element 19	Assistant Principal 9
Element 20*	Assistant Principal 10

[a]Notice how all of the principals are listed first and then all of the assistant principals are listed in this sampling frame. The sampling frame has been ordered according to administrative status (a categorical variable composed of principals and assistant principals).

50/50 split. Notice that you would be selecting individuals disproportional to their sizes in the population—that's why it is called disproportional stratified sampling. Disproportional stratified sampling in often used when the research interest lies more in comparing groups than in making generalizations about the total population. As we will mention later, if you use disproportional stratified sampling and also want to generalize to the total population, weighting procedures must be used. Disproportional stratified sampling is also sometimes used when certain groups in the population are very small; hence, you oversample these groups to ensure that you have adequate sample sizes.

Here is an example in which a disproportional stratified sample might be needed. Suppose you work at a traditionally female college of 5,000 students that recently started accepting males and the number of females still far outweighs the number of males. Let's assume that 90 percent of the students (4,500) are female and only 10 percent of the students (500) are male. If you are mainly interested in comparing males and females or in obtaining large samples of both females and males, then you might wish to select the same number of males as females. That is, you might opt for a disproportional stratified sample. Let's say you have the resources to obtain a sample size of 300. In this case, you might decide to select an equal number of females and males (150 females and 150 males). This way, comparisons between females and males will be based on similar sample sizes for both groups. Furthermore, we have fully 150 males and 150 females, which might be considered adequate sample sizes given your monetary resources.

It is important to understand that when disproportional stratified sampling is used, statements cannot be made about the total population without weighting because the relative sizes of the sample strata do not represent the relative sizes of the groups in the population. Weighting is something that statisticians do to provide less weight to the smaller strata so that they better represent the smaller strata in the population. Without weighting, you can make statements only about separate groups and make comparisons between the groups. Sometimes this is all researchers want to do.

An example should show the problem of trying to generalize to a total population from a disproportional stratified sample. If 150 females and 150 males are asked for their opinions about, say, female sports, it is quite possible that females and males will have different opinions on the subject. For example, assume that from interviews with the females we find out that fully 75 percent support equal funding for men's and women's basketball teams. However, on the basis of our interviews with the males, we find that only 25 percent of them support equal funding. At this point, we can state that, based on our sample, we believe that 75 percent of the females in the population support equal funding and only 25 percent of the males support equal funding. To find out what percentage of the support applies to the total population without specifying gender, a novice researcher might try to use the 300 people in the sample and calculate the total support. The conclusion would be that 50 percent of the people in the student population support equal funding. However, this number does not represent the total population of 5,000 students because we had far too many males in our sample. To get a more accurate reading of the population using our sample, we have to weight the sample to make it representative by giving females a weight of 90 percent and males a weight of 10 percent. When this is done, the new estimate of support in the population becomes fully 70 percent in support. The earlier estimate was much too low. The point here is that you cannot generalize to the full population using disproportional stratified sampling unless you adjust the sample sizes' weights.

Cluster Random Sampling

Cluster sampling is a form of sampling in which **clusters** (a collective type of unit that includes multiple elements, such as schools, churches, classrooms, universities, households, and city blocks) rather than single unit elements (such as individual students, teachers, counselors, administrators, and parents) are randomly selected. For example, a school is a cluster because it is composed of many individual students. At some point, cluster sampling always involves randomly selecting clusters (multiple-unit elements) rather than single-unit elements. For example, in cluster sampling one might randomly select classrooms. A classroom is a cluster because it is a collective unit composed of many single units (i.e., students). In the other sampling techniques discussed in this chapter, single units (individuals) were always the objects of selection, rather than collective units (clusters). Cluster sampling is just like simple random sampling except that rather than taking a random sample of *individuals* you take a random sample of *clusters*.

Cluster sampling requires a larger sample size than simple random sampling, systematic sampling, or stratified sampling. Nonetheless, there are many occasions when cluster sampling

■ **Cluster sampling**
Type of sampling in which clusters are randomly selected
■ **Cluster**
A collective type of unit that includes multiple elements

is preferred. In general, cluster sampling will be less accurate than simple random sampling, but at the same time, cluster sampling can be less costly. The tradeoff between cost and accuracy is prominent in cluster sampling situations. Often the importance of cost and time outweighs the loss in accuracy. For example, cluster sampling is often used when the elements in the population are geographically spread out. When you need to conduct in-person interviews, cluster sampling will result in reduced travel costs, reduced interviewer costs, and a reduced time period needed to physically interview all the people in the sample. If a population is geographically dispersed (as in the United States), the physical act of driving to every person's house in a simple random sample to conduct an interview will be very difficult to carry out. On the other hand, if you were conducting telephone interviews, you would *not* need to use cluster sampling. You could easily call from virtually anywhere in the United States.

An additional reason for cluster sampling is that sometimes a sampling frame of all the people in the population will not be available. When this is the case, you might be able to locate naturally occurring groups of sampling elements, such as classrooms, mental health agencies, census blocks, street maps, and voting districts. Lists of these clusters are usually available, or they can be developed without too much effort. After a sample of clusters is randomly selected from the list of all the clusters in the population, you only need to develop lists of the elements in the randomly selected clusters that were selected. There is no need to identify everyone in the entire population. Developing a list of the people in a subset of population clusters is much easier than developing a list of *all* people in all clusters (i.e., the entire population).

Now let's do some examples of cluster sampling. In the most simple case of cluster sampling, **one-stage cluster sampling,** a set of clusters is randomly selected from the larger set of all clusters in the population. For example, you might take a random sample of 10 schools from all of the schools in a city. Typically, simple random sampling, systematic sampling, or stratified random sampling is used to select the clusters. After the clusters are selected, all the elements (e.g., people) in the selected clusters are included in the sample. Sampling is therefore only conducted at one stage. Here's an example. Let's say you are interested in getting a sample of 250 fifth-grade students in a public school system composed of 80 classrooms. Further, assume there are 2,000 fifth-grade students in the system. Finally, assume that there are approximately 25 students in each classroom. To reduce interviewing and travel time you may choose to randomly select 10 clusters (10 fifth-grade classrooms) and interview all the students in these classes. You will have to visit only 10 classrooms. This will result in a sample including approximately 250 fifth-grade students (with completed sample size depending on the response rate). If, on the other hand, you had taken a simple random sample of students (rather than classrooms), you would have needed to go to far more than 10 classrooms.

In **two-stage cluster sampling,** sampling is done at two stages rather than at one. In stage one, a set of clusters is randomly selected from all of the clusters. In stage two, a random sample of elements is drawn from each of the clusters selected in stage one. For example, 25 classrooms (clusters) could be randomly sampled from the list of clusters. If all students in the 25 classrooms were included as in a one-stage cluster sample, the sample size would be 625 (25 classrooms times 25 students per classroom = 625). Just as before, however, we want to select a sample of size 250. Therefore, at stage two, 10 students could be randomly selected from each of the 25 classrooms. The outcome would be a cluster random sample of 250 students.

At this point, it is important to note that we have assumed that all the classrooms are composed of approximately 25 students. However, it is often *not* the case that clusters are of

■ **One-stage cluster sampling**
A set of randomly selected clusters in which all the elements in the selected clusters are included in the sample

■ **Two-stage cluster sampling**
A set of clusters is randomly selected and then a random sample of elements is drawn from each of the clusters selected in stage one

approximately equal sizes. As a result, in selecting clusters, a technique called **probability proportional to size** (PPS) is frequently utilized. Basically, this more advanced technique is used to give large clusters a larger chance of being selected and smaller clusters a smaller chance of being selected. Then a fixed number of individuals (e.g., 10) is randomly selected from each of the selected clusters. This approach, though more advanced, is the route that has to be taken to ensure that all people in the population have an equal chance of being selected. In other words, PPS is an equal probability selection method technique. And remember, equal probability selection methods produce representative samples. To use this advanced technique, you will need to go to a more advanced book on sampling or get help from a statistical consultant at your college or university. The important point for you to remember here is that if you want a representative sample, then probability proportional to size must be used when the clusters are unequal in size. For your convenience, we include a table with many useful web links relevant to quantitative research sampling (Table 7.1).

■ **Probability proportional to size**
A type of two-stage cluster sampling in which each cluster's chance of being selected in stage one depends on its population size

TABLE 7.1 Survey Research Sites Providing Useful Sampling Information and Links

Address	Name
www.isr.umich.edu/src	Survey Research Center at University of Michigan's Institute for Social Research
www.norc.uchicago.edu/homepage.htm	The National Opinion Research Center at the University of Chicago
www.wws.princeton.edu/~psrc	Survey Research Center at Princeton University
http://statlab.stat.yale.edu	Social Science Statistical Lab at Yale
www.indiana.edu/~csr	Indiana University Center for Survey Research
www2.irss.unc.edu/irss/home.asp	The Odum Institute for Research in Social Science at the University of North Carolina
http://filebox.vt.edu/centers/survey/index.html	Virginia Tech Center for Survey Research
http://members.bellatlantic.net/~abelson www.ku.edu/cwis/units/coms2/po/	These two sites provide many useful survey research links.
www.gallup.com	The Gallup Organization
www.surveysampling.com/ssi_home.html	Survey Sampling Inc.
www.aapor.org	The American Association for Public Opinion Research
www.ncpp.org	The National Council on Public Polls

R E V I E W

Q U E S T I O N S

7.5 How do you select a simple random sample?

7.6 What do all of the equal probability selection methods have in common?

7.7 What are the three steps for selecting a systematic sample?

7.8 How do you select a stratified sample?

7.9 What is the difference between proportional and disproportional stratified sampling?

7.10 When might a researcher want to use cluster sampling?

NONRANDOM SAMPLING TECHNIQUES

Convenience Sampling

■ **Convenience sampling**
People who are available, volunteer, or can be easily recruited are included in the sample

Researchers use **convenience sampling** when they include in their sample people that are available or volunteer or can be easily recruited and are willing to participate in the research study. That is, the researcher selects individuals who can be "conveniently selected." It should be noticed that technically speaking, we cannot generalize from a convenience sample to a population. First and most important, not everyone in a population has an equal chance of being included in the sample. Second, it is often not clear what specific population a convenience "sample" comes from.

When convenience samples are used, it is especially important that researchers describe the characteristics of the people participating in their research studies. Sometimes, researchers will even describe the "hypothetical population" that they believe most closely corresponds to their convenience sample. Ultimately, however, it is up to you, the reader of a research article, to examine the characteristics of a convenience sample and decide whom you believe the group of people may represent.

You might be surprised to learn that the majority of experimental researchers do not select random samples. Rather, they tend to use convenience samples. For example, some published research is conducted with undergraduate students enrolled in introductory psychology or educational psychology classes. Here is an example from a study by Turner, Johnson, and Pickering (1996):

> Seventy-nine college students (47 women and 32 men) were recruited from introductory psychology courses. Students participated in research as an option for course credit. The average of the sample was 23.7 yr. (Range = 17 to 52.) Seventy-three percent ($n = 58$) of the participants were Caucasian, 18% (or 14) were black, and the remaining 9% (or 7) were of other ethnic origins. (p. 1053)

Here is another example of a convenience sample:

> Fifty-five fourth-grade and 39 fifth-grade students from two public schools in western New York were included in the study, because their two principals and six teachers agreed to allow them to be pulled out of class individually and their parents gave written permission for their participation. (Gentile, Voelkl, Mt. Pleasant, & Monaco, 1995, p. 190)

Convenience samples are not the optimal way to go, especially when the researcher wants to generalize to a population on the basis of a single study. Nonetheless, researchers are often forced to use convenience samples because of practical constraints.

Quota Sampling

In **quota sampling,** the researcher identifies the major groups or subgroups of interest, determines the number of people to be included in each of these groups, and then selects convenience samples of people for each group. Quota sampling is so named because once the researcher decides how many of certain types of people to include in the sample, he or she then tries to "meet the quotas"; that is, the researcher tries to get the right number of people. If the researcher decides to make the sample proportional to the population on certain characteristics (e.g., gender), then this method of quota sampling will have an apparent similarity to proportional stratified sampling. For example, if a school is composed of 60 percent females and 40 percent males, the researcher might decide to make sure that his or her sample is also 60 percent female and 40 percent male. However, an important difference between quota sampling and stratified random sampling is that once the researcher decides how many people to include in each group, random sampling is *not* used. Although a quota sample might look similar to a population on some characteristics (e.g., the percentage of females and males), it is not a probability sample, and as a result, one's ability to generalize is severely limited.

> ■ **Quota sampling**
> The researcher determines the appropriate sample sizes or quotas for the groups identified as important and takes convenience samples from those groups

Purposive Sampling

In **purposive sampling** (sometimes called judgmental sampling), the researcher specifies the characteristics of a population of interest and then tries to locate individuals who have those characteristics (e.g., Johnson, 1995). For example, a researcher might be interested in adult females over the age of 65 who are enrolled in a continuing education program. Once the group is located, the researcher asks those who meet the inclusion criteria to participate in the research study. When enough participants are obtained, the researcher does not ask anyone else to participate. In short, purposive sampling is a nonrandom sampling technique in which the researcher solicits persons with specific characteristics to participate in a research study. Here is an example of purposive sampling from a published research article:

> ■ **Purposive sampling**
> The researcher specifies the characteristics of the population of interest and locates individuals with those characteristics

> A purposive sample of adult returning graduate students in two schools at a large midwestern university was selected for this study. Criteria for the sample were threefold: adult students were 25 years of age and older, were returning to school after an absence of at least 3 years, and were adding the student role to their other adult roles. Students in the sample were enrolled in a mix of day, evening, and weekend programs. (Flannery, 1991, p. 37)

Purposive sampling has the same limitations as any nonrandom sampling method. Specifically, the ability to generalize from a sample to a population on the basis of a single research study is severely limited. The optimal situation would be when the researcher specifies the criteria potential participants must meet to be included in a research study but then attempts to obtain a random sample of these people. However, this is not always possible or practical.

Snowball Sampling

■ **Snowball sampling**
Each research partici-
pant is asked to iden-
tify other potential
research participants

In **snowball sampling,** each research participant that volunteers to be in a research study is asked to identify one or more additional people who meet certain characteristics and may be willing to participate in the research study. Tallerico (1993) used snowball sampling to find 20 females who had once been school superintendents and four "informants" who had known a female superintendent so that they could study why females left this position. Only a few individuals might be identified in the beginning of a research study as being appropriate, willing, and able participants. Over time, however, as each new participant suggests someone else who might participate, the sample becomes larger and larger. The sample can be viewed metaphorically as a snowball that is rolling down a hill, getting bigger and bigger. This sampling approach can be especially useful when you need to locate members of hard-to-find populations or when no sampling frame is available.

> **R E V I E W**
>
> **Q U E S T I O N**
>
> **7.11** Are convenience samples used very often by experimental researchers?

RANDOM SELECTION AND RANDOM ASSIGNMENT

■ **Random selection**
Randomly selecting a
group of people from a
population

Random selection has been the focus of this chapter. Random selection is just another word that means random sampling. As you now know, simple random sampling is like pulling names from a hat. The names you pull out of the hat make up the random sample. We also discussed three specific methods of random sampling that are variations of simple random sampling (systematic sampling, stratified sampling, and cluster sampling). The purpose of random selection is to allow you to make generalizations from a sample to a population. Because the random selection methods produce representative samples, you are able to generalize from the sample to the population. This form of generalization is sometimes called statistical generalization.

■ **Random assignment**
Randomly assigning a
set of people to differ-
ent groups

Research
Navigator.c⊛m

random
assignment

On the other hand, we briefly discussed **random assignment** in Chapter 1 when we described experimental research. Random assignment involves taking a set of people and randomly *assigning* them to the groups in the experiment. Recall that random assignment is used in experimental research to make the groups being compared similar on "all possible factors" at the beginning of the experiment. Then, if the groups differ after they receive the different treatments, the researcher can attribute the difference to the independent variable because this was the only factor on which the groups systematically differed (e.g., one group may receive a pill and another group may receive a placebo). As we explained earlier in this chapter when we discussed convenience samples, many experiments are not based on random samples. Rather, they are frequently based on convenience samples. Therefore, although you *can* make a statement about the effect of the independent variable on the dependent variable (e.g., the effect of the experimental pill on behavioral outbursts) in an experiment that has random assignment but does not have random selection, you will *not* be able to directly generalize from such an experiment. There is a way out of this problem in experimental research, however: through the use of replication logic.

When experimental findings are *replicated* in different places at different times with different people, the findings about the causal effect of the independent variable on the dependent variable can be generalized to some degree, even when random selection is not used. That is because when we repeatedly see the same causal result (e.g., the experimental pill consistently reduces behavioral disorders), evidence that the causal relationship is real and that it applies to many people is obtained. Nonetheless, the results from a *single* research study based on a convenience sample cannot be statistically generalized to any known population. The strongest possible experimental design is one in which the participants are randomly selected from a population *and* are randomly assigned to groups.

7.12 If your goal is to generalize from a sample to a population, which is more important: random selection or random assignment?

REVIEW

QUESTION

DETERMINING THE SAMPLE SIZE WHEN RANDOM SAMPLING IS USED

When you design a research study, you will inevitably ask how big your sample should be. The simplest answer is that the larger the sample size, the better, because larger samples result in smaller sampling errors, which means that your sample values (the statistics) will be closer to the true population values (the parameters). In the extreme case, sampling error would be zero if you included the complete population in your study rather than drawing a sample. As a rule of thumb, we recommend using the whole population when the population is 100 or less in size. That way, without too much expense, you can be completely confident that you know about the total population. Our second answer to the question of sample size is that you may want to examine the research literature that is most similar to the research you hope to conduct and see how many research participants are used.

We have provided a table with recommended sample sizes for your convenience in Figure 7.5. The sample sizes provided there are usually adequate. The recommended sample sizes are given for populations ranging in size from very small (e.g., 10) to extremely large (e.g., 500 million). All you need to know to use the table is the approximate size of the population from which you plan on drawing your sample. You can see in Figure 7.5 that if the population is composed of 500 people, you need to randomly select 217 people. Likewise, if the population is composed of 1,500 people, you need to randomly select 306 people. We now make several additional points about random sampling from populations.

Research
Navigator.com

**sample size
and power**

1. If you examine the numbers in Figure 7.5, you will notice that a researcher must randomly select a large percentage of the population when the population is small. However, as the population becomes larger and larger, the percentage of the population needed becomes smaller and smaller.

FIGURE 7.5   Sample sizes for various populations of size 10 to 500 million

N stands for the size of the population. *n* stands for the size of the recommended sample. The sample sizes are based on the 95 percent confidence level.

N	n	N	n	N	n	N	n	N	n
10	10	110	86	300	169	950	274	4,500	354
15	14	120	92	320	175	1,000	278	5,000	357
20	19	130	97	340	181	1,100	285	6,000	361
25	24	140	103	360	186	1,200	291	7,000	364
30	28	150	108	380	191	1,300	297	8,000	367
35	32	160	113	400	196	1,400	302	9,000	368
40	36	170	118	420	201	1,500	306	10,000	370
45	40	180	123	440	205	1,600	310	15,000	375
50	44	190	127	460	210	1,700	313	20,000	377
55	48	200	132	480	214	1,800	317	30,000	379
60	52	210	136	500	217	1,900	320	40,000	380
65	56	220	140	550	226	2,000	322	50,000	381
70	59	230	144	600	234	2,200	327	75,000	382
75	63	240	148	650	242	2,400	331	100,000	384
80	66	250	152	700	248	2,600	335	250,000	384
85	70	260	155	750	254	2,800	338	500,000	384
90	73	270	159	800	260	3,000	341	1,000,000	384
95	76	280	162	850	265	3,500	346	10,000,000	384
100	80	290	165	900	269	4,000	351	500,000,000	384

Adapted from R. V. Krejecie and D. W. Morgan, "Determining Sample Size for Research Activities," *Educational and Psychological Measurement, 30*(3), p. 608, copyright © 1970 by Sage Publications, Inc. Reprinted by Permission of Sage Publications, Inc.

2. The more homogeneous a population, the smaller the sample size can be. A homogeneous population is one that is composed of similar people. In fact, if everyone were exactly alike, you would need only one person in your sample. Conversely, the more heterogeneous a population (the more dissimilar the people are), the larger the sample size needs to be.

3. The more categories or breakdowns you want to make in your data analysis, the larger the sample size needed. A researcher might be interested in determining the percentage of people in a city who plan on voting for a certain school superintendent candidate. But what if the researcher also wanted to know the percentage of females planning on voting for the candidate and the percentage of males planning on voting for the candidate? The original population has now been divided into two subpopulations of interest, and you would need an adequate sample size for each and every subpopulation. Therefore, a larger sample size would be needed. If you planned on making many additional breakdowns in your data analysis, the sample size would need to be increased quite sizeably.

4. In the later chapter on inferential statistics (Chapter 16), we will explain the idea of confidence intervals. For now, we will just say that sometimes researchers use a statistical procedure to estimate a population value, and they will provide an interval of values that they believe contains the population value. For example, you might hear a news reporter say that 55 percent of the people in a city support the school superintendent's decision to adopt school uniforms, *plus or minus 5 percent,* and that the "level of confidence" is 95 percent. The statement is that the true population value is probably somewhere between 50 and 60 percent. You will learn in a later chapter that the more people are included in a sample, the smaller the confidence interval will be. For example, if more people were included in the sample, one might be able to say that 55 percent of the people support the decision, *plus or minus 3 percent.* That is, the true population value is probably somewhere between 52 and 58 percent. The rule is, the larger the sample size the greater the precision of statements about the population based on the sample. That is, the bigger the sample the better.

5. Assume that you are planning to measure a relationship or the effect of an independent variable on a dependent variable. If you expect the relationship or effect to be relatively *weak,* then you will need a *larger* sample size. That's because there is less "noise" or "random error" in larger samples.

6. The more efficient the random sampling method, the smaller the sample size needs to be. As we discussed earlier in this chapter, stratified random sampling tends to need slightly fewer people than simple random sampling. On the other hand, cluster random sampling tends to require slightly more people than simple random sampling.

7. The last consideration mentioned here is that some of the people in your original sample will refuse to participate in your research study. In other words, your final sample may end up being smaller than you had intended. If you can guess approximately what percentage of the people will actually participate (the response rate), you can use the following formula to adjust your original sample size. The numerator is the number of people you want to have in your research study. The denominator is the proportion of people you believe will agree to participate.

$$\frac{\text{Desired sample size}}{\text{Proportion likely to respond}} = \begin{array}{l}\text{Number of people to include} \\ \text{in your original sample}\end{array}$$

For example, say that you want a sample of size 75 and you expect that only 80 percent of the people in your original sample will actually participate in your research study when you ask them. All you need to do is to divide 75 by .80, and you have the number of people you need to include in your sample. You will need 94 people. As another example, you want a sample of size 50 people, and you expect that 70 percent of them will participate. Can you get the number of people you need to include in your original sample? The numerator is 50, your desired sample size. The denominator is .70. And 50 divided by .70 is equal to 71. You will need 71 people. Just get your calculator, and you will not find this too difficult.

7.13 If your population size is 250,000, how many participants will you need, at a minimum, for your research study? (Hint: Look at Figure 7.5.)

REVIEW

QUESTION

SAMPLING IN QUALITATIVE RESEARCH

Qualitative researchers must first decide whom or what they want to study. This initial task is based on consideration of which populations or phenomena are relevant to the research focus being proposed or developed. The researcher typically defines a set of criteria or attributes that the people to be studied must possess and uses these criteria to distinguish the people of potential interest from those people who should be excluded from consideration. Once these inclusion boundaries are set, the researcher knows who he or she wishes to study and can then attempt to locate and obtain the sample.

Research
Navigator.c⊕m

qualitative research and sampling

Two well-known qualitative researchers, Margaret LeCompte and Judith Preissle (1993), call the overall sampling strategy used in qualitative research *criterion-based selection* because the researcher develops inclusion criteria to be used in selecting people or other units (e.g., schools). Another well-known qualitative researcher, Michael Patton (1987, 1990), uses the term *purposeful sampling* to describe the same process because individuals or cases are selected that provide the information needed to address the purpose of the research. The terms *criterion-based selection* and *purposeful sampling* are synonyms, and both describe what we earlier called *purposive sampling.* Purposive sampling is used in both quantitative and qualitative research. The other forms of nonprobability sampling previously discussed (snowball sampling, quota sampling, and convenience sampling) are also used in qualitative research.

Although the goal is always to locate information-rich individuals or cases, decisions about whom to study are also affected by logistical constraints, such as the availability of appropriate participants, the accessibility of the potential participants, and the costs of locating the people and enlisting their participation. Researchers virtually always face practical constraints such as these when they decide whom to include in their research studies. The researcher should pick a sample that can be used to meet the purpose of the research study and answer research questions while meeting cost and other constraints. Tradeoffs will always be present.

Many different types of sampling are used in qualitative research. We rely here mainly on the discussions by LeCompte and Preissle (1993) and Patton (1987, 1990). The first type is called **comprehensive sampling,** which means that all cases (individuals, groups, settings, or other phenomena) are examined in the research study. As you can see, this guarantees representativeness because everyone is included in the study. It can also be very expensive and quite impractical except for very small populations that are relatively easy to locate.

- **Comprehensive sampling**
  Including all cases in the research study
- **Maximum variation sampling**
  Purposively selecting a wide range of cases

Another form of sampling that qualitative researchers sometimes use is called **maximum variation sampling.** In this form of sampling, a wide range of cases (individuals, groups, settings, or other phenomena) are purposively selected so that all types of cases along one or more dimensions are included in the research. One reason for using this approach is to help ensure that no one can claim that you excluded certain types of cases. In addition, during data analysis, the qualitative researcher can search for a central theme or pattern that occurs across the cases. Something all the cases have in common might be identified. For example, while studying the organizational culture of a local school, an ethnographic researcher might identify certain core values and beliefs common to most, if not all, of the teachers in the school. Here is another example from a journal article by Fisher

(1993). Fisher was interested in describing the developmental changes experienced by older adults:

> Initially five sites were selected at which to conduct interviews: two senior centers in an urban county and two senior centers and a nursing home located in adjacent counties which combined suburban and rural characteristics. These sites were selected in order to increase the probability that persons available for interviewing would represent a broad age spectrum with diverse backgrounds and experiences. (p. 78)

In **homogeneous sample selection,** a relatively small and homogeneous case or set of cases is selected for intensive study. Focus group researchers commonly use this procedure. In focus group research, a small homogeneous group of around six or seven people is interviewed in a group situation on a topic of common interest. The group interview and discussion typically last about two hours. The focus group facilitator is able to gain an in-depth understanding of how the people in the group think about a topic by generating group discussion through the use of open-ended questions and targeted followups. In general, when specific subgroups are targeted for a research study or as a component of a larger study, the researchers may have relied on homogeneous sample selection.

- **Homogeneous sample selection**
  Selecting a small and homogeneous case or set of cases for intensive study

In **extreme case sampling,** the extremes, or poles, of some characteristic are identified, and then cases representing the extremes are selected for examination. The strategy is to select cases from the extremes and then to compare them. For example, you might examine a very large classroom and a very small classroom. Or perhaps you are interested in teacher stress, so you decide to interview teachers with very high stress and teachers with very low stress. The logic is that these extreme cases may provide particularly rich sources of information. In general, you might locate and compare "outstanding cases" with "notable failures" and attempt to determine what circumstances led to these outcomes (Patton, 1990). For example, you might compare the teaching environment created by an outstanding teacher with that created by a notably ineffective teacher.

- **Extreme-case sampling**
  Identifying the extremes or poles of some characteristic and then selecting cases representing these extremes for examination

In **typical-case sampling,** the researcher lists the criteria that describe a typical or average case and then finds an example to study. The researcher should speak to several experts to try to get a consensus on what example(s) is(are) typical of the phenomenon and should therefore be studied. For example, you might interview several people at your school and ask them how they would describe the typical first-grade school teacher. They might describe this person in terms of characteristics such as age, gender, teaching style, and number of years of experience. Sometimes even in a research study in which many cases are examined, illustrating a typical case in the final report helps the reader to make more sense of the findings.

- **Typical-case sampling**
  Selecting what are believed to be average cases

In **critical-case sampling,** cases that can be used to make a point particularly well or are known to be particularly important are selected for study. According to Patton (1990), "a clue to the existence of a critical case is a statement to the effect that 'if it happens there, it will happen anywhere,' or, vice versa, 'if it doesn't happen there, it won't happen anywhere.' " For example, consider a counseling center director who wants to use a new testing procedure and wants to see whether counselors can be trained in the testing procedure in a two-hour training session. The director might check to see whether the least talented

- **Critical-case sampling**
  Selecting what are believed to be particularly important cases

counselor can perform the test correctly after the two-hour training session. The director would be acting under the assumption that "if this person can do it, then I feel fairly confident that my other counselors will also be able to do it." Another example is a school superintendent who wants to make a change in a policy that may face resistance in the local schools. The superintendent might decide to select a school where he or she expects the greatest resistance to see whether enacting the policy is feasible in practice.

■ **Negative-case sampling**
Selecting cases that disconfirm the researcher's expectations and generalizations

In **negative-case sampling,** cases that disconfirm the researcher's expectations are purposively selected. For example, in the form of qualitative research called grounded theory, the qualitative researcher typically explores a phenomenon and attempts to inductively build a theory about it by checking out tentative hypotheses and hunches. As the researcher develops a tentative conclusion or generalization based on the data, however, it is important to search for instances in which the generalization does not hold in order to learn more about the boundaries of the generalization and about any potential problems that need to be addressed or qualifications that need to be made. If you are a careful and conscientious qualitative researcher, you must not overlook negative cases. You might find that your original expectation was not generally true and that you need to revise your generalization.

■ **Opportunistic sampling**
Selecting cases when the opportunity occurs

In **opportunistic sampling,** the researcher takes advantage of opportunities during data collection to select important cases. The cases might be critical, negative, extreme, or even typical. The important point is that qualitative research is an ongoing and emergent process, and the researcher might not be able to state in advance of the research everyone and everything that will be included in the study. The focus might change, and opportunities that could not be foreseen might occur. The effective researcher is one who is quick to discern whom to talk to and what to focus on while collecting the data in the field. The term *opportunistic sampling* was coined to refer to this process.

■ **Mixed purposeful sampling**
The mixing of more than one sampling strategy

The last form of sampling listed here is **mixed purposeful sampling.** This is a term that Patton coined to refer to the mixing of more than one sampling strategy. A researcher might, for example, conduct a quantitative survey research study based on a random sample but also use typical case selection to obtain an illuminating case to describe in the final report. Or a researcher might conduct a purely qualitative research study and start with maximum variation sampling, discover a general pattern or finding in the data, and then use negative-case selection to determine the generality of the pattern. Mixed purposeful sampling is also likely to be used when a researcher uses data triangulation—examining multiple data sources, which might be selected according to different sampling methods.

In concluding this section, note that the different sampling methods (quantitative and qualitative) can be used in any type of research and can be mixed in single research studies. For more detail on sampling in mixed method research you can consult the *Handbook of Mixed Methods Research* (Tashakkori & Teddlie, 2003).

REVIEW

QUESTION

7.14 Sampling in qualitative research is similar to which type of sampling in quantitative research?

SUMMARY

Sampling is the process of drawing a sample from a population. When we sample, we study the characteristics of a subset (called the sample) selected from a larger group (called the population) in order to understand the characteristics of the larger group (the population). If the researcher selects a sample from a population by using a random sampling technique, then the sample will be representative of the total population—it will be similar to the population. Therefore, after the researcher determines the characteristics of a randomly selected sample, he or she can generalize from the sample to the population; that is, the researcher can make statements about the population based on the sample. A sample is usually much smaller in size than a population; hence, sampling can save time and money. The major random sampling methods are simple random sampling, systematic sampling, stratified random sampling, and cluster random sampling. Each of these random sampling methods is an equal probability selection method, which means that each individual in the population has an equal chance of being included in the sample. Because each individual has an equal chance of being included in the sample, all of these sampling methods can be used to produce representative samples. Researchers do not always, however, use the most powerful sampling methods. Frequently, nonrandom samples are drawn. The four types of nonrandom sampling discussed are convenience sampling, quota sampling, purposive sampling, and snowball sampling. In addition, several kinds of sampling primarily used by qualitative researchers are discussed: purposive sampling, comprehensive sampling, maximum variation sampling, homogeneous sampling, extreme-case sampling, typical-case sampling, critical-case sampling, negative-case sampling, opportunistic sampling, and mixed purposeful sampling.

KEY TERMS

biased sample (p. 198)
census (p. 198)
cluster (p. 211)
cluster sampling (p. 211)
comprehensive sampling (p. 220)
convenience sampling (p. 214)
critical-case sampling (p. 221)
disproportional stratified
    sample (p. 209)
element (p. 199)
equal probability selection
    method (p. 200)
extreme-case sampling (p. 221)
generalize (p. 197)
homogeneous sample
    selection (p. 221)
k (p. 204)
maximum variation sampling (p. 220)

mixed purposeful sampling (p. 222)
N (p. 199)
n (p. 199)
negative-case sampling (p. 222)
one-stage cluster sampling (p. 212)
opportunistic sampling (p. 212)
parameter (p. 199)
periodicity (p. 207)
population (p. 199)
probability proportional to
    size (p. 213)
proportional stratified
    sampling (p. 207)
purposive sampling (p. 215)
quota sampling (p. 215)
random assignment (p. 216)
random selection (p. 216)
representative sample (p. 198)

response rate (p. 199)
sample (p. 199)
sampling (p. 197)
sampling error (p. 199)
sampling frame (p. 199)
sampling interval (p. 204)
simple random sample (p. 200)
snowball sampling (p. 216)
starting point (p. 204)
statistic (p. 199)
stratification variable (p. 207)
stratified sampling (p. 207)
survey research (p. 197)
systematic sample (p. 204)
table of random numbers (p. 201)
two-stage cluster sampling (p. 212)
typical-case sampling (p. 221)

DISCUSSION QUESTIONS

1. What is the difference between random selection and random assignment? Give an example of each.
2. Who do you think is more interested in using a random sampling method: a pollster running a political campaign or an experimental researcher who is studying a cause and effect relationship between two variables? Explain.
3. A local news radio station has people call in and voice their opinions on a local issue. Do you see any potential sources of bias resulting from this sampling approach?
4. Following are some examples of sampling. Identify the type of sample that is used in each.
   a. An educational psychology teacher uses all of her students to fill out her research questionnaire.
   b. An educational psychology teacher obtains a student directory that is supposed to include the students at your university. She determines the sampling interval, randomly selects a number

   from 1 to k, and includes every kth person in her sample.
   c. An educational researcher obtains a list of all the middle schools in your state. He then randomly selects a sample of 25 schools. Finally, he randomly selects 30 students from each of the selected schools. (That's a sample size of $25 \times 30 = 750$.) By the way, what are some potential problems with this procedure?
   d. A researcher takes a random sample of 100 males from a local high school and a random sample of 100 females from the same local high school. By the way, what are some potential problems with this procedure if the researcher wants to generalize from the 200 people to the high school population?
   e. Is simple random sampling the only equal probability sampling method? If not, what are some other equal probability sampling methods?

RESEARCH EXERCISES

1. Using the table of random numbers in Figure 7.1, draw a simple random sample of size 20 from the sampling frame in Figure 7.2.
   a. What is the average age of the 20 people in your sample?
   b. Now draw a systematic sample of size 20 from the sampling frame in Figure 7.2 and calculate the average age. What is the average age in your systematic sample?
   c. Compare the two sample averages you just obtained. Which one was closer to the population mean?
   d. Compare the sample averages you got above with the population parameter (i.e., the average age for all 60 people listed in Figure 7.2). What was the sampling error for your simple random sample? (Hint: If you subtract the sample average from the population average, you obtain the sampling error.) Finally, what was the sampling error for your systematic sample?
2. Go to Research Navigator (from the book's companion web page) and search the engine located there that is called "New York Times on the Web." Find some articles on an issue involving sampling, and write a short paper summarizing the positions. Be sure to include your own position.
3. During the 1990s, Congress discussed eliminating the process of enumerating every single individual in the United States and instead using random sampling techniques. What side are you on: the side that said "Do a census" or the side that said "Do a survey"? You might check out the following short papers at the American Statistical Association at these links: www.amstat.org/pressroom/technical.html and www.amstat.org/pressroom/prescorner.html.

RELEVANT INTERNET SITES

http://www.surveysystem.com/sscalc.htm
A sample size calculator.

http://www.randomizer.org/
A program that can be used for random selection and random assignment.

www.ssisamples.com/ssi.x2o$ssi_gen.faq_overview
Answers to some frequently asked questions about sampling from a sampling corporation.

www.graphpad.com/quickcalcs/randomize1.cfm
A program for conducting random assignment.

RECOMMENDED READING

Henry, G. T. (1990). *Practical sampling.* Thousand Oaks, CA: Sage.

Kalton, G. (1983). *Introduction to survey sampling.* Thousand Oaks, CA: Sage.

Schonlau, M., Fricker, R. D., & Elliott, M. N. (2002). *Conducting research surveys via e-mail and the Web.* Santa Monica, CA: Rand.

ENDNOTES

1. Sampling with replacement and sampling without replacement are both equal probability selection methods (EPSEM) (Cochran, 1977, p. 18; Kish, 1965, pp. 39–40). Sampling without replacement, however, is slightly more efficient in practice.

2. Systematic sampling is included as a type of random sampling for three reasons. First, the starting point is randomly selected. Second, it is an EPSEM (Kalton, 1983). Third, it is typically as good or better than a simple random sample of equal size (Scheaffer, Mendenhall, & Ott, 1996, pp. 252–254).

3. The sampling interval may not be a whole number in practice. A common solution is to round it off. If this does not work very well, see page 17 in Kalton (1983).

4. When lists are ordered in this way, they are said to be stratified. Often the researcher will stratify the list to improve the sampling results. Sometimes the list is already stratified without the researcher doing anything at all. This usually improves the sample because of a process called *implicit stratification* (Jaeger, 1984; Sudman, 1976).

5. The stratification variable has been categorical in our examples (e.g., grade level, gender). You can also select a proportional stratified sample with quantitative stratification variables (e.g., age, IQ). Just reorder the list by the quantitative stratification variable and take a systematic sample. For example, in the case of age, reorder the names in your original list from the youngest person to the oldest person and take a systematic sample from your new list.

6. It has been erroneously suggested by some methodologists that researchers should sample 10 percent of a population or 10 percent of the people in each group in a population. You should avoid this rule of thumb. Sampling experts make it clear that sample size should not be based on a percentage of a population. You can easily see the problem with the "10 percent rule" by applying it to a small population of 50 people and to a large population of 250 million people. In the former, the rule would say take a sample of size 5. In the latter, the rule would say take a sample of 25 million people!

8

Validity of
Research Results

LEARNING OBJECTIVES

To be able to

- Explain the meaning of confounding variables.
- Explain the meaning of statistical conclusion validity, internal validity, and external validity and their importance in the research process.
- Identify and explain the types of evidence that are needed to reach a causal conclusion.
- Explain the threats to internal validity and be able to identify when they might exist in a research study.
- Explain the threats to external validity and when they might exist in a research study.
- Explain the role of operationalization of constructs in research.
- Identify and explain the types of validity used in qualitative research.

For generations, the road to becoming a teacher has required a college degree with a major in education. Traditionally, this academic training has required a two- to three-month internship in a classroom. After the completion of the internship and the degree requirements, the aspiring teacher applies for a position in a school district or private school and reports for duty following the signing of a contract. In November 2001, the *Christian Science Monitor* (Savoye, 2001) reported that the Chicago public school district was going to try a different approach to the internship portion of the traditional training model. This altered approach was spurred by a general belief that the traditional internship was not long enough, intense enough, or comprehensive enough.

In September 2001, the Chicago public schools district opened the Chicago Academy with the objective of training prospective teachers over the course of a full school year. This training program will allow the student teachers to learn from many of the teachers at the school in addition to their own master teacher. To implement the most effective training, the academy was modified so that all classrooms have a small adjoining anteroom with mirrored, one-way glass that will allow the master teacher to step out of the classroom and observe the student teacher alone with the students. This observation phase was included to facilitate skill building that student teachers need but often do not receive such as learning to pause so that students can absorb a concept, refrain from calling on the same child too frequently, and learning how to move around the class rather than remaining stationary.

The goals of the initiative taken by the Chicago public schools are laudatory and to be commended. However, just because such an initiative is implemented and seems to be a worthy endeavor does not mean that the stated goals will be accomplished. The only way one can determine whether the stated goals are being met is to conduct a research study with the purpose of determining whether the quality of instruction is enhanced by providing the more intense, 10-month training program and whether students who participate in this program remain in the profession longer.

Let's assume that a study was conducted to test the benefit of providing prospective teachers with the more intensive 10-month internship program and the results of this study revealed that these students not only were better teachers, but also stayed in the profession longer. Such results would have important implications and would suggest that other teacher education programs should incorporate a similar program. Before drawing such a conclusion and recommending that teacher education programs incorporate a 10-month internship program, it is wise to carefully examine all facets of the study. There might be components of the study other than the intensive internship that could also account for the observed outcome. For example, assume that the students who were selected to participate in the program were the brighter and more motivated students. This selective participation and not the intensive internship might have produced the more effective teachers. Similarly, if the students participating in the experimental program were students who were more dedicated to the profession of teaching, this factor could account for their greater longevity in the teaching profession. In any study, such variables would be extraneous variables. These extraneous variables must be controlled to identify the effect of an independent variable. In this chapter, we will discuss some of the extraneous variables that can creep into a study and compromise the validity of the inferences that we can make from the data we collected.

To conduct a research study that will provide an answer to your research question, you must develop a plan, outline, or strategy to use in data collection. You naturally want to develop a plan or strategy that will allow you to collect data that will lead to a valid conclusion. To accomplish this goal, you must have knowledge of the factors that will lead to both valid and invalid conclusions. These factors are somewhat different depending on whether you are conducting a quantitative study or a qualitative study.

VALIDITY ISSUES IN THE DESIGN OF QUANTITATIVE RESEARCH

In Chapter 1, we stated that description, exploration, explanation, prediction, and influence represent the objectives of research. To accomplish these objectives, we must design research studies that allow us to collect uncontaminated data. This seems to be a straightforward requirement. In most quantitative studies, we want to identify the effect created by some independent variable and to be able to generalize the results beyond the confines of the study. However, in every study, there is the possibility that some variable other than the independent variable influenced the dependent variable or limited the ability to generalize the results. For example, if you are investigating the effect of parents' involvement in their child's education (independent variable) on the child's achievement test scores (dependent variable), you probably want to conclude that greater parent involvement results in high achievement test scores. However, if the parents with the greater involvement also have the brightest children, the higher achievement test scores could be due to the child's greater intellect. In such an instance, intellect would be an **extraneous variable,** a variable other than the ones you are specifically studying, which might have confounded the results of the study.

Extraneous variables might or might not introduce a confound. Extraneous variables are confounded when they systematically vary with the independent variable and also influence the dependent variable. It is impossible to draw clear and valid conclusions from the data collected when an uncontrolled **confounding variable** exists.

To illustrate how extraneous variables can confound the outcome of a study and produce ambiguous results, consider a hypothetical "Pepsi Challenge" study. Assume that Pepsi wants to conduct a study demonstrating that its product is preferred over Coke. In this study, research participants are given, in random order, Pepsi in a cup marked with an M and Coke in a cup marked with a Q. The research participants are to drink the beverage in each cup and then identify the one they like more. Now assume that 80 percent of the participants indicate that they prefer the beverage in the cup marked with an M. Pepsi would take this as an indication that their product was preferred over Coke. However, if people are more likely to choose something with the letter M over the letter Q, this could influence their selection of the beverage of choice. If the letter on the cup does influence choice, the results are ambiguous because it is impossible to tell whether the choice was due to the beverage or to the letter that appeared on the cup. This is the type of subtle extraneous variable that can systematically confound the outcome of a study and lead to ambiguous results.

The key component here is that the extraneous variable has to vary systematically with the independent variable and influence the dependent variable to represent a confound. There are many extraneous variables surrounding a study, but they do not represent a con-

■ **Extraneous variable**
Any variable other than the independent variable that might influence the dependent variable

■ **Confounding variable**
An extraneous variable that systematically varies with the independent variable and also influences the dependent variable

Research
Navigator.c⊕m

**confounding
variable**

founding influence. For example, the two beverages in the Pepsi Challenge study could be administered in glasses, paper cups, or Styrofoam containers. The type of container could influence a person's evaluation of the beverage; for example, glasses might result in a more positive evaluation than Styrofoam containers. The type of container could therefore represent an extraneous variable that could influence the beverage of choice. However, it would not be a confounding influence if both beverages were presented in identical containers. In other words, the influence of the extraneous variable of type of container would be constant across all participants. Extraneous variables are not confounding variables when they have the same influence on everyone in the study or are held constant across everyone in the study. Only when they systematically influence one group and not the other or have one influence on one research condition and another on another research condition are they confounding extraneous variables. This type of potential confound can be seen in the Pepsi Challenge study because the Pepsi beverage was contained in the cup with the M, and this might have resulted in people selecting this cup more than the cup with the Q, the one that contained the Coke beverage. Therefore, the letter on the cup was not held constant across participants, and it might have systematically influenced the individuals' choice of the desired beverage.

It is this type of confound that must be eliminated from research studies. Unfortunately, when we conduct research, we do not know which extraneous variables might be confounding variables. Therefore, we have to use our hunches, past research, and general intuition to identify potential confounding variables and then design a study that controls or eliminates the influence of these potential confounds. To eliminate such confounds and produce valid results, you must be aware of the criteria that must be met to conduct an uncontaminated study and have some knowledge of the type of variables that can represent confounding extraneous variables.

In quantitative research there are four types of validity—statistical conclusion, internal, construct, and external—that are used to evaluate the validity of the inferences that can be made from the results of a study.

In this chapter, we will discuss these four types of validity and present some of the threats to these validity types. In reading about these threats, you should realize that not all of them will occur in every study. The likelihood that any one will occur will vary with the context of the study. However, listing these threats serves the valuable function of increasing the probability of your anticipating their existence. If you can anticipate a threat before conducting the study, you can design it in such a way as to rule it out. If you cannot institute design controls, maybe you can measure the threat directly to determine whether it actually operated in the study and then conduct statistical analysis to find out whether it can plausibly account for the observed relationship.

Research Navigator.c⊕m

statistical conclusion validity

▬▬ STATISTICAL CONCLUSION VALIDITY

Statistical conclusion validity refers to the validity with which we can infer that two variables are related and the strength of that relationship. From this definition, you can see that statistical conclusion validity refers to statistical inferences. The first statistical inference is whether a relationship exists between the independent and dependent variables. The second

■ **Statistical conclusion validity**
The ability to infer that the independent and dependent variables are related and the strength of that relationship

statistical inference is an estimate of the magnitude of the relationship between the independent and dependent variables. Both of these inferences rely on statistical tests. Making an inference about whether the variables that are investigated in the study are related typically involves null hypothesis significance testing. We will discuss this in more depth in Chapter 16. Right now, all you need to know is that null hypothesis statistical testing involves making use of statistical tests to decide whether the independent and dependent variables are related. Making an inference about the magnitude of the relationship between the variables involves computing effect size estimates. Effect size estimates are obtained by computing a statistical index that gives an estimate of the strength of the relationship between the independent and dependent variables.

On the surface, it seems as though valid inferences should logically follow if the statistical tests are conducted correctly. However, there are a variety of reasons why a researcher might be wrong when making an inference about the existence of a relationship between two or more variables or the size of the relationship between these variables. We are not going to discuss these threats because they focus primarily on statistical issues that are beyond the scope of this textbook. We do want you to realize that the inferences you make from the results of statistical tests might or might not be valid and whether they are valid depends on the existence or nonexistence of a variety of threats. The interested reader can find these threats on the companion website for this book at www.ablongman.com/johnsonchristensen2e, under bonus material.

REVIEW

QUESTIONS

8.1 What is a confounding variable, and why do confounding variables create problems in research studies?

8.2 Identify and define the four different types of validity that are used to evaluate the inferences made from the results of quantitative studies.

8.3 What is statistical conclusion validity, and what is the difference between null hypothesis significance testing and effect size estimation?

Research
Navigator.com

internal validity

■ **Internal validity**
The ability to infer that a causal relationship exists between two variables

■ **Causal description**
Describing the consequences of manipulating an independent variable

INTERNAL VALIDITY

Internal validity is a term coined by Campbell and Stanley (1963). Cook and Campbell (1979) later refined the concept to refer to the "approximate validity with which we infer that a relationship between two variables is causal" (p. 37). Although research is conducted for the multiple purposes of description, exploration, explanation, prediction, and influence, most research focuses on the goal of attempting to determine whether a causal relationship exists between the variables being investigated.

Types of Causal Relationships

Shadish, Cook, and Campbell (2002) have pointed out that there are two different types of causal relationships: causal description and causal explanation. **Causal description** refers to describing the consequences of manipulating an independent variable. **Causal explanation** refers to explaining the mechanisms through which and the conditions under which a causal relationship holds. For example, assume that a study was conducted to investigate the benefit derived from incorporating a 10-month intensive internship program into the education of future teachers, as is being done by the Chicago public school district. Assume further that this study demonstrated that teachers who participated in this program were evaluated by their principals as being more effective than teachers who participated in the traditional two- to three-month internship. This study has therefore provided evidence of a causal relationship between teacher effectiveness and the length and intensiveness of the internship. This would be causal description because it would have described the causal relationship that exists between the more intensive internship and later teaching effectiveness.

This study would not, however, explain why this causal relationship exists. The teachers participating in this experimental program might be more effective for any of a number of reasons, such as the program giving them better skills to cope with difficult children, better organizational skills, better skills at presentation of material, more realistic expectations of the demands of the teaching profession, and so on. The only thing that the study would have demonstrated is the causal connection between the more intensive internship program and later teacher effectiveness. A full explanation of why the causal relationship exists, has to "show how the causally efficacious parts of the treatment influence the causally affected parts of the outcome through identified mediating processes" (Shadish, Cook, & Campbell, 2002, p. 9). In other words, causal explanation requires that you identify and show how the processes involved in the intensive internship caused a change in a person's later effectiveness as a teacher. Clearly, many factors are involved in the intensive internship program that influence the student's later teaching effectiveness, such as the student's motivation, the quality of instruction provided by the master teachers, and the support provided by the principal. Once a causal descriptive relationship has been found, most subsequent research is directed at explaining why and how the descriptive relationship exists, and this is causal explanatory research.

The practical importance of causal explanation can be seen if a subsequent study does not replicate the beneficial effect previously demonstrated from the 10-month internship program. If explanatory studies had been conducted, this information could be used to show how to fix the program that did not produce the beneficial results. However, identifying how and why a relationship exists is much more difficult than describing that relationship.

> ■ **Causal explanation**
> Explaining the mechanisms through which and the conditions under which a causal relationship holds

Criteria for Inferring Causation

Three types of evidence are needed to reach a causal conclusion. First, you need some evidence that the independent and dependent variables are related. In other words, do changes in the independent variable correspond to changes in the dependent variable? For example, assume that you want to know whether being absent from school, the independent variable, has any effect on the grades students make, the dependent variable. If there is no relationship between these two variables, then one obviously cannot affect the other. However, if there is some relationship between the independent and dependent variables, it is possible that they are causally related. Note that we said that it is *possible* that the two variables are causally related. We used the word *possible* because evidence of covariation or correlation does not provide sufficient evidence of causation. Evidence of covariation is necessary but not sufficient to infer causation.

The second source of evidence needed to infer causation is the temporal ordering of the variables being investigated, because a cause must precede an effect. This means that you need some knowledge of the time sequence of the events. For example, if you are studying the causal relationship between grades and number of absences from school, you might want to determine whether grades cause absences from school or whether absence from school has a causal influence on grades. At first glance, you might think that the direction of causality is from absence from school to grades, with fewer absences resulting in higher grades and more absences resulting in lower grades. However, it is also possible that the direction of causality is from grades to school absences. It might be that students with poor grades become frustrated and therefore miss school, whereas students with good grades enjoy school, so they demonstrate better attendance than do the students with poor grades. As you can see, the temporal order of the relationship has to be identified to reach a causal conclusion because the cause must precede the effect. It is logically impossible for an effect to occur before the existence of its cause.

The third type of evidence needed to reach a causal conclusion is that the variables being investigated are the ones that are causally related rather than being caused by some extraneous variable. In other words, we must look for variables other than the independent variable that might explain the change observed on the dependent variable. In the "Pepsi Challenge" experiment, the letter on the cup represents a logical explanation for participants' preference selection. In the example of student grades and attendance, it is possible that the grades students get and their attendance at school are caused by parents monitoring their children. Children whose parents do not monitor their children's behavior might have poorer grades and lower school attendance, whereas children who are monitored by their parents might get better grades and have fewer absences. In this instance, there is still a relationship between grades and school attendance, but the cause of this relationship is the third variable: parent monitoring. **Third variable** is simply another term to refer to a confounding extraneous variable.

■ **Third variable**
A confounding extraneous variable

This third-variable issue means that two variables may be correlated not because they are causally related, but because they are both related to some third variable. Consider the research that has attempted to relate coffee drinking to heart attacks (e.g., Brody, 1973). Some of these studies have found a positive correlation between the number of cups of coffee drunk and the incidence of heart attacks. From this positive relationship, it is tempting to make a causal inference that coffee consumption is contributing to the risk of having a heart attack. This would be a tenuous assumption because cigarette smoking is related to both heart attacks and coffee drinking. Cigarette smoking therefore could be the third variable that is related to and possibly causing both coffee drinking and heart attacks. Nonsmokers not only do not consume much coffee, but also have few heart attacks, whereas smokers consume large amounts of coffee and have a considerable number of heart attacks. Therefore, although there is a relationship between coffee consumption and heart attacks, this relationship could be caused by an underlying third variable of smoking.

As you can see from this example, a researcher cannot automatically assume causality just because two or more variables are related. Before such a causal connection can be made, the temporal ordering of the variables must be established, and some assurance must be provided that an extraneous variable is not causing the observed relationship. Establishing the temporal ordering of variables is easily accomplished in experiments because the experimenter actively manipulates and has control over the presentation of the independent variable, the causal variable, and observes the effect of this manipulation on the dependent variable, the effect. Because the independent variable is presented first and the dependent variable is measured after the occurrence of the independent variable, the time sequence of the events is established in experimental research.

Research studies other than experimental studies also frequently attempt to infer causality. In these studies, the direction of causality is more difficult to establish because of the difficulty in establishing the temporal sequencing of events and ruling out the influence of confounding variables.

8.4 What is internal validity, and why is it so important in being able to make causal inferences?

8.5 What are the two types of causal relationships, and how do these two types of causal relationships differ?

8.6 What type of evidence is needed to infer causality, and how does each type of evidence contribute to making a causal inference?

REVIEW
QUESTIONS

Threats to Internal Validity

To infer one variable was the cause of an effect observed in another variable, we must eliminate or control for all other possible causes. These other possible causes are the threats to internal validity because these threats represent rival and competing explanations for the results obtained. When these rival explanations exist, it is impossible to reach a causal explanation with any degree of certainty, leading to highly suspect results that cannot and should not be taken seriously. This is why it is necessary to control for and eliminate the systematic influence of these threats. These threats to the internal validity of a research study are greatest in a **one-group pretest-posttest design.** As Figure 8.1 illustrates, this is a research design in which one group of participants is pretested on some dependent variable and then administered a treatment condition. Some time after the treatment condition is administered, the group of participants is posttested on the dependent variable. For example, assume that you want to test the effects of a new drug on controlling the adverse behavior of children with ADHD. You first identify a group of children with ADHD and pretest them on some performance measure such as ability to perform a series of simple arithmetic computations in a fifteen-minute time period. You then give these children the treatment consisting of the new drug. After the children have taken the drug for two months, you posttest them on the arithmetic computations task to see whether their posttest performance is superior to the pretest performance. Although it might be tempting to interpret any improvement in performance from pretesting to posttesting as being due to the new drug, there are a number of

■ **One-group pretest-posttest design**
A research design in which a treatment condition is administered to one group of participants after pretesting but before posttesting on the dependent variable

■ **FIGURE 8.1** One-group pretest-posttest design

Pretest	Treatment	Posttest measure
O_1	X	O_2

▓ **F I G U R E   8 . 2**   Two-group design comparing an experimental group that receives a treatment condition with a control group that does not receive the treatment condition

	Treatment	Posttest
Group A	X	O_2
Group B	—	O_2

other variables that could exist during the interval between pretesting and posttesting that could also affect the posttest performance. These other variables represent threats to the internal validity of the study.

There are also a number of variables that can threaten the internal validity of a study that uses a multigroup research design. The most basic **multigroup research design** is the two-group design. As illustrated in Figure 8.2, this design has two groups of participants, one of which receives a treatment condition while the other does not. Both groups are posttested on the dependent variable following administration of the treatment condition, and the posttest results are compared to see whether the group that received the treatment condition responds differently on the posttest than does the group that did not receive the treatment condition. This design could, for example, be used to test the effect of a drug on controlling the behavior problems of children with ADHD. One group of children with ADHD is given the drug, and the other group is given a placebo (a pill that looks like the drug but does not contain the drug). Following drug administration, both groups of children with ADHD are posttested on measures such as the amount of time they spend out of their seat. The two groups are compared to determine whether the children that receive the drug stay in their seats for a longer period of time than do the children that do not receive the drug. There are a number of variables that can operate in this design and can threaten its internal validity, making it a very weak design. We now discuss some of the more obvious and common threats to the internal validity. We will begin our discussion with a threat that exists in some nonexperimental studies and then discuss threats that can exist in the one-group pretest-posttest design and the multi-group design.

■ **Multigroup research design**
A research design that includes more than one group of participants

Ambiguous Temporal Precedence   The **ambiguous temporal precedence** threat refers to the inability to specify which variable preceded which other variable. Remember that a cause must precede the effect, so to identify the causal variable, you have to know that it came first and the effect followed. In some nonexperimental studies, especially those that investigate the degree of relationship that exists between two variables, it is frequently unclear as to whether variable A preceded variable B or vice versa. For example, if we measured the degree of relationship that existed between the frequency of criminal behavior and frequency of incarceration, we would probably find that these two variables were correlated. On the surface, this might suggest that the causal direction would be from criminal behavior to incarceration. However, many individuals learn techniques for engaging in criminal behavior from association with other individuals while incarcerated, so being incarcerated might lead to more criminal behavior. In this case, it is difficult to identify which variable is the cause and which is the effect because it is difficult to identify which variable came first. This is why you frequently find the statement "correlation does not indicate causation," because a correlation between two variables only indicates their degree of relationship. This does not mean that a correlation between two variables cannot indicate causation,

■ **Ambiguous temporal precedence**
The inability to specify which variable is the cause and which is the effect

because sometimes one direction of causality is implausible, as might exist with the relationship between clogged arteries and heart attacks. It is implausible to assume that a heart attack caused a person's artery to clog up with plaque. So you can appropriately infer that the clogged artery came first. However, just because A precedes B does not justify claiming that A caused B. To make that statement, you must eliminate other possible causes for the observed relationship. This is why experiments were created. Only in experiments do we deliberately manipulate one variable before the other is measured and attempt to create an environment that rules out other confounding variables so that we can state that the variable we manipulated was the causal variable.

History A **history** effect may occur in a one-group pretest-posttest research design in which the pretest and posttest measurements of the dependent variable are separated by a rather lengthy time interval. History refers to the specific events, other than any planned treatment event, that occur between the first and second measurement of the dependent variable, as illustrated in Figure 8.3. These events, in addition to any treatment effect, can influence the postmeasurement of the dependent variable; therefore, these events are confounded with the treatment effect and become rival explanations concerning the change that occurred between the pretest and posttest measurements.

> ■ **History**
> Any event, other than a planned treatment event, that occurs between the pretest and posttest measurement of the dependent variable and influences the postmeasurement of the dependent variable

Consider a study investigating the effect of a peer tutoring procedure on spelling performance. This is a procedure in which one student serves as a tutor and the other as a tutee. Tutors dictate words to a tutee and provide feedback as to whether the tutee correctly spells the word and the correct spelling if the word is spelled wrong. After a given number of words, the students reverse roles and continue the tutoring procedure. One approach to investigating the efficacy of such a tutoring procedure is to test the students on the speed with which they can learn to correctly spell a list of words before the tutoring procedure is implemented. Then implement the tutoring procedure. After the students have had an opportunity to practice and become familiar with this procedure, test them again on the speed with which they learn to correctly spell a list of words equivalent to the list that they had previously been asked to learn. If they require less time to learn to correctly spell the list of words after the tutoring procedure is implemented than before it is implemented, this should indicate that the peer tutoring system is a more efficient method of spelling instruction.

The difficulty with making this assumption is that a time interval elapsed between the pretest and posttest measurements. It is possible that some event other than just the tutoring system has an effect on the participants during this time and this event influences their

FIGURE 8.3 Illustration of extraneous history events

Time interval between pretest and posttest measurements of the dependent variable, during which extraneous history events could occur

Pretest————————Posttest

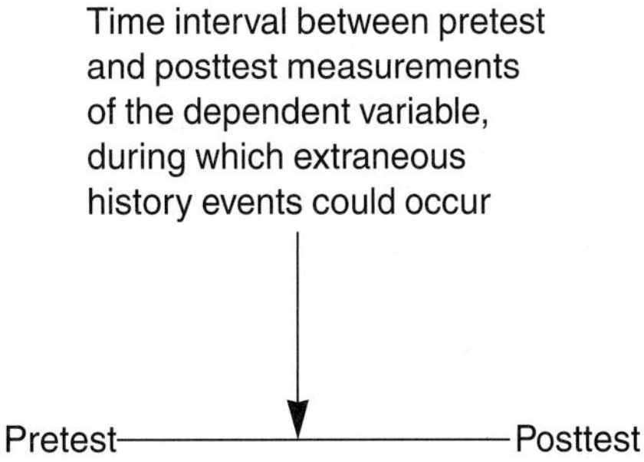

performance on the spelling test. For example, to implement the peer tutoring system, the teacher has to provide instruction to the students and constantly monitor their performance to ensure that they are conducting the peer tutoring correctly. This monitoring by the teacher might increase the students' motivation to learn to spell the list of words and affect their spelling performance. If the monitoring does influence the students' motivation and therefore their spelling performance, it represents a history variable and functions as a rival explanation for the cause of the students' enhanced spelling performance. Such history events represent threats to the internal validity of studies because they represent plausible rival explanations for the outcome of the study.

■ **Maturation**
Any physical or mental change that occurs over time that affects performance on the dependent variable

Maturation **Maturation** refers to physical or mental changes that may occur within individuals over time, such as aging, learning, boredom, hunger, and fatigue. Such changes can affect an individual's performance on the dependent variable. Because such changes might alter performance on the dependent variable, they represent threats to the internal validity of a study.

Consider a study in which Snowling, Goulandris, and Defty (1996) followed a group of children with dyslexia over a two-year period to track the development of their literary skills. Over this two-year time period, the children demonstrated an improvement in reading, spelling, and vocabulary. This improvement in the literary skills of the children with dyslexia may represent a maturation effect that could threaten the internal validity of a study. (Snowling et al. included two control groups to rule out maturation effects. The inclusion of these groups is not mentioned here to illustrate the maturation threat to internal validity.)

For example, assume that Snowling et al. wanted to assess the effect of a special instructional program on the development of literary skills of children with dyslexia. To test the effect of this program, they pretested a group of children with dyslexia on reading, spelling, and vocabulary before they entered the special instructional program and then tested them a second time after they had been in the program for two years. In comparing the pretest with the posttest scores, the investigators found that the children with dyslexia made significant advancements in literary skills. Although it might be tempting to attribute the improvement in literary skills to the special instructional program, all or part of the improvement could have been due to a maturation effect, or the improvement in learning that would have taken place without the special instructional program. That this natural or normal improvement could result from a maturational effect represents a rival explanation for the advancement in literary skills of the children with dyslexia and represents a threat to the internal validity of the study. To conduct an internally valid study, such maturation threats must be controlled.

■ **Testing**
Any change in scores obtained on the second administration of a test as a result of having previously taken the test

Testing **Testing** refers to changes that may occur in participants' scores obtained on the second administration of a test as a result of previously having taken the test. In other words, the experience of having taken a pretest may alter the results obtained on the posttest independent of any treatment effect or experimental manipulation intervening between the pretest and the posttest. Taking the pretest does a number of things that can alter a person's performance on a subsequent administration of the same test. Taking a test familiarizes you with the content of the test. After taking a test, you might think about errors you made that could be corrected if the test were taken over. When the test is administered a second time, you are already familiar with it and might remember some of your prior responses. This can lead to an enhanced performance that is entirely tied to the initial or pretest administration. Any alteration in performance as a result of a testing effect threatens the internal validity of a one-group study because it serves as a rival hypothesis to some treatment effect or experimental manipulation intervening between the pretest and posttest. Whenever the same test is administered on multiple occasions, some control needs to be implemented for testing rival hypotheses.

Snowling et al. (1996), for example, administered a number of reading, spelling, and vocabulary tests to children with dyslexia at the beginning of their study and two years later. Some of these tests were a little unusual, such as the Rhyme Sensitivity Test, which presented children with a string of four words (e.g., cot, hot, fox, pot) for which they were to identify the odd word in the rhyme segment (fox in this example). The unusual nature of this test suggests that it might be subject to a testing effect because it would seem as though, after participating in this test once, children would be more familiar with it and would be able to perform better on a subsequent administration of the test. If this familiarization effect did exist, it would account for some of the improvement in performance demonstrated by the dyslexic children. It would therefore serve as a rival explanation for any improvement demonstrated over the two years and preclude a clear explanation of the observed improvement. Snowling et al. (1996) did attempt to control for such a pretesting effect by administrating two practice sessions in which the children could become familiar with the test and minimize a pretesting effect. Such practice sessions do not necessarily eliminate a pretesting effect. However, including control groups that also experienced any testing effect would have controlled for this potential threat to internal validity. (If you read the Snowling et al. study, you will see that control groups were included. We did not mention them until now so that we could illustrate the testing threat to internal validity.)

Instrumentation

Instrumentation refers to any change that occurs in the measuring instrument. There are two primary ways in which an instrumentation threat may occur: An instrumentation threat can occur when the measurement instrument that is used during pretesting is different from that used during posttesting. If the tests used during pretesting and posttesting are not completely equivalent, a difference can occur between the two performance measures that is strictly due to the difference in the way the two tests are assessing performance. For example, assume that children with dyslexia are tested at time 1 with one test of rhyme sensitivity and are tested two years later with a different test of rhyme sensitivity. If a comparison is made of rhyme sensitivity from time 1 and two years later at time 2, any difference that is observed could be due to the children's enhanced development of rhyme sensitivity. However, it could also be due to the differences in the way the two tests measure rhyme sensitivity, which would be an instrumentation effect that would represent a rival explanation for any change observed in rhyme sensitivity. Instrumentation effects therefore represent threats to the internal validity of any study.

A second way in which an instrumentation effect could creep into a study is if the data were collected through observation. Many educational researchers use human observers to collect data. Human observers such as teachers are, unfortunately, subject to such influences as fatigue, boredom, and learning processes. In administering intelligent tests, the tester typically gains facility and skill over time and collects more reliable and valid data as additional tests are given. Observers and interviewers are also used to assess the effects of various experimental treatments. For example, Schafer and Smith (1996) had teachers and children view videotapes of children engaged in playful and real fights to make judgments as to whether the

■ **Instrumentation**
Any change that occurs in the way the dependent variable is measured

fights were real or play. As the observers and interviewers assess more and more individuals, they gain skill. Interviewers might, for example, gain additional skill with the interview or with observing a particular type of behavior, producing changes in the data collected that cannot be attributed to either the participant or any experimental conditions being tested in the study. This is why studies that use human observers to collect data typically use more than one observer and have each observer go through a training program. In this way, some of the biases that are inherent in making observations can be minimized, and the various observers can serve as checks on one another to ensure that accurate data are being collected. Typically, the data collected by the various observers must coincide before they are considered reliable.

■ **Regression artifacts**
The tendency of very high scores to become lower and very low scores to become higher on posttesting of other or the original measure

Regression Artifacts The concept of **regression artifact** refers to the fact that extreme scores will tend to regress or move toward the mean of a distribution on a second testing or assessment. Many educational research studies are designed in such a way that the research participants are tested before and after some experimental treatment condition is administered for the purpose of assessing change. Additionally, many of these studies investigate special groups of individuals such as children with learning disabilities or people with a specific deficiency such as poor reading or mathematical ability. These special groups of research participants are typically identified by having extreme scores such as low reading comprehension scores. After the research participants are selected, they are given some experimental treatment condition to improve this deficiency or ameliorate the special condition. Any positive change from pretesting to posttesting is frequently taken as evidence of the efficacy of the treatment program. However, the internal validity of a study such as this could be threatened because high-scoring research participants might score lower on posttesting or low-scoring research participants might score higher on posttesting not because of any experimental treatment effect but because of a regression artifact.

Regression artifacts occur because the first and second measurements of performance are not perfectly correlated. This lack of perfect correlation occurs because a person's test-taking performance is influenced by many variables in addition to ability. Think about the variables that could influence the score you receive on a reading comprehension test. There will undoubtedly be some questions that you cannot answer correctly. However, you guess; sometimes you guess correctly, and at other times you guess incorrectly. In addition to chance factors such as guessing, your test-taking performance could be influenced by other stresses in your life, such as not sleeping well the night before the test or having a fight with your spouse or significant other. You could also have misread questions, which might have led you to answer incorrectly. As you can see, there are many variables in addition to a person's ability that might influence the score obtained on a test.

To illustrate the regression effect, assume you want to test a technique that is supposed to increase the reading comprehension of young children. To test this technique, you give a reading comprehension test to a group of six- to ten-year-old children and select for your study all those children who received the lowest 10 percent of the scores on this test. Naturally, some of these individuals received low scores because they had very poor reading comprehension ability. However, others probably received low reading comprehension scores because they did not try very hard, were tired because they stayed up late the night before, or were especially stressed because of something like moving to another school or their parents' getting a divorce. These individuals would have artificially low scores because of these extraneous factors. On retesting, these children would be expected to do better because it is unlikely that these extraneous factors would again operate to the same extent to depress the reading comprehension scores. Consequently, the posttest scores would be higher. However, these higher scores would be the result of a regression phenomenon and not because of the experimental treatment meant to improve reading comprehension. In this case, regression would threaten the internal validity of the study.

Differential Selection **Differential Selection** is a threat to the internal validity of a study when a difference exists, at the outset of the research study, between the characteristics of the participants forming the various comparison groups. Participants in different comparison groups can differ in many ways, as illustrated in Table 8.1. One way in which this difference can occur is if you, as the researcher, have to use groups of participants that are already formed. For example, assume that you want to test a procedure for enhancing young children's motivation to learn. To test this procedure, you want to administer it to one group of fourth-grade children and compare their motivation to learn, after this procedure has been implemented, with a group of fourth-grade children who have not experienced this procedure. In conducting this study, you obtain permission from the local school district. However, you have to administer the experimental procedure to one fourth-grade class and compare its performance with that of another fourth-grade class. This might not seem to be a problem because they both represent fourth-grade students. However, there is no guarantee that the students in these two classes have the same motivation to learn before the study is conducted. If the class that receives the experimental procedure had a greater motivation to learn before conducting the study, they naturally show up as having a greater motivation to learn after the experimental procedure is implemented. Any difference in motivation to learn between the two fourth-grade classes could therefore be due entirely to a selection bias.

■ **Differential selection**
Selecting participants for the various treatment groups that have different characteristics

Additive and Interactive Effects **Additive and interactive effects** refers to the fact that the threats to internal validity can combine to produce complex biases. For example, a **selection-history** effect would occur if two comparison groups experienced a different

■ **Additive and interactive effects**
Refers to the fact that the threats to internal validity can combine to produce an additive or multiplicative bias.
■ **Selection-history effect**
Occurs when an event occurring between the pretest and posttest differentially affects the different comparison groups

■ **TABLE 8.1**   Characteristics on Which Research Participants Can Differ

Ability to do well on tests	Home environment	Reading ability
Age	Intelligence	Religious beliefs
Anxiety level	Language ability	Self-esteem
Attitudes toward research	Learning style	Socioeconomic status
Coordination	Maturity	Spelling ability
Curiosity	Motivation to learn	Stress level
Ethnicity	Personality type	Time spent on homework
Gender	Political beliefs	Vocabulary
Hearing ability	Quality of eyesight	

history event and the history effects they experienced resulted in their responding in different ways to the dependent variable. For example, assume that a joke was cracked at some time during the study in one of the comparison groups. In the other comparison group, one of the participants got very angry and frustrated at having to do the experimental task and voiced his disapproval aloud. Each of these two experiences represents a history effect, but the history effect occurring in each group would have been different. The different history effects, the joke or the expression of disapproval, would probably have affected the participants in each group very differently and might also have had a differential effect on their response to the dependent variable. If it did, this differential response would look like a treatment effect but would be a selection by history interaction effect.

■ **Selection-maturation effect**
Occurs when the different comparison groups experience a different rate of change on a maturation variable

To illustrate a **selection-maturation effect,** suppose you want to teach the concepts of good and bad to five-year-old children with and without hearing difficulties. In doing so, you find that the normal children learn these concepts much faster than do the children with hearing difficulties. From this study, you might conclude that the ability of children who have hearing difficulties to learn these concepts is somehow impaired. However, as Figure 8.4 reveals, Kusche and Greenberg (1983) revealed that the ability of children with hearing difficulties to gain an understanding of the concepts of good and bad develops or evolves more slowly than it does in children who can hear normally. Five-year-old children who cannot hear have not matured to the point at which they can understand these concepts as well as children who can hear normally. This difference in the evolution of the ability to understand these concepts is a maturational difference between the two groups of children and

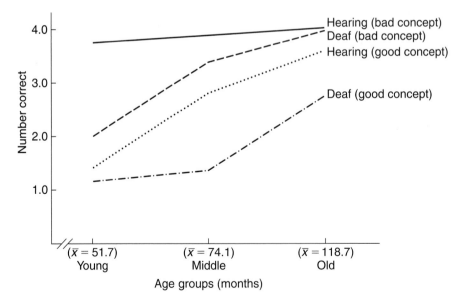

■ FIGURE 8.4   The evolution of good and bad concepts as a function of age and hearing status

Adapted from C. A. Kusche and M. T. Greenberg, "Evaluative Understanding and Role Taking Ability: A Comparison of Deaf and Hearing Children," *Child Development, 54,* pp. 141–147, © 1983 by The Society for Research in Child Development, Inc.

not an impairment in the ability of children who cannot hear to acquire these concepts. This indicates that a maturation-selection effect exists or that a maturational difference exists between these two groups of children in their ability to understand these two concepts. This maturational difference represents the most logical explanation for the difference observed in a study attempting to teach five-year-old children with and without hearing difficulties the concepts of good and bad and not a difference in ability to learn these concepts.

Differential Attrition   **Attrition** refers to the fact that some individuals do not complete the outcome measures. This can occur for any of a variety of reasons, such as failure to show up at the scheduled time and place or not participating in all phases of the study. **Differential attrition** refers to a bias that occurs when the people who do not complete the outcome measures are different in the various comparison groups. In conducting a research study, the typical procedure is to identify the individuals who agree to participate and schedule them to participate at a specific time and place. However, people fail to show up for a study for a variety of reasons ranging from just forgetting about the study to deciding that they don't want to participate.

■ **Attrition**
Loss of people who do not complete the experiment
■ **Differential attrition**
A differential loss of participants from the various comparison groups

   The loss of research participants from the research study does not, in and of itself, produce a bias. The bias results because the loss, when using a multigroup design, may produce differences between the comparison groups that cannot be attributed to the experimental treatment condition. To attribute a difference between comparison groups to the experimental treatment, the comparison groups have to be the same on all variables except the independent variable. The loss of research participants from the various comparison groups can create differences on variables other than the independent variable, producing a mortality threat to the internal validity of the study.

   For example, assume that you want to test the efficacy of a new technique for teaching mathematics to students. To test this new technique, you obtain permission from a school system to conduct the study. In conducting the study, one teacher teaches mathematics to one group of students by the traditional method and to another group of students by the new technique for one selected week of the school year. You know that research has revealed that older students perform better than younger students on mathematics, so you try to control for the age influence by having equal numbers of older and younger students in the two experimental groups. However, when you conduct the study, you find that half of the younger students assigned to the new technique group are sick and do not show up for class. When comparing the performance of the mathematical skills of the students in the two groups after the one week of instruction, you find that the new technique is superior to the traditional method. Can you conclude that the new technique is the superior teaching technique and that it should be used instead of the traditional method? This inference is incorrect because more older students were in the new technique group, and past research has indicated that older students do better in mathematics. This age difference and not the method of instruction may have produced the difference in the mathematical performance of the students in the two groups. If it did, then a differential attrition bias existed and represents a rival explanation for the performance difference observed in the two groups of students. From this example, you can see that differential attrition is really a type of differential selection bias because attrition can result in the various comparison groups being composed of people that differ on variables other than the independent variable.

8.7 What is an ambiguous temporal precedence threat, and why does it threaten internal validity?

8.8 What is a history threat, and how does it operate?

8.9 What is a maturation threat, and how does it operate?

8.10 What is a testing threat, and why does it exist?

8.11 What is an instrumentation threat, and when would this threat exist?

8.12 What is a regression artifact threat, and why does this threat exist?

8.13 What is a differential selection threat, and when would this threat exist?

8.14 What is meant by an additive and interactive effect as a threat to internal validity?

8.15 How does differential attrition threaten internal validity?

EXTERNAL VALIDITY

- **External validity**
  The extent to which the study results can be generalized to and across populations of persons, settings, times, outcomes, and treatment variations

Research Navigator.c⊕m

external validity

External validity is a term coined by Campbell and Stanley (1963) and extended by Shadish, Cook, and Campbell (2002) to refer to the extent to which the results of a study can be generalized to and across populations of persons, settings, times, outcomes, and treatment variations. In Chapter 1, we state that one of the basic assumptions of science is that there are regularities in human behavior and these regularities can be discovered through systematic research. Whenever we conduct a research study, we are attempting to discover these regularities. However, each research study is conducted on a specific sample of individuals in a specific setting with a specific independent variable, with specific outcomes, and at a specific point in time.

To generalize the results of a study, you must identify a target group of individuals, settings, times, outcomes, and treatment variations and then randomly select from these populations so that you will have a sample representative of these populations. Most studies cannot randomly sample from the populations of individuals, settings, times, outcomes, and treatment variations because of the expense, time, and effort involved as well as the fact that the populations of outcomes and treatment variations are probably not known and cannot, therefore, be adequately sampled. Therefore, all studies contain characteristics that threaten their external validity. We will discuss each of these threats so that you can be aware of some of the factors that limit the generalizability of a study.

Population Validity

- **Population validity**
  The ability to generalize the study results to individuals who were not included in the study

- **Target population**
  The larger population to whom the study results are to be generalized

Population validity refers to the ability to generalize from the sample of individuals on which a study was conducted to the larger target population of individuals and across different subpopulations within the larger target population. The **target population** is the larger population, such as all children with a learning disability, to whom the research study results are to be generalized. Within this larger target population, there are many subpopulations, such as male and female children with a learning disability. Population validity, therefore,

■ **FIGURE 8.5**　Two-step process involved in achieving external validity

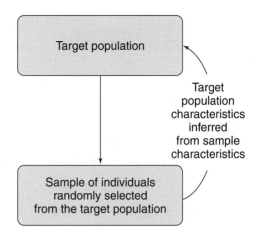

has the two components of generalizing from a sample to a target population and generalizing from a sample across types of persons in the target population.

Generalizing from a sample of individuals to the larger target population is a two-step process of defining the larger target population of individuals of interest and then randomly selecting a sample of individuals from this target population, as illustrated in Figure 8.5. Remember that random selection maximizes the probability that the sample will be representative of the target population. The characteristics of the population are then inferred from the characteristics of the sample. This is the ideal arrangement and the one that is sometimes achieved, primarily in survey research. It is also the type of sample that is needed when the goal of research is to identify population characteristics. Unfortunately, drawing a random sample from a target population is seldom possible because of practical considerations such as finances or practical limitations such as the fact that a list of all members of many target populations does not exist from which we can draw a sample (e.g., a list does not exist of all children with a learning disability). Therefore, we draw our sample from an accessible population.

The **accessible population** is the group of research participants that are available to the researcher for participation in research. This might be the college students taking a class in the researcher's department or children with a learning disability attending school in a specific school district that has granted the researcher permission to conduct his or her research.

Two inferential steps must be made in generalizing from the study sample results to the larger target population, as illustrated in Figure 8.6. First we have to generalize from the sample of individuals participating in the study to the accessible population. This step is easily accomplished if the individuals participating in the research study have been randomly selected from the accessible population. If the sample of participants is randomly selected, it should be representative, which means that the characteristics of the accessible population can be inferred from the sample. If a study is conducted on fifty children with learning disabilities randomly selected from the 200 attending the Cottage Hills School District, then the results obtained from the study can be generalized to all children with learning disabilities in that school district. However, more typical is a study conducted on participants who not only are accessible but who also volunteer.

■ **Accessible population**
The research participants who are available for participation in the research

▓ **FIGURE 8.6**   Inferential steps involved in generalizing from the study sample to the target population

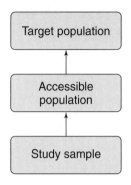

The second step in the generalization process involves inferring from the accessible population to the target population. This is the generalization you want to make but the one that you can seldom make with any degree of confidence because the accessible population is seldom representative of the target population. For example, if the study that you conducted demonstrated that you had developed a method for improving the reading skills of children with a reading disability, you would ideally want the results of your study to generalize to all children with a reading disability. To be able to make such a statement, the sample of children participating in your study would have had to have been randomly selected from the target population, which is rarely possible. Therefore, you probably have to settle for randomly selecting from an accessible population such as a specific school or a specific school district. One school, or even a school district, is seldom representative of the target population. For example, the school at which you conduct your study may consist primarily of children from an impoverished area of the city in which you work. Although this school might have a large percentage of children with learning disabilities, the children are certainly not representative of the target population consisting of all children in the United States with learning disabilities. Yet it is to the larger target population that you want to generalize. As you can see, generalizing the results of a study to the target population is frequently a tenuous process because the sample of participants used in most studies are not randomly selected from the target population.

Most of this discussion of external validity focuses on generalizing to a specific target population. However, we should not forget that external validity also focuses on the goal of generalizing across populations. In any target population, there are many subpopulations, as we mentioned earlier. When we talk about generalizing across populations, we are really asking the question of whether the results hold for each of the subpopulations within the larger target population. Assume that we conducted a study investigating a specific treatment enhancing the reading ability of children with dyslexia. Assume further that we did randomly select 500 children from the target population of children with dyslexia in the United States and found that the treatment was effective. Because we had randomly selected our sample (something that seldom occurs in this type of study), we could generalize back to the target population and conclude that children with dyslexia would, on the average, benefit from the treatment program.

The results would not, however, say anything about the effectiveness of the treatment for the many subpopulations within the larger target population. Can the results be generalized to both male and female children with dyslexia, to children with dyslexia coming from various socioeconomic groups, age groups, intellectual levels, and so forth? This is the issue of generalizing across populations. In fact, many studies that are conducted to test the generalization of a specific treatment across subpopulations, are attempting to identify the specific subpopulations to which a treatment can and cannot be generalized.

It is very important to understand the distinction between generalizing to and across populations. Survey research is the type of research that most often focuses on generalizing to target populations. Experimental and quasi-experimental research focuses more on generalizing across populations or identifying the populations to which a finding can and cannot be generalized.

Ecological Validity

Ecological validity refers to the ability to generalize the results of a study across settings. For example, one study might be conducted in a rural school in the South, using old computers that are slow and antiquated. If the results obtained from this study can be generalized to other settings, such as an urban school well equipped with state-of-the-art technology, then the study possesses ecological validity. Ecological validity therefore exists to the extent that the study results are independent of the setting in which the study was conducted.

- **Ecological validity**
  The ability to generalize the study results across settings

One of the subtle setting factors that can affect the ability to generalize the results of a study is participant's knowledge of the fact that they are participating in a study. This is known as a reactivity effect. **Reactivity** refers to the alteration in performance that can occur as a result of being aware that one is participating in a research study. It is similar to the effect many people have of being on television: Once you know the camera is on you, you shift to your "television" behavior. A similar phenomenon can occur in research studies. Once you know you are in a research study, you might change your behavior. A reactivity effect can therefore threaten both the internal and external validity of a study.

- **Reactivity**
  An alteration in performance that occurs as a result of being aware of participating in a study

Temporal Validity

Temporal validity refers to the extent to which the results of a study can be generalized across time. Temporal validity is an issue because most educational research studies are conducted during one time period. For example, Thokildsen, Nolen, and Fournier (1994) assessed children's views of several practices teachers use to influence motivation to learn. The data for this study were collected by interviewing 7- to 12-year-old children at one point in time. Although the data are valid for the time period in which they were collected, there is no assurance that the same results would hold true 10 years later. Frequently, it is assumed that the results of studies are invariant across time. Although this might exist for the results of some studies, it almost certainly does not exist for the results of others. Failure to consider the time variable can threaten the external validity of the study.

- **Temporal validity**
  The extent to which the study results can be generalized across time

Treatment Variation Validity

Treatment variation validity refers to the ability to generalize the results across variations of the treatment. Treatment variation validity is an issue because the administration of a treatment can vary from one time to the next. For example, many studies have been conducted demonstrating that behavior therapy is effective in treating depression. However,

- **Treatment variation validity**
  The ability to generalize across variations of the treatment

these studies have been typically been conducted in the context of a research study that has provided maximum assurance that the therapists were competent and delivered the therapy in the prescribed manner. Therapists who administer behavior therapy to the general public, however, vary considerably in their competency and the extent to which they deliver the therapy in the prescribed manner. This means that there is considerable variation in the way behavior therapy is administered. If behavior therapy produces a beneficial effect for the treatment of depression across these different variations in the way it is delivered, treatment generalization exists. If behavior therapy is beneficial only when administered exactly as prescribed by a competently trained therapist, then treatment generalization does not exist.

Outcome Validity

■ **Outcome validity**
The ability to generalize across different but related dependent variables

Outcome validity refers to the ability to generalize the results across different but related dependent variables. Many studies investigate the effect of some independent variable on one or more dependent variables. Outcome validity refers to the extent to which the independent variable influences a number of related outcome measures. For example, a job-training program is expected to increase the likelihood of getting a job after graduation. This is probably the primary outcome measure of interest. However, an equally important issue is maintaining the job. This means that the person must arrive on time, not miss work, and follow orders as well as demonstrate an acceptable level of performance. The effectiveness of the job-training program might increase the probability of getting a job but have no effect on job retention because it has little impact on these other essential adaptive job skills. Sometimes one outcome measure demonstrates that the treatment was effective. However, other outcome measures show no effect and maybe even a negative effect. Using several outcome measures is always desirable because this gives a more complete picture of the overall effect of the treatment. Fortunately, this is one of the easier design features to implement. You just need to include several related dependent variables in your study to answer questions about generalizability over outcomes.

REVIEW
QUESTIONS

8.16 What is external validity and why is it important?

8.17 What is population validity, and why is it difficult to achieve?

8.18 What is ecological validity?

8.19 What is temporal validity?

8.20 What is treatment variation validity, and why can this be a threat to external validity?

8.21 What is outcome validity?

CONSTRUCT REPRESENTATION

Up to this point in the chapter, we have discussed issues, such as internal validity, that are related to the validity of the design of an educational research study. Any educational research study involves the investigation of a set of variables such as televised instruction, the education of culturally diverse students, or the effect of stress on academic achievement. Additionally, we frequently want to conduct a study on a specific population of individuals such as children with attention deficit hyperactive disorder or dyslexia. Conducting a research study on variables or special populations such as these requires that they be assessed or measured. This creates some difficulty because many of the variables or characteristics of the special populations of interest represent abstract constructs. The educational researcher is faced with the task of identifying or devising some way of representing the constructs being investigated. This is a problem of construct validity. **Construct validity** refers to the extent to which a higher-order construct, such as help seeking, teacher stress, or dyslexia, is accurately represented in the particular study.

Research
Navigator.c⊛m
construct validity

■ **Construct validity**
The extent to which a higher-order construct is represented in a particular study

So how do we achieve construct validity? Construct validity is fostered by having a good definition and explanation of the meaning of the construct of interest. However, every construct, such as violence, has multiple features, and this creates a difficulty in identifying the prototypical features of a construct. For example, just hurting someone does not qualify as aggression or violence. There must be intent to harm. This problem is exacerbated in educational research because the explication of the prototypical features of many of the constructs we investigate has not occurred. This difficulty is partly because of the abstract nature of the constructs with which we work. Educational research focuses on issues such as intelligence, burnout, at-risk students, violence, abuse of testing in schools, lack of AIDS education, and stress. These are constructs that are hard to define precisely. Because of the abstract nature of many of the constructs we work with and the lack of a clear explanation of their meaning, there is typically an imperfect relationship between the way a construct is represented or measured in a research study and the higher-order construct we want to represent.

The multiple features of any construct and the lack of a clear explication of the prototypical features of a construct create difficulty for researchers when they try to represent constructs of interest in a research study. What is the researcher to do? The researcher must make use of the available knowledge and measures of the construct he or she is investigating and identify the specific way in which a construct will be represented in the study he or she is conducting. This is where the concept of operationalism enters and is useful as a communication tool for the researcher. **Operationalism** means that terms or constructs are represented by a specific set of steps or operations. For example, if stress is measured by the Stress in Teaching Questionnaire, then stress is represented by a score on this questionnaire. However, this set of operations might or might not accurately represent the construct of interest in the study because of the presence of any of a number of threats to construct validity. We are not going to discuss these threats because they are a little beyond the scope of this textbook. We have, however, listed them on the book's companion website at www.ablongman.com/johnsonchristensen2e under bonus material. We do want you to realize that the validity of inferences you make about constructs depends on the existence or nonexistence of such threats.

■ **Operationalism**
Representing constructs by a specific set of steps or operations

Operationism is the technique that most researchers use when conducting their studies. They select a specific operation or set of operations as their representation of the construct they are investigating. Manthei and Gilmore (1996) used the Stress in Teaching Questionnaire as their representation of teacher stress. Butler and Neuman's (1995) representation of help-seeking behaviors in second- and sixth-grade children was whether they asked the experimenter for assistance in solving puzzles.

Identifying the specific operations used to represent a construct is very convenient and is essential for communication. For example, Butler and Neuman's (1995) operationalization (i.e., their construct representation) of help seeking left little room for interpretation or question as to the way in which they had conceptualized and interpreted help-seeking. Note, however, that this is not the only way in which a person can seek help. Help can also be obtained by asking peers for help or going to the library and looking for reference material that would provide assistance. The important point to remember is that specification of a set of operations is for accuracy in communication. This is the beauty of operationalizations. They specify, in a concrete and specific way, how a construct is conceptualized and measured in a given study. This degree of specificity permits an exact communication of the construct and allows anyone else to repeat the steps and represent the construct in the same way.

Although the operationalization of constructs is necessary for educational researchers to communicate the way in which a construct is represented in a given research study, remember that seldom, if ever, does a given operationalization completely represent the construct being investigated. Consider, for example, the study by Manthei and Gilmore (1996) in which they operationally represented teacher stress as the response teachers provided on the Stress in Teaching Questionnaire. Although this questionnaire probably does measure some component of teacher stress, it would be foolish to assume that this single measure provides a completely accurate representation of the construct of teacher stress. Rather, stress of any type probably includes physiological reactions such as changes in heart rate and blood pressure as well as behavioral changes such as being less tolerant of the students, both of which are probably not adequately assessed by a questionnaire. Additionally, Campbell (1988) has pointed out that every observation is affected by factors that bear no relation to the construct that is being measured. For example, the Stress in Teaching Questionnaire probably does, in part, measure teacher stress. However, it is also a function of events that are irrelevant to the stress that occurs as a result of teaching, such as the type of questions asked, the interpretation of the questions by the teacher completing the questionnaire, the tolerance a teacher has for stress, and stress factors influencing the teacher that are not related to the profession of teaching.

The important point to remember is that there are many different ways of operationally representing a construct and that each operationalization represents only a portion of the construct. The most accurate representation of a construct would involve measuring it in several different ways. For example, teacher stress could be measured by a questionnaire, by the teacher's reaction to students, and by having others rate or identify factors influencing teacher stress. As more and more measures of the same construct are included, the probability of obtaining a more complete representation of the construct increases. The use of multiple measures of a construct is called **multiple operationalism,** which is the recommended approach to use in research studies (Campbell, 1988).

■ **Multiple operationalism**
The use of several measures of a construct

We also must point out that it is not sufficient to specify a set of operations as a representation of a construct and then assume that this is a valid measure of the intended construct or even some component of the construct of interest. Any set of operations does not have any necessary relationship to the construct being investigated. All operations do is state in specific and concrete terms the way in which the construct is being represented in a particular study. To drive this point home with a ridiculous example, assume that you want to investigate the effect of intelligence on learning. In this study, you operationally represent intelligence as a person's income on the assumption that more intelligent people make more money. This is obviously a poor representation of the construct of intelligence. However, it is operationalized in specific and concrete terms. This communicates how intelligence was represented in this study. However, it is a very poor measure and therefore a poor way of representing intelligence.

8.22 What is construct validity, and how is it achieved? **8.23** What is operationalism, and what is its purpose? **8.24** What is multiple operationalism, and why is it used?	**R E V I E W** **Q U E S T I O N S**

RESEARCH VALIDITY IN QUALITATIVE RESEARCH

Discussions of the term *validity* have traditionally been attached to the quantitative research tradition. Not surprisingly, reactions by qualitative researchers have been mixed regarding whether or not this concept should be applied to qualitative research. At the extreme, some qualitative researchers have suggested that the traditional quantitative criteria of reliability and validity are not relevant to qualitative research (e.g., Smith, 1984). Smith contends that the basic assumptions of quantitative and qualitative research are incompatible and that the concepts of reliability and validity should therefore be abandoned. Most qualitative researchers, however, do not hold this viewpoint, and neither do we. Most qualitative researchers argue that some qualitative research studies are better than others, and they frequently use the term *validity* to refer to this difference. When qualitative researchers speak of research validity, they are usually referring to qualitative research that is plausible, credible, trustworthy, and therefore defensible. We believe it is important to think about the issue of validity in qualitative research and to examine some strategies that have been developed to maximize validity. A list of these strategies is provided in Table 8.2. Keep in mind that most of these strategies can also be used in quantitative research.

research validity

One potential threat to validity that researchers must be careful to watch out for is called **researcher bias.** This problem is summed up in a statement a colleague of ours once made. She said, "The problem with qualitative research is that the researchers 'find' what they want to find, and then they write up their results." It is true that the problem of researcher bias is frequently an issue in qualitative research because qualitative research tends to be exploratory and is open-ended and less structured than quantitative research. (One would be remiss, however, to think that researcher bias is never a problem in quantitative research.) Researcher bias tends to result from selective observation and selective recording of information and also from allowing one's personal views and perspectives to affect how data are interpreted and how the research is conducted.

■ **Researcher bias**
Obtaining results consistent with what the researcher wants to find

The key strategy that is used to understand researcher bias is called **reflexivity,** which means that the researcher actively engages in critical self-reflection about his or her potential biases and predispositions (Table 8.2). Through reflexivity, researchers become more self-aware, and they monitor and attempt to control their biases. Many qualitative researchers

■ **Reflexivity**
Self-reflection by the researcher on his or her biases and predispositions

■ **T A B L E 8 . 2**   Strategies Used to Promote Qualitative Research Validity

Strategy	Description
Researcher-as-detective	A metaphor characterizing the qualitative researcher as he or she searches for evidence about causes and effects. The researcher develops an understanding of the data through careful consideration of potential causes and effects and by systematically eliminating rival explanations or hypotheses until the final case is made beyond a reasonable doubt. The detective can utilize any of the strategies listed here.
Extended fieldwork	To provide for both discovery and validation researchers should collect data in the field over an extended time period.
Low-inference descriptors	The use of description phrased very close to the participants' accounts and researchers' field notes. Verbatims (i.e., direct quotations) are a commonly used type of low-inference descriptors.
Triangulation	Cross-checking information and conclusions through the use of multiple procedures or sources. When the different procedures or sources are in agreement you have corroboration.
Data triangulation	The use of multiple data sources to help understand a phenomenon.
Methods triangulation	The use of multiple research methods to study a phenomenon.
Investigator triangulation	The use of multiple investigators (i.e., multiple researchers) in collecting, analyzing, and interpreting the data.
Theory triangulation	The use of multiple theories and perspectives to help interpret and explain the data.
Participant feedback	The feedback and discussion of the researcher's interpretations and conclusions with the actual participants and other members of the participant community for verification and insight.
Peer review	Discussion of the researcher's interpretations and conclusions with other people. This includes discussion with a disinterested peer, (e.g., with another researcher not directly involved). This peer should be skeptical and play the devil's advocate, challenging the researcher to provide solid evidence for any interpretations or conclusions. Discussion with peers who are familiar with the research can also help provide useful challenges and insights.
External audit	Using outside experts to assess the study quality.
Negative-case sampling	Locating and examining cases that disconfirm the researcher's expectations and tentative explanation.
Reflexivity	Involves self-awareness and critical self-reflection by the researcher on his or her potential biases and predispositions as these may affect the research process and conclusions.
Pattern matching	Predicting a series of results that form a distinctive pattern and then determining the degree to which the actual results fit the predicted pattern or "fingerprint."

include a distinct section in their research proposals entitled "Researcher Bias." In this section, they discuss their personal background, how it may affect their research, and what strategies they will use to address the potential problem. Another strategy that researchers use to reduce the effect of researcher bias is called **negative-case sampling** (Table 8.2). This means that researchers attempt carefully and purposively to search for examples that disconfirm their expectations and explanations about what they are studying. If you use this approach, you will find it more difficult to ignore important information and you will come up with more credible and defensible results.

- **Negative-case sampling**
  Locating and examining cases that disconfirm the researcher's expectations

Now let's look at some types of validity that are important in qualitative research. We start with three types of validity that are especially relevant to qualitative research (Maxwell, 1992, 1996): descriptive validity, interpretive validity, and theoretical validity. After discussing these three forms of validity, the traditional types of validity used in quantitative research, internal and external validity, are discussed.

Descriptive Validity

Descriptive validity refers to the factual accuracy of the account as reported by the researchers. The key questions that are addressed in descriptive validity are, Did what was reported as taking place in the group being studied actually happen? and Did the researchers accurately report what they saw and heard? In other words, descriptive validity refers to accuracy in reporting descriptive information (description of events, objects, behaviors, people, settings, times, places, and so forth). This form of validity is important because description is a major objective in nearly all qualitative research.

- **Descriptive validity**
  The factual accuracy of an account as reported by the researcher

One effective strategy used to obtain descriptive validity is **investigator triangulation** (Table 8.2). In the case of descriptive validity, investigator triangulation involves the use of multiple observers to record and describe the research participants' behavior and the context in which they were located. The use of multiple observers allows cross-checking of observations to make sure the investigators agree about what took place. When corroboration (agreement) of observations across multiple investigators is obtained, it is less likely that outside reviewers of the research will question whether something occurred. As a result, the research will be more credible and defensible.

- **Investigator triangulation**
  The use of multiple investigators in collecting and interpreting the data

Interpretive Validity

Interpretive validity refers to accurately portraying the meaning attached by participants to what is being studied by the researcher. More specifically, it refers to the degree to which the research participants' viewpoints, thoughts, feelings, intentions, and experiences are accurately understood by the qualitative researcher and portrayed in the research report. An important part of qualitative research is understanding research participants' "inner worlds" (i.e., their subjective worlds), and interpretive validity refers to the degree of accuracy in presenting these inner worlds. Accurate interpretive validity requires that the researcher get inside the heads of the participants, look through the participants' eyes, and see and feel what they see and feel. In this way the qualitative researcher can understand things from the participants' perspectives and thus provide a valid account of these perspectives.

- **Interpretive validity**
  Accurately portraying the meaning given by the participants to what is being studied

■ **Participant feedback**
Discussion of the
researcher's conclu-
sions with the actual
participants

Some strategies for achieving interpretive validity are provided in Table 8.2. **Participant feedback** (or member checking) is perhaps the most important strategy (see Table 8.2). By sharing your interpretations of participants' viewpoints with the participants and other members of the group, you may clear up areas of miscommunication. Do the people being studied agree with what you have said about them? Although this strategy is not perfect, because some participants may attempt to put on a good face, useful information is frequently obtained and inaccuracies are often identified.

■ **Low-inference
descriptors**
Description that is
phrased very similarly
to the participants' ac-
counts and the re-
searchers' field notes

When writing the research report, using many **low-inference descriptors** is also helpful so that the reader can experience the participants' actual language, dialect, and personal meanings (Table 8.2). In this way, the reader can hear how the participants think and feel about issues and experiences. A *verbatim* is the lowest inference descriptor of all because the participants' exact words are provided in direct quotations. Here is an example of a verbatim from a high school dropout who was part of an ethnographic study of high school dropouts:

> I wouldn't do the work. I didn't like the teacher and I didn't like my Mom and Dad. So, even if I did my work, I wouldn't turn it in. I completed it. I just didn't want to turn it in. I was angry with my Mom and Dad because they were talking about moving out of state at the time. (Okey & Cusick, 1995, p. 257)

This verbatim provides some description (i.e., what the participant did), but it also provides some information about the participant's interpretations and personal meanings (which is the topic of interpretive validity). The participant expresses his frustration and anger toward his parents and teacher and shares with us what homework meant to him at the time and why he acted as he did. By reading verbatims like this one, readers of a report can experience for themselves the participants' perspectives. Again, getting into the minds of research participants is a common goal in qualitative research, and Maxwell calls our accuracy in portraying this "inner content" interpretive validity.

Theoretical Validity

■ **Theoretical validity**
The degree to which a
theoretical explanation
fits the data

Theoretical validity refers to the degree to which a theoretical explanation developed from a research study fits the data and is therefore credible and defensible. As we discuss in Chapter 1, theory usually refers to discussions of *how* a phenomenon operates and *why* it operates as it does. Theory is usually more abstract and less concrete than description and interpretation. Theory development moves beyond "just the facts" and provides an explanation of the phenomenon. In the words of Joseph Maxwell (1992):

> one could label the student's throwing of the eraser as an act of resistance, and connect this act to the repressive behavior or values of the teacher, the social structure of the school, and class relationships in U.S. society. The identification of the throwing as "resistance" constitutes the application of a theoretical construct . . . the connection of this to other aspects of the participants, the school, or the community constitutes the postulation of theoretical relationships among these constructs. (p. 291)

In this example, the theoretical construct called resistance is used to explain the student's behavior. Maxwell points out that the construct of resistance may also be related to other theoretical constructs or variables. In fact, theories are often developed by relating theoretical constructs.

A strategy for promoting theoretical validity is **extended fieldwork** (Table 8.2), which means that you should spend a sufficient amount of time studying your research participants and their setting so that you can have confidence that the patterns of relationships you believe are operating are stable and so that you can understand why these relationships occur. As you spend more time in the field collecting data and generating and testing your interpretations, your theoretical explanation might become more detailed and intricate. You may decide to use the strategy called **theory triangulation** (Table 8.2; Denzin, 1989). This means that you would examine how the phenomenon being studied would be explained by different theories and perspectives. The various theories might provide you with insights and help you develop a more cogent explanation. In a related way, you might also use investigator triangulation and consider the ideas and explanations generated by additional researchers studying the research participants.

As you develop your theoretical explanation, you should make some predictions based on the theory and test the accuracy of those predictions. When doing this, you can use the **pattern matching** strategy (Table 8.2). In pattern matching, the strategy is to make several predictions at once; then, if all of the predictions occur as predicted (i.e., if the pattern or "fingerprint" is found), you have evidence supporting your explanation. As you develop your theoretical explanation, you should also use the negative-case sampling strategy mentioned earlier (Table 8.2). That is, you must always search for cases or examples that do not fit your explanation so that you do not simply find data that support your developing theory. As a general rule, your final explanation should accurately reflect the majority of the people in your research study. Another useful strategy for promoting theoretical validity is called **peer review** (Table 8.2), which means that you should try to spend some time discussing your explanation with your colleagues so that they can identify any problems in it. Each problem must then be resolved. In some cases, you will find that you will need to go back to the field and collect additional data. Finally, when developing a theoretical explanation, you must also think about the issues of internal validity and external validity, to which we now turn.

> ■ **Extended fieldwork**
> Collecting data in the field over an extended period of time
>
> ■ **Theory triangulation**
> The use of multiple theories and perspectives to help interpret and explain the data
>
> ■ **Pattern matching**
> Predicting a pattern of results and determining whether the actual results fit the predicted pattern
>
> ■ **Peer review**
> Discussing one's interpretations and conclusions with one's peers or colleagues

Internal Validity

You are already familiar with internal validity, which is the fourth type of validity in qualitative research of interest to us. As you know, internal validity refers to the degree to which a researcher is justified in concluding that an observed relationship is causal. Often qualitative researchers are not interested in cause-and-effect relationships. Sometimes, however, qualitative researchers are interested in identifying potential causes and effects. In fact, qualitative research can be very helpful in describing how phenomena operate (i.e., studying process) and in developing and testing preliminary causal hypotheses and theories (Campbell, 1979; Johnson, 1994; LeCompte & Preissle, 1993; Strauss, 1995; Yin, 1994). However, after potential causal relationships are studied using qualitative research, they should be tested and confirmed by using experimental methods when this is feasible. In this way, more conclusive evidence about cause and effect can be obtained.

When qualitative researchers identify potential cause-and-effect relationships, they must think about many of the same issues discussed earlier in this chapter when we talked about internal validity and about the strategies that are used for obtaining theoretical validity. The qualitative researcher takes on the role of the "detective" searching for the true cause(s) of a phenomenon, examining each possible "clue," and attempting to rule out each rival explanation generated (see **researcher-as-detective** in Table 8.2). When trying to identify a causal relationship, the researcher makes mental comparisons. The comparison might be to a hypothetical control group. Although a control group is rarely used in qualitative research, the researcher can think about what would have happened if the causal factor had not occurred. The researcher can sometimes rely on his or her expert opinion, as well as published research studies, when available, in deciding what would have happened. Furthermore, if the event is something that should occur again the researcher can determine whether the causal factor precedes the outcome. In other words, when the causal factor occurs again, does the effect follow?

> ■ **Researcher-as-detective**
> Metaphor applied to the researcher when searching for cause and effect

When a researcher believes that an observed relationship is causal, he or she must also attempt to make sure that the observed change in the dependent variable is due to the independent variable and not to something else (e.g., a confounding extraneous variable). The successful researcher will always make a list of rival explanations or rival hypotheses that are possible or plausible reasons for the relationship other than the originally suspected cause. One way to identify rival explanations is to be a skeptic and think of reasons why the relationship should *not* be causal. Each rival explanation must be examined after the list has been developed. Sometimes you will be able to check a rival explanation with the data you have already collected through additional data analysis. At other times, you will need to collect additional data. One strategy would be to observe the relationship you believe to be causal under conditions in which the confounding variable is not present and compare this outcome with the original outcome. For example, if you concluded that a teacher effectively maintained classroom discipline on a given day but a critic maintained that it was the result of a parent visiting the classroom on that day, then you should try to observe the teacher again when the parent is not present. If the teacher is still successful, you have some evidence that the original finding was not because of the presence of the parent in the classroom.

All the strategies shown in Table 8.2 are used to improve the internal validity of qualitative research. Now we will explain the only two strategies not yet discussed: methods triangulation and data triangulation. When using **methods triangulation** (Table 8.2), the researcher uses more than one method of research in a single research study. The word *methods* is used broadly here, and it refers to different methods of research (ethnography, correlational, experimental, and so forth) as well to different methods of data collection (e.g., interviews, questionnaires, focus groups, observations). You can intermix any of these methods (e.g., ethnography and survey research methods, interviews and observations, or experimental research and interviews). The logic is to combine different methods that have nonoverlapping weaknesses and strengths. The weaknesses (and strengths) of one method will tend to be different from those of a different method, which means that when you combine two or more methods, you will have better evidence. In other words, the whole is better than its parts.

> ■ **Methods triangulation**
> The use of multiple research methods

Here is an example of methods triangulation. Perhaps you are interested in why students in an elementary classroom stigmatize a certain student named Brian. A stigmatized student is an individual who is not well liked, has a lower status, and is seen as different from the "normal" students. Perhaps Brian has a different haircut from the other students, is dressed differently, or doesn't act like the other students. In this case, you might decide to observe how students treat Brian in various situations. In addition to observing the students, you will probably decide to interview Brian and the other students to understand their beliefs and feelings about Brian. A strength of observational data is that you can actually see the students' behaviors. A weakness of interviews is that what the students say and what they actually do may be different. However, using interviews, you can delve into the students' thinking and reasoning, whereas you cannot do this using observational data. Therefore, the whole will likely be better than the parts.

When using **data triangulation** (Table 8.2), the researcher uses multiple data sources in a single research study. "Data sources" does not mean using different methods. Data triangulation does refer to the use of multiple data sources using a single method. For example, the use of multiple interviews would provide multiple data sources while using a single method (i.e., the interview method). Likewise, the use of multiple observations is another example of data triangulation; multiple data sources would be provided while using a single method (i.e., the observational method). Another important part of data triangulation involves collecting data at different times, at different places, and with different people.

■ **Data triangulation**
The use of multiple data sources

Here is an example of data triangulation. Perhaps a researcher is interested in studying why certain students are apathetic. It would make sense to get the perspectives of several different kinds of people. The researcher might interview teachers, interview students identified by the teachers as being apathetic, and interview peers of apathetic students. Then the researcher could check to see whether the information obtained from these different data sources was in agreement. Each data source may provide additional reasons as well as a different perspective on the question of student apathy, resulting in a more complete understanding of the phenomenon. The researcher should also interview apathetic students at different class periods during the day and in different types of classes (e.g., math and social studies). Through the rich information gathered (from different people, at different times, at different places), the researcher can develop a better understanding of why students are apathetic than if only one data source is used.

External Validity

As you know, external validity is important when you want to generalize from a set of research findings to other people, settings, times, treatments, and outcomes. Typically, generalizability is not the major purpose of qualitative research. There are at least two reasons for this view. First, the people and settings examined in qualitative research are rarely randomly selected, and as you know, random selection is the best way to generalize from a sample to a population. As a result, qualitative research is virtually always weak in the form of population validity focused on "generalizing to" populations.

Second, some qualitative researchers are more interested in documenting "particularistic" findings than "universalistic" findings. In other words, in certain forms of qualitative research, the goal is to describe a certain group of people or a certain event in a specific context, rather than to generate findings that are broadly applicable. At a fundamental level, many qualitative researchers do not believe in the presence of "general laws" or "universal laws." General laws are things that apply to many people, and universal laws are things that apply to everyone. As a result, qualitative research is frequently considered weak on the "generalizing across populations" form of population validity (i.e., generalizing to different kinds of people), and on ecological validity (i.e., generalizing across settings), and temporal validity (i.e., generalizing across times).

■ **Naturalistic generalization**
Generalizing on the basis of similarity

Other experts argue that rough generalizations can be made from qualitative research. Perhaps the most reasonable stance toward the issue of generalizing is that we can generalize to other people, settings, times, and treatments to the degree to which they are similar to the people, settings, times, and treatments in the original study. Stake (1997) uses the term **naturalistic generalization**[1] to refer to this process of generalizing on the basis of similarity. The bottom line is this: The more similar the people and circumstances in a particular research study are to the ones that you want to generalize to, the more defensible your generalization will be and the more readily you should make such a generalization.

To help readers of a research report know when they can generalize, qualitative researchers should provide the following kinds of information: the number and kinds of people in the study, how they were selected to be in the study, contextual information, the nature of the researcher's relationship with the participants, information about any "informants" who provided information, the methods of data collection used, and the data analysis techniques used. This information is usually reported in the methodology section of the final research report. Using the information included in a well-written methodology section, readers will be able to make informed decisions about to whom the results may be generalized. They will also have the information they will need if they decide to replicate the research study with new participants.

■ **Replication logic**
The idea that the more times a research finding is shown to be true with different sets of people, the more confidence we can place in the finding and in generalizing beyond the original participants

Some experts show another way to generalize from qualitative research (e.g., Yin, 1994). Qualitative researchers can sometimes use **replication logic,** just like the replication logic that is commonly used by experimental researchers when they generalize beyond the people in their studies, even when they do not have random samples. According to replication logic, the more times a research finding is shown to be true with different sets of people, the more confidence we can place in the finding and in the conclusion that the finding generalizes beyond the people in the original research study (Cook & Campbell, 1979). In other words, if the finding is replicated with different kinds of people and in different places, then the evidence suggests that the finding applies very broadly. Yin's key point is that there is no reason why replication logic cannot be applied to certain kinds of qualitative research.[2]

Here is an example. Over the years, you might observe a certain pattern of interactions between boys and girls in a third-grade classroom. Now you decide to conduct a qualitative research study and you find that the pattern of interaction occurs in your classroom and in two other third-grade classrooms you study. Because your research is interesting, you decide to publish it. Then other researchers replicate your study with other people and they find that the same relationship holds in the third-grade classrooms they study. According to replication logic, the more times a theory or a research finding is replicated with other people, the greater the support for the theory or research finding. Now assume that other researchers find that the relationship holds in classrooms at several other grade levels. If this happens, the evidence suggests that the finding generalizes to students in other grade levels, adding additional generality to the finding.

8.25 What is meant by research validity in qualitative research?

8.26 Why is researcher bias a threat to validity, and what strategies are used to reduce this effect?

8.27 What is the difference between descriptive validity, interpretive validity, and theoretical validity?

8.28 What strategies are used for promoting descriptive, interpretative, and theoretical validity?

8.29 How is external validity assessed in qualitative research, and why is qualitative research typically weak on this type of validity?

R E V I E W

QUESTIONS

SUMMARY

When we conduct a study, we develop a plan, outline, or strategy to use that will allow us to collect data that will lead to a valid conclusion. In any study, there are a number of extraneous variables that could systematically vary with the independent variable and confound the results making it impossible to assess the effect of the independent variable. To eliminate potentially confounding extraneous variables, we must design our study so that we can make valid inferences about the relationship between independent and dependent variables. In quantitative studies, there are four types of validity that are used to evaluate the accuracy of the inferences that can be made from the study results.

Statistical conclusion validity refers to the validity with which we can infer that two variables are related and the strength of that relationship. Internal validity refers to the validity with which we can infer that the relationship between two variables is causal. This causal relationship can be a causal descriptive relationship or a causal explanatory relationship.

To make this causal connection between the independent and dependent variables, we need evidence that they are related, that the direction of effect is from the independent variable (the cause) to the dependent variable (the effect), and that the observed effect on the dependent variable is due to the independent variable and not to some extraneous variable. Internal validity is related to the ability to rule out the influence of extraneous variables. A study is internally valid when the effect observed on the dependent variable is due to the independent variable. However, there are many extraneous variables that can creep into a study and confound the results. The influence of these extraneous variables must be controlled or eliminated. A number of the more obvious threats to the internal validity of a study are the following:

1. Ambiguous temporal precedence—the inability to specify which variable preceded which other variable.
2. History—specific events, other than the independent variable, that occur between the first and second measurement of the dependent variable.
3. Maturation—the physical or mental changes that may occur in individuals over time such as aging, learning, boredom, hunger, and fatigue.

4. Testing—changes in the score a person makes on the second administration of a test that can be attributed entirely to the effect of having previously taken the test.

5. Instrumentation—any change that occurs in the measuring instrument between the pretesting and posttesting.

6. Regression artifact—the tendency of extreme scores to regress or move toward the mean of the distribution on a second testing.

7. Differential selection—differences that exist in the comparison groups at the outset of the research study and are not due to the independent variable.

8. Additive or interactive effects—differences that exist in the comparison groups because one of the threats, such as maturation or history, affects the groups differently.

9. Differential attrition—difference that exists in the comparison groups because the participants that drop out of the various comparison groups have different characteristics.

In addition to trying to meet the criteria of internal validity, the researcher must attempt to meet the criteria of external validity. In most studies, we want to be able to generalize the results and state that they hold true for other individuals in other settings and at different points in time. External validity is achieved if we can generalize the results of our study to the larger target population, at other points in time, in other settings across different treatment variations, and across different outcomes.

Threats to external validity include a lack of population validity, ecological validity, temporal validity, treatment variation validity, and outcome validity. Population validity refers to the ability to generalize to and across subpopulations in the target population. Ecology validity refers to the ability to generalize the results of a study across settings. Temporal validity refers to the extent to which the results of a study can be generalized across time. Treatment variation validity refers to the extent to which the results of the study can be generalized across different variations of the treatment condition. Outcome validity refers to the extent to which the results of the study can be generalized across different outcomes that should be influenced by the treatment condition.

When we conduct a research study, we also need to select measures of the variables we are investigating. This is frequently a difficult process because the variables we study often represent abstract constructs and we must devise some way of measuring these constructs. The technique that most researchers use is operationalism, or selecting a specific operation or set of operations as the representation of the construct they are investigating. Although operationalism is necessary for communicating the way a construct is represented, seldom, if ever, does it provide a complete representation of the construct. Each operationalization of a construct represents only a portion of the construct. This is a problem of construct validity, or the extent to which a higher-order construct is represented in the study.

The majority of this chapter focused on validity in traditional quantitative research, especially experimental research. However, validity is also an important issue in qualitative research. Three types of validity in qualitative research are descriptive validity, interpretive validity, and theoretical validity. Descriptive validity refers to the factual accuracy of the account as reported by the qualitative researcher. Interpretive validity is obtained to the degree that the participants' viewpoints, thoughts, intentions, and experiences are accurately understood and reported by the qualitative researcher. Theoretical validity is obtained to the degree to which a theory or theoretical explanation developed from a research study fits the data and is therefore credible and defensible. Internal validity and external validity are also important to qualitative research when the researcher is interested in making cause and effect statements and generalizing, respectively. Twelve strategies that are used to promote validity in qualitative research were discussed.

KEY TERMS

accessible population (p. 243)
additive and interactive effects (p. 239)
ambiguous temporal
   precedence (p. 234)
attrition (p. 241)
causal description (p. 230)
causal explanation (p. 231)
confounding variable (p. 228)
construct validity (p. 247)
data triangulation (p. 255)
descriptive validity (p. 251)
differential attrition (p. 241)
differential selection (p. 239)
ecological validity (p. 245)
extended fieldwork (p. 253)
external validity (p. 242)
extraneous variable (p. 228)
history (p. 235)

instrumentation (p. 237)
internal validity (p. 230)
interpretive validity (p. 251)
investigator triangulation (p. 251)
low-inference descriptors (p. 252)
maturation (p. 236)
methods triangulation (p. 254)
multigroup research design (p. 234)
multiple operationalism (p. 248)
naturalistic generalization (p. 256)
negative-case sampling (p. 251)
one-group pretest-posttest
   design (p. 233)
operationalism (p. 247)
outcome validity (p. 246)
participant feedback (p. 252)
pattern matching (p. 253)
peer review (p. 253)

population validity (p. 242)
reactivity (p. 245)
regression artifact (p. 238)
reflexivity (p. 249)
replication logic (p. 256)
researcher-as-detective (p. 254)
researcher bias (p. 249)
selection-history effect (p. 239)
selection-maturation effect (p. 240)
statistical conclusion validity (p. 229)
target population (p. 242)
temporal validity (p. 245)
testing (p. 236)
theoretical validity (p. 252)
theory triangulation (p. 253)
third variable (p. 232)
treatment variation validity (p. 245)

STUDY TIP   Visit the companion website for *Educational Research* at www.ablongman.com/johnsonchristensen2e for study questions and multiple-choice questions to see how well you have mastered the material in this chapter. Also look at the other activities we have included to promote your mastery of the material in this chapter.

DISCUSSION QUESTIONS

1. In this chapter, we listed and discussed four different types of validity. We also stated that it is unlikely that a researcher will be able to attain all four types in a single study. If only three of the different types of validity can be achieved, which three should the researcher strive for? Does this mean that the one type that is disregarded is less important?

2. In this chapter, we have discussed several criteria for inferring causation. Can we ever be sure that

we have met these criteria? What type of evidence is needed to ensure that each of the criteria have been met?

3. In what type of studies would each of the various threats to internal validity be most prevalent?

4. Why do qualitative and quantitative researchers refer to different concepts when referring to research validity?

5. Is it ever possible to attain interpretive validity in a qualitative research study?

RESEARCH EXERCISES

Using Research Navigator, find a quantitative or qualitative research article in an area in which you are interested, such as teacher burnout. When selecting an article, make sure it is about a cause-and-effect issue. Read the article, and then answer questions 1 through 4. If you selected a qualitative article, also answer questions 5 and 6.

1. Is the study a causal descriptive or causal explanatory study? Explain why it is one and not the other.
2. Identify the threats to internal validity that might exist in this study.
3. Identify the constructs that are used in this study and the operations used to define these constructs.
4. What problems might exist in trying to generalize the results of the study, and to whom and what conditions might the results be generalized?
5. Does the study have descriptive validity, interpretive validity, or theoretical validity? If it has any of these, how does the author demonstrate this type of validity?
6. Is internal or external validity an issue in the study, and how are these handled?

RELEVANT INTERNET SITES

http://trochim.human.cornell.edu/kb/intval.htm
A website that provides a discussion of internal validity.

www2.chass.ncsu.edu/garson/pa765/validity.htm
A website that provides an extended discussion of validity as it is applied to drawing conclusions from data.

www.nova.edu/ssss/OR/OR4-3/winter.html
A website that provides a discussion of validity in both quantitative and qualitative research.

RECOMMENDED READING

Campbell, D. T. (1988). Definitional versus multiple operationism. In E. S. Overman (Ed.), *Methodology and epistemology for social science: Selected papers* (pp. 31–36). Chicago: University of Chicago Press.

Maxwell, J. A. (1992). Understanding and validity in qualitative research. *Harvard Educational Review, 62*(3), 279–299.

Shadish, W. R., Cook, T. D., & Campbell, D. T. (2002). *Experimental and quasi-experimental designs for generalized causal inference.* Boston: Houghton Mifflin. (Chapters 2 and 3 discuss the various types of validity and threats to these types of validity.)

ENDNOTES

1. Donald Campbell (1988) makes a similar point, and he uses the term *proximal similarity* to refer to the degree of similarity between the people and circumstances in the original research study and the people and circumstances to which you wish to apply the findings. Using Campbell's term, your goal is to check for proximal similarity.

2. The late Donald Campbell, perhaps the most important research methodologist over the past fifty years, approved of Yin's (1994) book. See, for example, his introduction to this book.

9

Experimental Research

LEARNING OBJECTIVES

To be able to

- Explain the way in which the educational experiment produces evidence of causality.
- Describe the different ways in which an independent variable can be manipulated.
- Explain the importance of control in experimental research and how control is achieved.
- Explain the different ways of controlling the influence of potentially confounding variables.
- Explain why some experimental research designs are weak designs and others are strong designs.
- Compare and contrast factorial and repeated-measures designs.
- Explain the concept of interaction.

One of the rituals that seems to be performed every 10 to 15 years in the hallowed halls of academia is curriculum reform. Seldom, if ever, is there complete agreement about the curriculum that undergraduates should complete. This lack of agreement initiates a movement to reform a current curriculum. For example, Richard R. Beeman, the dean of the University of Pennsylvania's School of Arts and Sciences, has stated that the university's current curriculum "isn't perfect." Others at the university have described the current curriculum as "a shambles" and "a Hodgepodge" in serious need of overhaul (Bartlett, 2002).

When curriculum reform is initiated, it is frequently hashed out in committees. This committee approach is often hamstrung by poor management and a failure to build consensus. For example, when the University of Pennsylvania started discussing reform in the undergraduate curriculum in 1998, almost everyone had a vision. The problem was that everyone's vision was different. The result is frequently a half-hearted compromise, with idealism giving way to political horse-trading that typically results in another revision in another 10 to 15 years.

Curriculum reform is a task for which the educational researcher should be well suited because educational researchers are the experts in conducting research on educational issues. From a research perspective, curriculum reform should be just as amenable to a research study as any other educational issue. This is exactly the approach taken by the University of Pennsylvania. The university's president, Judith Rodin, has stated that these important changes should be approached in the same manner and with the same seriousness as any other scholarly activity (Bartlett, 2002).

As a result, the University of Pennsylvania decided to conduct an experimental study to investigate the outcome of students' taking different curricula. To conduct this experimental study, the researchers had to design a research study that would provide knowledge of the effect of following different curricula. This means that they had to make decisions about the independent and dependent variables as well as the control techniques to be used had to be identified. The independent variable in this study was the different curricula followed by the students. The students in the control group were to follow the standard curriculum, and the students in the experimental group were allowed more freedom in selecting their courses but were also required to take a series of interdisciplinary courses, many of which were team taught.

The dependent variables in this study involved the results of focus groups, interviews, questionnaires, grades achieved, and skills tests as well the courses selected by students in the experimental group. Control over many extraneous variables was accomplished by randomly assigning the volunteer students to either a control or an experimental group. These are the types of decisions that have to be made to construct a research design that will provide information that will help answer your research question. In this chapter, we will discuss the decisions that must be made in developing a good research design and present the most basic research designs used in experimental studies.

The experimental research approach is the research method designed to ferret out cause-and-effect relationships. Causal relationships can be identified when using the experimental research approach because it allows us to observe, under controlled conditions, the effect of systematically changing one or more variables. It is this ability that represents the primary advantage of the experimental approach because it permits greater control over confounding extraneous variables. The greater the degree of control, the greater the degree of internal validity of the study, and the greater our confidence in our claims about causality. However, the more control that is exerted over confounding extraneous variables, the more unnatural the study becomes, which threatens the external validity of the study. Experimental research therefore frequently sacrifices external validity for enhanced internal validity. In spite of this disadvantage, experimental research is a valuable methodology for the educational researcher.

THE EXPERIMENT

■ **Experiment**
An environment in which the researcher objectively observes phenomena that are made to occur in a strictly controlled situation in which one or more variables are varied and the others are kept constant

Experimental research is carried out within the context of an experiment. An **experiment** is defined as the development of an environment in which the researcher, typically called the experimenter, objectively observes "phenomena which are made to occur in strictly controlled situations in which one *or more* variables are varied and the others are kept constant" (Zimney, 1961, p. 18; italics ours). This seems to be one of the better definitions, so let's take a closer look at what it is saying. First, it is saying that we must attempt to make impartial and unbiased observations. This is not always possible because experimenters can unintentionally influence the outcome of an experiment. However, we must realize that we are capable of some unintentional influence and strive to make observations that are free of this bias.

In conducting experiments, we make observations of "phenomena that are made to occur." The term *phenomena* refers to some observable event. In educational research, this means that we observe events such as responses to an interview, test, questionnaire, or actions or statements made by the participants in an experimental research study. These phenomena are "made to occur" because we present a set of conditions to the research participant and record the effect of these conditions on their behavior. This is the way in which we ferret out cause-and-effect relationships through use of the experiment. We present a set of stimulus conditions—the independent variable—and then observe the effect of this independent variable presentation on the dependent variable.

The observations must be made in a strictly controlled situation. This means that we must eliminate the influence of confounding extraneous variables. Controlling for variables confounded with the independent variable is necessary to achieve internal validity.

The last component of the definition of experiment that needs to be examined is that "one or more variables are varied and the others are kept constant." This means that we deliberately vary the independent variable(s) along a defined range and attempt to make sure that all other variables do not vary. For example, if you want to test the effect of eating breakfast on the ability to solve math problems, you might want to vary the independent variable of breakfast by having a group of participants that eats breakfast and a group that does not eat breakfast. On the other hand, you might want to vary the type of breakfast that the participants eat. You might feed some participants a high-carbohydrate, low-protein breakfast and feed others a high-protein, low-carbohydrate breakfast. The point is that you must vary the independent variable in some way, but the nature of the variation you create will depend on your research question and hypothesis. Regardless of the type of variation produced, you must keep all variables other than the independent variable constant. In other words, you must make sure that variables other than the independent variable do not vary. This is in effect saying that when you conduct an experiment, you must create a set of conditions in which extraneous variables are controlled and not confounded with the independent variable.

INDEPENDENT VARIABLE MANIPULATION

The independent variable is the variable that is manipulated by the experimenter and presumed to cause a change in the dependent variable. In any given study, there are many possible independent variables that can be used. The independent variable or variables used in a given study are specified by the research question(s). For example, one of the research questions Breznitz (1997) asked was "Does accelerated reading among dyslexic children partially account for changes in their short-term memory processing?" Breznitz wanted to determine the effect that increasing reading speed has on short-term memory, so reading speed has to be the independent variable. This means that reading speed has to be varied in some way. Breznitz hypothesized that readers with dyslexia who engaged in fast-paced reading relative to self-paced reading would show significant performance gains in short-term memory. This hypothesis specifies the nature of the variation that has to be created in the independent variable. There have to be at least two levels of variation of the independent variable of reading speed; these two levels are fast-paced and self-paced reading. Although the research question may identify the independent variable, it is not always easy to create the needed variation. For example, Breznitz had to develop a procedure that would allow for the manipulation of reading speed and in such a way that the experimenter could increase the speed of reading over that of the self-paced reading of the children with dyslexia.

From this brief discussion, you should be able to see that there are many decisions that must be made regarding the manipulation of the independent variable. You must identify the variable that will represent the independent variable, and then you must decide how to manipulate the independent variable to provide an answer to your research question.

Ways to Manipulate an Independent Variable

The research question, as we have just discussed, identifies the independent variable. However, it does not specify the way in which the independent variable is to be manipulated. There are at least three different ways, illustrated in Figure 9.1, in which you can manipulate an independent variable. The first way is by a **presence or absence technique.** This technique is exactly what the name implies. One group of research participants receives a treatment condition, and the other group does not. For example, assume that you want to determine whether a review session will improve the mathematics test grades of high school students taking algebra. You can manipulate the independent variable using the presence or absence technique by having one group of algebra students take an examination without the aid of a review session and the other group take the same examination after they have participated in a review session.

A second way in which you can manipulate the independent variable is by an **amount technique.** This technique involves administering different amounts of the independent variable to several groups of participants. For example, you might think not only that a review session helps to improve the examination scores of students taking an algebra test, but

■ **Presence or absence technique**
Manipulating the independent variable by presenting one group the treatment condition and withholding it from the other group

■ **Amount technique**
Manipulating the independent variable by giving the various comparison groups different amounts of the independent variable

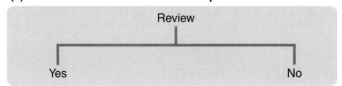

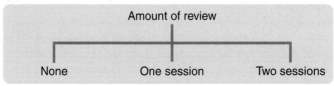

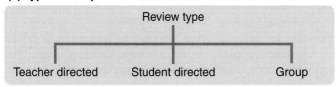

■ **FIGURE 9.1**   Three different ways of manipulating the independent variable

also that several review sessions during the week preceding the examination provide an additional benefit. This would essentially involve varying the amount of review the students receive. You could manipulate the amount of review by having one group of students take the algebra examination without the aid of a review session. A second group would be given one review session, a third group would receive two review sessions, and a fourth group would receive three review sessions.

■ **Type technique**
Manipulating the independent variable by varying the type of variable presented to the different comparison groups

A third way of manipulating the independent variable is by a **type technique.** Using this technique involves varying the type of variable presented to the participants. For example, rather than varying the amount of review the participants received, you might think that the type of review is the important variable. You could, for example, have a teacher-directed review session, a student-directed review session, or a group review session. Once you have identified the types of review sessions you want to investigate, you would expose a different group of research participants to each type of review session prior to their taking the examination.

CONTROL OF CONFOUNDING VARIABLES

In Chapter 8 we discussed a number of the more obvious extraneous variables that can threaten the internal validity of an experiment. These are the types of extraneous variables that must be controlled within an experiment to enable us to reach causal conclusions. There are a number of ways in which confounding extraneous variables can be controlled. Before we discuss several of these control techniques, we want to briefly discuss the meaning of **experimental control.**

When you first consider controlling for potentially confounding extraneous variables, you probably think about totally eliminating the influence of these variables. For example, if noise is a potential confound in an experiment, you naturally consider controlling this potential confound by constructing an environment void of noise, perhaps by having the participants complete the experiment in a soundproof room. However, most variables that can influence the outcome of an educational experiment, such as intelligence, age, motivation, and stress, cannot be eliminated. Control of these variables comes through the elimination of any differential influence that they may have. **Differential influence** refers to influence that is different for different comparison groups of participants. For example, intelligence would have a differential influence if one comparison group was made up of bright individuals and the other comparison group was made up of individuals with average intelligence. We want to keep the influence of variables such as intelligence constant across the comparison groups, or equate the groups on such variables so that any difference noted on the dependent variable would be due to the manipulation of the independent variable. For example, Wade and Blier (1974), in their study of the effect of two methods of learning on the retention of a list of words, had to control for the association the participants had with these words because participants who had more association with the words would probably learn them faster and retain them longer. To control for association value, Wade and Blier selected words that had previously been shown to have the same average association value. In this way, they held the association value of the words constant across the two groups of participants and eliminated any differential influence this variable might have had.

As you can see from this example, control is frequently obtained by designing the study in such a way that the influence of the potential extraneous variables does not vary across the comparison groups. When constancy is obtained, the extraneous variable exerts an equal influence on the dependent variable across all comparison groups. When an equal influence in exerted, the effect of the extraneous variable on the dependent variable is the same for all comparison groups. Any difference noted on the dependent variable would therefore be attributable to the independent variable. Therefore, the influence of the extraneous variable would have been controlled. Control, as you can see, generally refers to achieving constancy. The question that must be answered is how to achieve this constancy. We now turn our attention to some of the more general techniques for achieving constancy of effect of potentially confounding variables.

- **Experimental control**
  Eliminating any differential influence of extraneous variables

- **Differential influence**
  When the influence of an extraneous variable is different for the various comparison groups

9.1 What is an experiment and what are the significant components of this definition?

9.2 What are the different ways a researcher could use to manipulate an independent variable?

9.3 What is meant by the term *experimental control,* and how is experimental control related to *differential influence* within the experiment?

R E V I E W

Q U E S T I O N S

Random Assignment

Random assignment is a procedure that makes assignments to conditions on the basis of chance. Because it makes assignments on the basis of chance, random assignment maximizes the probability that potentially confounding extraneous variables, known and unknown, will not systematically bias the results of the study. Because random assignment has the ability to control for both known and unknown potentially confounding extraneous variables, it is a procedure that should be used whenever and wherever possible. Do not confuse random assignment with random selection or random sampling. Random selection or random sampling involves selection of units from a population by chance so that the sample selected will be similar to the population. Random assignment starts with a sample, often a convenience sample, and then makes assignments to groups on the basis of chance to maximize the probability that the groups generated will be similar.

Ideally, in any research study, you should select participants randomly from the population because this provides maximum assurance that a systematic bias does not exist in the selection process and that the selected participants are representative of the population. Remember that "representative" means that the sample participants have characteristics similar to that of the population and can, therefore, stand for the population. If the average IQ in the population is 110, then the average IQ in the sample should be about 110. The sample can say something about the population only when it is representative of the population.

Once participants have been randomly *selected* from the population, they should be randomly *assigned* to the various comparison groups, as illustrated in Figure 9.2. Although randomly selecting the sample of participants from the population and then randomly assigning the participants to the various comparison groups is the ideal arrangement, seldom is it possible to randomly select research participants from the population. Just think of the

FIGURE 9.2   The ideal procedure for obtaining participants for an experiment

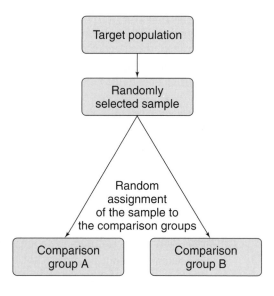

difficulty of randomly selecting a sample of high school English teachers from all English teachers within the United States. This would be not only difficult but next to impossible to do unless you had a large research grant that allowed you either to go to the high school in which they were teaching or pay to have them come to your university. Consequently, random selection of participants from the population is an ideal that is seldom achieved. Fortunately, random selection of participants is not the crucial element needed to achieve control over the influence of confounding variables in an experiment. Random assignment to the comparison groups provides maximum assurance that the extraneous variables are controlled because it makes the groups similar on all extraneous variables.

When research participants are randomly assigned to various comparison groups, each research participant has an equal probability of being assigned to each group. This means that chance determines which person gets assigned to each comparison group. Remember that each person brings with him or her certain variables, such as intelligence. If we want to control for a variable such as intelligence, we want individuals with approximately the same intelligence level in each comparison group. This is exactly what random assignment does. When participants are randomly assigned, the variables they bring with them are also randomly assigned. The result is that variables such as intelligence are randomly assigned to the comparison groups when we randomly assign the participants. Therefore, the comparison groups are similar on these variables, and any differences that do exist will be due to chance. Random assignment therefore produces control by virtue of the fact that the variables to be controlled are distributed in approximately the same manner in all comparison groups at the beginning of the experiment. If the comparison groups are similar on the extraneous variables, the groups are expected to perform approximately the same on the dependent variable *when* the independent variable has no effect on the participants. If the participants respond differently on the dependent variable, this difference can be attributed to the independent variable. Randomly assigning participants to groups is illustrated on the companion website for this textbook at www.ablongman.com/johnsonchristensen2e under bonus material.

Random assignment is the most important technique to use to control potentially confounding extraneous variables. However, this does not mean that random assignment will always give us the needed control. It is possible that the comparison groups will not be similar even with random assignment because chance determines the way in which the variables are distributed. In most instances, particularly when you randomly assign a large number of individuals, the comparison groups will be similar. However, because chance determines which people are assigned to each comparison group, it is possible that the groups will not be similar. For example, it is possible that random assignment would result in the brightest individuals being assigned to one comparison group and individuals with average intelligence being assigned to another comparison group. The smaller the number of research participants, the greater the risk that this will happen. However, random assignment minimizes the probability of this happening even with small samples. Since the probability of the groups being equal is so much greater with than without random assignment, it is a very powerful method for generating similar groups and eliminating the threat of confounding variables. Because random assignment is the only method for controlling for the influence of unknown variables, it is necessary to randomize whenever and wherever possible, even when other control techniques are used.

Matching

Matching is a control technique for equating the comparison groups on one or more variables that are correlated with the dependent variable. The most commonly used matching
procedure is to match participants in the various comparison groups on a case-by-case basis
for each of the selected extraneous variables. For example, assume that you want to conduct
an experiment testing the effectiveness of three different methods of instruction in algebra on
algebra test performance. You know that variables such as IQ and gender are variables that
probably affect test performance, so you want to control for the influence of these variables.
One way to obtain the needed control is to match individual participants in the three comparison groups so that each group contains individuals with about the same IQ and gender. In
other words, if the first participant who volunteers for the study is a male with an IQ of 118,
then we have to find two other males with IQs very close to 118. It would be very difficult to
find individuals with exactly the same IQ, so the criterion is that the participants have to be
very similar on the variables on which they are matched. Once you have identified three individuals who are similar on the matched variables, you randomly assign these three individuals to the three comparison groups. Note the use of random assignment even when we are
using the control technique of matching. This follows the rule we stated earlier of randomiz-
ing whenever and wherever possible, even when other control techniques, such as matching,
are used. Once these three individuals have been matched and randomly assigned, you would
find another group of three individuals matched on IQ and gender and randomly assign them
to the comparison groups. This procedure, as illustrated in Figure 9.3, is continued until you
have the desired number of participants in each comparison group. The end result is that the
participants in the comparison groups are identical or very similar on the matched variables.
The influence of these variables on the dependent variable is, therefore, constant across the
comparison groups. This is the desired type of control in an experiment.

The matching technique just described is an *individual* matching approach because individuals are matched. It is also possible to engage in *group* matching. With group matching, you would want the groups of participants to have similar average scores and a similar
distribution of scores. In other words, if you were matching on intelligence and one group
of participants had an average IQ of 118 and a standard deviation of IQ scores of 6, you
would want to select participants for the other two groups with an average IQ of about 118
and a standard deviation of IQ scores of about 6.

Holding the Extraneous Variable Constant

Another frequently used technique is to hold the extraneous variable to be controlled constant across the comparison groups. This means that the participants in each comparison
group will have approximately the same amount or type of the extraneous variable. For example, assume you want to test the efficacy of using ebonics in teaching reading. This approach was developed for use with African American individuals, so you would probably
want to eliminate the extraneous variable of including other ethnic groups in the study by
including only African American students. The extraneous variable of ethnic group would
be controlled by holding the ethnic background of the research participants constant across
the comparison groups. After selecting a sample of only African American students, you

■ **FIGURE 9.3**   The matching control technique

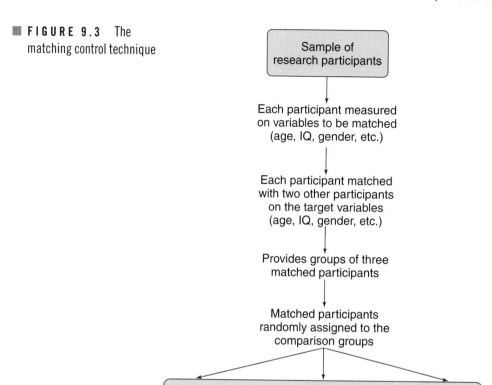

should include the control technique of randomly assigning these students to the comparison groups, as illustrated in Figure 9.4. Again, this follows the principle of randomly assigning whenever and wherever possible.

Building the Extraneous Variable into the Research Design

Extraneous variables can be controlled by being built into the research design. When this is done, the extraneous variable becomes another independent variable. For example, in the hypothetical study investigating the use of ebonics in teaching reading to African American children, you want to control for the effects of intelligence. It would not make much sense to use the control technique of holding intelligence constant and include only individuals with IQs of a given range such as 105–110. It seems more appropriate to include individuals with a wider spectrum of intelligence levels. One way to accomplish this goal and at the same time control for the extraneous variable of intelligence, is to select individuals with several IQ levels, such as 90–99, 100–109, and 110–119, and treat these IQ levels as an independent variable, as illustrated in Figure 9.5.

Although building the extraneous variable into the research design is an excellent technique for achieving control, it is recommended only if you are interested in the differences produced by the various levels of the extraneous variable. In the hypothetical ebonics study,

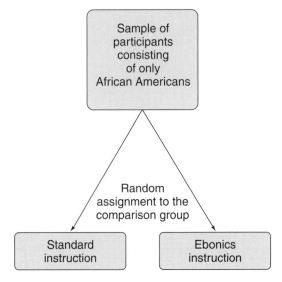

■ **FIGURE 9.4**   Control exercised by
holding the extraneous variable constant

you might be interested in seeing whether the efficacy of teaching reading using this method is more effective with individuals of different intellectual levels. In this case, this control technique is excellent because it identifies the effect produced by the extraneous variable while, at the same time, controlling for its influence on the other independent variable of interest. In other words, it takes an extraneous variable that could bias the experiment and makes it focal in the experiment as an independent variable.

Counterbalancing

■ **Counterbalancing**
Administering the experimental treatment conditions to all comparison groups but in a different order

■ **Sequencing effects**
Biasing effects that can occur when each participant must participate in each experimental treatment condition

■ **Order effect**
A sequencing effect that occurs from the order in which the treatment conditions are administered

Counterbalancing refers to administering the experimental treatments to all comparison groups but in a different order. It is often used in repeated measures research designs. It is a technique that is used to control for **sequencing effects,** which are effects that can occur when the design of an experiment requires each participant to participate in each of several experimental comparison groups, as illustrated in Figure 9.6. Two types of sequencing effects can occur when every person participates in each comparison group. The first is an **order effect,** which arises from the order in which the treatment conditions are administered. Supposed you are interested in the effect of caffeine on learning to spell based on the fact that caffeine is assumed to increase attention and alertness. To test the effect of caffeine, you could administer caffeine on one day and a placebo on another day. This means that the research participants would get one of two possible orders of the treatment conditions: caffeine on the first day and placebo on the second day or placebo on the first day and caffeine on the second day.

In a study such as this, on the first experimental day, the research participants might be unfamiliar with the experimental procedure, participating in an educational experiment, or the surroundings of the experiment. If they are administered the placebo condition on the first day, the participants might not perform effectively because their attention will not be

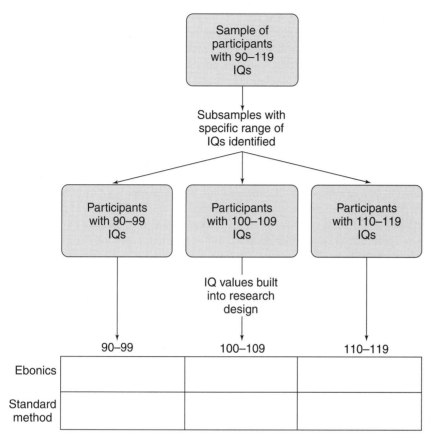

	90–99	100–109	110–119
Ebonics			
Standard method			

■ **FIGURE 9.5**   Control of an extraneous variable by building it into the research design

■ **FIGURE 9.6**   Type of design that may include sequencing effects

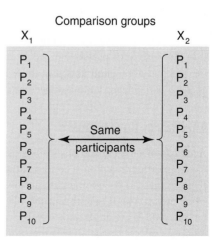

focused totally on the spelling task. On the second day, when they are administered caffeine, this familiarity will exist, increasing the chances that the participant can focus more on the spelling task, which could enhance performance. The result is that the participants might perform better under the caffeine treatment condition administered on the second day not because it is any more effective, but because the participants are more familiar with the experiment and the experimental surroundings and can focus more attention on learning the list of spelling words. This type of effect is an order effect because it occurs strictly because of the order of presentation of the experimental treatment conditions.

The second type of sequencing effect that can occur is a carryover effect. A **carryover effect** occurs when performance in one treatment condition is partially dependent on the conditions that precede it. For example, if in the caffeine experiment caffeine was administered on the first day, it is possible that the caffeine was not completely metabolized and cleared from the body before the participants consumed the placebo on the next day. Any effect of the prior day's dose of caffeine would therefore carry over to the next day and affect performance. Therefore, the performance on the day that participants consumed the placebo would be any placebo effect plus any carryover from the prior day's consumption of caffeine.

One of the ways of controlling for the carryover and order effects is to counterbalance the order in which the treatment conditions are administered to the participants. Basically, counterbalancing involves administering each experimental treatment condition to all groups of research participants but in a different order. For example, in the caffeine experiment, assume that we wanted to test the effect of three different doses of caffeine (100, 200, and 300 mg of caffeine) against no caffeine or a placebo group. One way of counterbalancing would be to have groups of participants equal to the number of levels of the independent variable. In this caffeine experiment, there are four levels of caffeine ranging from no caffeine to 300 mg, so there would be four experimental groups. Each group would receive the four treatment conditions but in a different order, as follows:

> Group 1—placebo, 100 mg, 300 mg, 200 mg
> Group 2—100 mg, 200 mg, placebo, 300 mg
> Group 3—200 mg, 300 mg, 100 mg, placebo
> Group 4—300 mg, placebo, 200 mg, 100 mg

This establishes the different counterbalanced orders. The important point to remember is that each group of participants takes each experimental treatment condition, so, in effect, the study is replicated as many times as there are groups of participants. To learn more about establishing counterbalanced sequences, see Christensen (2001, pp. 212–218).

Analysis of Covariance

Analysis of covariance is a statistical method that can be used to equate groups that are found to differ on a pretest or some other variable or variables. It is useful when the participants in the various comparison groups differ on a pretest variable that is related to the dependent variable. If the pretest variable is related to the dependent variable, differences can be observed in the dependent variable that are due to the differences on the pretest variable. Analysis of covariance adjusts the scores on the dependent variable for the differences ob-

■ **Carryover effect**
A sequencing effect that occurs when performance in one treatment condition is influenced by participation in a prior treatment condition(s)

■ **Analysis of covariance**
A statistical method that can be used to statistically equate groups that differ on a pretest or some other variable

served on the pretest variable and in this way statistically equates the participants in the various comparison groups. For example, if you are conducting a study on gender differences in solving mathematics problems, you will want to make sure that the male and female students are of equal ability level. If you measure the IQ of the participants and find that the male students are brighter than the female students, the mathematics performance could be due to this difference in ability and not anything related to gender. You could use analysis of covariance to adjust the mathematics scores for this difference in intelligence and in this way create two groups of participants that are equated, at least on this variable.

9.4 What is random assignment, and what is the difference between random assignment and random selection?

9.5 How does random assignment accomplish the goal of controlling for the influence of confounding variables?

9.6 How would you implement the control technique of matching, and how does this technique control for the influence of confounding variables?

9.7 How would you use the control technique of holding the extraneous variable constant?

9.8 When would you want to build the extraneous variable into the research design?

9.9 What is counterbalancing and when would you use it?

9.10 What is the difference between a carryover effect and an order effect?

9.11 What is analysis of covariance, and when would you use it?

REVIEW

QUESTIONS

EXPERIMENTAL RESEARCH DESIGNS

Research design refers to the outline, plan, or strategy you are going to use to seek an answer to your research question(s). In other words, when you get to the stage of designing your experiment, you have to identify the plan or strategy to be used in collecting the data that will adequately test your hypotheses. Planning a research design means that you must specify how the participants are to be assigned to the comparison groups, how you are going to control for potentially confounding extraneous variables, and how you are going to collect and analyze the data.

How do you go about designing an experiment that will test your hypotheses and provide an answer to your research questions? This is no simple task, and there is no set way to tell others how to do it. Designing a research study requires thought about the components to include and pitfalls to avoid. However, it helps to have some knowledge of the general types of research designs that can be used. Some of these research designs are weak in the sense that they do not provide for maximum control of potentially confounding variables. Others are strong in that they provide for the maximum control of potentially confounding variables. We will first discuss the weak designs and point out their deficiencies. We then discuss stronger experimental designs that represent ones that you should model when designing your research study.

■ **Research design**
The outline, plan, or strategy that is used to answer a research question

Weak Experimental Research Designs

We present three experimental research designs that are designated weak designs because they do not control for many potentially confounding extraneous variables. Remember that in an experimental research study, we want to identify the effect produced by the independent variable. Any uncontrolled confounding variables threaten our ability to do this and can render the experiment useless in the worst case and, in the best of circumstances, jeopardize our ability to reach a valid conclusion. This is not to say that these weak experimental designs do not provide any valuable information. They can provide some useful information. However, whenever a researcher uses one of them, he or she must be alert to the influence of potentially confounding extraneous variables that can threaten the internal validity of the study. Table 9.1 provides a summary of some of the threats to internal validity that may operate in each of these three designs.

■ **One-group posttest-only design**
Administering a posttest to a single group of participants after they have been given an experimental treatment condition

One-Group Posttest-Only Design In the **one-group posttest-only design,**[1] a single group of research participants is exposed to an experimental treatment and then measured on the dependent variable to assess the effect of the treatment condition, as illustrated in Figure 9.7. This design might be used if a school system wanted to find out whether implementation of a new reading program enhances students' desire to read. After implementation of the program for an entire school year, a survey is given to all students in the program to assess their attitude toward reading. If the results indicate that the students' attitude is positive, the program is assumed to engender a positive attitude toward reading.

The problem with reaching such a conclusion is that you cannot attribute the students' attitudes toward reading to the new reading program. It is possible that the students had a positive attitude toward reading before participating in the program and that the program actually had no impact on their attitude toward reading. The important point is that it is impossible to determine whether the new reading program had any effect or what that effect was without some sort of comparison. Because the students were not pretested, the researcher does not know anything about what the students were like prior to implementation of the reading program. From a scientific point of view, this design is of almost no value because, without pretesting or comparing the students in the program to students who did not participate in the reading program, it is impossible to determine whether the treatment produced any effect. Even if it did produce an effect, it is impossible to determine whether that effect was caused by the treatment program or by some extraneous variable such as history, maturation, or statistical regression.

■ **One-group pretest-posttest design**
Administering a posttest to a single group of participants after they have been pretested and given an experimental treatment condition

One-Group Pretest-Posttest Design Most individuals quickly recognize that the one-group posttest-only design is ineffective because of the lack of some type of comparison. The first response in many instances is to state that a pretest is needed to be able to compare the pretreatment response with the posttreatment response. This design, illustrated in Figure 9.8, is an improvement over the one-group posttest-only design and is typically called the **one-group pretest-posttest design.** A group of research participants is measured on the dependent variable, O, prior to administration of the treatment condition. The independent variable, X, is then administered, and the dependent variable, O, is again measured. The difference between the pretest and posttest scores is taken as an index of the effectiveness of the treatment condition.

TABLE 9.1   Summary of the Threats to Internal Validity of Weak Experimental Designs

Designs	Ambiguous Temporal Precedence	History	Maturation	Testing	Instrumentation	Regression Artifact	Differential Selection	Differential Attrition	Additive and Interactive Effects
One-group posttest-only design $X_T \quad O_2$	+	−	−	NA	NA	NA	NA	NA	NA
One-group pretest-posttest design $O_1 \quad X_T \quad O_2$	+	−	−	−	−	−	NA	NA	NA
Posttest-only design with nonequivalent groups $\dfrac{X_T \quad O_2}{X_C \quad O_2}$ (no random assignment)	+	+	?	+	+	+	−	−	−

A negative sign (−) indicates a potential threat to internal validity, a positive sign (+) indicates that the threat is controlled, a question mark (?) indicates that the threat may or may not be controlled depending on the characteristics of the study, and NA indicates that the threat does not apply to that design. X_T designates a treatment condition, X_C designates a control or standard treatment condition, O_1 designates a pretest, O_2 designates a posttest, and a dashed line indicates *no* random assignment to groups.

FIGURE 9.7   One-group posttest-only design in which X_T is the treatment and O_2 is the posttest assessment

Treatment	Posttest measure
X_T	O_2

FIGURE 9.8   One-group pretest-posttest design in which X_T is the treatment and O_1 and O_2 represent the pretest and posttest assessment

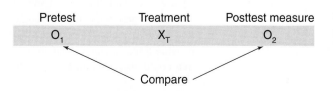

Although the one-group pretest-posttest design does represent an improvement over the one-group posttest-only design, any change in the posttest scores over the pretest scores cannot automatically be taken as an index of an effect produced by the independent variable. Many potentially confounding extraneous variables, such as history, maturation, instrumentation, and regression artifacts, can influence the posttest results. To the extent that they do, these extraneous variables represent rival hypotheses explaining any difference between the pretest and posttest scores.

To illustrate the way in which these potential rival hypotheses can operate when using this design, consider a hypothetical study in which an educational researcher wants to test a new instructional program for teaching reading to slow learners in the fifth grade. At the beginning of the school year, slow learners are identified by administering the Metropolitan Achievement Tests to all fifth-grade students in the New Approach elementary school. Those fifth-grade students who score at least two years below the fifth-grade level (pre-O) are considered slow learners and placed in an experimental classroom where the new reading instructional program is administered. At the end of two years the Metropolitan Achievement Tests are again administered and the reading grade placement score received by the students at this time (post-O) is compared with their pre-O score. Now let's assume that this comparison indicates that the slow learners have improved an average of 2.2 years in reading grade placement, indicating that the students made nice advancement during the two years that they were in the experimental classroom. It is tempting to attribute this improvement to the experimental reading program. However, if you think about it for a moment, you can probably identify several rival hypotheses that could have accounted for this change in performance.

History is a very real possibility. The students were placed in an experimental classroom, which means that they were singled out and given special attention. The special effort made by the school system may have motivated the parents of these children to encourage them to read and perform their homework assignments. This parental encouragement could have enhanced the students' reading performance in addition to the experimental program. Similarly, two years elapsed between the pretest and posttest assessments. The students were two years older, and maturation would predict that some of the improvement would occur just because the students were older and thus had matured during the intervening two years. A testing effect could exist because the students took the Metropolitan Achievement Tests during pretesting and posttesting, which means that the tests may have been more familiar on the second testing occasion. However, a testing effect would be more likely if a shorter time lapse had occurred between the pretesting and posttesting. Finally, a regression artifact is a very real possibility because the students selected for the experimental classroom were those who scored lowest on the initial pretest. A regression artifact, would predict that some of these students would improve on posttesting because their low scores on the pretest were in part due to chance factors.

As you can see, the one-group pretest-posttest design is problematic in that many potentially confounding extraneous variables, in addition to the independent variable, can reasonably account for any change in behavior, making it a weak design. Although the one-group pretest-posttest design is weak, it does provide some information in that it lets you know if a change occurred between pretesting and posttesting. However, it does not provide a reasonable explanation of the cause of this change because of the many threats that could also account for the behavioral change. When using this design, you should always be cautious about interpreting any effect as being due to the independent variable and constantly seek evidence that would rule out the existence of threats to the internal validity of the design.

The Posttest-Only Design with Nonequivalent Groups The **posttest-only design with non-equivalent groups** is a design in which one group of research participants is administered a treatment and is then compared, on the dependent variable, with another group of research participants who did not receive the experimental treatment, as illustrated in Figure 9.9. The dashed line in Figure 9.9 indicates that intact or nonrandomly assigned groups are formed; X_1 indicates the experimental treatment condition; and X_2 indicates the control comparison condition. For example, if you want to determine whether including a computer-assisted drill and practice lab enhances learning and performance of students taking an educational statistics course, you might have one class take the statistics course without the computer laboratory (X_2) and the other class take statistics with the computer laboratory (X_1). Both classes would be taught by the same instructor, so there would not be an effect of different instructors. At the end of the course you would compare the two classes in terms of their statistics performance (O). If the class that includes the computer laboratory performs better than the class that does not have computer laboratory practice, this should indicate that the addition of the computer laboratory enhanced statistics performance. Unfortunately, this might not be true because there are some potentially confounding extraneous variables that can creep into this design and threaten its internal validity.

The posttest-only design with nonequivalent groups might seem to be adequate on the surface because a comparison group is included that provides for a comparison of the performance of participants who were and were not exposed to the computer laboratory. Additionally, the same instructor taught the two courses, so there should be little difference in instructional quality. Why, then, is the design included as an example of a weak design? The reason is that the two classes of research participants were not equated on variables other than the independent variable. The two classes were formed on the basis of the students who signed up for them at the two times offered and were not randomly assigned to the comparison groups, as the dashed line in Figure 9.9 illustrates. This could have resulted in having students in the two classes who were very different on many variables other than the presentation of the independent variable. For example, the students taking the course that included the computer laboratory might have been brighter or older and more motivated to do well than the students in the comparison group that did not have exposure to the computer

▓ **FIGURE 9.9** The posttest-only design with nonequivalent groups in which X_T = experimental treatment, X_C = control or standard treatment, and O_2 represents the posttest assessment

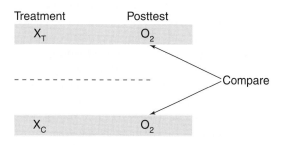

laboratory. Either or both differences could have contributed to the final outcome and serve as rival hypotheses explaining the outcome.

To achieve maximum assurance that two or more comparison groups are equated, participants must be randomly assigned. There are, however, times when intact groups are the only groups available. In this instance, the posttest-only design with nonequivalent groups might be the only type of design that can be used so you must be aware of the threats that exist to internal validity. Because a comparison group is included, threats such as history and instrumentation are probably controlled, and maturation might be. However, given that the two groups might not be equivalent, one group may be maturing faster than the other. Differential attrition could also influence the dependent variable and represent a possible threat to internal validity.

REVIEW
QUESTIONS

9.12 What is a research design, and what are the elements that go into developing a research design?

9.13 When would the one-group posttest-only design be used, and what are the problems encountered in using this design?

9.14 When would you use the one-group pretest-posttest design, and what are the potential rival hypotheses that can operate in this design?

9.15 When would you use the posttest-only design with nonequivalent groups, and what are the potential rival hypotheses that can operate in this design?

Strong Experimental Research Designs

The designs just presented are considered weak because they do not provide a way of isolating the effect of the independent variable from the influence of potentially confounding variables. A strong experimental research design is one in which the influence of confounding extraneous variables has been controlled. Table 9.2 summarizes the threats to internal validity that are controlled by the strong experimental designs. A strong experimental research design therefore is one that has internal validity. In most experimental research designs, the most effective way to achieve internal validity and eliminate rival hypotheses is to include one or more of the control techniques discussed earlier in this chapter and to include a control group.

Of the many control techniques that are available to the researcher, random assignment is the most important, and its importance cannot be overemphasized because it is the only means by which unknown variables can be controlled. Also, statistical reasoning is dependent on the randomization process, so we emphasize again: *Randomize whenever and wherever possible.*

Control of confounding extraneous variables is also achieved by including a control group. In all strong experimental research designs, there are at least two comparison groups: an experimental group and a control group. The **experimental group,** as you might expect, is the group that receives the experimental treatment condition. The **control group** is the group that does not receive the experimental treatment condition. This might mean that nothing was done to the control group or that the control group got what might be viewed as a standard or typical condition. If you were investigating the efficacy of a new method of teaching reading, the experimental group would be exposed to the new reading method and

■ **Experimental group**
The group that receives the experimental treatment condition

■ **Control group**
The group that does not receive the experimental treatment condition

TABLE 9.2 Summary of the Threats to Internal Validity That Are Controlled by the Strong Experimental Designs

Designs	Ambiguous Temporal Precedence	History	Maturation	Testing	Instrumentation	Regression Artifact	Differential Selection	Differential Attrition	Additive and Interactive Effects	Sequencing
Pretest-posttest control-group design	+	+	+	+	+	+	+	?	+	NA
Posttest-only control-group design	+	+	+	+	+	+	+	?	+	NA
Factorial design	+	+	+	+	+	+	+	?	+	NA
Repeated-measures design*	+	?	?	?	?	?	NA	?	NA	?
Factorial design based on a mixed model	+	+	+	+	+	+	+	?	+	?

Pretest-posttest control-group design

$$R \Big\langle \begin{matrix} O_1 & X_C & O_2 \\ O_1 & X_T & O_2 \end{matrix}$$

Posttest-only control-group design

$$R \Big\langle \begin{matrix} X_C & O_2 \\ X_T & O_2 \end{matrix}$$

Factorial design

$$R \Big\langle \begin{matrix} X_{T_1} & Z_{T_1} & O_2 \\ X_{T_1} & Z_{T_2} & O_2 \\ X_{T_2} & Z_{T_1} & O_2 \\ X_{T_2} & Z_{T_2} & O_2 \end{matrix}$$

Repeated-measures design*

$$\left| X_{T_1} \quad O_2 \right| X_{T_2} \quad O_2 \left| X_{T_3} \quad O_2 \right|$$

Same participants take every
level of the treatment condition

Factorial design based on a mixed model

$$R \Big\langle \begin{matrix} X_{T_1} \ Z_{T_1} \ O_2 | X_{T_2} \ Z_{T_1} \ O_2 | X_{T_3} \ Z_{T_1} \ O_2 \\ X_{T_1} \ Z_{T_2} \ O_2 | X_{T_2} \ Z_{T_2} \ O_2 | X_{T_3} \ Z_{T_2} \ O_2 \end{matrix}$$

All participants receive all levels of the X
treatment variable, but different participants are
randomly assigned to the two levels of the Z
treatment variable

*With counterbalancing, this design controls for all applicable threats except possibly differential attrition.

A positive sign (+) indicates that the threat is controlled, a question mark (?) indicates that the threat may or may not be controlled depending on the characteristics and control techniques included in the study, and NA indicates that the threat does not apply to that design. X_T designates a treatment condition, X_C designates a control or standard treatment condition, O_1 designates a pretest, O_2 designates a posttest, $X_{T_1-T_3}$ designate three levels of one independent variable, $Z_{T_1-T_2}$ designate two levels of a second independent variable, and R designates random assignment to groups.

the control group would be exposed to the typical or standard way of teaching reading. If you were testing a new drug on children with ADHD based on the hypothesis that it would reduce their level of ADHD and permit them to learn more effectively, the experimental group would receive the drug and the control group would receive either a placebo or the standard or commonly administered drug for treating ADHD. In this type of study, you might even have three groups: a group that received the placebo, another that received the standard drug, and a third that received the experimental drug.

A control group is necessary because of the functions it serves. First, it serves as a comparison. To determine whether some treatment condition or independent variable had an effect, we must have a comparison or control group. Consider a situation in which one group of students in your classroom is repeatedly talking to each other. This is disruptive not only to these children, but also to others in the classroom. To control this behavior, you keep these students in during recess and also move them to different areas in the classroom. To your delight, this stops them from talking and allows you to continue teaching without this disruption. You attribute this change in behavior to having kept these students inside during recess. However, you also changed their seating location, and it might be that being seated together promoted their talking. When you moved their locations in the classroom, you might have placed each person in a spot where the student was surrounded by people he or she knew but who were not the student's friends, so a rival hypothesis is that the talking was prompted by their being surrounded by friends. To determine whether keeping the students in during recess or moving them to other locations was the factor in producing the change in behavior, a control group who would be moved to other locations in the classroom but not be kept in during recess would have to be included. If both groups changed their behavior and stopped talking to others around them, we would know that being kept in during recess was probably not the variable causing the elimination of talking behavior.

This hypothetical example also demonstrates that a control group serves to control for rival hypotheses, its second function. All variables operating on the control and experimental groups must be identical except for the independent variable manipulated by the experimenter. The change in location in the classroom variable was held constant across the students who were and the students who were not allowed to go out during recess and therefore did not confound the results. You must realize, however, that a control group can control for rival hypotheses only if the participants in the control and experimental groups are similar. If this condition does not exist, the control group cannot stand for the responses that members of the experimental group would have given if they did not receive the experimental treatment condition. The participants in the two groups must be as similar as possible so that theoretically they would yield identical scores in the absence of the introduction of the independent variable.

Pretest-Posttest Control-Group Design   The **pretest-posttest control-group design,** as illustrated in Figure 9.10, is a design in which a group of research participants is randomly assigned to an experimental and control group and then pretested on the dependent variable, O. The independent variable, X, is then administered to the experimental group, and the experimental and control groups are posttested on the dependent variable, O. The pretest and posttest data can be analyzed using difference scores, analysis of covariance, or a statistical technique called analysis of variance based on a mixed model to determine whether the in-

■ **Pretest-posttest
control-group design**
A research design that
administers a posttest
to two randomly as-
signed groups of par-
ticipants after both
have been pretested
and one of the groups
has been administered
the experimental treat-
ment condition

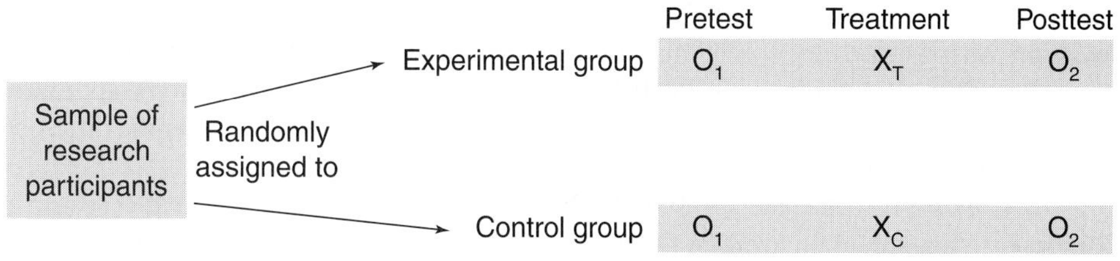

		Pretest	Treatment	Posttest
Experimental group		O_1	X_T	O_2
Control group		O_1	X_C	O_2

Sample of research participants — Randomly assigned to

FIGURE 9.10   Pretest-posttest control-group design in which X_T represents the treatment condition, and X_C represents the control or standard treatment condition, and O_1 and O_2 represent the pretest and posttest assessment of the dependent variable

dependent variable produced an effect. The method that was used in the past was to compute a pretest to posttest difference score for both the experimental and control groups and then statistically compare the difference scores to determine whether the experimental group's difference score is significantly different from the control group's difference score. This method has been criticized (e.g., Cronbach & Furby, 1970) as being inappropriate because such difference scores have low reliability. Although this view is not supported by all investigators (e.g., Rogosa, 1988), Cook and Campbell (1979) contend that the use of difference scores is less precise than either analysis of covariance or analysis of variance based on a mixed model (we will discuss this briefly later in this chapter). At the present time, either of these latter two methods of analysis is the preferred method.

Figure 9.10 reveals that the pretest-posttest control-group design is a two-group design containing one control and one experimental group. However, this design could be, and frequently is, expanded to include more than one experimental group, as illustrated in Figure 9.11. For example, if you want to determine which of three different ways of teaching reading—the standard way or two new, recently introduced ways—was most effective, you

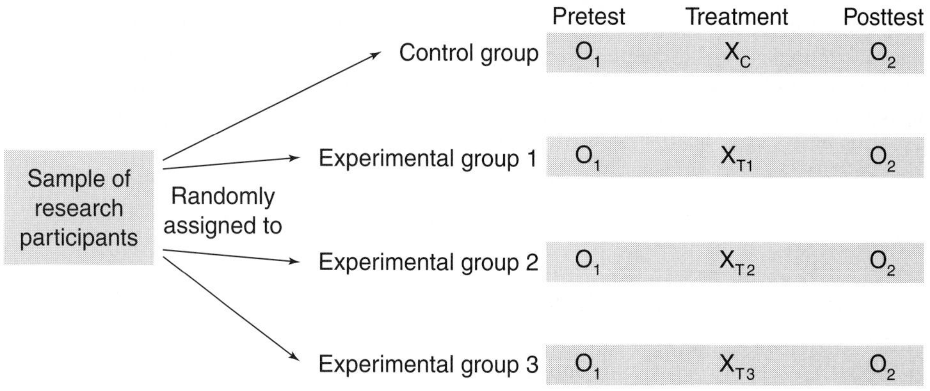

	Pretest	Treatment	Posttest
Control group	O_1	X_C	O_2
Experimental group 1	O_1	X_{T1}	O_2
Experimental group 2	O_1	X_{T2}	O_2
Experimental group 3	O_1	X_{T3}	O_2

Sample of research participants — Randomly assigned to

FIGURE 9.11   Pretest-posttest control-group design with more than one experimental group in which O_1 and O_2 represent the pretest and posttest assessment, X_C is the control or standard condition, and X_{T1}–X_{T3} represent three experimental treatment conditions

would randomly assign the participants to three different groups and then pretest each prior to administering the different reading programs. After the reading programs have been administered, the participants are posttested, and the data are analyzed by one of the appropriate statistical techniques, such as analysis of covariance, to determine whether the different reading programs produced different results.

The pretest-posttest control-group design is an excellent experimental design because it does an excellent job of controlling for rival hypotheses that would threaten the internal validity of the experiment. History and maturation are controlled because any history event or maturation effect that occurred in the experimental group would also occur in the control group unless the history event affected only one of the two groups. In this case, the history event would not be controlled because it would not have affected both groups. Instrumentation and testing are controlled because both the experimental and control groups were exposed to the pretest, so any effect of the pretest should exist in both groups. Regression and differential attrition variables are controlled because participants were randomly assigned to the experimental and control groups. Random assignment provides maximum assurance that the two groups are equated at the outset of the experiment. Although random assignment does not provide 100 percent assurance of initial equality of the experimental and control groups, it is the technique that provides the best assurance and therefore the technique that provides the best control for potential biases such as regression and differential attrition.

■ **Posttest-only control-group design**
Administering a posttest to two randomly assigned groups of participants after one group has been administered the experimental treatment condition

Posttest-Only Control-Group Design

The **posttest-only control-group design,** illustrated in Figure 9.12, is an experimental design in which the research participants are randomly assigned to an experimental group and a control group. The independent variable is administered to the experimental group, and then the experimental and control groups are measured on the dependent variable. The posttest scores of the experimental and control groups are statistically compared to determine whether the independent variable produced an effect.

This is an excellent experimental design because of the control it provides to the threats to internal validity. Because the posttest-only control-group design includes a control group and randomly assigned participants to the experimental and control group, it controls for all potential threats to internal validity in the same way as the pretest-posttest control-group design did. Neither group, however, provides an effective control for differential attrition because this potential threat involves the differential loss of participants from the two comparison groups. If one group loses participants with characteristics that are dif-

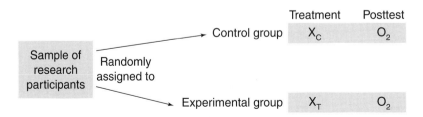

■ **F I G U R E 9 . 1 2**   Posttest-only control-group design in which X_C is the control condition, X_T is the treatment condition, and O_2 is the posttest assessment

ferent from those that are lost in the other comparison group, a difference could be found on posttesting because the differential loss produced two groups of participants who are no longer equivalent on all variables other than the independent variable. Because the pretest-posttest control-group design includes a pretest, it is possible to compare the control and experimental group participants who dropped out on this variable. If no difference existed, some basis would exist to argue that the attrition did not produce an inequality of the comparison groups. However, this argument is based only on a comparison of the pretest and not on other unknown variables that may also represent a confound. The bottom line is that there is no effective control for the potential threat that differential attrition can produce.

The two-group posttest-only control-group design presented in Figure 9.12 is only one variation of this design. There are many times when more than two groups are needed for comparison in a study; then the posttest-only control-group design can be expanded to include as many comparison groups as are needed. The same structure is maintained in that participants are randomly assigned to groups. After the experimental treatment is administered, the participants are posttested and compared, using analysis of variance, to determine whether a difference exists among the groups, as illustrated in Figure 9.13.

REVIEW

QUESTIONS

9.16 What makes a design a strong experimental design?

9.17 What is the difference between an experimental and a control group?

9.18 What functions are served by including a control group into a research design?

9.19 What potentially confounding extraneous variables are controlled in the pretest-posttest control-group design, and how does the design control for them?

9.20 What potentially confounding extraneous variables are controlled in the posttest-only control-group design, and how does the design control for them?

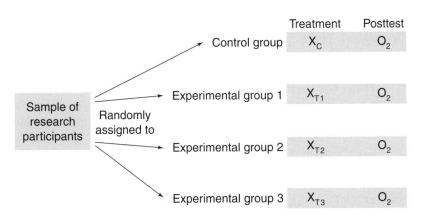

■ **FIGURE 9.13**   Posttest-only control-group design with more than one experimental group in which X_C is the control or standard treatment condition, X_{T1}–X_{T3} represent three treatment conditions, and O_2 is the posttest assessment

Factorial Designs

■ **Factorial design**
A design in which two or more independent variables, at least one of which is manipulated, are simultaneously studied to determine their independent and interactive effects on the dependent variable

factorial design

A **factorial design** is a strong experiential design in which two or more independent variables, at least one of which is manipulated, are simultaneously studied to determine their independent and interactive effects on the dependent variable. The experimental designs we have discussed up to this point have all been limited to investigating only one independent variable. For example, assume that you want to identify the most effective way of teaching mathematics and have identified four different types of instruction: computer-assisted, lecture, discussion, and programmed text. In designing this study, you have one independent variable—method of instruction—and four different levels of that independent variable—the four types of instruction. Because there is only one independent variable, either the pretest-posttest control-group design or the posttest-only control-group design could be used. The design selected would depend on whether a pretest was included. In educational research, we are often interested in the effect of several variables acting in concert. Most variables of significance to educators do not act independently. For example, one type of instruction might be more effective for large classes and another type for small classes. Similarly, a student's anxiety level might hinder effective performance when a discussion format is used, whereas a computer-assisted format might allow the student to relax and perform better. This is where factorial designs come in because they allow us to investigate simultaneously several independent variables and the interaction between them.

If you are interested in investigating the effect of anxiety level and type of instruction on teaching of mathematics, you are obviously investigating two independent variables. Let's further assume that you want to investigate the effect of two levels of anxiety—high and low—and three types of instruction—computer-assisted, lecture, and discussion. This means that you have two independent variables: anxiety level and type of instruction. The anxiety variable has two levels of variation—high and low—and the type of instruction variable has three levels of variation corresponding to the three different types of instruction. Figure 9.14 depicts this design, which reveals that there are six combinations of the two independent variables: high anxiety and computer-assisted instruction, low anxiety and computer-assisted instruction, high anxiety and lecture, low anxiety and lecture, high anxiety and discussion, and low anxiety and discussion.

■ **Cell**
A combination of two or more independent variables in a factorial design

Each of these independent variable combinations is referred to as a **cell,** which means that there are six cells to which research participants are assigned. Let's assume that we are measuring level of anxiety with an anxiety test, and we separate people into those with high and low anxiety. The high- and low-anxiety individuals are then randomly assigned to the cells corresponding to the three types of instruction. The participants randomly assigned to a given cell would receive the combination of independent variables corresponding to that cell. After the research participants have received their appropriate combination of independent variables and responded to the dependent variable, their dependent variable responses would be analyzed to identify two types of effects: main effects and interaction effects. A

■ **Main effect**
The effect of one independent variable

main effect refers to the influence of an independent variable. The design depicted in Figure 9.14 has two main effects: anxiety level and type of instruction. Statistical analysis of the main effect of anxiety level tells us whether anxiety level had a statistically significant influence on performance in mathematics or whether there was a statistically significant difference in performance depending on whether a person experienced high or low anxiety.

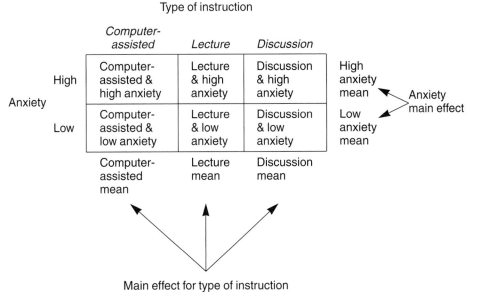

Type of instruction

FIGURE 9.14   Factorial design with two independent variables.

The main effect of type of instruction tells us whether the method of providing mathematics instruction influenced performance or whether there was a statistically significant difference in performance depending on the type of mathematics instruction the research participants received.

A factorial design also allows us to investigate interaction effects. An **interaction effect** exists when the effect of one independent variable depends on the level of another independent variable. The concept of interaction is rather difficult for most students to grasp, so we will spend some time on this issue. First, we demonstrate an outcome in which the two main effects of anxiety level and type of instruction are present, but the interaction is not. Look at Figure 9.15(a). The scores in the cells represent the mean, or average, posttest score for each group of participants (e.g., the high-anxiety participants who received computer-assisted instruction had a mean score of 10). The hypothetical posttest scores represent the mean dependent variable score, such as number of mathematics problems correctly answered. The **marginal means,** or the mean of the scores in the cells of a column or row, shown here outside the cells, represent the mean posttest scores across the cells (e.g., the mean score of 15 for the high-anxiety participants is the average of the scores in the three cells of the high-anxiety participants). In this example, the mean score for the high-anxiety individuals is 15, and the mean score for the low-anxiety participants is 25, indicating that there is a main effect of participant anxiety level on performance. Similarly, there is a difference between the mean scores of individuals given different types of instruction, indicating that there is an instructional main effect that also influences performance. The difference in the mean mathematics performance scores of high- and low-anxiety individuals indicates that individuals with low anxiety performed better than individuals with high anxiety. The difference in the

interaction effect

- **Interaction effect**
  When the effect of one independent variable depends on the level of another independent variable

- **Marginal mean**
  The mean of scores in the cells of a column or a row

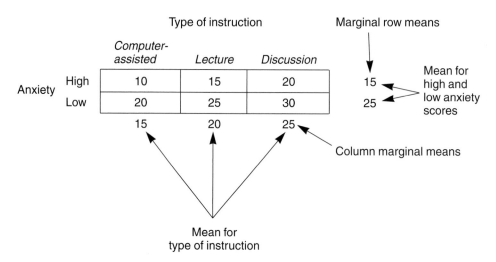

■ **F I G U R E   9 . 1 5 (a)**   Tabular representation of data showing significant main effect for both independent variables but not the interaction

mean mathematics performance scores of individuals receiving the different types of instruction indicates that individuals receiving the computer-assisted instruction performed the
worst and those receiving the discussion instruction performed the best.

Now look at Figure 9.15(b), which graphically illustrates the main effect for both independent variables. In particular, take note of the fact that the two lines are parallel. Whenever

■ **F I G U R E   9 . 1 5 (b)**   Graphic illustration of a significant main effect for both independent variables

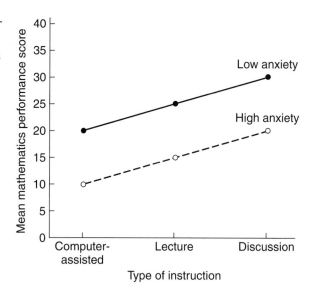

this happens, an interaction cannot exist, because an interaction means that the effect of one variable, such as anxiety level, depends on the level of the other variable being considered, such as the three different types of instruction, and this would produce nonparallel lines. In this example, individuals with low anxiety levels were always better than those with high anxiety levels regardless of the type of instruction received, indicating an anxiety main effect. Similarly, programmed-text instruction resulted in the best performance regardless of the participants' anxiety level, again indicating a main effect but no interaction effect.

Let us now look at an interaction effect. If you look at Figure 9.15(c), you will see that there is no difference between the marginal mean scores of individuals with different anxiety levels or with individuals receiving different types of instruction, indicating that these two main effects did not influence mathematics performance. However, if you look at the scores in the cells, you can see that high-anxiety participants received the highest scores when receiving computer-assisted instruction and the lowest scores when receiving discussion instruction. Low-anxiety participants, on the other hand, got the lowest scores under computer-assisted instruction and the highest scores when receiving discussion instruction. In other words, the effect of type of instruction depended on the participants' anxiety level, or an interaction existed between type of instruction and participant anxiety level. If you look at Figure 9.15(d), you will see that the lines for high- and low-anxiety individuals cross. Whenever the lines cross like this, you have a **disordinal interaction effect.** Performance increases under low anxiety levels and decreases under high anxiety levels as you move from computer-assisted instruction to discussion. Therefore, the effectiveness of the type of instruction depends on whether a person has a high or low level of anxiety, which is an interaction effect.

Before leaving this section on interaction, we need to point out that a possible interaction exists whenever the lines on the graph are not parallel even if they do *not* cross. The

■ **Disordinal interaction effect**
An interaction effect that occurs when the lines on a graph plotting the effect cross

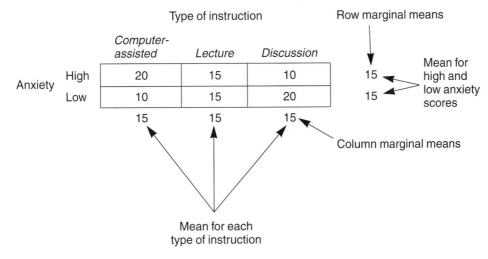

■ **FIGURE 9.15(c)**   Tabular representation of data showing nonsignificant main effects but a significant interaction effect

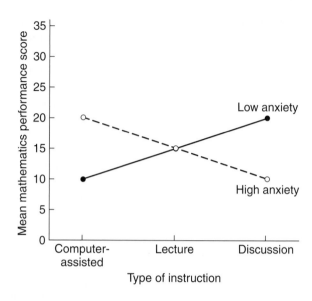

FIGURE 9.15(d) Graphic illustration of a significant disordinal interaction effect

classic interaction effect is one in which the lines cross, as we have illustrated in Figure 9.15(d). Now look at Figure 9.15(e), and you will see a graph in which the lines do not cross, but they are also not parallel. This is an **ordinal interaction effect.** Performance increases under low anxiety levels and decreases under high anxiety levels as we move from computer-assisted instruction to discussion. Again, the effectiveness of type of instruction depends on the level of anxiety a person has, which is an interaction effect.

So far, the discussion of factorial designs has been limited to those with two independent variables. There are times when it would be advantageous to include three or more in-

■ **Ordinal interaction effect**
An interaction effect that occurs when the lines on a graph plotting the effect do not cross

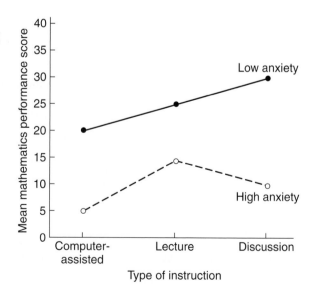

FIGURE 9.15(e) Graphic illustration of a significant ordinal interaction

dependent variables in a study. Factorial designs enable us to include as many independent variables as we consider important. Mathematically or statistically, there is almost no limit to the number of independent variables that can be included in a study. Practically speaking, however, there are several difficulties associated with increasing the number of variables. First, there is an associated increase in the number of research participants required. In an experiment with two independent variables, each of which has two levels of variation, a 2 × 2 arrangement is generated, yielding four cells. If ten participants are required for each cell, the experiment requires a total of forty participants. In a three-variable design, with two levels of variation per independent variable, a 2 × 2 × 2 arrangement exists, yielding eight cells, and eighty participants are required in order to have ten participants per cell. Four variables mean that sixteen cells and 160 participants are required. As you can see, the required number of participants increases rapidly with an increase in the number of independent variables.

A second difficulty with factorial designs incorporating more than two independent variables arises when higher-order interactions are statistically significant. In a design with three independent variables, it is possible to have a significant interaction among the three variables. Consider a study that investigates the effect of the independent variables of type of instruction, anxiety level, and participant gender on performance in mathematics. A three-variable interaction means that the effect of type of instruction on mathematics performance depends on people's anxiety level and whether they are male or female. In other words, the two-way interaction between type of instruction and anxiety level is different for males and females. If you conduct this study, you must look at this triple interaction and interpret its meaning, deciphering what combinations produce which effect, and why. Triple interactions can be quite difficult to interpret, and interactions of an even higher order tend to become unwieldy. Therefore, it is advisable to restrict a research design to no more than three variables. In spite of these problems, factorial designs are very popular because they permit the investigation of more than one independent variable and of the interactions that may exist among these variables.

Repeated-Measures Designs

In a **repeated-measures design,** as illustrated in Figure 9.16, the same research participants participate in all experimental treatment conditions. Another way of stating this is that all participants are repeatedly measured under each treatment condition. Carr and Jessup (1997) used this design in one part of their study investigating variables that contributed to gender differences in first-graders' mathematics strategy use. First-grade children were interviewed individually outside the classroom in October, January, and May of the school year to determine the strategies they used when solving addition and subtraction problems. In other words, the participants' strategies (the dependent variable) were repeatedly investigated at three different times (the independent variable) during the school year to determine whether strategy use changed over the course of the school year.

The repeated-measures design has the benefit of requiring fewer participants than the factorial design because all participants participate in all experimental conditions. Remember that in the factorial design, the number of participants needed is equal to the number needed in one-cell or experimental condition × the number of experimental conditions or

■ **Repeated-measures design**
A design in which all participants participate in all experimental treatment conditions

Research
Navigator.c✦m

repeated measures

■ **FIGURE 9.16**

Repeated-measures design

Experimental treatment conditions

A	B	C
P_1	P_1	P_1
P_2	P_2	P_2
P_3	P_3	P_3
P_4	P_4	P_4
.	.	.
.	.	.
.	.	.
P_n	P_n	P_n

All research participants
are in all conditions; n = number
of participants in the study.

cells. In the repeated-measures design, the number of participants needed is equal to the number needed in one experimental condition because all participants participate in all experimental conditions, just as all the children in the Carr and Jessup (1997) study participated in the interviews conducted in October, January, and May.

With the repeated-measures design, the investigator does not have to worry about the participants in the different groups being equated because the same participants participate in all experimental conditions. The participants therefore serve as their own control, which means that the participants in the various experimental conditions are perfectly matched.

With all these advantages, you might think that the repeated-measures design would be used more than the factorial design. Actually, the reverse is true because the repeated measures design has the serious disadvantage of a confounding influence of a sequencing effect. Remember that this is an effect that can exist when participants participate in more than one experimental condition. Because this is the primary characteristic of a repeated-measures design, a sequencing rival hypothesis is a real possibility. In some studies, such as that by Carr and Jessup (1997), sequencing effects are not a problem and represent an integral part of the study. Carr and Jessup looked for changes in strategy use over the course of the year, so the sequencing effect was something they were studying. In other studies, sequencing would represent a confound. To overcome sequencing effects, investigators should use the counterbalancing control technique discussed earlier and illustrated in Figure 9.17.

As you can see, there are some serious problems associated with the repeated-measures design. These problems are generally more difficult to control than those that exist with the factorial design even when counterbalancing is included as a control technique. As a result, the factorial design is used more frequently. However, remember that the repeated-measures design is a strong experimental design and the one that must be used when sequencing effects are an integral part of the study.

■ **FIGURE 9.17**   Repeated measures
design with counterbalancing in which
X_1–X_3 represent three treatment conditions
administered to all groups in a different
counterbalanced order, and O represents
the dependent variable measured after
each treatment condition

Group I	X_1	O	X_2	O	X_3	O
Group II	X_2	O	X_3	O	X_1	O
Group III	X_3	O	X_1	O	X_2	O

Factorial Designs Based on a Mixed Model

There are times in educational research when one or more of the variables of interest fits
into a repeated-measures design and the other variable(s) of interest fits into a posttest-only
control-group design. These variables can be combined into one study by using a factorial
design based on a mixed model. The simplest form of this design involves an experiment
using two independent variables. One independent variable requires several comparison
groups, one for each level of variation of the independent variable. The other independent
variable is constructed in such a way that all participants have to take each level of variation
of the independent variable. Therefore, the first independent variable requires a posttest-only control-group design, and the second independent variable requires a repeated-measures design. When the two independent variables are included in the same scheme, it
becomes a **factorial design based on a mixed model,** as illustrated in Figure 9.18.

In this design, participants are randomly assigned to the different comparison groups
required by the one independent variable. All participants then take each level of variation
of the repeated-measures independent variable. This gives us a strong experimental design
with the advantage of being able to test for the effects produced by each of the two independent variables as well as for the interaction between the two independent variables. Additionally, we have the advantage of needing fewer participants because all participants take
all levels of variation of one of the independent variables.

■ **Factorial design
based on a mixed
model**
A factorial design in
which different participants are randomly assigned to the different
levels of one independent variable but all
participants take all
levels of another independent variable

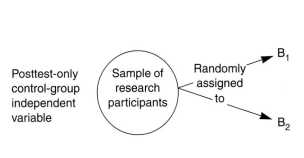

■ **FIGURE 9.18**   Factorial design based on a mixed model

We have limited our discussion of the factorial design based on a mixed model to two independent variables. This does not mean that the design cannot be extended to include more than two independent variables. As with the factorial design, we can include as many independent variables as are considered necessary.

REVIEW

QUESTIONS

9.21 What is a factorial design, and what is the advantage of this design over the two-group posttest-only design?

9.22 What is a main effect?

9.23 What is an interaction effect, and what is the difference between an ordinal and a disordinal interaction?

9.24 What is the difference between a factorial and a repeated-measures design?

9.25 What are the advantages and disadvantages of factorial and repeated-measures designs?

9.26 What is a factorial design based on a mixed model, and when would it be used?

SUMMARY

The experimental approach to conducting research is used to identify cause-and-effect relationships. This type of research is conducted within the context of an experiment, which is an environment in which the experimenter attempts to objectively observe phenomena that are made to occur in a strictly controlled environment in which one or more variables are varied and the others are kept constant.

Conducting an educational experiment involves manipulating the independent variable so that the effect of this manipulation can be observed on the dependent variable. The independent variable can be manipulated using a presence or absence technique, varying the amount of the independent variable that is administered, or varying the type of the independent variable.

Conducting an educational experiment necessitates control of the effect of potentially confounding extraneous variables. Control is achieved in most studies by eliminating any differential influence of the extraneous variables across the comparison groups. The most effective method for controlling the differential influence of potentially confounding extraneous variables is to randomly assign the research participants to the various comparison groups.

In addition to random assignment, control of potentially confounding extraneous variables is achieved by matching individual participants, holding extraneous variables constant, building the extraneous variable into the research design, counterbalancing, and using analysis of covariance. However, none of these control techniques takes the place of random assignment. Even if one or more of these other control techniques is used, you should still randomly assign whenever and wherever possible.

The next step in conducting a research study is to design the study. Research design refers to the outline, plan, or strategy used in conducting the study. There are a number of research designs that can be used. Some are weak designs because they do not control for the effect of potentially confounding extraneous variables. These designs include the one-group posttest-only design, the one-group pretest-posttest design, and the posttest-only design with nonequivalent groups. Other designs—the pretest-posttest control-group design and the posttest-only control-group design—are strong experimental designs because they control for the effect of potentially confounding extraneous variables. This control is achieved primarily through the inclusion of a control comparison group and random assignment of participants to the comparison groups.

Factorial designs are frequently used in education research because they permit the simultaneous assessment of two or more independent variables. Use of a factorial design has the advantage of permitting us to investigate simultaneously the effect of several independent variables and the interaction between these independent variables. Investigation of the interaction allows us to determine whether the effect that one independent variable has on the dependent variable is dependent on the level of the other independent variable, which permits the investigation of complex relationships.

A repeated-measures design is used when the same research participants must participate in all experimental treatment conditions. Although the repeated-measures design has the advantage of needing fewer research participants and ensures that participants are equated across treatment conditions, it has the potentially major disadvantage of including sequencing effects. Counterbalancing can be used to control for sequencing effects in some but not all studies. Because sequencing effects are such a serious potential confound, this design is used less frequently than the factorial design.

There are times when one of the independent variables of interest would fit into a repeated-measures design and the other independent variable would fit into a posttest-only control-group design. When such an instance exists, a factorial design based on a mixed model is appropriate. When using this design, participants are randomly assigned to the different comparison groups required by the one independent variable. All participants then take each level of variation of the second independent variable.

KEY TERMS

amount technique (p. 265)
analysis of covariance (p. 274)
carryover effect (p. 274)
cell (p. 286)
control group (p. 280)
counterbalancing (p. 272)
differential influence (p. 267)
disordinal interaction effect (p. 289)
experiment (p. 264)
experimental control (p. 267)
experimental group (p. 280)
factorial design (p. 286)

factorial design based on a mixed model (p. 293)
interaction effect (p. 287)
main effect (p. 286)
marginal mean (p. 287)
matching (p. 270)
one-group posttest-only design (p. 276)
one-group pretest-posttest design (p. 276)
order effect (p. 272)
ordinal interaction effect (p. 290)

posttest-only control-group design (p. 284)
posttest-only design with non-equivalent groups (p. 279)
presence or absence technique (p. 265)
pretest-posttest control-group design (p. 282)
random assignment (p. 268)
repeated-measures design (p. 291)
research design (p. 275)
sequencing effects (p. 272)
type technique (p. 266)

DISCUSSION QUESTIONS

1. What are you trying to do when you incorporate control techniques such as matching and random assignment, and how do these control techniques accomplish this?
2. What are the strengths and weaknesses of matching?
3. Shouldn't the control group used in the posttest-only design with nonequivalent groups control for most extraneous variables and enable a researcher using this design to effectively test the effect of an independent variable?
4. Why is a factorial design more powerful than the posttest-only control-group design?
5. Why is the posttest-only design control-group design used more frequently than the repeated-measures design?

RESEARCH EXERCISES

To give you some experience in identifying the elements that go into conducting an experimental research study, use Research Navigator and identify an experimental study in any area such as teacher stress, distance education, violence in schools, or burnout among teachers.

Read the article and then answer the following questions.

1. What makes this study an experimental research study? _____
2. What research questions and hypotheses are posed by the researchers? _____
3. What are the independent and dependent variables? _____
4. What control techniques were used? _____
5. What research design did the researchers use? _____

RELEVANT INTERNET SITES

http://trochim.human.cornell.edu/tutorial/tutorial.htm
This site discusses many topics related to research methods. Go to the list of topics under "Research Design and Internal Validity" and find the topic "Introduction to research design, Choosing a research design." Click on this topic, and it will link you to a discussion of research design. After you have finished reading this, click on the topics on the left sidebar; this will provide a discussion of additional issues related to research design.

http://trochim.human.cornell.edu/kb/design.htm
This site discusses both experimental and quasi-experimental designs. If you connect to this site, stick to the information relating to experimental design; we will get to quasi-experimental designs in the next chapter.

http://trochim.human.cornell.edu/kb/expfact2.htm
This site will give you additional exposure to factorial designs as well as viewing and interpreting main effects and interactions. We highly recommend that you spend some time with this site.

RECOMMENDED READING

Campbell, D., & Stanley, J. (1966). *Experimental and quasi-experimental designs for research.* Chicago: Rand McNally. This is the original classic book that discussed the primary experimental research designs.

Shadish, W. R., Cook, T. D., & Campbell, D. T. (2002) *Experimental and quasi-experimental designs for general-ized causal inference.* Boston: Houghton Mifflin. Read Chapter 8, which discusses randomized experiments. This is the third edition of Campbell and Stanley (1966). It includes recent advances not discussed in Campbell and Stanley (1966).

ENDNOTE

1. In some texts, this design is called the one-shot case study, which is incorrect.

10

Quasi-Experimental and Single-Case Designs

LEARNING OBJECTIVES

To be able to

- Explain the difference between strong experimental research designs and quasi-experimental research designs.
- Explain the limitations of quasi-experimental designs in making causal inferences.
- Explain the characteristics of the nonequivalent comparison-group quasi-experimental design and how to search for rival hypotheses that may explain the obtained results.
- Explain the characteristics of the interrupted time-series designs.
- Explain how the regression discontinuity design assesses the effect of a treatment.
- Explain how time-series and single-case research designs attempt to rule out confounding variables.
- Explain how a treatment effect is demonstrated in single-case research designs.
- Explain the limitations of each of the single-case research designs.
- Recognize and understand the methodological issues in single-case research designs.

In 1995, Zipora Jacob took a day trip to Disneyland, where she hopped on the Indiana Jones Adventure, a roller coaster that was slower than most but had high-tech hydraulics that made it seem speedier and jerkier. When the ride stopped, Jacob said she felt as though her head was exploding. "By the next morning, she was in a coma from a massive brain bleed. She endured surgeries and memory loss, and still has a permanent shunt draining fluid from her brain" (Rosenberg, 2002, p. 49).

Although Jacob has settled a lawsuit with Disney, the roller-coaster industry denies the fact that a roller coaster is a risky thrill ride. Instead, the industry states that it is "one of the safest family activities you can engage in" and that millions of people enjoy rides on roller coasters every year without incident. Yet some scientists are concerned that the G-forces and the rapid jerking of the head can cause serious injury. However, the link between G-forces and injuries has not been scientifically supported. Even without this evidence, there is a movement to regulate the G-force permitted on roller coasters in the belief that excessive G-force experienced on a roller coaster can place a person at risk.

Rather than basing laws and regulations on individual cases such as Zipora Jacob's, laws should be based on sound scientific evidence. However, conducting a randomized experimental study to determine whether a given G-force in combination with rapid jerking of the head causes head injury would mean that some individuals would have to suffer the G-force and rapid head jerking experienced on a roller coaster ride. Others would experience lower levels of G-force and head jerking to determine not only whether the amount experienced on roller coasters caused head injury, but also how much could be tolerated before head injury occurred.

Conducting such an experiment would place the individuals in the experiment at potential serious risk and would therefore be unethical and not permitted. Recall from the chapter on ethics (Chapter 4) that the potential benefit derived from a study must be greater than the risk to the participants for the study to be permitted. The possibility of serious and permanent brain injury is a risk that definitely exceeds the benefit that could be derived. In cases such as this, however, researchers need not throw up their hands and abandon the research. Rather, they must turn to the use of quasi-experimental designs—designs that enable researchers to investigate problems that preclude the use of some of the procedures required by a strong or randomized experiment. These are the type of designs we will discuss in this chapter, along with single-case designs, which are designs that can be used when you have only one or a couple of participants or a single intact group on which to test your research question.

In the previous chapter, we discussed the characteristics of experimental research and presented a number of strong experimental research designs that can be used to test causal hypotheses. However, as the vignette at the beginning of this chapter reveals, there are times when researchers are confronted with situations in which not all of the demands of experimental research can be met. For example, sometimes it is not possible to randomly assign participants to groups, a requirement of strong experimental research. On other occasions, a researcher might have access to only a single intact group, such as a classroom of individuals with learning disabilities, or to only one or two participants, such as a student with school phobia. In these instances, it would be impossible to use one of the strong research designs discussed in Chapter 9 because these designs require the random assignment of participants to at least two groups.

When this occurs, researchers must use quasi-experimental and single-case research designs. These are the types of designs that are discussed in this chapter.

QUASI-EXPERIMENTAL RESEARCH DESIGNS

■ **Quasi-experimental research design**
An experimental research design that does not provide for full control of potential confounding variables primarily because it does not randomly assign participants to comparison groups

Research
Navigator.c☉m

quasi-experimental

A **quasi-experimental research design** is an experimental research design that does not provide for full control of potential confounding variables. In most instances, the primary reason that full control is not achieved is because participants cannot be randomly assigned to groups. For example, assume that you want to conduct a study investigating the efficacy of several different ways of teaching reading to third-grade students. To control for the influence of confounding variables, ideally you want to randomly assign the third-grade students to the various groups or classrooms in which the different reading techniques are being taught. Sometimes it is not possible to randomly assign students to classrooms because of a variety of factors; for example, the school year might have already begun and the school system might not be willing to allow you to reassign students to different classrooms. This means that you would have to conduct the study making use of existing classes of students, which precludes the use of random assignment.

When random assignment is not possible, you must make use of a quasi-experimental research design. The important issue that must be considered in using a quasi-experimental design is whether it is possible to reach a valid causal conclusion using one of these designs, because they do not rule out the influence of all confounding variables. To make a causal inference from a quasi-experiment, you must meet the same basic requirements that are needed for any causal relationship: Cause must covary with the effect, cause must precede effect, and rival hypotheses must be implausible. The first two requirements, cause preceding effect and cause covarying with effect, are easy to handle because quasi-experiments, like strong or randomized experiments, manipulate conditions so that the cause is forced to precede the effect, and covariation between the cause and effect is tested, typically through statistical analysis. The third requirement, ruling out rival hypotheses, is frequently difficult because quasi-experiments do not use random assignment. This means that rival hypotheses or alternative explanations for the observed effect frequently exist when quasi-experiments are conducted.

Causal inferences can be made using quasi-experimental designs, but these inferences are made only when data are collected that make rival explanations implausible. For example, assume that you have a son who made a perfect score of 100 on a multiple-choice history test. If he had studied diligently for several days before taking the test, you would probably attribute the good grade to the diligent study. He could also have made the perfect score in a number of other ways (sheer luck in selecting the correct answer on each question, for example), but such alternative explanations might not be accepted because they are not plausible, given their unlikely occurrence and the fact that your son had spent so much time studying. In like manner, causal interpretations are made from quasi-experiments only when rival explanations have been shown to be implausible. The difficulty is identifying the plausible rival explanations. There are several ways to address rival explanations and demonstrate that they are implausible. We will focus attention on identification and study of plausible threats to internal validity in this chapter. Discussion of the other approaches is beyond the scope of this textbook. Shadish, Cook, and Campbell (2002) have an extended discussion of these two principles.

10.1 What is a quasi-experimental design, and when would you use such a design?

10.2 What requirements must be met to reach a valid causal inference when using a quasi-experimental design?

REVIEW

QUESTIONS

Nonequivalent Comparison-Group Design

Shadish, Cook, and Campbell (2002) identified a number of quasi-experimental designs. Probably the most commonly used quasi-experimental design is the **nonequivalent comparison-group design,** depicted in Figure 10.1. This design consists of giving an experimental and a control group a pretest and then a posttest after the experimental treatment condition has been administered to the experimental group. The responses of the two groups are then analyzed in one of two ways. The responses could be analyzed by comparing the pretest to posttest difference scores of the two groups or by comparing the experimental and control groups' posttest scores after they have been adjusted for any differences that may exist on their pretest scores using analysis of covariance (ANCOVA). Although both approaches have been used, ANCOVA is the one that is usually recommended, although pretest to posttest difference scores are still used to analyze the results of this design.

Consider the study conducted by Brown, Pressley, Van Meter, and Schuder (1996), which investigated the effect of using a specific type of instruction, called transactional strategies, for enhancing students' comprehension of the text that they read. In conducting this study, the investigators identified a group of accomplished teachers who used the transactional-strategies instructional method in their classrooms and a group of teachers in the same school district with reputations as excellent reading teachers who taught reading using the regular literacy curriculum. The investigators did not randomly assign the

■ **Nonequivalent comparison-group design**
A design consisting of a treatment group and a nonequivalent untreated comparison group both of which are administered pretest and posttest measures

Research
Navigator.c⊕m

nonequivalent comparison-group design

■ **FIGURE 10.1** Non-equivalent comparison-group design. The dashed line indicates nonrandom assignment to comparison groups.

	Pretest measure	Treatment	Posttest measure
Experimental group	O_1	X_1	O_2
	- - - - - - - - - - - - - - - - - - - -		
Control group	O_1	X_2	O_2

teachers to provide reading instruction by either the transactional strategy or the regular lit-eracy curriculum because it takes several years to become an accomplished transactional-strategies instruction teacher. The researchers felt that it was inappropriate to ask these teachers to alter their instructional strategy for a year. Additionally, the second-grade stu-dents who participated in the study (those reading below a second-grade level at the begin-ning of the school year) were not randomly assigned to classes that taught the transactional-strategies or regular literacy curriculum. The researchers did, however, select students from the various classes that were matched on reading comprehension at the begin-ning of the study. However, this equates the students only on initial reading comprehension. Because many teachers were used in the study and they, as well as the students, were not randomly assigned to groups, a quasi-experimental design had to be used.

Brown, Pressley, Van Meter, and Schuder (1996) selected the nonequivalent comparison-group research design with matching of participants in the two groups, as illustrated in Figure 10.2. Both groups, each consisting of several classes, were interviewed at the beginning of the academic year to identify the strategy the students used to assist in their comprehension of the material read and were pretested on several outcome measures, such as a test of reading com-prehension. After matched samples of students (students who had similar reading comprehen-sion scores) were identified, one group was taught reading by using the transactional strategy, and the other group was taught by using the regular literacy curriculum. At the end of the aca-demic year, the students in each group were posttested on the outcome measures. Analysis of the results revealed that the students who received transactional-strategies instruction im-proved in reading comprehension more than the students taught by the conventional reading method.

■ **FIGURE 10.2**   Design of the Brown, Pressley, Van Meter, and Schuder study (1996)

	Pretest measure	Treatment conditioning	Posttest measure
Classes in the experimental condition	Reading comprehension	Teach reading using the transactional strategy	Reading comprehension
Matched on initial reading comprehension			
Classes in the control condition	Reading comprehension	Teach reading using the regular literacy curriculum	Reading comprehension

The results of the Brown, Pressley, Van Meter, and Schuder study (1996) demonstrated that the performance of the students receiving transactional-strategy instruction was superior to that of the students receiving conventional reading instruction. Because a nonequivalent comparison-group quasi-experimental design was used, the groups are potentially nonequivalent on variables other than the one matched variable of reading comprehension. Therefore, biases may be present that would threaten the validity of the study. Table 10.1 identifies the type of biases that can exist in this design.

The students in the two groups were matched in terms of initial reading comprehension, so some basis exists for asserting that the results were not due to the differences in initial reading comprehension. However, the teachers were not randomly assigned to the two groups, nor was there any attempt to equate the teachers in terms of teaching effectiveness. The authors state that the teachers who used the transactional-strategies method were excellent teachers who offered rich language arts experiences for their students. Consequently, these teachers would seem to represent very effective teachers. The investigators did select comparison teachers who were recommended by school principals and district reading specialists on the basis of four criteria, such as fostering student involvement in reading and providing motivating learning activities. However, no attempt was made to ensure that the teachers providing instruction in the two methods were equated in ability to teach reading. Therefore, there could be a difference in the ability of these teachers to motivate and/or provide instruction in reading. Therefore, the events occurring between the pretest and posttest would be different for the two groups of students, creating a selection-history bias. Such differences could have accounted for some or all of the difference in reading comprehension of the two groups of students.

Shadish, Cook, and Campbell (2002) have pointed out that rival explanations arising from the use of designs such as the nonequivalent comparison-group design are "dependent on the joint characteristics of the design, on extra study knowledge about the threats, and on

---

■ **T A B L E   1 0 . 1**   Potential Biases That Exist in the Nonequivalent Comparison-Group Design

- *Selection Bias*—Because groups are nonequivalent, there will always be a potential differential selection bias. However, the pretest allows exploration of the possible size and direction of the bias on any variables measured at pretesting.

- *Selection-Maturation*—A selection-maturation bias may exist if one group of participants becomes more experienced, tired, or bored than participants in the other group.

- *Selection-Instrumentation*—A selection-instrumentation bias may exist if the nature of the dependent variable or the way it is measured varies across the nonequivalent groups.

- *Selection-Regression*—A selection-regression bias may exist if the two groups are from different populations such as the experimental treatment group being from a population of individuals with low reading scores and the comparison group being from a population of individuals with high reading scores.

- *Selection-History*—A selection-history bias may exist if an event occurring between the pretest and posttest affects one group more than the other group.

the pattern of observed results" (p. 139). Therefore, just because a threat is possible, it does not mean that it is plausible. The primary way of determining if a threat is plausible is to look at the pattern produced by the results because the plausibility of a threat tends to be related to the results obtained.

For example, look at Figure 10.3, which illustrates hypothetical results that might have been obtained from using the nonequivalent comparison-group design. This figure reveals that the control group did not change from pretesting to posttesting. The experimental group, however, started at a higher level and showed a significant positive change. This outcome would seem to suggest that the experimental treatment was effective. However, this outcome could also have been due to a selection-maturation effect.

In the Brown, Pressley, Van Meter, and Schuder study (1996), a selection-maturation effect would have been present if the participants in the experimental condition were developing intellectually and motivationally more rapidly than the participants in the control group and increased their reading comprehension from pretesting to posttesting because of these maturational factors and not because of the type of instruction they received. If this were the case, the posttest improvement in reading comprehension of the experimental group would be due to maturational factors and not to the experimental treatment effect.

Many investigators attempt to eliminate threat of bias from the selection-maturation effect by matching experimental and control participants on important variables. Brown, Pressley, Van Meter, and Schuder (1996) matched on initial reading comprehension, equating the groups on this variable. Ideally, this equality will persist over time, so any difference observed during a posttest is attributed to the experimental treatment condition. However, Campbell and Boruch (1975) have revealed that this assumption could be erroneous because a statistical regression phenomenon could occur within the two groups of matched participants, accounting for part or all of the difference observed between the two groups upon posttesting. This difference could be misinterpreted as being due to a treatment effect. If you conduct a study using a nonequivalent comparison-group design with matching during pretesting, you should consult Campbell and Boruch's article (1975).

The nonequivalent comparison-group design, as we have just discussed, is susceptible to producing biased results because of the potential for a number of threats to internal validity. The existence of these potential threats suggests that the results obtained from this quasi-experimental design are likely to be biased and produce results that are different from that which would be obtained from one of the strong experimental designs. Heinsman and Shadish

■ **FIGURE 10.3**   Hypothetical results that might be obtained from a study using a nonequivalent comparison-group design

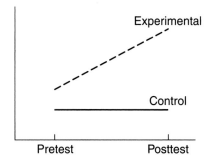

(1996) conducted a meta-analysis comparing the effect size estimates from randomized designs, or strong experimental designs, and nonrandomized designs, or the nonequivalent comparison-group design, to determine the extent to which similar results would be obtained from studies using these two designs. This analysis suggested that if the strong experimental design and the nonequivalent comparison-group design were equally well designed and executed, they would yield about the same effect size. In other words, the nonequivalent comparison-group design would give about the same results as the strong experimental design.

The results of this meta-analysis is a strong endorsement of the nonequivalent comparison-group design. However, this strong endorsement exists only when the nonequivalent comparison-group design is as well designed and executed as the strong experimental design. As Heinsman and Shadish (1996) have pointed out, it is probably very difficult, in many studies, to design and execute the nonequivalent comparison-group design as well as the strong experimental designs. Therefore, in many studies, the nonequivalent comparison-group design will give biased results.

There seem to be two design components on which researchers must focus in designing and conducting quasi-experiments to ensure that results are not biased. The first component focuses on the way in which participants are assigned to groups. To obtain unbiased results, you must not let the participants self-select into groups or conditions. The more they self-select into the treatment conditions, the more biased the results will be. The second component focuses on pretest differences. Big differences at the pretest will lead to big differences at the posttest. This means that the researcher should try to reduce any pretest differences by matching the comparison groups on variables that are correlated with the dependent variable. When it is not possible to match, you should consider statistically adjusting the posttest scores for any pretest differences (e.g., using ANCOVA). Focusing on these two design characteristics will mean that the results obtained from the nonequivalent comparison-group design will be a closer approximation to those of a strong experimental research design.

10.3 What is a nonequivalent comparison-group design, and what are the essential features of this design?

10.4 How are rival explanations addressed when using the nonequivalent comparison-group design?

10.5 What types of biases can exist when using the nonequivalent comparison-group design?

10.6 What is the best way of determining whether a threat is plausible when using the nonequivalent comparison-group design?

REVIEW

QUESTIONS

Interrupted Time-Series Design

In educational research, there are times when it is difficult to find an equivalent group of participants to serve as a control group. When only one group of participants is available, you can make use of the one-group pretest-posttest design. However, as we discussed earlier, there are many confounding variables that threaten the internal validity of this design. To control for these potentially confounding variables in situations in which we have only one group of research participants, we must think of mechanisms other than the use of a control group. These other control mechanisms are part of the interrupted time-series design.

In the **interrupted time-series design,** a single group of participants is pretested a number of times during the A, or baseline, phase; exposed to a treatment condition; and then posttested a number of times during the B, or treatment, phase, as depicted in Figure 10.4. Baseline refers to the observation of a given behavior before the presentation of any treatment designed to alter behavior. The baseline phase is therefore the period during which the participants' behavior is recorded in its freely occurring state. After the baseline behavior is recorded, a treatment is implemented, and behavior is recorded while this treatment is applied. The treatment effect is demonstrated by the discontinuity in the pretest versus the posttest responses. This discontinuity could be represented by a change in the level of the pretest and posttest responses. For example, pretest responses might consist of a group of children emitting an average of eight to ten disruptive behaviors during a given class period, and the posttest responses might consist of an average of only three to five disruptive behaviors, indicating a change, or decline, in the level of response. This discontinuity could also be demonstrated by a change in the slope of the pretest and posttest responses. A change in the slope would occur if the pretest responses demonstrated a change in one direction, such as a gradual increase in the number of disruptive behaviors during a class period, and the posttest responses demonstrated a change in the opposite direction, such as a gradual decrease in these behaviors.

To illustrate this design, consider the study conducted by Mayer, Mitchell, Clementi, Clement-Robertson, and Myatt (1993). One of the relationships they investigated was how making the classroom environment more positive affected the percentage of students who were engaged in their assigned activities. Mayer et al. identified ninth-grade students who had low grade point averages and were frequently absent from the schools. All these students attended an experimental classroom for at least one period each school day, so there was a single intact group of participants available for experimentation, which meant that some form of a time-series design had to be used. In this experimental classroom, emphasis was placed on the positive. For example, classroom rules were stated positively (e.g., show courtesy and respect to others), and points and praise were given to the students when they followed the rules. While in this experimental classroom, the experimenters assessed the percentage of students that were engaged in their assigned activities, defined as being "on-task," at ten and forty minutes into the class period. The percentage of students who were on-task was repeatedly measured before and after the teachers focused on making the classroom more positive.

Figure 10.5 illustrates the percentage of students who were on-task at both ten and forty minutes into the class period. From this figure, you can see that the percentage of students who were on-task was assessed multiple times before and after implementation of the positive classroom environment, making it an interrupted time-series design. This assessment reveals that the percentage of students who were on-task remained rather constant

■ **Interrupted time-series design**

A design in which a treatment condition is assessed by comparing the pattern of pretest responses with the pattern of posttest responses obtained from a single group of participants

Research
Navigator.c⊛m

interrupted time-series design

■ **FIGURE 10.4**
Interrupted time-series design

Multiple pretests	Treatment	Multiple posttests
O_1 O_2 O_3 O_4 O_5	X_1	O_6 O_7 O_8 O_9 O_{10}

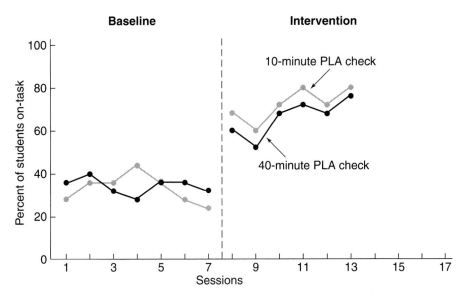

FIGURE 10.5   Percentage of students who are on-task at 10 minutes and 40 minutes into the class period. The figure presented here depicts the results of one of five classrooms investigated by Mayer et al. Only one classroom is presented here to illustrate a time-series design, whereas Mayer et al. used five classrooms and a multiple-baseline design. PLA refers to planned activity.

Adapted from G. R. Mayer, L. K. Mitchell, T. Clementi, E. Clement-Robertson, & R. Myatt (1993). "A dropout prevention program for at-risk high school students: Emphasizing consulting to promote positive classroom climates," *Education and Treatment of Children, 16,* 135–146. Reprinted by permission.

during the first seven baseline class sessions, or the class sessions before implementation of the positive classroom environment. After implementation of the positive classroom environment, the percentage of on-task students consistently rises over the next six class sessions, suggesting that the implementation of the positive approach had a beneficial effect on the students' behavior. This conclusion, however, is based on visual inspection. Now it is necessary to ask two questions. First, did a significant change occur following the introduction of the treatment condition? Second, can the observed change be attributed to the treatment condition?

Visual inspection of the pattern of preintervention and postintervention behavior can be very helpful in ruling out some potentially confounding variables and in determining whether an experimental treatment had an effect. Figure 10.6 illustrates a number of possible patterns of behavior that can be obtained from time-series data. Look at the first three patterns: A, B, and C. Pattern A reveals a continuous increase in response before intervention, and this pattern of continuous increase is maintained during posttesting. Such a response pattern could reflect an instrumentation or a maturation effect rather than a treatment effect. Similarly, response patterns B and C reveal that the pattern of responses established during pretesting continued during posttesting. Response patterns A, B, and C, therefore, do not reveal a treatment effect because the postintervention pattern of responses

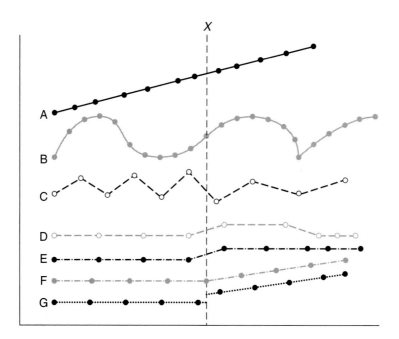

■ **F I G U R E 1 0 . 6**   Possible pattern of behavior of a time-series variable. *X* designates introduction of the experimental intervention.

Adapted from J. T. Caporaso, *The structure and function of European integration,* © 1974 by Goodyear Publishing Company.

represents a continuation of the preintervention pattern of responses. If several pretests and posttests had not been obtained, it would be tempting to infer that a treatment effect had occurred. Look at the response immediately preceding and immediately following the intervention in patterns A and B. In these patterns, you can see that the preintervention response was lower than the postintervention response, indicating an improvement in behavior. In pattern C, the postintervention response was lower than the preintervention response, indicating a decline in response. Without taking repeated assessments before and after intervention, you would not know that the postintervention response represented a continuation of the preintervention pattern of response.

Response patterns D, E, F, and G appear to represent true changes in behavior because the posttest response pattern was different than the pretest response pattern. Additionally, the change in the response pattern continued, with the exception of pattern D, during the entire posttesting period. It is this change in the posttest pattern of responses, particularly if it is a continuous change, that gives some assurance of the fact that a change in response occurred.

Even with this visual inspection of the data, it is important to determine whether the change in response pattern is statistically significant, which involves a test of significance. The most widely used and appropriate significance test seems to be the autoregression moving average model (Box & Jenkins, 1970; Glass, Willson, & Gottman, 1975). Basically, this method consists of determining whether the pattern of postresponse measures differs from the pattern of preresponse measures. Use of this statistical method requires obtaining at least fifty data points (Glass et al., 1975), which frequently cannot be accomplished. Fortunately, Tryon (1982) and Cosbie (1993) have developed statistical procedures that can be used with as few as ten data points so that valid statistical analysis can be conducted on the data collected on most time-series studies.

After the data are analyzed and an assessment is made as to whether the preresponse pattern differs from the postresponse pattern, it is important to determine whether the change was due to the experimental intervention or to some confounding variable. For example, Mayer et al. (1993) had to determine whether the implementation of the positive classroom environment led to the increase in on-task behavior or whether some extraneous variable was responsible. This means that you have to look at the data and identify the possible confounding variables that could have produced the behavioral change. The primary rival hypothesis that exists in the interrupted time-series design is a history effect. If some extraneous variable that increased the percentage of students engaged in on-task behaviors occurred at the same time as the implementation of the positive classroom environment, this extraneous variable would serve as a rival explanation for the change in the students' behavior. A researcher using the interrupted time-series design must consider all other events taking place at the time of implementation of the experimental treatment and determine whether they might be rival explanations.

10.7 What are the essential design characteristics of an interrupted time-series design?

10.8 How is a treatment effect demonstrated when using an interrupted time-series design?

10.9 How are potential confounding variables ruled out when using the interrupted time-series design?

REVIEW
QUESTIONS

Regression-Discontinuity Design

Research
Navigator.c⊕m

The **regression-discontinuity design** is a design that is used to determine if individuals meeting some predetermined criteria profit from receiving some special treatment. This design, depicted in Figure 10.7, consists of measuring all participants on a preassignment

regression
discontinuity
design

■ **Regression-discontinuity design**
A design that assesses the effect of a treatment condition by looking for a discontinuity in regression lines between individuals who score lower and higher than some predetermined cutoff score

| Experimental group | O_p | C | X | O_2 |
| Control group | O_p | C | | O_2 |

■ **FIGURE 10.7** Structure of the regression-discontinuity design in which O_p is the preassignment measure, C indicates the preassignment measure cutoff score used to assign participants to conditions in which participants with scores above the cutoff are assigned to the treatment condition and participants with scores below the cutoff are assigned to the control condition, X refers to a treatment condition, and O_2 refers to the posttest measure or the outcome or dependent variable

measure and then selecting a cutoff score based on this measure. All participants who score above the cutoff score receive the special treatment and participants who score below the cutoff score do not receive the special treatment. After the special treatment is administered, the posttest measure is obtained, and the two groups are compared on the outcome measure to determine whether the special treatment was effective. However, the way in which the two groups are compared in the regression discontinuity design is different from that of any other design we have considered so far. A treatment effect is demonstrated by a discontinuity in the regression line that would have been formed if no treatment effect existed.

To illustrate what we are talking about with reference to a discontinuity in the regression line, take a look at Figure 10.8. This figure represents a continuous increase of scores from a low of about 41 to a high of about 58 and a cutoff score of 50 separating the control group from the treatment group. The straight line pushed through these scores represents the regression line. Note that this regression line is continuous and that the individuals that received the special treatment made a score of higher than 50 on the preassignment variable. The continuous regression line indicates that there was no effect of the treatment because the scores of the people above the cutoff of 50 and receiving the treatment continued the pattern of scores of people below the cutoff of 50 who did not receive the treatment.

Now look at Figure 10.9. This figure reveals that the regression line for the people above the cutoff score of 50 is not a continuation of the regression line established for the people with a cutoff score below 50. In other words, there is a discontinuity of the regres-

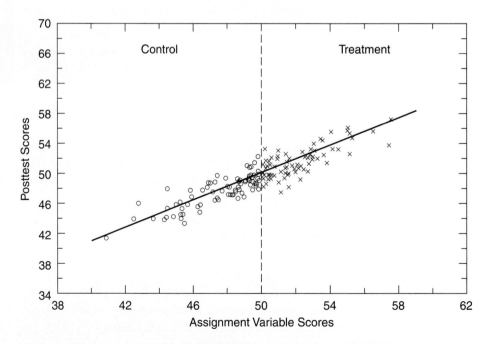

FIGURE 10.8   Regression discontinuity experiment with no treatment effects

From W. R. Shadish, T. D. Cook, and D. T. Campbell, *Experimental and Quasi-Experimental Designs for Generalized Causal Inference.* Copyright © 2002 by Houghton Mifflin Company. Reprinted by permission.

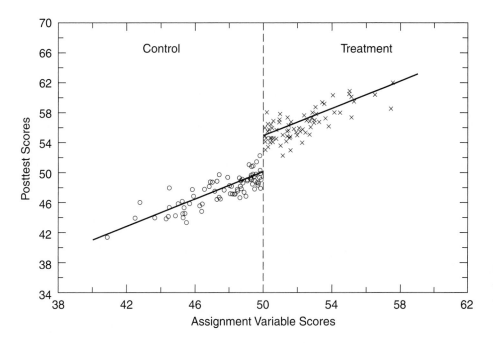

FIGURE 10.9   Regression discontinuity experiment with an effective treatment

From W. R. Shadish, T. D. Cook, and D. T. Campbell, *Experimental and Quasi-Experimental Designs for Generalized Causal Inference.* Copyright © 2002 by Houghton Mifflin Company. Reprinted by permission.

sion line for the people with a cutoff score below and above 50. This discontinuity indicates that the treatment had an effect because if no treatment effect had existed, there would be no discontinuity of the regression line as illustrated in Figure 10.8.

Braden and Bryant (1990) used the regression discontinuity design to determine whether a program for gifted students enhanced their achievement more than regular school placement. The cutoff score to be admitted into the gifted program was set at two or more standard deviations above the mean on the Stanford-Binet or WISC-R intelligence tests. Students who received this cutoff score were admitted to the gifted program, and students who were referred to the program but did not receive the cutoff score represented the control group and remained in the regular classroom. Three years after initiation of the gifted program, outcome data were collected by using the California Achievement Test total battery percentile. Statistical analysis of the outcome data demonstrated that a significant discontinuity of the regression lines for the two groups of students did not exist, indicating that the gifted program did not enhance the bright students' academic achievement.

The regression discontinuity design is an excellent design that can be used when researchers want to investigate the efficacy of some program or treatment but cannot randomly assign participants to comparison groups. However, there are a number of criteria, listed in Table 10.2, that must be adhered to for the design to effectively assess the effectiveness of a treatment condition. When these criteria are met, the regression discontinuity design is a very good design to use for testing the effect of a treatment condition and typically more powerful than other quasi-experimental designs.

■ **TABLE 10.2**   Requirements of the Regression Discontinuity Design

- Assignment to comparison groups must be based only on the cutoff score.

- The assignment variable must be at least an ordinal variable and is best if it is a continuous variable. It cannot be a nominal variable such as sex, ethnicity, religious preference, or status as a drug user or nonuser.

- The cutoff score ideally should be located at the mean of the distribution of scores. The closer the cutoff score is to the extremes, the lower the statistical power of the design.

- Assignment to comparison groups must be under the control of the experimenter to avoid a selection bias. This requirement rules out most retrospective uses of the design.

- The relationship between the assignment and outcome variables (whether it is linear, curvilinear, etc.) must be known to avoid a biased assessment of the treatment effect.

- All participants must be from the same population. With respect to the regression discontinuity design, this means that it must have been possible for all participants to receive the treatment condition. Therefore, the design would not be appropriate if the experimental participants were selected from one school and control participants were selected from another school.

Any threat to the validity of the regression discontinuity design would have to cause a sudden discontinuity in the regression line that coincides with the cutoff. As Shadish et al. (2002) have pointed out, this is implausible, though possible. The primary threat that could produce such an effect is a contemporaneous history effect. However, this history effect would have to be one that affected only participants on one side of the cutoff, which makes it quite unlikely. Of the other threats to internal validity that we discussed in Chapter 8, attrition is about the only other serious threat. However, this is a threat to any design including experiments with random assignment.

SINGLE-CASE EXPERIMENTAL DESIGNS

■ **Single-case experimental designs**
Designs that use a single participant to investigate the effect of an experimental treatment condition

Research Navigator.c⊕m

single-case experimental design

Single-case experimental designs use a single participant in the experimental design to investigate the efficacy of an experimental treatment condition. The necessity of conducting a study that investigates a single individual can occur any time you want to investigate some phenomenon but have access to only one or two individuals who demonstrate that phenomenon. For example, assume that you have an unusually bright student in your class and you want to study this person's learning strategies. Because only one student with this ability level is in your class, you have to use a single-case design.

All single-case experimental designs are some form of a time-series design, because these designs require repeated measurement on the dependent variable prior to and following implementation of the experimental treatment condition. The pretreatment responses are used as the comparison responses for assessing the effect of the independent variable. Additionally, the multiple pretreatment and posttreatment responses permit us to rule out many extraneous variables, such as history and maturation, that could confound the results.

The way in which this is accomplished is identical to that which we discussed under the topic of interrupted time-series design earlier in this chapter.

As we discuss the single-case experimental research designs, you should realize that these designs can be, and frequently are, used with an intact group of participants as well as with single participants. There are times when you cannot break a group of participants, such as a class, into a control and experimental group but still want to investigate the efficacy of an independent variable. In these instances, you can treat the class as a single case and use one of the single-case experimental designs.

A-B-A and A-B-A-B Designs

The **A-B-A design** is a single-case design involving three phases, as illustrated in Figure 10.10. The first phase, the first A of this design, is the baseline condition during which the target response is repeatedly recorded before any experimental intervention. The second phase, the B part of this design, is the experimental treatment condition. During this phase, some treatment condition is deliberately imposed to try to change the response of the participant. This treatment phase is typically continued for the same length of time as the original baseline phase, or until some substantial and stable change occurs in the behaviors being observed. After the treatment condition has been introduced and the desired behavioral change has occurred, the second A phase is introduced. The second A phase of this design represents a return to the baseline conditions. In other words, the treatment condition is withdrawn, and whatever conditions existed during baseline are reinstated. This second A phase is reinstated to determine whether the behavior will revert back to its original pretreatment level. This reverting back to the original pretreatment level is very important for demonstrating that the treatment condition, and not some other extraneous variable, produced the behavioral change observed during the B phase when the experimental treatment condition was in effect. If the response reverts back to the original baseline level when the treatment condition is withdrawn, rival hypotheses such as history become less plausible.

To illustrate the use of this design, consider the study conducted by Gunter, Shores, Jack, Denny, and DePaepe (1994). These researchers investigated the effect of using a teaching method that involved providing information that would ensure correct responses on the disruptive behavior of a twelve-year-old student named Tom. Tom was selected to participate in the study because his participation in a prior study identified him as having a high rate of disruptive behavior during academic instruction. A baseline rate of occurrence of disruptive behaviors (defined as making inappropriate noises, talking out without permission, walking away from the instructional area without permission, and making nondirected negative verbalizations) was recorded for ten class periods. Baseline recording for each class began when the teacher gave Tom his math assignment and ended with the completion of the math activity or the expiration of thirty minutes of continuous observation.

■ **A-B-A design**
A single-case experimental design in which the response to the experimental treatment condition is compared to baseline responses taken before and after administering the treatment condition

Research Navigator.c⊕m

A-B-A design

Baseline (A)	Treatment (B)	Baseline (A)
$O_1\ O_2\ O_3\ O_4\ O_5$	$O_6\ O_7\ O_8\ O_9\ O_{10}$	$O_{11}\ O_{12}\ O_{13}\ O_{14}\ O_{15}$

■ **FIGURE 10.10** A-B-A time-series design

Intervention was then implemented that consisted of the teachers providing Tom with the information that would ensure his getting a correct response prior to presenting him with the task he was to perform. For example, during intervention the teacher would say, "Tom, 6 × 4 is 24. What is 6 × 4?" if he had miscalculated this problem. After Tom had completed seventeen class periods under intervention conditions, the teacher reverted to her baseline behavior of not providing information that would ensure a correct response.

You can see a display of the per minute rate of disruptive behaviors Tom displayed for each session in Figure 10.11. From this figure, you can see that Tom displayed a number of disruptive behaviors during every session of the first baseline (A) condition. When the treatment condition (B) of giving Tom information that ensured his giving a correct response was implemented, the disruptive behaviors declined, and during several of the sessions, Tom did not display any disruptive behaviors. When baseline conditions (A) were reinstated and Tom no longer received the information he needed to provide a correct response, disruptive behaviors became more frequent.

In looking at the results of this study, it appears that the use of the A-B-A design provides a rather dramatic illustration of the influence of the experimental treatment condition. However, there are several problems with this design (Hersen & Barlow, 1976). The first problem is that the design ends with the baseline condition. From the standpoint of an educator who desires a positive behavioral change, this might be unacceptable because the ben-

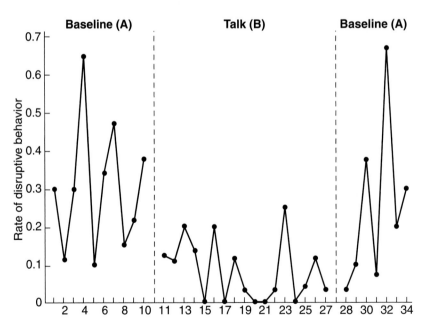

■ **FIGURE 10.11**   Rate of Tom's disruptive behaviors during baseline and intervention. This figure depicts the first three phases of the design used by Gunter et al. to illustrate the A-B-A design.

Adapted from P. L. Gunter, R. E. Shores, S. L. Jack, R. K. Denny, & P. A. DePaepe (1994). "A case study of the effects of altering instructional interactions on the disruptive behavior of a child identified with severe behavior disorders," *Education and Treatment of Children, 17,* 435–444. Reprinted by permission.

efits of the treatment condition are denied. Fortunately, this limitation can be handled easily by adding a fourth phase to the A-B-A design in which the treatment condition is reintroduced. This makes it an A-B-A-B design, as illustrated in Figure 10.12. When using the **A-B-A-B design,** the participant ends the experiment with the full benefit of the treatment condition. Actually, Gunter, Shores, Jack, Denny, and DePaepe (1994) used the A-B-A-B design. In Figure 10.12 you can see that they reinstated the treatment conditions. When the treatment condition was reinstated a second time, the disruptive behaviors declined once again. Tom, their experimental participant, did therefore end the study with the positive effects of the experimental treatment condition.

■ **A-B-A-B design**
An A-B-A design that
is extended to include
the reintroduction of
the treatment condition

A second problem with using the A-B-A design is the necessity of the dependent variable response to revert to baseline conditions when the experimental treatment condition is withdrawn to rule out rival explanations such as history. If Tom's disruptive behavior did not revert to its baseline level when the treatment condition was withdrawn, it would have been impossible to determine whether the behavioral change was due to the treatment condition or to a history variable that occurred at the same time that the treatment condition was introduced. Reversal is therefore essential to rule out rival hypotheses.

The problem with the A-B-A and A-B-A-B designs is that a reversal to baseline does not occur with all dependent variable responses. Without the reversal, the researcher cannot be sure that the change in response following introduction of the treatment condition was not caused by some extraneous variable. Failure to reverse might be due to a carryover

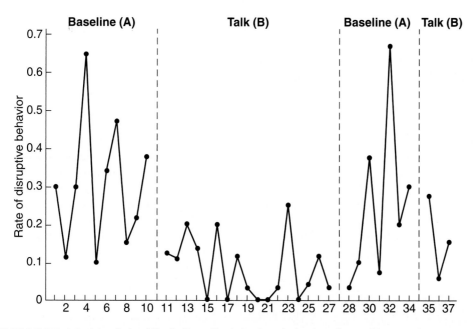

■ **FIGURE 10.12**   Rate of Tom's disruptive behaviors during baseline and intervention

Adapted from P. L. Gunter, R. E. Shores, S. L. Jack, R. K. Denny, & P. A. DePaepe (1994). "A case study of the effects of altering instructional interactions on the disruptive behavior of a child identified with severe behavior disorders," *Education and Treatment of Children, 17,* 435–444. Reprinted by permission.

effect across phases, whereby the treatment condition was maintained so long that a relatively permanent change in behavior took place. For example, if you were investigating the effect of reinforcing students every time they correctly completed their mathematics homework, either by giving them praise, granting them additional recess time, or allowing them to chat with their friends for ten minutes during class time, you might find that the reinforcer worked so well that the students found that successful completion of their homework and receiving a good grade was reinforcing by itself. This would sustain the behavior of completing homework without any teacher intervention. In such a case, the teacher intervention could be removed and the students' behavior of completing their homework would continue, which would mean that the students' behavior would not reverse. Because of the possibility of such a carryover effect, Bijou, Peterson, Harris, Allen, and Johnston (1969) recommend that short experimental periods be used to facilitate obtaining a reversal effect. Once the influence of the experimental treatment has been demonstrated, attention can be placed on its persistence.

Before leaving the A-B-A design, we need to point out that in implementing this design, the return to baseline conditions sometimes involves a withdrawal of the treatment condition, and at other times it involves the implementation of another treatment condition in which the intent is to reverse the behavior. Reversing the behavior would involve attempting to create an alternative but incompatible behavior. For example, assume that you want to increase the play behavior of a socially withdrawn female child. Baseline would consist of recording the percentage of time the child spends interacting with other children as well as with adults, such as the teachers, during a specific time period, such as during recess. Treatment might consist of praising the child whenever she interacted with other children and not with adults to see whether the percentage of time she spent with other children but not with adults increased over baseline. During the second A phase of the design, you could attempt to demonstrate the effect of the reinforcement by withdrawing the praise and seeing whether the child reverted to being socially withdrawn and interacting less with other children. You could also have implemented a reversal during this second A phase. If a reversal was implemented, you might praise the child whenever she interacted with teachers and ignore her whenever she interacted with other children. This reversal phase would be implemented to see whether the percentage of time the child spent with teachers would increase and the percentage of time the child spent with other children would decrease. If it did, then the child's behavior would have reversed from focusing on other children to focusing on teachers. If this reversal did take place, it would represent a dramatic demonstration of the power of the effect of reinforcement. Although a reversal to an alternative behavior can reveal dramatic results, it is more cumbersome and thus is used less frequently than the more adaptable withdrawal of the treatment condition.

REVIEW

QUESTIONS

10.10 What are the essential characteristics of the A-B-A design?

10.11 How does the A-B-A design rule out rival hypotheses and demonstrate the effect of an experimental treatment condition?

10.12 What are the primary problems that can exist when using the A-B-A design, and how can they be solved?

Multiple-Baseline Design

The primary limiting component of the A-B-A and the A-B-A-B designs is their inability to eliminate the rival hypothesis of history when the target behavior does not revert to baseline following withdrawal of the treatment condition. If you suspect that such a situation exists, you should select a design that does control for a history rival hypothesis. In this situation, the multiple-baseline design is a logical alternative because it does not entail withdrawing the treatment condition. Therefore, its effectiveness does not hinge on a reversal of behavior to baseline level.

The **multiple-baseline design,** as depicted in Figure 10.13, focuses on two or more different behaviors in the same individual, on the same behavior exhibited by two or more individuals, or on the same behavior exhibited by one individual but in different settings.

Let's focus on the same behavior exhibited by four different individuals. With this focus, the first phase of this design involves collecting baseline behavior on all four individuals. During the second phase, the treatment condition is administered to the first individual, and baseline behavior is maintained on the other three individuals. For each subsequent phase, the treatment condition is successively administered to the next two individuals. If the individual who is exposed to the treatment condition demonstrates a change in behavior and no behavioral change exists for those who continue the baseline behavior, evidence exists supporting the efficacy of the treatment condition.

Gilbert, Williams, and McLaughlin (1996) used this design to investigate the effect that an assisted reading program would have on correct oral reading rates of three elementary school children with learning disabilities. These investigators collected baseline reading rates on the children by having them read independently for four minutes into a tape recorder after having practiced silently reading a designated passage over a forty-five-minute time period. The assisted reading treatment program consisted of having the students listen to recorded passages using earphones while they followed the lines of print with their fingers and then reading the passage three times aloud while listening to the tape recorder. While reading the passage, the students were praised and encouraged for their effort. The morning after the assisted reading, the students read the passage independently for four minutes into a tape recorder. The number of words that were read correctly for each minute of the four-minute tape recordings represented the dependent variable.

From Figure 10.14, it can be seen that baseline was maintained for fourteen days for the first student, after which the assisted reading program was implemented. The assisted reading program was introduced for the second student after sixteen baseline days and after

Research
Navigator.c⊛m

multiple baseline design

- **Multiple-baseline design**
  A single-case experimental design in which the treatment condition is successively administered to different participants or to the same participant in several settings after baseline behaviors have been recorded for different periods of time

▓ **F I G U R E   1 0 . 1 3**   Multiple-baseline design

		Phase 1	Phase 2	Phase 3	Phase 4	Phase 5
Different people, different behaviors, or different settings	A	Baseline	Treatment	Treatment	Treatment	Treatment
	B	Baseline	Baseline	Treatment	Treatment	Treatment
	C	Baseline	Baseline	Baseline	Treatment	Treatment
	D	Baseline	Baseline	Baseline	Baseline	Treatment

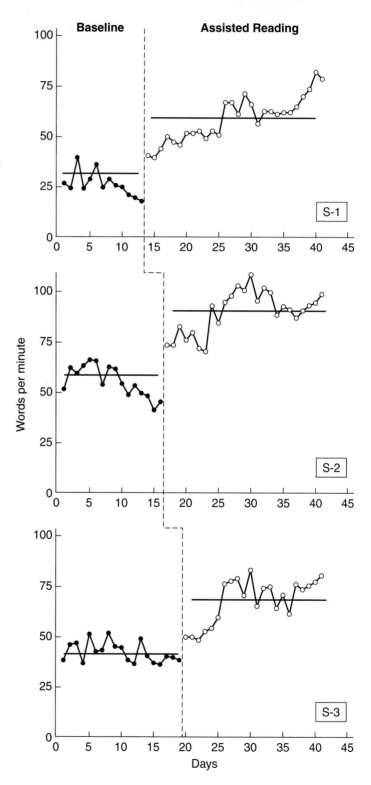

FIGURE 10.14 The correct reading rates during baseline and assisted reading for each participant. Solid horizontal lines indicate condition means. The assisted reading treatment is staggered, first being provided to participant 1, second to participant 2, and third to participant 3. Notice the change in behavior in all three cases after the introduction of the treatment condition.

From L. M. Gilbert, R. L. Williams, & T. F. McLaughlin (1996). "Use of assisted reading to increase reading rates and decrease error rates of students with learning disabilities," *Journal of Applied Behavior Analysis, 29,* 255–257. Reprinted by permission.

nineteen baseline days for the third student. Figure 10.14 reveals that the number of correct words read for each student remained stable or declined slightly during all baseline days. However, immediately after the introduction of the assisted reading program the number of words that were correctly read increased over baseline for all three individuals. The important point is that the change in number of correct words read did not change until the assisted reading program was implemented, providing evidence that it was the assisted reading program that caused the improvement in reading.

Although the multiple-baseline design can provide convincing evidence for the efficacy of a treatment and avoids the problem of reversibility, it has another basic difficulty. For this design to be effective in evaluating the efficacy of a treatment, the target behaviors must not be highly interrelated. This means that the behaviors must not be interdependent such that a change in one behavior alters the other behaviors. Borden, Bruce, Mitchell, Carter, and Hall (1970), for example, used a multiple-baseline design and found that reinforcement not only changed the inattentive behavior of the target participant but also changed that of an adjacent peer. When interdependence exists, it destroys much of the power of this design because its power is dependent on its ability to demonstrate change when the treatment condition is administered to a given behavior, individual, or setting. If administering the experimental treatment to one behavior, individual, or setting results in a corresponding change in the other behaviors, individuals, or settings, then it will have less impact and produce less change in the remaining behaviors, individuals, or settings because the behavior had previously been altered. In this case, it would not be clear what caused the change in behavior. All this means is that when considering the use of a multiple-baseline design, you must also determine whether the behaviors, individuals, or settings are independent, and if you think they might not be, you must collect data to ensure that they are independent. Different behaviors of the same individual are probably most likely to be interdependent. If you have data indicating that the target behaviors (e.g., talking out and being out of seat) are interdependent, you should use different individuals or different settings because these will probably be more distinct than different behaviors of the same individual.

Changing-Criterion Design

The changing-criterion design is presented because it is particularly useful for investigating educational problems that require shaping of behavior over a period of time or in cases where a step-by-step increase in accuracy, frequency, or amount are the goals of the research. The **changing-criterion design,** depicted in Figure 10.15, requires an initial baseline measure on a single target behavior. A treatment condition is then implemented and continued across a series of intervention phases. During the first intervention or treatment phase, an initial criterion of successful performance is established. When the participant achieves the established level of performance, the experiment moves to the second phase, where a new and more difficult criterion level is established while the treatment condition is continued. When behavior reaches this new criterion level and is maintained, the next phase, with its more difficult criterion level, is introduced. In this manner, each successive phase of the experiment requires a step-by-step increase in the criterion measure. Experimental control and elimination of rival explanations are demonstrated by the successive change in the target behavior with each stepwise change in the criterion.

Research
Navigator.c✦m

**changing
criterion design**

■ **Changing-criterion
design**
A single-case experimental design in which a participant's behavior is gradually altered by changing the criterion for success during successive treatment periods

■ FIGURE 10.15
Changing criterion
design

Phase A	Phase B	Phase C	Phase D
Baseline	Treatment and initial criterion	Treatment and criterion increment	Treatment and criterion increment

Hall and Fox (1977) provide a good illustration of the changing-criterion design in a study of a child named Dennis, who refused to complete arithmetic problems. To overcome this resistant behavior, the investigators first obtained a baseline measure of the average number of assigned arithmetic problems (4.25) that he would complete during a forty-five-minute session. Then Dennis was told that a specified number of problems had to be completed correctly during the subsequent session. If he completed them correctly, he could take recess and play with a basketball; if he did not, he would have to miss recess and remain in the room until they were correctly completed. During the first treatment phase, the criterion number of problems to be solved was set at five, which was about one more than the mean number completed during the baseline phase. After successfully achieving this criterion performance on three consecutive days, Dennis had to finish an additional problem to take recess and play with a basketball. The results of this experiment, shown in Figure 10.16, reveal

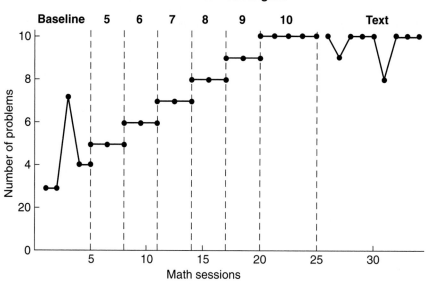

FIGURE 10.16   Number of math problems solved in a changing-criterion design

Adapted from R. V. Hall, & R. G. Fox (1997). *Changing-criterion designs: An alternative applied behavior analysis procedure. New Developments in Behavioral Research: Theory, Method, and Application.* In honor of Sidney W. Bijou, edited by C. C. Etzel, G. M. LeBlanc, and D. M. Baer, 1977. Hillsdale, NJ: Lawrence Erlbaum Associates. Copyright © 1977 by Lawrence Erlbaum Associates. Reprinted by permission of the publisher and the authors.

that Dennis's performance increased as the acceptable criterion level was increased. When a change in behavior parallels the criterion change, it demonstrates the effects of the treatment.

Successful use of the changing-criterion design does require attention to the length of the baseline and treatment phases, the amount of change in criterion, and the number of changes in the criterion. Ideally, the treatment phases should be of different lengths, or if they are of a constant length, the baseline phase should be longer than the treatment phases. This is necessary to ensure that the step-by-step changes in behavior are caused by the experimental treatment and not by some history or maturational variable that occurs simultaneously with the criterion change. Each treatment phase should be long enough to allow the behavior to change to its new criterion level and then to stabilize. If the behavior fluctuates between the new and old criterion level, stability has not been achieved, and it is difficult to determine which criterion level has been achieved. The criterion change should be large enough to detect a behavioral change but small enough so that it can be achieved. This requirement is a logical one because an unachievable criterion change would doom the experiment to failure and not permit an assessment of the efficacy of the experimental treatment.

10.13 How does the multiple-baseline design demonstrate a treatment effect?

10.14 What is the primary problem that can be encountered in using the multiple-baseline design?

10.15 When would you use the changing-criterion design?

10.16 What are the essential characteristics of the changing-criterion design?

REVIEW

QUESTIONS

METHODOLOGICAL CONSIDERATIONS IN USING SINGLE-CASE DESIGNS

The discussion of the single-case experimental designs we have just presented by no means represents an exhaustive survey but shows the most basic and commonly used designs. If you are interested in other single-case designs, you should consult Barlow and Hersen's (1992) book. Regardless of the design used, there are several methodological issues that must be considered in attempting to conduct a single-case study. These issues are summarized in Table 10.3.

SUMMARY

Quasi-experimental designs are used when not all the demands of experimental research can be met. For example, these designs are used when it is impossible to randomly assign research participants to the various comparison groups. This means that a confounding variable might be present that would make the interpretation of the results ambiguous. Therefore, whenever you use a quasi-experimental design, you must be alert for the influence of extraneous variables that could confound the results.

■ **TABLE 10.3**   Methodological Issues in Single-Case Studies

1. **Baseline**—The behavior of the participant before the administration of the experimental treatment condition. Baseline serves as the standard for assessing change induced by the experimental treatment condition, and to serve as this standard, it must be stable. A stable baseline is characterized by (a) an absence of trend or baseline data that does not increase or decrease over time and (b) little variability, which is defined by Sidman (1960) as only a 5 percent variability.

2. **Changing One Variable at a Time**—In single-case studies, only one variable can be changed from one phase of the experiment to the next. This is necessary to be able to isolate the effect produced by that variable.

3. **Length of Phases**—Agreement does not exist with regard to the length of phases. Some researchers state that the various phases should be of equal length, and others state that each phase should be continued until some degree of stability has been achieved.

4. **Assessment of Treatment Effect**—There are two approaches to assessing the effect of an experimental treatment:

   a. Visual inspection—Looking at the data generated in the various phases is sufficient to identify a treatment effect if the baseline and intervention data do not overlap (there is a change in the level of the baseline and intervention phases) or if the trend of the data in the baseline phase is different from that which exists in the intervention phase.

   b. Statistical analysis—A statistical analysis such as a time series analysis is necessary if there is a great deal of variability in the data. In general, the statistical analysis is not needed if there is little variability in the data and the baseline data is very stable. When these two conditions do not exist, a statistical analysis should be used.

There are many designs, such as the nonequivalent comparison-group design and the interrupted time-series design, that fall under the rubric of quasi-experimental designs. The most frequently used design is the nonequivalent comparison-group design, which consists of giving an experimental and a control group a pretest and then a posttest after an experimental treatment condition has been administered to the experimental group. The interrupted time-series design consists of taking multiple pretests, introducing a treatment condition, and then taking multiple posttests. The regression discontinuity design consists of administering an experimental treatment condition to participants who score above some preset cutoff score. A treatment effect is assumed to exist if there is a discontinuity of the regression lines from the participants above and below the cutoff score.

Single-case designs are all some type of a time-series design. Two of the most frequently used single-case designs are the A-B-A design and the multiple-baseline design. The A-B-A design assesses the effect of an independent variable by determining whether the dependent variable responses are different from the baseline responses following implementation of the experimental treatment and whether they revert to baseline level when the independent variable is removed. The A-B-A design rules out history by demonstrating that the dependent variable response reverts to baseline when the treatment condition is withdrawn. The multiple-baseline design assesses the effect of an independent variable by demonstrating that a change in behavior occurs only when the treatment effect is successively administered to different individuals, different behaviors, or to the same behavior in different settings.

The changing-criterion design can be used when the goal is to increase the amount, accuracy, or frequency of some behavior. After a baseline is established, a treatment condition is administered following attainment of a specific criterion of initial successful performance. When this performance criterion has been achieved, the criterion is progressively increased until the desired behavior is attained. The treatment condition is administered only after the criterion of successful performance is attained.

There are a number of methodological issues that must be considered in designing a single-case study. These involve consideration of the baseline—that only one variable can be changed at a time, the length of phases—and how to assess the treatment effect.

KEY TERMS

A-B-A design (p. 313)
A-B-A-B design (p. 315)
changing-criterion design (p. 319)
interrupted time-series
  design (p. 306)

multiple-baseline design (p. 317)
nonequivalent comparison-group
  design (p. 301)
quasi-experimental research
  design (p. 300)

regression-discontinuity
  design (p. 309)
single-case experimental
  designs (p. 312)

DISCUSSION QUESTIONS

1. Reread the definition of selection effects in Chapter 10. Is selection a problem in the nonequivalent comparison-group design? If so, what can a researcher do to minimize the problem of selection?
2. What type of design from this chapter would you select for each of the following hypothetical studies? Briefly list the strengths and weaknesses of the design.
   a. You want to compare two different ways of teaching college algebra to college students. One group uses calculators, and the other group carries out hand calculations.
   b. You want to study the effect of a new training program, and you are able to rigidly divide people into two groups based on a cutoff score on the quantitative variable called *achievement pretest*.
   c. You want to study the effect of a curriculum implemented a few years ago. You have located baseline data (on the dependent variable) before implementation of the new curriculum and continue to record data after the intervention.
   d. You want to determine the usefulness of a behavioral reinforcement technique for keeping a student on-task.
   e. You have only three or four people to study, and you want to determine the impact of a technique for teaching students how to perform multiplication.
3. List any problems you identify for each of the following hypothetical studies:
   a. A researcher uses the nonequivalent comparison-group design. She compares the achievement scores of a third-period high school

English class taught by Ms. Turner using the discussion method with the scores obtained by the students in a different third-period high school English class that is taught by Mr. Newman using the lecture method.

b. A researcher uses the nonequivalent comparison-group design. The researcher compares the achievement scores of a third-period high school English class taught by an instructional computer program with a class taught by the lecture method. The instructional period is equal for both the computer and lecture treatments.

c. A school economist uses the interrupted time series design to study the impact of a new program aimed at increasing donations to the PTA. The program was implemented in January 2002. The school economist has five years of pretest data and will collect annual data for the next five years. (Hint: Note that in 2002, the stock market took a major downturn.)

d. A teacher uses the A-B-A design to study the impact of her new strategy for teaching multiplication.

RESEARCH EXERCISES

To gain some experience in reading and identifying quasi-experimental and single-case designs, use Research Navigator to find one of the following articles:

Copland, M. A. (2000). Problem-based learning and prospective principals' problem-framing ability. *Educational Administration Quarterly, 36*(4), 585–607.

Hitendra, P. (1998). An investigation of the effect of individual cognitive preferences on learning through computer-based instruction. *Educational Psychology, 18*(2), 171–182.

Moore, D. W., Prebble, S., Robertson, J., Waetford, R., & Anderson, A. (2001). Self-recording with goal setting: A self-management programme for the classroom. *Educational Psychology, 21*(3), 255–265.

Once you have selected your article, read it carefully and answer the following questions:

1. What is the primary research question that the study addresses?
2. What are the independent and dependent variables in the research design?
3. What type of design was used in the study to answer the research question?
4. Why do you think the researchers used the design they selected?
5. What limitations exist for the design used in the research study?
6. What could the researchers have done to improve the research design?

RELEVANT INTERNET SITES

http://trochim.human.cornell.edu/kb/quasiexp.htm
Bill Trochim's presentation on quasi-experiments.

www.envmed.rochester.edu/wwwrap/behavior/jeab/jeabhome.htm
Journal of the Experimental Analysis of Behavior: has short videos and you can print out reprints of selected articles.

www.unlv.edu/Colleges/Education/EP/scsadsgn.htm
A site that focuses on single-case designs.

RECOMMENDED READING

Braden, J. P., & Bryant, T. J. (1990). Regression disconti-nuity designs: Applications for school psychologists. *School Psychology Review, 19,* 232–239.

Campbell, D. T., & Russo, M. J. (1999). *Social experimen-tation.* Thousand Oaks, CA: Sage.

Eckert, T. L., Ardoin, S. P., Daiesy, D. M., & Scarola, M. D. (2000). Empirically evaluating the effectiveness of reading interventions: The use of brief experimental analysis and single case designs. *Psychology in the Schools, 37*(5), 463–473.

Reichardt, C. S., & Mark, M. M. (1998). Quasi-experimen-tation. In L. Bickman & D. J. Rog (Eds.), *Handbook of applied social research methods* (pp. 193–228). Thousand Oaks, CA: Sage.

Shadish, W. R., Cook, T. D., & Campbell, D. T. (2002). *Ex-perimental and quasi-experimental designs for gen-eralized causal inference.* New York: Houghton Mifflin.

11

Nonexperimental Quantitative Research

LEARNING OBJECTIVES

To be able to

- State the definition of nonexperimental quantitative research.
- Identify categorical and quantitative independent variables that cannot be manipulated by a researcher.
- Describe the limitations of the simple cases of causal-comparative and correlational research.
- Evaluate evidence for cause and effect using the three necessary conditions for cause-and-effect relationships.
- Explain the third-variable problem.
- List and briefly describe the three major techniques of control that are used in nonexperimental research.
- Compare and contrast cross-sectional research, longitudinal research, and retrospective research.
- Compare and contrast the three types of longitudinal research.
- Identify descriptive research studies, predictive research studies, and explanatory research studies when examining published research.
- Explain the difference between a direct effect and an indirect effect.

In 1962, Surgeon General Dr. Luther Terry assembled the U.S. Surgeon General's Advisory Committee. The mission for this group of experts was to examine all of the research on the association between smoking and cancer. Their job was clear: They were to provide the nation with an answer to the question, Does smoking cause cancer of the lungs? Because it was not possible to experimentally study smoking and cancer with humans, most of the research was nonexperimental research, which is more controversial when trying to make statements about causes and effects. Over the next two years, the Advisory Committee reviewed the vast research literature and they examined all known plausible alternative explanations for the association between smoking and lung cancer.

In 1964, the committee's landmark conclusion was made public: "Cigarette smoking is causally related to lung cancer in men; the magnitude of the effect of cigarette smoking far outweighs all other factors. The data for women, though less extensive, point in the same direction" (U.S. Office of the Surgeon General, 1964, p. 37).

Despite the Surgeon General's Report, scientists working for the tobacco industry did not give up. They repeatedly espoused the view that one can "prove" that smoking causes lung cancer only through the conduct of experimental research. They argued that the association between smoking and cancer was an artifact due to some hidden and unknown factor. They argued that smokers and nonsmokers probably differed on some genetic factor that caused them to smoke and caused lung cancer. The scientists working for the tobacco industry were capitalizing on the limitation of nonexperimental research: This type of research does not eliminate the influence of extraneous variables as easily and successfully as does experimental research. However, over time, the nonexperimental research studies continued to demonstrate the relationship between lung cancer and smoking when all other plausible extraneous variables were taken into account. The evidence for a causal relationship became so strong that it revealed that the critics working for the tobacco industry were wrong. Smoking did and does cause lung cancer.

In March 1997, the first cigarette company, Liggett Group, admitted that the wealth of evidence, including decades of their own research, supported the conclusion that smoking does indeed cause lung cancer. Three years later, two more of the top five cigarette companies joined. As of May 24, 2000, the nation's leading cigarette company, Philip Morris, as well as another top five company, R. J. Reynolds, had yet to admit that smoking causes lung cancer.

In this chapter, we will discuss a number of nonexperimental research designs and show you why these designs are not as effective as experimental designs in demonstrating a causal relationship. We will also show you what needs to be done to arrive at a causal conclusion when using these designs.

Researchers are interested in the issue of causality because they want to learn how the world operates and obtain information about how to make it work better. You have learned in earlier chapters that experimental research is the strongest research method for providing evidence of a causal relationship between two variables. Sometimes, however, researchers are interested in causality, but they cannot conduct an experiment, either because the independent variable cannot be manipulated or because it would be unethical to manipulate it.

For example, let's say that you want to determine whether cigarette smoking causes lung cancer. What kind of research would you choose? Would you set up the following experiment? Select 500 newborn babies, and randomly assign them to two groups, an experimental group ($n = 250$) that would be forced to smoke cigarettes and a control group ($n = 250$) that would not be allowed to smoke cigarettes. Then you would measure the rates of lung cancer in the two groups many years later. Obviously, you could never conduct this experiment because it would be highly unethical. So what must you do instead? Should you give up on scientific research because you can't manipulate the independent variable? Of course not. The research problem is much too important. What you have to do in cases like this is use a *non*experimental research method and attempt to establish the best evidence that you can given your practical constraints.

■ **Nonexperimental research**
Research in which the independent variable is not manipulated and there is no random assignment to groups

Here is the formal definition of **nonexperimental research** used in this chapter (Kerlinger, 1986):

> Nonexperimental research is systematic empirical inquiry in which the scientist does not have direct control of independent variables because their manifestations have already occurred or because they are inherently not manipulable. Inferences about relations among variables are made, without direct intervention, from concomitant variation of independent and dependent variables. (p. 348)

You can see in Kerlinger's definition that the researcher does not manipulate the independent variable in nonexperimental research (i.e., "the scientist does not have direct control of independent variables"); the researcher can look back at what naturally happened in the past, or he or she can move forward and observe what happens over time (i.e., "because their manifestations have already occurred or because they are inherently not manipulable"); and the researcher observes how variables relate to one another (i.e., "Inferences about relations among variables are made . . . from concomitant variation of independent and dependent variables"). The independent and dependent variables can be categorical and/or quantitative in nonexperimental research. In this chapter, you should assume that the dependent variable is quantitative unless we tell you otherwise. However, the logic that is explained in this chapter equally applies to a research study with a categorical dependent variable.[1]

Manipulation of an independent variable and random assignment to groups are missing in *non*experimental research studies. This means that nonexperimental researchers must study the world as it naturally occurs. Because nonexperimental researchers cannot directly manipulate their independent variables or randomly assign research participants to experimental and control groups, a red flag should always pop up in your mind reminding you that nonexperimental research cannot provide evidence for causality that is as strong as the evidence obtained in experimental research. Evidence for causality in nonexperimental research is more tentative, more exploratory, and less conclusive.

Despite its limitations, nonexperimental research is very important to the field of education because many important educational variables cannot be manipulated or created in the laboratory, and it is difficult if not impossible to create many real-life settings using experiments. Here is the way one leading research methodologist put it:

> It can even be said that nonexperimental research is more important than experimental research. This is, of course, not a methodological observation. It means, rather, that most so-

cial scientific and educational research problems do not lend themselves to experimentation, although many of them do lend themselves to controlled inquiry of the nonexperimental kind. Consider Piaget's studies of children's thinking, the authoritarianism studies of Adorno et al., the highly important study *Equality of Educational Opportunity,* and McClelland's studies of need for achievement. If a tally of sound and important studies in the behavioral sciences and education were made, it is possible that nonexperimental studies would outnumber and outrank experimental studies. (Kerlinger, 1986, pp. 359–360)

Kerlinger was trying to emphasize the importance of nonexperimental research in this quote despite the fact that he actually preferred experimental to nonexperimental research. He was careful to point out that his reasoning was not based on a methodological observation because, again, other things being equal, you should prefer an experiment when you are interested in studying causality. It is a cardinal rule in research, however, that *your research questions should drive your research.* This means that you first determine your research questions and then select the strongest research method available to address those questions. In education, this often means that we have to conduct nonexperimental research to address important questions.

STEPS IN NONEXPERIMENTAL RESEARCH

The typical steps in nonexperimental research are similar to the steps in experimental research. (1) The researcher determines the research problem and the research hypotheses to be tested. (2) The researcher selects the variables to be used in the study. (3) The researcher collects the data. (4) The researcher analyzes the data. (5) The researcher interprets the results of the study. The researcher specifically determines whether the hypotheses are supported. The researcher also typically explores the data to generate additional hypotheses to be tested in future research studies. It is important that the researcher follow these steps when conducting nonexperimental research in order to avoid the post hoc fallacy.

The **post hoc fallacy** reads "*Post hoc, ergo propter hoc.*" In English, this says, "After this, therefore because of this." (Now you know a little Latin!) We engage in the post hoc fallacy if we argue after the fact that because A preceded B, A must have caused B. For example, you get the flu and attribute it to your friend's sniffling child, who visited your home yesterday. This kind of reasoning is more informally known as "twenty-twenty hindsight." We are all pretty good at explaining, after the fact, why something happened. Although this kind of reasoning is fine for generating ideas, it is far from conclusive scientific evidence. An especially egregious form of the post hoc fallacy would occur if a researcher analyzed some data, found some statistically significant correlations or group differences, and then acted as if he or she had predicted those relationships. The point is that in explanatory research, you must test your hypotheses with empirical data to make sure that they work.

■ **Post hoc fallacy**
Making the argument that because A preceded B, A must have caused B

INDEPENDENT VARIABLES IN NONEXPERIMENTAL RESEARCH

Independent variables used in nonexperimental research frequently cannot be manipulated, either because it is impossible to manipulate them or because it would be unethical to manipulate them. Nonexperimental research is also sometimes done on independent variables that can be but are not manipulated because the researcher wants to explore how the independent variable is related to other variables before doing an experiment or the researcher wants to replicate a result that has been previously demonstrated with experimental research. All these forms of nonexperimental research can make a contribution to the educational research literature.

Now let's look at some examples of categorical and quantitative independent variables that might be used in nonexperimental research because they cannot be manipulated. Some categorical independent variables that cannot be manipulated by the researcher are gender, parenting style, student learning style, ethnicity, retention in grade (i.e., retained or not retained), drug or tobacco use, and any enduring personality trait that is operationalized as a categorical variable (e.g., high extroversion versus low extroversion). If you try, you can probably think of some additional categorical independent variables that cannot be manipulated by the researcher. Some quantitative independent variables that cannot be manipulated by the researcher are intelligence, aptitude, age, GPA, any enduring personality trait that is operationalized as a quantitative variable (e.g., degree of extroversion varying from a low value of 1 to a high value of 100), and so forth. Again, you can probably think of some additional quantitative independent variables that can't be manipulated by the researcher if you think about it for a moment.

Researchers sometimes turn inherently quantitative independent variables into categorical independent variables. For example, you could take the quantitative variable aptitude and categorize it into three groups (high, medium, and low motivation). Another example is in the previous paragraph, where we pointed out that extroversion could be operationalized as either a categorical variable or a quantitative variable. Categorizing an independent variable makes the research study look like an experiment because the independent variable is usually categorical in experimental research studies. Do *not* be misled, however. If the independent variable is not manipulated, then it is not an experiment. Most experts contend that categorizing quantitative independent variables is a poor practice that should be discontinued (e.g., Kerlinger, 1986, p. 558; Pedhazur & Schmelkin, 1991, p. 308). The problem is that you lose some information about the relationship between the independent and dependent variables when you categorize a quantitative variable. Also, if only two categories are used (e.g., high versus low), then only linear (straight line) relationships can be examined. You can solve this last problem by simply using three categories rather than two categories. The problem of loss of information cannot be avoided. In short, we recommend that researchers generally avoid turning quantitative variables into categorical variables.

SIMPLE CASES OF CAUSAL-COMPARATIVE AND CORRELATIONAL RESEARCH

You learned in Chapter 2 that the term *causal-comparative research* is sometimes applied to nonexperimental research in which the primary independent variable of interest is categorical, and the term correlational research is sometimes applied to nonexperimental research in which the primary independent variable of interest is quantitative (Fraenkel & Wallen, 1996). In practice, most published nonexperimental research studies are a cross between causal-comparative and correlational because the researchers include one or more categorical independent variables and one or more quantitative independent variables in the same research study. It is also important to realize that many published research studies are a cross between experimental and nonexperimental research. This happens when the researcher manipulates one variable (e.g., method of teaching) but includes another independent variable that is not manipulated (e.g., intelligence).

The distinction between causal-comparative and correlational research is artificial because one can easily transform a correlational research study into a causal-comparative research study by simply categorizing the independent variable. (We gave examples of categorizing the variables *aptitude* and *extroversion* earlier.) We recommend, however, that researchers *not* categorize inherently quantitative independent variables. Students and researchers need to understand that what is *essential* when addressing the issue of causation is not whether an independent variable is categorical or quantitative, but how effectively the researcher deals with the three *necessary conditions for causation* (discussed later and in Chapter 8). Furthermore, we point out that many published research articles are a cross between causal-comparative and correlational. Nonetheless, it is instructive to learn about what are called the **simple cases** of causal-comparative and correlational research (i.e., nonexperimental research designs with only one independent variable and one dependent variable) when you are first learning about research because it allows you to start with the most basic forms of nonexperimental research.

In the **simple case of causal-comparative research,** there is one categorical independent variable and one quantitative dependent variable. For example, perhaps a researcher examined the relationship between gender and math performance and found out that, on average, the males did slightly better than the females. This is a simple case of causal-comparative research because there is one categorical independent variable (gender) and one quantitative dependent variable (math performance). In the simple case of causal-comparative research, the researcher compares the two group means (males versus females) to see whether the groups differ on the dependent variable (math performance). The researcher also uses a statistical test to determine whether the relationship between the independent and dependent variables is statistically significant. The researcher would specifically use either a *t*-test or an ANOVA (explained in Chapter 16) to determine whether the difference between the two group means is **statistically significant** (i.e., Is the difference between the groups greater than what one would expect to see by chance?). Group means that are very different are usually statistically significant, and if they are, the researcher concludes that there is a relationship between the independent and dependent variables. (We will carefully explain the ideas of *t*-test, ANOVA, and statistical significance in Chapter 16. So don't worry about knowing any more than the basics for now! We just wanted to use these terms here to show you where they fit into the overall research process.)

In the **simple case of correlational research,** there is one quantitative independent variable and one quantitative dependent variable. For example, perhaps a researcher examined the relationship between students' level of motivation and their math performance and found out that lower levels of motivation predicted lower math performance and higher levels of motivation predicted higher math performance (i.e., there was a positive correlation). In the simple case of correlational research, the researcher first plots his or her data to determine whether the relationship is linear or curvilinear. Examples of linear and curvilinear relationships are shown in Figure 11.1. As you can see, a linear relationship follows a straight-line pattern and a curvilinear relationship follows a curved-line pattern. If the relationship between the variables is linear, then the researcher computes the

----

■ Simple cases
When there is only one independent variable and one dependent variable

■ Simple case of causal-comparative research
When there is one categorical independent variable and one quantitative dependent variable

■ Statistically significant
A research finding is probably not attributable to chance

■ Simple case of correlational research
When there is one quantitative independent variable and one quantitative dependent variable

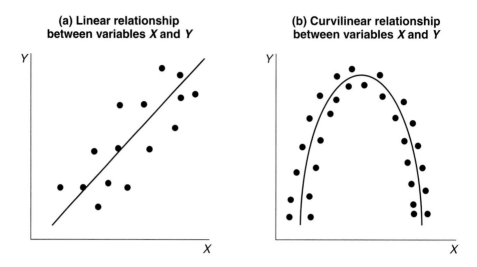

FIGURE 11.1   Linear and curvilinear relationships

Pearson Product Moment correlation coefficient. This is the most commonly used correlation coefficient (discussed in Chapter 2), and it is the one that researchers are usually referring to if they say they computed the "correlation." If the relationship is curvilinear, the researcher must rely on an alternative measure of the relationship between two variables known as η (Greek eta) (for details, see Howell, 1997, pp. 331–333) or use curvilinear regression (for details, see Pedhazur & Schmelkin, 1991, pp. 451–458).

After determining the correlation between the single independent variable and the single dependent variable in the simple case of correlational research, the researcher usually conducts a statistical test to determine whether the correlation is statistically significant. A correlation coefficient is said to be statistically significant when it is larger than would be expected by chance. Correlation coefficients that are much larger than zero are usually statistically significant.

Assume now that a researcher found that the relationship between the two variables was statistically significant in our examples of the simple cases of causal-comparative and correlational research. *It is important for you to remember that both of these simple cases of nonexperimental research are seriously flawed if you want to make a causal attribution* (i.e., if you want to conclude that gender affects math performance or if you want to conclude that level of motivation affects math performance). The biggest problem is that there are too many uncontrolled extraneous variables that may be the reason for the observed relationship. For example, can you think of some alternative explanations for an observed relationship between gender and math achievement (e.g., perhaps females are socialized to deemphasize mathematics and males are socialized to emphasize mathematics)? Can you think of some reasons why level of motivation might not be causally related to math achievement (e.g., perhaps math achievement is due to amount of time spent studying and ability rather than motivation)?

The key point is that you cannot draw a conclusion about cause and effect from either the simple case of causal-comparative research or the simple case of correlational research because *observing a relationship between two variables is not nearly enough evidence to conclude that the relationship is causal.* In the next sections, we explain how you can establish firmer evidence of causation. For example, you can design superior nonexperimental research studies by also collecting data on extraneous variables that represent plausible alternative explanations. In practice, you should avoid the simple cases of causal-comparative and correlational research whenever you are interested in studying cause and effect. The terms *causal comparative* and *correlational* also are not very useful when describing more advanced cases of nonexperimental research. We recommend simply using the term *nonexperimental* and then describing your study on the characteristics of time and objective as discussed later in this chapter. Our goal in this chapter is to show you how to design and conduct *high-quality* nonexperimental research studies.

THREE NECESSARY CONDITIONS FOR CAUSE-AND-EFFECT RELATIONSHIPS

Whenever your goal is to provide evidence about the existence of a cause-and-effect relationship between two variables, you must check for the presence of the **three necessary conditions** for concluding that changes in variable A tend to produce (cause) changes in variable B (Asher, 1983; Cook & Campbell, 1979). Notice that we said "tend to" in the previous sentence. We used those words to remind you that educational researchers are interested in **probabilistic cause** (i.e., changes in variable A tend to cause changes in variable B), not perfect causation (i.e., changes in variable A always produce the same changes in variable B). The idea of probabilistic cause should make sense to you because you know that, for example, a technique of teaching might work quite well for many students but it does not work well for a few of your students. Counselors know that a certain type of therapy might work well for many clients but not for a few of their clients. It is also true that the same individual might not always react the same way to the same stimulus. For these reasons, when educational researchers talk about causation, they are almost always talking about probabilistic causation rather than about perfect or absolute causation.

The three necessary conditions that you must always consider if you want to establish that changes in variable A tend to *cause* changes in variable B are discussed in Chapter 8. They are shown again in Table 11.1. As you can see in the table, condition 1 states that variable A and variable B must be related. This is the relationship condition: If there is no relationship whatsoever between two variables, then one variable cannot affect the other variable. Condition 2 states that proper time order must be established. This condition should be obvious, because if changes in variable A are to cause changes in variable B, the changes in variable A must precede the changes in variable B.

Condition 3 says that the relationship between variable A and variable B must not be due to a confounding extraneous or third variable. This means that alternative or rival explanations must be eliminated. A common rival explanation states that an observed relationship was due to an extraneous variable (i.e., a third variable) that was not controlled for in the research study. This rival explanation is sometimes called the **third-variable problem** because it states that the relationship between A and B is actually due to C. We discuss the third-variable problem in more depth later. The key point for now is that because you want to conduct a strong research study, you must identify extraneous variables that operate as rival explanations, and

■ **Three necessary conditions**
Three things that must be present if you are to contend that causation has occurred

■ **Probablistic cause**
Changes in variable A tend to produce changes in variable B

Research
Navigator.c⊛m

causal

■ **Third-variable problem**
An observed relationship between two variables that may be due to an extraneous variable

TABLE 11.1
The Three Necessary
Conditions for
Causation

Researchers must establish three conditions if they are to conclude that changes in variable A cause changes in variable B.

Condition 1:   Variable A and variable B must be related (the relationship condition).

Condition 2:   Proper time order must be established (the temporal antecedence condition).

Condition 3:   The relationship between variable A and variable B must *not* be due to some confounding extraneous or "third" variable (the lack of alternative explanation condition).

you should identify those variables during the planning and designing phases of the study so the problem can be prevented. After a study has been completed, it is usually too late to do anything about an extraneous variable.

Some terminology is potentially confusing. First, the terms *confounding variables* and *third variables* are used interchangeably in this chapter because they are synonyms. Both terms refer to extraneous variables that researchers need to identify before they collect their data so that they can attempt to eliminate the variables as rival explanations for an observed relationship. You can eliminate or minimize the influence of third variables by using one of the approaches discussed in the section on techniques of control in nonexperimental research. Second, the terms *alternative explanation, rival explanation,* and *rival hypothesis* are also synonyms. These terms are used to refer to new reasons for an observed relationship other than the reason originally stated by a researcher (i.e., the new reasons operate as alternatives or rivals). Whenever you identify a flaw or problem with a research study finding, you are stating a rival explanation.

A technique for identifying rival explanations is called the **method of working multiple hypotheses** (Chamberlin, 1965). Chamberlin explains the method of working multiple hypotheses this way:

■ **Method of working multiple hypotheses**
Attempting to identify all rival explanations

> The effort is to bring up into view every rational explanation of new phenomena, and to develop every tenable hypothesis respecting their cause and history. The investigator thus becomes the parent of a family of hypotheses; and, by his parental relation to all, he is forbidden to fasten his affections unduly upon any one. (cited in Kerlinger, 1986, p. 357)

If you conduct a research study, remember to use the method of working multiple hypotheses when you are *planning* the study, not after you have completed it and someone has identified the potential flaw. This way you can obtain conclusions that are defensible.

The three necessary conditions for cause and effect that we just discussed are truly general. They apply to both experimental and nonexperimental research. In fact, the criteria apply whenever you want to establish evidence that a relationship is causal, regardless of your research method (e.g., the conditions apply in qualitative research if you are interested in causality). You learned in previous chapters that strong experimental research designs (i.e., designs with manipulation and random assignment) perform extremely well on the three conditions for causation. Now we examine how well nonexperimental research performs on the three necessary conditions for causality.

APPLYING THE THREE NECESSARY CONDITIONS FOR CAUSATION IN NONEXPERIMENTAL RESEARCH

Neither manipulation nor random assignment is present in nonexperimental research. Let's examine the implications this fact has for establishing evidence of cause and effect. We start with the simple cases of causal-comparative and correlational research discussed earlier. Recall that in the simple cases, there is a single independent variable and a single dependent variable. In an earlier example, we saw that a relationship was observed between gender and math performance in our causal-comparative example, and a relationship was observed between level of motivation and math performance in our correlational example. The problem that we run into with the two simple cases is that observing a relationship is clearly not sufficient grounds for concluding that a relationship is causal. Let's apply the three necessary conditions for causation to the two simple cases.

In the case of gender and math performance, a relationship was observed. This means that condition 1 is met (i.e., a relationship between the two variables must be observed). We can also assume that gender occurs before math performance as measured in the research study if we assume that gender is a measure of one's biological sex. That's because biological sex is fixed at birth. In this case, condition 2 also appears to be met (i.e., gender comes before math performance). Note that one might argue that gender is much more than biological sex. If one makes this argument, however, it would be wise to specifically measure the important aspects of gender and study how they relate to the dependent variable. One would then have to consider the issue of time order for each new aspect studied.

Our biggest problem, based on the three necessary conditions, is with condition 3. There are many alternative explanations for an observed relationship between gender and math performance. As we pointed out earlier, perhaps males and females are socialized differently regarding mathematics. Or perhaps females are just as good at math as males except that they tend to have higher math anxiety than males, which lowers their math performance. Socialization and math anxiety represent uncontrolled third variables that are confounded (entangled) with the independent variable gender. Therefore, we cannot know for sure whether math performance is due to gender or whether it is due to socialization or to math anxiety (or to some other unnamed third variable). This problem is an example of the *third-variable problem* that is omnipresent in nonexperimental research. The third-variable problem is present whenever there are uncontrolled and therefore potentially confounding extraneous variables present.

Now let's move to the case of level of motivation and math performance. Once again, a relationship was observed (the higher the motivation, the higher the math performance). Therefore, condition number 1 is met (relationship between the two variables is present). We can't know for sure whether level of motivation or math performance occurred first, since we assume that the researchers measured both variables at the same time in this example. (Later in this chapter, we discuss some nonexperimental designs in which participants are studied at more than one time point.) We might assume on theoretical grounds that the level of motivation was to some degree present before the students took the test measuring their math performance. It is reasonable to assume, for example, that students who are more motivated will attend class regularly and study harder and that attending class and studying for exams occur before the actual exams. On the other hand, we cannot know time ordering for sure because it is also reasonable to believe that math performance has some impact on level of motivation. In short, condition 2 (proper time order) is only partially met because the proper time order is only assumed or hypothesized to occur, and no direct evidence exists that the proper time order did occur.

As was the case in the gender study example, condition 3 is a major problem. There are alternative explanations for the observed relationship between level of motivation and math performance. We listed two rival explanations earlier: Perhaps the students' math performance was due to amount of time spent studying or to ability rather than to level of motivation. The problem of alternative or rival explanations is omnipresent in nonexperimental research. In a nonexperimental study, the researcher can never know for sure whether an observed relationship can be explained away by some uncontrolled extraneous or third variable that a researcher failed to identify.

The most serious problem that we run into in the simple cases of nonexperimental research is that the observed relationship might be due to an extraneous variable (condition 3). We have called this the third-variable problem. When the relationship between two variables is due to another variable, researchers sometimes call it a **spurious relationship.** A spurious relationship is a completely noncausal relationship. When the relationship between two variables is only partially due to another variable, the relationship is said to be **partially spurious** (Davis, 1985). If a third variable is to cause the third-variable problem, it must be related to both the independent and the dependent variable.

Did you know that the amount of fire damage to houses and the number of fire trucks responding to fires is positively related? Should we conclude based on this observed relationship that calling more fire trucks to a fire will cause more fire damage to occur because this is a spurious relationship? No. The real cause of the relationship between fire damage and the number of trucks responding is the *size of the fire.* More fire trucks respond to larger fires, and more damage results from larger fires. However, if you examined only the relationship between number of fire trucks and amount of fire damage without considering the size of fire, you would find a clear, positive relationship [see part (a) in Figure 11.2].

Researchers frequently check to see whether relationships are due to third variables by controlling for these variables. You have controlled for a third variable when you have provided evidence that the relationship between two variables is not due to a third variable. In particular, *the original relationship between two variables will actually disappear when controlling for the third variable if the relationship is totally spurious,* as in the case of fire damage and fire trucks.[2] In part (b) of Figure 11.2, we controlled for size of fire by examining the original relationship separately for small, medium, and large fires (i.e., we examined the relationship within levels of the extraneous variable). As you can see, there is no relationship between fire damage and number of trucks when you look only at small fires. There is no relationship when you look only at medium fires. Likewise, there is no relationship when you look only at large fires. Therefore, the original relationship between variables fire damage and number of fire trucks responding disappears when you control for the size of fire. In other words, there is no longer a relationship between the variables fire damage and number of fire trucks responding after you control for the third variable size of fire. Examining a relationship within the different

■ **Spurious relationships**
When the relationship between two variables is due to one or more third variables

■ **Partially spurious**
When the relationship between two variables is partially due to one or more third variable

(a) Before controlling for size of fire

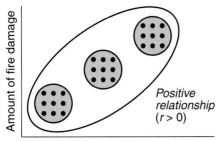

Amount of fire damage

Positive relationship (r > 0)

Number of fire trucks responding

(b) After controlling for size of fire

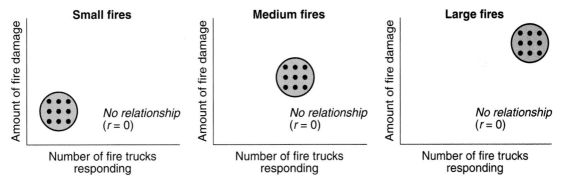

Small fires

Amount of fire damage

No relationship (r = 0)

Number of fire trucks responding

Medium fires

Amount of fire damage

No relationship (r = 0)

Number of fire trucks responding

Large fires

Amount of fire damage

No relationship (r = 0)

Number of fire trucks responding

FIGURE 11.2 Relationship between amount of fire damage and number of trucks responding before and after controlling for size of fire. We controlled for size of fire by examining the original relationship at different levels of size of fire. The original relationship disappears.

levels of a third variable such as we just did is an important strategy of controlling for an extraneous variable. This strategy is one type of what we refer to as *statistical control.*

We have provided a list of some additional spurious relationships in Table 11.2. We think that you will find the list quite entertaining! For example, did you know that there is a positive relationship (i.e., a positive correlation) between the number of police officers in an area and the number of crimes in the area? Obviously, we cannot conclude on the basis of this observed relationship that having more police officers causes crime. The completely spurious relationship is due to the third variable, population density. There are more crimes and more police officers in areas with many people, and there are fewer crimes and fewer police officers in areas with fewer people. Once the researcher controls for the third variable (population density), the original relationship will disappear. For example, if the researcher examined the relationship between police officers and crime within the different levels of population density (low, medium, and high population density), the relationship would disappear. Each of the spurious relationships shown in Table 11.2 will disappear if the researcher controls for the third variable causing the spurious relationship. None of the relationships is causal.

■ **TABLE 11.2**   Examples of Spurious Relationships

Observed Spurious Relationship*	Reason for the Relationship (the Third Variable)
Amount of ice cream sold and deaths by drownings (Moore, 1993)	Season: Ice cream sales and drownings tend to be high during the warm months of the year.
Size of left hand and size of right hand	Genetics: The size of both hands is due to genetic makeup.
Height of sons and height of daughters (Davis, 1985)	Genetics: Heights of sons and daughters are both due their parents' genetic makeup.
Ministers' salaries and price of vodka	Area (i.e., urban or rural): In urban areas, prices and salaries tend to be higher.
Shoe size and reading performance for elementary school children	Age: Older children have larger shoe sizes and read better.
Number of doctors in region and number of people dying from disease	Population density: In highly dense areas, there are more doctors and more people die.
Number of police officers and number of crimes (Glass & Hopkins, 1996)	Population density: In highly dense areas, there are more police officers and more crimes.
Number of homicides and number of churches	Population density: In highly dense areas, there are more homicides and more churches.
Number of storks sighted and the population of Oldenburg, Germany, over a six-year period (Box, Hunter, & Hunter, 1978)	Time: Both variables were increasing over time.
Number of public libraries and the amount of drug use	Time: Both were increasing during the 1970s.
Teachers' salaries and the price of liquor (Moore and McCabe, 1993)	Time: Both tend to increase over time.
Tea drinking and lung cancer	Smoking: Tea drinkers have a lower risk only because they smoke less.

*All but one of the spurious relationships in the first column shows a positive relationship. That is, as one of the variables increases, the other variable also increases. The one negative relationship is the relationship between tea drinking and lung cancer.

R E V I E W

QUESTIONS

11.1 Why is experimental research much stronger than nonexperimental research when the researcher is interested in making cause-and-effect statements?

11.2 Why must a researcher sometimes conduct nonexperimental research rather than experimental research?

11.3 Why must researchers watch out for the post hoc fallacy?

11.4 Name a potential independent variable that cannot be manipulated.

11.5 Explain the problems with the simple cases of causal-comparative and correlational research. Why is a researcher *not* justified in making a cause-and-effect claim from these two cases?

11.6 Explain exactly how strong experimental research fulfills each of the three necessary conditions for cause and effect.

11.7 On which of the three necessary conditions for cause and effect is nonexperimental research especially weak? On which one of the three necessary conditions is nonexperimental research strong?

11.8 Explain why you cannot make a defensible causal claim based on an observed relationship between two variables (e.g., gender and achievement) in nonexperimental research.

TECHNIQUES OF CONTROL IN NONEXPERIMENTAL RESEARCH

You learned in the previous section that the third-variable problem is usually present in nonexperimental research. This means that the threat of confounding extraneous variables is virtually always present in nonexperimental research. Now we discuss the major techniques that researchers use to control for extraneous variables in nonexperimental research. You have already been introduced to most of these ideas in earlier chapters (e.g., see Chapters 8 and 9). Appropriate use of these control techniques helps to improve the rigor and credibility of nonexperimental research.

Matching

As was discussed in earlier chapters, one way to control for extraneous variables is to use matching. To perform matching you must first select one or more **matching variables.** The matching variable(s) are extraneous variable(s) that you want to eliminate as threats to the presumed causal relationship between your independent and dependent variables. The second step in matching is to select participants to be in your study in such a way that your independent and matching variables will be unrelated (i.e., uncorrelated, or unconfounded). If your independent variable is categorical, this simply involves constructing comparison groups that are similar on the matching variable but different on the independent variable. This is exactly the same goal that you had in experimental research.

   For example, assume that your independent variable is gender and your dependent variable is math performance. Also assume that you want to match the groups on interest in mathematics because you think the relationship that is sometimes observed between gender and math performance is due to the fact that boys are socialized to be interested in mathematics. That is, perhaps boys are more interested in mathematics because of gender socialization, and as a result, boys try harder and perform better in mathematics. To match on interest in mathematics, you could give an interest in mathematics test to all the students in your local high school. You could find twenty-five boys whose interest levels varied from low to high. Then, for each of these twenty-five boys, you would locate a girl with a similar score on the interest in mathematics test. When you were done, you would have twenty-five boys and twenty-five girls who were matched on interest in mathematics (for a total of fifty research participants). The two groups would be similar on the variable interest in mathematics (the extraneous variable you were worried about), but they would differ on gender (the independent variable). To complete this nonexperimental research study, you would

■ **Matching variable**
The variable the researcher matches to eliminate it as an alternative explanation

measure the dependent variable *math performance* for the twenty-five boys and twenty-five girls to see whether they differed. If they did differ, it would not be because of interest in mathematics because the groups were similar on interest in mathematics.

Matching can also be used when the independent variable is quantitative. Assume that your independent variable is level of mathematics motivation (a quantitative variable varying from a low value of one to a high value of ten); your dependent variable is actual math performance; and the extraneous variable you want to eliminate as a rival explanation is grade point average (i.e., GPA is a proxy for overall academic achievement). Your research hypothesis is that higher motivation leads to higher math performance. In this example, you could match on the extraneous variable (GPA) by finding students with high, medium, and low GPAs at each of the ten levels of mathematics motivation. That is, for low-motivation students, you would locate students with high, medium, and low GPAs. Then for the next higher level of motivation, you would locate students with high, medium, and low GPAs. You would continue this process for all ten levels of motivation.[3] After completing this process, you would have your research participants. Furthermore, your independent variable (motivation) and your matching variable (GPA) would be uncorrelated and therefore unconfounded. If you still observed a relationship between motivation and math performance, you would conclude that it is not due to GPA because you eliminated GPA as a threat through the matching technique.

The key idea is that matching is used to strengthen nonexperimental research studies on condition 3 of the necessary conditions for causation (Table 11.1). That is, it is used to eliminate alternative explanations due to extraneous variables. Matching unfortunately has a number of weaknesses that limit its use. We conclude our discussion by listing the seven major limitations:

1. Matching can be cumbersome because you must search for individuals who meet the criteria for inclusion in the research study. This is a serious limitation unless you have a very large pool of potential participants to select from and you have access to information about them.
2. Researchers frequently cannot find matches for many potential research participants. These potential participants are eliminated or excluded from the research study.
3. There is usually more than one alternative explanation for the relationship of interest, so you need to match on more than one variable.
4. You must know what the relevant extraneous variables are in order to match.
5. You never know for sure that you have matched on all of the appropriate variables.
6. If you match groups from different populations (e.g., disadvantaged and advantaged groups matched on pretest achievement based on extreme scores, then the threat to internal validity, called regression to the mean, can be a problem in studies occurring over time.
7. Matching can create an unrepresentative sample because the participants are selected for the purpose of matching rather than for the purpose of being representative of a population. Therefore, the generalizability might be compromised.

Holding the Extraneous Variable Constant

When using this technique of control, researchers turn the extraneous variable into a constant. They do this by restricting the research study to a particular subgroup. For example, if you are concerned that gender might operate as a confounding extraneous variable, then you can turn gender into a constant by including only female participants in your research study. If everyone is a female, then gender does not vary (it is a constant). Most important, if all participants are of one gender, then gender cannot possibly confound the relationship between the independent and dependent variables. If you were concerned that age is a confounding extraneous variable, you could limit your research study to young people, middle-aged people, or older people. You could even limit the study to sixteen-year-olds. Unfortunately, there is a serious problem with the technique of restricting your research study to a certain subpopulation. The researcher cannot generalize to the kinds of people that are excluded from the study. In other words, the generalizability (the external validity) of the study is restricted. For example, if the study were done only with sixteen-year-olds, then the researcher could generalize only to sixteen-year-olds.

Statistical Control

Statistical control is the most commonly used technique for controlling for extraneous variables in nonexperimental research. When statistically controlling for one or more extraneous variables, the researcher uses a statistical technique to remove the influence of the extraneous variable(s). Most techniques of statistical control are spinoffs of a mathematical procedure called the **general linear model,** or the GLM (Knapp, 1978; Tabachnick & Fidell, 1996; Thompson, 1998). All you need to know about the general linear model is that it is the "parent" of many statistical techniques (i.e., the "children") that are used in education. More formally, many statistical procedures commonly used to control for extraneous variables are called special cases of the general linear model.

One **special case of the general linear model** is called **partial correlation,** which is used to examine the relationship between two quantitative variables controlling for one or more quantitative extraneous variables (Cohen, 1968; Cohen & Cohen, 1983). It is called a partial correlation because the effect of the third variable is "partialled out" or removed from the original relationship. Typically, all the variables used in partial correlation analysis must be quantitative rather than categorical. Here is a relatively easy way to think about partial correlation. If you determine the regular correlation between your independent variable and your dependent variable *at each of the levels* of your extraneous variable, you will have several correlations (e.g., if your extraneous variable had ten levels, then you would have ten correlations; if your extraneous variable had one hundred levels, then you would have one hundred correlations). The partial correlation coefficient is simply the average of those correlations (Pedhazur, 1997). The range of a partial correlation coefficient is the same as a regular correlation coefficient (i.e., −1.00 to +1.00, with zero signifying no relationship at all). As a general rule, if a researcher used a regular correlation coefficient (the correlation between two variables) rather than a partial correlation coefficient (the correlation between two variables controlling for one or more additional variables), then you can be pretty sure that he or she was not thinking about extraneous variables. On the other hand, if a researcher used a partial correlation coefficient (or another control technique), you can be pretty sure that he or she was thinking about controlling for extraneous variables. As a general rule, you should upgrade your evaluations of research articles in which the authors controlled for extraneous variables.

Another special case of the general linear model is called **analysis of covariance** (ANCOVA), which was discussed in earlier chapters. ANCOVA is used to determine the

■ **General linear model**
A mathematical procedure that is the "parent" of many statistical techniques

■ **Special case of the general linear model**
One of the "children" of a broader statistical procedure known as the general linear model (GLM)

■ **Partial correlation**
Used to examine the relationship between two quantitative variables controlling for one or more quantitative extraneous variables

■ **Analysis of covariance**
Used to examine the relationship between one categorical independent variable and one quantitative dependent variable, controlling for one or more extraneous variables

relationship between one categorical independent variable and one quantitative dependent variable controlling for one or more quantitative extraneous variables (Pedhazur & Schmelkin, 1991). For example, there is a relationship between gender (a categorical variable) and income (a quantitative variable) in the United States. Men earn more money, on average, than do women. You might decide, however, that you want to control for education; that is, you want to make sure that the difference is not due to education. You could eliminate education as a rival explanation (i.e., you could control for it) by comparing the average income levels of males and females at each of the levels of education in your data. You could also have the computer analyze your data using the ANCOVA technique to tell you whether gender and income are still related after controlling for education. If gender and income are still related, then the researcher can conclude that education has been eliminated as a rival hypothesis. The details of ANCOVA and partial correlation are beyond the scope of this book, but you can remember that ANCOVA shows the relationship between a categorical independent variable (e.g., gender) and a quantitative dependent variable (e.g., income level) controlling for a quantitative extraneous variable (e.g., level of education).

An advantage of statistical control (compared to matching) is that researchers can base their research on samples of participants who are randomly selected from a population (Pedhazur & Schmelkin, 1991). (You don't have to throw out cases from the data as you do in matching when you can't find a match for an individual.) In order to statistically control for one or more extraneous variables, a researcher must collect data on the extraneous variables in addition to data on the independent and dependent variables (i.e., collect data on all the important variables). In effect, the researcher incorporates the extraneous variables into the design of the research study. Then, after collecting the data, the researcher controls for the extraneous variables during data analysis (using ANCOVA, partial correlation, or another technique).

REVIEW

QUESTION

11.9 What is the purpose of the techniques of control in nonexperimental research?

TIME DIMENSION IN RESEARCH

It is important to have an understanding of the time dimension for at least two reasons. First, we often want to study how variables change over time (e.g., what happens to children as they get older). Second, the second necessary condition for establishing cause and effect is if variable A affects variable B, then variable A must occur before variable B. In other words, when studying cause and effect, researchers must establish proper time order. This means that we are concerned about the time dimension whenever we talk about a cause and effect. Nonexperimental research is classified into three types of research that address the time dimension issue quite differently: cross-sectional research, longitudinal research, and retrospective research (see Figure 11.3).

■ **FIGURE 11.3**   Depiction of cross-sectional, longitudinal, and retrospective research designs

Design Type	Depiction	Example
Cross-sectional	O_1	Data are collected at one point in time on several variables such as gender, income, and education.
Longitudinal	$O_1 \quad O_2 \ldots O_n$	Data are collected in a forward direction over time on one or more variables such as gender (O_1), IQ (O_1), discipline problems in middle school (O_1), high school GPA (O_2) and dropout status (O_2).
Retrospective	$O_{T-n} \ldots O_{T-1} \quad O_T$	Data are collected that represent present and past status on variables such as dropout (O_T), use of drugs (O_{T-1}), and GPA (O_{T-1}).

O stands for collection of data on independent variables, control variables, and/or dependent variables. n stands for the final time period data are collected for the longitudinal design, "T" stands for the current time, "T–1" stands for a time in the past, and "T–n" stands for the beginning time point in the past examined in the retrospective design.

Cross-Sectional Research

In **cross-sectional research,** data are collected from the research participants at a single point in time or during a single, relatively brief time period (i.e., a period long enough to collect data from all of the participants selected to be in the study). The data are typically collected from multiple groups or types of people in cross-sectional research. For example, data in a cross-sectional study might be collected from males and females, from people in different socioeconomic classes, from multiple age groups, and from people with different abilities and accomplishments. The major advantage of cross-sectional research is that data can be collected on many different kinds of people in a relatively short period of time.

Cross-sectional research has several weaknesses. One disadvantage is that it is difficult to establish time order (condition 2 of the necessary conditions for causality). If you collect data from research participants at a single time point only, you can't directly measure changes that are occurring in them over time. Time order can be partially established in cross-sectional research through theory, through past research findings, and through an understanding of the independent variable (e.g., you can safely assume that an adult's biological sex occurs before the amount of education they have because biological sex is set at birth). These techniques for establishing time order are weaker than actually observing people over time. A related disadvantage is that the study of developmental trends (changes in people as they get older) can be misleading when using cross-sectional data.

Suppose that you collected cross-sectional data from 1,000 adults who were ages eighteen or older. When analyzing the data, suppose that you found that age and political conservatism were positively correlated (the older the participants are, the more conservative they tend to be). You cannot safely conclude in this case that aging causes conservatism

■ **Cross-sectional research**
Data are collected at a single point in time.

Research
Navigator.c⊕m

cross-sectional data

because you have not established proper time order (necessary condition 2), and you have not ruled out rival explanations (necessary condition 3). Remember this important point: In a cross-sectional study, people at different ages are not the same people. Therefore, you are not able to observe your participants change over time and properly establish time order. In addition, the older and younger people may differ on important extraneous variables (e.g., they might differ on education and experience of certain historical events). An alternative explanation for the relationship between age and political conservatism is that the people in the earlier generations of your data (the older people) have always been more conservative than the more recent generations (the younger people), perhaps because of some historical effect. The younger people lived in different historical times during their formative years, and they may turn out differently when they are older. Thus, you can't make a strong conclusion that age causes people to become more conservative.

Research Navigator.c☉m

longitudinal data

- **Longitudinal research**
  Data are collected at multiple time points and comparisons are made across time

- **Trend study**
  Independent samples are taken from a population over time and the same questions are asked

- **Panel study**
  Study in which the same individuals are studied at successive points over time

- **Prospective study**
  Another term applied to a panel study

- **Cohort**
  Any group of people with a common classification or characteristic

Longitudinal Research

In **longitudinal research,** the data are collected at more than one time point or data-collection period, and the researcher is interested in making comparisons across time. Although longitudinal research requires a minimum of two time periods, data can be collected over as many time periods as needed to address the research questions. The term *longitudinal research* refers to research that occurs over time. There are two major variations of longitudinal research: trend studies and panel studies. For some examples of longitudinal research, many of which are still ongoing, see Young, Savola, and Phelps's book *Inventory of Longitudinal Studies in the Social Sciences* (1991). Although not discussed in this chapter, longitudinal research can also be done in qualitative research (e.g., see Huber & Van de Ven, 1995).

A **trend study** is a form of longitudinal research in which independent samples (samples composed of different people) are taken from a general population over time and the same questions are asked of the samples of participants. In a trend study, you might, for example, take a new sample each year for five consecutive years of U.S. citizens who are 18 years or older (i.e., adults). An example of a survey that has been used in many trend studies is the General Social Survey (GSS), which has been conducted annually since 1972 by interviewers working for the National Opinion Research Center, based in Chicago. The interviewers document the status of approximately 1,500 randomly selected adult (18 years or older) participants on an extensive number of variables each year (Davis & Smith, 1992).

The second major type of longitudinal research is a **panel study.**[4] The defining characteristic of a panel study is that the *same individuals* are studied at successive points over time. The researcher's goal is to understand why the panel members change over time. Because the researcher starts in the present and moves forward in time, the term **prospective study** is also applied by some researchers. For example, if you select 200 beginning teachers and follow them over the next ten years (e.g., interviewing them every other year), you have a panel, or prospective, study. You would be studying the same people over time. The individuals in a panel study are often selected from several age cohorts to strengthen the design. A **cohort** is defined as any group of people with a common classification or characteristic. For example, a researcher might follow individuals from three age cohorts for three consecutive years. If the children in the study were ages five, seven, and nine in the first year of the study, they would be ages six, eight, and ten in the second year of the study (assuming the study was conducted at the same time of year), and they would be ages seven, nine, and eleven in the third year, or "third wave" of the study. As you can see, individuals in panel studies grow older over time. This means that the average age of the people in the study will increase over time, and at some point it will be impossible to continue a panel study because all of the participants will have died of old age!

Let's say that you interview 1,500 randomly selected participants who are representative of the United States in the year 2000. This group of people will become more and more unrepresentative of the United States at later dates (e.g., in 2005, 2010, and 2015) because the U.S. population is constantly changing (e.g., people are constantly born into and move into and out of the United States). No new people are added to the panel study over time.[5] The point is that even if no one ever dropped out of your panel study, the panel and the current population can become very different over time. This is a threat to external validity because it limits your ability to generalize from the panel to the current population.

Perhaps an even greater problem is **differential attrition,** which occurs when participants do not drop out of the study randomly (i.e., when the people who drop out do not resemble the people who remain). In other words, the problem occurs when certain types of people drop out of the research study. Differential attrition can reduce external validity because after certain types of people drop out of the panel, the panel no longer resembles the population. Differential attrition can also reduce internal validity (the ability to firmly establish evidence of cause and effect). Assume, for example, that you are studying children's use of effective study strategies as they age. Your hypothesis is that age has a causal influence on effective strategy use (i.e., older children will use more effective study strategies than younger children). A problem might occur, however, if the less motivated and lower strategy users (i.e., children who use immature or inefficient strategies) drop out of your panel. You might erroneously conclude that effective strategy use increases with age simply because the lower strategy users drop out over time and the effective strategy users remain in the study. Because of the problems caused by differential attrition, researchers should always provide information about the kinds of people who dropped out of their research study and the potential implications this event has for their conclusions.

■ **Differential attrition**
Participants who drop out are different from those who stay

Panel studies also have some important strengths. First, you are better able to establish necessary condition 2 (proper time order) because you actually study the people over a period of time. Therefore, panel studies are superior to cross-sectional studies (studies in which data were collected at a single time point). Panel studies are also more powerful than trend studies because changes can be measured at the level they occur (within the individuals who change). Remember that in a trend study you are limited to comparing different people at different times, but in a panel study you can study the same individuals over time. One strategy in panel studies is to divide the original sample into groups based on the independent variable, follow the participants over time, and document what happens to them. Another strategy is to identify participants who change on a variable and the participants who do not change on the variable and then investigate the factors that help explain this change or lack of change.

You might, for example, decide to test the research hypothesis that students who begin using drugs in the tenth grade are more likely to drop out of high school than are students who do not use drugs during their high school years. To test this hypothesis, you could select a sample of ninth-grade students and then interview them each year for the next five years. You could identify the students who begin drug use during the tenth grade and compare them with the other students over the next several years, looking for differences between the two groups. You might also want to test the hypothesis that students who start drug use earlier in high school (e.g., the ninth or tenth grade) are more likely to drop out than students who start drug use later in high school or students who never use drugs at all during the high school years. You would divide your sample during data analysis as before, this time to see whether the early users were more likely to drop out than the later users or the nonusers to determine whether the hypotheses are supported. You could also analyze the data to test additional hypotheses or to locate additional behaviors and attitudes that are associated with drug use (e.g., peers who use drugs, poor grades, low self-esteem, family problems).

Medical researchers have effectively used prospective panel studies to help establish that smoking causes lung cancer (Gail, 1996). In a typical study, two groups of individuals (smokers and nonsmokers) are matched on multiple extraneous variables and are then followed forward in time. Researchers use matching to make the two groups as similar as possible, with the ultimate (but probably unattainable) goal being that the only important difference between the two groups is the participants' status on the independent variable. Then they follow these two groups over time, documenting their relative rates of lung cancer. The researchers also check for a dose-response relationship; that is, they check to see whether there is a positive correlation between the number of cigarettes smoked and the onset of lung cancer.

Prospective studies such as this cancer study are relatively strong on the first two conditions of causation. The relationship between smoking and lung cancer can be clearly established because different rates of lung cancer are found in the two groups and because a dose-response relationship is found. Time order is fairly well established because individuals are observed before and after the onset of cancer. Researchers use a variety of control techniques to help establish condition 3 (i.e., to rule out alternative explanations). As noted earlier, matching is used to create similar groups. Then, during data analysis, statistical control is used to further control for extraneous variables. Although prospective studies can be used to rule out many alternative explanations, they cannot rule out all of them. The key is that no *plausible* alternative explanation exists for the relationship between smoking and lung cancer.

The scientific opinion that smoking causes lung cancer (Gail, 1996) is based on the evidence obtained from a multitude of research studies. The most important human studies used in establishing this causal relationship have been prospective panel studies. Remember that *the panel study is a relatively powerful nonexperimental method for examining causality.* Unfortunately, prospective research is usually quite expensive and can take a long time to complete. Therefore, it should not be surprising that longitudinal studies are less common than cross-sectional studies. Prospective studies are often done at large universities by faculty members with federal funding and large staffs to help them conduct their research.

Retrospective Research

■ **Retrospective research**
The researcher starts with the dependent variable and moves backward in time

In **retrospective research,** the researcher typically starts with the dependent variable (i.e, with an observed result or outcome) and then "moves backward in time," locating information on variables that help explain individuals' status on the dependent variable. Retrospective research was one of the earliest kinds of research used to suggest smoking led to lung cancer (Gail, 1996). Medical researchers compared the smoking habits of people who currently had lung cancer with people who did not currently have lung cancer and found that smokers had higher rates of cancer than nonsmokers (Wynder & Graham, 1950). Retrospective research may be based on actual data collected in the past, or, frequently, researchers use retrospective questions to learn about the participants' pasts. **Retrospective questions** ask people to recall something from an earlier time in their life. In a smoking study, a retrospective question might ask current smokers how old they were when they first started smoking cigarettes. Another question might ask what type of cigarettes they smoked when they first started smoking.

■ **Retrospective questions**
Questions asking people to recall something from an earlier time

Here are some retrospective questions you might ask if you are studying drug use among high school students: Did you use drugs when you were in high school? What drug did you use most often? How frequently did you use that drug? Who first introduced you to the drug? Did your grades decline after you began using drugs? What was your grade level when your grades started declining? You must be careful when using retrospective questions because individuals' accounts of their past are not always entirely accurate. If possible, you should try to verify retrospective accounts by collecting additional corroborative information. For example, if someone said that his or her grades started declining in the tenth grade, you could check the student's school records for corroboration. Obviously, researchers cannot always corroborate each finding. You should, however, upgrade your evaluation of research studies in which corroboration was done for some or many of the research findings.

Research
Navigator.c☀m

retrospective data

CLASSIFYING NONEXPERIMENTAL RESEARCH METHODS BY RESEARCH OBJECTIVE

A very useful way to classify nonexperimental research is by the primary objective or research purpose. After determining that a research study is nonexperimental (because there is no manipulation or random assignment), you should try to determine the primary research objective.[6] We discuss five major research objectives in Chapter 1: exploration, description, prediction, explanation, and influence. Nonexperimental quantitative research often takes one of three forms: descriptive research, predictive research, or explanatory nonexperimental research. We now explain each of these kinds of research and provide some examples.

Descriptive Research

The primary purpose of **descriptive research** is to provide an accurate description or picture of the status or characteristics of a situation or phenomenon. The focus is not on how to ferret out cause-and-effect-relationships but rather on describing the variables that exist in a given situation, and, sometimes, on how to describe the relationships that exist among those variables. An examination of the research questions or the author's stated purpose in each research article you look at will help you know when you should apply the label *descriptive research.* Researchers doing descriptive research commonly follow these three steps: (1) randomly select a sample from a defined population, (2) determine the sample characteristics, and (3) infer the characteristics of the population based on the sample.

■ **Descriptive research**
Research focused on providing an accurate description or picture of the status or characteristics of a situation or phenomenon

Educators sometimes conduct descriptive research to learn about the attitudes, opinions, beliefs, behaviors, and demographics (e.g., age, gender, ethnicity, education) of people. Although the survey method of data collection is commonly used in descriptive research, keep in mind that this method (i.e., the use of questionnaires and/or interview protocols as discussed in Chapter 6) can also be used in predictive and explanatory research (see Babbie, 1990; Finkel, 1995; Kerlinger, 1986; Kiecolt & Nathan, 1985; Rosenberg, 1968; Stolzenberg & Land, 1983). Another research area that is primarily descriptive is in the field of tests and measurement. Test developers are constantly developing and refining tests and other measurement instruments, and they base many decisions on validity and reliability coefficients. On the basis of this descriptive information, they establish evidence about how well their tests operate with different kinds of people under a variety of circumstances.

An example of a published descriptive research study by Sears, Kennedy, and Kaye (1997) is titled "Myers-Briggs Personality Profiles of Prospective Educators." These researchers administered the Myers-Briggs personality test to 4,483 undergraduate university students who were considering majoring in education. Their major purpose was to provide descriptive information about prospective teachers based on the popular Myers-Briggs personality test. They also checked student records several years later to see which of the students graduated and what area of education they selected as their majors.

They found that the predominant personality profile of the prospective educators who later graduated with degrees in elementary education was SFJ (sensing, feeling, and judging). They describe SFJs as "warm, sociable, responsible, and caring about people" (Sears et al., 1997, p. 201). In contrast, the personality profile of the students who graduated with degrees in secondary education was NTJ (intuitive, thinking, and judging). They described NTJs as "oriented to the theoretical, disposed to investigate possibilities and relationships; and drawn to complexity, innovation, and change" (Sears et al., 1997, p. 201). Because of these personality traits, the researchers predicted that the secondary education majors would be more likely than the elementary majors to advance educational innovation and reform once they became teachers (Sears et al., 1997, p. 291). If the researchers tested this prediction in a future research study, they would have an example of predictive research, which we discuss next. Remember, the key to descriptive research is that the researchers collect data used for description.

Predictive Research

Predicitve research
Research focused on predicting the future status of one or more dependent variables based on one or more independent variables

Predictive research is done so that we can predict the future status of one or more dependent (or criterion) variables on the basis of one or more independent (or predictor) variables (Pedhazur, 1997). For example, college admissions officers might be interested in predicting student performance based on variables such as high school GPA, scores on admissions tests, gender, and type of school attended (e.g., public, private). Insurance companies are interested in predicting who will have auto accidents, who will get sick, who will be injured, and who will die of old age. (That's why auto insurance rates are higher for males and for adolescents.) Employers are interested in predicting who will be a happy and productive employee. An economist might want to predict the performance of the United States economy using "leading indicators." Educators are often interested in predicting who is at risk for problems like poor academic performance, drug use, dropping out of high school, and skipping class. The key point is that if a researcher wants to see how well he or she can predict some outcome based on one or more independent or predictor variables, then the research study is labeled predictive research.

Dykeman, Daehlin, Doyle, and Flamer (1996) provide an example of predictive research published in a journal article titled "Psychological Predictors of School-Based Violence: Implications for School Counselors." The researchers wanted to find out whether three psychological constructs could be used to predict violence among students in grades five through ten. The first psychological predictor was a measure of impulsivity. The researchers' hypothesis was that the more impulsive children are, the more prone to violence they will be. The second predictor was a measure of empathy. The researchers believed that delinquents were less likely to have empathic skills, which would result in greater aggression. Their hypothesis was therefore that there would be a negative relationship between empathy and violence (i.e., the more empathy students have, the less prone they are to violence). The third psychological predictor variable was locus of control. People with an internal locus of control tend to view their own experiences as resulting from their own actions and decisions. People with an external locus of control tend to view their experiences as resulting from luck, chance, or destiny. The researchers hypothesized that people with internal locus of control would be less prone to violence than people who had more external locus of control. The researchers used a special case of the general linear model called multiple regression to determine how well the three variables predicted violence. It turned out that all three of the predictive hypotheses were supported. Impulsivity was the most important of the three predictor variables. The authors concluded that the aim of a violence prevention program might be "(a) to change group norms about violence, (b) to enhance family relationship characteristics, (c) to improve peer relationship skills, (d) to decrease substance abuse, (e) to lessen impulsivity, (f) to increase empathy, and (g) to engender internal locus of control" (Dykeman et al., 1996, p. 44). The last three points were directly based on the data from this research study.

Explanatory Research

In **explanatory research,** researchers are interested in testing hypotheses and theories that explain how and why a phenomenon operates as it does (Pedhazur, 1997). The researcher's goal is to understand the phenomenon being studied. The researcher is also interested in establishing evidence for cause-and-effect relationships. Although experimental research is the strongest form of explanatory research for providing evidence of cause and effect, you have learned in this chapter that many important independent variables cannot be manipulated, which means that these variables must be investigated using nonexperimental explanatory research.

■ **Explanatory research**
Testing hypotheses and theories that explain how and why a phenomenon operates as it does

A good example of explanatory nonexperimental research is "A Prospective, Longitudinal Study of the Correlates and Consequences of Early Grade Retention," by Jimerson, Carlson, Rotert, Egeland, and Sroufe (1997). It is important to understand the effects of early grade retention (not promoting a child). However, it would be unethical to manipulate this independent variable (i.e., you cannot randomly assign students to be either retained in their grade or promoted). Therefore, nonexperimental explanatory research must be used to study the effects of grade retention.

In the Jimerson et al. study, a retained group was identified from the participants in a larger, long-term study of at-risk children and their parents. A group of similar low-achieving promoted students (the nonretained group) was also identified from the project participants for a comparison group. The retained and nonretained groups were matched on academic ability and academic performance because the researchers wanted to compare retained students who are low achieving with promoted students who are low achieving in order to learn about the effects of retention/promotion. The researchers also used the control technique called statistical control (discussed earlier in this chapter) when making some of their comparisons to further equate the groups on additional variables. The practical question driving the research was whether a low achieving student should be retained or promoted.

Key results from the research study include the following. The retained students showed a short-term improvement in math achievement. However, that improvement disappeared once new material was taught. The retained and nonretained students did not differ on most measures of social and personal adjustment or on a measure of behavior problems. The one difference found was that the promoted students were more emotionally adjusted several years after being promoted. The researchers concluded that "Essentially, the retained and low-achieving promoted students did not differ . . . despite an extra year, and [they] continued to remain comparable years after the promotion or retention" (Jimerson et al., 1997, p. 18). In short, this research study confirmed the results of many additional studies suggesting that elementary grade retention produces few if any of its promised effects. In general, retention appears to be an ineffective strategy for improving the achievement levels or psychological adjustment of children or for reducing behavior problems.

Another form of explanatory research increasing in popularity is called causal modeling (Asher, 1983; Maruyama, 1998; Pedhazur, 1997; Schumacker & Lomax, 1996). Although many of the details of causal modeling are beyond the scope of this book, we cover some of the basic conceptual ideas here. **Causal modeling** is a procedure in which a researcher hypothesizes a causal model and then empirically tests the model to determine how well the model fits the data. The researcher develops or constructs the causal model based on past research findings and on theoretical considerations. Causal models depict the interrelationships among two or more variables and are used to explain how some theoretical process operates. Some synonyms for the term *causal model* are *path model, structural model,* and *theoretical model.* Many researchers use these terms interchangeably.

A hypothetical causal model with four variables is shown in Figure 11.4. The four variables in the causal model are parental involvement, student motivation, teaching quality (of the school teachers), and student achievement. You can understand this model by realizing that each of the arrows stands for a hypothesized causal relationship. The type of causal rela-

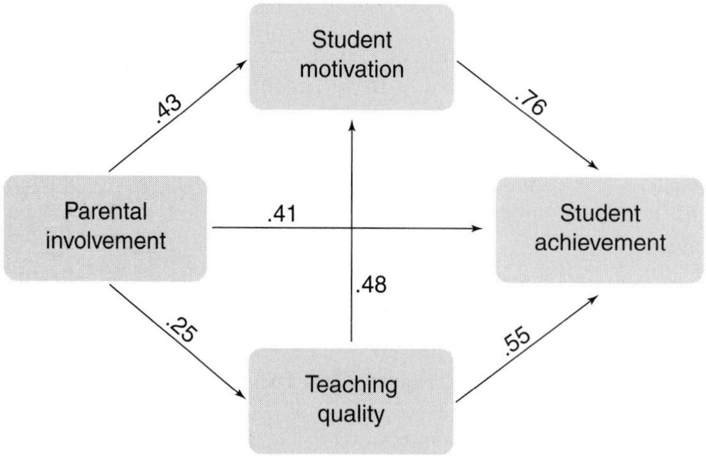

■ **Causal modeling**
A form of explanatory research in which the researcher hypothesizes a causal model and then emperically tests the model

FIGURE 11.4   A causal model of student achievement

tionship between any two variables connected by an arrow is known as a **direct effect,** which is the effect of the variable at the origin of an arrow on the variable at the receiving end of the arrow. For example, look at Figure 11.4 and you will see that there is an arrow going from parental involvement to student motivation (parental involvement → student motivation). This means that parental involvement is hypothesized to have a direct effect on student motivation. It is important to realize that the assumption that parental involvement affects student motivation (rather than student motivation affecting parental involvement) is based on theory. In the absence of experimental research data, assumptions like this will always be tentative.

The numbers on the arrows are called **path coefficients,** and they provide quantitative information about the direct effects based on the data collected in a research study. If the coefficient is positive, then the relationship between the two variables is positive (i.e., as one variable increases the other variable increases). If the coefficient is negative, then the relationship is negative (i.e., as one variable increases, the second variable decreases). You can interpret the strength of the relationship by looking at the size of the coefficient, just as with correlation coefficients (i.e., coefficients that are close to +1.00 or −1.00 are very strong, and coefficients that are near zero are very weak). Looking at Figure 11.4, you see the number .76 on the path from student motivation to student achievement. This suggests that there is a strong positive relationship between student motivation and student achievement.

Take a moment now to look at the other arrows in the causal model. Try to answer these questions. First, what two variables are hypothesized to have direct effects on student motivation? Second, what variable is hypothesized to have a direct effect on teaching quality? Third, what three variables are hypothesized in the model to have direct effects on student achievement? [The answers are that (1) student motivation is shown to be influenced by parental involvement and teaching quality; (2) teaching quality is influenced by parental involvement; and (3) student achievement is influenced by parental involvement, teaching quality, and student motivation.]

In addition to showing hypothesized direct effects, causal models also show hypothesized indirect effects. An **indirect effect** occurs when one variable affects another variable indirectly; that is, an indirect effect occurs when a variable affects another variable by way of an **intervening variable.** We defined intervening variables (which are also called *mediator variables*) and indirect effects in Chapter 2. According to the causal path A → B → C, variable B is an intervening variable (it occurs in between A and C). Furthermore, variable A has an indirect effect on variable C by way of the intervening variable B. Whenever a variable falls in between two other variables in a causal chain, it is called an intervening variable.

Now that you know what an indirect effect is, see whether you can find some indirect effects in the causal model shown in Figure 11.4. As you can see, teaching quality has an indirect effect on student achievement through student motivation. In this case, student motivation is the intervening variable. You can see that teaching quality also has a direct effect on student achievement because there is an arrow going from teaching quality to student achievement. In other words, a variable can have both a direct effect and an indirect effect. Also, parental involvement indirectly influences student achievement through teaching quality and through student motivation. There are quite a few relationships (indirect and direct) in even a relatively small causal model.

Figure 11.5 shows another example of a causal model, which was reported in the *Journal of Educational Psychology.* This model was developed and tested by Karabenick and Sharma (1994). It shows the effects of several variables on the likelihood of students asking

■ **Direct effect**
The effect of the variable at the origin of an arrow on the variable at the receiving end of the arrow

■ **Path coefficient**
A qualitative index providing information about a direct effect

Research
Navigator.c⚛m

causal model

■ **Indirect effect**
An effect occurring through an intervening variable
■ **Intervening variable**
A variable occurring between two other variables in a causal chain

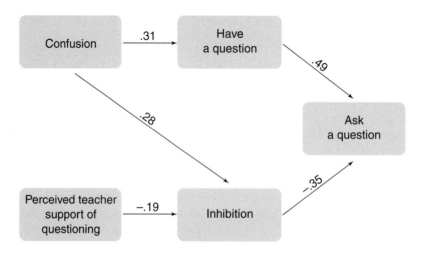

■ **FIGURE 11.5**   A causal model of question asking

(Adapted from Karabenick and Sharma, 1994, p. 98. Copyright © 1994 by the American Psychological Association. Adapted with permission.)

questions during lectures. Look at the model, and see whether you think they have done a good job explaining what factors cause students to ask or not ask questions. The researchers collected data to test their model from 1,327 undergraduate college students. After collecting the data, they used a statistical program called LISREL to calculate the path coefficients (the numbers on the arrows).

The original theoretical model developed by the researchers looked like the model shown in Figure 11.5 except that it included an arrow from "Perceived teacher support of questioning" to "Ask a question." Because this particular path turned out to be unimportant on the basis of the data collected in the research study (it was not statistically significant), the researchers eliminated it from the final model shown in Figure 11.5. It is a common practice in the field of causal modeling to exclude arrows that turn out to be unimportant based on the data. This process of eliminating arrows is sometimes called *theory trimming.* The other arrows in the model in Figure 11.5 were correctly predicted by the researchers to be important.

You can determine the strength and direction of the direct effects by looking at the path coefficients on the arrows. For example, the path coefficient from inhibition to asking a question is –.35. This means that the effect of inhibition on asking a question (controlling for having a question) is small to moderate in size and the relationship operates in the negative direction. Recall from your study of correlation that a negative relationship exists when two variables move in opposite directions. In this case, the more inhibition students feel, the less likely they are to ask questions. Not surprisingly, the relationship between confusion and having a question (+.31) is moderately small, and the relationship is positive (i.e., the more confusion students have, the more likely they are to have questions). You can interpret the other path coefficients in the model in a similar way.

You can also find the indirect effects in Figure 11.5 by noting when variables affect other variables through intervening variables. For example, perceived teacher support of questioning does not affect students asking questions directly (i.e., there is no direct arrow). However, it does affect asking questions indirectly by way of the intervening variable called inhibition. Likewise, confusion indirectly affects asking questions through having a question and through inhibition. In other words, confusion has two indirect effects on asking questions. This is complex, but its complexity is also a strength because it more closely approximates how a small part of the real world actually operates. Also, researchers can communicate all of the relationships suggested by their theory in a picture.

We discussed causal modeling in this chapter because these complex models are usually used in nonexperimental research, although they are occasionally tested in experimental research. Note also that although causal models are most frequently based on cross-sectional data (data collected at a single time), they are more and more frequently being based on longitudinal data (data collected at two or more time points). As a general rule, causal models based on experiments provide the most solid evidence for cause and effect; causal models based on longitudinal data are second best; and causal models based on cross-sectional data are the weakest. Even when based on cross-sectional data, however, causal models represent drastic improvements over the simple cases of causal-comparative and correlational research.

CLASSIFYING NONEXPERIMENTAL RESEARCH BY TIME AND RESEARCH OBJECTIVE

We have discussed the two major dimensions that are used to classify nonexperimental research (i.e., the *time* dimension and the *research objective* dimension). To put this together, we have crossed these two dimensions into a matrix (shown in Table 11.3) to create a typology of

TABLE 11.3   Types of Research Obtained by Crossing Research Objective and Time Dimension

Research Objective	Time Dimension		
	Retrospective	Cross-Sectional	Longitudinal
Descriptive	retrospective, descriptive study. (type 1)	cross-sectional, descriptive study. (type 2)	longitudinal, descriptive study. (type 3)
Predictive	retrospective, predictive study. (type 4)	cross-sectional, predictive study. (type 5)	longitudinal, predictive study. (type 6)
Explanatory	retrospective, explanatory study. (type 7)	cross-sectional, explanatory study. (type 8)	longitudinal, explanatory study. (type 9)

Source: Adapted from Johnson (2001).

nine types of nonexperimental research (Johnson, 2001). To use this classification, all you have to do is answer these two questions:

1. How are the data collected in relation to time (i.e., are the data retrospective, cross-sectional, or longitudinal)?
2. What is the primary research objective (i.e., description, prediction, or explanation)?

Your answer to these two questions will lead you to one of the nine cells shown in Table 11.3.

11.10 Which form of nonexperimental research tends to be the best for inferring cause and effect: cross-sectional research, trend studies, cohort studies, panel studies (i.e., prospective studies), or retrospective research studies? Why?

11.11 Explain the difference between a direct effect and an indirect effect.

11.12 List an advantage and a disadvantage of causal modeling.

SUMMARY

The researcher does not manipulate independent variables in nonexperimental research. The researcher does study relationships among variables. If the researcher's questions concern independent variables that cannot be manipulated, nonexperimental research is the logical choice. A few independent variables that cannot be manipulated are gender, parenting style, grade retention, ethnicity, and intelligence. Researchers must be very careful when using the nonexperimental research method, however, if they wish to obtain evidence of cause-and-effect relationships. The three necessary conditions for concluding that the relationship between variable A and variable B is causal are that (1) there must be a relationship between variable A and variable B, (2) variable A must occur before variable B, and (3) alternative explanations must be eliminated. Unfortunately, the third necessary condition is virtually always a problem in nonexperimental research. Researchers must attempt to control for any extraneous, or third, variables that might potentially explain the relationship between two variables when they want to obtain evidence that the relationship is causal. The three key techniques of control that are used in nonexperimental research are (1) matching, (2) restricting the study to a subpopulation, and (3) statistical control.

Nonexperimental research is sometimes classified on the basis of the time dimension. If the data are collected at a single time point or data-collection period, it is a cross-sectional study. If the data are collected at multiple time points over time, it is a longitudinal study. If the data are collected backwards in time, it is a retrospective study. Nonexperimental research is also classified on the basis of the researcher's primary research objective. The purpose of descriptive research is to provide an accurate description or picture of the status or characteristics of a situation or phenomenon. The purpose of predictive research is to predict the future status of one or more dependent or outcome variables on the basis of one or more independent or predictor variables. The purpose of explanatory nonexperimental research is to test hypotheses and theories explaining how and why a phenomenon operates as it does. Causal modeling is a form of explanatory research in which the researcher develops a causal model and empirically tests the model to determine how well the model fits the data.

KEY TERMS

analysis of covariance (p. 341)
causal modeling (p. 350)
cohort (p. 344)
cross-sectional research (p. 343)
descriptive research (p. 347)
differential attrition (p. 345)
direct effect (p. 351)
explanatory research (p. 349)
general linear model (GLM) (p. 341)
indirect effect (p. 351)
intervening variable (p. 351)
longitudinal research (p. 344)
matching variable (p. 339)

method of working multiple hypotheses (p. 334)
nonexperimental research (p. 328)
panel study (p. 344)
partial correlation (p. 341)
partially spurious (p. 336)
path coefficient (p. 351)
post hoc fallacy (p. 329)
predictive research (p. 348)
probabilistic cause (p. 333)
prospective study (p. 344)
retrospective questions (p. 347)
retrospective research (p. 346)

simple case of causal-comparative research (p. 331)
simple case of correlational research (p. 331)
simple cases (p. 331)
special case of the general linear model (p. 341)
spurious relationship (p. 336)
statistically significant (p. 331)
third-variable problem (p. 333)
three necessary conditions (p. 333)
trend study (p. 344)

DISCUSSION QUESTIONS

1. What kind of nonexperimental quantitative study would you find most interesting: a descriptive study, a predictive study, or an explanatory study? Why?
2. Why do methodologists and researchers emphasize the point that association does not prove causation?
3. How should researchers approach the issue of cause and effect in nonexperimental quantitative research? How do researchers meet each of the three necessary conditions for cause and effect? How do they strengthen their designs to move beyond the simple cases of correlational and causal-comparative research?

4. Can you think of two variables that are associated but are not causally related. (Hint: You might want to take a look at Table 11.2 to get started.)
5. Which kind of data do you think provides the most solid evidence of necessary condition 2 (proper time order): retrospective, cross-sectional, or longitudinal?
6. On the book's companion website (under Bonus Materials for this chapter) you will find a file titled "How Do Epidemiologists Determine Causality?" What do you think about this list? Which criteria do you believe are most important? Do you think it adds much to the three necessary conditions discussed in this chapter?

RESEARCH EXERCISES

1. Think of a hypothetical example of a nonexperimental educational research study that would be interesting to you for each of the following research objectives. Be sure to explain why it is nonexperimental rather than experimental:
   a. Explanatory
   b. Predictive
   c. Descriptive

2. Search ContentSelect or another database at your library. Find and then list the titles of nonexperimental articles that appear to be based primarily on each of the following research objectives.
   a. Prediction
   b. Explanation
   c. Description
   Provide an annotated bibliography of the three articles, and briefly explain why you think the article is of a certain type.

3. It is helpful to examine published examples of nonexperimental research so that you can see more concretely how to carry out nonexperimental research. As an exercise, read and write up a two-page review of one of the following nonexperimental research articles:

Eckenrode, J., Laird, M., & Doris, J. (1993). School performance and disciplinary problems among abused and neglected children. *Developmental Psychology, 29*(1), 53–62.

Turner, L. A., & Johnson, B. (2003). A model of mastery motivation for at-risk preschoolers. *Journal of Educational Psychology, 95*(3).

When you write up your article review, organize it into the following general sections:

1. Purpose
2. Methods
3. Results
4. Strengths and weaknesses of the research.

RELEVANT INTERNET SITES

www.eval.org/EvaluationLinks/links.htm
Program evaluation links.

http://bama.ua.edu/archives/semnet.html
You can find many discussions of causality issues when using nonexperimental data in these archives of a popular academic discussion group.

RECOMMENDED READING

Berk, R. A. (1988). Causal inference for sociological data. In N. J. Smelser (Ed.), *Handbook of Sociology* (pp. 155–172). Newbury Park, CA: Sage.

Bullock, H. E., Harlo, L. L., & Mulaik, S. A. (1994). Causation issues in structural equation modeling research. *Structural Equation Modeling, 1*(3), 253–257.

Johnson, R. B. (2001). Toward a new classification of nonexperimental quantitative research. *Educational Researcher, 30*(2), 3–13.

Kaufman, J. S., & Poole, C. (2000). Looking back on "causal thinking in the health sciences." *Annual Review of Public Health, 21,* 101–119.

Reynolds, A. J. (1998). Confirmatory program evaluation: A method for strengthening causal inference. *American Journal of Evaluation, 19*(2), 203–221.

Susser, M. (1991). What is a cause and how do we know one? A grammar for pragmatic epidemiology. *American Journal of Epidemiology, 133,* 635–648.

ENDNOTES

1. The only thing that changes is the type of statistical analysis used after the data are collected.

2. The relationship also will disappear when the variable is an intervening variable. Therefore, the use of theory is

very important in determining whether the variable is a confounding variable or an intervening variable.

3. If the quantitative independent variable has more than ten levels, then we recommend that you collapse it into fewer categories for the purposes of matching.

4. Panel studies can also be used in experimental research. A panel study with manipulation is more powerful than a panel study without manipulation when you are interested in studying cause and effect.

5. There is a type of panel study, called the revolving panel design, in which new people are added to the panel (see Menard, 1991).

6. When you examine published research articles, keep in mind that some research studies may have more than one objective.

12

Qualitative Research

LEARNING OBJECTIVES

To be able to

- List the major characteristics of qualitative research.
- Compare and contrast the four main approaches to qualitative research: phenomenology, ethnography, case study, and grounded theory.
- Define and explain phenomenology.
- Define and explain ethnography.
- Define and explain case study research.
- Define and explain grounded theory.

On April 20, 1999, Denver police officer John Lietz received a phone call shortly after 11:00 A.M. that will stay with him for the rest of his life. He picked up the phone to hear Matthew Depew, the son of a fellow police officer, say that he and seventeen other Columbine High School students were trapped in a storage room off the school cafeteria, hiding from kids with guns. Bursts of gunfire could be heard in the background as Lietz told the kids to barricade the door with chairs and sacks of food. As Lietz and Depew spoke, Lietz could hear the shooters trying to break in on several occasions. At one point, they pounded on the door, prompting Depew to calmly tell Lietz that he was sure he was going to die.

The shooters, Eric Harris and Dylan Klebold, had started their day as they always did, attending a bowling class at 6:15 A.M. When either of them hit a strike or spare, they shouted "Sieg Heil!" in celebration, something they had done in the past. By 11:00 A.M., Harris and Klebold were walking toward the Columbine cafeteria wearing their trademark black trench coats and wraparound shades. Denny Rowe, sitting on a knoll not far from the cafeteria's entrance, watched one of them take off his coat, revealing something that looked like grenades. The other lit some firecrackers and threw them toward the school entrance. One of the boys then brandished a semiautomatic rifle, pointed it toward a seventeen-year-old freshman male, and shot the freshman in the thigh and then in the back as he tried to run away. The killers then turned toward Rowe and his friends, shooting one of them in the knee and another in the chest as they proceeded toward the cafeteria, where there were some 500 students. By the time the terror ended with the killers committing suicide, twelve students and a teacher were dead, and twenty-three students were wounded, several critically.

Following such a tragic incident, the overarching question in the minds of many Americans is "Why?" Eric Harris and Dylan Klebold were bright kids who came from seemingly stable, affluent homes. Almost immediately, a variety of possible explanations emerged. Violence on network television and in cartoons, comic books, music, video games, and movies might have been contributors. The availability of information on the Internet about such things as how to make bombs may have contributed. The access that teenagers have to guns in our society is also seen as a potential contributor (Dority, 1999).

With so many possibilities, how can one identify the most likely causes of Eric Harris and Dylan Klebold's killing spree? Although we might never know all of the causes, psychologists will conduct extensive qualitative interviewing of the killers, study their life histories, and interview the killers' friends, classmates, teachers, and family to obtain some evidence. One day, through the study of multiple cases, perhaps psychologists and educators will come up with a viable theory about why such events occur and what parents, teachers, and students can do to prevent future outbreaks of violence. Qualitative research approaches are very useful in exploring situations like this and in developing explanations that can be further developed over time. This chapter will acquaint you with the four major types of qualitative research.

In Chapter 2, we defined **qualitative research** as research relying primarily on the collection of qualitative data (nonnumerical data such as words and pictures). Qualitative

Research
Navigator.c◈m

**qualitative
research**

researchers tend to rely on the inductive mode of the scientific method, and the major objective of this type of research is exploration or discovery. This means that qualitative researchers generally study a phenomenon in an open-ended way, without prior expectations, and they develop hypotheses and theoretical explanations that are based on their interpretations of what they observe. Qualitative researchers prefer to study the world as it naturally occurs, without manipulating it (as in experimental research). While observing, qualitative researchers try not to draw attention to themselves. That is, they try to be unobtrusive so that they will have little influence on the naturally occurring behavior being studied. Qualitative researchers view human behavior as dynamic and changing, and they advocate studying phenomena in depth and over an extended period of time. The product of qualitative research is usually a narrative report with rich description (vivid and detailed writing) rather than a statistical report (a report with a lot of numbers and statistical test results).

In Figure 12.1, we list the eight common steps in a qualitative research study. In a simple qualitative research study, the researcher might move directly through the steps, and the study will be completed. It is important that you understand, however, that the qualitative researcher does not always follow the eight steps in a linear fashion (i.e., step 1, then step 2, then step 3, and so on). Typically, the qualitative researcher selects a topic and generates preliminary questions at the start of a research study. The questions can be changed or modified, however, during data collection and analysis if any of the questions are found to be naive or less important than other questions. This is one reason that qualitative research is often said to be an *emergent* or fluid type of research. During the conduct of a qualitative re-

■ **F I G U R E   1 2 . 1**   Steps in a qualitative research study. The steps are *not* always linear or sequential.

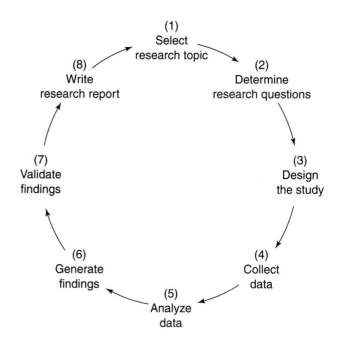

search study the researcher acts like a detective or novelist and goes wherever interesting and enlightening information may be.

Data collection and analysis (steps 4 and 5) in qualitative research have a longitudinal character because qualitative research often takes place over an extended period of time. The researcher purposely selects people to interview and/or observe at early points as well as at later points in a research study. Data collection and data analysis (steps 4 and 5 in Figure 12.1) are often done concurrently or in cycles in qualitative research (e.g., the researchers collect some data, analyze those data, collect more data, analyze those data, and so on). The researcher also attempts to validate the data and his or her interpretations throughout the research study (steps 6 & 7). For example, the researcher should attempt to establish the kinds of qualitative research validity you learned about in Chapter 8 (descriptive validity, interpretative validity, theoretical validity, internal validity, and external validity). At the end of the research study, the researcher finishes the research report (step 8).

For further extension of your knowledge about qualitative research, we include Patton's (1990) list of twelve major characteristics of qualitative research in Table 12.1. Patton did a good job of succinctly summarizing what he saw as the ten key characteristics of qualitative research, and the list should be helpful as you learn about qualitative research. Although not all qualitative research studies will have all of the characteristics mentioned by us and by Patton, they are very typical of qualitative research.

The purpose of the remainder of this chapter is to introduce you to the different types of qualitative research. Although you already understand qualitative research as a general type of research, *qualitative research* is actually a very general term because there are many different types of qualitative research. We discuss what we believe to be the four most important types: phenomenology, ethnography, case study, and grounded theory. A list showing the major characteristics of these four approaches is given in Table 12.2. You might want to preview the list now and then review it again after you finish reading this chapter. Each approach has a different history, and each is currently used in the field of education.

Because the four research approaches discussed in this chapter fall under the heading of qualitative research, the characteristics of qualitative research reviewed earlier will usually apply. This means that the approaches will have much in common. At the same time, each approach is different and distinct from the others in important ways (e.g., compare the four research purposes shown in Table 12.2). We describe the four major qualitative research approaches in detail now so that you can understand qualitative research articles and books based on these approaches and so that you can consider which approach you would choose to use if you ever wanted to conduct a qualitative research study on your own.

12.1 What are the key characteristics of qualitative research?

12.2 Explain the role of induction in qualitative research.

12.3 Why is it said that qualitative research does *not* follow a series of steps in a linear fashion?

12.4 Why is qualitative research important for educational research?

REVIEW
QUESTIONS

■ **TABLE 12.1**   Twelve Major Characteristics of Qualitative Research

Design Strategies

1. *Naturalistic inquiry*—Studying real-world situations as they unfold naturally; nonmanipulative and noncontrolling; openness to whatever emerges (lack of predetermined constraints on findings).

2. *Emergent design flexibility*—Openness to adapting inquiry as understanding deepens and/or situations to change; the researcher avoids getting locked into rigid designs that eliminate responsiveness and pursues new paths of discovery as they emerge.

3. *Purposeful sampling*—Cases for study (e.g., people, organizations, communities, cultures, events, critical incidences) are selected because they are "information rich" and illuminative, that is, they offer useful manifestations of the phenomenon of interest; sampling, then, is aimed at insight about the phenomenon, not empirical generalization from a sample to a population.

Data-Collection and Fieldwork Strategies

4. *Qualitative data*—Observations that yield detailed, thick description; inquiry in depth; interviews that capture direct quotations about people's personal perspectives and experiences; case studies; careful document review.

5. *Personal experience and engagement*—The researcher has direct contact with and gets close to the people, situation, and phenomenon under study; the researcher's personal experiences and insights are an important part of the inquiry and critical to understanding the phenomenon.

6. *Empathic neutrality and mindfulness*—An empathic stance in interviewing seeks vicarious understanding without judgment (neutrality) by showing openness, sensitivity, respect, awareness, and responsiveness; in observation it means being fully present (mindfulness).

7. *Dynamic systems*—Attention to process; assumes change as ongoing whether focus is on an individual, an organization, a community, or

an entire culture; therefore, mindful of and attentive to system and situation dynamics.

Analysis Strategies

8. *Unique case orientation*—Assumes that each case is special and unique; the first level of analysis is being true to, respecting, and capturing the details of the individual cases being studied; cross-case analysis follows from and depends on the quality of individual case studies.

9. *Inductive analysis and creative synthesis*—Immersion in the details and specifics of the data to discover important patterns, themes, and interrelationships; begins by exploring, then confirming, guided by analytical principles rather than rules, ends with a creative synthesis.

10. *Holistic perspective*—The whole phenomenon under study is understood as a complex system that is more than the sum of its parts; focus on complex interdependencies and system dynamics that cannot meaningfully be reduced to a few discrete variables and linear, cause-effect relationships.

11. *Context sensitivity*—Places findings in a social, historical, and temporal context; careful about, even dubious of, the possibility or meaningfulness of generalizations across time and space; emphasizes instead careful comparative case analyses and extrapolating patterns for possible transferability and adaptation in new settings.

12. *Voice, perspective, and reflexivity*—The qualitative analyst owns and is reflective about her or his own voice and perspective; a credible voice conveys authenticity and trustworthiness; complete objectivity being impossible and pure subjectivity undermining credibility, the researcher's focus becomes balance—understanding and depicting the world authentically in all its complexity while being self-analytical, politically aware, and reflexive in consciousness.

Source: From M. Q. Patton, *Qualitative Research and Evaluation Methods,* Third Edition, pp. 40–41, copyright 2002 by Sage Publications, Inc.

■ **TABLE 12.2**   Characteristics of Four Qualitative Research Approaches

	Qualitative Research Approach			
Dimension	Phenomenology	Ethnography	Case Study	Grounded Theory
Research purpose	To describe one or more individuals' experiences of a phenomenon (e.g., the experience of the death of a loved one).	To describe the cultural charac- teristics of a group of people and to describe cultural scenes.	To describe one or more cases in-depth and address the re- search questions and issues.	To inductively gen- erate a grounded theory describing and explaining a phenomenon.
Disciplinary origin	Philosophy.	Anthropology.	Multidisciplinary roots, including business, law, social sciences, medicine, and education.	Sociology.
Primary data- collection method	In-depth interviews with up to 10–15 people.	Participant ob- servation over an extended pe- riod of time (e.g., one month to a year). Inter- views with informants.	Multiple methods are used (e.g., inter- views, observations, documents).	Interviews with 20–30 people. Ob- servations are also frequently used.
Data analysis approach	List significant state- ments, determine mean- ing of statements, and identify the essence of the phenomenon.	Holistic descrip- tion and search for cultural themes in data.	Holistic description and search for themes shedding light on the case. May also include cross-case analysis.	Begin with open coding, then axial coding, and end with selective coding.
Narrative report focus	Rich description of the essential or invariant structures (i.e., the common characteristics, or essences) of the experience.	Rich description of context and cultural themes.	Rich description of the context and op- eration of the case or cases. Discussion of themes, issues, and implications.	Description of topic and people being studied. End with a presentation of the grounded theory. May also list propositions.

PHENOMENOLOGY

Foundational question: What is the meaning, structure, and essence of the lived experience of this phenomenon by an individual or by many individuals?

■ **Phenomenology**
The description of one or more individuals' consciousness and experience of a phenomenon

■ **Life-world**
An individual's inner world of immediate experience

Research
Navigator.c⊕m

phenomenology

Phenomenology refers to the description of one or more individuals' consciousness and experience of a phenomenon, such as the death of a loved one, viewing oneself as a teacher, the act of teaching, the experience of being a minority group member, or the experience of winning a soccer game. The purpose of phenomenological research is to obtain a view into your research participants' life-worlds and to understand their personal meanings (i.e., what something means to them) constructed from their "lived experiences." **Life-world** is the translation of the German term *Lebenswelt* used by the founder of phenomenology, philosopher Edmund Husserl (1859–1938), to refer to the individual's "world of immediate experience." It is the individual's inner world of consciousness and experience. You are in your life-world right now as you read this chapter and as you exist wherever you are. In other words, your life-world is in your mind. It is your combination of feelings, thoughts, and self-awareness at any moment in time. The purpose of phenomenology is to gain access to individuals' life-worlds and to describe their experiences of a phenomenon.

To experience phenomenology firsthand, try describing your own personal experience of a phenomenon. To do this effectively, you must give it your full attention—the following poem by Moffitt[1] makes this point quite eloquently (cited in Moustakas, 1990):

> To look at any thing
> If you would know that thing,
> You must look at it long:
> To look at this green and say
> "I have seen spring in these
> Woods," will not do—you must
> Be the thing you see:
> You must be the dark snakes of
> Stems and ferny plumes of leaves,
> You must enter in
> To the small silences between
> The leaves,
> You must take your time
> And touch the very place
> They issue from.

When you want to experience something to its fullest, you must stop what you are doing, focus on what you are experiencing at that meaningful moment, and experience the thoughts, sensations, and feelings associated with that experience. Phenomenologists point out that to experience something in its purest form, you need to **bracket,** or suspend, any preconceptions or learned feelings that you have about the phenomenon. This is because they want you to experience the phenomenon "as it is." When you bracket your preconceptions, you set aside your taken-for-granted orientation toward it, and your experience of the phenomenon becomes part of your consciousness.

■ **Bracket**
To suspend your preconceptions or learned feelings about a phenomenon

Examples of Phenomenology

Here are brief descriptions of a few phenomenological research studies, any of which you can look up and read if you need to learn more about phenomenological research. Only one of these articles was based on a single individual's experiences (Green, 1995). First, Cross and Stewart (1995) studied what it is like being a gifted student in a rural high school in an article entitled "A Phenomenological Investigation of the Lebenswelt of Gifted Students in Rural High Schools." Cross and Stewart also compared rural students' experiences with the experiences of urban school students based on previous research. This is an exemplary phenomenological research article if you want to read just one article. Green (1995) studied a teacher's meaning and experience of utilizing an experiential learning approach with her students in an article entitled "Experiential Learning and Teaching." Brown (1996) examined children's experiences of being in a mathematics classroom in an article entitled "The Phenomenology of the Mathematics Classroom." Finally, Muller (1994) studied the meaning and experience of empowering other people from the perspective of the person doing the empowering, in this case, six women who had been identified as leaders in the article entitled "Toward an Understanding of Empowerment: A Study of Six Women Leaders." Again, we remind you that one of the best ways to learn about qualitative research is to read qualitative research journal articles.

Types of Phenomenology

Phenomenology can be used to focus on the unique characteristics of an individual's experience of something. We all know that events, objects, and experiences can mean different things to different people. For example, different individuals may view a single event differently. The hiring of a new principal at a school might mean the school is moving in the right direction and offer solace to one teacher, while to another teacher, the change might arouse anger and result in restlessness because of its uncertainty. In counseling, the phenomenological method is often used to understand each client's unique perspective of some life event or personal condition. The counselor assumes that each client's perspective is unique to that individual and attempts to empathetically understand that perspective. In education, a tenet of constructivist teaching is that teachers need to understand the unique perspective of each student in order to be in touch with the students and to better understand each individual student and his or her needs. Thus, there is a phenomenological component to this theory.

Phenomenological researchers do not, however, generally assume that individuals are completely unique. More technically speaking, phenomenological researchers do not just study the variant structures of an experience (the unique part of an individual's experience that varies from person to person). Phenomenologists generally assume that there is some commonality in human experience, and they seek to understand this commonality. This commonality of experience is called an **essence,** or invariant structure, of the experience (a part of the experience that is common or consistent across the research participants). An essence is an essential characteristic of an experience. It is universal and is present in particular instances of a phenomenon (van Manen, 1990). Consider the experience of the death of a loved one. Certainly, each of us reacts to and experiences this event somewhat differently (i.e., the idiosyncratic or variant structure). However, there are probably essences to this experience that are common to everyone (i.e., the common or invariant structures). For example, in the case of the death of a loved one, grief and sorrow would probably be elements of the common experience. You can search for the essential structures of a phenomenon by studying multiple examples of it and finding what experiences the different people have in common. An essence will often be more abstract than literal descriptions of the particular

■ **Essence**
An invariant structure of the experience

experiences (e.g., general sorrow is more abstract than being "sad that your Uncle Bob is no longer around" to provide love and friendship).

The search for the essences of a phenomenon is probably the defining characteristic of phenomenology as a research technique. An example of a rich description of the essences of the experience of guilt is given in Exhibit 12.1. Are your experiences of guilt similar to the ones described in the exhibit? The description is from Yoder's (1990) doctoral dissertation.

■ EXHIBIT 12.1 The Essence of Guilt

Feelings of guilt are signs of significant turbulence, flaring up within the person. They come like a storm with lightning and cold winds. "It felt like mists, cold wind, dark streets, uncomfortable things. Stormy clouds in the sky. Occasional flashes of lightning. Empty beaches on a cold day. A cold wind from the water."

Guilt feelings close in. They are an imprisonment in which there is no way out. "You feel closed in when you are really feeling guilty. You feel cramped, very claustrophobic, limited, constricted, walled in."

The feeling of guilt is sharp and jagged. It is "being on the hook," a "knife," a pain as sharp as a surgical incision. The feeling of guilt is fast. "I'm thinking of lightning because it is a jab."

Guilt feelings are "a heavy weight." They are experienced as a "crushing blow." The feeling of guilt pushes, removes, evokes withdrawal, a sinking enormously heavy feeling. It comes in waves. "This intense push that jolts me back." "I'm gonna sink down. It's like this weight is on me."

Feeling guilty is "being in a shell," an invisible agent in a "world of strangers." Guilt feelings send one adrift into space where time is unending and the link with others is severed and closed. There is no hope of repair, renewal, belonging, no chance of even recognizing a genuine self.

The experience of feeling guilty is the experience of being forcibly removed from the flow of everyday life, from the world of ordinary human sharing and warmth. When we feel guilty, we are cast into a painful, frozen, inner-focused world that takes over the self and creates a reality of its own. Guilt feelings sever our sense of connectedness with everyday things, with other people and with ourselves. In the experience of feeling guilty, time stands still. All exits are closed. We are isolated and trapped within ourselves.

In guilt feelings, self-respect deteriorates, a sense of physical ugliness often awakens. Real emotions are hidden. Masked ways of being show themselves in pleasing others. In everyday and in ultimate moments, "The real me is not good enough. Not ever."

Time is experienced as slowed down and unchangeable. Clock time goes haywire. Everything churns and then freezes. Only the crystallized moment of guilt endures. The past is relived over and over again, an endless recycling, a movie that repeats itself without any genuine change or realization.

In guilt feelings, the relationship to the body is also affected. The body becomes distant, moves like a robot. It is in pain, anxious to move somehow, yet, at the same time, fearful that any action will reawaken the scenes of guilt.

In spite of the torturous feelings and helpless, endless, sense of guilt, there is still within the self, the possibility of recovering oneself and regaining the sense of harmonious flow with life. There is the potential to come to terms with the guilt, accept it, share it with another and, in this acceptance, find a way to peace. What is required is the courage to take the first step and risk scornful judgment and the pain of acknowledging one's limitations. There is no guarantee that if one freely and honestly expresses the guilt, and recognizes the vulnerability and limitedness of the self, that the guilty feelings will be excised permanently, but for some of my co-researchers this acceptance and sharing enabled them to reclaim themselves and reestablish inner tranquility.

Reprinted from Yoder, 1990.

Data Collection, Analysis, and Report Writing

In a typical phenomenological research study, the researcher collects data from several individuals and depicts their experience of something. The data are usually collected through in-depth interviews. Using the interview data, the researcher attempts to reduce the statements to the common core or essence of the experience as described by the research participants. For research participants to explore their experience, they must be able to relive it in their minds, and they must be able to focus on the experience and nothing else. This is what you must get your research participants to do if you conduct a phenomenological research study.

One effective strategy for eliciting data from participants is to tell each participant to recall a specific experience he or she has had, to think about that specific experience carefully, and then to describe that experience to you. You might use the following general question to get participants talking about their experience: "Please carefully describe your experience with _____." You might also say, "When you think of your experience with _____ what comes into your mind?" You might find that you need to prompt the respondent during the interview for greater detail, and you should do so. Remember that your goal is to get your participants to think about their specific experience and to describe it in rich detail. Rather than having each research participant describe the meaning and structure of his or her experience to you in an in-person interview, you can also have them write about their experience and then give you their written narrative. Both approaches work well.

During data analysis, the researcher searches for significant statements. These are statements (a few words or phrase, a sentence, or a few sentences) that have particular relevance to the phenomenon being studied. For example, perhaps you asked a kindergarten student to describe what school is like and one of her statements was that "We are all like a family at my school." If this statement seemed to fit her other statements, then the statement is probably a significant statement. In general, to determine whether a statement is significant, you should ask yourself, "Does the statement seem to have meaning to the participant in describing his or her experience? Is the statement descriptive of the experience? Does the statement tap into the participant's experience?" Many researchers like to record the significant statements verbatim (i.e., in the actual words of the participants). Some researchers also like to interpret and describe the meanings of the significant statements at this point by making a list of the *meanings*. For example, in the case of the kindergarten student's statement, you might conclude that the child sees school as being like a family because there is a teacher (the head of the family) and other students (family members) at school and the family does things together as a unit (play, eat, take naps). This is an interpretative process that is done by the researcher and should be verified by the participants (i.e., use the member-checking technique discussed in Chapter 8).

After constructing the lists of significant statements and meanings, the researcher searches for *themes* in the data. In other words, what kinds of things did the participants tend to mention as being important to them? The researcher might find that certain individuals or groups (e.g., males and females) tend to describe an experience somewhat differently. This information is useful in understanding individual and group differences. However, the phenomenological researcher is usually most interested in describing the fundamental structure of the experience (the essence) for the total group. It is here that the researcher describes the fundamental features of the experience that are experienced in common by virtually all the participants. Finally, researchers should use member checking as a validity check whenever possible in this process. This means that the researcher should have the original participants review the interpretations and descriptions of the experience, especially the statement of the fundamental structure of the experience.

In a research chapter entitled "The Essential Structure of a Caring Interaction: Doing Phenomenology," Riemen (1986) reported hospital patients' experiences of "caring" and "noncaring" nurses. We have included Rieman's description of the "essential structure" of her hospital patients' experiences of caring and noncaring nurses in Exhibits 12.2 and 12.3. Riemen also compared males' and females' significant statements and meanings. This is an excellent example of phenomenological research and a good model to follow.

The final report in a typical phenomenological study is a narrative that includes a description of the participants in the study and the methods used to obtain the information from the participants (usually interviews), a rich description of the fundamental structure of the experience, and a discussion of the findings. The researcher might also describe any in-

---

■ EXHIBIT 12.2   Description of a Caring Nurse

In a caring interaction, the nurse's existential presence is perceived by the client as more than just a physical presence. There is the aspect of the nurse giving of oneself to the client. This giving of oneself may be in response to the client's request, but it is more often a voluntary effort and is unsolicited by the client. The nurse's willingness to give of oneself is primarily perceived by the client as an attitude and behavior of sitting down and really listening and responding to the unique concerns of the individual as a person of value. The relaxation, comfort, and security that the client experiences both physically and mentally are an immediate and direct result of the client's stated and unstated needs being heard and responded to by the nurse.

From Creswell (1998), p. 289.

■ EXHIBIT 12.3   Description of a Noncaring Nurse

The nurse's presence with the client is perceived by the client as a minimal presence of the nurse being physically present only. The nurse is viewed as being there only because it is a job and not to assist the client or answer his or her needs. Any response by the nurse is done with a minimal amount of energy expenditure and bound by the rules. The client perceives the nurse who does not respond to this request for assistance as being noncaring. Therefore, an interaction that never happened is labeled as a noncaring interaction. The nurse is too busy and hurried to spend time with the client and therefore does not sit down and really listen to the client's individual concerns. The client is further devalued as a unique person because he or she is scolded, treated as a child, or treated as a nonhuman being or an object. Because of the devaluing and lack of concern, the client's needs are not met and the client has negative feelings, that is, frustrated, scared, depressed, angry, afraid, and upset.

From Creswell (1998), p. 289.

teresting individual or group differences. A well-written report will be highly descriptive of the participants' experience of the phenomenon, and it will elicit in the readers a feeling that they understand what it would be like to experience the phenomenon themselves. This kind of feeling is called a vicarious experience.

12.5 What are the key characteristics of phenomenology?

12.6 How does the researcher analyze the data collected in a phenomenology?

Research
Navigator.c⊛m

ethnography

ETHNOGRAPHY

Foundational questions: What are the cultural characteristics of this group of people or of this cultural scene?

Ethnography is an approach to qualitative research that originated in the discipline of anthropology around the turn of the twentieth century. Ethnography literally means "writing about people" (*ethnos* means people, race, or cultural group, and *graphia* means writing or representing) (LeCompte & Preissle, 1993). Because of the importance of the concept of culture to the discipline of anthropology, **ethnography** is traditionally or classically defined as the discovery and comprehensive description of the culture of a group of people. Educational ethnographers also focus on cultural description as done in classical ethnography. The main difference is that anthropologists usually describe small cultures across the world (especially in less developed nations), and educational ethnographers usually study the cultural characteristics of small groups of people or other cultural scenes as they relate to educational issues.

The Idea of Culture

Culture is a system of shared beliefs, values, practices, perspectives, folk knowledge, language, norms, rituals, and material objects and artifacts that members of a group use in understanding their world and in relating to others. So that you can better understand this definition, here are the definitions of several important words in it. **Shared beliefs** are the specific cultural conventions or statements that people who share a culture hold to be true or false. **Shared values** are the culturally defined standards about what is good or bad or desirable or undesirable. **Norms** are the written and unwritten rules that specify appropriate group behavior (e.g., "Raise your hand when you have a question" is a common norm in a classroom).

If you look at the definition of culture, you will notice it includes a nonmaterial component (the shared beliefs, values, norms, and so forth of the members of a group) and a material component (the material things produced by group members, such as buildings, books, classroom bulletin boards, and art). Ethnographers sometimes refer to these two components as *material culture* and *nonmaterial culture*. Although ethnographers do not

- **Ethnography**
  The discovery and comprehensive description of the culture of a group of people
- **Culture**
  A system of shared beliefs, values, practices, perspectives, folk knowledge, language, norms, rituals, and material objects and artifacts that members of a group use in understanding their world and in relating to others
- **Shared beliefs**
  The specific cultural conventions or statements that people who share a culture hold to be true or false
- **Shared values**
  The culturally defined standards about what is good or bad or desirable or undesirable
- **Norms**
  The written and unwritten rules that specify appropriate group behavior

usually specify whether they are referring to the material or nonmaterial component of culture or both, the intention is usually clear from the context of the statement. When one is attempting to understand and explain human behavior, the nonmaterial component is usually the focus of attention.

Individuals become members of a culture through the socialization process by which they learn and are trained about the features of the culture. During socialization, they usually internalize the culture; that is, they take the values and beliefs to be their own. Over time, people identify so strongly with their culture that the ways of doing things in their own culture might seem natural to them, and the ways of doing things in other cultures might seem strange. You might have heard the term *culture shock,* which refers to an experience people have when they observe different cultural practices. Cultures are maintained over time through socialization and through a social sanctioning process through which members of a culture stigmatize people who break group norms, and they praise and associate with the members who follow the appropriate cultural norms. In general, as people become members of any new group, they learn the culture of that group so that they can become fully functioning and accepted members of the group. The people who follow the norms of a group or society are often called normal, and those who deviate from the cultural norms are called deviant.

Although we often think of a culture as being associated with a very large group such as a society (e.g., the culture of the United States), the concept of culture can be used on a much smaller scale. In fact, culture can be viewed as varying on a continuum, with macro culture on one end and micro culture on the other end. At the macro level, we might study the cultural characteristics (the shared values, beliefs, and norms) of U.S. citizens, Japanese adolescents, or the Ohio Amish. On a more micro level, we might study the cultural characteristics of a group of Sikh immigrants (first-generation Americans originally from a province in India) attending an American high school. Other micro-level groups we might study include the members of the Chicago Bears football team, the band members at a local high school, Spanish-speaking students at a local middle school, or the students in Ms. Smith's first-grade classroom. Educational ethnographers are most likely to study cultures or the cultural characteristics of groups much smaller than an entire nation like the United States or Japan. That is, they usually (but not always) study relatively small or micro cultures.

In an educational ethnography conducted at a clearly micro level, a researcher might choose to study a classroom culture. For example, the researcher might want to study the culture of one elementary schoolteacher's home room students to find out how and why the teacher has been successful in helping these students learn to read. Ethnographic concepts (shared values, beliefs, group norms, etc.) and procedures (observations and interviews) will be very useful in understanding this classroom. You might ask questions such as, What norms do the students follow while they are in this classroom? What values do they adopt while they are in the classroom? How does the teacher interact with the students? How do the students interact with one another? Are all of the students usually doing the same thing or are there several clusters of interacting students at a time? What seems to motivate the students to work so hard? What classroom values have the students internalized? What teaching practices and strategies does the teacher use to teach? This list of questions is unlimited because an ethnography should be a relatively comprehensive description of the group's culture and the important cultural scenes.

Sometimes the term **subculture** is used to refer to a culture that is embedded within a larger culture. For example, a high school can be viewed as containing several subcultures (e.g., a teacher culture and various student group cultures). However, researchers usually continue to use the more general term *culture* even for these smaller groups (i.e., they say the school is composed of several cultures) rather than using the more specific term *subculture*. If you want to make the point that a group of people is composed of two or more smaller but distinct groups, then you may use the term *subculture*. Otherwise, using the more general term *culture* is fine. In general, humans are members of and are affected by multiple cultures or subcultures simultaneously. For example, the members of the school band at a suburban high school are probably affected by the overall U.S. culture, by the adolescent culture within the United States by a suburban culture, by their own school culture, and by any cultural characteristics they share by virtue of their membership in the band.

■ **Subculture**
A culture embedded within a larger culture

Examples of Ethnographic Research

Now that you know what ethnography and culture are, we briefly describe several published research articles that use ethnographic techniques. As with all of the qualitative research approaches discussed in this chapter, the best way to learn more about them is to read some published articles or book-length examples. In "An Ethnographic Study of Norms of Inclusion and Cooperation in a Multiethnic Middle School," Deering (1996) studied the culture in a middle school that was known to be supportive of inclusion. Deering defined inclusion as "the degree to which all persons and their aspirations and interests are incorporated into a given social context" (p. 22). Deering studied the school over a two-year period by observing and talking to teachers, administrators, students, parents, and other community members. He described the school culture, the peer culture, and parent and community involvement. It was remarkable how well students from different groups got along at this particular school. Some reasons were the leadership provided by the principal, a norm of respect applied to everyone in the school, and an expectation of positive involvement by all groups in the school.

In "The Content of Conversations about the Body Parts and Behaviors of Animals during Elementary School Visits to a Zoo and the Implications for Teachers Organizing Field Trips," Tunnicliffe (1995) observed and listened to children while they were at a zoo. She provided a description of what the children said, she classified those statements by topic, and she provided some quotes from the children (e.g., "It's showing its teeth." "Miss Wicks, look! Their hands are like ours!" "There's a baby one."). This study took the reader into a small part of the children's culture and described it to the reader. It is an example of a cultural scene.

In "An Ethnographic Study of Cross-Cultural Communication with Puerto Rican–American Families in the Special Education System," Harry (1992) observed and interviewed parents from twelve Spanish-speaking Puerto Rican American families who had children in the special education system. She also interviewed several educators. She found that cultural differences seemed to lead to communication breakdowns between the educators and the Puerto Rican American parents. For example, the parents expected the educational professionals to treat them as friends (i.e., as *mi amiga* or "my friend") as in Puerto Rico, but they did not perceive this to be happening. They felt that the American school system was impersonal, and they did not trust it. Much of the communication about their children and the Individual Education Plan (IEP) was written, and this tended to further alienate the parents. Sometimes the parents didn't understand the language and jargon used by the educators (e.g., the term *IEP* was sometimes misunderstood). Feeling a lack of power, the parents often withdrew from the communication process and deferred to the professionals, who, as a result, felt the parents were apathetic. In sum, the educators and the parents tended to come from different cultures, and they often misunderstood one another.

Types of Ethnographic Research

■ **Ethnology**
The comparative study of cultural groups

There are two other types of ethnographic work that are closely related to classical ethnography. These are called ethnology and ethnohistory. An **ethnology** is the comparative study of cultural groups. It involves conducting or comparing a series of separate ethnographic studies of the same or different cultural groups to uncover general patterns and rules of social behavior. For example, ethnology might involve the comparison of family practices or educational practices in several different cultures. The ethnologist would look for similarities and differences among the groups. As an example, sociologists and anthropologists have found that all societies have some form of the family institution. However, the extended family pattern, in which parents, children, and other kin such as grandparents and aunts and uncles interact a great deal, is more common in traditional agrarian societies (e.g., El Salvador and Bangladesh) and the nuclear family pattern, in which one or two parents and their children interact the most, is more common in modern industrial societies (e.g., the United States and Sweden). Because there is greater interest in general patterns (what many people have in common) in ethnology than in particular patterns (the unique characteristics of each group), this form of research tends to have greater external validity than a single ethnography.

An example of an educational ethnology is LeCompte and Preissle's (1992) chapter entitled "Toward an Ethnology of Student Life in Schools and Classrooms: Synthesizing the Qualitative Research Tradition." LeCompte and Preissle have been conducting educational ethnographies for over two decades, and in this ethnology, they compare the findings from a large number of ethnographic studies over that time period. Their goal was to find some common themes across the educational ethnographies. We mention only three of their findings. First, they found that children's focus of attention changes over time (e.g., from kindergarten to high school). "Younger children conceptualize school experience as types of activity [e.g., work and play] and the structures that support them. Older students shift their attention from structures, tasks, and schedules to relationships with people" (p. 823). Not surprisingly, students' and teachers' perspectives about what is important tended to be different. Second, they also found that teacher expectations for different kinds of students tended to affect student behavior. Third, they found that "Students who are better integrated into their home culture achieve higher success in school, even if they are members of stigmatized minority groups" (p. 846).

■ **Ethnohistory**
The study of the cultural past of a group of people

The other form of ethnographic research is **ethnohistory,** which is the study of the cultural past of a group of people. An ethnohistory is often done during the early stages of an ethnography to uncover the group members' cultural roots and to study how the group has changed (or not changed) over time. This information provides the researcher with a deeper sense of the people being studied. The researcher relies on data such as official documents, oral histories, journals and newspapers, and information gathered from talking with the older people in the group to learn about how things used to be and how things are different now. The ethnohistory can be the end purpose of a research study, but it is usually part of a larger ethnographic study.

Data Collection, Analysis, and Report Writing

Ethnography relies on extended fieldwork. This means that the researcher spends a long time in the field with the people being studied. The researcher typically becomes a participant or nonparticipant observer. In fact, extended fieldwork and participant observation are the distinguishing characteristics of a classical or ideal type ethnography. Spending six months to a year in the field is not at all uncommon. As you can see, this type of research can be quite demanding!

Data collection and data analysis in ethnography are said to be concurrent, or alternating. This means ethnographers typically collect some data and analyze those data, then return to the field to collect more data and analyze those data, and so on. This process cycles during most of the time spent in the field. The researcher needs to look at the data and analyze them while he or she is still fresh out of the field and also to know where and what kinds of data need to be collected next.

Ethnography is an emergent, fluid, and responsive approach to qualitative research because the original research questions sometimes change. For example, Holland and Eisenhart (1990) spent several years studying females attending college. They were originally interested in the influence of peer groups on females' role identities and how peer groups affected the women's choices of college majors. They realized over time that the women's peers knew very little about how or why they chose their college major. The researchers decided that the more important questions emerging from their study were how the women responded to their college culture, how they specifically responded to the patriarchal conditions that they faced, and what important subcultural differences existed among the women. Although an ethnographer might think he or she knows exactly what to study in the field, it is always possible that it becomes clear during extended fieldwork that the original research questions were naive, unimportant, or not researchable or that other issues and questions were more important.

The researcher collects data during fieldwork that might help in understanding the group of people. Ethnographers talk to people, observe their behavior in their natural day-to-day environments, and examine documents kept by the group members. They also take extensive field notes of what they see on an ongoing basis, and they write memos to themselves, recording their thoughts and interpretations about the developing ethnographic description. Video and audio recording devices are frequently helpful because of their accuracy and because the tapes can be reviewed at a later time.

One of the cardinal rules in doing ethnographic research is not to be ethnocentric toward the people you are studying. **Ethnocentrism** means judging people from a different culture or group according to the standards of your own culture or group. An example of ethnocentric behavior would be going to another country and being judgmental about what they eat (e.g., Why would anyone eat snails?!). When we are being ethnocentric, we don't try to understand people who are different from us. Therefore, when doing ethnographic research,

■ **Ethnocentrism**
Judging people from a different culture according to the standards of your own culture

you must take a nonjudgmental stance toward the people you are studying in order to gain useful information.

Ethnographers also try to take on the emic and etic perspectives during data collection and analysis. The **emic perspective** is the insider's perspective. It includes the meanings and views of the people in the group being studied. Taking the emic perspective also means considering questions and issues for study that are important to insiders. The researcher documenting the emic perspective must try to get inside of the heads of the group members. Therefore, this aspect of ethnography is very phenomenological in approach. To understand the emic perspective, it is helpful if you can learn the local language and forms of expression used by the people being studied. Special words or terms used by them are called **emic terms.** Some emic terms used by high school students in a middle-sized Southern city to refer to the more academic-type students were *brains, advanced, intellectuals, nerds, geeks, dorks,* and *smarties* (Smith, 1997). A larger list of emic terms identified by Smith for various groups in high schools is shown in Table 12.3.

Ethnographers use the term **etic perspective** to refer to an external, social scientific view of reality (Fetterman, 1998). This is the perspective of the objective researcher studying a group of people. The goal is to move beyond the perspectives of the people being studied and use social science concepts, terms (i.e., **etic terms**), and procedures to describe the people and explain their behavior. Researchers using the etic perspective also bring their research questions from the outside (e.g., issues are considered important on the basis of a review of the research literature). They tend to take an instrumental view, wanting to study the participants in order to answer a specific question or to produce a specific product.

Effective ethnographers are able to utilize both perspectives. If a researcher only took the emic perspective, he or she would risk what is called **going native,** which means that the researcher identifies so completely with the group that he or she can no longer remain objective. Someone who goes native has basically become an insider. That person overidentifies with the group and can view things only from the viewpoint of the insiders. On the other hand, if researchers took only the etic viewpoint, they would risk not understanding the people from the native perspective. They would also risk imposing their own predetermined beliefs and categories on their interpretations about the participants. We believe that effec-

---

■ Emic perspective
The insider's perspective

■ Emic terms
Special words or terms used by the people in a group

■ Etic perspective
An external, social scientific view of reality

■ Etic terms
Outsider's words or special words that are used by social scientists

■ Going native
Identifying so completely with the group being studied that you can no longer remain objective

---

■ **T A B L E   1 2 . 3**   Selected Emic Terms Used by High School Students

Losers	Rebels	Skanks	Jocks	Prep	Holy Rollers
Retards	Rednecks	Bubbas	Mechanics	Vo Techs	Goody-Goodies
Hippies	Peacers	Gangsters	Druggies	Burnouts	Clowns
Grubbies	Loners	Roaches	Wannabes	Woodies	Azalea Trail Maids
Surfers	Whammers	Punks	Airheads	Rockers	Brains
Geeks	Dorks	Duds	Book worms	Grunge	Band

Source: From Smith, Heather J. 1997. *The Role of Symbolism in the Structure, Maintenance, and Interaction of High School Social Groupings.* Masters Thesis. University of South Alabama Department of Sociology and Anthropology. Used by permission.

tive researchers must walk the fine line between the emic and etic perspectives and must periodically delve into the world of each perspective in order to gather insights and produce a good ethnography.

Because of the reliance on observational and interview data, ethnographers should constantly triangulate their observations and data sources to corroborate their research findings. For example, if a participant or informant says that some event took place, the ethnographer does not take that single participant's account at face value. Instead, the ethnographer searches for other participants who experienced (or observed or heard about) the same event and listens to their accounts and interpretations. In this way, evidence for descriptive validity is improved. During the later months in the field, ethnographers frequently begin composing and writing their final report. This way, the written description and interpretation can be shown to the participants for their review and validation. Recall that this process is called *participant review* or *member checking.*

When writing the final report, ethnographers contextualize their study. That is, they carefully examine the context in which the group is situated, and they write this up in the report. For example, ethnographers describe the particulars of the physical and social settings, including the time, the place, and the situation in which a study was conducted. Contextualization helps make the ethnographer more aware of the relationship between the context and the observed behavior, and it helps readers of the research report to know where and to whom they can apply the research results.

When describing a group, ethnographers also try to be holistic. **Holism** was discussed briefly in Chapter 2 and also in Table 12.1 (characteristic 10). Although the concept of holism is summed up in the statement "The whole is greater than its parts," holistic description does not ignore the parts of the whole because an analysis of the parts is essential to understanding the whole. The ethnographer consciously works back and forth between the parts and the whole, ultimately creating a picture of the cultural group or scene. For example, a high school band is composed of individuals who come together as a unit and create a holistic product (music). In a typical ethnography, holistic description involves examining the characteristics of the individuals in a group (e.g., what the individuals are like); it involves examining how the individuals in the group interact with one another (e.g., when they interact and what they do); and it involves examining how the individuals come together to form the group (e.g., what they have in common, what their group norms and rituals are, and what the group identity is). In short, when composing a holistic description, you must study the parts of the whole in addition to describing the whole. The final ethnographic report typically includes rich and holistic description of the group. It also usually includes many verbatims (direct quotations from group members).

■ **Holism**
The idea that the whole is greater than the sum of its parts

▬▬▬▬ CASE STUDY RESEARCH

Foundational question: What are the characteristics of this single case or of these comparison cases?

Merriam (1988) tells us that "case study research is nothing new" (p. xi), pointing out that the idea of studying cases has been around for a long time and across many different disciplines (e.g., medicine, law, business, the social sciences). During the late 1970s and the 1980s, however, authors such as Robert Stake (1978), Robert Yin (1981), and Sharan Merriam (1988) delineated case study research as a specific type of research. Although Stake and Merriam have a qualitative orientation toward case study research (preferring an inductive or generative approach) and Yin has a more quantitative orientation (preferring a more deductive or testing approach), what these case study researchers have in common is that they choose to call their objects of study cases, they collect primarily qualitative data, and they organize their research efforts around the study of those cases (e.g., Merriam, 1988; Stake, 1995; Yin, 1998). We define **case study research** simply as research that provides a detailed account and analysis of one or more cases.[2]

- **Case study research**
  Research that provides a detailed account and analysis of one or more cases

- **Case**
  A bounded system

Research
Navigator.c⊕m

qualitative
case study

What Is a Case?

A **case** is defined as a bounded system. In the words of one prominent case study researcher, Robert Stake (1997), "Lou Smith used a fancy name, 'bounded system,' to indicate that we are going to try to figure out what complex things go on within that system. The case study tells a story about a bounded system" (p. 406). Note that a *system* is a set of interrelated elements that form an organized whole. Using the system metaphor, cases are seen as holistic entities that have parts and that act or operate in their environments. *Bounded* is added to emphasize that you should identify the outline or boundaries of the system—you must determine what the case is and what it is not.

Typical cases are a child with a learning disability, a pupil with a special need, a language arts classroom, a charter school, and a national program (e.g., the Head Start Program). Some case study researchers are very inclusive in what they call cases (e.g., Cresswell, 1998; Merriam, 1988; Yin, 1998). For them, a case is not just an object or entity with a clear identity (e.g., a group, a person, a classroom, or an organization), but can also include an event (e.g., a campus protest), an activity (e.g., learning to play softball), or a process (e.g., becoming a professional teacher during one's first year of teaching). When you read case study articles, you should check early on to see what kind of case the authors are examining.

For example, Gallo and Horton (1994) conducted a case study of one high school in East Central Florida. Here the high school was the case. The research focused on the process and results of having access to the Internet at the high school. The authors concluded that Internet access could have many positive effects on teachers (e.g., incorporation of technology into the classroom, increased self-esteem, development of positive attitudes toward computers), especially if the teachers were given adequate training in how to use the Internet and how to incorporate it into their classrooms. Valentine and McIntosh (1990) examined the characteristics of an organization (the case) in which women held all the positions of power. They found that the organization took on a *gemeinschaft* (a local community) type of character rather than a *gesellschaft* (citylike, impersonal) character. Van Haneghan and Stofflett (1995) conducted case studies of four fifth-grade teachers (four cases). They determined how each teacher implemented an innovative videodisc curriculum focused on problem solving. These authors developed a heuristic model based on their observations that could be used to train teachers to implement the new curriculum into their classrooms.

Because case study researchers define a case as a bounded system, it should not be surprising that they study how the system operates. As a result, they are interested in holistic description. Almost all systems are made up of components or parts, and it is important to understand how the parts operate together in order to understand the system (i.e., the case). For example, a high school is made up of teachers, buildings, students, classrooms, and books (among many other things). You can also view an individual as being composed of many different components or parts (e.g., cognitive, emotional, physiological). How the parts come together (i.e., their synergism) is of utmost interest to a case study researcher.

Case study researchers also view each case as having an internal and an external context. Take a school as an example. Internally, a researcher might examine the organizational climate at a school, the leadership style used by the principal, and the condition of the physical and instructional facilities. Externally, the school will be situated in a geographical area with specific social, economic, and demographic characteristics. If the school is a public school, it will be situated within a public school system with additional characteristics. The point is that case study researchers carefully examine the contexts of the case in order to better describe and explain the functioning of the case.

Types of Case Study Research Designs

There are three different kinds of case studies according to Stake (1995): intrinsic case studies, instrumental case studies, and collective case studies. In an **intrinsic case study** the researcher's primary interest is in understanding a specific case. This design is the classic, single-case design. Here the researcher describes, in depth, the particulars of the case in order to shed light on the case. For example, a researcher might want to understand a student who is having difficulty in class or a researcher might want to understand how the local PTA operates. The goal is to understand the case as a holistic entity as well as to understand its inner workings. A secondary goal is to understand a more general process based on an analysis of the single case.

> ■ **Intrinsic case study**
> Interest is in understanding a specific case

The intrinsic case study is very popular in education. It is also popular with program evaluators, whose goal is to describe a program and to evaluate how effectively the program is operating (e.g., an evaluator might evaluate a local drug education program for at-risk middle and high school students). Finally, the intrinsic case study is often used in exploratory research in which the researcher attempts to learn about a little-known phenomenon by studying a single case in depth. The advantage of the intrinsic case study is that researchers can put all their time and resources into the study of a single case and can therefore develop an in-depth understanding. A weakness is that generalizing from a single case can be very risky.

In an **instrumental case study,** the researcher's primary interest is in understanding something other than the particular case. The case is seen as important only as a means to an end. In other words, the researcher studies the case to learn about something more general

> ■ **Instrumental case study**
> Interest is in understanding something more general than the particular case

(e.g., teenage drug use in general rather than teenage drug use at a particular high school, or discipline in general rather than discipline in a particular teacher's classroom). The goal tends to be less particularistic and more universalistic. That is, researchers doing instrumental case studies are less interested in making conclusions that are specific to the case and its particular setting than they are in making conclusions that apply beyond a particular case.

In the instrumental case study design, the researcher is usually interested in how and why a phenomenon operates as it does. That is, the researcher chooses the case to develop and/or test a theory or to better understand some important issue. Explanation is a key goal. The specific case can be selected because it is extreme or unique in some way (and can be used to test theoretical predictions) or because it is typical (and can be used to understand the general case). The instrumental case study is popular with many academic researchers when they are interested in generalizing and extending the findings in research literatures on various topics.

■ **Collective case study**
Studying multiple cases in one research study

In the **collective case study,** the researcher believes that he or she can gain greater insight into a research topic by concurrently studying multiple cases in one overall research study. The collective case study is also called the multiple-case design (e.g., Yin, 1994). Several cases are usually studied in a collective case study. For example, two or three cases might be studied when a relatively in-depth analysis of each case is required and when resources are limited. When less depth is required and when greater resources are available, collective case studies of around ten cases are common. The cases in the collective case study are usually studied instrumentally rather than intrinsically. For example, a researcher might select several cases to study because he or she is interested in studying the effects of inclusion of children with mild mental retardation in general education classes. Rather than studying the outcomes in a single classroom, the researcher studies the impact in several different classrooms.

There are several advantages to studying more than one case. First, a comparative type of study can be conducted in which several cases are compared for similarities and differences. For example, a public school might be studied and compared with a private school. Second, one can more effectively test a theory by observing the results of multiple cases. Third, one is more likely to be able to generalize the results from multiple cases than from a single case. Yin (1994) points out that replication logic can be used when one has multiple cases. In experimental research, we have more confidence in a finding when it has been replicated many times. Here is what Yin (1994) says about this idea and its relevance for case study research:

> Thus, if one has access only to three cases of a rare, clinical syndrome in psychology or medical science, the appropriate research design is one in which the same results are predicted for each of the three cases, thereby producing evidence that the three cases did indeed involve the same syndrome. If similar results are obtained from all three cases, replication is said to have taken place. (p. 45)

In Yin's example mentioned in this quote, the theory that predicted the same result for each case was supported. Therefore, compared to a single case study, the researcher would have greater confidence that a similar result would happen in a new case.

A disadvantage of studying multiple cases is that depth of analysis will usually have to be sacrificed because of the breadth of analysis obtained from studying more than one case.

This is the classic depth versus breadth tradeoff, and it is a common tradeoff in case study research. In other words, because of limited resources (e.g., money and time) available in most research studies, you will be forced to make a choice between "depth and detail" and "breadth and comparative information." It takes considerable time to study one case in depth, but you end up with a deep understanding of the case. On the other hand, if you are going to study multiple cases, you will have to reduce the amount of time spent on each case but you get important comparative information. As you can see, there are advantages and disadvantages to both sides of this tradeoff. You will ultimately have to make the final judgment about how to deal with this tradeoff if you conduct a research study.

Data Collection, Analysis, and Report Writing

Case study research methodologists (those researchers who write books about doing case study research) tend to be pragmatic and advocate the use of multiple methods and multiple data sources (i.e., methods and data triangulation). These methodologists recommend that you take an eclectic approach and rely on any data that will help you understand your case and answer your research questions. Any of the methods of data collection (observation, interviews, questionnaires, focus groups, tests, and secondary data such as documents) discussed in Chapter 6 can be used when they help answer your research questions. Qualitative versions of these methods (such as participant observation, in-depth interviews, open-ended questionnaires) do, however, tend to be the most popular in educational case studies.

Research questions (or research "issues," according to Stake) and the relevant findings are presented for each question. During analysis and writing, the researcher will always examine and report on the case (e.g., a school) because the case is always the primary unit of analysis in case study research. Other units of analysis that are embedded in the case might also be examined (e.g., within a school, some embedded units of analysis could be the classrooms, the teachers, and the students). If multiple cases are used, then each case is usually first examined in total, and then the different cases are compared in a **cross-case analysis** for similarities (patterns that cut across the cases) as well as differences. When people or groups of people are studied, an attempt is usually made to reconstruct the participants' realities and portray the multiple viewpoints existing in the case (e.g., you might portray the different viewpoints of the teachers in a school).

■ Cross-case analysis
Searching for similarities and differences across multiple cases.

The final report is usually written to present a rich (vivid and detailed) and holistic (i.e., describes the whole and its parts) description of the case and its context. An example of rich description is given in Exhibit 12.4. Research questions (or research "issues" according to Stake) and the relevant findings are presented. The findings should be related back to similar findings in the research literature when possible. When people or groups of people are studied, an attempt is usually made to reconstruct the participants' realities and portray the multiple viewpoints existing in the case (e.g., you might portray the different viewpoints of the teachers in a school). When a collective case study is conducted (i.e., studying multiple cases), the report might be organized case by case with a separate section integrating the findings from all of the cases. Through data collection, analysis, and report writing, the researcher should use the validity strategies discussed in Chapter 8, such as the different types of triangulation, to help increase the validity or trustworthiness of the case study findings.

■ **EXHIBIT 12.4** **An Example of Rich Description in a Case Study**

That first morning, I reached Harper [School] a few minutes after 8 A.M., in time to see most of the students arriving. It was a nippy morning, the day following Martin Luther King's birthday. Many youngsters were bundled in Chicago Bulls gear. All were walking, almost all from the adjacent high-rise housing. Residents called it "The Place."

A middle-school youngster wearing a crossing-guard sash courteously escorted me to an unmarked door. Also unmarked—by graffiti or weather—was the white brick face of the building, lettered simply Frances Harper School. Just inside the door, Mr. Carter, the security captain, pointed the way to the office. A janitor and several kids took notice of my arrival.

The office clerk, with a large smile, introduced me to "the boss." Principal Lyda Hawkins's greeting also was warm. We moved into her room for a lengthy conversation—in spite of mounting traffic. First we commented on yesterday's Denver confrontation between King marchers and Klansmen. I said, "How could it be?" She said, "Some things don't change."

Lyda Hawkins had taught in this part of Chicago since the 1950s and had been principal of this school for over 16 years. She knew her neighborhood. We talked about change, about the Chicago school reform plan, about its orientation to governance more than to teaching and learning. "To many, it was license to get the principal," she said with feeling. She spoke of Local School Councils, noting that she had a good council. She spoke of unrealistic expectations of reform groups about readiness of parents to assume school governance responsibilities, the lack of experience before election, the insufficiency of orientation after. One of her council members had said, "How do you expect us to understand a $2 million budget? I can't manage $460 a month!"

Community involvement in Harper School was not high. Only a few parent volunteers worked with teachers. It was even difficult to get Local School Council members to come to council meetings. In the words of Mattie Mitchell, teacher and school community representative, "Who wants to make decisions? Who is ready to make decisions? Not many."

Reprinted from R. E. Stake, *The Art of Case Study Research,* pp. 138–139, copyright © 1995 by Sage Publications, Inc. Reprinted by Permission of Sage Publications, Inc.

REVIEW QUESTIONS

12.11 What are the key characteristics of case study research?

12.12 What is a case?

12.13 Define intrinsic case study, instrumental case study, and collective case study.

GROUNDED THEORY

Research
Navigator.com

grounded theory

Foundational question: What theory or explanation emerges from an analysis of the data collected about this phenomenon?

Barney Glaser and Anselm Strauss wrote a book in 1967 on what they called *grounded theory.* These two sociologists contended that theory should emerge inductively from empirical data. They said we need to "discover theory from data" (p. 1). Although this was not an entirely new idea in the field of research, Glaser and Strauss wanted to counter what they saw as a tendency in their field to focus on *theory confirmation* (testing hypotheses developed from previous theories) rather than on *theory generation* and construction (developing new theories grounded in new data). They thought that the discipline of sociology had stagnated because of a reliance on older theories. They also thought that current research was too quantitative and had become too far removed from the empirical reality that it sought to explain. They believed that many of the popular theories at that time were not grounded in real data but were, instead, based on the thinking of a few famous theorists. Since publication of Glaser and Strauss's important book in 1967, grounded theory has become a popular approach to qualitative research in many different disciplines, including education, counseling, and nursing.

"**Grounded theory** is a *general methodology* for developing theory that is grounded in data systematically gathered and analyzed" (Strauss & Corbin, 1994, p. 273). The product of the grounded theory methodology is frequently called a grounded theory. Therefore, when you do grounded theory research, your goal is to construct a grounded theory. It is important to understand that *a grounded theory is not generated a priori* (i.e., based only on reasoning). Rather, a grounded theory is based on concepts that are generated directly from the data that are collected in one or more research studies. This is another way of saying that the theory is inductively derived. Figuratively speaking, you can think of inductive analysis as "getting into your data" (during data collection and analysis), "living there" or "hanging out there for a while," and developing an understanding of the phenomenon based on the data. For example, if someone outside of education wanted to learn about teaching, this person could go to a real classroom, observe a teacher for several weeks, and then draw some tentative, data-based conclusions about teaching. Induction is a bottom-up approach based on original data (i.e., you start with the data and then make your generalizations after looking at your data). Strauss and Corbin (1990) point out the inductive nature of grounded theory research when they say that "One does not begin with a theory, then prove it. Rather, one begins with an area of study and what is relevant to that area is allowed to emerge" (p. 23). During a particular grounded theory research study, some data are collected and analyzed and, as the theory is being developed, additional data are collected and analyzed to further clarify, develop, and validate the theory.

> ■ **Grounded theory**
> A general methodology for developing theory that is grounded in data systematically gathered and analyzed

Characteristics of a Grounded Theory

Glaser and Strauss (1967) list four important characteristics of a grounded theory. They are fit, understanding, generality, and control. First, the theory must fit the data if it is to be useful. Glaser and Strauss make an important point when they say that a researcher "often develops a theory that embodies, without his realizing it, his own ideals and the values of his occupation and social class, as well as popular views and myths, along with his deliberate efforts at making logical deductions from some formal theory to which he became committed as a graduate student" (p. 238). The point is that theory must correspond closely to the real-world data, not to our personal wishes or biases or predetermined categories. Second, the theory should be clearly stated and readily understandable to people working in the substantive area, even to nonresearch types. One reason for this is that practitioners might need to use the theory or employ someone else to use the theory one day. If the theory is not understandable to them, it might never be used. Glaser and Strauss point out, "Their understanding the theory tends to engender a readiness to use it, for it sharpens their sensitivity to the problems that they face and gives them an image of how they can potentially make matters better" (p. 240).

Third, the theory should have generality. This means that the scope of the theory and its conceptual level should not be so specific that the theory only applies to one small set of people or to only one specific situation. Such a theory would rarely be of use. Furthermore, it would be practically impossible to develop a new theory for every single person and situation. A strategy for avoiding such specificity is to conceptualize the concepts in the theory at a level abstract enough to move beyond the specifics in the original research study. The fourth characteristic of a good grounded theory as discussed by Glaser and Strauss is control. If someone uses the theory, he or she should have some control over the phenomenon that is explained by the theory. In the words of Glaser and Strauss (1967), "The substantive theory must enable the person who uses it to have enough control in everyday situations to make its application worth trying" (p. 245). As a result, it is a good idea to identify controllable variables and build them into your grounded theory.

As you can see, meeting the criteria of fit, understanding, generality, and control is a lot to expect from a grounded theory, especially if the theory is developed from a single research study. That is why the development of a grounded theory is a neverending process. In a single research study the researcher should try to collect as extensive data as feasible. During the study the researcher will interact with the data and collect additional data when questions arise and need answering. A grounded theory should be further elaborated and modified in future research studies; the key strategy, again, is that the developing theory should be grounded in the data. Practitioners who attempt to use the theory should also be involved in making suggestions for theory modifications. As Glaser and Strauss (1967) say, "The person who applies the theory becomes, in effect, a generator of theory" (p. 242).

Example of a Grounded Theory

So that you will have a better idea about a real grounded theory research study, we will now describe a study conducted by Creswell and Brown (1992) entitled "How Chairpersons Enhance Faculty Research: A Grounded Theory Study." The article is easy to read, and it is a good example of a grounded theory based on a single research study.

Creswell and Brown (1992) studied how college and university department chairpersons interact with their faculty members. They conducted "semi-structured telephone interviews with thirty-three chairpersons" (p. 42). They found that the chairpersons actually performed many different roles. The roles identified were labeled "providing, enabling, advocating, acting as a mentor, encouraging, collaborating, and challenging." They also found that the chairpersons performed different roles at different times, depending on the level of the faculty member they were interacting with. The important levels identified in the study were beginning faculty (faculty who had been in the department from one to three years), pretenured faculty (faculty who had been in the department from three to five years), posttenured faculty (faculty who had not yet been promoted to full professor), and senior faculty (faculty who were full professors). They found, for example, that beginning faculty needed extra time for writing and publishing, and the chairperson would provide additional resources and try to enable the faculty member by providing a favorable schedule and a reduction in committee work. If this strategy were successful, the outcome would be more publications by the faculty member, which would help improve the faculty member's chance of getting tenure. You can see Creswell and Brown's depiction of their grounded theory in Figure 12.2. As shown there, the type of faculty issue that a chairperson is concerned with depends on the career stage of the faculty member and other signs such as a lack of productivity. Given a faculty member who is at a specific stage and the presence of certain signs, the department chairperson performs certain roles (strategies) to help the faculty member develop. These actions result in specific outcomes (e.g., improved productivity, an improved attitude toward the department). Finally, the general process operates within a context, which can also affect how the chairperson works with the faculty member.

Data Collection, Analysis, and Report Writing

Data analysis in grounded theory starts at the moment of initial contact with the phenomenon being studied, and it continues throughout the development of a grounded theory. In other words, data collection and analysis in grounded theory are concurrent and continual activities. The most popular data-collection method in grounded theory is the open-ended interview, although other strategies, especially direct observations, are often used to collect original data. Technically, any data-collection method is allowed in developing a grounded theory. Remember that what is always required in a grounded theory research study is that the theory be grounded in the data.

Data analysis in grounded theory is called the **constant comparative method,** and it involves the constant interplay between the researcher, the data, and the developing theory. Because of the active role of the researcher in this process, it is important that the researcher have **theoretical sensitivity,** a characteristic of the researcher that is present when the researcher is effective at thinking about what kinds of data need to be collected and what aspects of the already collected data are the most important for the grounded theory. It involves a mixture of analytic thinking ability, curiosity, and creativity. The theoretically sensitive researcher is able to continually ask questions of the data in order to develop a deeper and deeper understanding of the phenomenon. Over time, the theoretically sensitive researcher will be able to develop a grounded theory that meets the criteria discussed earlier (i.e., fit, understanding, generality, and control). The more research experience you get, the more theoretically sensitive you will become. If you like to ask questions, then it is very possible that you have what it takes!

The theoretically sensitive researcher attempts continually to learn by observing and listening to research participants and by examining and thinking about the data. As was just mentioned, the researcher must constantly ask questions of the data to learn what the data are saying. During analysis, ideas and hypotheses are generated and then provisionally tested, either with additional data that have already been collected or by collecting more data. When a grounded theory study involves extended fieldwork (spending many months in the field), there will be plenty of time to collect additional data to fill in gaps in the developing grounded theory. There will also be time to verify and test propositions based on the theory. As you can see, extended fieldwork is a optimal situation because you can continue to collect important data. If all the data have to be collected in one short period of time, then the conditions for developing a convincing grounded theory are not nearly as favorable.

- **Constant comparative method**
  Data analysis in grounded theory research
- **Theoretical sensitivity**
  When a researcher is effective at thinking about what kinds of data need to be collected and what aspects of already collected data are the most important for the grounded theory

Nonetheless, you still may be able to develop a tentative grounded theory that can be further developed in later research.

One of the unique parts of the grounded theory research approach is its approach to data analysis. The three types or stages of data analysis are called open coding, axial coding, and selective coding (Strauss & Corbin, 1990). **Open coding** is the first stage in grounded theory data analysis. It begins after some initial data have been collected, and it involves examining the data (usually reading transcripts line by line) and naming and categorizing discrete elements in the data. In other words, it involves labeling important words and phrases in the transcribed data. For example, let's say that you have collected interview data from twenty participants. You are reading an interview transcript and it says, "I believe that two important properties of a good teacher are caring about your students and motivating them to learn." From this phrase, you might generate the concepts teaching techniques, caring about students, and motivating students. Open coding means finding the concepts like this in your data. As you continue open coding, you would continue to see whether teaching techniques are reflected again in future comments by the same person or by another person in another interview.

Axial coding follows open coding. During **axial coding,** the researcher develops the concepts into categories (i.e., slightly more abstract concepts) and organizes the categories. The researcher then looks to see what kinds of things the participants mentioned many times (i.e., what themes appeared across the interviews). The researcher also looks for possible relationships among the categories in the data. A goal is to show how the phenomenon operates (i.e., showing its process). The researcher also asks questions like, How is the phenomenon manifested? What are its key features? What conditions bring about the phenomenon? What strategies do participants use to deal with the phenomenon? What are the consequences of those strategies? Creswell and Brown (1992) addressed many of these questions in their grounded theory. For example, looking at Figure 12.2, you will see that the characteristics of the phenomenon are listed under the title "Phenomena." The conditions that bring about the phenomenon are listed under "Causal conditions." Strategies are listed under "Strategies." And the consequences of the strategies are listed under "Outcomes."

Selective coding is the stage of data analysis in which the researcher puts the finishing touches on the grounded theory for the current research study. In particular, this is where the grounded theorist looks for the story line of the theory (i.e., the main idea) by reflecting on the data and the results that were produced during open coding and axial coding. The researcher will usually need to continue to analyze the data, but with more focus on the central idea of the developing theory. Ultimately, it is during selective coding that the researcher writes the story, explaining the grounded theory. It is here that the researcher fleshes out the details of the theory. Selective coding also involves rechecking the theory with the data to make sure that no mistakes were made. The researcher also goes to the published literature during selective coding for additional ideas to consider in developing the grounded theory and in understanding its broader significance. The grounded theorist has finished analyzing the data when **theoretical saturation** occurs. This occurs when no new information or concepts are emerging from the data and when the grounded theory has been thoroughly validated with the collected data.

A grounded theory research report reflects the process of generating a grounded theory. The major research question or topic is discussed first. The participants who were se-

■ **Open coding**
The first stage in grounded theory data analysis

■ **Axial coding**
The second stage in grounded theory data analysis

■ **Selective coding**
The final stage in grounded theory data analysis

■ **Theoretical saturation**
Occurs when no new information or concepts are emerging from the data and the grounded theory has been validated

Causal conditions

Signs
Who identifies the problem (chair or faculty member) Overt signs (e.g., lack of tenure, lack of productivity) Problems in other areas than research

Phenomena

Strategies

Outcomes

Stages of career
Beginning faculty member (1–3 years) Pretenure faculty member (3–5 years) Posttenure faculty member (before full professor) Senior faculty member (full professor to retirement)

Types of faculty issues
Getting started with research Lacks interest in research Needs to modify research agenda Needs to refocus energies Needs to strengthen promotion & tenure file Needs to revive scholarship

Administrative:
Provider Enabler **Advocate:** Advocate **Interpersonal:** Mentor Encourager Challenger Collaborator

For the faculty member (more productive, more accepting of criticism, better colleague) For the department's morale or overall productivity Too early to tell (timeframe for change) Degree of change (significant to little)

The context

Institutional expectations	Good for the individual (strength or drawbacks)
Unique discipline character	Responsibility of the chair
Whether the person can be helped	Good of the department or institution

■ **FIGURE 12.2** Creswell and Brown's model for chairpersons' role in enhancing faculty research performance

From: J. W. Creswell and M. L. Brown. "How Chairpersons Enhance Faculty Research: A Grounded Theory Study." *Reviews of Higher Education,* vol. *16*(1), p. 57. © 1992. The Association for the Study of Higher Education. Reprinted by permission of the Johns Hopkins University Press.

lected for the study and why they were selected are also discussed early in the report. Then the methods of data collection are discussed. As you know, interviews and observations are the most popular data-collection methods. The results section is the most lengthy section in the report because a grounded theory is usually based on extensive information learned in a research study. Ultimately, the final grounded theory is discussed. Glaser and Strauss, the founders of grounded theory, usually wrote book-length expositions of their grounded theories. Today, grounded theories are commonly reported in journal articles. By way of summary, we have provided an example of a grounded theory in Exhibit 12.5.

REVIEW

QUESTIONS

12.14 What are the key characteristics of grounded theory?

12.15 What are the four important characteristics of grounded theory according to Glaser and Strauss?

12.16 When does the researcher stop collecting data in grounded theory research?

■ EXHIBIT 12.5 A Grounded Theory of Instructional Leadership

Harchar and Hyle (1996) were interested in the process of instructional leadership by administrators in elementary schools. They studied known leaders (most were principals who were nominated because of their leadership abilities), and they determined what these leaders did when they were leading. Although there is much more to this journal article, we provide a quote in which they discuss their procedures first, and then we provide a quote in which they summarize their grounded theory:

> Grounded Theory served as both the theoretical structure and research design. Data collection, analysis and theory development followed Strauss and Corbin's Grounded Theory. Loosely-structured, open-ended interviews served as the primary data collection strategy. Following transcription, we subjected the data to three coding procedures: open, axial and selective. In open coding, the information was labeled, classified, and named, and categories developed in terms of their properties and dimensions, simultaneously and, at times, randomly. Through axial coding, the researcher arranged the data in new ways through the exploration of elements of context, intervening conditions, action/interaction strategies and consequences to those strategies. Selective coding, the last analytic process, resulted in the development of a story line, the gist of the phenomenon under study. On the basis of these related concepts, a theory was developed which described elementary instructional leadership. (p. 16)

Here is Harchar and Hyle's final description of their grounded theory.

Through collaborative power, instructional leaders balance power inequities in the school and school community. . . . School environments are fraught with power inequities, both experiential and knowledge-based, ranging from educational and district/building experience to knowledge and preparation expertise. Within this environment, the elementary instructional leader works to develop a common vision across staff and throughout the community. Through visioning, each organizational and community supporter is empowered with direction and purpose. The principal recognizes and supports positive behaviors and confronts and defuses negative behaviors. Trust, respect and collegiality form the foundation of the school environment as all work for the development of a quality school where staff, students and community share and work toward common, dynamic goals. The importance of all organizational members is recognized and an even playing field developed from which all can and must contribute. Consistency, honesty, and visibility are key constants. The principal must demand that all teachers voice their opinions and ideas, thus fostering problem solving, constructive discourse and ownership in an equitable school environment. Even though all principals did not use the same strategies, there were general tactics used to balance power. The strategies are not linear; they occur both simultaneously and at varying times, building on each other. (pp. 26–27)

SUMMARY

We started by summarizing the major characteristics of qualitative research. Next we discussed the four most prominent approaches to qualitative research in education. These approaches are phenomenology, ethnography, case study, and grounded theory. Although each approach follows the qualitative research paradigm, the focus of each approach is different from the others. In a phenomenology, the researcher is interested in obtaining a vivid description of individuals' experiences of some phenomenon. In ethnography, the researcher is also interested in getting into the heads of the people being studied. However, ethnographers are specifically interested in studying cultural groups, and they focus on cultural description and on relating cultural characteristics to human behavior. Case study research is a very general and inclusive approach to qualitative research. What case study researchers have in common is that they choose to call their objects of study "cases" and organize their research efforts around the study of those cases. The focus is usually on describing the characteristics of one or more cases, describing how the case or cases operate, and answering specific research questions about the case(s). In the grounded theory approach to qualitative research, researchers focus on generating a grounded theory to explain some phenomenon. Important characteristics of a grounded theory are fit, understanding, generality, and control.

KEY TERMS

axial coding (p. 384)
bracket (p. 364)
case (p. 376)
case study research (p. 376)
collective case study (p. 378)
constant comparative method (p. 383)
cross-case analysis (p. 379)
culture (p. 369)
emic perspective (p. 374)
emic terms (p. 374)
essence (p. 365)

ethnocentrism (p. 373)
ethnography (p. 369)
ethnohistory (p. 372)
ethnology (p. 372)
etic perspective (p. 374)
etic terms (p. 374)
going native (p. 374)
grounded theory (p. 381)
holism (p. 375)
instrumental case study (p. 377)
intrinsic case study (p. 377)

life-world (p. 364)
norms (p. 369)
open coding (p. 384)
phenomenology (p. 364)
qualitative research (p. 359)
selective coding (p. 384)
shared beliefs (p. 369)
shared values (p. 369)
subculture (p. 371)
theoretical saturation (p. 384)
theoretical sensitivity (p. 383)

DISCUSSION QUESTIONS

1. Which qualitative method or methods do you think would be most appropriate for studying a teacher who constantly excels above all others in his or her school?
2. What are some examples of a macro culture? What are some examples of a micro culture?
3. Do you think you have any tendency toward ethnocentrism? Can you think of an example?
4. If you are a teacher, what are some emic terms used by students at your school?
5. If you were interested in conducting an explanatory qualitative research study and you wanted to probe the issue of cause and effect, which qualitative method would you select? Why?

RESEARCH EXERCISES

1. Think of a hypothetical example of a qualitative research study that would interest you for each of the following qualitative research methods. Write a paragraph or two about each example.
   a. Phenomenology
   b. Ethnography
   c. Grounded theory
   d. Case study
2. Search ContentSelect or another database at your library. Find and then list the titles of a phenomenology, an ethnography, a grounded theory, and a case study. Also provide a brief (one paragraph) summary of each article.
3. This exercise will help you to experience phenomenology. Think about a time in your past when you were afraid. For example, you might have been afraid of the dark when you were a child. You might have been accosted by a stranger. You might have been in an accident. Try to remember how you felt, and write this down in rich detail. Compare your description with some others, and search for the essential characteristics of the phenomenon of being afraid.
4. We have pointed out repeatedly that one of the best ways to learn about research is to read published research articles. Here are several good examples of qualitative research articles. Go to the library and look at each article. Then choose *one* article to review.

Ethnography example

Deering, P. D. (1996). An ethnographic study of norms of inclusion and cooperation in a multiethnic middle school. *The Urban Review, 28*(1), 21–39.

Case study example

Abell, S. K., & Roth, M. (1994). Constructing science teaching in the elementary school: The socialization of a science enthusiast student teacher. *Journal of Research in Science Teaching, 31*(1), 77–90.

Phenomenology example

Cross, T. L., & Stewart, R. A. (1995). A phenomenological investigation of the *lebenswelt* of gifted students in rural high schools. *The Journal of Secondary Gifted Education, 6*(4), 273–280.

Grounded theory example

Neufeldt, S. A., Karno, M. P., & Nelson, M. L. (1996). A qualitative study of experts' conceptualization of supervisee reflectivity. *Journal of Counseling Psychology, 43*(1), 3–9.

Exercise Sheet

If you are proposing or conducting a qualitative study, answer the following questions.
1. Write out the tentative title of your study.
2. What do you hope to learn in your study?
3. List your research questions.
4. Who will you study? Where will you study them? How many people will you study? How long will you study them?
5. What data collection methods will you use?
6. What validity strategies will you use to help ensure the trustworthiness of your data and conclusions? (Hint: see the strategies discussed in Chapter 8.)

RELEVANT INTERNET SITES

www.groundedtheory.com/
The Grounded Theory Institute.

www.lcweb.loc.gov/folklife/other.html
The Library of Congress Resources in Ethnographic
Studies page.

www.ualberta.ca/~vanmanen/
Web page of an important writer in phenomenology,
Max Van Manen.

http://writing.colostate.edu/references/research/
casestudy/pop2b.cfm
Case studies page.

RECOMMENDED READING

Moustakas, C. (1994). *Phenomenological research methods.* Thousand Oaks, CA: Sage.

Preissle, J., LeCompte, M. D., & Tesch, R. (1997). *Ethnography and qualitative design in educational research.*
New York: Academic Press.

Schwandt, T. A. (2001). *Qualitative inquiry: A dictionary
of terms.* Thousand Oaks, CA: Sage.

Stake, R. E. (1995). *The art of case study research.* Thousand Oaks, CA: Sage.

Strauss, A. L., & Corbin, J. (1998). *Basics of qualitative research: Techniques and procedures for developing
grounded theory.* Newbury Park, CA: Sage.

Van Manen, M. (1990). *Researching the lived experience.*
London: University of Western Ontario.

Yin, R. K. (2002). *Case study research: Design and methods.* Newbury Park, CA: Sage.

ENDNOTES

1. Reprinted by permission of John Moffitt Papers, Special
   Collections, University of Virginia Library.
2. Don't be surprised if you see journal articles in which the
   authors claim to be performing case study research as
   well as another research method. The term *case study* is
   not used consistently. For example, it is not uncommon
   for ethnographers to refer to their groups as "cases"
   (LeCompte & Preissle, 1993). Similarly, other qualitative
   researchers may call the individuals or groups in their
   study "cases."

13

Historical Research

LEARNING OBJECTIVES

To be able to

- Explain what is meant by historical research.
- Explain the various reasons for conducting historical research.
- Explain how historical research is conducted.
- Differentiate between primary and secondary sources.
- Explain the meaning of external and internal criticism and why they are important when conducting historical research.
- Differentiate between positive and negative criticism.
- Recognize and explain the methodological problems that must be avoided when synthesizing the data collected and preparing the narrative account of this data.

In the United States, we frequently view adolescence as an exciting but challenging stage for the adolescent and his or her family. It spans nearly a decade, involves independence from the family, questioning and or forming one's identity, and making important decisions about the paths to be pursued in adulthood. Often, it is also a time when risky behaviors such as drug use and unprotected sex occur.

How has our definition of this stage changed through history? Think back in your own family: What were your great-grandparents doing when they were seventeen? How does the adolescence of your great-grandparents compare to your own adolescence?

In the United States, the twentieth century ushered in several changes in our culture that had an immeasurable impact on the stage of adolescence. First, secondary education became the norm (and the law) rather than the exception. In the late 1800s, only about 6 percent of 14- to 17-year-olds were enrolled in school. Obviously, that has changed dramatically with all states now having laws requiring mandatory secondary education, usually to age 16. Second, juvenile justice systems were formed. They identified juveniles as distinct from adults and in need of differential treatment. Finally, in 1938, the Fair Labor Standards Act was passed that prevented many types of child labor. In fact, for some types of work (hazardous work), the worker has to be at least 18 years of age.

As these legal and cultural changes were lengthening the time for adolescence, puberty was also occurring earlier and lengthening this life stage. In effect, childhood was ending sooner, and adulthood was beginning later. So adolescence as we know it is a relatively new phenomenon. Having this knowledge is important for several reasons. Having a historical perspective on adolescence, as this example illustrates, gives us a better understanding of this developmental stage and shows how it has changed and developed over time. It also demonstrates the importance of social and cultural factors in constructing ideas or concepts (such as adolescence) that are important to us. Historical perspectives such as this one are provided by individuals who are engaged in historical research. These are the individuals who are interested in looking back at our past to provide us with a perspective on where we have been and on how many things we take for granted change over time. As you go through this chapter, you will gain information about the way in which historical research is conducted as well as the importance of historical research.

In reading the title of this chapter, you might wonder why a chapter on historical research is included in a textbook on educational research methods. Historical research obviously has to focus on events occurring in the past, and our primary concern is with improving the current and future educational process. Throughout this book, we discuss research methods that enable us to answer research questions that focus on current educational issues. This would seem to further indicate that focusing on past events has little, if any, relevance to the solution of current educational problems. However, as we discuss later in this chapter, the past does have significance for present and future events, and historical research provides a means for capitalizing on the past. In this chapter, we discuss the methodology of historical research, how it is useful to professional educators, and the relevance it has to current educational problems.

WHAT IS HISTORICAL RESEARCH?

■ **Historical research**
The process of system-
atically examining past
events or combinations
of events to arrive at an
account of what hap-
pened in the past

Historical research is the process of systematically examining past events or combinations of events to arrive at an account of what has happened in the past (Berg, 1998). In constructing this account, it is important to realize that historical research involves much more than an accumulation of facts, dates, figures, or a description of past events, people, or developments. Historical research is interpretative. Its presentation is much more than the mere retelling of past facts. Instead it is a flowing, fluid, dynamic account of past events that attempts to recapture the complex nuances, individual personalities, and ideas that influenced the events being investigated (Berg, 1998). This does not mean that the historical researcher does not use incidents, facts, dates, and figures. Rather, the historical researcher uses this type of information but also attempts to reconstruct and present the facts and figures in a way that communicates an understanding of the events from the multiple points of view of those who participated in them. In presenting these multiple points of view, the historian's own interpretation is also very much a part of history. In fact, that is the very heart of historical interpretation. Historians openly acknowledge their own biases in a way few other scholars do. Whether the historian is liberal or conservative, black or white, male or female matters a great deal in the account of the historical event being investigated and the interpretation of the facts and incidents surrounding that event.

To illustrate this use of facts and data, look at Fultz's (1995) account of the African American schools in the south from 1890–1940.

> 93.4 percent of the 24,079 African American schools in fourteen southern states in 1925–26 were rural. Of the total, more than three-fourths (82.6 percent) were one-teacher (63.8 percent) or two-teacher (18.8 percent) facilities. Moreover, almost three-fourths (73.9 percent) of the African American teachers in these states taught in rural schools. (p. 402)

Now look at the way in which Fultz (1995) continued this discussion of African American schools by moving into the interpretative phase, which provides a dynamic and fluid account not only of the condition of the schools, but also of the effect that these conditions had on the delivery of instructional services.

> In addition, the literature is replete with references to the deplorable physical condition of many African American schools, a pervasive state of disrepair that potentially undermined the delivery of instructional services. Among the signs of neglect were rickety benches with and without backs, holes in the floor and the roof, inadequate heating, poor lighting, unpainted walls, dilapidated steps, unkempt surroundings, and a lack of desks and other educational supplies and materials. (p. 403)

This narrative account of events and accompanying interpretations presented as a story provides far more than just a retelling of the facts. It provides a rich account of the development of the historical events and gives the reader an idea of the circumstances that shaped the events of the past.

SIGNIFICANCE OF HISTORICAL RESEARCH

Why should we want to study the history of education? If you are a history buff, you realize that events that happened in the past are often very interesting. For example, it is very interesting to read an account detailing the educational system that existed in rural America in the 1800s and the difficulties that children and families of that time had to endure to receive even a minimal education. Berg (1998) has identified five reasons for conducting historical research:

1. To uncover the unknown
2. To answer questions
3. To identify the relationship that the past has to the present
4. To record and evaluate the accomplishments of individuals, agencies, or institutions
5. To aid in our understanding of the culture in which we live

Some of these reasons mgiht seem very apparent and logical, and others might not. For example, uncovering the unknown might seem somewhat strange because historical research focuses on past events, and past events should already be known. For any of a variety of reasons, however, significant events often go unrecorded. For example, Fultz (1995) observed that the content of the journals devoted to information about African Americans in the early 1900s virtually ignored any discussion of black teachers and their social roles and community contributions. Without the systematic investigation and documentation of these events and roles, we would have little knowledge or appreciation of the contributions made by black teachers in the early part of the twentieth century.

Providing answers to questions is probably one of the most logical and apparent reasons for conducting historical research. As a teacher or student, you might have wondered what it was like to go to school in the 1800s or just how severely teachers disciplined children in the early part of the twentieth century. These are obviously questions that require historical research. Many other questions could be asked about past educational practices, policies, or events.

Historical research is also conducted to identify the relationship that the past has to the present. It might seem strange that we should conduct historical research to find out something about the present. However, the past can give us a perspective for current decision making and help to avoid the phenomenon of trying to reinvent the wheel. The past can also provide information about what strategies have and have not worked. In other words, it allows us to discover those things that have been tried and found wanting and those things that have been inadequately tried and still might work. For example, a neighbor of one of the authors (Christensen) was a historian engaged in documenting the history of one of the banks in Houston, Texas. Christensen asked why the bank would want someone to record its history. The neighbor stated that prior historical analysis of various banks has indicated that bank officials tend to repeat mistakes and having a record of their history and the mistakes they had previously made should help them avoid such mistakes in the future. Kaestle (1997), in his discussion of the history of American education, pointed out school decentralization—making community boards responsible for making many of the decisions involved in the operation of regular elementary and secondary education rather than having these decisions made at a central education agency—was debated vigorously in the 1960s. Advocates of decentralization used information from the past to point out that centralization was used by the social elites in the early twentieth century to control urban education, protect the social structure, and impose certain values on the children of that time. Centralization, it was argued, was an undemocratic means of social control. This is just one example of individuals using past experience as an argument for present policy on the assumption that the experience of the past would be repeated if similar policies were implemented again. Those responsible for educational policy and planning might be able to profit from knowing what has and has not worked in the past. Frequently, past events can be used in the formulation of current policy and procedure by allowing individuals to capitalize on what has and has not been effective.

Historical research is frequently conducted to record the accomplishments of a noted individual or the history of an agency or institution. For example, an educational researcher might be interested in documenting the development and growth of private, church-supported schools. Historically, Catholic churches have operated schools and provided education primarily for children of the Catholic faith. However, other denominations have increasingly moved into the educational field and participated in the education of the youth of the United States. Other educational researchers may be interested in recording the accomplishments of a noted individual in the field of education. Jonathan Messerli (1972), for example, profiled the life of Horace Mann, the individual who has been viewed as the founder of public education.

Historical research is also conducted to assist us in understanding the culture in which we live. Education has always been a part of our history. It is as much a part of our culture as anything we could possibly imagine. In discussing the history of U.S. education, Kaestle (1997) points out that before the 1950s, individuals writing about the history of American education focused almost entirely on the public school system. However, the history of education is a broader phenomenon that must include the history of schooling, which includes agencies of instruction other than schools, such as the family, the workplace, and the churches (Kaestle, 1997). In the broadest definition of education, it includes every aspect of socialization, which means it is a cultural event.

REVIEW

QUESTIONS

13.1 What is historical research?

13.2 Why would someone want to do historical research?

13.3 How can historical research tell us anything about the present?

HISTORICAL RESEARCH METHODOLOGY

How is historical research conducted? The uninformed individual seems to think that historical research is divided into two phases (Carr, 1963), collecting and reading material related to the topic of the research and writing the manuscript or book from the notes taken on the material that was collected. Carr (1963) points out that this is a very unrealistic picture of the methodology followed. For Carr (1963) the process is one of back-and-forth between reading and writing. After reading some of the primary sources, Carr begins writing—and not necessarily at the beginning. After writing a certain amount, he returns to reading about additional sources relating to his chosen topic. Carr finds that the writing helps direct the reading because the more he writes, the more he knows what he is looking for and what he needs to read.

This is an overview of just one person's approach, and Carr acknowledges that others probably use a somewhat different approach. Some individuals conduct an exhaustive search for historical information and read and digest this information before organizing and writing the historical account. Kaestle (1992, 1997) has even stated that there is no agreed-on methodology for conducting historical research, and historians are constantly looking to other disciplines for methods or theories. This does not mean that there is no consistency in the way in which historical research is conducted. Its general methodology has much in common with the other research methods we have discussed in this book. In general, historical research adheres to the following steps, although there is overlap and a movement back and forth between these steps.

1. Identification of the research topic and formulation of the research problem or question
2. Data collection or literature review
3. Evaluation of materials
4. Data synthesis
5. Report preparation or preparation of the narrative exposition

We discuss each of these steps in some detail.

IDENTIFICATION OF THE RESEARCH TOPIC AND FORMULATION OF THE RESEARCH PROBLEM OR QUESTION

As with any type of educational research, the first step is to identify a topic you wish to investigate and then formulate the research problem or question you wish to answer. The research topics chosen by investigators can be stimulated by any of a variety of sources. Current issues in education are frequently the stimulus for a research study. For example, during the decade of the 1990s, there was a movement away from affirmative action policies in college admission. You might want to know what led to the affirmative action policy in the first place and why this policy, which was implemented for decades, is now being reversed.

A research topic could also result from an interest in the impact of a specific individual, institution, or social movement on educational policy and/or reform. For example, you might know of someone who has spent his or her professional life working for the improvement of the education of children from the ghetto. If this individual made significant strides in this direction in the face of continued adversity, a record of his or her accomplishments and the process of gaining these accomplishments may be of significance to the field of education and worthy of investigation.

You might also be interested in exploring the relationship among different events. For example, during the 1960s, busing—moving children from one neighborhood school to another in an attempt to create a specific racial/ethnic mix of children in each public school—was initiated. A number of questions could be asked about the effect of implementing this policy. What effect did busing have on the quality of education that the children received? Did busing have any effect on the decisions that many parents made about where their children were educated? Parents could go along with the busing decision, for example, or they could send their children to private school. Why is busing no longer being implemented?

You might even think that past events that have been presented by educational historians can be interpreted in a different and more appropriate way. Kaestle (1997), for example, has observed that during the past twenty-five to thirty years, the traditional methods and assumptions of American historians have increasingly come under attack. Until about 1950, the assumption of most American educational historians was that the history of education was almost exclusively related to the history of public school systems and that public universal schooling was a good thing. Since that time, this view has increasingly come under attack as more recent American educational historians have focused on education being delivered by agencies (e.g., church, family) other than the public school. Additionally, some American educational historians have questioned the notion that public education was universally good.

Research topics leading to historical research can come from a variety of sources and can focus on many different topics and events. Table 13.1 lists examples of research studies conducted by educational historians. As you can see, these topics cover many diverse areas in the field of education.

TABLE 13.1 Examples of Research Studies Conducted by Educational Historians

- Cleverly, J. (1991). *The schooling of China: Tradition and modernity in Chinese education.* North Sydney, Australia: Allen and Unwin.
- Fultz, M. (1995). African American teachers in the south, 1890–1940: Powerlessness and the ironies of expectations and protest. *History of Education Quarterly, 37,* 401–422.
- Galenson, D. W. (1995). Determinants of the school attendance of boys in early Chicago. *History of Education Quarterly, 37,* 371–400.
- Mitch, D. F. (1992). *The rise of popular literacy in Victorian England: The influence of private choice and public policy.* Philadelphia: University of Pennsylvania Press.
- Osgood, R. L. (1997). Undermining the common school ideal: Intermediate schools and ungraded classes in Boston, 1838–1900. *History of Education Quarterly, 37,* 375–398.
- Reuben, J. A. (1997). Beyond politics: Community civics and the redefinition of citizenship in the progressive era. *History of Education Quarterly, 37,* 399–420.
- Rosner, L. (1991). *Medical education in the age of improvement: Edinburgh students and apprentices, 1760–1826.* Edinburgh: Edinburgh University Press.
- Tomiak, J., ed. (1991). *Schooling, educational policy, and ethnic identity: Comparative studies on governments and non-dominant ethnic groups in Europe, 1850–1940* (vol. 1). New York: New York University Press.

DATA COLLECTION OR LITERATURE REVIEW

Once you have decided on a research topic, the next step is to identify the sources that will contain information about your research topic and then locate these sources. The identification, location, and collection of related information make up the data collection or literature review stage of historical research. This stage is similar to the literature review you would conduct for other types of educational research, because in qualitative and quantitative studies, you conduct a literature review to locate studies that have been conducted in the past. These studies tell you what is known about your given research topic. In historical research, a similar process takes place. However, the sources containing the information you need are quite different from those of other types of educational research. In historical research, the information you seek may be contained in documents, records, photographs, relics, and interviews rather than in professional journals and books.

The documents or records that are of interest to the educational historian typically consist of written or printed materials such as diplomas, cartoons, diaries, memoirs, newspapers, yearbooks, memos, periodicals, reports, files, attendance records, census reports, budgets, maps, and tests. Actually, just about anything that is printed or written down and relating to the chosen research topic would represent a document or record that you would want to obtain and, perhaps, use in your final narrative account of your chosen topic.

Oral histories or oral records are another source of information the educational historian might want to use. **Oral histories** or records consist of interviews that the educational historian may conduct with a person who has had direct or indirect experience with or knowledge of the chosen topic. Rand Evans, a psychological historian who was gathering information on E. B. Titchener, an individual who was influential in the development of the field of psychology, had gathered a wealth of information from available records and documents. However, he also wanted to talk to someone who knew Titchener personally. The only problem was finding such a person. From the information Evans had collected, he knew where Titchener resided at the time of his death, so he placed an advertisement in that city's newspaper asking any relative of Titchener to contact him. After placing several of these advertisements and getting no response, Evans was discouraged and assumed that he was not going to make contact with a relative of Titchener. A friend of Evans encouraged him to try one more time, which he did. This time, one of Titchener's relatives saw the advertisement and contacted Evans, much to his delight. Evans then proceeded to set up a time and place to interview this individual and obtain an oral record of information about Titchener. Oral records are not, however, limited to interviews with people. They may also consist of stories, tales, songs, or other forms of oral expression.

Relics can also be used as a source of information. A relic is any object whose physical or visual characteristics can provide information about the past. Relics may be articles of clothing, buildings, books, architectural plans, desks, or any other object that may provide information about the past.

■ **Oral histories**
Interviews with a person who has had direct or indirect experience with or knowledge of the chosen topic

Research
Navigator.com

oral history

HOW TO LOCATE HISTORICAL INFORMATION

Libraries, particularly the larger university libraries such as the one that exists at the University of Texas, are good sources of information because they typically have collections of things such as rare books, letters, periodicals, personal papers, and old maps. Once in such a library, you can make use of reference books such as *Reference Sources in History: An Introductory Guide,* by Fritze, Coutts, and Vyhnanek (1990); *Guide to Historical Literature* by Norton (1995); and *Biographical Dictionary of American Educators* by Ohles (1978) to locate relevant information.

If you are not close to a large library, you may want to first identify a repository that may contain the information you desire. The National Historical Publications and Records Commission publishes the *Directory of Archives and Manuscript Repositories in the United States* (1988), which contains a list of repositories in the United States. Additionally, the *National Inventory of Documentary Sources in the United States* provides a list of federal documents and libraries.

One very good source of historical information is the National Archives, which contains records of the U.S. government. The National Archives is an extremely valuable resource containing documents, cartographic items, video and sound recordings, photographs, and reels of motion picture film all created by various government agencies since the creation of our nation. These documents and other historical items exist in various record centers, presidential libraries, and regional archives.

In locating historical information about a given topic, you must remember that you are conducting an educational study. Therefore, you should also consider local courthouses and school board central offices as well as individual schools as possible information sources. Additionally, oral histories should not be forgotten, because they can provide information that frequently cannot be obtained in any other way (Yow, 1994). Oral histories can provide insight and an understanding of the cause or motive for an event that might not be accessible in any other form because the information was not recorded. However, there are limitations in the use of oral histories. Oral histories tend to focus on personal experiences, but these experiences take place in the larger context of a specific sociopolitical climate. It is important to consider the local, national, or international trends taking place at the time of the targeted event and consider the relationship between these events and the personal experiences reported by the individual or individuals providing the oral history.

Oral histories are naturally limited to individuals who are still alive, and these individuals tend to be older people. The oral history is therefore confined to the experiences, memory, and interpretations of a selected group of individuals who must rely upon their memory to relay past events. Recall of events changes with the passage of time and every individual selectively remembers past events. To overcome some of these biases, Yow (1994) recommends interviewing a range of individuals from the most confident and articulate to those with compromised verbal skills. In conducting this interview, Yow (1994) recommends that you include questions such as the following:

- If you were writing this study, what would you include?
- Who would you recommend I interview?
- If you were writing this history, what would you consider important?
- Who was present at that event?
- Who was instrumental in making this happen?
- Who was affected by this?

Although these are obviously not all the questions you would want to ask, they do represent some of the ones that might be overlooked and can lead to focusing on important issues and interviewing other individuals who may provide important insights and information.

Primary versus Secondary Sources

As you locate and acquire the documents, records, oral histories, or other sources needed to prepare your narrative of the topic or event you have selected to research, you need to classify these sources as primary or secondary. A **primary source** is a source in which the creator was a direct witness or in some other way directly involved or related to the event. Examples of primary sources are a diary, an original map, a song or ballad, a transcript of an oral interview conducted with a person who participated in an event, the minutes of a board meeting, court decisions and the arguments that accompany them, and a photograph of a World War II battle scene. A **secondary source** is a source that was created from primary sources, other secondary sources, or some combination of primary and secondary sources. A secondary source is therefore a source that is at least one step removed from direct contact, involvement, or relationship with the event being researched. The most useful and accurate secondary sources are probably those that have been created by scholarly historians using primary sources. Scholarly historians have written articles and books about all types of events ranging from battles and court decisions to accounts of ethical violations such as the Tuskegee experiments that we discussed in the chapter on ethics (Chapter 4). Other secondary sources are history textbooks or encyclopedias. However, history textbooks and encyclopedias are secondary sources that are even more removed from the actual event being described and frequently viewed as the least useful sources of information.

- **Primary source**
  A source in which the creator was a direct witness or in some other way directly involved or related to the event
- **Secondary source**
  A source that was created from primary sources, secondary sources, or some combination of the two

13.4 What are the steps involved in the conduct of historical research?

13.5 Identify the sources of historical research topics?

13.6 What type of information is used when conducting a historical research study?

13.7 Where would you find the information needed for a historical study?

13.8 What is the difference between a primary source and a secondary source?

REVIEW

QUESTIONS

EVALUATION OF HISTORICAL SOURCES

An educational researcher who is engaged in a historical study must evaluate every source of information obtained for its authenticity and accuracy regardless of whether that source is a document, map, photograph, or oral history. Every piece of material has to be tested for its truthfulness because any source can be affected by factors such as prejudice, social or economic conditions, political climate, and religious background. These are the kinds of biases that color every historian's interpretation. This means that a document might be slanted to reflect a particular bias of its author. An old photograph or document might appear to represent a given event when, in fact, it has been forged, deliberately altered, or even falsified. Even if a document has not been deliberately altered or falsified, it could be affected by the particular bias a person may have or the political or economic climate existing at the time. For example, an educational historian writing about an educational event during the Depression would probably have his or her view and interpretation of the event colored by the depressed economy of that time. Educational historians must therefore view every source with a critical eye, and every source must pass two kinds of evaluations before it is used to construct the narration of the event being researched. Every source must be evaluated in terms of external and internal criticism.

External Criticism

■ **External criticism**
The validity, trustworthiness, or authenticity of the source

External criticism refers to the validity, trustworthiness, or authenticity of the source. In other words, was the document, diary, or memo really created by the author to whom it was attributed? Was the photograph or map really produced at the time specified and does it depict the events occurring at that time? In other words, the historian has to determine whether the document, record, or other source is what it claims to be or has been falsified in some way. Unfortunately, throughout history there have been notable examples of hoaxes. For example, in the early 1980s, two men sold sixty volumes of what were supposed to be Adolf Hitler's diaries to the German magazine *Stern* for the tidy sum of $3 million dollars. Several years later, *Stern* discovered that the diaries were false and sued the sellers, resulting in their returning the money and being sent to prison (Hitler diaries, 1985). Obviously, if *Stern* had been more diligent about checking the authenticity of the volumes, they would never have purchased the forged diaries. Hoaxes such as this are quite rare and, as is evident from the case just mentioned, typically motivated by financial gain.

Sometimes the validity of documents or other sources can be easily established by handwriting; age of the paper on which the documents are written; signatures; and, particularly, if they have been filed, collected, and archived under the name of the author(s) (Christy, 1975). In other instances, it is more difficult to validate a source because, for example, a document could be ghostwritten. Although you can never be completely certain about the validity of your sources, you can attempt to acquire information that will maximize the probability that the sources used are valid. For example, you can attempt to get answers to questions such as who wrote a particular document, when the document was written, and whether different versions of the document exist. At times, it might be necessary to obtain the services of specialists such as handwriting experts or linguists who are knowledgeable about the dialects or writing style of a given period. You might even want to carbon-date a particular source to ensure that it was produced during a given era. In most instances, it is not necessary to go to such extremes because, as with other areas of research, authors attempt to be as accurate and valid as possible. In most instances, the documents and other information sources used by the educational historian are authentic, which means that historians typically spend little time focusing on the phase of external criticism.

Internal Criticism

After the educational historian has done everything possible to ensure that his or her documents and other sources are valid and authentic and, if secondary sources are used, that they are true to the original, the researcher is ready for the process of internal criticism. **Internal criticism** refers to the reliability or accuracy of the information contained in the sources collected. In making an assessment of reliability or accuracy, the educational historian must first engage in positive criticism (Christy, 1975). By **positive criticism** we mean that the educational historian must be sure that he or she understands the statements made or the meaning conveyed in the various sources. For example, Supreme Court decisions must frequently be converted into policy at the local level. This means that the agencies and people affected by a decision must interpret its text and meaning. The words, terms, and phrases of the decision must be interpreted properly for the decision to be carried out appropriately. This interpretation becomes even more difficult for the historian because words and colloquialisms may take on new meanings over time or be foreign to the investigator. Kaestle (1997) states that this is a problem of vagueness and presentism. **Vagueness** refers to uncertainty in the meaning of words or phrases. As an example of vagueness, Kaestle (1997) points out that it is commonplace in educational history to see the notion that industrialization caused educational reform. However, this statement has the potential of communicating different things to different people unless the terms *industrialization* and *educational reform* are defined. Additionally, it is difficult to assess and document the relationship between industrialization and educational reform without a strict definition of these terms.

Presentism refers to the assumption that the present-day connotations of terms also existed in the past. It is not uncommon for the meaning of terms to change over time. There are examples of terms that have a specific present-day meaning or connotation that either did not exist in the past or was something totally different. For example, a person who was called "square" in the early 1900s was considered to be honest, upright, or trustworthy. Fifty years later, the connotation was that a "square" person was someone who was unsophisticated or had conservative tastes (Christy, 1975). Similarly, in the eighteenth century, a public educational institution was an institution where children learned collectively, and the educational endeavor was for the public good as opposed to selfish gain. The educational institutions of that time were financed by tuition and were considered and called "public" institutions. Present-day terminology would have labeled them "private" institutions (Kaestle, 1997) because they were financed by tuition rather than being state supported.

Once the researcher has satisfied the criterion of positive criticism, he or she moves to the phase of negative criticism (Christy, 1975). **Negative criticism** refers to establishing the reliability or authenticity and accuracy of the content of the documents and other sources used by educational historians. The negative criticism phase is the more difficult because it requires the educational historian to make a judgment about the authenticity and accuracy of what is contained in the source. Although most authors attempt to be as accurate as possible in their production of documents, photographs, maps, or other sources of evidence, there are times when inaccurate statements are made. For example, in June 1974 (Holy Horatio, 1974), a brief article appeared in *Time* magazine revealing that the biography Herbert Mayes had written of Horatio Alger in the 1920s was filled with contradictions, absurd fabrications, and invented events and occurrences derived totally from his imagination. This biography had served as the standard reference work on Alger for more than forty years and was quoted by historians and scholars during this time. Fortunately, such inaccurate statements are rare because historians typically make every effort possible to avoid making inaccurate statements.

Firsthand accounts by witnesses to an event are frequently assumed to be the most reliable and accurate. However, eyewitness accounts can be biased, and there is a tendency for

■ **Internal criticism**
The reliability or accuracy of the information contained in the sources collected

■ **Positive criticism**
Ensuring that the statements made or the meaning conveyed in the various sources is correct

■ **Vagueness**
Uncertainty in the meaning of words or phrases

■ **Presentism**
The assumption that the present-day connotations of terms also existed in the past

■ **Negative criticism**
Establishing the reliability or authenticity and accuracy of the content of the documents and other sources used by the researcher

memory to fade over time and the gaps in memory to be filled in with plausible details. To get an example of the differences that can exist in memory, all you have to do is ask two or more people to recall the details of some event such as an automobile accident or a school board meeting. This does not mean that there is any deliberate attempt to distort the event that was witnessed. Rather, each person has different motivations and attends to different components of an event.

Just think of a physician, a law enforcement officer, and an insurance agent witnessing a car accident and then making reports on it. The physician will probably focus on the severity of the injuries sustained by the passengers. The law enforcement officer will most likely focus on the speed the car was traveling, road conditions, and traffic conditions. The insurance agent will probably focus on the amount of damage the automobile sustained. Because of his or her training, prejudices, or prior experience, each person will focus on different aspects of the event, which will lead to very different reports. The educational historian attempts to take the background and prior experience that color a report of an event into account when establishing the accuracy of the contents of a document.

If eyewitness accounts represent a biased account, how does the educational historian establish the accuracy of his or her source material? Wineburg (1991), in his analysis of the way in which historians handle evidence, concluded that three heuristics—corroboration, sourcing, and contextualization—were used in evaluating documents. **Corroboration** refers to comparing documents to each other to determine whether they provide the same information or reach the same conclusions. For example, several of the documents used in Wineburg's (1991) study focused on the size of the colonial force that assembled on Lexington Green in Massachusetts. One document listed the size of the force at 300 to 400 men. This document was compared with other documents that provided indirect information about the size of the colonial force, but this information suggested that the size of the force was considerably smaller.

Sourcing, the second heuristic identified by Wineburg (1991), refers to information that identifies "the source or attribution of the document" (p. 79). In other words, sourcing refers to identifying the author, the date of creation of the document, and the place it was created. This information allows the historian to dismiss information created by a novelist or from a secondary source such as a textbook written long after the event occurred. Additionally, it allows the historian to identify the distance in time between the documentation of an event and its actual occurrence. For example, a historian might well consider an account of a battle recorded as the battle was being fought to be more accurate than a participant's account several days after the battle was fought. Sourcing therefore provides information that is used in judging the trustworthiness and accuracy of the content of a document.

Contextualization, the third heuristic identified by Wineburg (1991), refers to the identification of when and where an event took place. The "when" component of this heuristic involves placing events in chronological order and requires historians to focus on the sequencing of events. The "where" component of this heuristic involves identifying where an event took place as well as identifying the conditions that existed at the time of occurrence, such as the weather, landscape, and geography of the surrounding area. The contextualization heuristic is very important because it not only identifies order of the events that took place, but it also assists in the interpretative phase of the narration of the event. For example, one of the historians in Wineburg's (1991) study used information about the time

■ **Corroboration**
Comparing documents to each other to determine whether they provide the same information or reach the same conclusion

■ **Sourcing**
Information that identifies the source or attribution of the document

■ **Contextualization**
The identification of when and where an event took place

of occurrence of an event in one of the documents "to reconstruct the intelligence network of the Minutemen, making inferences about when the colonists must have learned that the British were setting out from Boston" (p. 82).

The three heuristics identified by Weinburg (1991) are important in the evaluation of historical documents. Although historians probably do make use of methods and procedures other than those identified by Weinburg, his study did identify three important characteristics of the historical method. In evaluating documents, historians compare information sources, give critical attention to the sources of their documents, and attend to the chronological and geographical context in which the event took place.

DATA SYNTHESIS AND REPORT PREPARATION

The last task the educational historian must accomplish is synthesizing, or putting together the materials collected, and writing the narrative account of the topic or event selected. **Synthesis,** therefore, refers to the selection, organization, and analysis of the materials collected. The information that has passed the test of internal and external criticism is sorted and categorized into topical themes and central ideas or concepts. These themes and ideas are then pulled together so that there is a continuity between them. A chronological ordering of events is frequently helpful.

■ **Synthesis**
The selection, organization, and analysis of the materials collected

As the researcher is synthesizing the material collected, he or she will typically begin the narrative account of the topic or event selected. This will consist of a narration of the patterns, connections, and insights uncovered from the synthesis of the documents and other source materials collected. In synthesizing the material collected and preparing the narrative account, the educational researcher should always be aware of four methodological problems that must be avoided (Kaestle, 1997). The first problem is the confusion of correlation and causation. In statistics courses and methods courses such as this one, you will repeatedly hear the admonition to make sure that you do not try to infer causation from correlational evidence. Just because two phenomena occur together or one proceeds another does not mean that one caused the other. For example, urban Irish families in the United States during the 1800s did not send their children to school as often as did parents of other ethnic groups (Kaestle, 1997). However, this does not mean that being Irish caused low school attendance. Obviously, many other factors, such as socioeconomic status, could have contributed to the low school attendance. Whenever we deal with correlational evidence, we must avoid the temptation of inferring causation regardless of how tempting it may be or how logical it seems.

A second problem that must be attended to is the problem of defining and interpreting key words, terms, and phrases. As we discussed earlier in this chapter, this boils down to the dual issues of vagueness and presentism. Not only must terms be defined so as to avoid ambiguity, but also close attention should be paid to the connotation of terms as they existed during the time in which the historical event took place.

A third problem identified by Kaestle (1997) is that educational historians should make sure that they differentiate between evidence indicating how people should behave and evidence indicating how they did in fact behave. For example, Kaestle (1997) points out that educators and physicians in the late 1830s in the northeastern part of the United States encouraged parents to keep children under age five or six at home. These professionals believed that school attendance of children this age was unwise, dangerous to their health, and a nuisance to teachers. This evidence might lead one to infer that children began school at age five or six. However, such an inference would be incorrect, because census data and statistical school reports revealed that parents sent three- and four-year-old children to school until local regulations enacted in the 1850s and 1860s forced them to keep these children at home. This example demonstrates that there was a lag between the opinion of the professionals and popular behavior, and educational historians must be alert to such differences.

The final problem that educational historians must avoid when constructing their narrative account is maintaining a distinction between intent and consequences. Historians, because they conduct their research after events have taken place, run the risk of assuming that the historical actors were aware of the full consequences of their ideas and actions. In other words, there is the risk of assuming that the consequences observed from some policy or activity were the consequences intended. For example, school busing for racial balance, which was implemented in the 1960s, led to the growth of private schools in many parts of the United States. To assume that this consequence was one of the intents of busing would be totally inaccurate. This is the type of inappropriate connection that must be avoided by the educational historian.

Constructing the narrative account of a historical event is a difficult process requiring the synthesis of a wealth of information. In reading and synthesizing this information, the educational historian must not only make judgments regarding the accuracy and authenticity of his or her information, but also avoid making certain assumptions such as those just discussed.

When writing the narrative account of a historical event, you should adhere to the style presented in *The Chicago Manual of Style* (University of Chicago Press, 1993). Most quantitative and qualitative research reports make use of the writing style presented in the *Publication Manual of the American Psychological Association* (1994), although some of these journals will accept research reports prepared according to either style. Historical studies, however, are usually prepared following *The Chicago Manual of Style.*

REVIEW

QUESTIONS

13.9 What is the difference between external criticism and internal criticism?

13.10 What is meant by positive criticism?

13.11 What is meant by vagueness and presentism, and how do these relate to positive criticism?

13.12 What is meant by negative criticism, and how does a person conducting a historical study achieve negative criticism?

13.13 What methodological problems might a person encounter when synthesizing material and preparing the narrative report?

SUMMARY

Historical research attempts to arrive at an account of what has happened in the past by systematically examining past events or combinations of events. This account represents a flowing, fluid, and dynamic account of facts, dates, people, and figures as well as an interpretation of them to capture the nuances, personalities, and ideas that influenced the events being investigated.

Historical research is conducted for multiple reasons. It is conducted to uncover the unknown; to answer questions; to identify the relationship that the past has to the present; to record and evaluate the accomplishments of individuals, agencies, or institutions; and to aid in our understanding of the culture in which we live. Conducting historical research involves a series of activities, including the identification of the research topic and formulating the research problem or research question, reviewing the available literature or collecting the information related to the research topic, evaluating the collected information, synthesizing the information, and preparing the narrative exposition.

Historical research topics can originate from any of a variety of sources, such as a current educational issue or the impact of an individual, institution, or social movement on the field of education. Research topics can also originate from an interest in investigating the relationship between several historical events or from a desire to look at a different way of interpreting a historical event. The point is that historical research topics can originate from many different sources.

Collecting information on a historical topic involves locating documents, records, and relics. This information can generally be found in university libraries or repositories such as the National Archives. Oral histories are also valuable sources of information about many historical topics. They can provide insight and an understanding of the cause or motive for an event that may not be available from other sources. Oral histories are, however, confined to the experiences, memory, and interpretations of the individuals who provide them and might be biased by the passage of time and the selective memory for events.

The information sources collected are classified as primary or secondary. Primary sources are those in which the creator was a direct witness or was in some other way directly involved in or related to the event. A secondary source is one that was created from primary sources. Primary sources are generally viewed as the more valuable sources of information.

Regardless of whether an information source is primary or secondary, it must be evaluated for its accuracy and authenticity. This means that each information source must pass the test of external criticism and internal criticism. External criticism refers to the validity, trustworthiness, or authenticity of the source. Internal criticism refers to the reliability or accuracy of the information contained in the material collected. In making this assessment of reliability and accuracy, the educational historian must engage in positive and negative criticism. Positive criticism means that the educational historian must be sure he or she understands the statements made and the meaning conveyed in the source material. Negative criticism refers to the accuracy or authenticity of the statements made or the content of the source materials. In establishing the accuracy of his or her source material, historians use the three heuristics of corroboration, sourcing, and contextualization.

The final task of the educational historian is to synthesize the data collected and write the narrative account of the historical event or issue researched. In preparing this narrative account, the educational historian must avoid the methodological problems of confusing correlation and causation, misinterpreting key terms, words, and phrases, failing to differentiate between evidence indicating how people should behave and how they did behave, and failing to maintain a distinction between intent and consequences.

KEY TERMS

contextualization (p. 402)
corroboration (p. 402)
external criticism (p. 400)
historical research (p. 392)
internal criticism (p. 401)

negative criticism (p. 401)
oral histories (p. 397)
positive criticism (p. 401)
primary source (p. 399)
presentism (p. 401)

secondary source (p. 399)
sourcing (p. 402)
synthesis (p. 403)
vagueness (p. 401)

> **STUDY TIP**   Visit the book's companion website at www.ablongman.com/johnsonchristensen2e for study questions and multiple-choice questions to find out how well you have mastered the material in this chapter. Also look at the other activities we have included to promote your mastery of the material in this chapter.

DISCUSSION QUESTIONS

1. How do you believe historical researchers approach or should approach the issue of cause and effect in history?
2. What do you see as the advantages and disadvantages of primary sources?
3. What do you see as the advantages and disadvantages of secondary sources?
4. Which do you trust more: external or internal criticism? Why?
5. How strongly do you believe historical writings are influenced by the historian doing the writing? What kinds of checks and balances are in place? Should others be added?

RESEARCH EXERCISES

1. The following article is one that is representative of the type of research conducted by educational historians. Get this article from the library, and read it to gain some idea of historical research conducted in the field of education.

   Murphy, M. F. (1997). Unmaking and remaking the "One Best System." London, Ontario, 1852–1860. *History of Education Quarterly, 37,* 291–309.

   After reading this article, answer the following questions.

   a. What was the author's purpose in conducting this historical research?
   b. How does the presentation of this historical research differ from the presentation of quantitative research?
   c. Identify at least one primary and one secondary source used by the author.
2. Using Research Navigator, locate an educational history journal article and answer the following questions:
   a. What were the topic and purpose of the research?
   b. What kinds of data were collected?
   c. Briefly summarize the narrative findings.
   d. Locate an example in which the writer provides evidence of the trustworthiness of the data based on external criticism and based on internal criticism.
   e. What is your overall evaluation of this manuscript?

RELEVANT INTERNET SITES

www.dohistory.org/
Award-winning site on doing history.

**http://maple.lemoyne.edu/~hevern/
nr-method.html#oralhistory**
Oral history.

**http://maple.lemoyne.edu/~hevern/
nr-method.html#oralhistory**
The 10 Commandments of Good Historical Writing.

RECOMMENDED READING

Gray, W. (1991). *Historian's handbook: A key to the study and writing of history.* Prospect Heights, IL: Waveland.

Iggers, G. (1997). *Historiography in the twentieth century: From scientific objectivity to the postmodern challenge.* Middletown, CT: Wesleyan.

Prevenier, W., & Howell, M. C. Howell (2001). *From reliable sources: An introduction to historical methods.* Cornell, NY: Cornell University Press.

14

Mixed Method and Mixed Model Research

LEARNING OBJECTIVES

To be able to

- List the major strengths and weaknesses of qualitative research.
- List the major strengths and weaknesses of quantitative research.
- Define mixed research, mixed model research, and mixed method research.
- Explain the difference between mixed method and mixed model research.
- Explain how to use the notational system that is used to depict mixed method designs.
- Compare and contrast the mixed model research designs.
- Compare and contrast the nine mixed method research designs.
- List the five purposes or rationale for conducting a mixed research study.
- Describe the eight major steps in the mixed research process.
- Explain the strengths and limitations of mixed research.

One evening in December 2001, Garmzaban was with two of his friends in a mall food court in Baltimore, Maryland, when they were approached by 16-year-old Christopher Williams and 18-year-old Richard Rodriguez. Williams and Rodriguez told Garmzaban that they wanted to purchase some marijuana. Although Garmzaban did not know either of them, he agreed to sell Williams and Rodriguez the marijuana. Williams said that his car was on the south side of the mall and the money he needed to pay for the marijuana was in the car. Garmzaban agreed to drive Williams to his car. When they arrived at his car, Williams pulled out a gun and told Garmzaban to hand over the marijuana he was carrying. Garmzaban, a former high school wrestler, started to fight with Williams. However, Williams had the gun, and he fatally shot Garmzaban in the chest (O'Brien, 2002).

Drug-related deaths such as this one are not uncommon, as Thomasina Piercy knows firsthand. Her oldest son died of a heroin overdose, stimulating her to action. In 2001, she started a drug awareness program at all of the schools in the county where she lives (McMenamin, 2002). She set up a 24-hour crisis hot line for students, an ambitious program of parent presentations, and an encyclopedic volume of substance abuse information that she publishes in school newsletters each month. She and her team of community leaders also added skits designed to shock complacent parents who think that drug abuse will never afflict their children. As you can see, the Piercy Drug Program has several components.

As of 2002, the Piercy Drug Program had not been formally examined for its effectiveness. Some evidence of effectiveness has come from participants who saw the skits (which brought tears to the eyes of some parents), letters from parents, and counting the number of parents who had picked up *Not My Kid* brochures (McMenamin, 2002). Although this information provides some useful information, it is limited.

If you wanted to get some evidence that this program was working, you could take several approaches. For example, if you were lucky, you might find secondary data that provide estimates of the percentage of kids at the county schools who were involved with drugs before and after the introduction of the program. You could have children and parents rate the program using five-point rating scales. You could interview parents to find out how their lives had changed and what changes they have made in their relationships with their children. You could interview children to determine their awareness and ask them about the program and their relationship with their parents. Although you could take either a qualitative or a quantitative approach to assessing the effect of the program, it would be wise to take a more multifaceted approach by collecting qualitative and quantitative data. Often, as you will learn in this chapter, the use of both qualitative and quantitative approaches is a more complete way to learn about phenomena we are interested in, such as the Piercy Drug Program.

In Chapter 2, we introduced you to the three major research paradigms that are currently used in education: quantitative research, qualitative research, and mixed research. In the previous chapters in this part of your book, we extensively discussed the two major methods of quantitative research (experimental and nonexperimental research) and the five methods

Research
Navigator.c⊛m

**mixed method
research**

Research
Navigator.c⊛m

**multimethod
research**

Research
Navigator.c⊛m

**quantitative and
qualitative
research**

■ **Mixed research**
Research in which
quantitative and quali-
tative techniques are
mixed in a single study

■ **Compatibility thesis**
The idea that quan-
titative and qual-
itative methods are
compatible

■ **Pragmatist
philosophy**
A philosophy that says
to use what works

Research
Navigator.c⊛m

pragmatism

of qualitative research (phenomenology, ethnography, case study, grounded theory, and his-torical research).

We now move to the mixed research paradigm, a paradigm that in some ways uses ideas from both quantitative and qualitative research. To get you oriented, take a moment (yes, right now) and review Table 2.1 (on page 31). Chapter 2 is where we first introduced you to quantitative, qualitative, and mixed research. You need to review the main character-istics of quantitative and qualitative research (shown in Table 2.1 in Chapter 2) so that you can begin to think about mixing the different research approaches. By the way, so that you don't get confused when you read published research articles, note that various authors refer to mixed research as *mixed methods research, mixed method research, mixed method-ology, multimethod research,* and *multiplism.* You will be glad to know that you can treat all of these terms as synonyms.

As Tables 14.1 and 14.2 show, both quantitative and qualitative research methods have strengths and weaknesses. For example, quantitative research, especially experimental re-search, is very useful for establishing cause-and-effect relationships (strength). When based on random samples, quantitative research is very useful for making generalizations about populations (strength). Quantitative research typically is less useful for exploring new phe-nomena or for documenting participants' internal perspectives and personal meanings about phenomena in their lives (weakness). On the other hand, qualitative research almost always studies behavior in naturalistic settings, which helps to yield holistic insights into educational processes that exist within specific settings (strength). Qualitative research pro-vides in-depth and rich information about participants' worldviews and their personal meanings (strength). Qualitative research also can provide detailed information about why a phenomenon occurs (strength). However, qualitative research is typically based on small, nonrandom samples and often is used more for exploratory or discovery purposes than for hypothesis testing and validation purposes, which means that qualitative research findings are often not very generalizable beyond the local research participants (weakness).

Because of the strengths and weaknesses of both quantitative and qualitative research, more and more researchers are advocating that studies be conducted that combine these re-search traditions within the same investigation. These studies represent what is called mixed research. **Mixed research** is the class of research studies in which a researcher mixes or combines quantitative and qualitative research techniques into a single research study. Proponents believe that mixed research helps to improve the overall quality of research. Proponents also advocate the **compatibility thesis,** which simply says that quantitative and qualitative methods are compatible and can be mixed (e.g., Brewer & Hunter, 1989; Mor-gan, 1998; Pring, 2000; Reichardt & Cook, 1979; Reichardt & Rallis, 1994; Tashakkori & Teddlie, 1998). As was mentioned in Chapter 2, researchers who conduct mixed research studies often adhere to the **pragmatist philosophy,** in which the researcher mixes research components in any way he or she believes will work for the given research problem, re-search question, and research circumstance. The pragmatist is not overly concerned about many longstanding philosophical arguments and is much more concerned about doing "what works."

Mixed researchers view the use of multiple perspectives, theories, and research meth-ods as a strength in educational research. Moreover, they believe that mixed research can produce a study that is superior to one produced by either quantitative research or qualita-

■ **TABLE 14.1**   Strengths and Weaknesses of Quantitative Research

Strengths

- Testing and validating already constructed theories about how and why phenomena occur
- Testing hypotheses that are constructed before the data are collected
- Can generalize research findings when the data are based on random samples of sufficient size
- Can generalize a research finding when it has been replicated on many different populations and subpopulations
- Useful for obtaining data that allow quantitative predictions to be made
- The researcher may construct a situation that eliminates the confounding influence of many variables, allowing one to more credibly establish cause-and-effect relationships
- Data collection using some quantitative methods is relatively quick (e.g., telephone interviews)
- Provides precise, quantitative, numerical data
- Data analysis is relatively less time consuming (using statistical software)
- The research results are relatively independent of the researcher (e.g., statistical significance)
- It may have higher credibility with many people in power (e.g., administrators, politicians, people who fund programs)
- It is useful for studying large numbers of people

Weaknesses

- The researcher's categories that are used might not reflect local constituencies' understandings
- The researcher's theories that are used might not reflect local constituencies' understandings
- The researcher might miss out on phenomena occurring because of the focus on theory or hypothesis testing rather than on theory or hypothesis generation (called the *confirmation bias*)
- Knowledge produced might be too abstract and general for direct application to specific local situations, contexts, and individuals

---

tive research alone. As was noted in Chapter 2, when mixing research or when you read and evaluate research that involves mixing, you should always be sure to consider the **fundamental principle of mixed research.** According to this principle, researchers should collect multiple sets of data using different approaches and methods in such a way that the resulting mixture or combination has complementary strengths and nonoverlapping weaknesses (Brewer & Hunter, 1989; Johnson & Turner, 2002; Webb et al., 1981).

■ **Fundamental principle of mixed research**
The researcher should use a mixture or combination of methods that has complementary strengths and nonoverlapping weaknesses

▓ **TABLE 14.2**   Strengths and Weaknesses of Qualitative Research

Strengths

- Data based on the participants' own categories of meaning
- Useful for studying a limited number of cases in depth
- Useful for describing complex phenomena
- Provides individual case information
- Can conduct cross-case comparisons and analysis
- Provides understanding and description of people's personal experiences of phenomena (i.e., the emic or insider's viewpoint)
- Can describe in rich detail phenomena as they are situated and embedded in local contexts
- The researcher almost always identifies contextual and setting factors as they relate to the phenomenon of interest
- The researcher can study dynamic processes (i.e., documenting sequential patterns and change)
- The researcher can use the primarily qualitative method of grounded theory to inductively generate a tentative but explanatory theory about a phenomenon
- Can determine how participants interpret constructs (e.g., self-esteem, IQ)
- Data are usually collected in naturalistic settings in qualitative research
- Qualitative approaches are especially responsive to local situations, conditions, and stakeholders' needs
- Qualitative researchers are especially responsive to changes that occur during the conduct of a study (especially during extended fieldwork) and may shift the focus of their studies as a result
- Qualitative data in the words and categories of participants lend themselves to exploring how and why phenomena occur
- You can use an important case to vividly demonstrate a phenomenon to the readers of a report
- Determine idiographic causation (i.e., determination of causes of a particular event)

Weaknesses

- Knowledge produced might not generalize to other people or other settings (i.e., findings might be unique to the relatively few people included in the research study).
- It is difficult to make quantitative predictions.
- It is more difficult to test hypotheses and theories with large participant pools.
- It might have lower credibility with some administrators and commissioners of programs.
- It generally takes more time to collect the data when compared to quantitative research.
- Data analysis is often time consuming.
- The results are more easily influenced by the researcher's personal biases and idiosyncrasies

For example, you have learned that experiments can provide very strong conclusions about the presence of a cause-and-effect relationship. Experiments, however, are usually based on convenience (i.e., nonrandom) samples. Experiments tend to be strong on internal validity (i.e., causal validity) but weaker on external validity (generalizing validity). You might decide to check your experimental research finding using a survey based on a probability sample (if the research question can be studied this way). If the finding is corroborated (i.e., the same research finding is obtained in both the experimental data and the survey data), then you will have increased the generalizability of the research finding. You can sometimes improve experiments even further by conducting in-depth interviews and focus groups (i.e., collecting some qualitative data) to get at the research participants' perspectives and meanings that lie behind the experimental research findings and numbers.

In practice, mixed research has been conducted for many years. It is only recently, however, that a paradigm or community of researchers advocating mixed research has come to the fore, and now it appears that mixed research is becoming more and more accepted by the vast majority of practicing researchers. We predict that this trend will continue in the future until mixed research is just as commonly accepted as quantitative research or qualitative research. We have provided a list of the strengths and weaknesses of mixed research in Table 14.3.

14.1 What position does the mixed researcher take on the compatibility thesis and pragmatist philosophy?

14.2 Why is the fundamental principle of mixed research important?

REVIEW

QUESTIONS

THE RESEARCH CONTINUUM

Mixed research provides a framework for conducting a study that incorporates quantitative and qualitative research approaches. In each mixed research study, a combination of quantitative and qualitative data is collected, analyzed, and interpreted using systematic principles. As shown in Figure 14.1, mixed research takes most of the space on the research continuum that varies from not mixed (i.e., what is called *monomethod*) to fully mixed. A monomethod research study, at the far left of the continuum, involves the exclusive use of either a quantitative or qualitative research approach. As long as both quantitative and qualitative research approaches are used within the same investigation, the study moves from being monomethod to at least a partially mixed method, even if one of the research approaches is used only minimally. As you move to the right on the research continuum, mixing or integration of elements of quantitative and qualitative research becomes greater and greater.

For example, the following study would be situated relatively far to the left on the research continuum (i.e., not strongly mixed): The researcher conducts a primarily quantitative research study and includes one open-ended question on a data collection instrument to provide some limited qualitative data. In an example of a more strongly mixed research study, a research team could collect extensive qualitative and quantitative data on a topic

TABLE 14.3   Strengths and Weaknesses of Mixed Research

Strengths

- Words, pictures, and narrative can be used to add meaning to numbers.
- Numbers can be used to add precision to words, pictures, and narrative.
- Can provide quantitative and qualitative research strengths (see strengths listed in Tables 14.1 and 14.2).
- Researcher can generate and test a grounded theory.
- Can answer a broader and more complete range of research questions because the researcher is not confined to a single method or approach.
- The specific mixed research designs discussed in this chapter have specific strengths and weaknesses that should be considered (e.g., in a two-phase sequential design, the phase one results can be used to develop and inform the purpose and design of the phase two component).
- A researcher can use the strengths of an additional method to overcome the weaknesses in another method by using both in a research study (this is the principle of complementarity).
- Can provide stronger evidence for a conclusion through convergence and corroboration of findings (this is the principle of triangulation).
- Can add insights and understanding that might be missed when only a single method is used.
- Can be used to increase the generalizability of the results.
- Qualitative and quantitative research used together produces more complete knowledge necessary to inform theory and practice.

Weaknesses

- It can be difficult for a single researcher to carry out both qualitative and quantitative research, especially if two or more approaches are expected to be done concurrently (i.e., it might require a research team).
- The researcher has to learn about multiple methods and approaches and understand how to appropriately mix them.
- Methodological purists contend that one should always work within either a qualitative or a quantitative paradigm.
- It is more expensive.
- It is more time consuming.
- Some of the details of mixed research remain to be fully worked out by research methodologists (e.g., problems of paradigm mixing, how to qualitatively analyze quantitative data, how to interpret conflicting results).

FIGURE 14.1 The research continuum

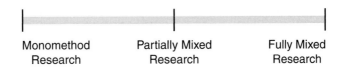

Monomethod Research   Partially Mixed Research   Fully Mixed Research

and integrate the results during data analysis and interpretation to provide a full picture of the phenomenon being studied. There are probably an infinite number of ways in which qualitative and quantitative techniques can be mixed, but each single study can be placed on the research continuum showing the degree of mixing. In the next section, we will introduce you to some specific methods of mixed research.

TYPES OF MIXED RESEARCH METHODS

Mixed research is a growing field. As such, many mixed research designs are still being developed. In Chapter 2, we discussed the two major methods of mixed research. They are *mixed model* research and *mixed method* research. Below, we will review our earlier discussion of these two methods, and we will extend that discussion by presenting some of the key research designs that exist within each of the two mixed research methods.

Mixed Model Research

The **mixed model method** involves mixing components or stages from qualitative and quantitative research (Tashakkori & Teddlie, 1998). To understand this method of mixing, however, you first need to become familiar with a simplified (three-stage) view of the research process. (Note: If we included more stages in the research process, things would get more complex, and, of course, we do not want to raise your blood pressure!) For the purpose of thinking about mixed model research, let's view a typical research study as involving three major stages:

■ **Mixed model research method** Quantitative and qualitative approaches are mixed within or across the stages of the research process

1. Selecting the research objective (based on your research questions)
2. Collecting the research data
3. Analyzing the research data (to help answer your research questions)

Let's look at how qualitative and quantitative research would fall out on these three stages if the models (i.e., paradigms) were *not* mixed. In qualitative research paradigm, the primary research objectives are exploration and description, the primary type of data collected is qualitative data (e.g., such as words and images), and the primary mode of analysis is qualitative analysis (e.g., inductively searching the collected data to discover categories, themes, and patterns). This is design 1 in Figure 14.2. In contrast, in quantitative research, the primary research objectives are explanation, prediction, and description; the primary type of data collected is quantitative data (e.g., such as numbers and variables); and the primary mode of analysis is quantitative analysis (e.g., analyzing the data with a statistical software program and testing hypotheses about relationships in the numerical data). This is design 8 in Figure 14.2. Another important distinction between qualitative and quantitative

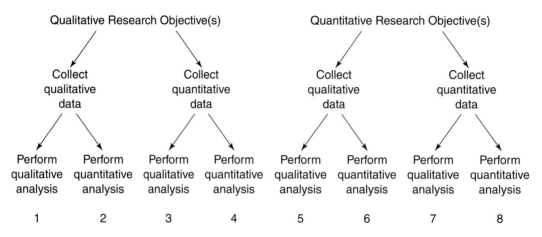

■ **FIGURE 14.2**   Monomethod and mixed model designs

Designs 1 and 8 on the outer edges are the monomethod designs. The mixed model designs are designs 2, 3, 4, 5, 6, and 7.

research is that the former relies more on the discovery oriented or inductive mode of the scientific method and the latter relies more on the hypothesis testing or deductive mode of the scientific method. (Note: If you found this paragraph difficult, please look one more time at Table 2.1 in Chapter 2, which summarizes the characteristics of pure qualitative research and pure quantitative research. Also look at Figure 1.2, which visually shows the difference between the inductive and the deductive methods.)

Now that you know how pure qualitative and pure quantitative research follow the three stages of research (i.e., research objective, data collection, data analysis), you can more easily envision how these pure models can be mixed. There are two primary ways in which you can mix the qualitative and quantitative models. The first way involves the use of both qualitative and quantitative research *within* one or more of the three stages of a single research study that we just discussed: (1) selecting the research objective, (2) collecting the research data, and (3) analyzing the research data. The second way involves the use of both qualitative and quantitative research *across* any of the three stages. These two classes of mixed model research are called, respectively, within-stage and across-stage mixed model research.

In **within-stage mixed model research,** the researcher mixes or combines quantitative and qualitative research approaches at one or more of the three major research stages (i.e., research objective, data collection, data analysis). This research involves mixing within at least one stage of a single study. For example, you could mix within the research objective stage by designing a research study to answer a research question (or a set of related questions) that suggests or requires both exploration (qualitative) and hypothesis testing or confirmation (quantitative). You could mix within the type of data stage by using a mode of data collection that provides both qualitative and quantitative data (e.g., a questionnaire that includes open- and closed-ended items). Finally, you could mix within the type of analysis stage by examining narrative data both qualitatively (searching for major themes) and quantitatively (counting the number of times key words occur) or by examining numeric data both quantitatively (computing descriptive statistics) and qualitatively (forming categories based on the descriptive statistics).

■ **Within-stage mixed model research**
Quantitative and qualitative approaches are mixed within one or more of the stages of research

An example of a within-stage mixed model design is a study conducted by Daley and Onwuegbuzie (in press), who investigated male juvenile delinquents' causal attributions for others' violent behavior (i.e., what causes others to act violently) and the kind of information these delinquents used in forming their attributions. The 82 male juvenile offenders who participated in the study were incarcerated at a correctional facility at the time of the research. The researchers developed a 12-item questionnaire to assess attributions made by juveniles for the behavior of others involved in violent acts. Each item consisted of a vignette followed by three possible attributions (i.e., person, stimulus, circumstance) presented in a multiple-choice format. The questionnaire also included an open-ended question asking the juveniles their reasons for choosing the responses that they did. By collecting quantitative (multiple-choice) and qualitative (open-ended) data with the same instrument, the researchers mixed models within the type of data stage. The researchers also did some within-stage mixing in the data analysis stage, using some cutting-edge mixed method data analysis techniques. Remember, the key to within-stage mixing is that the researcher mixes quantitative and qualitative approaches *within* at least one of the stages of research (research objective, data collection, data analysis).

In **across-stage mixed model research,** the researcher mixes or combines quantitative and qualitative research approaches across at least two of the three research stages in a single research study. For example, you could use an exploratory approach as the research study's objective (qualitative), collect qualitative data (qualitative), but then analyze your data using quantitative techniques (quantitative). In this example, the ordering through the three stages was qualitative, qualitative, quantitative; it is design 2 in Figure 14.2. Perhaps the easiest way to understand across-stage mixed model research is by looking at the six across-stage mixed model research designs shown in Figure 14.2 (i.e., designs 2, 3, 4, 5, 6, and 7).

- **Across-stage mixed model research**
  Quantitative and qualitative approaches are mixed across at least two of the stages of research

A published example of an across-stage mixed model research study was conducted by Roberts and Le-Dorze (1994). These researchers were interested in studying the verbal fluency of patients with aphasia. The objective of the study was qualitative, specifically exploratory and inductive. Qualitative data were collected via interviews. Specifically, two groups of aphasia patients were interviewed on an individual basis: patients with recent aphasia and patients with chronic aphasia. The interview involved asking each patient to name as many words as possible that belonged to a category. Each patient was interviewed twice, six to eight weeks apart. Quantitative analysis of the qualitative data revealed that the recent aphasia group listed fewer correct words than did the chronic aphasia group. Also, both groups performed better on the second interview. In this example, the research objective was qualitative (exploring), the data collected were qualitative (words), and the analysis was quantitative (counting), yielding mixed model design 2 in Figure 14.2. In this design, the model mixing occurs across stages two and three.

Mixed Method Research

In **mixed method research,** the researcher systematically uses the qualitative research paradigm for one phase of a research study and the quantitative research paradigm for another phase of the research study. In contrast to mixed model research, in mixed method research the qualitative phase (which includes a qualitative objective, qualitative data collection, and qualitative data analysis) and the quantitative phase (which includes a quantitative objective,

- **Mixed method research**
  A quantitative phase and a qualitative phase are included in the overall research study

quantitative data collection, and quantitative data analysis) are kept intact and separate from one another. This means that in mixed method research, a qualitative research study and a quantitative research study essentially are conducted as part of a larger, overall study. In mixed method research, the mixing generally is done more at the level of interpretation of the results.

Our review of the various available mixed research designs has led us to conceptualize mixed method research as a function of the following two dimensions: time orientation of the qualitative and quantitative phases (concurrent versus sequential) and paradigm emphasis (equal status versus dominant status). Time orientation refers to whether the qualitative and quantitative phases of the study occur at approximately the same point in time (i.e., concurrently) or whether these two phases occur one after the other (i.e., sequentially). Paradigm emphasis refers to whether the qualitative and quantitative parts of the study have approximately equal emphasis (i.e., equal status) with regard to answering the research question(s) and interpreting the results or whether one paradigm clearly has more weight than the other (i.e., dominant status). The key idea in mixed method studies is that you must make two major decisions: You decide whether you want to operate largely within one dominant paradigm or not, and you decide whether you want to conduct the phases concurrently or sequentially.

Crossing the two dimensions (i.e., paradigm emphasis and time order) produces a 2 (equal status versus dominant status) by 2 (concurrent versus sequential) matrix that yields four cells. This matrix is shown in Figure 14.3. To understand the specific designs shown in these four cells, however, you must become familiar with some basic notation that is commonly used in mixed research (Morse, 1991). The symbol system works like this:

- The letters qual or QUAL stand for qualitative research.
- The letters quan or QUAN stand for quantitative research.
- Capital letters denote priority or increased weight.
- Lowercase letters denote lower priority or weight.
- A plus sign (+) represents a concurrent collection of data.
- An arrow (→) represents a sequential collection of data.

■ FIGURE 14.3   Mixed method design matrix. Mixed method research designs are shown in the four cells.

Time Order Decision

		Concurrent	Sequential
	Equal Status	QUAL + QUAN	QUAL → QUAN
			QUAN → QUAL
Paradigm Emphasis Decision	Dominant Status	QUAL + quan	QUAL → quan
			qual → QUAN
			QUAN → qual
		QUAN + qual	quan → QUAL

For example, the combination of symbols QUAL + QUAN indicates a design in which the qualitative and quantitative paradigms are given equal weight or equal status (both are in caps) and are conducted concurrently (see the plus sign). The combination of symbols QUAL→quan says that the qualitative paradigm is the dominant paradigm used in the research study (QUAL is in capital letters, and quan is in lowercase) and a follow-up quantitative component is included in the study (see the arrow between QUAL and quan). Now you try it. What would this set of symbols indicate: qual→QUAN? (The answer is that it indicates that quantitative paradigm dominates the study and that a qualitative phase is followed sequentially by a quantitative phase in the study.) Now you know a new symbol system. Don't forget to share it with your friends!

Now you can examine the nine designs shown in Figure 14.3. As you can see, some of the cells include more designs than others (e.g., there is only one equal-status concurrent design, but there are four dominant-status sequential designs). In actual research practice, some designs are more commonly used than others. For example, many researchers are trained in a single research paradigm, and if they conduct mixed research, they tend to use one of the dominant-status designs. For example, predominantly qualitative researchers will often include a quantitative component in their research without changing their overall paradigm or approach to research. Likewise, predominantly quantitative researchers will often include a qualitative component without changing their overall paradigm or approach to research.

A published example of a study based on an *equal-status concurrent design* (i.e., QUAL + QUAN) was conducted by Onwuegbuzie and DaRos-Voseles (2001). The title of their study was "The Role of Cooperative Learning in Research Methodology Courses: A Mixed-Methods Analysis." These researchers investigated the effectiveness of cooperative learning (CL) and individual learning (IL) with graduate students enrolled in an educational research course. There were 81 students in the sections in which cooperative learning groups were formed to undertake the major course requirements and 112 students in the sections in which assignments were undertaken individually (IL). The quantitative part of the study involved comparing the CL and IL groups' performance on the midterm and final exams. In the qualitative part of the study, students in both the CL and IL groups wrote reflective journals about their experiences in their respective research classes. This study is based on an equal-status concurrent design because both parts of the study were given approximately equal weight (equal status), and the quantitative and qualitative portions of the study occurred at approximately the same point in time (i.e., concurrently). The quantitative and qualitative portions of the study were mixed after both data types had been collected and analyzed.

A published example of a study based on a *dominant-status concurrent design* was conducted by Senne and Rikard (2002) in a study entitled "Experiencing the Portfolio Process during Internship: A Comparative Analysis of Two PETE Portfolio Models." These researchers compared PETE portfolio models (curricular interventions during the student teacher experience) to determine their effect on intern (i.e., student teacher) perceptions of the utility of the teaching portfolio and intern professional growth. They specifically used a QUAL + quan design. The quantitative phase of the study, the component with the least weight, involved administering a measure of developmental growth (i.e., principled thinking and moral judgment reasoning). The qualitative phase of the study, which took place concurrently, had the dominant status because more qualitative data were collected than quantitative data and the qualitative data were collected for a longer period of time than were the quantitative data. The qualitative phase involved the interns recording their 15-week teaching experiences in weekly reflection logs. In addition, the interns were asked to complete an eight-item questionnaire. This questionnaire was designed for interns to evaluate the portfolio process, the teacher education program, and the student teaching experience. This instrument also asked the interns to describe their accomplishments and overall professional growth. The quantitative and qualitative data were analyzed separately before being compared at the end of the study.

Up to this point, all of the examples of mixed research that we have provided were carried out in a single research study. Although technically a mixed design requires that a study be carried out in a single research study, we are going to stretch that rule slightly in the next example. The researchers formed a team, but they published the results of their *equal-status sequential design* in two different reports. They specifically used a QUAN→QUAL design. The first part of this study was conducted by Bos et al. (1999) in an article entitled "New Hope for People with Low Incomes: Two-Year Results of a Program to Reduce Poverty and Reform Welfare." These researchers conducted phase 1 of an evaluation of the New Hope program.

New Hope was a two-year voluntary antipoverty initiative that took place in selected inner-city neighborhoods in Milwaukee, Wisconsin. In this program, residents from these neighborhoods who worked for 30 hours a week received, when appropriate, a wage subsidy, health insurance, and child care benefits. Bos et al. (1999) evaluated this phase of the project using quantitative research techniques. Specifically, a randomized experiment was used, focusing on causal explanations of targeted program outcomes. These targeted outcomes included poverty reduction, full-time employment, and child and family well-being. Bos et al. collected administrative records and family and teacher surveys both at baseline and at the end of the two-year program. The experimental and control groups were compared on the quantitative data.

At the two-year point of the New Hope program, the qualitative phase was implemented. This phase consisted of an ethnographic study, with the goal of obtaining an in-depth understanding of the meaningfulness of the participants' experiences over the first two years of the program (Weisner, 2000). Approximately half of the treatment and control group members were interviewed, and their responses were compared. In this sequential study (i.e., phases one and two), the quantitative and qualitative data sets were analyzed separately, and mixing took place in interpreting the final results. In this study, the quantitative data and design provided evidence that the New Hope Program worked. The qualitative, ethnographic data provided useful insights into how the members of the different groups viewed their participation and their circumstances. The qualitative data complemented and corroborated the quantitative data.

An example of a study based on a *dominant-status sequential design* was conducted by Way, Stauber, Nakkula, and London (1994) in a study entitled "Depression and Substance Use in Two Divergent High School Cultures: A Quantitative and Qualitative Analysis." They specifically used a QUAN→qual design. In the first phase, a structured questionnaire was administered to students in suburban and urban high schools. The questionnaires measured student depression, substance abuse, and several demographic variables. During data analysis, the researchers found a positive correlation between depression and substance abuse (i.e., the higher the depression, the higher the substance abuse) for students in the suburban high schools but not for the students in the urban high schools. In the second phase, the researchers conducted follow-up qualitative interviews with the most depressed students from both urban and suburban high schools to explore why the relationship was present only for suburban students. They found that suburban students saw drugs as a way to escape problems. In contrast, the urban students saw drugs more as a cause of their problems. Phase 2 was used in a complementary way; specifically, phase 2 results helped to clarify the phase 1 finding about the relationship between depression and substance abuse.

14.3 Give an example of a within-stage mixed model research study.

14.4 Give an example of an across-stage mixed model research study.

14.5 What is the difference between mixed model research and mixed method research?

14.6 What kind of study does this notation imply: qual → QUAN → qual? Can you think of why a researcher might use such a design?

14.7 What is the difference between a sequential and a concurrent design feature?

R E V I E W

QUESTIONS

STAGES OF THE MIXED RESEARCH PROCESS

The mixed research process discussed in this chapter follows eight distinct steps:

1. Determine whether a mixed design is appropriate.
2. Determine the rationale for using a mixed design.
3. Select the mixed method or mixed model research design.
4. Collect the data.
5. Analyze the data.
6. Validate the data.
7. Interpret the data.
8. Write the research report.

These steps are shown in Figure 14.4. Although all research starts with one or more research questions and an objective, the rest of the steps can vary in order (i.e., they are not necessarily linear as implied by the figure). Writing the research report is the last step in the research process, although some preliminary writing or the writing of some sections of a report often occurs before the end of a research project. The arrow leading back to the first step is included to emphasize that the research objective(s) can be reformulated during a single research study or subsequent studies. Each of these steps is discussed in more detail below.

Step 1: Determine Whether a Mixed Design Is Appropriate

You learned in Chapter 3 that all empirical research starts by selecting a research topic (i.e., the broad subject matter area to be investigated), identifying a research problem (the educational issue or problem within a broad topic area), determining the research purpose (i.e., a statement of the intent or objective of the study), and finally coming up with the research question (i.e., the very specific question that you have determined needs to be answered).

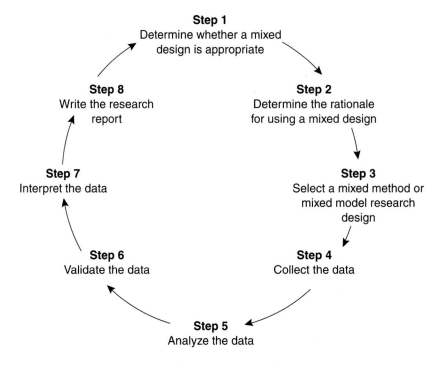

FIGURE 14.4 Important steps in a mixed research study

Although the steps are numbered, researchers often move around in the circle in multiple directions (especially steps 4 through 7).

Sometimes, especially in quantitative research, a statement of the hypothesis is also made (i.e., the researcher makes a prediction about the research outcome). You must go through similar steps when proposing a mixed research study.

Once you have identified your research questions, it is helpful to determine the objective of your research. As we discussed in Chapter 1, there are five major research objectives in educational research: exploration, description, explanation, prediction, and influence. These five objectives are as pertinent in mixed research as they are when using monomethods. Furthermore, it is common in mixed research to have more than one objective for your research study. As a reminder, exploration uses primarily inductive methods to explore a concept, phenomenon, or situation with the goal of developing tentative hypotheses, generalizations, and conclusions. Description involves identifying and describing the nature and attributes of phenomena. Explanation involves the testing of a hypothesis or theory in an attempt to clarify the relationship among phenomena and to determine reasons and causes of outcomes. Prediction involves using certain known information to determine what will occur at a later point in time. Finally, influence involves the manipulation of the situation or variable to produce a desired outcome.

What is unique in mixed research is that the research problem and your research questions suggest to you that a mixed design is appropriate. For example, you might need to explore the language of a group of people and then develop a standardized questionnaire that will work for them. Or perhaps you want to develop a grounded theory, but after developing it, you want to empirically test the theory on an independent group of people. Both of these examples imply a mixed research study.

If you are willing to go the route of mixed research, this means that you are willing to take a pragmatic position toward your research and that you do not view any single method dogmatically. You probably adhere to the compatibility thesis rather than the incompatibility thesis. Although you might feel that one paradigm tends to have the best overall approach for studying educational problems, if you use a mixed design, it is apparent that you are also open to collecting both quantitative and qualitative data to help answer your research question(s).

An important consideration, before making the final conclusion that you want to design an actual mixed study, is to make sure that the study you are planning is feasible. Mixed designs mean that you must collect quantitative and qualitative data or mix models in ways that might not be currently well established in practice. Mixed methods studies are typically more expensive, so if expense is a major issue, you might decide to do just one part of your study now and wait until later to do the other part (i.e., you might decide to mix methods across your research program, rather than mixing methods in a single study).

Step 2: Determine the Rationale for Using a Mixed Design

Once you have decided that a mixed design is needed for your research, the next step is to determine the rationale for using a mixed design. What do you want to achieve by mixing quantitative and qualitative approaches? How will mixing approaches help you in answering your research questions? In answering these questions, we recommend that you use Greene, Caracelli, and Graham's (1989) framework (see Table 14.4). Their framework is based on using

TABLE 14.4   Greene, Caracelli, and Graham's List of Purposes for Mixed Research

Purpose	Explanation
Triangulation	Seeks convergence, corroboration, correspondence of results from different methods
Complementarity	Seeks elaboration, enhancement, illustration, clarification of the results from one method with the results from the other method
Development	Seeks to use the results from one method to help develop or inform the other method, where development is broadly construed to include sampling and implementation, as well as measurement decisions
Initiation	Seeks the discovery of paradox and contradiction, new perspectives of frameworks, the recasting of questions or results from one method with questions or results from the other method
Expansion	Seeks to extend the breadth and range of inquiry by using different methods for different inquiry components

Source: Based on Greene, Caracelli, and Graham (1989).

one of the following five broad purposes as the rationale for a mixed research study: (1) triangulation, (2) complementarity, (3) development, (4) initiation, and (5) expansion.

Research
Navigator.c⊛m

triangulation

Triangulation is the term given when the researcher seeks convergence and corroboration of results from different methods studying the same phenomenon. When you want to make a statement with confidence, you want your pieces of evidence to converge on the correct answer. Triangulation can substantially increase the credibility or likelihood of the correctness of a research finding. The purpose is said to be *complementarity* when the investigator seeks elaboration, enhancement, illustration, and clarification of the results from one method with results from the other method. This helps you in understanding the overlapping and different facets of a phenomenon. *Development* is the name given when the researcher uses the results from one method to help inform the other method. *Initiation* refers to discovering paradoxes and contradictions as well as providing different perspectives that may lead to a reframing of the research question or results. Finally, the purpose of research is called *expansion* when the investigator attempts to expand the breadth and range of inquiry by using different methods for different inquiry components. For example, you might use qualitative research to study an educational program's process (i.e., how it works) and use quantitative research to study the outcomes of the program.

Determining the mixed research purpose using Greene et al.'s framework helps further to form or select a mixed research design. For example, if the purpose of the research is triangulation, then, at the very least, mixing should occur during data interpretation and report writing. If the purpose is development, then a sequential design is needed.

Step 3: Select the Mixed Method or Mixed Model Research Design

When constructing a mixed design, researchers have all the research methods, research designs, and research strategies at their disposal that are discussed in the other chapters of this book. That's part of the beauty of mixing. You are not bound by any particular philosophy, style, or method. You are free to be creative, as long as the design that you create is useful and is appropriate for your research questions. For example, an experimental approach in a quantitative phase of a mixed research study could be followed up with qualitative interviews to get at the participants' insights and experiences regarding their participation in the experiment (as a manipulation check or validity check). In the mixed research world, one could even conduct an experiment (a quantitative research method) by collecting qualitative data, although such a study might be difficult and time consuming in practice.

Once you have decided that a mixed research design is needed, you must next determine whether a mixed model design or a mixed method design (or a combination of the two) is more appropriate. If a mixed model design is called for, then consider selecting one of the mixed model designs shown in Figure 14.2. If none of those designs fits your specific needs and circumstances, you will need to configure a more unique design using the ideas you have learned in this chapter and book.

If a mixed method design seems more appropriate, then answer these two questions:

1. Is the qualitative or quantitative paradigm going to be given priority, or will they be given equal status in your study?
2. Should the qualitative and quantitative components be carried out concurrently or sequentially?

Your answer to those two questions leads you to one of the four cells shown in Figure 14.3. Next you can check to see whether one of the nine mixed method designs in Figure 14.3 is appropriate for your study. If your study requires a more complex design, then you can still use the ones in Figure14.3 as a starting point and configure your own unique design. For example, you might decide that you first need to collect some exploratory qualitative data, then conduct an explanatory and confirmatory quantitative stage, and then follow this with qualitative interviews to explore or help interpret the earlier findings. In this case, you would use a qual → QUANT → qual design. You can also modify your design during the conduct of a study. For example, perhaps your early findings or results provide a serendipitous insight and suggest a change in the kind of data you need to collect or the sequence of your activities.

Step 4: Collect the Data

Data in mixed research designs can be collected on the same sample or on different samples. You can use any of the various ways of selecting samples in quantitative and qualitative research, which are classified (Chapter 7) as random sampling (i.e., simple, stratified, systematic, and cluster) and nonrandom sampling (i.e., convenience, quota, purposive, network, snowball, comprehensive, maximum variation, negative case) techniques. Any combination of random sampling and nonrandom sampling can be used in mixed research. For example, random sampling can be used in the quantitative phase and nonrandom sampling in the qualitative phase.

Mixed researchers also have the full complement of data collection methods at their disposal. Specifically, as presented in Chapter 6, all six major methods of data collection (i.e., tests, questionnaires, focus groups, observations, interviews, and secondary data) should be considered. You must determine the most appropriate combination of data collection methods, depending on your research questions, your research objective(s), and your rationale for using mixed research.

Step 5: Analyze the Data

When analyzing quantitative data, mixed researchers can utilize the whole range of techniques available. Mixed researchers can use the array of quantitative data analysis procedures that you will learn about in Chapters 15 and 16 as well as qualitative data analysis procedures discussed in Chapter 17. Your choice of analysis should be driven by the research objective(s), research purpose, research questions/hypotheses, and type of data collected.

In mixed model research, researchers sometimes conduct quantitative analyses of qualitative data and/or perform qualitative analyses of quantitative data. The former can be accomplished by undertaking what Tashakkori and Teddlie (1998) call quantitizing data. **Quantitizing** data involves converting qualitative data into numerical codes and then using statistical analysis techniques with the data. For example, a researcher who is interviewing students to find out their experiences in an educational research class could construct a frequency distribution that shows the number of times words such as *anxiety* or *fun* are used during the interviews. Thus, words or themes are converted to numbers. Conversely, qualitative analyses of quantitative data can be undertaken by converting quantitative data to narrative data, or **qualitizing** (Tashakkori & Teddlie, 1998). For instance, quantitative scales can be converted to categories based on the numeric scores. For example, you might take scores

- **Quantitizing**
Converting qualitative data into quantitative data

- **Qualitizing**
Converting quantitative data into qualitative data

based on a four-point agreement scale—(1) agree strongly, (2) agree, (3) disagree, (4) strongly disagree—and decide to merge options 1 and 2 and merge options 3 and 4. Then you have categorized participants' responses into "agree" or "disagree." For additional information on conducting mixed research data analysis, see Onwuegbuzie and Teddlie (2002).

Step 6: Validate the Data

In Chapter 8, we discuss validity issues in quantitative and qualitative research, and throughout this book, we have emphasized the importance of assessing validity when using both approaches. As a reminder, the primary quantitative research validity types are internal validity, external validity, construct validity, and statistical conclusion validity (see Table 8.1 on page 239). In qualitative research, the primary types are descriptive validity, interpretative validity, and theoretical validity (see pages 249–253). We have a list of specific strategies for promoting qualitative research validity in Table 8.2 (p. 250) In mixed research, you will need to establish the trustworthiness of your data by demonstrating evidence of a combination of these validity types. Furthermore, in mixed research, assessment of research validity often is a cyclical, interactive process. An initial assessment of data and conclusion validity may lead to more data being collected (e.g., extended fieldwork and participant feedback).

The techniques of triangulation (i.e., data triangulation, investigator triangulation, theory triangulation, and methods triangulation as discussed in Chapter 8) are especially helpful in establishing the credibility of your mixed data. In data triangulation, the researcher uses multiple sets of data to cross-validate and corroborate findings. In investigator triangulation, multiple investigators are used for corroboration. In theory triangulation, multiple perspectives and theories are used in understanding the data. In methods triangulation, the investigator uses multiple methods of data collection and/or research methods. When mixing data and methods, you should use the fundamental principle of mixed research; that is, you should design your study so that the weaknesses of one method or set of data are minimized by the use of another method or set of data. As Denzin (1978) noted, through triangulation, "the bias inherent in any particular data source, investigators, and particularly method will be canceled out when used in conjunction with other data sources, investigators, and methods" (p. 14), and "the result will be a convergence upon the truth about some social phenomenon" (p. 14). Triangulation can result in corroboration or convergence as well as inconsistency and contradiction. Regardless, knowledge should be increased and direction will be provided about the kind of data that need to be collected in the next stage of a study or in a future research study. By using any of the designs presented in this chapter, mixed researchers are in a position to introduce more rigor into their studies than are those who conduct monomethod studies. Thus, mixed researchers can be more confident about the validity of their findings.

Step 7: Interpret the Data

It is important to remember that data interpretation begins as soon as the very first data are collected, and it continues throughout a research study. Once most or all of the data have been collected, analyzed, and validated, the mixed researcher is in a position to begin the formal process of interpreting the data. In a sequential study, the data collected in phase one are interpreted before the researcher moves on to phase two. For example, interpretations made here might be used developmentally to help inform phase two data collection and interpretation. Phase two data collection and interpretations in a sequential design may also be done for one of the additional rationales discussed earlier, such as collecting more data for the purpose of triangulation, complementarity, initiation, and/or expansion.

In a concurrent mixed research study, the qualitative and quantitative data can be interpreted separately or together depending on the research purpose and rationale. However, more often than not, some integration or comparison occurs during data interpretation because this type of mixing can help the researcher to identify convergence, inconsistency, and contradiction in the data. The ultimate goal of the mixed researcher, as with monomethod researchers, is to form trustworthy conclusions after ruling out as many rival hypotheses as possible. Therefore, data validation and data interpretation are extremely interactive, reciprocal, and important to forming accurate and defensible conclusions.

Step 8: Write the Research Report

Once all conclusions have been formulated and assessed for validity, the mixed researcher is ready to write the report. The researcher can write separate reports for the quantitative and qualitative phases. For example, in the New Hope study, the quantitative data (Bos et al., 1999) and qualitative data (Weisner, 2000), were written up separately. However, the two phases are more likely to be integrated in one report either by presenting the two sets of findings and interpretations in separate sections or by fully integrating them in the same section. In any case, mixed research reports contain the same features as do most monomethod reports, including the review of the related literature, methods, results, and discussion. Typically, the results section is the longest section in the report because it contains both the quantitative and qualitative findings. A well-written report will be highly descriptive of all eight phases of the mixed research process. Even when the quantitative phase is dominant, mixed researchers should always contextualize their reports; that is, they should carefully communicate the context in which the mixed research study took place. Contextualization not only helps the mixed researcher to examine how the quantitative and qualitative findings relate to one another, but also helps readers to know the extent to which they can generalize the findings. Also, where possible, mixed research reports should be holistic, both the parts of the whole and the whole being described adequately.

In writing a report, the mixed researcher should always be aware of four potential problems that must be addressed. The first problem stems from the fact that quantitative research and qualitative research traditionally have yielded different styles of writing. In particular, quantitative reports have traditionally been relatively impersonal and formal, whereas qualitative reports tend to be more personal and informal. Thus, a challenge to mixed researchers is for them to strike a balance between the two forms of writing without compromising the integrity of either the quantitative or the qualitative sections of the report.

A second problem that must be addressed is the problem of writing to audiences that likely are not sufficiently versed in both qualitative and quantitative techniques. Therefore, the mixed researcher should not take highly specialized quantitative, qualitative, or mixed research terms for granted and should define any research terms that are likely to be unknown to the audience and provide useful references for readers who want to expand their understanding of the related concepts. Endnotes can play a useful role here.

A third problem pertains to the length of mixed research studies. Because mixed research studies involve two or more components or phases, the reports tend to be longer than reports stemming from monomethod studies. This is a problem when the mixed researcher attempts to publish their reports because most journals have strict page limits. Fortunately, more and more reputable on-line journals are emerging, which often are more liberal in the number of pages allowed. Mixed researchers also should consider publishing their reports as monographs, book chapters, and books, which will give them more page space for writing. Additionally, it might be appropriate for mixed researchers to publish the different phases of their studies separately, especially if the phases are sequential over a long period of time, as was the case in the New Hope evaluation study.

The final problem that mixed researchers may face is the fact that mixed research is still a somewhat controversial and emerging field. Therefore, some readers, especially pure qualitative or pure quantitative researchers, might not be very open to mixed research reports and might read them with negative biases. This is a particular problem with manuscripts that are being read by skeptical journal editors and reviewers, who might reject the manuscript because of their philosophical orientation, regardless of the quality of the mixed research report. Encouragingly, several journals that routinely publish mixed research are now available (e.g., *Field Methods, Quality and Quantity, Evaluation, Evaluation Practice, Educational Evaluation & Policy Analysis,* and *Research in Nursing & Health*), and the list is growing. In an effort to gain more credibility, it is essential that mixed researchers show the highest degree of organization and rigor. We believe that using mixed research frameworks such as those outlined in this chapter will help in this quest.

REVIEW

QUESTIONS

14.8 What are the eight stages of the mixed research process?

14.9 Explain each of Greene, Caracelli, and Graham's five rationales for conducting a mixed research study.

14.10 What is the difference between quantitizing and qualitizing, and are these used in mixed method or mixed model designs?

14.11 What kinds of validity might be relevant in a mixed design?

LIMITATIONS OF MIXED RESEARCH

Although mixed research studies have great potential for enhancing understanding of the issues facing educational research, there are several limitations. First and foremost, because they use more complex designs than do monomethod studies, they tend to require more time and resources to undertake. Second, mixed methods research requires expertise in designing and implementing both qualitative and quantitative phases. For this reason, several pragmatist researchers (e.g., Rossman & Wilson, 1994) recommend that more than one researcher be engaged in a mixed research study, each bringing a unique methodological expertise to the team.

Third, some mixed research studies yield contradictory findings, especially between the quantitative and qualitative phases. Although viewed as a weakness, this can also be deemed a strength because conflicting findings can motivate replication studies or new studies in which the research objective, purpose, and/or questions are reframed. However, such extensions require additional investment of time, expertise, resources, and effort. Moreover, when stakeholders and policymakers are dependent on a single mixed research study to set policy, conflicting findings not only make it difficult to form firm recommendations, but also can potentially promote division among interested parties. Therefore, mixed researchers must deliberate carefully about how to report contradictory findings to users of the results.

Fourth, little is known about the relative merits of the different types of mixed research designs proposed in this chapter and elsewhere. Research methodologists need to systematize this knowledge and make it readily available to other researchers. Such information is needed so that researchers will be in a position to choose a design that has the most potential to address their mixed research objective(s). Nevertheless, as the number of mixed research studies increases, this information will become available.

14.12 What are the four potential problems involved in writing and attempting to publish a mixed research report?

R E V I E W

QUESTION

SUMMARY

This chapter has provided a framework for conducting mixed research. We started by describing the two types of mixed research: mixed model research and mixed method research. We briefly summarized the philosophy of pragmatism (which says to use any combination of method or research techniques that works in answering your research question(s). Also, we reviewed the fundamental principle of mixed research (which prescribes that you to use a mixture or combination that has complementary strengths and nonoverlapping weaknesses). To help you in using the fundamental principle, you can use Tables 14.1 and 14.2 (which show the strengths and weaknesses of quantitative and qualitative research). You should also use the tables showing the strengths and weaknesses of the different methods of data collection that are provided in Chapter 6 bonus materials.

We pointed out that mixed model research studies involve the mixing of quantitative and qualitative techniques within or across one or more stages of the research process (e.g., objective, data collection, data analysis). In contrast, in mixed method research, the researcher uses the qualitative research sequence (qualitative or exploratory objective, collect qualitative data, analyze data using qualitative techniques) for one part or phase of the study and the quantitative research sequence (quantitative or explanatory, or predictive, or confirmatory objective, collect quantitative data, and statistically analyze the data) for a different part or phase of the research study. Typically, in a mixed method study, mixing occurs at the interpretation and writing stages. The exception to this is in sequential studies in which interpretations at one phase are used to develop or in some way inform the design of the second phase. Even in this form, mixing occurs again at the interpretation and writing stages in a research study.

We next specified and described the eight steps in the mixed research process: Determine whether a mixed design is appropriate, determine the rationale for using a mixed design, select the mixed method or mixed model research design, collect the data, analyze the data, validate the data, interpret data, and write the research report. The final section of the chapter contained a presentation of the major limitations of mixed research. In this section, we noted that mixed researchers must be cognizant of these limitations, especially those that pertain to time, expertise, resources, and effort expended. Therefore, there are clearly a number of methodological issues that must be considered before a mixed research study is conducted. Nevertheless, the potential gains achieved by mixing methods are great: greater diversity and collaboration among researchers with different orientations, more comprehensive findings, increased confidence in results, increased conclusion validity, more insightful understanding of the underlying phenomenon, greater value consciousness, promotion of more creative ways of collecting data, and increased synthesis or integration of theories. Therefore, the limitations of mixed research should be weighed against the potential benefits of this approach.

KEY TERMS

across-stage mixed model
   research (p. 417)
compatibility thesis (p. 410)
fundamental principle of mixed
   research (p. 411)

mixed method research (p. 417)
mixed model research
   method (p. 415)
mixed research (p. 410)
pragmatist philosophy (p. 410)

qualitizing (p. 425)
quantitizing (p. 425)
within-stage mixed model
   research (p. 416)

DISCUSSION QUESTIONS

1. Which of the following do you tend to like the best: qualitative research, quantitative research, or mixed research? Why?
2. How could you apply the fundamental principle of mixed research? Give an example.
3. Which method do you think is harder to conduct: mixed model or mixed method research? Why?

4. Which of the rationales for conducting mixed research do you think is the most important in the area of research that is most important to you (triangulation, complementarity, development, initiation, or expansion)? Why?
5. Try to think of a hypothetical study design that includes features of both mixed model and mixed methods. What would you call the design?

RESEARCH EXERCISES

1. If you are proposing or conducting a mixed research study, answer the following questions, to help clarify your thinking.
   a. What are your research questions and/or hypotheses?
   b. What is the rationale for using a mixed design in your research study?
   c. What mixed method or mixed model research design will you use?
   d. What methods of data collection will you use? If there is an ordering (i.e., sequence) to your data collection, please explain it.

    e. How will you analyze your data?

    f. How will you validate your data?

    g. How and when will you interpret your data?

    h. Write out your anticipated table of contents (i.e., the important headings you expect to use in your report).

2. Locate a published article on ContentSelect that is based on mixed research. Explain how the study relates to each of the eight steps of mixed research:

    a. Was a mixed design appropriate, given the research questions and objectives?

    b. Which of the five rationales for using a mixed design (shown in Table 14.4) best fits your research article?

    c. What mixed method or mixed model design did the researcher use?

    d. What kind of data were collected?

    e. How did the researchers analyze the data?

    f. How did the researchers validate the data?

    g. When and how do you suspect the researchers interpreted the data?

    h. How was the journal article organized and written?

3. Using design 2, 3, 4, 5, 6, or 7 in Figure 14.2, design your own simple mixed model study. State whether a qualitative or quantitative approach is used for the study's objective, type of data collected, and data analysis.

RELEVANT INTERNET SITES

www.fiu.edu/~bridges/
Bridges: Mixed Methods Network for Behavioral, Social, and Health Sciences.

www.ehr.nsf.gov/EHR/REC/pubs/NSF97-153/ start.htm
A free book entitled "User Friendly Handbook for Mixed Method Evaluation."

www.fiu.edu/~bridges/glossary.htm
Glossary of mixed methods terms.

RECOMMENDED READING

Brewer, J., & Hunter, A. (1989). *Multimethod research: A synthesis of styles.* Newbury Park, CA: Sage.

Greene, J. C., & Caracelli, V. J. (Eds.). (1997). *Advances in mixed-method evaluation: The challenges and benefits of integrating diverse paradigms.* New Directions for Evaluation, no. 74. San Francisco, CA: Jossey-Bass.

Newman, I., & Benz, C. R. (1998). *Qualitative-quantitative research methodology: Exploring the interactive continuum.* Carbondale, IL: Southern Illinois University Press.

Pring, R. (2000). The "false dualism" of educational research. *Journal of Philosophy of Education, 34*(2), 247–260.

Tashakkori, A., & Teddlie, C. (1998). *Mixed methodology: Combining qualitative and quantitative approaches.* Applied Social Research Methods Series (Vol. 46). Thousand Oaks, CA: Sage.

Tashakkori, A., & Teddlie, C. (Eds.). (2002), *Handbook of mixed methods in social and behavioral research.* Thousand Oaks, CA: Sage.

15

Descriptive Statistics

LEARNING OBJECTIVES

To be able to

- Explain the purpose of descriptive statistics.
- Distinguish between inferential and descriptive statistics.
- Explain the difference between a frequency distribution and a grouped frequency distribution.
- Read and interpret bar graphs, line graphs, and scatterplots.
- Calculate the mode, median, and mean.
- List the strengths and weaknesses of the mode, median, and mean.
- Explain positive skew and negative skew.
- Explain the impact of skewness on the measures of central tendency.
- Describe and interpret the different measures of variability.
- Calculate the range, variance, and standard deviation.
- Explain percentile ranks and z-scores.
- Explain how to construct and interpret a contingency table.
- Explain the difference between simple and multiple regression.
- Explain the difference between the Y-intercept and the regression coefficient.

During the 1960s and 1970s and continuing into this century, there has been concern about discrimination and ensuring that it does not exist. The following vignette is a simplified version of what happened at the University of California at Berkeley in 1973. In particular, the admissions data suggested gender discrimination, but when the data were examined more carefully, it was clear that discrimination did not exist. We will show you the kind of data that suggested discrimination and the kind that did not. This case is written up in *Science* (Bickel, 1975).

Assume that you work in the College of Education admissions office at your local university. You find that the acceptance rate for men is 55 percent (i.e., 55 percent of the men who apply to your school are accepted) and the acceptance rate for women is 44 percent. What would you conclude? Would you conclude that gender discrimination *might* be occurring? After all, men are being accepted at a significantly higher rate than are women.

Let's say that the numbers for your university are shown in the following table:

	Number Applied	Number Admitted	Percentage Admitted
Men	360	198	**55%**
Women	200	88	**44%**

The key statistic in this table is that men have a higher admissions rate than women have.

You, however, know a little bit about statistics and decide to delve further into the data. There only are two departments in your College of Education, so you decide to look at the admissions rates for each of the two departments. These results are shown below. Here is what you find when you look at the acceptance rate for both departments: Women (not men) are more likely to be admitted in both departments!

	DEPARTMENT A				DEPARTMENT B		
	Number Applied	Number Admitted	Percentage Admitted		Number Applied	Number Admitted	Percentage Admitted
Men	120	18	**15%**	Men	240	180	**75%**
Women	120	24	**20%**	Women	80	64	**80%**

In other words, when you look at your data more carefully, you find out that women are more likely to be admitted, and it is clear now that the claim of discrimination against women is unlikely. In this example, the overall data suggested one thing, but when the data were more carefully examined, a completely different conclusion was apparent. One reason for the surprising result is because men were more likely to apply to the department that was easy to get into and women were more likely to apply to the department that was harder to get into. Our purpose for this chapter is to show how to accurately describe your data so that you can inform your audience and not mislead them.

The field of statistics is a branch of mathematics that deals with the analysis of numerical data. It can be divided into two broad categories called descriptive statistics and inferential statistics. In **descriptive statistics,** the goal is to describe, summarize, or make sense of a particular set of data. The goal of **inferential statistics** is to go beyond the immediate data and to infer the characteristics of populations based on samples. As you can see in Figure 15.1, inferential statistics may be subdivided into estimation and hypothesis testing, and estimation may be divided into point and interval estimation. In this chapter, we focus on descriptive statistics, and in the next chapter, we focus on inferential statistics. Our discussion requires very little mathematical background, so don't worry! We focus more on interpretation than on calculation. We do, however, show you how to perform a few basic calculations, so get your calculator handy.

- **Descriptive statistics**
  Statistics that focus on describing, summarizing, or explaining data
- **Inferential statistics**
  Statistics that go beyond the immediate data and infer the characteristics of populations based on samples

DESCRIPTIVE STATISTICS

- **Data set**
  A set of data

Descriptive statistics starts with a set of data, sometimes called a **data set.** The researcher attempts to convey the essential characteristics of the data by arranging the data into a more interpretable form (e.g., by forming frequency distributions and generating graphical displays) and by calculating numerical indexes such as averages, percentile ranks, and measures of spread. The researcher can summarize the variables in a data set one at a time. He or she can also examine how the variables are interrelated (e.g., by examining correlations). The key question in descriptive statistics is how we can communicate the essential characteristics of the data. An obvious way would be to supply a printout of the complete set of data. However, we can do much better than that!

We have included a data set (i.e., a set of data) in Table 15.1 that we will use in several of our examples in this chapter and the next. We refer to this data set as the "college student data set." The hypothetical data are for twenty-five recent college graduates. Data values are

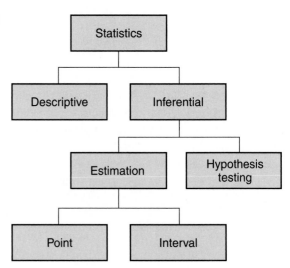

FIGURE 15.1 Major divisions in the field of statistics

▓ **TABLE 15.1**   Hypothetical Set of Data for Twenty-Five Recent College Graduates

Person	Starting Salary	GPA	College Major	Gender	GRE Verbal
1	31,000	2.9	2	1	520
2	32,000	3.6	1	1	600
3	33,000	3.7	1	1	610
4	28,000	2.4	2	0	450
5	37,000	3.4	3	0	500
6	32,000	3.0	3	0	500
7	33,000	3.1	2	0	520
8	25,000	2.5	1	1	450
9	38,000	3.0	3	0	650
10	33,000	2.7	2	0	490
11	30,000	3.0	2	1	500
12	32,000	2.6	1	0	580
13	32,000	3.1	2	1	480
14	31,000	3.1	1	1	530
15	24,000	2.5	1	1	460
16	40,000	3.3	3	0	630
17	31,000	3.3	1	1	510
18	38,000	3.2	2	1	620
19	35,000	3.1	3	1	680
20	32,000	3.2	2	0	550
21	41,000	3.5	3	0	680
22	34,000	3.0	3	1	590
23	28,000	3.0	1	1	650
24	30,000	2.9	2	0	480
25	36,000	3.5	2	0	570

Note: For the categorical variable college major, the value labels are 1 = education, 2 = arts and sciences, 3 = business. For the categorical variable gender, the value labels are 0 = male and 1 = female.

provided for three quantitative variables—starting salary, grade point average, and GRE verbal scores—and for two categorical variables—college major and gender. Take a look at Table 15.1 now to see what a data set looks like. Notice that the data set is structured so that the cases (i.e., individuals) are represented in rows and the variables are represented in columns. This cases-by-variables arrangement is the standard way of organizing data after data collection has been completed.

15.1 What is the difference between descriptive statistics and inferential statistics?

REVIEW

QUESTION

▬▬▬ FREQUENCY DISTRIBUTIONS

One of the most basic ways to describe the data values of a variable is to construct a frequency distribution. A **frequency distribution** is a systematic arrangement of data values in which the data are rank ordered and the frequencies of each unique data value are shown. Just follow these steps, and you can construct a frequency distribution for the data values of any variable:

■ **Frequency distribution**
Arrangement in which the frequencies of each unique data value are shown

1. List each unique number in ascending order in column 1. If a particular number appears more than once, remember to list it only once. For example, even if the number 3 appears five times, list it only once. If a number does not appear in the data, you don't need to list it.
2. Count the number of times each number listed in column 1 occurs, and place the results in column 2.
3. (Optional). Construct a third column by converting column 2 into percentages by dividing each number in column 2 by the total number of numbers.

The first column shows the unique data values, the second column shows the frequencies, and the third column shows the percentages.

For example, look at Table 15.2. This frequency distribution is for the variable starting salary from the college student data set provided in Table 15.1. You can see in column 1 that the lowest starting income is $24,000 and the highest starting income is $41,000. The frequencies are shown in column 2. For example, the most frequently occurring starting income for our recent college graduates was $32,000. Percentages are shown in column 3. For

▨ **TABLE 15.2**
Frequency Distribution of Starting Salary

(1) Starting Salary (X)	(2) Frequency (f)	(3) Percentage (%)
24,000	1	4.0
25,000	1	4.0
28,000	2	8.0
30,000	2	8.0
31,000	3	12.0
32,000	5	20.0
33,000	3	12.0
34,000	1	4.0
35,000	1	4.0
36,000	1	4.0
37,000	1	4.0
38,000	2	8.0
40,000	1	4.0
41,000	1	4.0
	$n = 25$	100.0%

Note: Column 2 shows the frequency distribution. Column 3 shows the percentage distribution.

■ **TABLE 15.3**
Grouped Frequency
Distribution of Starting
Salary

Starting Salary (X)	Frequency (f)	Percentage (%)
20,000–24,999	1	4.0
25,000–29,999	3	12.0
30,000–34,999	14	56.0
35,000–39,000	5	20.0
40,000–44,999	2	8.0
	$n = 25$	100.0%

example, 20 percent of the students started at $32,000 per year, and 4 percent started at $41,000 per year.

When a variable has a wide range of data values, interpretation may be facilitated by collapsing the values of the variable into intervals. The result is called a **grouped frequency distribution** because the data values are clustered, or grouped, into intervals. Researchers typically construct around five to eight equal-size intervals. We constructed a grouped frequency distribution for starting income, which you can see in Table 15.3. Column 1 shows the intervals. As before, the frequencies are shown in column 2, and the percentages are shown in column 3. You can see that the most frequent interval is $30,000–$34,999. This interval includes 14 of the data values, which make up 56 percent of all starting income data values.

In constructing a grouped frequency distribution, it is important that the intervals are **mutually exclusive.** This means that there should not be any overlap among the intervals. (The intervals $20,000–$25,000 and $25,000–$30,000 are not mutually exclusive because a person earning $25,000 can be placed into two intervals.) It is also important that the intervals are **exhaustive.** A set of intervals is exhaustive when it covers the complete range of data values. If all the data values fall into the set of intervals, the intervals are exhaustive.

■ **Grouped frequency distribution**
The data values are clustered or grouped into separate intervals and the frequencies of each interval are given

■ **Mutually exclusive**
The property that intervals do not overlap

■ **Exhaustive**
The property that a set of intervals covers the complete range of data values

GRAPHIC REPRESENTATIONS OF DATA

Graphs are pictorial representations of data in two-dimensional space. Many graphs display the data on two dimensions or *axes*. These two axes are the X- and Y-axes, where the X-axis (also called the abscissa) is the horizontal dimension and the Y-axis (also called the ordinate) is the vertical dimension. If you are graphing the data for a single variable, the values of this variable are represented on the X-axis and frequencies or percentages are represented on the Y-axis. If you are examining two variables, the values of the independent variable are put on the X-axis and the values of the dependent variable are put on the Y-axis. Graphs can also be constructed for more than two variables.

Bar Graphs

A **bar graph** is a graph that uses vertical bars to represent the data. You can see a bar graph of college major in Figure 15.2. The data are from Table 15.1, our college student data set. Notice that the X-axis represents the variable called college major and the Y-axis represents

■ **Bar graph**
A graph that uses vertical bars to represent the data

■ **FIGURE 15.2**   A bar graph of
college major

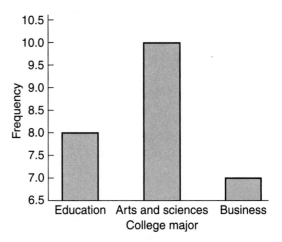

frequency of occurrence. The bars provide graphical representations of the frequencies of
the three different college majors. Arts and sciences was the most common major ($n = 10$),
education was the second most common ($n = 8$), and business was the least common ($n = 7$).

Histograms

■ **Histogram**
A graphic that shows
the frequencies and
shape that characterize
a quantitative variable

Bar graphs are used when your variable is a categorical variable. However, if your variable is
a quantitative variable, a histogram is preferred. A **histogram** is a graphic presentation of a
frequency distribution. It is especially useful (compared to a frequency distribution) because
it shows the shape of the distribution of values. We used the computer program called SPSS
to generate the histogram of starting salary (shown in Figure 15.3). Notice that, in contrast to
bar graphs, the bars in histograms are set next to each other with no space in between.

■ **FIGURE 15.3**   A histogram of
starting salaries

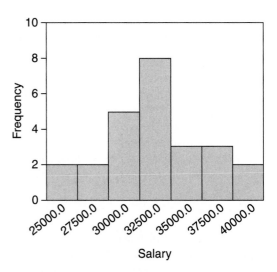

Line Graphs

One useful way to draw a graphical picture of the distribution of a variable is to construct a **line graph.** A line graph is a format for illustrating data that relies on the drawing of one or more lines. You can see a line graph of grade point average (from the college student data set) in Figure 15.4. GPA data values around 3.0 are near the center of the distribution and they occur the most frequently (i.e., low B grades occur the most frequently). You can also see that there are quite a few GPA data values that are higher and lower than 3.0. In other words, the GPA data values are somewhat spread out.

■ **Line graph**
A graph that relies on the drawing of one or more lines

In the previous example, the line graph was given for a single variable: grade point average. It is important to understand that line graphs can also be used with more than one variable. For example, look back at Figure 9.15(b) (page 288), and you will see the type of line graph that is commonly constructed in factorial research designs. The dependent variable is placed on the vertical axis, one of the independent variables is placed on the horizontal axis, and the categories of a second independent variable are represented by separate lines.

Another common use of line graphs is to show trends over time. In this case, the variable that you wish to observe changing over time is placed on the vertical axis, and time is placed on the horizontal axis. The key point is that there is not just one type of line graph. Line graphing is a versatile tool that you might want to use in the future.

Scatterplots

A **scatterplot,** or scatter graph, is a very useful way to visualize the relationship between two quantitative variables. The dependent variable is represented on the vertical axis, and

■ **Scatterplot**
A graph used to depict the relationship between two quantitative variables

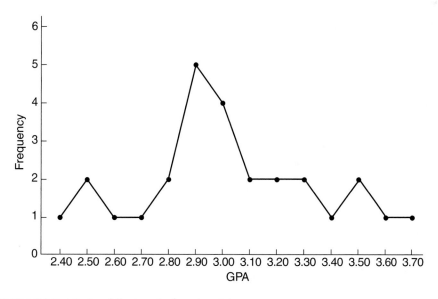

■ **FIGURE 15.4**   A line graph of grade point average

the independent variable is represented on the horizontal axis. Dots are plotted within the graph to represent the cases (i.e., individuals).

A scatterplot of grade point average by starting salary is shown in Figure 15.5. These quantitative variables are from our college student data set. There are a total of twenty-five data points in the graph (i.e., one data point for each of the twenty-five individuals in the data set). If you examine the graph in Figure 15.5, you will clearly see that there is a positive relationship between GPA and starting salary. We calculated the correlation coefficient and found that it is equal to +0.628. This moderately strong, positive correlation coefficient confirms our observation that as GPA increases, starting salary also tends to increase. In short, there is a clear linear relationship between GPA and starting salary.

When you examine a scatterplot, it is helpful to consider the following questions:

- Does there appear to be a relationship between the two variables?
- Is it a linear relationship (a straight line) or a curvilinear relationship (a curved line)? (Linear relationships are much more common than curvilinear relationships.)
- If a linear relationship is present, is it a positive relationship or a negative relationship? The relationship is positive if the data points move in a southwest-to-northeast direction. The relationship is negative if the data points move in a northwest-to-southeast direction.
- If there is a relationship, how strong does it appear to be? The more the data points look like a straight line, the stronger is the relationship. The more they look like a circle or the more dispersed the data are, the weaker is the relationship.

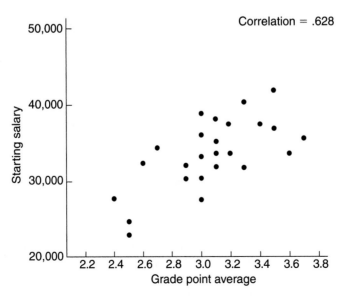

■ **FIGURE 15.5**   A scatterplot of starting salary by grade point average

REVIEW

QUESTIONS

15.2 List the three steps in constructing a frequency distribution.

15.3 What types of graphical representations of data were discussed in the chapter?

15.4 Which graphical representation is used to examine the correlation between two quantitative variables?

MEASURES OF CENTRAL TENDENCY

A **measure of central tendency** is the single numerical value that is considered the most typical of the values of a quantitative variable. For example, if someone asked a teacher how well his or her students did on their last exam, a measure of central tendency would provide an indication of what score was typical. If someone wanted to know how much money people tend to earn annually in the United States, a measure of central tendency would again be called for. Finally, in an experiment, a researcher might be interested in comparing the average performance (which is a measure of central tendency) of the experimental group with the average performance of the control group. We now discuss the three most commonly used measures of central tendency: the mode, the median, and the mean.

■ **Measure of central tendency**
The single numerical value considered most typical of the values of a quantitative variable

Mode

The **mode** is the most frequently occurring number. For example, if you had the numbers

1, 2, *3, 3,* 4

the mode is 3 because 3 occurs more often than any other number. The number 3 occurs twice, and the other numbers only occur once. Therefore, the number 3 is the most frequently occurring number. Suppose you had this set of numbers:

1, 1, 3, 3, 4

In this case, you have two modes: 1 and 3. When you have two modes like this, you can use the term *bimodal* to describe the data. (If you have three or more modes, some researchers use the term *multimodal* as a descriptor.) If you had this set of numbers:

1, 3, 5, 8

you would conclude that you have multiple modes because all the numbers occur an equal number of times. For practice, determine the mode in this set of numbers:

1, 4, 6, 7, 7, 7, 9, 9, 11, 11, 30

The mode is 7 because 7 is the most frequently occurring number. For a more challenging exercise, find the mode of the variable called starting salary in our earlier data set. You will see that the mode is equal to $32,000.

■ **Mode**
The most frequently occurring number

Median

■ **Median**
The fiftieth percentile

The **median,** or fiftieth percentile, is the middle point in a set of numbers that has been arranged in order of magnitude (either ascending order or descending order). If you have an odd number of numbers, the median is defined as the middle number. Here is a simple example. If you had the numbers

2, 9, 1, 7, 10

you would first put them in ascending order of magnitude as follows:

1, 2, 7, 9, 10

Now you can easily see that the median is equal to 7 because 7 is the middle number. (If you "slice" the number 7 down the center, you have the middle point.)

If you have an even number of numbers, the median is defined as the average of the two innermost numbers. For example, if you had the numbers

3, 4, 1, 10

you would first put them in ascending order:

1, 3, 4, 10

Because there is no center number, you take the average of the two innermost numbers (i.e., take the average of the numbers 3 and 4). You can see that the median is 3.5 because that is the average of the two innermost numbers [i.e., $(3 + 4)/2 = 3.5$].

Before moving on, check to make sure that you can find the median in a set of numbers. Here is an easy one: What is the median of 1 and 2? Right, it is 1.5. Now find the median for this set of numbers: 1, 5, 7, 8, 9. The median is 7, because 7 is the middle number. As a more challenging check on your understanding, find the median of starting salary in the college student data set (Table 15.1). The median is equal to $32,000.

Mean

■ **Mean**
The arithmetic average

The **mean** is the arithmetic average, or what most people call the average. You probably already know how to get the average. For example, find the average of these three numbers: 1, 2, and 3. The average is 2. That wasn't hard, was it? Here is what you did, according to the formula for the mean:

$$\text{Mean} = \frac{\Sigma X}{n}$$

This formula is not hard to use once you learn what the symbols stand for. The symbol X stands for the variable whose observed values are 1, 2, and 3 in our example. The symbol Σ (the Greek letter sigma) means "sum what follows." Therefore, the numerator (the top part) in the formula says "sum the X values." The n in the formula stands for the number of numbers. You get the average by summing the observed values of your variable and dividing that sum by the number of numbers. If the numbers are 1, 2, and 3, you would use the formula as follows:

$$\text{Mean} = \frac{\Sigma X}{n} = \frac{1+2+3}{3} = \frac{6}{3} = 2$$

Now don't say that you can't do this because you already know how to get the average of these three numbers. You do need to carefully note the symbols that are used, however, since they are probably new to you. For practice, use the formula now and get the average of 2, 3, 6, 7, and 2. (The average is 4.) You could also calculate the mean of starting salary from the college student data set (Table 15.1). If you add up all the numbers and divide by the total number of numbers, you will find that the mean starting salary is equal to $32,640.

A Comparison of the Mean, Median, and Mode

In this section, we are going to introduce the normal distribution and the concept called skewness. Afterward we show the impact that the shape of a distribution of scores has on the mean, median, and mode. We also provide some commentary on the properties of the mean, median, and mode. Let's start with the idea of the normal curve.

The **normal distribution,** or normal curve, is a unimodal, symmetric, bell-shaped distribution that is the theoretical model used to describe many physical, psychological, and educational variables. You can see an example in Figure 15.6(b). The normal distribution is unimodal because it has only one mode. It is symmetrical because the two sides of the distribution are mirror images. It is said to be bell-shaped because it is shaped somewhat like a bell (i.e., the curve is highest at the center and tapers off as you move away from the center). The height of the curve shows the frequency or density of the data values. Now, remember this important characteristic of the normal distribution: The mean, the median, and the mode are the same number.

■ **Normal distribution**
A unimodal, symmetric, bell-shaped distribution that is the theoretical model of many variables

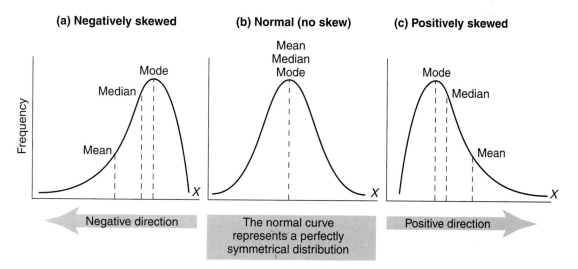

FIGURE 15.6   Examples of normal and skewed distributions

■ **Skewed**
Not symmetrical

■ **Negatively skewed**
Skewed to the left

■ **Positively skewed**
Skewed to the right

The other two distributions shown in Figure 15.6 are not normally distributed [see the distributions in parts (a) and (c)]. These two distributions are **skewed,** which means that they are not symmetrical. A distribution is skewed when one tail is stretched out longer than the other tail, making the distribution asymmetrical. The numbers in the longer tail occur less frequently than the numbers in the "mound" of the distribution. If one tail appears to be stretched or pulled toward the left, the distribution is said to be skewed to the left, or **negatively skewed** (i.e., stretched in the negative direction, where numbers are decreasing in numerical value). The scores on an easy test will tend to be negatively skewed. If a tail appears to be stretched or pulled toward the right, the distribution is said to be skewed to the right, or **positively skewed** (i.e., stretched in the positive direction, where numbers are increasing in numerical value). The scores on a very difficult test will tend to be positively skewed.

Something interesting happens when a distribution is skewed. In particular, the mean, the median, and the mode are different when a distribution is skewed. In the negatively skewed distribution shown in Figure 15.6, the numerical value of the mean is less than the median, and the numerical value of the median is less than the mode (i.e., mean < median < mode). In the positively skewed distribution shown in Figure 15.6, the numerical value of the mean is greater than the median, which is greater than the mode (i.e., mean > median > mode).

Why does the mean change more than the other measures of central tendency in the presence of a skewed distribution? The answer is because the mean takes into account the magnitude of all of the scores. In contrast, the median takes into account only the number of scores and the values of the middle scores.

Here is a demonstration. If you have these five numbers,

1, 2, 3, 4, 5

you can see that the median and the mean are both equal to 3. However, look at what happens if the last number is changed from 5 to 1,000. Here are the new numbers:

1, 2, 3, 4, 1,000

This time, the mean is 202 rather than 3. That is quite a dramatic change. The median, however, is unchanged. The median is still 3. The point is that the mean uses the magnitude of all the scores and is affected by the scores in the tails of a distribution (i.e., by the large numbers and by the small numbers), whereas the median is affected only by the middlemost scores. This means that the mean is pulled more to the left in a negatively skewed distribution (the small values pull the mean down) and the mean is pulled more to the right in a positively skewed distribution (the large values pull the mean up). Because of this pattern, you should remember this general rule:

■ If the mean is less than the median, the data are skewed to the left.
■ If the mean is greater than the median, the data are skewed to the right.

This rule is helpful because it allows you to obtain a rough indication of skewness simply by comparing the mean and the median. If they are very different, the data are probably skewed.[1]

You might wonder which measure of central tendency is the best. As a general rule, the mean is the best measure because it is the most precise. The mean takes into account the magnitude of all scores. The median and the mode do not do this. The mean is also the most stable from sample to sample. As you know, the median takes into account only the number of scores and the values of the middle scores. The mode is usually the least desirable because it provides information only about what data value occurs the most often. Therefore, you should use the mode only when you believe that it is important to express which single number or category occurs the most frequently. Otherwise, the mean or the median is usually the preferred measure of central tendency.

There is one situation in which the median is preferred over the mean. The median is usually preferred when your data are highly skewed. This is because the median is less affected by extreme scores. We use measures of central tendency when we want to describe what is typical for a set of numbers.

Here is an example in which the median would be preferred. Assume that the annual incomes for the ten families living in a small residential neighborhood are as follows:

$16,000
$18,000
$18,000
$18,000
$19,000
$19,000
$20,000
$21,000
$21,000
$500,000

Nine of the families earn somewhere between $16,000 and $21,000. There is, however, an **outlier**, a number that is very atypical of the other numbers in a distribution. One family in the neighborhood earns $500,000. (Think of it like this: If Bill Gates lived in your neighborhood, his income would certainly be an outlier!) The median income in this example is $19,000, and the mean income is $67,000. Which of these two numbers do you believe best describes the "typical family income"? Many would argue that the median better represents these ten families. The median is much closer than is the mean to the actual incomes of 90 percent of the people in this example. Ninety percent of these families are basically under some financial constraints because of low income levels. The mean provides an overly optimistic assessment of the income levels by suggesting that the average or typical family income is $67,000. This is why researchers usually use the median rather than the mean when they are reporting annual income and, more important, why they often use the median when their data are highly skewed.

■ **Outlier**
A number that is very atypical of the other numbers in a distribution

---

15.5 What is a measure of central tendency, and what are the common measures of central tendency?

15.6 When is the median preferred over the mean?

15.7 If the mean is much greater than the median, are the data skewed to the right or skewed to the left?

REVIEW
QUESTIONS

▬▬▬ **MEASURES OF VARIABILITY**

■ **Measure of variability**
A numerical index that provides information about how spread out or how much variation is present

A **measure of variability** is a numerical index that provides information about how spread out or dispersed the data values are or how much variation is present. In other words, measures of variability tell you how similar or different people are with respect to a variable. For example, do the individuals in our earlier data set tend to have very similar or very different grade point averages? The variability in grade point average in our data set was visually shown by the line plot in Figure 15.4. Measures of variability provide a numerical indication of the amount of variability and therefore provide another type of information when you are describing a set of numbers.

If all the numbers were the same, there would be no variability at all. For example, if the set of numbers was

7, 7, 7, 7, 7, 7, 7, 7

you would conclude that there was no variability for the simple reason that there is no variation in the data: All the numbers are the same. On the other hand, the following set of numbers does have some variability:

1, 3, 7, 10, 12, 15, 17, 20

■ **Homogeneous**
A set of numbers with little variability
■ **Heterogeneous**
A set of numbers with a great deal of variability

When there is very little variability in a set of numbers, we sometimes say that the numbers are **homogeneous.** If, on the other hand, there is a great deal of variability, we describe the numbers as being **heterogeneous.** When a set of numbers is relatively homogeneous, you can place more trust in the measure of central tendency (mean, median, or mode) as being typical. Conversely, when a set of numbers is relatively heterogeneous, you should view the measure of central tendency as being less typical or representative of the data values.

Following are examples of relatively low variability and relatively high variability:

Data for group A: 53, 54, 55, 55, 56, 56, 57, 57, 58, 59
Data for group B: 4, 8, 23, 41, 57, 72, 78, 83, 94, 100

You can see that the numbers for group B are more spread out (and have higher variability) than the numbers for group A. You might be surprised to learn that the mean is actually the same in both of these sets of data! The mean is 56 for both. When the numbers are not very spread out, the mean is more representative of the set of numbers than when the numbers are quite spread out. Therefore, a measure of variability should usually accompany measures of central tendency. We now discuss the three most commonly used indexes of variability: the range, the variance, and the standard deviation.

Range

■ **Range**
The difference between the highest and lowest numbers

The **range** is simply the difference between the highest and lowest numbers. In the following formula, the range is the highest (i.e., largest) number minus the lowest (i.e., smallest) number in a set of numbers:

Range = $H - L$

where

 H is the highest number, and
 L is the lowest number.

Find the range for the distributions for group A and group B shown in the previous section. The range in distribution A is 6 (i.e., $59 - 53 = 6$). The range in distribution B is 96 (i.e., $100 - 4 = 96$). The range seems to work in this case because we knew that distribution B had more variability than distribution A. Although the range is very easy to calculate, its use is limited. In fact, the range is not used very often by researchers. One problem with the range is that it takes into account only the two most extreme numbers. A related problem is that it is severely affected by the presence of a single extreme number. To see this problem, change the highest number from 59 to 101 in distribution A. The range changes from 6 to 48; it becomes eight times larger on the basis of changing a single number.

Variance and Standard Deviation

The two most popular measures of variability among researchers are the variance and standard deviation because these measures are the most stable and are the foundations of more advanced statistical analysis. These measures are also based on all the data values of a variable and not just the highest and lowest numbers, as was the case with the range. They are essentially measures of the amount of dispersion or variation around the mean of a variable.

 The **variance** is a measure of the average deviation from the mean in squared units. To turn the variance back into more appealing units, you just take the square root. When you take the square root of the variance, you obtain the standard deviation. You can view the **standard deviation** as an approximate indicator of how far the numbers tend to vary from the mean. The variance and standard deviation will be larger when the data are spread out (heterogeneous) and smaller when the data are not very spread out (homogeneous).

 We show you how to calculate the variance and standard deviation in Table 15.4. We also explain it to you in words here. To get the variance and standard deviation, follow these five steps:

■ **Variance**
A measure of the average deviation from the mean in squared units
■ **Standard deviation**
The square root of the variance

1. Find the mean of a set of numbers. As illustrated in Table 15.4, add the numbers in column 1 and divide by the number of numbers. (Note that we use the symbol "X-bar" (i.e., $\bar{X}$) to stand for the mean.)
2. Subtract the mean from each number. As illustrated in Table 15.4, subtract the mean from each number in column 1 and place the result in column 2.
3. Square each of the numbers you obtained in the last step. As illustrated in Table 15.4, square each number in column 2 and place the result in column 3. (To square a number, multiply the number by itself. For example, 2 squared is 2×2, which is equal to 4.)
4. Put the appropriate numbers into the variance formula. As illustrated in Table 15.4, insert the sum of the numbers in column 3 into the numerator (the top part) of the variance formula. The denominator (the bottom part) of the variance formula is the number of numbers in column 1. Now divide the numerator by the denominator and you have the *variance*.

TABLE 15.4
Calculating the
Variance and
Standard Deviation

(1)* X	(2) $(X - \bar{X})$	(3) $(X - \bar{X})^2$
1	−2	4
2	−1	1
3	0	0
4	1	1
5	2	4
15	0	10
↑	↑	↑

Sums $\sum X$ $\sum(X - \bar{X})$ $\sum(X - \bar{X})^2$

**(4) Variance $= \dfrac{\sum(X - \bar{X})^2}{n} = \dfrac{10}{5} = \dfrac{2}{1} = 2$

(5) Standard deviation $= \sqrt{\text{variance}} = \sqrt{2} = 1.41$

*The mean of column 1 $= \bar{X} = \dfrac{\sum X}{n} = \dfrac{15}{5} = \dfrac{3}{1} = 3$

**Note:* If the variance is used in inferential statistics (i.e., where the sample variance is used as the estimate of the population variance), then you need to use $n - 1$ rather than n in the denominator for technical reasons. When you use $n - 1$, the variance is referred to as the sample variance.

5. You obtained the variance in the previous step. Now take the square root of the variance and you have the *standard deviation*. (To get the square root, type the number into your calculator and press the square root [$\sqrt{\ }$] key.)

Standard Deviation and the Normal Distribution

Now that you understand the idea of standard deviation, we can point out another important characteristic of the normal distribution that we did not mention earlier. The following will always be true *if* the data fully follow a normal distribution:

- 68.26 percent of the cases fall within *one* standard deviation.
- 95 percent fall within 1.96 standard deviations.
- 95.44 percent fall within *two* standard deviations.
- 99.77 percent fall within *three* standard deviations.

A good rule for approximating the area within one, two, and three standard deviations is what we call the "68, 95, 99.7 percent rule" (Figure 15.7). Don't forget, however, that you can only use this rule when you know that the data are normally distributed. The rule is a

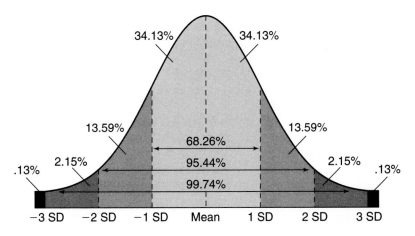

■ **FIGURE 15.7**   Areas under the normal curve. SD = standard deviation.

useful approximation, for example, when you are talking about things like height, weight, and IQ. You should be careful, however, when you have collected your own data, because a distribution usually does not become normally distributed (even if the underlying distribution is normal) until many, many cases have been collected. If you want to apply the 68, 95, 99.7 percent rule, check to see that the data are normally distributed. Do not automatically assume that the rule is applicable.

15.8 What is a measure of variability, and what are the common measures of variability?	**REVIEW**
15.9 How are the variance and standard deviation mathematically related?	
15.10 If a set of data is normally distributed, how many of the cases fall within one standard deviation? How many fall within two standard deviations? How many fall within three standard deviations?	**QUESTIONS**

■ **Measures of relative standing**
Provide information about where a score falls in relation to the other scores in the distribution of data
■ **Percentile ranks**
Scores that divide a distribution into 100 equal parts
■ **Standard scores**
Scores that have been converted from one scale to another to have a particular mean and standard deviation

MEASURES OF RELATIVE STANDING

The raw scores of many research and assessment instruments are not inherently meaningful. How would you feel, for example, if someone told you that your raw scholastic aptitude score was 134? Likewise, how would you compare your score to a score of 119? Without more information, you obviously would not know exactly how to interpret your raw score of 134. This is why standardized test makers rarely report raw scores. Instead, they report various **measures of relative standing,** which provide information about where a score falls in relation to the other scores in the distribution of data. We focus on two types of relative standing: **percentile ranks** (scores that divide a distribution into 100 equal parts) and **standard scores** (scores that have been converted from one scale to another so that they

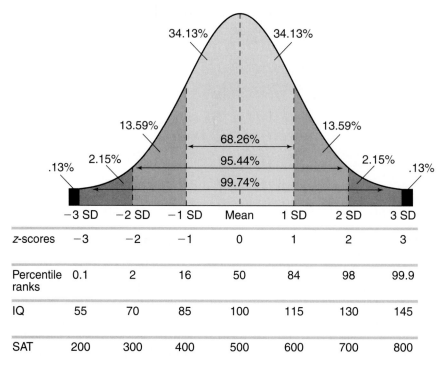

FIGURE 15.8   Percentile ranks and standard scores in relation to the normal curve. SD = standard deviation.

have a particular mean and standard deviation that are believed to be more interpretable). Our following discussion of standard scores focuses on z-scores, although two additional types of standard scores are shown in Figure 15.8. We have included IQ scores (which usually have a mean of 100 and a standard deviation of 15) and SAT scores (which have a mean of 500 and a standard deviation of 100) for your comparison.

Percentile Ranks

■ **Percentile rank**
The percentage of scores in a reference group that fall below a particular raw score

■ **Reference group**
The norm group that is used to determine the percentile ranks

A **percentile rank** is interpreted as the percentage of scores in a reference group that fall below a particular raw score (Crocker and Algina, 1986; Cronbach, 1984; Educational Testing Service, 2002). Percentile ranks help individuals to interpret their test scores in comparison to others. The reference group is often referred to as the norm group or the standardization sample. A **reference group** is the group of people that is used to determine the percentile ranks. A reference group might be a national sample, a sample of a particular aged child, or all of the students in a school district. As a general rule, percentile ranks should be used only when the reference group is quite large.

To interpret the meaning of a score using a percentile rank, let's say that you made a raw score of 680 on the Graduate Record Examination Verbal Test. This score of 680 corre-

■ **TABLE 15.5**
GRE General Test
Interpretive Data

Scaled Score	Percentile Ranks*		
	Verbal Ability	Quantitative Ability	Analytical Ability
800	99	94	97
780	99	89	95
760	99	84	92
740	99	80	89
720	98	75	85
700	97	71	81
680	95	68	76
660	93	64	71
640	91	59	66
620	88	55	61
600	85	50	56
580	80	46	52
560	76	42	47
540	70	37	42
520	65	34	38
500	59	29	33
480	54	25	29
460	48	22	25
440	42	18	21
420	36	15	17
400	30	12	14
380	25	10	11
360	19	7	9
340	14	6	6
320	9	4	4
300	5	3	3
280	3	2	2
260	1	1	1
240		1	
220			
200			
Mean	469	584	560
Standard deviation	117	148	139
Number of examinees	1,082,718	1,082,416	1,080,935

*Based on the performance of all examinees who were tested between October 1, 1998, and September 30, 2001.

sponds to a percentile rank of 95, which means that 95 percent of the individuals in the norm group made scores less than your score. For another example, assume that a friend of yours got a verbal score of 420. Because this score corresponds to a percentile rank of 36, only 36 percent of the individuals made a score lower than your friend. You can see the list of other GRE verbal test standard scores and the corresponding percentile ranks in Table 15.5. As a final example, how would you interpret a verbal score of 580? As you can see in Table 15.5, this score corresponds to the percentile rank of 80.

z-Scores

■ **z-score**
A raw score that has been transformed into standard deviation units

A **z-score** is defined as a raw score that has been transformed into standard deviation units. This means that *a z-score tells you how many standard deviations a raw score is from the mean.* If a raw score is above the mean, the z-score will be positive; if a raw score is below the mean, the z-score will be negative; if a raw score is equal to the mean, the z-score will equal zero (because the mean of a set of z-scores will always be zero).

The z-score standardization transforms any set of raw scores into a new set of scores that has a mean of zero and a standard deviation of one. *The z-score transformation does not impact the overall shape of the data distribution.* If the data are normal (not skewed) before the z-score transformation, then they will still be normal after the z-score transformation, and if the data are skewed before the z-score transformation, then they will still be skewed after the z-score transformation. The new, transformed scores are called "z-scores."

For example, let's say that Jenny has a z-score of +2.00 on some standardized test (e.g., the GRE, the MAT, the SAT). This means that Jenny scored two standard deviations above the mean. Remember, z-scores tell you where a person's score stands in relation to the mean. Jenny obviously did better than the average person. Let's say that Jay has a z-score of –2.00; therefore, Jay scored two standard deviations below the mean. In other words, Jay did worse than the average person. John's z-score is zero; therefore, John's raw score is equal to the mean (i.e., the overall average). John was exactly average. Jean's z-score is +3.50. Jean's raw score falls 3½ deviations above the mean, which is far above the average and better than Jenny's score, which was two standard deviations above the mean.

If the underlying data are normally distributed, then z-scores communicate additional information. In Figure 15.8, we show the normal distribution along with percentile ranks and several standard scores (z-scores, IQ scores, and SAT scores). Because we are now as-suming that the scores are normally distributed, we have additional information about Jenny's score of +2.00. Because a z-score of +2.00 has a percentile rank of 98 when the data are normally distributed, we know that Jenny's score is better than the scores of 98 percent of the people taking the standardized test. Jay's score has a percentile rank of 2, which means that he did better than only 2 percent of the people. John was right at the median (i.e., the fiftieth percentile). Jean did better than virtually everybody, including Jenny.

You can compute a z-score by taking the difference between a particular raw score and the overall mean and then dividing by the standard deviation. You would use this formula:

$$z\text{-score} = \frac{\text{raw score} - \text{mean}}{\text{standard deviation}} = \frac{X - \bar{X}}{SD}$$

To use this formula, you need the raw score that you wish to transform into a *z*-score, and you need to know the mean and standard deviation of all of the scores. Most IQ tests have a mean of 100 and a standard deviation of 15. Therefore, the *z*-score for Maria, who scored 115 on an IQ test, would be determined as follows:

$$z\text{-score} = \frac{115 - 100}{15} = \frac{15}{15} = 1$$

We put Maria's IQ of 115 into the formula, along with the IQ mean (100) and standard deviation (15). The resulting *z*-score is equal to one (+1.00), which means Maria's IQ is one standard deviation above the mean. That's all you do if you want to use the *z*-score formula!

An advantage of *z*-scores is that they can be used to compare raw scores between two different tests that have different means and standard deviations. To compare a person's scores on two different tests, you simply convert the two raw scores into *z*-scores and compare them. For example, assume that Maria got an SAT score of 700. Did Maria do better on the SAT or on the IQ test? You already know that Maria's IQ score results in a *z*-score of 1. An SAT score of 700 results in a *z*-score of +2.00. (If you want to calculate the *z*-score for an SAT score of 700, put these values into the formula: raw score = 700, mean = 500, and standard deviation = 100. The result will be a *z*-score of +2.00.) Obviously, a *z*-score of +2.00 is better than a *z*-score of +1.00, which means that Maria did better on the SAT than she did on the IQ test.

15.11 What is a measure of relative standing, and what are the common measures of relative standing?

15.12 How do you calculate a *z*-score?

R E V I E W

QUESTIONS

EXAMINING RELATIONSHIPS AMONG VARIABLES

Throughout this book, we have been talking about relationships among variables. This is because researchers are seldom satisfied with describing the characteristics of single variables. Research becomes much more interesting when the relationships among variables are also described. We have already talked about comparing means in earlier chapters (e.g., see discussion of analysis of variance in Chapter 9) and about interpreting correlation coefficients (e.g., see discussion of correlation coefficients in Chapter 2). There are two more topics, however, that you need to know about. These topics are contingency tables and regression.

Research
Navigator.c⊛m

**correlation
coefficient**

Contingency Tables

A **contingency table** (also called a cross-tabulation) displays information in cells formed by the intersection of two or more categorical variables. In a two-dimensional contingency table, the rows represent the categories of one variable, and the columns represent the

■ **Contingency table**
A table displaying information in cells formed by the intersection of two or more categorical variables

▓ **TABLE 15.6**   Party Identification by Gender Contingency Tables

(a) Contingency Table Showing Cell Frequencies (Hypothetical Data)

Political Party Identification	Gender		Total
	Males	*Females*	*Total*
Democrat	92	390	482
Republican	16	169	185
Total	108	559	667

(b) Contingency Table Showing Column Percentages (based on the data in Part (a))*

Political Party Identification	Gender	
	Males	*Females*
Democrat	85.2%	69.8%
Republican	14.8%	30.2%
Total Column %	100%	100%

*The column percentage 85.2 percent was obtained by dividing 92 by 108 (and multiplying by 100 to get a percentage); 14.8 percent was obtained by dividing 16 by 108; 69.8 percent was obtained by dividing 390 by 559; 30.2 percent was obtained by dividing 169 by 559. Note that both columns in part (b) sum to 100 percent. [If you want to obtain row percentages, just divide the number of cases in each cell in part (a) by the corresponding row total. Then each row will sum to 100%.]

categories of the other variable. Various kinds of information can be put into the cells of a contingency table (e.g., observed cell frequencies, row percentages, column percentages). You can see a contingency table with cell frequencies in Table 15.6(a). You can see a contingency table with column percentages in Table 15.6(b).

Look at the contingency table in Table 15.6(a). You can see that the row variable is political party identification and the column variable is gender. The numbers in the cells are the observed cell frequencies, which indicate the number of people in each cell. For example, 92 people in the hypothetical set of data were Democrat and male, and 390 were Democrat and female. A table with cell frequencies is a good starting point in constructing a contingency table, but you should not stop there because it is very difficult to detect a relationship between the variables when you examine only the cell frequencies.

Look at the contingency table in Table 15.6(b). This table was constructed in the following way. We made the independent or predictor variable the column variable; we made the dependent variable the row variable; and we obtained column percentages by calculating the percentages down the columns. This is an appropriate table construction because it will allow us to make our comparisons across the levels of the independent variable (gender). We explain exactly where the numbers came from in a footnote to the table. Whenever you obtain *column* percentages, each column will sum to 100 percent, just as the columns do in part (b). After you construct your table in this way, you should make your comparisons across the rows.

When you convert your data to column percents like this, the table is composed of rates, which you should use for comparison purposes. A **rate** shows the percentage (or proportion) of people in a group who have a specific characteristic. For example, in Table 15.6(b), you can see that the rate of membership in the Democratic party for males is 85.2 percent, and that for females is 69.8 percent. In short, males have a higher rate of membership in the Democratic party than do females. (Remember that our data are hypothetical!)

When group comparisons are presented in the news, they are usually calculated in this way; that is, you will often hear that members of one group are more likely than members of another group to have some characteristic. For example, the poverty rate is higher for unwed mothers than for mothers who are married, the rate of lung cancer is higher for smokers than for nonsmokers, the rate of cirrhosis of the liver is higher for heavy drinkers than for light drinkers, and so forth. Comparing across cells helps the researcher to determine whether there is a relationship between the two categorical variables in the contingency table (e.g., marriage status is related to poverty, smoking is related to cancer, and getting cirrhosis of the liver is related to the amount people drink, and in our hypothetical example, gender is related to political party).[2] If there is no relationship between the variables, the rates will be the same.

Here is a simple rule for you to use whenever you want to determine whether the variables in a contingency table are related:

- If the percentages are calculated down the columns, compare across the rows.
- If the percentages are calculated across the rows, compare down the columns.

This simple rule will help you to see very quickly whether there is a relationship between two variables in a contingency table. It is also easy to memorize.

You can extend the ideas presented here by adding more categorical variables to the mix. If you have three categorical variables, the strategy is to examine the original two-dimensional table separately for each level of the third categorical variable. If you want to see an example of this process or learn more about higher-level contingency tables (i.e., tables based on three or more variables), we recommend reading Babbie (1998, pp. 378–383 and Chapter 16) and Frankfort-Nachmias and Nachmias (1992, pp. 403–412). We also have an example at the book's companion website. Now we introduce a technique called regression analysis.

Regression Analysis

Regression analysis is a set of statistical procedures used to explain or predict the values of a dependent variable based on the values of one or more independent variables. In regression analysis, there is always a single quantitative dependent variable. Although the independent variables can be either categorical or quantitative, we discuss only the case in which the independent variables are quantitative. The two main types of regression are called **simple regression,** in which there is a single independent variable, and **multiple regression,** in which there are two or more independent variables.

■ **Rate**
The percentage of people in a group who have a specific characteristic

■ **Regression analysis**
A set of statistical procedures that are used to explain or predict the values of a dependent variable on the basis of the values of one or more independent variables

■ **Simple regression**
Regression based on one dependent variable and one independent variable

■ **Multiple regression**
Regression based on one dependent variable and two or more independent variables

- **Regression equation**
  The equation that defines the regression line
- **Regression line**
  The line that best fits a pattern of observations

The basic idea of simple regression is that you obtain a **regression equation.** The regression equation defines the **regression line** that best fits a pattern of observations. The two important characteristics of any line (including a regression line) are the slope of the line and the Y-intercept of the line. The slope of a line basically tells you how steep the line is. The Y-intercept tells you where the line crosses the Y-axis. These are the two key components of the regression equation. Here is the simple regression equation formula:

$$\hat{Y} = a + bX$$

where

$\hat{Y}$ (called y-hat) is the predicted value of the dependent variable,
a is the Y-intercept,
b is the regression coefficient or slope, and
X is the single independent variable.

Researchers rarely calculate regression equations by hand. Most researchers use a computer program such as SPSS or SAS. All of this might seem complicated, but it will become clearer with an example. Let's use our college student data set (Table 15.1) to see whether we can predict starting salary using our knowledge of grade point average. If you look at Figure 15.9, you can see the regression line that resulted when we used the computer program SPSS to fit the regression line to the data. You can see from looking at the regression line that the relationship is positive (i.e., as grade point average increases, starting salary increases). You can also use the regression line to make approximate predictions.

Here is what to do if you want to use the regression line to make an approximate prediction. You can visually examine the regression line to see what value of Y (the dependent variable) corresponds to a particular value of X (the independent variable). For example,

FIGURE 15.9 The regression line showing the relationship between starting salary and GPA

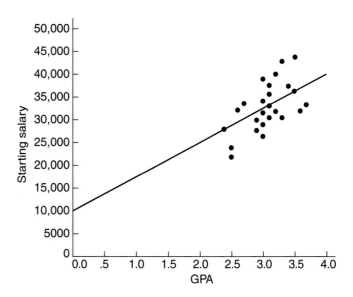

first find the value 3.00 for grade point average on the horizontal axis. Then mark the point on the regression line that corresponds to this grade point average of 3.00. Third, determine what starting salary (i.e., what point on the vertical axis) corresponds to this point on the regression line. It looks as though the predicted starting salary is about halfway between $30,000 and $35,000, so our guess is that the predicted starting salary is about $32,000.

Rather than making predictions by visually examining the regression line, we usually obtain the regression equation and insert values of X and obtain the predicted values of Y. We will show you how to insert values in a moment. Now look at the regression equation that was provided by the computer program:

$$\hat{Y} = 9{,}234.56 + 7{,}638.85(X)$$

The Y-intercept is equal to $9,234.56. The **$Y$-intercept** is defined as the point where the regression line crosses the Y-axis. In Figure 15.9, the X-axis is grade point average and the Y-axis is starting salary. The value of Y at the point where the regression line touches the Y-axis is $9,234.56. It is the value of the Y variable (the dependent variable) that would be predicted if the independent variable (X) were equal to zero.

The regression coefficient in the regression equation is equal to $7,638.85. The regression coefficient, or slope, tells you how steep the regression line is. The **regression coefficient** is more formally defined as the predicted change in Y given a one-unit change in X. A large regression coefficient implies a steep line, and if a line is very steep, Y will change quite a lot given a one-unit change in X. A small regression coefficient implies a line that is not very steep, and if a line is not very steep, Y will not change much given a one-unit change in X. In our example, the regression equation tells us that if someone's GPA increased by one full unit (it went from a C to a B or it went from a B to an A), then we would expect his or her starting salary to increase by $7,638.85. In sum, you can see in Figure 15.9 that the variables starting salary and grade point average are related, and the regression coefficient tells you how much, on average, starting salary increases given a one-unit increase in grade point average.

Now we will show you something you will probably find interesting: You can use a simple regression equation to make predictions. In our example, the dependent variable Y is starting salary. We can obtain a predicted value of starting salary by inserting a value for grade point average into the equation and solving. Let's find the predicted starting salary for someone who has a B grade point average (for someone whose grade point average is 3.00). First we write down the equation:

$$\hat{Y} = 9{,}234.56 + 7{,}638.85(X)$$

Now we insert the value for X (grade point average) and see what predicted value for Y we obtain:

$\hat{Y} = 9{,}234.56 + 7{,}638.85(3.00)$ We inserted the GPA value of 3.00.

$\hat{Y} = 9{,}234.56 + 22{,}916.55$ We multiplied $7,638.85 and 3.00.

$\hat{Y} = 32{,}151.11$ We added $9,234.56 and $22,916.55.

■ **Y-intercept**
The point where the regression line crosses the Y-axis

■ **Regression coefficient**
The predicted change in Y given a one-unit change in X

Our predicted value of starting salary is $32,151.11 when grade point average is a 3.00 (i.e., B). In short, on the basis of our hypothetical college student data, we expect B students to have a starting salary of $32,151.11. We have now used our regression equation to make a prediction.

You should try to make a prediction now. Determine what starting salary you would predict college students with a grade point average of 3.8 to have on the basis of our data. All you need to do is take the equation $\hat{Y} = 9{,}234.56 + 7{,}638.85(X)$ and insert the value of 3.8 where it says X. Then do the arithmetic and find the result. You will find that the predicted value is $38,262.19. You can insert other grade point averages into the equation to find other predicted starting salaries.

When you use a regression equation such as the one we just used from our college student data set, you need to remember that you should use it only for values of X that are in the range of the X values in your data set. In our case, we should *not* use our equation for grade point averages that are below a C or higher than an A because we do not have any data on these grade levels. All the students in our data set had grades in the C to A range. In fact, it is impossible for a student to get a grade higher than an A, so you would never insert a value greater than 4.00 into the equation. Researchers must be very careful when using a regression equation to make predictions.

Multiple regression is similar to simple regression except that there are two or more independent variables. The main difference is that the regression coefficients in multiple regression are called **partial regression coefficients,** and they show the predicted change in Y given a one-unit change in the independent variable *while controlling for the other independent variable(s) in the equation.* The regression coefficients still show the relationship between an independent variable and the dependent variable. However, the multiple regression coefficients also take into account the fact that other independent variables are included in the regression equation. Multiple regression coefficients are similar to partial correlation coefficients, discussed in Chapter 12.

Let's use our college student data set one more time. We let starting salary be our dependent variable, and we use two independent variables: grade point average and GRE verbal scores. Here is the multiple regression equation that was provided by our statistical program, SPSS:

$$\hat{Y} = 3{,}890.05 + 4{,}675.41(X_1) + 26.13(X_2)$$

where

X_1 is grade point average, and
X_2 is GRE verbal.

According to this equation, starting salary increases by $4,675.41 for a one-unit increase in grade point average, when you control for GRE verbal performance. Also, starting salary increases by $26.13 for a one-unit increase in GRE verbal performance when you control for grade point average.

You can also use the multiple regression equation to find the predicted starting salary for a set of values for the two independent variables that you choose. Let's say you want to know the predicted starting salary when a student is a B student (i.e., the student's GPA is 3.00) and the student earned a 500 on the GRE verbal test. All you have to do is insert 3.00

■ **Partial regression coefficient**

The regression coefficient obtained in multiple regression

Research
Navigator.c⊛m

**multiple
regression**

for GPA and 500 for GRE verbal and then find the predicted value for Y, the predicted starting income:

$\hat{Y} = 3{,}890.05 + 4{,}675.41(3.00) + 26.13(500)$	We inserted the two values.
$\hat{Y} = 3{,}890.05 + 14{,}026.23 + 26.13(500)$	We multiplied 4,675.41 times 3.00.
$\hat{Y} = 3{,}890.05 + 14{,}026.23 + 13{,}065.00$	We multiplied 26.13 times 500.
$\hat{Y} = 30{,}981.28$	

If a recent college graduate has a grade point average of 3.00 and a GRE verbal score of 500, we predict that his or her starting salary will be \$30,981.28. You can put any other valid values into the regression equation and obtain the predicted starting salary. For example, you might want to know the predicted starting salary for someone with a GPA of 3.8 and a GRE verbal of 700. All you need to do is insert these two values into the equation and get the predicted salary.

15.13 What are some of the different ways to examine the relationships among variables?

15.14 If you calculate percentages in a contingency table down, then should you make your comparisons down the columns or across the rows?

15.15 What is the difference between simple regression and multiple regression?

15.16 How is the regression coefficient interpreted in simple regression?

15.17 How is the regression coefficient interpreted in multiple regression?

REVIEW

QUESTIONS

SUMMARY

The goal of descriptive statistics is to describe or summarize a set of data. Typically, variables are summarized one at a time. Some common ways to describe the values of a variable are to construct a frequency distribution or a grouped frequency distribution. Graphical representations, such as bar graphs, histograms, and line graphs, are also useful in describing data. Scatterplots are useful when you want to examine the relationship between two quantitative variables. Measures of central tendency (mean, median, and mode) provide the numerical value that is considered most typical of the values of a quantitative variable. The mean takes into account the magnitude of the scores and is usually considered the best measure of central tendency. However, the median is sometimes the preferred measure of central tendency if the data are severely skewed (not symmetrical). Measures of variability tell you how spread out or dispersed the data values are. The most useful measures are the variance and the standard deviation. When data are normally distributed, you can apply the following approximate rule: 68 percent of the cases will fall within one standard deviation, 95 percent of the cases will fall within two standard deviations, and 99.7 percent of the cases will fall within three standard deviations. Measures of relative standing tell you where a score falls in relation to other scores. The most important measures of relative standing are percentile ranks and z-scores. Some important ways to examine and describe the relationships among variables are scatterplots, contingency tables, and regression analysis.

KEY TERMS

bar graph (p. 437)
contingency table (p. 453)
data set (p. 434)
descriptive statistics (p. 434)
exhaustive (p. 437)
frequency distribution (p. 436)
grouped frequency
   distribution (p. 437)
heterogeneous (p. 446)
histogram (p. 438)
homogeneous (p. 446)
inferential statistics (p. 434)
line graph (p. 439)
mean (p. 442)
measure of central tendency (p. 441)

measure of variability (p. 446)
measures of relative standing (p. 449)
median (p. 442)
mode (p. 441)
multiple regression (p. 455)
mutually exclusive (p. 437)
negatively skewed (p. 444)
normal distribution (p. 443)
outlier (p. 445)
partial regression coefficient (p. 458)
percentile rank (p. 450)
percentile ranks (p. 449)
positively skewed (p. 444)
range (p. 446)
rate (p. 455)

reference group (p. 450)
regression analysis (p. 455)
regression coefficient (p. 457)
regression equation (p. 456)
regression line (p. 456)
scatterplot (p. 439)
simple regression (p. 455)
skewed (p. 444)
standard deviation (p. 447)
standard scores (p. 449)
variance (p. 447)
Y-intercept (p. 457)
z-score (p. 452)

DISCUSSION QUESTIONS

1. When do you think the use of descriptive statistics is important?
2. Some statisticians say that a measure of central tendency such as the mean should be accompanied by a measure of variability. Why do you think they say this?
3. Which measure (or measures) of relative standing should teachers use when communicating students' test score results to parents? Why?
4. Name a variable that you think is normally distributed. Does it have all of the characteristics of the normal curve? For example, does it precisely follow the 68, 95, 99.7 percent rule? Do the tails of the curve ever completely touch the bottom axis (which is also a characteristic of the normal curve)?

5. For each of the following cases, list the procedure shown in this chapter that is used to examine the relationship between two variables:
   a. You have two categorical variables.
   b. You have two quantitative variables.
   c. You have a quantitative dependent variable and one or more quantitative independent variables.
   d. To foreshadow what is coming up in the next chapter, note the following: When you have a quantitative dependent variable and one categorical independent variable, the procedure is called a *one-way analysis of variance.* When you have one quantitative dependent variable and two categorical independent variables, it is called a *two-way analysis of variance.*

RESEARCH EXERCISES

1. Determine the mean, median, and mode of the following numbers: 1, 2, 2, 2, 3, 3, 3, 3, 4, 4, 4, 9, 1650. Are these data skewed to the left (negatively skewed) or skewed to the right (positively skewed)? Which measure of central tendency do you think best represents the central tendency of the data?
2. In Table 15.4, we calculated the standard deviation of the following set of numbers: 1, 2, 3, 4, 5. Now calculate the z-score for each of the five numbers. You will recall that we claimed that the mean is zero and the standard deviation is 1 for any complete set of z-scores. Is this true for your set of z-scores?

3. If someone tells you that his or her IQ is 145, how rare is this event? (*Hint:* Calculate the *z*-score, and interpret it in relation to the normal curve.)

4. In the chapter, we provided a simple regression equation showing the relationship between grade point average and starting salary. The regression equation is: $\hat{Y} = 9{,}234.56 + 7{,}638.85(X)$. What starting salary would you predict (using the regression equation) for someone who has a GPA of 4.00 (a student who has all A's)?

5. In Table 15.6(a), we showed a contingency table with cell frequencies. In Table 15.6(b), we showed a contingency table that had been percentaged down the columns. There is a new set of cell frequencies in the table that follows.

Party Identification	Gender		
	Males	Females	Total
Democrat	390	920	1310
Republican	569	160	729
Total	959	1080	2039

Calculate percentages in this new table down the columns, and interpret the results.

RELEVANT INTERNET SITES

www.psychstat.smsu.edu/sbk00.htm
An on-line statistics textbook.

http://wise.cgu.edu/ and
http://wise.cgu.edu/linksf.shtml
Lots of statistics-related links.

RECOMMENDED READING

Henry, G. T. (1995). *Graphing data: Techniques for display and analysis.* Thousand Oaks, CA: Sage.

Huff, D. (1993). *How to lie with statistics.* New York: Norton. (Original work published 1954).

Koomey, J. G. (2001). *Turning numbers into knowledge: Mastering the art of problem solving.* Oakland, CA: Analytics Press.

Vogt, W. P. (1999). *Dictionary of statistics and methodology: A nontechnical guide for the social sciences.* Thousand Oaks, CA: Sage.

ENDNOTES

1. Note that you cannot necessarily conclude that the data are normal when the mean and the median are the same.

2. If you form the ratio of the rates, you can obtain what is called the *relative risk,* which is also frequently given on the national news. In our example, the relative rate is 85.2/69.8 = 1.22. This rate of 1.22 means that males are 22 percent more likely than females to be Democrats. If the relative rate were 2.00, then males would be twice as likely to be Democrats; if the rate were 15.00, males would be fifteen times as likely.

16

Inferential Statistics

Over the past 10 to 15 years a number of studies have compared smaller with larger schools and found that students in smaller schools "come to class more often, drop out less, earn better grades, participate more often in extracurricular activities, feel safer, and show fewer behavior problems" (Viadero, 2001). One of the studies contributing to this conclusion is the study funded by the Chicago-based Joyce Foundation (Wasley, Fine, King, Powell, Holland, Gladden, & Mosak, 2000). This was a two-year study in which the Chicago public schools were classified into different types, the primary distinction being small schools with fewer than 350 students versus larger schools with more than 350 students. Over two years, the researchers collected data on a variety of indicators of school performance such as dropout rates, attendance rates, retention rates, school grades, and standardized test scores. Following completion of the study, the researchers had to analyze this large data set in a way that would provide answers to the research questions that directed the study. One of the questions was whether there was a relationship between school size and student achievement. They also wanted to find out whether the effect of school size differed between elementary schools and high schools.

How did these researchers go about analyzing their data to answer their research questions? To appropriately analyze any set of quantitative data requires knowledge of statistics. Note that these researchers were not just interested in the schools that they studied but were asking a general question regarding the effect of school size. They wanted to use the information to make a more general statement about the effect of school size. In other words, they wanted to be able to generalize from the results of their study to other schools in similar circumstances. To be able to make such statements requires the use of inferential statistical techniques. This is the type of statistical techniques that we will discuss in this chapter. It is also the type of statistical analysis that Wasley et al. (2000) used when they analyzed the results of their study.

In descriptive statistics, researchers attempt to describe the numerical characteristics of their data. In **inferential statistics** researchers attempt to go beyond their data. In particular, they use the laws of probability to make inferences about populations based on sample data. In the branch of inferential statistics known as estimation, researchers want to estimate the characteristics of populations based on their sample data. To make valid statistical estimations about populations, they use random samples (i.e., "probability" samples). In the branch of inferential statistics known as hypothesis testing, researchers test specific hypotheses about populations based on their sample data. You can see the major divisions of the field of statistics by reviewing Figure 15.1 (page 434).

Let's start with four important points about inferential statistics. First, the distinction between samples and populations is essential. You will recall that a **sample** is a subset of cases drawn from a population, and a **population** is the complete set of cases. A population might be all first-grade students in the city of Ann Arbor, Michigan, and a sample might consist of 200 first-grade students selected from this population. The researcher should always define the population of interest.

- **Inferential statistics**
  Use of the laws of probability to make inferences and draw statistical conclusions about populations based on sample data

- **Sample**
  A subset of cases drawn from a population
- **Population**
  The complete set of cases

■ **Statistic**
A numerical character-
istic of a sample
■ **Parameter**
A numerical character-
istic of a population

Second, a **statistic** (also called a sample statistic) is a numerical characteristic of a sample, and a **parameter** (also called a population parameter) is a numerical characteristic of a population. Some examples of numerical characteristics that interest researchers are means (averages), proportions (or percentages), variances, standard deviations, correlations, and regression coefficients. Here is the main idea: If a mean or a correlation (or any other numerical characteristic) is calculated from sample data, it is called a statistic; if it is based on all the cases in the entire population (such as in a census), it is called a parameter.

Third, in inferential statistics, we study samples when we are actually much more interested in populations. We don't study populations directly because it would be cost prohibitive and impossible to study everyone in a population for every single research study. Because we study samples rather than populations, our conclusions will sometimes be wrong. The solution provided by inferential statistics is that we can assign probabilities to our statements, and we can make conclusions that are very likely to be correct.

Fourth, random sampling is assumed in inferential statistics. You will recall from our earlier chapter on sampling that random sampling produces representative samples (i.e., samples that are similar to the populations from which they are selected). The assumption of random sampling is important in inferential statistics because it allows researchers to utilize the probability theory that underlies inferential statistics. Basically, statisticians have studied the behavior of sample statistics when these statistics are based on random samples.

Now you need to become familiar with some symbols that are used to represent several commonly used statistics and parameters. Researchers and statisticians use different symbols for *statistics* and *parameters* because they want to communicate whether their research is based on sample or population data. Statisticians usually use Greek letters to symbolize population parameters and Roman letters (i.e., English letters) to symbolize sample statistics. (This is probably why some students say, "Statistics is like Greek to me!") This convention goes quite far back in the history of statistics. Please take a moment now and examine the symbols shown in Table 16.1. In the next paragraph, we are going to ask you a few questions about the symbols shown in Table 16.1.

Let's say that you have calculated the average reading performance of a sample of 100 fifth-grade students. What symbol would you use for this sample mean? The most com-

▨ **TABLE 16.1**
A List of Symbols Used
for Statistics and
Parameters

Name	Sample Statistic	Population Parameter
Mean	$\bar{X}$	μ (mu)
Variance	SD^2	σ^2 (sigma squared)
Standard deviation	SD	σ (sigma)
Correlation	r	ρ (rho)
Proportion	p	π (pi)
Regression coefficient	b	β (beta)

Note: Statistics are usually symbolized with Roman letters and parameters with Greek letters.

monly used symbol is $\overline{X}$ (it's called *X*-bar). Now assume that you have conducted a census of all fifth-grade students in the United States and you have calculated the average reading performance of all these students. What symbol would you use? As you can see in Table 16.1, the correct symbol for the population mean is μ (mu). The average is calculated in exactly the same way for both a sample and a population. The only difference is the symbol that is used to stand for the mean.

Now assume that you also calculated the correlation between math performance and reading performance for the 100 students in your sample of fifth-graders. What symbol would you use? The correct symbol for the sample correlation coefficient is *r*. If you conducted a census of all the fifth-grade students in the U.S. population and calculated the correlation between math performance and reading performance, what symbol would you use? The appropriate symbol is ρ (which is called rho). The important point is that when you calculate numerical indexes such as means, percentages, and correlations, you should use the appropriate symbol, and the correct symbol depends on whether you are analyzing sample data or population data. Statistics and parameters are *usually* calculated in exactly the same way. For example, the mean is calculated the same way for sample and population data. The key exception to this rule is that researchers use $n-1$ rather than n in the denominator of the variance and standard deviation formulas when they are analyzing sample data. (You don't need to worry about the technical reason for this exception to the rule.[1])

16.1 What is the difference between a statistic and a parameter?

16.2 What is the symbol for the population mean?

16.3 What is the symbol for the population correlation coefficient?

SAMPLING DISTRIBUTIONS

The theoretical notion of sampling distributions is what allows researchers to make probability statements about population parameters based on sample statistics. The **sampling distribution** of a statistic is defined as the theoretical probability distribution of the values of a statistic that results when all possible random samples of a particular size are drawn from a population. More simply, a sampling distribution is the distribution of a sample statistic that comes from **repeated sampling** (i.e., drawing a sample, calculating the statistic, drawing *another* sample, calculating the statistic, drawing *another* sample, and so forth, until *all* possible samples have been selected). The sampling distribution is an important idea to know about because it explains how sample statistics operate over repeated sampling.

The idea of a sampling distribution is a very general one because a sampling distribution can be constructed for any sample statistic. For example, a sampling distribution can be constructed for the mean (the sampling distribution of the mean), a percentage (the sampling distribution of the percentage or proportion), a correlation (the sampling distribution of the correlation coefficient), a variance (the sampling distribution of the variance), and even the difference between two means. Can you guess what this last type of sampling distribution is

- **Sampling distribution**
  The theoretical probability distribution of the values of a statistic that results when all possible random samples of a particular size are drawn from a population
- **Repeated sampling**
  Drawing many or all possible samples from a population

called? (It's called the sampling distribution of the difference between two means.) You will be glad to know that you will never have to actually construct a sampling distribution! Mathematical statisticians have already constructed the sampling distributions for every common statistic that educational researchers currently use. You need to know only the definition of a sampling distribution given above and to understand the concept of sampling distributions.

It is important that you remember the following point: Researchers do *not* actually construct sampling distributions when they conduct their research. A researcher typically selects only *one* sample, not all possible samples, from a population, and then uses a computer program such as SPSS or SAS to analyze the data collected from the people in the sample. Remember that a sampling distribution is based on all possible samples, not the single sample that the researcher studies. The computer program does, however, use sampling distributions. In particular, the computer uses the idea of a sampling distribution to determine certain probabilities that we will discuss shortly. You should therefore think of a sampling distribution as a theoretical distribution because there is a sampling distribution underlying each inferential statistical procedure that a researcher uses.

A sampling distribution demonstrates that *the value of any sample statistic* (such as a mean or a correlation coefficient) *varies from sample to sample.* Think of it like this: If you selected several random samples from a population and calculated the value of a statistic (such as a mean) for each of the samples, wouldn't you expect the sample values to be a little different from one another? You would *not* expect all of your sample values to be *exactly* the same number. This chance variation from sample to sample results in sampling error.

- **Sampling error**
  The difference between a sample statistic and the corresponding population parameter

Sampling error is the difference between a sample statistic and the corresponding population parameter, and it is virtually always present in research because researchers rarely study everyone in a population. The presence of sampling error does not mean that random sampling doesn't work or that a researcher has made a mistake. It simply means that the values of statistics calculated from random samples will tend to vary because of chance fluctuations.

Researchers sometimes need an indicator of the amount of sampling error (i.e., variation) present in a sampling distribution. That is, they need to know what is called the standard error of a sampling distribution. The **standard error** is nothing more than the standard deviation of a sampling distribution. Recall from Chapter 15 that the standard deviation tells you how much variation there is in a distribution of data. The variation of a sampling distribution can also be described by determining the standard deviation. However, statisticians like to call this special type of standard deviation (the standard deviation of a *sampling distribution*) the standard error. It tells you how much variation there is in the scores that make up a sampling distribution. Whenever you hear the word *standard error,* you should therefore think of the variation in a sampling distribution.

- **Standard error**
  The standard deviation of a sampling distribution

When there is a lot of sampling error in a sampling distribution, the standard error will be large, and when there is not much sampling error, the standard error will be small. For example, if a sampling distribution is based on large random samples (e.g., all possible samples of size 1,500), the standard error will be smaller than if the sampling distribution is based on small random samples (e.g., all possible samples of size 20). That's because, on average, large samples provide values closer to the population parameter than small samples do. In short, researchers prefer a small standard error, and a good way to get a small standard error is to select a large sample.

There is one more characteristic of sampling distributions to remember: If you construct a sampling distribution, you see that *the average of the values of the sample statistic is equal to the population parameter.* For example, if you took all possible samples from a population and calculated the correlation for each sample, the average of all those sample correlations would equal the correlation in the entire population. The reason is that a sample statistic value will sometimes overestimate the population value and will sometimes underestimate the population value. Most important, a sample statistic will not be consistently too large or too small. The result is that the average of all the possible sample statistic values is equal to the population parameter.

Sampling Distribution of the Mean

Now let's make things a little more concrete by considering the sampling distribution of a particular statistic. Let's think about the sampling distribution of the mean. Let's say that you just drew a random sample of 100 people from the population of a city. *For the purpose of this example, we are telling you that the average income of the population is $50,000.* (In practice you would *not* know the population mean.) What value would you expect to obtain if you calculated the mean income of the 100 people in your randomly selected sample? You would expect the sample mean to be around $50,000 (since you happen to know that the population mean is $50,000). Let's say, however, that your sample mean turns out to be $45,600. Your mean is a little less than the population mean, and the amount of sampling error is $4,400 (i.e., $50,000 − $45,600 = $4,400). Your sample mean is not exactly the same as the population mean.

Now assume that you select another random sample of 100 people from the same city population. What value would you expect for the sample mean this time? Again, you would expect the sample mean to be about $50,000. This time, however, the sample mean is equal to $52,000. Now draw *another* random sample of 100 people. Let's say this sample mean is $49,800. Now, let's say, hypothetically speaking, that you continued this process (of selecting a random sample of a specified size and calculating the sample mean on each sample) until all possible samples have been examined. You would obviously have a lot of sample means resulting from your exercise in repeated sampling! The line graph constructed from all of these means would form a normal curve, and the overall average of this sampling distribution would be $50,000 (which is the same as the population parameter). The name of this theoretical distribution of sample means is the **sampling distribution of the mean.**

You can see a picture of our hypothetical sampling distribution of the mean in Figure 16.1. We assume that the standard error is $10,000. This means that the standard deviation of our hypothetical sampling distribution of the mean is $10,000. If you look at the line graph in Figure 16.1, you see that the sampling distribution of the mean is normally distributed. Because the distribution is normally distributed, we know that most of the randomly selected sample means will be close to the population mean but a few of them will be farther away. Basically, random sampling works well most of the time but not all of the time.

The mean of the sampling distribution of the mean is equal to the true population mean because random sampling is an unbiased sampling process (i.e., random sampling does not produce sample statistics that are systematically larger or smaller than the population parameter). If you take all possible random samples and calculate the mean of each sample, the

■ **Sampling distribution of the mean**
The theoretical probability distribution of the means of all possible random samples of a particular size drawn from a population

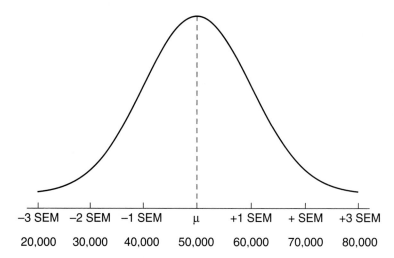

−3 SEM	−2 SEM	−1 SEM	μ	+1 SEM	+ SEM	+3 SEM
20,000	30,000	40,000	50,000	60,000	70,000	80,000

F I G U R E 1 6 . 1   The sampling distribution of the mean. SEM stands for standard error of the mean. *Standard error* is the term used to refer to the standard deviation of a sampling distribution.

means will fluctuate randomly around the population mean and they will form a normal distribution. Some of these means will fall above the population mean, and some will fall below the population mean, but the average of all of these sample means will equal the true population mean. That's how random sampling operates. It is a chance process. You now have the important ideas of sampling distributions. Sampling distributions are important in estimation and hypothesis testing, the major divisions of inferential statistics.

R E V I E W

QUESTIONS

16.4 What is the definition of a sampling distribution?

16.5 How does the idea of repeated sampling relate to the concept of a sampling distribution?

ESTIMATION

People often make estimations. For example, if your best friend asks you what time you're coming to his house Sunday for a visit, you will provide an estimate. You might say to your friend, "I'll probably come over about two o'clock." In other words, your estimate is "two o'clock." Researchers use inferential statistics to make an estimation of a population parameter. The key question in the field of statistical estimation is

Based on my random sample, what is my estimate of the population parameter?

There are two different kinds of estimation procedures in inferential statistics. If you use a single number (the value of your sample statistic) as your estimate (your best guess) of the population parameter, then you are engaged in point estimation. If you use a range of numbers that you believe includes the population parameter, then you are engaged in interval estimation. As an analogy, let's say that you take your car in for a repair, and the service manager gives you an estimate of how much the repair will cost. If the manager says that the cost will probably be $300, then the manager has provided a point estimate (a single number). If the manager says that the cost will probably be "somewhere between $250 and $350" then the manager has provided an interval estimate (a range of numbers that is likely to include the true cost). That's the basic idea. Now we will explain these two ideas a little further.

Point Estimation

Point estimation is defined as the use of the value of a sample statistic as the estimate of the value of a population parameter. You might use the sample mean to estimate the population mean, the sample percentage to estimate the population percentage, or the sample correlation to estimate the population correlation. The specific value of the statistic is called the **point estimate,** and it is the estimated value of the population parameter. The point estimate is your best guess about the likely value of the unknown population parameter.

Let's see whether you can now engage in point estimation. Let's say that the average income of the people in a random sample of 350 teachers from San Antonio, Texas, is $39,000. What is your point estimate of the population mean? You would estimate the value in the population of teachers in San Antonio to be $39,000 because that was the mean in your random sample. Now let's say that 59 percent of the 350 teachers in your sample say that they support bilingual education. What is the point estimate of the population percentage? You would estimate the percentage in the population of teachers in San Antonio to be 59 percent because that was the percentage in your random sample. In sum, your point estimates are $39,000 (for income) and 59 percent (for bilingual education).

Point estimation is used whenever a researcher uses the value of the sample statistic as his or her estimate of the population parameter. Because of the presence of sampling error, however, a point estimate will rarely be exactly the same value as the population parameter. Think of it like this. If the average income in a population is $35,000, would you expect your sample value to be exactly $35,000, or would you expect it to be some number near $35,000? You should expect that it would be a number near but not exactly equal to $35,000. An insight from our earlier study of sampling distributions is that *the value of a statistic varies from sample to sample.* That's why a point estimate is usually wrong. Because of the presence of sampling error, many researchers recommend the use of interval estimation.

Interval Estimation

When researchers use interval estimation, they construct confidence intervals. A **confidence interval** is a range of numbers inferred from the sample that has a certain probability or chance of including the population parameter. The endpoints of a confidence interval are called **confidence limits;** the smallest number is called the **lower limit** and the largest number is called the **upper limit.** In other words, rather than using a point estimate (which is a single number), the researcher uses a range of numbers, bounded by the lower and upper limits, as the interval estimate. This way, researchers can increase their chances of capturing the true population parameter.

- **Point estimation**
The use of the value of sample statistic as the estimate of the value of a population parameter
- **Point estimate**
The estimated value of a population parameter
- **Confidence interval**
A range of numbers inferred from the sample that has a certain probability or chance of including the population parameter
- **Confidence limits**
The endpoints of a confidence interval
- **Lower limit**
The smallest number on a confidence interval
- **Upper limit**
The largest number on a confidence interval

■ **Level of confidence**
The probability that a confidence interval to be constructed from a random sample will include the population parameter

Researchers are able to state the probability (called the **level of confidence**) that a confidence interval to be constructed from a random sample will include the population parameter. We use the future tense because our confidence is actually in the long-term process of constructing confidence intervals. For example, 95 percent confidence intervals will capture the population parameter 95 percent of the time (the probability is 95 percent), and 99 percent confidence intervals will capture the population parameter 99 percent of the time (the probability is 99 percent). This idea is demonstrated in Figure 16.2.

In the top part of Figure 16.2, you see a hypothetical sampling distribution of the mean. Recall from our earlier discussion that the sampling distribution of the mean is normally distributed and its mean is equal to the population mean. Also, a key idea of the sampling distribution of the mean is that the values of individual sample means vary from sample to sample because of sampling error. Now look at the twenty sample means (the dots) surrounded by their confidence intervals below the sampling distribution in Figure 16.2. These twenty means randomly jump around the population mean just as you would expect. Notice, however, that nineteen out of the twenty confidence intervals covered the population mean. Only one of the confidence intervals missed the true population mean. The process worked as we would expect for these twenty samples.

Most of the time confidence intervals will include the population parameter, but occasionally, they will miss it. In Figure 16.2, the process worked nineteen times out of twenty. Because the intervals were 95 percent confidence intervals, that is exactly what we expected would happen. We expected to be right about 95 percent of the time, and we were (nineteen out of twenty is 95 percent). The bottom line is that if you construct 95 percent confidence intervals, then you will capture the population parameter 95 percent of the time in the long run.

You are probably wondering why a researcher would use 95 percent confidence intervals rather than 99 percent confidence intervals. After all, the researcher will make a mistake 5 percent of the time with 95 percent confidence intervals but only 1 percent of the time with 99 percent confidence intervals. The reason is because 99 percent confidence intervals are wider than 95 percent confidence intervals, and wider intervals are less precise (e.g., the interval from 20 to 80 is wider and less precise than the interval from 45 to 55). That is the tradeoff. Fortunately, there is a way out of it. *An effective way to achieve both a higher level of confidence and obtain a more narrow (i.e., more precise) interval is to increase the sample size.* Bigger samples are therefore better than smaller samples. As a general rule, most researchers use 95 percent confidence intervals, and as a result, they make a mistake about 5 percent of the time. Researchers also attempt to select sample sizes that produce intervals that are narrow (i.e., precise) enough for their needs.

Now we want to give you an intuitive explanation of how a confidence interval is constructed. Here is the general formula for a confidence interval:

Confidence interval = point estimate ± margin of error

■ **Margin of error**
One-half the width of a confidence interval

where the symbol ± means plus or minus. As you can see, a confidence interval is a point estimate (a sample mean, a sample percentage, a sample correlation, and so forth) plus or minus the margin of error. The **margin of error** is simply one-half the width of the confidence interval. A confidence interval is constructed by taking a point estimate and surrounding it by the margin of error. For example, if you wanted a confidence interval for the mean, you could find the sample mean and surround it on each side by the margin of error.

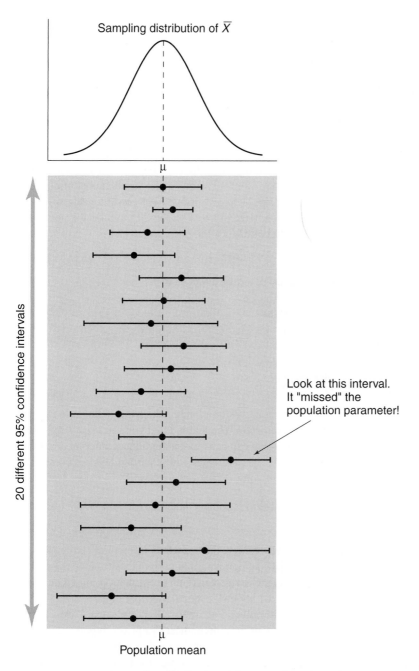

FIGURE 16.2 A sampling distribution of the mean (based on all possible samples of size 100) and an illustration of the 95 percent confidence intervals for twenty possible samples. The width of the intervals will be slightly different because they are estimated from different random samples. In the long run, 95 percent of confidence intervals will capture the population mean.

To find out how to calculate the margin of error, you will need to consult a statistics book (e.g., Moore & McCabe, 1993, p. 503). Fortunately, researchers rarely need to calculate their confidence intervals by hand because confidence intervals are easily obtained through the use of statistical computer programs such as SPSS and SAS.

Now we will show you an example of a confidence interval based on the college student data set that we introduced in Table 15.1. Using the statistical computer program called SPSS, we obtained the point estimate and the 95 percent confidence interval for starting salary. The average starting salary for the twenty-five recent college graduates in our data set was $32,640. Therefore, $32,640 is the point estimate. (If we had to pick *one* number as our estimate, $32,640 is the number we would pick.) We found that the margin of error for the 95 percent confidence interval was $1,726.29. Therefore, the 95 percent confidence interval is the range of values from $30,913.71 to $34,366.29. We conclude that we are 95 percent confident that the interval from $30,913.71 to $34,366.29 includes the population mean. Now you know how to interpret a confidence interval correctly!

REVIEW

QUESTIONS

16.6 Which of the two types of estimation do you like the most? Why?

16.7 What are the advantages of using interval estimation rather than point estimation?

HYPOTHESIS TESTING

In the preceding section, we introduced you to estimation, in which the goal was to use sample statistics to estimate population parameters. You learned that you can use a single number as the estimate (a point estimate) or you can construct a confidence interval around the point estimate, allowing you to estimate the parameter with a certain level of confidence. The key question in estimation is the following:

- Based on my random sample, what is my (point or interval) estimate of the true population parameter?

■ **Hypothesis testing**
The branch of inferential statistics that is concerned with how well the sample data support a null hypothesis and when the null hypothesis can be rejected

In this section, we introduce **hypothesis testing,** the branch of inferential statistics that is concerned with how well the sample data support a particular hypothesis called the null hypothesis and when the null hypothesis can be rejected. Unlike estimation, in which the researcher usually has no clear hypothesis about the population parameter, in hypothesis testing, the researcher constructs a priori null and alternative hypotheses and uses inferential statistics to help make a decision about these hypotheses (a priori hypotheses are hypotheses that are stated by the researcher before the data are collected). For now, just think of the null hypothesis as the hypothesis that states "there is no effect present," and the alternative hypothesis as the hypothesis that states "there is an effect present."

This is the key question that is answered in hypothesis testing:

- Is the value of my sample statistic unlikely enough (*assuming* that the null hypothesis is true) for me to reject the null hypothesis and tentatively accept the alternative hypothesis?

For example, a researcher might do an experiment to compare a new method of counseling (given to the experimental group) to no counseling at all (the control group). In this case, the null hypothesis says that there is no effect (i.e., the treatment group is *not* any better than the control group after the treatment) and the alternative hypothesis says that there is an effect (i.e, the treatment and control groups do differ after the treatment). If the two groups are very dissimilar after the treatment, the researcher might be able to reject the null hypothesis and accept the alternative hypothesis.[2] The goal of hypothesis testing is to help a researcher make a probabilistic decision about the truth of the null and alternative hypotheses. Ultimately, the researcher hopes the research data will allow him or her to reject the null hypothesis and support the alternative hypothesis.

In the next section, we carefully explain the null hypothesis and the alternative hypothesis because these two hypotheses are the foundation of hypothesis testing. In Exhibit 16.1, we show you that hypothesis testing has some similarities to the courtroom. The material in Exhibit 16.1 provides a preview of the material that follows.

Research
Navigator.c⊛m

**null hypothesis
significance
testing**

Research
Navigator.c⊛m

NHST

Null and Alternative Hypotheses

The starting point for hypothesis testing is to state the null and the alternative hypotheses. The **null hypothesis,** represented by the symbol H_0, is a statement about a population parameter and states that some condition concerning the population parameter is true. In most educational research studies, the null hypothesis (H_0) predicts no difference or no relationship in the population. It is the null hypothesis that is the hypothesis directly tested using probability theory. In particular, hypothesis testing operates under the *assumption* that the null

■ **Null hypothesis**
A statement about a
population parameter

■ **E X H I B I T   1 6 . 1   An Analogy from Jurisprudence**

The U.S. criminal justice system operates on the assumption that the defendant is innocent until proven guilty beyond a reasonable doubt. In hypothesis testing, this assumption is called the null hypothesis. That is, researchers assume that the null hypothesis is true until the evidence suggests that it is not likely to be true. The researcher's null hypothesis might be that a technique of counseling does not work any better than no counseling. The researcher is somewhat like a prosecuting attorney, who brings someone to trial when he or she believes that there is some evidence against the accused; the researcher brings a null hypothesis to "trial" when he or she believes that there is some evidence against the null hypothesis (i.e., the researcher actually believes that the counseling technique does work better than no counseling). In the courtroom, the jury decides what constitutes reasonable doubt, and it makes a decision about guilt or innocence. The researcher uses inferential statistics to determine the probability of the evidence under the assumption that the null hypothesis is true. If this probability is low, the researcher is able to reject the null hypothesis and accept the alternative hypothesis. If this probability is not low, the researcher is not able to reject the null hypothesis. No matter what decision is made, things are still not completely settled, because a mistake could have been made. In the courtroom, decisions of guilt or innocence are sometimes overturned or found to be incorrect. Similarly, in research, the decision to reject or not reject the null hypothesis is based on probability, so researchers sometimes make a mistake. However, inferential statistics gives researchers the probability of their making a mistake.

hypothesis is true. Then, if the results obtained from the research study are very different from that expected under the assumption that the null hypothesis is true, the researcher rejects the null hypothesis and then tentatively accepts the alternative hypothesis. The null hypothesis is the focal point in hypothesis testing because it is the hypothesis that is directly tested.

■ **Alternative hypothesis**
Statement that the population parameter is some value other than the value stated by the null hypothesis

The **alternative hypothesis,** represented by the symbol H_1, states that the population parameter is some value other than the value stated by H_0. The alternative hypothesis typically asserts the opposite of the H_0 and usually represents a statement of a difference or a relationship that is consistent with what the researcher actually believes is true. The null and alternative hypotheses are logically contradictory because they cannot both be true at the same time. Remember that the alternative hypothesis is consistent with the researcher's research hypothesis, which means that the researcher is interested in supporting the alternative hypothesis, not the null hypothesis. You can see several examples of research questions, null hypotheses, and alternative hypotheses in Table 16.2. Later in this chapter, we will test several of these null hypotheses using our college student data set from Table 15.1.

Many students are curious why researchers use the term *null hypothesis.* It was developed by a famous statistician, Sir Ronald Fisher (1890–1962), who invented the procedure of

▨ **TABLE 16.2**   Examples of Null and Alternative Hypotheses in Inferential Statistics

Research Question	Verbal Null (H_0) Hypothesis	Symbolic H_0 Hypothesis	Verbal Alternative (H_1) Hypothesis	Symbolic H_1 Hypothesis
Do teachers score higher on the GRE verbal than the national average?	The teacher population GRE verbal mean is equal to the national average of 476.	$H_0: \mu_{GREV} = 476$	The teacher population GRE verbal mean is different from the national average of 476.	$H_1: \mu_{GREV} \neq 476$
Do males or females tend to score better on the GRE verbal?	The male and female population means are not different.	$H_0: \mu_M = \mu_F$	The male and female population means are different.	$H_1: \mu_M \neq \mu_F$
Do education, arts and sciences, and business students have different starting incomes?	The education, arts and sciences, and business student populations have the same mean starting incomes.	$H_0: \mu_E = \mu_{A\&S} = \mu_B$	At least two of the three population means are different.	H_1: Not all equal
Is there a correlation between GPA (X), and starting salary (Y)?	The population correlation between GPA and starting salary is equal to zero.	$H_0: \rho_{XY} = 0$	The population correlation between GPA and starting salary is not equal to zero.	$H_1: \rho_{XY} \neq 0$
Is there a relationship between GRE verbal (X_1), and starting salary (Y), controlling for GPA (X_2)?	The population regression coefficient is equal to zero.	$H_0: \beta_{YX_1 \cdot X_2} = 0$	The population regression coefficient is not equal to zero.	$H_1: \beta_{YX_1 \cdot X_2} \neq 0$

hypothesis testing. The idea is to set up a hypothesis to be "knocked down," or rejected. Researchers do this because the convention is to assume no effect or no difference from the hypothesized null value until sufficient evidence to the contrary is provided. You can therefore view the null hypothesis as the no-change or the no-effect hypothesis. You can also view it as the status quo or the "nothing new" or the "business as usual" hypothesis. The key point is that the null hypothesis is what researchers *assume* until they can demonstrate otherwise.

Here is how Harnett (1982) explains the null hypothesis:

> The term "null hypothesis" developed from early work in the theory of hypothesis testing, in which this hypothesis corresponded to a theory about a population parameter that the researcher thought did *not* represent the true value of the parameter (hence the word "null," which means invalid, void, or amounting to nothing). The *alternative hypothesis* generally specified those values of the parameter that the researcher believed did hold true. (p. 346)

According to the logic of hypothesis testing, you should assume that an effect is *not* present until you have good evidence to conclude otherwise. The researcher states a null hypothesis but hopes ultimately to be able to reject it. In other words, the null hypothesis is the hypothesis that the researcher hopes to be able to nullify by conducting the hypothesis test.

As an example, let's assume that we are interested in knowing which teaching method works better: the discussion teaching method or the lecture teaching method. Here are the null and alternative hypotheses:

Null hypothesis: $\quad\quad\quad\quad H_0: \mu_D = \mu_L$

Alternative hypothesis: $\quad\quad H_1: \mu_D \neq \mu_L$

where

$\quad\mu_D$ is the symbol for the discussion group population mean and

$\quad\mu_L$ is the symbol for the lecture group population mean

This null hypothesis says that the average performance of students in discussion classes is equal to the average performance of students in lecture classes. This null hypothesis is called a point or exact hypothesis because it contains an equals sign (=). As you can see, the alternative hypothesis states the opposite of the null hypothesis (i.e., that the discussion and lecture population means are *not* equal).

It is a good idea to remember the following three points about hypothesis testing. First, the alternative hypothesis can never include an equals sign (=). Second, the alternative hypothesis is based on one of these three signs: $\neq$ (not equal to), $<$ (less than), or $>$ (greater than). Third, the null hypothesis is based on one of these three signs: = (equal to), $\leq$ (less than or equal to), or $\geq$ (greater than or equal to). As you can see, the equality sign is always a part of the null hypothesis.

Directional Alternative Hypotheses

Sometimes the researcher will state an alternative hypothesis in a directional form rather than in a nondirectional form. A **nondirectional alternative hypothesis** includes a not

■ **Nondirectional alternative hypothesis**
An alternative hypothesis that includes the not equal sign

■ **Directional alterna-tive hypothesis**
An alternaitve hypoth-esis that contains ei-ther a greater than sign (>), or a less than sign

equal to sign (≠). A **directional alternative hypothesis** contains either a greater than sign (>) or a less than sign (<).

For example, the researcher in our previous example could have stated this set of hypotheses:

Null hypothesis: $H_0: \mu_D \leq \mu_L$
Alternative hypothesis: $H_1: \mu_D > \mu_L$

You can see that the alternative hypothesis states that the discussion group population mean is greater than the lecture group population mean. In other words, a directional alternative hypothesis was stated. The null hypothesis was also changed so that all possible outcomes were included in the two hypotheses. Note that the null hypothesis still has the equality in it (i.e., the sign ≤ means less than or *equal* to).

The researcher could have also stated this set of hypotheses:

Null hypothesis: $H_0: \mu_D \geq \mu_L$
Alternative hypothesis: $H_1: \mu_D < \mu_L$

Once again, a directional alternative hypothesis is given. This time, however, the alternative hypothesis states that the discussion group population mean is less than the lecture group population mean. In other words, it is hypothesized that students learning by lecture do better, on average, than do students learning by discussion.

Although the use of directional alternative hypotheses might seem attractive, there is a major drawback. If a researcher uses a directional alternative hypothesis and a large difference in the *opposite* direction is found, the researcher must conclude that *no* relationship exists in the population. That is the rule of hypothesis testing. Therefore, when you read journal articles, the vast majority of the alternative hypotheses will be nondirectional. In fact, if a researcher has used a *directional* alternative hypothesis, he or she is obliged to tell you (Pillemer, 1991). If a researcher does not state the type of alternative hypothesis used, you can assume that it was a nondirectional alternative hypothesis.

Examining the Probability Value and Making a Decision

Now you are going to learn how the researcher makes the decision to reject or fail to reject the null hypothesis. As we told you earlier, it is the null hypothesis that is directly tested in the hypothesis testing procedure. When a researcher states a null hypothesis, the researcher is able to use the principles of inferential statistics to construct a probability model about what would happen *if the null hypothesis were true*.[3] This probability model is nothing but the sampling distribution that would result for the sample statistic (mean, percentage, correlation) over repeated sampling if the null hypothesis were true. In practice, the researcher uses a computer package, such as SPSS or SAS, that automatically selects the correct sampling distribution for the particular statistical test. For example, if you tested a null hypothesis about the mean, SPSS would use information about the sampling distribution of the mean for your statistical test. All you have to do is know what null hypothesis you want to test and then select the appropriate statistical test.

After the researcher states the null hypothesis, collects the research data, and selects a statistical test using SPSS, the computer program analyzes the research data and provides something called a probability value as part of the computer output. The **probability value** is the probability of the result of your research study or an even more extreme result assuming that the null hypothesis is true. Obtaining the probability value is a key idea in hypothesis testing because the researcher uses this value to make a decision about the null hypothesis. In particular, the researcher uses the probability value that is based on his or her research results to determine whether the observed value of the sample statistic (mean, percentage, correlation, and so forth) is probable or improbable, assuming that the null hypothesis is true.

- **Probability value**
  The probability of the result of your research study, assuming that the null hypothesis is true

For example, suppose a researcher wants to determine who has the higher starting salary: recent male college graduates or recent female college graduates. Let's say that you construct these two statistical hypotheses for your research study:

| Null hypothesis: | H_0: $\mu_{\text{Males}} = \mu_{\text{Females}}$ |
| Alternative hypothesis: | H_1: $\mu_{\text{Males}} \neq \mu_{\text{Females}}$ |

As you can see, you want to test the null hypothesis that the average starting salaries for the males and females are the same in their respective populations. The alternative hypothesis says the average starting salaries are *not* the same. You have randomly selected samples of males and females, and you have calculated the starting salaries for these individuals in your research study.

If the average starting salary was $43,000 for the males and $27,000 for the females in your research study, the probability value would be small because such a large difference would be unlikely if the null hypothesis were true. When the probability value is small, the researcher rejects the null hypothesis because the research results call into question the null hypothesis. When the researcher rejects the null hypothesis, the researcher decides to accept the alternative hypothesis. (We will explain in a moment when you should consider a probability value to be small.) If you did reject the null hypothesis and therefore tentatively accepted the alternative hypothesis, you would also make the claim that the finding is **statistically significant.** Researchers claim their finding is statistically significant when they do *not* believe their observed result was due only to chance or sampling error.

- **Statistically significant**
  Claim made when the evidence suggests an observed result was probably *not* due to chance

On the other hand, if the average starting salary was $33,000 for the males in your study and $31,000 for the females in your study, the difference between $33,000 and $31,000 could simply be due to chance (i.e., sampling error). In this case, the probability value would be larger than that in the previous example because this time the difference is not so unlikely under the assumption that the null hypothesis is true. If the probability value is large, the researcher will fail to reject the null hypothesis. The researcher will also make the claim that the research finding is not statistically significant (i.e., the observed difference between the two means may simply be a random or chance fluctuation).

We told you that you can use a computer program such as SPSS to find out how likely or unlikely your sample result is *assuming that the null hypothesis is true.* You make this determination using the probability value that you get from the computer printout. If the probability value is small, then your sample result is unlikely (assuming that the null hypothesis is true). If the probability value is large, then your sample result is not unlikely (assuming

that the null hypothesis is true). You are probably wondering, "When do I consider a probability value to be small?" and "When do I consider a probability value to be large?" The answer is that most researchers consider a probability value that is less than or equal to .05 to
be small and a probability value that is greater than .05 to be relatively large.

For example, assume that the probability value (based on your computer analysis of
the research data) was .03 when the male and female incomes were very different ($43,000
versus $27,000). Because this probability value is less than .05, the researcher would reject
the *null hypothesis* that the two population means are the same ($H_{0:}$ $\mu_{Males} = \mu_{Females}$), and
the researcher would accept the alternative hypothesis that the two population means are
different ($H_{1:}$ $\mu_{Males} \neq \mu_{Females}$). The researcher would also claim that the difference between the two sample means is statistically significant.

On the other hand, assume that the probability value (based on your computer analysis
of the data) was .45 when the male and female incomes were similar ($33,000 versus
$31,000). In this case, the probability value is greater than .05. Therefore, the researcher
would *fail to reject the null hypothesis.* The researcher would also claim that the difference
between the two sample means is not statistically significant. Note that the researcher cannot claim that the two population means are the same. The researcher can only claim that he
or she has failed to reject the null hypothesis. Basically, whenever the researcher is unable
to reject the null hypothesis, he or she is left in an ambiguous situation.

This number .05 that we just used is the significance level that we chose to help us decide when the probability value was small or large. In other words, a researcher selects a
significance level to aid in making the decision about the size of the probability value obtained from the analysis of the research data. The **significance level** (also called the alpha
level) is the cutoff that the researcher uses for deciding when to reject the null hypothesis:
(1) when the probability value is less than or equal to the significance level, the researcher
rejects the null hypothesis and (2) when the probability value is greater than the significance level, the researcher fails to reject the null hypothesis. It is important to understand
that a significance level does not always have to be .05. The researcher can select any significance level to use in a research study as long as he or she can justify why a particular significance level was used.

You might wonder why educational researchers usually select a significance level of
.05 and why they believe that a probability value that is less than or equal to .05 is small
enough to reject the null hypothesis and that a probability value greater than .05 is not small
enough (is too large) to reject the null hypothesis. There are no ultimate answers to these
questions. Basically, the significance level of .05 has become a widespread convention
among researchers in education and every other social and behavioral science. In other
words, it is the significance level that researchers have decided to adopt. Historically, Sir
Ronald Fisher originally used the .05 significance level, and ever since then, the .05 significance level has been popular with many researchers. Remember, however, that the .05 significance level is not used by all researchers; it is only the most commonly used significance
level.

What exactly does a significance level of .05 mean? A significance level of .05 means
that if the observed sample result occurs only 5 percent of the time or less (when the null hypothesis is true), then the researcher will consider the observed sample result to be an unlikely
event, and therefore, the researcher will make the decision to reject the null hypothesis. Re-

■ **Significance level**
The cutoff the re-
searcher uses to decide
when to reject the null
hypothesis

member this point: The significance level is the value that the researcher compares the probability value with.

First, the researcher selects a significance level that he or she wants to use in the research study. The significance level is a value (such as .05) that the researcher chooses to use in deciding when the probability value is small enough to call into question the null hypothesis. Be careful not to get the probability value and the significance level mixed up! Then the researcher gets the probability value from the computer printout. The probability value is based on the statistical analysis of the research data. It tells the researcher how likely the observed value of the sample statistic is, under the assumption that the null hypothesis is true. Remember that the probability value is based on the empirical research data collected by the researcher and analyzed by the computer program.

When you engage in hypothesis testing, you follow these two rules:

- *Rule 1:* If the probability value (which is a number obtained from the computer printout and is based on your research results) is *less than or equal to* the significance level (the researcher usually uses .05), then the researcher rejects the null hypothesis and tentatively accepts the alternative hypothesis. The researcher also concludes that the observed relationship is statistically significant (i.e., the observed difference between the groups is not just due to chance fluctuations).
- *Rule 2:* If the probability value is *greater than* the significance level, then the researcher cannot reject the null hypothesis. The researcher can only claim to fail to reject the null hypothesis and conclude that the relationship is not statistically significant (i.e., any observed difference between the groups is probably nothing but a reflection of chance fluctuations).

If you memorize rules 1 and 2, the rest of the material in this chapter is going to be easier than you might expect! These two rules are stated more concisely in Table 16.3. At this point you should review the steps in hypothesis testing summarized in Table 16.3 so that you can remember the logic of hypothesis testing (also called the logic of significance testing). Because of the importance of the concepts of probability value and significance level, we explain them in an intuitive way in Exhibit 16.2.

The Hypothesis-Testing Decision Matrix

Because samples are studied in inferential statistics rather than complete populations, hypothesis testing is based on incomplete data. Because hypothesis testing is based on sample data, it relies on probability theory to inform the decision-making process. As a result, decision-making errors will inevitably be made some of the time. The four possible hypothesis-testing outcomes are illustrated in Table 16.5.

Across the top of Table 16.5 are the two possible conditions that can exist in the population: The null hypothesis is true, or the null hypothesis is false. Across the rows of the table are the two possible decisions that a researcher can make: A researcher can reject the null hypothesis, or a researcher can fail to reject the null hypothesis. You will see in Table 16.5 that these two sets of conditions result in four possible outcomes. Two of the outcomes are good (they are correct decisions), and two of the outcomes are bad (they are incorrect decisions).

▨ **TABLE 16.3**   Steps in Hypothesis Testing

1. State the null and alternative hypotheses.
2. Set the *significance level* before the research study.
   (Most educational researchers use .05 as the significance level. Note that the significance level is also called the *alpha level* or, more simply, *alpha*.)
3. Obtain the *probability value* using a computer program such as SPSS.
4. Compare the probability value to the significance level and make the statistical decision.

Step 4 includes two decision-making rules:

Rule 1:

If: Probability value ≤ significance level (i.e., probability value ≤ alpha)

Then: Reject the null hypothesis.

And: Conclude that the research finding is statistically significant.

In practice, this usually means:

If: Probability value ≤ .05

Then: Reject the null hypothesis.

And: Conclude that the finding is statistically significant.

Rule 2:

If: Probability value > significance level (i.e., probability value > alpha)

Then: Fail to reject the null hypothesis.

And: Conclude that the research finding is not statistically significant.

In practice this usually means:

If: Probability value > .05

Then: Fail to reject the null hypothesis.

And: Conclude that the research finding is not statistically significant.

5. Interpret the results. That is, make a substantive, real-world decision and determine practical significance.
   This means that you must decide what the results of your research study actually mean. Statistics are only a tool for determining statistical significance. If you obtain statistical significance, you must now interpret your results in terms of the variables used in your research study. For example, you might decide that females perform better, on average, than males on the GRE verbal test or that client-centered therapy works better than rational emotive therapy, or that phonics and whole language in combination work better than phonics only.

   You must also determine the *practical significance* of your findings. A finding is practically significant when the difference between the means or the size of the relationship is big enough, in your opinion, to be of practical use. For example, a correlation of .15 would probably not be practically significant, even if it was statistically significant. On the other hand, a correlation of .85 would probably be practically significant. *Effect-size indicators* (p. 484) are important aids when you are making a judgment about practical significance.

■ EXHIBIT 16.2   Understanding Probability Value and Significance Level

The ideas of probability value and significance level are extremely important. A coin-tossing example might help you to gain a deeper understanding of the ideas of significance level and probability value.

Let's suppose that your research teacher decides to test the null hypothesis that a particular coin is fair. A fair coin has an equal chance of coming up heads or tails on a given toss. The coin that your teacher is using looks like a normal coin, but you can see it only from a distance. Next, your research teacher tells you that she is going to check to see whether the assumption that the coin is fair seems to be justified. The two hypotheses in this example are as follows:

Null hypothesis: H_0: The coin is fair.
Alternative hypothesis: H_1: The coin is biased.

Your teacher tells you that she is going to flip the coin ten times and record the number of heads. Obviously, if the coin is fair, you would expect to get about as many heads as tails over the ten flips of the coin. Your teacher flips the coin for the first time, looks at it, and says, "It was heads." She puts a check on the board to record the result. She flips the coin again, looks at it, and says, "It was heads." She puts another check on the board. Once again, your teacher flips the coin, looks at it, and says, "It was heads." She puts yet another check on the board. Your teacher contin-

ues this coin-flipping exercise seven more times, and each time she tells you that the coin flip resulted in heads! Is this coin fair? The teacher flipped the coin ten times, and it came up heads every single time. That is ten heads in a row. Does this seem like a likely or an unlikely result?

Most students reject the null hypothesis that the coin in this exercise is fair, and they claim that the coin must be biased. Some students will start questioning the assumption that the coin is fair after only three or four heads have come up in a row. By the time heads has come up ten times in a row, virtually everyone rejects the null hypothesis that the coin is fair. Basically, each student has the concepts of significance level and probability in his or her head. The cutoff point (the point at which the student decides the coin is not fair) is the student's significance level. The student's perception of how likely the particular observed result would be assuming the coin is fair is the probability value. Students compare this probability value to the significance level. When the probability value reaches the student's significance level (the point where the student decides that the fair-coin hypothesis appears to be too improbable to believe), the student rejects the null hypothesis. The student rejects the original assumption that the coin is fair.

In Table 16.4, you can see the actual probability values of getting heads under the assumption that

■ TABLE 16.4
Coin Toss Probabilities

Number of Tosses	Probability Value of Consecutive Heads	
1	.50000	Probability of heads
2	.25000	Probability of two heads in a row
3	.12500	Probability of three heads in a row
4	.06250	Probability of four heads in a row
5	.03125	Probability of five heads in a row
6	.01563	Probability of six heads in a row
7	.00781	Probability of seven heads in a row
8	.00391	Probability of eight heads in a row
9	.00195	Probability of nine heads in a row
10	.00098	Probability of ten heads in a row

(continued)

■ **EXHIBIT 16.2   Continued**

the coin is fair. The probability of getting ten heads in a row is .00098. What this probability value means is that if the coin is fair, the rules of probability inform us that we will get ten heads in a row only about once every thousand times. That means that getting ten heads in a row is quite unlikely. Formal hypothesis testing works a lot like this coin-tossing example. Researchers compare the actual probability value (which they get from the computer printout) to the significance level that they choose to use. As you know, researchers usually use a significance level of

.05. In our coin-tossing example, we would have rejected the null hypothesis (that the coin is fair) because the probability value (.00098) is clearly less than the significance level (.05). Remember that the *probability value* is the mathematical probability of an observed result, under the assumption that the null hypothesis is true. The *significance level* is the cutoff point that the researcher chooses to use when deciding how unlikely an event must be in order to reject the null hypothesis.

Can you locate the two correct decisions in Table 16.5? Type A correct decisions occur when the null hypothesis is true and you do not reject it (i.e., you fail to reject the null hypothesis). This is exactly what you hope to do when the null hypothesis is true. Type B correct decisions occur when the null hypothesis is false and you reject it. Again, this is exactly what you hope to do when the null hypothesis is false. If the null hypothesis is false, you always want to reject it. Researchers hope for a Type B correct decision because they hope to reject their null hypotheses and be able to claim that their research findings are statistically significant.

■ **Type I error**
Rejecting a true null hypothesis

Now look at the two "errors" in Table 16.5. These errors are called Type I errors and Type II errors. A **Type I error** occurs when the researcher rejects a true null hypothesis. Remember: If the null hypothesis is true it should *not* be rejected. Type I errors are called false

■ **TABLE 16.5**   The Four Possible Outcomes in Hypothesis Testing

		The True (but Unknown) Status of the Null Hypothesis	
		The null hypothesis is true (It should not be rejected.)	The null hypothesis is false (It should be rejected.)
Your Decision*	Fail to reject the null hypothesis	Type A Correct decision!	**Type II Error** (false negative)
	Reject the null hypothesis	**Type I Error** (false positive)	Type B Correct decision!

*Remember that if the null hypothesis is true, it should *not* be rejected, but if the null hypothesis is false, it *should* be rejected. The problem is that you will not know if the null hypothesis is true or false. You only have the probabilistic evidence obtained from your sample data.

positives because the researcher has falsely concluded that there is a relationship in the population. The researcher has claimed statistical significance in error. Here is an analogy. In medicine, the null hypothesis is "the patient is not ill." Therefore, a false positive occurs when a medical test says that you have a disease, but you really don't. As another analogy, in the criminal justice system, the defendant is presumed to be innocent until found guilty by a judge or jury. Hence, a Type I error occurs when an innocent person is found guilty.

A **Type II error** occurs when the researcher fails to reject a false null hypothesis. Remember, if the null hypothesis is false, it is supposed to be rejected. Type II errors are sometimes called false negatives because the researcher has falsely concluded that there is no relationship in the population. That is, the researcher has claimed it to be not statistically significant in error. In a medical analogy, a false negative occurs when a medical test says that you do not have a disease, but you really do. In the courtroom, a Type II error occurs when a guilty person is found to be not guilty.

> ■ **Type II error**
> Failing to reject a false null hypothesis

Traditionally, researchers have been more concerned with avoiding Type I errors than Type II errors. In fact, the significance level that we have been discussing is defined as the probability of making a Type I error that the researcher is willing to tolerate. If a researcher uses .05 as the significance level, the researcher is saying that he or she is only willing to tolerate making a Type I error 5 percent of the time. In other words, the researcher is willing to tolerate making false positives (claiming there is an effect when there is none) only 5 percent of the time. This attitude suggests that researchers are conservative people when it comes to making claims from their research data. They are willing to *incorrectly* claim that they have an effect only 5 percent of the time.

Controlling the Risk of Errors

We pointed out in the previous section that the significance level used by a researcher is the probability of making a Type I error that a researcher is willing to accept. When a researcher uses the .05 significance level, for example, the researcher is willing to make Type I errors only 5 percent of the time. You might wonder, therefore, why researchers don't just use a smaller significance level. For example, why don't researchers just use a significance level equal to .01 rather than a significance level equal to .05? After all, a researcher who uses this smaller level will make fewer Type I errors.

The problem with using a smaller significance level is that Type I errors and Type II errors tend to be inversely related. In other words, when you try to *decrease* the likelihood of making a Type I error, you usually *increase* the likelihood of making a Type II error. In particular, if you use a smaller significance level, say, .01 rather than .05, you will make it harder to reject the null hypothesis. This reduces the frequency of Type I errors. However, when you make it harder to reject the null hypothesis this way, you are also more prone to making Type II errors. That is, you are more likely to fail to reject the null hypothesis when you should have rejected it. That is the tradeoff. In short, when you try to make a false positive less likely, you tend to make a false negative more likely.

You will be glad to know that there is a solution. The solution is to include more participants in your research study. In other words, you need to increase your sample size. Larger samples provide a more sensitive or **powerful** test. If you increase the sample size, you are less likely to make a hypothesis-testing error, and that is exactly what we all want! So

> ■ **Power**
> The likelihood of rejecting the null hypothesis when it is false

remember, "the bigger the sample size, the better."[4] Larger sample sizes are better than smaller sample sizes because you will be more likely to draw the correct conclusion.

If you are able to use large sample sizes and you also happen to obtain statistical significance (you reject the null hypothesis), you must also make sure that your finding is **practically significant** (the difference between the means is large or the correlation is strong enough to be of practical importance). This is because even small deviations from the null hypothesis are sometimes found to be statistically significant when large sample sizes are used. Scriven (1993) made this point when he quoted a Harvard statistician as follows:

> Fred Mosteller, the great applied statistician, was fond of saying that he did not care much for statistically significant differences; he was more interested in *interocular differences,* the differences that hit us between the eyes. (p. 71)

For example, perhaps you compared two techniques for teaching spelling, and the two means in your study turned out to be 86 and 85 percent correct on the spelling test after the intervention. The difference between these two means is quite small and is probably not practically significant; however, this difference might end up being statistically significant if you have a very large number of people in each of the two treatment groups. Likewise, a small correlation might be statistically significant but not practically significant if you have a very large number of people in your research study. This does *not* mean that larger samples are bad. The bigger the sample size, the better rule still applies. It simply means that you must always make sure that a finding is practically significant in addition to being statistically significant.

A useful tool for helping you to determine when a finding is practically significant is to examine an effect-size indicator. An **effect-size indicator** is a statistical measure of the strength of a relationship. It tells you how big an effect is present. Some effect-size indicators are Cohen's standardized effect size, eta squared, omega squared, Cramer's *V,* and the correlation coefficient squared. (If you want to learn more about effect-size indicators, you can refer to a statistics book such as Hays, 1994; Howell, 1997; or Huck and Cormier, 1996.) All you need to know now is that effect-size indicators tell you how big or how strong an effect is. You also need to understand that hypothesis testing is only a tool that the researcher uses to determine whether the null or the alternative hypothesis provides the better explanation of the data. Knowing that a finding is statistically significant does *not* tell you anything about the effect size or the practical importance of a research finding. Statistical significance only tells you that a finding is not just a chance occurrence. That's why it is so important to determine whether a finding is practically significant (see step 5 in Table 16.3).

■ **Practical significance**
A conclusion made when a relationship is strong enough to be of practical importance

practical significance

■ **Effect-size indicator**
A measure of the strength of a relationship

effect size

REVIEW
──────────
QUESTIONS

16.8 What is a null hypothesis?

16.9 To whom is the researcher similar in hypothesis testing: the defense attorney or the prosecuting attorney? Why?

16.10 What is the difference between a probability value and the significance level?

16.11 Why do educational researchers usually use .05 as their significance level?

16.12 State the two decision-making rules of hypothesis testing.

16.13 Do the following statements sound like typical null or alternative hypotheses? (a) The coin is fair. (b) There is no difference between male and female incomes in the population. (c) There is no correlation in the population. (d) The patient is not sick (i.e., is well). (e) The defendant is innocent.

16.14 What is a Type I error? What is a Type II error? How can you minimize the risk of both types of errors?

16.15 If a finding is statistically significant, why is it also important to consider practical significance?

HYPOTHESIS TESTING IN PRACTICE

When you read educational journal articles, you will quickly notice that researchers frequently test hypotheses and therefore report on the statistical significance of their findings. You will recall that when a null hypothesis is rejected, the finding is said to be statistically significant, and when a null hypothesis is not rejected, the finding is said to be not statistically significant. Researchers do this to add credibility to their conclusions. Researchers do not want to interpret findings that are not statistically significant because these findings are probably nothing but a reflection of sampling error (i.e., chance fluctuations). On the other hand, researchers do want to interpret research findings that are statistically significant. A commonly used synonym for the term *hypothesis testing* is the term **significance testing,** because when you engage in hypothesis testing you are also checking for statistical significance.

■ **Significance testing**
A commonly used synonym for hypothesis testing

We now show some examples of several commonly used significance tests. Keep in mind that we use the .05 significance level for all of our statistical tests. For a more exhaustive introduction to significance testing, you will need to examine a statistics textbook (e.g., Glass & Hopkins, 1996; Hays, 1994; Howell, 1997; Huck & Cormier, 1996; Knoke & Bohrnstedt, 1994; Moore & McCabe, 1993).

Before we get started, you need to review the two hypothesis testing rules discussed earlier and shown in Table 16.3.

- *Rule 1.* If the probability value is less than or equal to the significance level, then reject the null hypothesis, tentatively accept the alternative hypothesis, and conclude that the finding is statistically significant.
- *Rule 2.* If the probability value is greater than your significance level, then you must fail to reject the null hypothesis and conclude that the finding is not statistically significant.

The key to conducting a significance test is to set your significance level (most people use .05) and get the probability value. The significance level is set by the researcher (usually at .05). The probability value is based on the computer analysis of the data from your research study, and the researcher gets the probability value from the computer printout. Finally, you compare the probability value to the significance level and determine whether rule 1 or rule 2 applies. In all of the following examples, we will follow these two rules.

We use the same college student data set that we used in Table 15.1. The data set includes the hypothetical data for twenty-five recent college graduates on several variables (starting salary, gender, GRE verbal, GPA, and college major). Because we will use these data for inferential statistics in this chapter, we *assume* that the twenty-five individuals are a random sample from a larger population of recent college graduates. In practice, a sample of only twenty-five people would be quite small. However, our data set is for illustration only.

The *t*-Test for Independent Samples

■ **t-test for independent samples**
Statisical test used to determine whether the difference between the means of two groups is statistically significant

One of the most common statistical significance tests is called the *t*-test for independent samples. The **t-test for independent samples** is used with a quantitative dependent variable and a dichotomous (i.e., composed of two levels or groups) independent variable. The purpose of this test is to see whether the difference between the means of two groups is statistically significant. The reason this test is called a *t*-test is that the sampling distribution used to determine the probability value is known as the *t*-distribution. The *t*-distributions (there is a separate *t*-distribution for each sample size) look quite a bit like the normal curve shown in Chapter 15. The main difference is that for relatively small sample sizes, the *t*-distribution is a little flatter and a little more spread out than the normal curve. The mean of the *t*-distribution is equal to zero. Just like the normal curve, the *t*-distribution is symmetrical, it is higher at the center, and it has a "right tail" and a "left tail" that represent extreme events.

The *t*-distribution is the sampling distribution under the *assumption* that the null hypothesis is true. Therefore, the researcher rejects the null hypothesis when the value of *t* is large (i.e., when it falls in one of the two tails of the *t*-distribution). Typically, *t* values that are greater than +2.00 (e.g., +2.15) or less than –2.00 (e.g., –2.15) are considered to be large *t* values. When we say *large,* we mean that the value is not near the center of the distribution; instead, the value is in a tail of the distribution. As an analogy, think about the normal curve. Values that are more than two standard deviations out from the center of the normal curve are considered to be extreme because fewer than 5 percent of the cases fall beyond these points. It is exactly the same way with the *t*-distribution. That is, when the *t* value of the sample result falls in one of the two tails of the *t*-distribution (i.e., in the left tail or in the right tail), it is considered to be an unlikely event (under the assumption that the null hypothesis is true). Therefore, the researcher rejects the null hypothesis and claims that the alternative hypothesis is the better explanation of the results.

We used the sample data in our college student data set (Table 15.1) to examine the following research question: Is the difference between the average starting salary for males and the average starting salary for females statistically significant? The dependent variable is starting salary and the independent variable is gender. The two statistical hypotheses are

Null hypothesis: $H_0: \mu_M = \mu_F$

Alternative hypothesis: $H_1: \mu_M \neq \mu_F$

As you can see, the null hypothesis states that the male and female population means are the same. The alternative hypothesis states that the male and female population means are different (i.e., they are not equal). Assuming that our male and female data were randomly selected, we can legitimately test the null hypothesis.

The average starting salary for the males in our data set was $34,333.33, and the average starting salary for the females in our data set was $31,076.92. Obviously, these two sample means are different. Remember, however, that whenever sample data are used, sampling error will be present. This means that the observed difference in the sample means could be due to chance. The key question is whether the sample means are different enough for us to conclude that the difference is probably not due to random sampling error (i.e., chance), and that there is a real difference between male and female starting salaries in the population from which the data came.

Using SPSS (a very popular computer package that is used to analyze data), we conducted the *t*-test for independent samples on our student data. The *t* value was 2.08, and because this *t* value falls in the right tail of the *t*-distribution, it is an unlikely value. (If the *t* value had been –2.08, then it would have fallen in the left tail of the *t*-distribution, which would have also been an unlikely value.) Because the *t* value is relatively unlikely, assuming that the null hypothesis is true, the probability value was small. We got the probability value from the computer printout based on the analysis of our data. The probability value was equal to .049. Because this probability value (.049) is less than the significance level (.05), we reject the null hypothesis and we accept the alternative hypothesis (using rule 1 from Table 16.3).

We conclude that the observed difference between the male and female means is statistically significant. We do not believe that the observed difference between our sample means was due to chance. Rather, we believe that there is a real difference between the starting salaries of males and females in the population. The male mean is higher than the female mean, the effect size eta squared is .16 which means that gender explains 16 percent of the variance in salary. We conclude that males have a higher starting salary, on average, than females and that, if this were true, it would be important for policymakers to know. It is practically significant.

One-Way Analysis of Variance

One-way analysis of variance (one-way ANOVA) is used to compare two or more group means. It is appropriate whenever you have one quantitative dependent variable and one categorical independent variable. (Two-way analysis of variance is used when you have two categorical independent variables; three-way analysis of variance is used when you have three categorical independent variables; and so forth.) Analysis of variance techniques use what is called the *F*-distribution. This is the name of the sampling distribution that is used in analysis of variance techniques. Don't be surprised if you sometimes hear analysis of variance techniques referred to as *F*-tests. The *F*-distribution looks like the distribution shown in Figure 15.6(c), which was skewed to the right (i.e., the tail was pulled or stretched out to the right). You don't have to worry much about the *F*-distribution because the statistical computer programs take care of that for you.

Here is the research question that we were interested in for our example: Is there a statistically significant difference in the starting salaries of education majors, arts and sciences

■ **One-way analysis of variance**
Statistical test used to compare two or more group means

majors, and business majors? The dependent variable is starting salary, and the independent variable is college major.

The two statistical hypotheses are

Null hypothesis:	$H_0: \mu_E = \mu_{A\&S} = \mu_B$
Alternative hypothesis:	H_1: Not all equal

The null hypothesis states that the education, the arts and sciences, and the business student populations all have the same mean starting income. The alternative hypothesis states that at least two of the population means are different from one another. The alternative hypothesis does not state which two of the population means are different from one another.

Once again we used SPSS to obtain our results. The F value was equal to 9.66, which is quite an extreme value. (When there is no relationship, the F value is theoretically equal to 1.0.) Our F value of 9.66 is quite a bit bigger than 1.0, which means our sample result falls in the right tail of the F-distribution. Therefore, the probability value was small (i.e., the sample result was unlikely *assuming* the null hypothesis is true). The probability value, which we got from the SPSS printout, was equal to .001. Because we are using a significance level of .05, we reject the null hypothesis and conclude that the relationship between college major and starting income is statistically significant. That's because our probability value (.001) was less than our significance level (.05) (from rule 1). The effect-size indicator eta squared was .47, which means that college major explains 47 percent of the variance in salary. We can conclude that at least two of the college major means are significantly different and that follow-up tests are needed to determine which means are significantly different.

Post Hoc Tests in Analysis of Variance

One-way analysis of variance tells the researcher whether the relationship between the independent and dependent variables is statistically significant. In our example, college major and starting income were significantly related. We therefore concluded that at least two of the means were significantly different. If you want to know which means are significantly different, you have to use what is called a **post hoc test,** a follow-up test to analysis of variance that is used to determine which means are significantly different. If an independent variable has only two levels, you don't need a post hoc test. You just need to look to see which mean is bigger. If an independent variable has three or more levels, you will need post hoc testing.

Many different post hoc tests are available to a researcher. All of them provide appropriate probability values for a researcher to use in determining statistical significance. Some of the popular post hoc tests are the Newman-Keuls Test, the Tukey Test, the Scheffe Test, and the Bonferroni Test. We used the Bonferroni procedure to see which of the means in our previous example were significantly different.

Here are the mean incomes for our example:

- Average starting salary for education majors is $29,500.
- Average starting salary for arts and sciences majors is $32,300.
- Average starting salary for business majors is $36,714.29.

■ Post hoc test
A followup test to the analysis of variance

These are the sample means. The question is, Which of these means are significantly differ-ent from each other? We must check for statistical significance because the differences be-tween our sample means *could be* due to chance (i.e., sampling error).

First, we checked to see whether the education and the arts and sciences means were significantly different. The Bonferroni-adjusted probability value (obtained from the SPSS printout) was .233. Our significance level is .05. As you can see, our probability value (.233) is greater than the significance level (.05). Therefore, we use rule 2. We fail to reject the null hypothesis (that the population means are the same), and we conclude that the dif-ference between the two means is *not* statistically significant. We can't really say whether the education or the arts and sciences mean is larger in the population.

Second, we checked to see whether the education and the business majors' means were significantly different. The Bonferroni-adjusted probability value was .001. Our significance level is .05. You can see that our probability value (.001) is less than the significance level (.05). Therefore, we use rule 1. We reject the null hypothesis (that the population means are the same), and we conclude that the difference between the two means is statistically signifi-cant. We believe that business majors have a higher starting salary than education majors, and because this difference is so large, it also appears to be practically significant.

Third, we checked to see whether the arts and sciences and the business majors' means were significantly different. The Bonferroni-adjusted probability value was .031. Our sig-nificance level is .05. Therefore, we use rule 1. We reject the null hypothesis (that the popu-lation means are the same), and we conclude that the difference between the two means is statistically significant. We conclude that the starting salary for business majors is greater than the starting salary for arts and sciences in the population. This difference is sizable and would be practically significant.[5]

The *t*-Test for Correlation Coefficients

Correlation coefficients are usually used to show the relationship between a quantitative de-pendent variable and a quantitative independent variable. In inferential statistics, the re-searcher wants to know whether an observed correlation coefficient is statistically significant. The ***t*-test for correlation coefficients** is the statistical test that is used to deter-mine whether a correlation coefficient is statistically significant. We called this procedure a *t*-test for correlation coefficients because the sampling distribution used to test the null hy-pothesis (that the population correlation coefficient is zero) is the same *t*-distribution that we used earlier. The *t*-distribution is used for many different statistical tests.

Using our college student data set, we decided to answer this research question: Is there a statistically significant correlation between GPA (X) and starting salary (Y)? The sta-tistical hypotheses are as follows:

Null hypothesis: $H_0: \rho_{XY} = 0$
Alternative hypothesis: $H_1: \rho_{XY} \neq 0$

The null hypothesis says that there is no correlation between GPA and starting salary in the population from which the data were selected. The alternative hypothesis says that there is a correlation in the population.

■ *t*-test for correlation coefficients
Statistical test used to determine whether a correlation coeffi-cient is statistically significant

Our sample correlation between GPA and starting salary was +.63, which suggests that there is a moderately strong positive correlation between GPA and starting salary. However, we wanted to know whether this correlation was statistically significant. Our probability value (based on the analysis of our data and obtained from the SPSS printout) was equal to .001. Once again, we are using a significance level of .05. Because the probability value is less than the significance level, our correlation is statistically significant. We conclude that GPA and starting salary are correlated in the population. We also conclude that this correlation is practically significant because of its relatively large magnitude (i.e., .63). A correlation of .63 means that almost 40 percent of the variance in salary is accounted for by GPA. (That's because, with a simple correlation, you obtain the percentage of variance in a dependent variable that is explained by the independent variable by squaring the correlation coefficient and converting it to a percentage: .63 times .63 equals .397, and moving the decimal place two points to the right we obtain 39.7 percent.)

The *t*-Test for Regression Coefficients

We point out in Chapter 15 that simple regression is used to test the relationship between one quantitative dependent variable and one independent variable. We also point out that multiple regression is used to test the relationship between one quantitative dependent variable and two or more independent variables. The **t-test for regression coefficients** uses the *t*-distribution (sampling distribution) to test each regression coefficient for statistical significance.

t-test for regression coefficients
Statistical test used to determine whether a regression coefficient is statistically significant

Because we introduced you to simple and multiple regression in Chapter 15, we do not repeat that material here. Rather, we take the multiple regression equation discussed in Chapter 15 and now test the two regression coefficients in that equation for statistical significance. Look at the equation from Chapter 15 once again:

$$\hat{Y} = 3{,}890.05 + 4{,}675.41(X_1) + 26.13(X_2)$$

where

$\hat{Y}$ is predicted starting salary,
X_1 is grade point average,
X_2 is GRE verbal,
3,890.05 is the Y-intercept,
4,675.41 is the value of the regression coefficient for X_1. It shows the relationship between starting salary and GPA (controlling for GRE verbal), and
26.13 is the value of the "regression coefficient" for X_2. It shows the relationship between starting salary and GRE verbal (controlling for GPA).

The key point for you to understand is that researchers usually test their regression coefficients for statistical significance. A researcher will not trust a coefficient that is not statistically significant because the coefficient might simply be due to chance (sampling error). If a coefficient is statistically significant, a researcher can conclude that there is a real relationship in the population from which the data came.

Our first research question relates to the first regression coefficient (4,675.41):

- *Research question 1.* Is there a statistically significant relationship between starting salary (Y) and GPA (X_1) [controlling for GRE verbal (X_2)]?

The two statistical hypotheses for this first research question are as follows:

Null hypothesis: $H_0: \beta_{YX_1 \cdot X_2} = 0$

Alternative hypothesis: $H_1: \beta_{YX_1 \cdot X_2} \neq 0$

The null hypothesis says that the population regression coefficient is equal to zero (i.e., there is no relationship). The alternative hypothesis says that the population regression coefficient is not zero (i.e., there is a relationship).

Using SPSS, we computed the *t*-test and obtained the probability value corresponding to the regression coefficient, showing the relationship between starting salary and GPA. The probability value was equal to .035. Because this probability value (.035) is less than our significance level (.05), we reject the null hypothesis and accept the alternative hypothesis. The semipartial correlation squared ($(sr)^2$) was equal to .10, which says that 10 percent of the variance in starting salary was uniquely explained by GPA. We conclude that the relationship between starting salary and GPA (controlling for GRE verbal) is statistically and practically significant.

This is the research question for the second regression coefficient (26.13):

■ *Research question 2.* Is there a statistically significant relationship between starting salary (Y) and GRE verbal (X_2) [controlling for GPA (X_1)]?

The two statistical hypotheses for research question two are

Null hypothesis: $H_0: \beta_{YX_2 \cdot X_1} = 0$

Alternative hypothesis: $H_1: \beta_{YX_2 \cdot X_1} \neq 0$

Using SPSS, we computed the *t*-test and obtained the probability value corresponding to the regression coefficient showing the relationship between starting salary and GRE verbal. The probability value was equal to .014. Because this probability value (.014) is less than our significance level (.05), we reject the null hypothesis and accept the alternative hypothesis. The semipartial correlation squared was .15, which says that 15 percent of the starting salary variance was uniquely explained by GRE verbal. We conclude that the relationship between starting salary and GRE verbal (controlling for GPA) is statistically and practically significant.

The Chi-Square Test for Contingency Tables

The **chi-square test for contingency tables** is used to determine whether a relationship observed in a contingency table is statistically significant. In Chapter 15, we taught you how to construct and interpret the numbers in contingency tables. We told you that contingency tables are used when both variables are categorical. The two categorical variables in our college student data set are gender and college major. Therefore, let's see whether these two variables are significantly related. We used the computer package called SPSS to produce the contingency table shown in Table 16.6. The row variable is college major, and the column variable is gender. Within the body of the table are the counts (the number of people in each

■ **Chi-square test for contingency tables**
Statistical test used to determine whether a relationship observed in a contingency table is statistically significant

TABLE 16.6   Contingency Table of College Major by Gender*

			Gender		
			Male	Female	Total
College Major	Education	Count	1	7	8
		Expected count	3.8	4.2	8.0
		% of gender	8.3% ⟶	53.8%	32.0%
	Arts and sciences	Count	6	4	10
		Expected count	4.8	5.2	10.0
		% of gender	50.0% ⟶	30.8%	40.0%
	Business	Count	5	2	7
		Expected count	3.4	3.6	7.0
		% of gender	41.7% ⟶	15.4%	28.0%
Total		Count	12	13	25
		Expected count	12.0	13.0	25.0
		% of gender	100.0%	100.0%	100.0%

*Because the percentages are calculated down, you should compare across the rows, as indicated by the arrows.

cell), the expected counts (the number of people that would be expected to be in each cell *if the variables were not related*), and the "percent of gender" (the column percentages).

How can you determine whether the variables in this contingency table are related? These are the rules from the last chapter:

- If the percentages are calculated down the columns, compare across the rows.
- If the percentages are calculated across the rows, compare down the columns.

You can see that we calculated the percentages down the columns in Table 16.6. Therefore, you can determine whether college major and gender are related by reading across the rows. If you do this, you will see that the variables appear to be related. Looking at the first row, you can see that 53.8 percent of the females were education majors but only 8.3 percent of the males were education majors. Obviously, females have the higher rate. Also, fully 50 percent of the males were arts and sciences majors, but only 30.8 percent of the females were arts and sciences majors. Finally, 41.7 percent of the males were business majors, and only 15.4 percent of the females were business majors. College major and gender are clearly related.

The inferential statistics question is, Is the observed relationship between college major and gender in the contingency table statistically significant? The null hypothesis says that college major and gender are *not* related in the population from which the data were selected. The alternative hypothesis says that college major and gender *are* related in the population. The sampling distribution used for contingency tables is called the chi-square distribution. The computed value of chi-square in our example is 6.16. The probability value is .046. Our probability value of .046 is less than our significance level of .05. Therefore, we reject the null hypothesis (there is no relationship) and accept the alternative hypothesis (there is a relationship). The effect size indicator for contingency tables that we used is called Cramer's V. The size of Cramer's V can be interpreted just like the size of a correlation coefficient. Cramer's V was .496, which suggests that the relationship between college major and gender was moderately large. We conclude that there is a relationship between college major and gender, that the relationship is statistically significant, and that the relationship appears to be practically significant.

Other Significance Tests

Believe it or not, you have come a long way! There are many additional significance tests that we could discuss. In fact, we mentioned several other statistical analyses in earlier chapters. For example, we discussed two-way analysis of variance in Chapter 9, we discussed analysis of covariance in Chapter 9 and in Chapter 11, and we discussed partial correlation coefficients in Chapter 11. If you ever need to refresh yourself on any of these procedures, you can review that material. If you run across a significance test that is not discussed in this book, go to our book's companion website, where we have an extensive listing of statistical tests. The key point is that the ideas that you have learned in this chapter apply to any significance test (including two-way ANOVA, ANCOVA, and partial correlation). In other words, you can determine whether the observed relationship is statistically significant.

Here is some good news. You now understand the fundamental **logic of significance testing.** You state the null and alternative hypotheses. Then you determine the probability value and compare it to the significance level. You decide whether the finding is statistically significant or not statistically significant using the two rules shown in Table 16.3. Then you interpret the results and determine practical significance. This fundamental logic will carry you quite a long way when you read journal articles or begin conducting your own research. If you run across a significance test that is not mentioned in this book, you can consult a textbook focused on statistics (e.g., Glass & Hopkins, 1996; Hays, 1994; Howell, 1997; Huck & Cormier, 1996; Knoke & Bohrnstedt 1994; Moore & McCabe, 1993). However, the idea of statistical significance will remain the same.

■ **Logic of significance testing**
Understanding and following the steps shown in Table 16.3

16.16 How do you write the null and alternative hypotheses for each of the following? (a) The *t*-test for independent samples, (b) one-way analysis of variance, (c) the *t*-test for correlation coefficients, (d) the *t*-test for a regression coefficient.

REVIEW
QUESTION

SUMMARY

The purpose of inferential statistics is to estimate the characteristics of populations and to test hypotheses about population parameters. Randomization (random sampling or random assignment) is required when using the probability theory underlying inferential statistics, which is based on the idea of sampling distributions. A sampling distribution is the theoretical probability distribution of the values of a statistic that results when all possible random samples of a particular size (e.g., all possible samples of size 100 or all possible samples of size 500) are drawn from a defined population. Sampling distributions make it clear that the value of a sample statistic varies from sample to sample. The sampling distribution constructed for the sample mean is called the sampling distribution of the mean. It shows the distribution of the sample mean when many samples are taken. Other sample statistics (e.g., proportions, correlation coefficients) also have their own sampling distributions.

There are two types of estimation. In point estimation, the researcher uses the value of a sample statistic as the estimate of the population parameter. In interval estimation, the researcher constructs a confidence interval (a band of numbers) that will include the population parameter a certain percentage of the time in the long run. For example, 95 percent confidence intervals will capture the population parameter 95 percent of the time.

Hypothesis testing is the branch of inferential statistics concerned with testing hypotheses about population parameters. Hypothesis testing follows a very specific logic, called the logic of significance testing. Basically, the researcher sets up a null hypothesis that he or she hopes to ultimately reject in order to accept the alternative hypothesis. It is the null hypothesis (not the alternative hypothesis) that is directly tested using probability theory. To engage in hypothesis testing, you must understand the difference between the probability value and the significance level. The *probability value* is the probability of the sample results under the assumption that the null hypothesis is true. The *significance level* is the cutoff point that the researcher believes represents an unlikely event. Using these ideas, the researcher follows these decision-making rules:

- *Rule 1.* If the probability value is less than or equal to the significance level, then reject the null hypothesis, tentatively accept the alternative hypothesis, and conclude that the finding is statistically significant.
- *Rule 2.* If the probability value is greater than the significance level, then you must fail to reject the null hypothesis and conclude that the finding is not statistically significant.

A statistically significant finding is a finding that the researcher does *not* believe is due to chance. A finding is statistically significant when the evidence supports the alternative hypothesis rather than the null hypothesis. The logic of significance testing will carry you a long way because the basic logic applies to all significance tests, and significance tests are frequently reported in published research.

KEY TERMS

alternative hypothesis (p. 474)
chi-square test for contingency tables (p. 491)
confidence interval (p. 469)
confidence limits (p. 469)
directional alternative hypothesis (p. 476)

effect-size indicator (p. 484)
hypothesis testing (p. 472)
inferential statistics (p. 463)
level of confidence (p. 470)
logic of significance testing (p. 493)
lower limit (p. 469)
margin of error (p. 470)

nondirectional alternative hypothesis (p. 475)
null hypothesis (p. 471)
one-way analysis of variance (p. 487)
parameter (p. 464)
point estimate (p. 469)
point estimation (p. 469)

DISCUSSION QUESTIONS

1. What exactly does it mean when a researcher reports that a finding is statistically significant?
2. What do you think is more important: statistical significance or practical significance?

3. How does one determine practical significance?
4. What is the difference between null and alternative hypotheses?

RESEARCH EXERCISES

1. Many quantitative research articles in education do not provide the exact probability values. Rather, they include statements of probability values such as $p < .05$, $p < .01$, $p < .03$, $p < .001$, and so forth. Remember that the significance level used in most articles is .05. For each of the following possible probability values, indicate whether the result would be statistically significant or not statistically significant. Assume that the significance level is set at .05. (*Hint:* If a probability value is less than or equal to the significance level, the result is statistically significant. Otherwise, it is not statistically significant.) Place a check in the box to the left of each of your answers.

Probability Value	Your Statistical Decision	
$p > .05$	☐ Statistically significant	☐ Not statistically significant
$p < .05$	☐ Statistically significant	☐ Not statistically significant
$p < .03$	☐ Statistically significant	☐ Not statistically significant
$p < .01$	☐ Statistically significant	☐ Not statistically significant
$p < .001$	☐ Statistically significant	☐ Not statistically significant
$p < .0001$	☐ Statistically significant	☐ Not statistically significant

2. Let's now assume that the researcher is using a more conservative significance level. In particular, assume that the researcher is using the .01 significance level rather than the .05 significance level. For each of the following probability values, indicate whether the result would be statistically significant or not statistically significant.

Probability Value	Your Statistical Decision	
$p > .05$	☐ Statistically significant	☐ Not statistically significant
$p < .05$	☐ Statistically significant	☐ Not statistically significant
$p < .03$	☐ Statistically significant	☐ Not statistically significant
$p < .01$	☐ Statistically significant	☐ Not statistically significant
$p < .001$	☐ Statistically significant	☐ Not statistically significant
$p < .0001$	☐ Statistically significant	☐ Not statistically significant

3. Find a quantitative journal article (you can use the one linked in Appendix A if you want to) and note where the author(s) talk about statistical significance. (*Note:* Some researchers still say significant when they actually mean statistically significant.) Did the author(s) report probability values when they claimed that a finding was statistically significant? Were any of the findings in the research article you examined *not* statistically significant? Did the author(s) adequately address the issue of practical significance in addition to statistical significance?

4. There has been a widespread debate among researchers about the importance or lack of importance of statistical significance testing. One point in this debate is that if researchers report effect sizes (which show the magnitude or size of a relationship) then statistical significance testing (i.e., the use of p values to rule out chance as an explanation of the result) is not needed. Another group says that significance testing is essential because if a finding is not statistically significant, then we might simply be observing a chance event. Do you think we need significance testing? Do you think we need to report effect sizes (which indicate the strength of a relationship or effect)? Do we need both? Find an article on ContentSelect that supports your viewpoint. Also find an article that goes against your viewpoint.

Exercise Sheet

1. Rewrite the research questions and hypotheses for your proposal or research study.
2. If you are going to use inferential statistics, are you planning to use confidence intervals or significance testing (or both)?
3. List the inferential statistical procedure you will use for each of your hypotheses.
4. If you are using significance testing, write out the null and alternative hypotheses for each of the statistical tests you just listed.
5. How will you decide if your findings are practically significant?

RELEVANT INTERNET SITES

www.ruf.rice.edu/~lane/stat_sim/index.html and **www.anu.edu.au/nceph/surfstat/surfstat-home/applets.html**
Demonstrations of statistical concepts.

http://davidmlane.com/hyperstat/index.html
An excellent on-line statistics textbook and related materials.

http://roberts.ed.psu.edu/users/droberts/sigtest.htm
A special issue of the journal *Research in the Schools* that was devoted to the controversy over using significance testing.

www.cas.lancs.ac.uk/glossary_v1.1/main.html
Explanations of most of the concepts discussed in this chapter.

RECOMMENDED READING

Grimm, L. G., & Yarnold, P. R. (1995). *Reading and understanding multivariate statistics.* Washington, DC: American Psychological Association.

Harlow, L. L., Mulaik, S. A., & Steiger, J. H. (Eds.). (1997). *What if there were no significance tests?* Mahwah, NJ: Lawrence Erlbaum Associates.

Huck, S. W. (2004). *Reading statistics and research.* Boston: Allyn & Bacon.

Kirk, R. E. (2001). Promoting good statistical practices: Some suggestions. *Educational and Psychological Measurement, 61*(2), 213–218.

ENDNOTES

1. In case you are curious, researchers use $n - 1$ because statisticians have shown that the use of n provides an underestimate of the population parameter.

2. Although we sometimes say that you "accept" the alternative hypothesis, remember that whenever you reject the null hypothesis, you can only tentatively accept the alternative hypothesis because you could have made a mistake.

3. Don't forget that the research participants must be randomly selected or randomly assigned whenever inferential statistics is used. That is, without randomization, the probability model will have no meaning.

4. At some point, a sample size becomes large enough. In other words, it would become wasteful to include more participants in the research study. You might want to review our discussion in Chapter 7 on how big a sample is big enough.

5. Some statisticians suggest *not* following the procedure we just explained (i.e., conducting an analysis of variance and following it up with post hoc tests). Instead, they suggest that researchers should conduct what are called *planned comparisons*. That is, they suggest that researchers plan, before they collect their data, the exact hypotheses that they want to test.

17

Data Analysis in Qualitative Research

LEARNING OBJECTIVES

To be able to

- Understand the terminology surrounding qualitative data analysis.
- Describe the process of coding.
- List the different types of codes.
- Know what it means to analyze data inductively.
- Code some text data.
- Know some of the common types of relationships found in qualitative data.
- Describe the procedures used to analyze qualitative data.
- List the three most popular computer programs that are used to analyze qualitative data.
- Know the advantages and disadvantages of using computer programs for qualitative data analysis.

In the latter half of 2002, Josh Max got one of the nicest experiences of his life. He was allowed to test drive that year's hottest bike, a Harley-Davidson V-Rod. As he climbed on the bike and took off, he had what he said was "a moment of pure mechanical joy" (Max, 2002). Not only did the bike carve every twist and turn, but it looked great doing it. He had the bike for a total of eight hours and rode it for all but 15 minutes of that time, sailing for miles past the Pacific Ocean, winding up and down deserted side roads. This was the most fun he had had in a long time, taking all day to go nowhere.

Obviously, for motorcycle riders, the new Harley-Davidson V-Rod is a great bike. However, there seems to be a mystique associated with owning a Harley-Davidson motorcycle that goes beyond the quality of the bike or the experience of riding a motorcycle. For example, every year in August, a bike rally is held in Sturgis, South Dakota, that is attended by about 250,000 motorcyclists, most of whom are Harley-Davidson owners. At this rally and many other places you see Harley-Davidson riders, you will see that they tend to wear a similar biker "uniform" consisting of some combination of jeans, black boots, T-shirts, a black leather jacket, and a vest that might carry insignias of club affiliation. Wearing anything else would cast you as something other than a member of the Harley-Davidson club. The rally and ownership of a Harley-Davidson attract people of all walks of life. For example, not only was the late Malcolm Forbes of *Forbes* magazine a Harley enthusiast, but the whole Forbes clan is replete with riders (Forbes Family, 2002).

To John Schouten, Professor of Marketing at University of Portland, and James McAlexander, Professor of Marketing at Oregon State University, this tremendous identification with Harley-Davidson objects and activities suggested that a subculture of consumption had been created. They decided to document this subculture (Schouten & McAlexander, 1995) by conducting an ethnographic analysis specifically of "new bikers" defined as Harley-Davidson owners who did not belong to known outlaw organizations.

Over a three-year period, Schouten and McAlexander attended the rally in Sturgis, South Dakota; attended the Daytona bike week; bought BMW and Honda motorcycles initially and later purchased Harley-Davidson motorcycles; attended the Iowa BMW rally, the ABATE rally, and the western HOG rally; conducted interviews with individuals at Harley-Davidson headquarters; and became active HOG members. They also went to dealerships, club meetings, bars, and restaurants where there were other Harley-Davidson owners. While appearing at these events and riding with other Harley-Davidson motorcycle owners, Schouten and McAlexander observed the behavior of these "other" owners and jotted down their observations, they interviewed many Harley-Davidson motorcycle owners and took pictures of many of these individuals in a variety of situations. The result was that over the three years, Schouten and McAlexander accumulated a mass of diverse information. At the end of the three-year data collection period, they had to decide how to synthesize and summarize this wealth of information so that it made sense and, in this case, presented a picture of the subculture of consumption that exists among Harley-Davidson motorcycle owners. The process of summarizing and making sense of qualitative data such as that collected by Schouten and McAlexander is a very difficult and time-consuming one. However, there are specific techniques and recommendations that can help to make it manageable. The purpose of the present chapter is to acquaint you with these techniques.

Formal qualitative research has been conducted since the early twentieth century. Qualitative data analysis, however, is still a relatively new and rapidly developing branch of research methodology. Writing in 1984, two pioneers in qualitative data analysis, Matthew Miles and Michael Huberman, noted that "we have few agreed-on canons for qualitative data analysis" (p. 16). In 1994, they noted, "Today, we have come far from that state of affairs. . . . Still, much remains to be done." (Huberman & Miles, p. 428). Over recent years, many qualitative researchers have realized the need for more systematic data analysis procedures, and they have started to write more about how to conduct qualitative research data analysis (e.g., Bryman & Burgess, 1994; Dey, 1993; Huberman & Miles, 1994; LeCompte & Preissle, 1993; Lofland & Lofland, 1995; Miles & Huberman, 1994; Patton, 1990; Silverman, 1993; Strauss & Corbin, 1990). In this chapter, we introduce you to the terminology surrounding qualitative data analysis, show you the basics of qualitative data analysis, and briefly discuss the use of computer software in the analysis of qualitative data.

Research Navigator.com

qualitative analysis

▬▬ INTERIM ANALYSIS

Data analysis begins early in a qualitative research study, and during a single research study, qualitative researchers alternate between data collection (e.g., interviews, observations, focus groups, documents, physical artifacts, fieldnotes) and data analysis (creating meaning from raw data). This cyclical or recursive process of collecting data, analyzing the data, collecting additional data, analyzing those data, and so on throughout the research project is called **interim analysis** (Miles & Huberman, 1994).

■ **Interim analysis**
The cyclical process of collecting and analyzing data during a single research study

Interim analysis is used in qualitative research because qualitative researchers usually collect data over an extended time period, and they need to continually learn more and more about what they are studying during this time frame. In other words, qualitative researchers use interim analysis to develop a successively deeper understanding of their research topic and to guide each round of data collection. This is a strength of qualitative research. By collecting data at more than one time, qualitative researchers are able to collect data that help to refine their developing theories and test their inductively generated hypotheses (i.e., hypotheses developed from examining their data or developed when they are in the field). Qualitative researchers basically act like detectives when they carefully examine and ask questions of their data and then reenter the field to collect more data to help answer their questions. Interim analysis continues until the process or topic the researcher is studying is understood (or until the researcher runs out of resources!). Grounded theorists use the term *theoretical saturation* to describe the situation in which understanding has been reached and there is no current need for more data. We have summarized the qualitative data collection process in Figure 17.1.

REVIEW QUESTION

17.1 What is interim analysis?

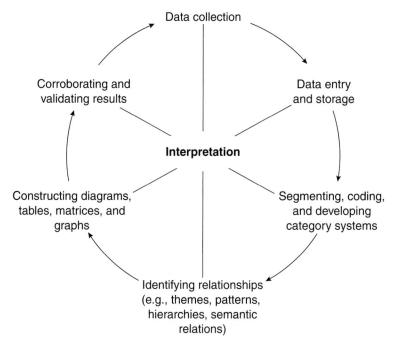

FIGURE 17.1   Data analysis in qualitative research

MEMOING

A helpful tool for recording ideas generated during data analysis is called **memoing** (writing memos). Memos are reflective notes that researchers write to themselves about what they are learning from their data. The content of memos can include notes about anything, including thoughts on emerging concepts, themes or patterns found in the data, the need for further data collection, a comparison that needs to be made in the data, and virtually anything else. Memos written early in a project tend to be more speculative, and memos written later in a project tend to be more focused and conclusive. Memoing is an important tool to use during a research project to record insights gained from reflecting on data. Because qualitative data analysis is an interpretative process, it is important that you keep track of your ideas. You should try to record your insights as they occur so that you do not have to rely on your memory later.

■ **Memoing**
Recording reflective notes about what you are learning from the data

17.2 What is memoing?

REVIEW

QUESTION

DATA ENTRY AND STORAGE

■ **Transcription**
Transforming qualitative data into typed text

To carefully analyze qualitative data, we recommend that you transcribe your data. **Transcription** is the process of transforming qualitative research data, such as audio recordings of interviews or field notes written from observations, into typed text. The typed text is called a transcript. If the original data source is an audio recording, transcription involves sitting down, listening to the tape recording, and typing what was said into a word processing file. If the data are memos, open-ended questionnaires, or observational field notes, transcription involves typing the handwritten text into a word processing file. In short, transcription involves transferring data from a less usable to a more usable form. After you transcribe your data, you should put your original data somewhere for safekeeping.

Some qualitative researchers use one of the voice recognition computer programs that are available on the market, which can make transcribing relatively easy. These programs create transcriptions of data while you read the words and sentences into a microphone attached to your computer. Two popular programs are IBM's ViaVoice and Dragon's Naturally Speaking. The main advantage of voice recognition software is that it is easier to talk into a microphone than it is to type. Time savings are not currently large in comparison with typing, but the efficiency of these programs will continue to improve over time.

The principles discussed in this chapter also apply when your qualitative data do not directly lend themselves to text (e.g., videotapes of observations, still pictures, and artifacts). You cannot directly transcribe these kinds of data sources. What you can do, however, is use the same principles of coding (discussed in the next section) and put the codes and your comments into text files for further qualitative data analysis.

REVIEW QUESTION

17.3 Why is it important to transcribe qualitative data when possible?

SEGMENTING, CODING, AND DEVELOPING CATEGORY SYSTEMS

■ **Segmenting**
Dividing data into meaningful analytical units

Segmenting involves dividing the data into meaningful analytical units. When you segment text data, you read the text line by line and continually ask yourself the following kinds of questions: Do I see a segment of text that has a specific meaning that might be important for my research study? Is this segment different in some way from the text coming before and after it? Where does this segment start and end? A meaningful unit (i.e., segment) of text can be a word, a single sentence, several sentences, or it might include a larger passage such as a paragraph or even a complete document. The segment of text must have meaning that the researcher thinks should be documented.

■ **Coding**
Marking segments of data with symbols, descriptive words, or category names

Coding is the process of marking segments of data (usually text data) with symbols, descriptive words, or category names. Here is how Miles and Huberman (1994, p. 56) explain it: "*Codes* are tags or labels for assigning units of meaning to the descriptive or inferential information compiled during a study. Codes usually are attached to 'chunks' of varying size—words, phrases, sentences, or whole paragraphs. . . . They can take the form of a straightforward category label or a more complex one." When a researcher finds a meaningful segment of text in a transcript, he or she assigns a code or category name to signify or identify that particular segment. As you can see, segmenting and coding go hand in hand because segmenting involves locating meaningful segments of data and coding involves marking or labeling those segments with codes or categories.

An example of a coded interview transcript is shown in Table 17.1. The narrative in the transcript is from an interview with a college teacher (CT) by a researcher (R). If you look at Table 17.1, you can see that the researcher read the text line by line and placed descriptive words or phrases in the left-hand margin next to the segments of text. The researcher also placed brackets around the segments of data to make it clear where each segment started and ended. Some other ways to mark segments are to use line numbers or to underline the relevant text rather than using brackets as in Table 17.1. In this example, a college teacher was asked about the experiences her students had when they visited elementary school classrooms as a course requirement in an educational psychology course. The teacher believes

■ **TABLE 17.1**   Example of Coded Text Data

	R: Well, let's start with the impact of early field experiences in the schools for undergraduate education majors. What kind of an impact do you see these experiences having on your students?
Book learning	**CT:** I think it gives them a needed view into the classroom in the real world. [It's one thing to read about teaching in books;] [it is another to actually go into a real classroom, with real students, and actually try to teach them something. Basically, I think that there is something to learning by experience.] [My students can try out the
Experiential learning Classroom management Teaching strategies	classroom management principles] and the [teaching strategies] I teach them about in my educational psychology course. My students can also learn that all elementary students are not alike.
Common student needs Individual student needs	[The kids have a set of common needs], but [they also have a set of needs unique to each individual in the classroom].
	R: Are there any other results from going into the classroom?
Career choice	**CT:** Yes. Most of my students have not been in a real classroom since they were in school themselves. Things have changed in the schools in many ways since then. [The vocational experience of going into the classroom has helped some of my students decide that teaching really was not for them.] I hate to lose potential
Timing of vocational learning	teachers, but [it is probably better that they decide now than wait until they have completed four years of education learning to be a teacher and then decide they don't want to be in a classroom.]

that the visitation experiences provide experiential learning and provide her students (potential future teachers) with information that helps them to make career choices.

As new codes are developed during coding, they must be added to the master list of codes if they are not already on the list. A **master list** is simply a list of all the codes used in the research study. The master list should include each code followed by the full code name and a brief description or definition of the code. A well-structured master list will enable other researchers working on the project to readily use the list.

During coding, the codes on the master list should be reapplied to new segments of text each time an appropriate segment is encountered. For example, one category from the master for the data in Table 17.1 would be "career choice." Therefore, when the data analyst for this research study encountered another segment of data in which the same or a different person being interviewed made a comment about career choice, the researcher would reapply the label "career choice." Every time a segment of text was about career choice, the researcher would use the code career choice to refer to that segment.

Here is an example of coding based on data from a consulting project done by one of this book's authors. The members of a public organization filled out an open-ended questionnaire in which one of the questions asked, What are some specific problems needing action in your organization? The participants' responses are shown in Table 17.2. Take a look at the responses for a moment, and decide whether you notice any meaningful categories of information. Then look at Table 17.3 and see how the data were coded. As you can see, the answers to the open-ended question are segmented into six categories in Table 17.3. The codes are shown in the left-hand margin. The members of the organization listed a number of problems in their organization, and these problems fell into the categories of management issues, physical environment, personnel practices, employee development, intergroup and interpersonal relations, and work structure. These six categories were determined by examining the responses and sorting them into these inductive categories.

If you think that you or someone else might have coded the responses from the previous example differently, you are probably right. When you have high consistency among different coders about the appropriate codes, you have **intercoder reliability.** Intercoder reliability is a type of inter-rater reliability (discussed in Chapter 5; also see Miles & Huberman, 1994, p. 64). Intercoder reliability adds to the objectivity of the research, and it reduces errors due to inconsistencies among coders. Achieving high consistency requires training and a good deal of practice. **Intracoder reliability** is also important. That is, it is also important that each individual coder be consistent. To help you remember the difference between intercoder reliability and intracoder reliability, remember that the prefix *inter-* means "between" and the prefix *intra-* means "within." Therefore, intercoder reliability means reliability, or consistency, between or across coders, and intracoder reliability means reliability within a single coder. If the authors of qualitative research articles that you read address the issues of intercoder and intracoder reliability, you should upgrade your evaluation of their research.

If you want to code your own data and develop category names, you should start with words that describe the content of the segments of data. You will often want the category name to be more abstract than the literal text so that the same category name can be applied to other, similar instances of the phenomenon that you encounter as you read more text. For example, in Table 17.3, the category name "physical environment" was used rather than

■ **Master list**
A list of all the codes used in a research study

■ **Intercoder reliability**
Consistency among different coders

■ **Intracoder reliability**
Consistency within a single individual

■ **TABLE 17.2** Unordered List of Responses to the Open-Ended Question, What are some specific problems needing action in your organization?

Participant Responses

There is not enough space for everyone.
Our office furniture is dated and needs replacing.
We need a better cleaning service for the office.
We need more objective recruitment and hiring standards.
We need objective performance appraisal and reward systems.
We need consistent application of policy.
There are leadership problems.
Nonproductive staff members should not be retained.
Each department has stereotypes of the other departments.
Decisions are often based on inaccurate information.
We need more opportunities for advancement here.
Our product is not consistent because there are too many styles.
There is too much gossiping and criticizing.
Responsibilities at various levels are unclear.
We need a suggestion box.
We need more computer terminals.
There is a lot of "us and them" sentiment here.
There is a lack of attention to individual needs.
There is favoritism and preferential treatment of staff.
More training is needed at all levels.
There needs to be better assessment of employee ability and performance so that promotions can be more objectively based.
Training is needed for new employees.
Many employees are carrying the weight of other untrained employees.
This office is "turf" oriented.
There is a pecking order at every level and within every level.
Communication needs improving.
Certain departments are put on a pedestal.
There are too many review levels for our product.
Too many signatures are required.
There is a lot of overlap and redundancy.
The components of our office work against one another rather than as a team.

"office furniture" so that other aspects of the physical environment, in addition to office furniture, could be included in the category. This ability comes with practice. You might not get the best category name on your first try. If you don't, all you have to do is generate a new category name and use the new category name on the transcripts. When you actually code some written text, you will find that this process of coding is easier than you might think.

Full descriptive words or phrases are not always used in coding. Some researchers prefer to use abbreviations of category names as their codes. Using abbreviations can save time

■ **TABLE 17.3**   Categorization of Responses to the Open-Ended Question, What are some specific problems needing action in your organization?

Inductive Categories	Participant Responses
Management issues	There are leadership problems. We need a suggestion box. There is a lack of attention to individual needs. There is favoritism and preferential treatment of staff. Decisions are often based on inaccurate information. We need consistent application of policy.
Physical environment	We need a better cleaning service for the office. Our office furniture is dated and needs replacing. We need more computer terminals. There is not enough space for everyone.
Personnel practices	We need more objective recruitment and hiring standards. We need objective performance appraisal and reward systems. Nonproductive staff members should not be retained. There needs to be better assessment of employee ability and performance so that promotions can be more objectively based.
Employee development	More training is needed at all levels. Training is needed for new employees. Many employees are carrying the weight of other untrained employees. We need more opportunities for advancement here.
Intergroup and interpersonal relations	This office is "turf" oriented. There is a lot of "us and them" sentiment here. There is a pecking order at every level and within every level. Communication needs improving. There is too much gossiping and criticizing. Certain departments are put on a pedestal. Each department has stereotypes of the other departments.
Work structure	There are too many review levels for our product. Too many signatures are required. Responsibilities at various levels are unclear The components of our office work against one another rather than as a team. There is a lot of overlap and redundancy. Our product is not consistent because there are too many styles.

compared to writing out full category names every time a category appears in the data. Other researchers develop complex symbol systems for coding their data. When you code some data for yourself you must decide whether you want to use full words, phrases, abbreviations, or a complex symbolic coding system.

An example of data coded using a symbolic coding system is shown in Table 17.4. The transcript is an excerpt from an observational study done by educational ethnographer Margaret LeCompte, who was studying norms in the elementary school classroom. LeCompte placed the time in the left column every five minutes or when an activity changed. She placed teacher talk in quotes and placed student talk and information recorded by the researcher in parentheses. The type of activity is indicated in the left margin. The code R stands for teacher talk that establishes rules, the code T stands for teacher talk focused on organizing a time schedule for the students, and the code W stands for teacher talk that is focused on student tasks or student work. Although the codes that are used in the table are not very clear to the outside reader, they had very precise meaning to LeCompte. LeCompte inductively developed her coding system early in her research study, and she used it in her later data analysis.

TABLE 17.4   Symbolic Coding System Used on Field Note Transcript

(Children are playing outside the classroom; a few are standing on the porch. The teacher arrives.)

8:55			"Come in, girls first." (There's some messing around before
8:57			they line up.) (They come in and move toward their seats.)
		T2A	(T2A) "Mrs. Smith is ready to start." (She's sitting on the
	Getting	R1A	desk in the front of the room.) (R1A) "Mrs. Smith is
	settled	R2B	waiting." (R2B) "I like the way Bernie is sitting down, and
		R1A	Atocha." (R1A) "Please, people, do not throw snowballs at
		R4B	one another." (R4B) "There isn't enough snow on the
			ground and you pick up rocks with it. If we have a lot of
			snow we'll have a snowball fight, but please don't throw the
		R4A	snow when there isn't much . . . " (R4A) "If you go along
			with me and don't throw now, as soon as there's good stuff
		R4B	we'll have a snowball fight." (R4B) "It isn't just that you
			hurt people, but you'll get in trouble too."
9:03		T2A	(T2A) "All right, the girls will go to bake cookies at recess."
		W1B	(W1B) "Boys, come back here if you aren't done; if you
			can't work alone you can go into Mrs. Dvorak's game
	Getting	W2B	room." (W2B) "I expect if you come in here to work I
	organized	R1A	expect you to work." (R1A) "I want everybody to bring a
			nickel by Monday." (Is it for the girl's surprise?) "No, it's
			for everybody."

Note: Teacher talk is recorded in quotations; pupil talk and locational description are enclosed in parentheses.

Source: From M. D. LeCompte, J. Preissle, and R. Tesch, *Ethnography and Qualitative Design in Educational Research,* p. 260, copyright © 1993 by Academic Press. Reprinted by permission of Academic Press and the authors.

Inductive and a Priori Codes

- **Inductive codes**
  Codes that are generated by a researcher by directly examining the data

Because of the inductive nature of most qualitative research, qualitative researchers traditionally generate their codes or category names directly from their data. When you develop codes this way, you are actually generating **inductive codes,** which are defined as codes that are generated by the researcher by directly examining the data during the coding process. Inductive codes can be based on emic terms (terms that are used by the participants themselves). For example, high school students might use the emic term *jocks* to refer to students who play sports. Inductive codes can also be based on social science terms that a researcher is familiar with. For example, a social science term for *jocks* might be *athletic role.* Finally, inductive codes might be good, clear, descriptive words that most people would agree characterize a segment of data (e.g., we might agree that the segment of data refers to athletes).

- **A priori codes**
  Codes that were developed before examining the current data

Sometimes researchers bring an already developed coding scheme to the research project. These codes are called **a priori codes** or preexisting codes because they were developed before or at the very beginning of the current research study. A priori codes are used when a researcher is trying to replicate or extend a certain line of previous research. Researchers may also establish some a priori codes before data collection based on their relevance to the research questions. When researchers bring a priori codes to a research study, they come in with a start list of codes—an already developed master list that they can use for coding. During coding, however, the researcher should apply these codes only when they clearly fit segments of data. The codes should not be forced onto the data, and new codes should be generated when data segments are found that do not fit any of the codes on the list. In practice, many researchers employ both preexisting and inductive codes.

Co-Occurring and Facesheet Codes

In our discussion so far, we have used just one descriptive category for any given segment of data. If you code transcripts, however, it is very possible that the codes will overlap. In other words, more than one topic or category might be applied to the same set of data. If the categories are intertwined, you simply allow the codes to naturally overlap, and the result is what is called co-occurring codes. **Co-occurring codes** are sets of codes (i.e., two or more codes) that partially or completely overlap. Co-occurring codes might merely show conceptual redundancy in coding (i.e., the two codes mean basically the same thing). More interestingly, co-occurring codes might suggest a relationship among categories within a set of text for a single individual (e.g., an interview transcript) or across multiple sets of text for different individuals (i.e., across several interview transcripts).

- **Co-occurring codes**
  Codes that partially or completely overlap

An example of co-occurring codes within an individual's transcript is shown in Table 17.5. If you look at the text in the table, you will see that "mood" is the category marking lines 8–13, "positive" is the category for lines 11–20, "like" is the category for lines 16–20, "don't like" is the category for lines 21–29, "miss" is the category for lines 30–40, and "they" is the category for lines 32–34. As you can see, some of these categories overlap. More specifically, lines 32–34 are coded with two co-occurring codes. The two codes "miss" and "they" co-occur for these three lines. Also, lines 16–20 are coded with the codes "like" and "positive." Therefore, these are also co-occurring codes. The key point to remember is that you can allow codes to overlap when coding data.

▓ **TABLE 17.5**   Text with Overlapping Codes

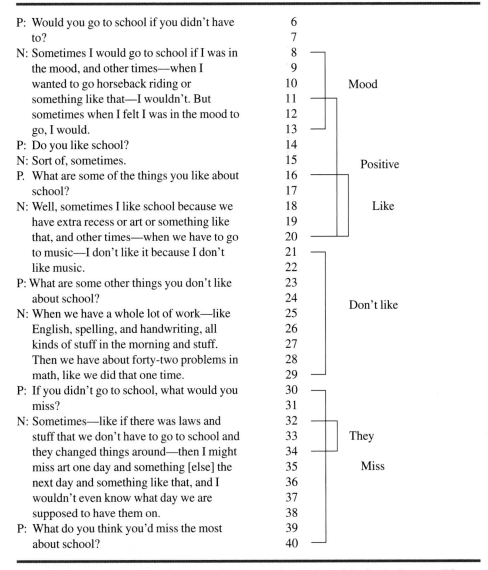

P: Would you go to school if you didn't have to?	6 7
N: Sometimes I would go to school if I was in the mood, and other times—when I wanted to go horseback riding or something like that—I wouldn't. But sometimes when I felt I was in the mood to go, I would.	8 9 10 Mood 11 12 13
P: Do you like school?	14
N: Sort of, sometimes.	15 Positive
P. What are some of the things you like about school?	16 17
N: Well, sometimes I like school because we have extra recess or art or something like that, and other times—when we have to go to music—I don't like it because I don't like music.	18 Like 19 20 21 22
P: What are some other things you don't like about school?	23 24 Don't like
N: When we have a whole lot of work—like English, spelling, and handwriting, all kinds of stuff in the morning and stuff. Then we have about forty-two problems in math, like we did that one time.	25 26 27 28 29
P: If you didn't go to school, what would you miss?	30 31
N: Sometimes—like if there was laws and stuff that we don't have to go to school and they changed things around—then I might miss art one day and something [else] the next day and something like that, and I wouldn't even know what day we are supposed to have them on.	32 33 They 34 35 Miss 36 37 38
P: What do you think you'd miss the most about school?	39 40

Source: From M. D. LeCompte, J. Preissle, and R. Tesch, *Ethnography and Qualitative Design in Educational Research,* p. 294, copyright © 1993 by Academic Press. Reprinted by permission of Academic Press and the authors.

A researcher can also attach codes to an entire document, interview, or set of lines. For example, lines 6–40 in Table 17.5 (i.e., all the given lines) could have been given a code such as "school" because that was the topic of discussion in all of the lines. If you had several interview transcripts, you might decide to attach the code "female" or "male" to each

■ **Facesheet codes**
Codes that apply to a
complete document
or case

transcript to signify the participant's gender. Codes that apply to a complete document or case (e.g., to an interview) are called **facesheet codes.** The origin of the term *facesheet* probably comes from researchers attaching a sheet of paper to each transcript with codes listed that apply to the whole transcript. Demographic variables are frequently used as facesheet codes (e.g., gender, age, race, occupation, school). Researchers might later decide to sort their data files by facesheet codes to search for group differences (e.g., differences between older and younger teachers) or other relationships in the data.

17.4 What is the difference between segmenting and coding?

17.5 What is the difference between inductive codes and a priori codes?

17.6 What is the difference between co-occurring codes and facesheet codes?

ENUMERATION

■ **Enumeration**
The process of quanti-
fying data

We have talked about the importance of transcribing data, and we have shown you the basics of assigning codes to qualitative data. At this point, a data analyst might decide to determine how frequently words or coded categories appear in the data. This process of quantifying data is called **enumeration.** Enumeration helps qualitative researchers to communicate concepts such as "amount" or "frequency" when writing up the results. Often a reader needs to know how much or how often, in addition to knowing that something happened. Weber (1990), for example, reports the word frequencies used in the 1980 Democratic and Republican platforms. The five most common words in the Democratic platform were *our* (430 occurrences), *must* (321), *Democratic* (226), *federal* (177), and *support* (144). The most common words in the Republican platform were *our* (347), *their* (161), *administration* (131), *government* (128), and *Republican* (126). Word or code frequencies can help researchers to determine the importance of words and ideas. Listing frequencies can also help in identifying prominent themes in the data (e.g., What kinds of things did the participants say many times?).

When numbers are reported in qualitative research reports, you must always be sure to check the basis of the numbers being used, or you could be misled. For example, in the Democratic and Republican platform example, the basis was all words in the document (e.g., 144 of the words in the Democratic platform were *support*). A number such as this simply points out the emphasis placed on a word by the writer of the document. If several interview transcripts are analyzed, the basis of a reported number might be the number of words mentioned by all of the participants. If a word had a high frequency in this case, you might be inclined to believe that most of the participants used the word frequently. However, a high frequency of a particular word could also mean that a single participant used the particular word many times. In other words, a word might have a large frequency simply because one or two research participants used the word many times, not because a large number of different participants used the word. Enumeration can be helpful in qualitative data analysis, but always be careful to recognize the kinds of numbers that are being reported.

17.7 Explain the process of enumeration.

CREATING HIERARCHICAL CATEGORY SYSTEMS

Categories are the basic building blocks of qualitative data analysis because qualitative researchers make sense of their data by identifying and studying the categories that appear in their data. You can generally think of the set of categories for a collection of data as forming a classification system characterizing those data. Rather than having to think about each sentence or each word in the data, the researcher will, after coding the data, be able to focus on the themes and relationships suggested by the classification system. You learned earlier how to find categories in qualitative data, and you also learned that you may want to count these categories for suggestive themes.

Sometimes categories can be organized into different levels. That is, a set of subcategories might fall beneath a certain category, and that certain category might itself fall under an even higher level category. Think about the category called *fruit*. In this case, some possible subcategories are oranges, grapefruit, kiwi, apples, and bananas. These are subcategories of fruit because they are "part of" or "types of" the higher level category called *fruit*. The category fruit may itself be a subcategory of yet a higher category called *food group*. Systems of categories like this are called hierarchies because they are layered or fall into different levels.

An example of a hierarchical classification system can be found in a research article by Frontman and Kunkel (1994). These researchers were interested in when and how counselors believed a session with a client was successful. They interviewed sixty-nine mental health workers from various mental health fields, including counseling psychology, clinical psychology, marriage and family therapy, social work, and school psychology. After an initial session with a client, the participants filled out an open-ended questionnaire asking them to describe what they felt was successful in the session. A team of researchers analyzed the transcripts and came up with a rather elaborate hierarchical classification system. Frontman and Kunkel report that they developed their hierarchy in a bottom-up fashion, which means that the lowest level categories are the closest to the actual data collected in the study. This bottom-up, or inductive, strategy is the most common approach used by qualitative researchers (Weitzman & Miles, 1995).

We have reproduced a small part of Frontman and Kunkel's (1994) classification system in Figure 17.2 to give you a feel for hierarchical coding. When looking at the figure, be sure to realize that many of the categories in Frontman and Kunkel's hierarchical system are left out; the downward arrows indicate where additional levels and categories were excluded. All forty-four categories in their full hierarchical classification system are given in the article.

You can see that the higher levels of the hierarchy shown in Figure 17.2 are more general than the lower levels. That is, a higher-level category includes or subsumes the categories falling under it. The highest level of the hierarchy in Figure 17.2 includes the very

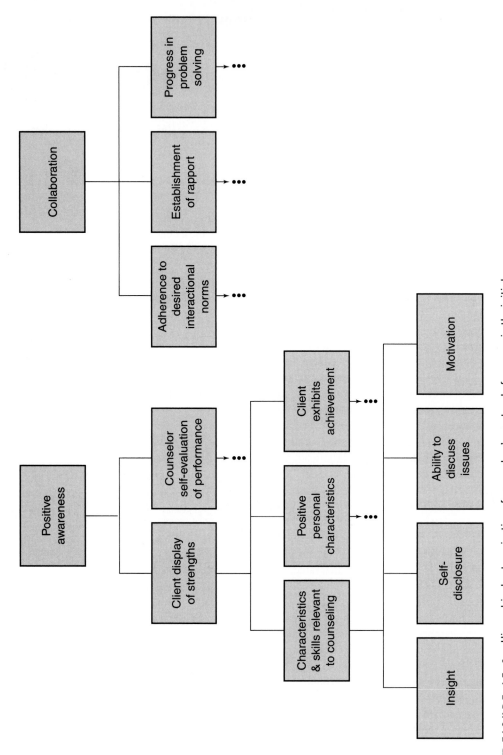

FIGURE 17.2 Hierarchical categorization of counselors' construal of success in the initial session. The vertical ellipses show where we have left out subcategories.

general categories called positive awareness and collaboration. Frontman and Kunkel tell us that they decided near the conclusion of their research project that these two general categories subsumed the sets of categories falling below them. At the second highest level of the hierarchy in Figure 17.2, you can see that the researchers categorized counselors' construal of success into five categories. The five categories with brief explanations are as follows:

1. Client display of strengths ("The skills, actions, and characteristics expressed by the client that the counselor connotes as indication of success.")
2. Counselor self-evaluation of performance ("Counselor assesses success through evaluating the quality of his or her performance during the session.")
3. Adherence to desired interactional norms ("Success is determined by the presence of particular interactional patterns in the session.")
4. Establishment of rapport ("Success defined as indication that rapport between counselor and client is being established.")
5. Progress in problem solving ("Success is attributed to client making progress toward establishing and implementing direct steps in solving a problem.") (Frontman & Kunkel, 1994, pp. 498–499).

The first two of the five categories we just listed are part of positive awareness, and the last three are part of collaboration. At the second lowest level of the hierarchy, we provide the categories falling under client display of strengths. At the lowest level of the hierarchy, we show the categories falling under characteristics and skills relevant to counseling. As you can see, there is a total of four levels in the hierarchy shown in Figure 17.2. We find Frontman and Kunkel's hierarchy interesting because it provides a direct picture of the hierarchical structure of their data. It is also interesting to see what counselors believe makes therapy successful.

17.8 What is a hierarchical category system, and why can it be useful to construct hierarchical systems?

R E V I E W

QUESTIONS

IDENTIFYING RELATIONSHIPS AMONG CATEGORIES

In this section, we show you some ways to explore relationships in qualitative research data. When qualitative researchers use the term *relationship,* they have a slightly different meaning than when quantitative researchers use the term. You learned in earlier chapters that quantitative researchers focus their efforts on examining the relationships among variables. Qualitative researchers, however, attach a much broader meaning to the term *relationship.* The hierarchical system just shown in Figure 17.1 is one type of relationship. Qualitative researchers use the term *relationship* to refer to many different kinds of relations or connections between things, including but not limited to variables. This is not better or worse; it is just different.

A summary of several kinds of relationships identified by one well-known qualitative researcher named James Spradley (1979) is given in Table 17.6. Take a moment to examine the nine relationships because you might identify some of these relationships when you are reading transcripts or when you are examining categories generated from your data. Spradley's list is not exhaustive, but it is suggestive. You will undoubtedly find additional kinds of relationships if you analyze some transcribed data.

Suppose you were reading an interview transcript and you came across the following text: "When I just ignore Johnny's acting out, he becomes more aggressive toward the other students in my classroom. But if I walk over and stand beside him, he will usually quiet down for a little while." This text suggests a possible causal process operating among several categories. (In Table 17.6, this is called a cause-effect relationship.) It is suggested, in particular, that ignoring Johnny's behavioral outbursts results in aggressive behavior and proximity results in less aggressive behavior. Obviously, two sentences like this in a transcript do not provide solid evidence of a general cause-and-effect relationship; however, statements like this do have a causal form, and they might suggest that you do additional analysis and data collection to further explore the relationship.

Now recall the hierarchical categorization that we showed you in Figure 17.2. If you look at the figure again you will see that one of the categories was "characteristics and skills relevant to counseling." That category has four characteristics falling under it. They are insight, self-disclosure, ability to discuss issues, and motivation. You can view these four subcategories as following Spradley's strict inclusion relationship because they are "kinds of" characteristics or skills. Strict inclusion is a very common form of relationship in qualitative data analysis.

Educational researchers often use the term *typology* to refer to categories that follow Spradley's strict inclusion form of relationship. A **typology** is a classification system that breaks something down into its different types or kinds. A typology is basically the same thing as a taxonomy. You might remember what a taxonomy is from your high school or college biology class. (Okay, I know it has been a long time!) In biology, the levels of the animal taxonomy are kingdom, phylum, class, order, family, genus, and species. (Here's a memory aid: **K**ings **P**lay **C**hess **O**n **F**iber **G**lass **S**tools.) Bailey (1994) points out that "the term *taxonomy* is more generally used in the biological sciences, while *typology* is used in the social sciences" (p. 6). Typologies are useful because they help make sense out of qualitative data.

Typologies can be simple or complex. You might, for example, be interested in the different types of cliques in schools, types of teaching strategies used by teachers, or types of

■ **Typology**
A classification system that breaks something down into different types or kinds

Research
Navigator.c⊛m

typology

■ **TABLE 17.6**		
Spradley's Universal Semantic Relationships	**Title**	**Form of Relationship**
	1. Strict inclusion	X is a kind of Y
	2. Spatial	X is a place in Y; X is a part of Y
	3. Cause-effect	X is a result of Y; X is a cause of Y
	4. Rationale	X is a reason for doing Y
	5. Location for action	X is a place for doing Y
	6. Function	X is used for Y
	7. Means-end	X is a way to do Y
	8. Sequence	X is a step (stage) in Y
	9. Attribution	X is an attribute (characteristic) of Y

Source: Adapted from J. P. Spradley, 1979, p. 111. Used by permission.

student lifestyles. These would be fairly simple, one-dimensional typologies. At a more complex level, you could view the hierarchical classification in Figure 17.2 as one big typology, showing the types of counselors' construal of success. To construct a typology, it is helpful to construct mutually exclusive and exhaustive categories. **Mutually exclusive categories** are categories that are clearly separate or distinct; they do not overlap. **Exhaustive categories** classify all the relevant cases in your data. Exhaustiveness of categories can be difficult in qualitative research because some cases simply don't fit into a typology. However, the more cases there are that fit into your typology, the better.

■ **Mutually exclusive categories**
A set of categories that are separate or distinct

■ **Exhaustive categories**
A set of categories that classify all of the relevant cases in the data

Another interesting typology was constructed by Patton (1990) when he was helping a group of high school teachers to develop a student dropout prevention program. Patton observed and interviewed teachers, and here is what he found:

> The inductive analysis of the data suggested that teachers' behaviors toward dropouts could be conceptualized along a continuum according to the extent to which teachers were willing to take direct responsibility for doing something about the problem. This dimension varied from taking responsibility to shifting responsibility to others. The second dimension concerned the teachers' views about the effective intervention strategies. The inductive analysis revealed three perspectives among the teachers. Some teachers believed that a rehabilitation effort was needed to help kids with their problems; some teachers preferred a maintenance or caretaking effort aimed at just keeping the school running, that is, maintaining the system; and still other teachers favored finding some way of punishing students for their unacceptable and inappropriate behaviors, no longer letting them get away with the infractions they had been committing in the past. (pp. 411–412)

You can see from this quote that Patton found two simple or one-dimensional typologies that were related to dropout prevention: (1) teachers' beliefs about how to deal with dropouts and (2) teachers' behaviors toward dropouts.

Patton then decided to cross these two simple typologies into a two-dimensional matrix to relate the two dimensions. When he did this, he found a typology that made a lot of sense to the teachers in the research study. The typology included six types of teacher roles in dealing with the high school dropout problem. The roles are shown in the six cells of the matrix in Figure 17.3. The different types of teacher roles shown in the figure are counselor/friend, traffic cop, old-fashioned schoolmaster, referral agent, ostrich, and complainer. You might know some of these kinds of teachers at your own school. Remember, when analyzing qualitative data, you can sometimes find new and interesting information by cross-classifying two or more dimensions.

Now let's look at an example of Spradley's "sequence" type of relationship (Table 17.6). This example comes from an article titled, "A Framework for Describing Developmental Change among Older Adults," by Fisher (1993). Fisher pursued this research because he was interested in determining whether older adulthood could be categorized into a set of meaningful stages. He decided not to rely on the stages presented in popular developmental psychology books because many of these lists were dated. Also, some of these lists lumped all older people into a single developmental stage called *old age*. Fisher decided that he wanted to explore the concept of old age using qualitative research.

Fisher conducted in-depth interviews with seventy-four adults whose ages ranged from sixty-one to ninety-four years old. Using in-depth, open-ended interviews, he asked

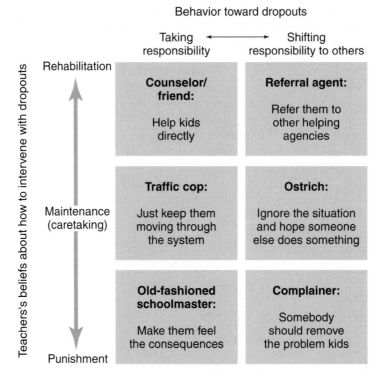

his participants what kinds of experiences they had in their lives. An interesting theme in his research findings was a tendency by all of the older adults toward adaptation to their life circumstances, no matter what the circumstances were. Fisher also generated five core categories from his data that could be ordered by time. These categories resulted in the following sequence of old age: (1) continuity with middle age, (2) early transition, (3) revised lifestyle, (4) later transition, and (5) final period. You can see the defining characteristics of each of these five stages in Table 17.7.

Drawing Diagrams

■ **Diagramming**
Making a sketch, drawing, or outline to show how something works or to clarify the relationship between the parts of a whole

A useful tool for showing the relationships among categories is called **diagramming** (i.e., making diagrams). A diagram is "a plan, sketch, drawing, or outline designed to demonstrate or explain how something works or to clarify the relationship between the parts of a whole" (American Heritage Dictionary). Figures 17.2 and 17.3, which we discussed in the previous section, are examples of diagrams. Diagrams are very popular with visually oriented learners and can be used to effectively demonstrate relationships for the readers of reports. The use of diagrams can also be helpful during data analysis when you are trying to make sense out of your data.

▧ **TABLE 17.7**
Categories Ordered
by Time

Category I: Continuity with Middle Age

Characteristics: Retirement plans pursued
Middle-age lifestyle continued
Other activities substituted for work

Category II: Early Transition

Characteristics: Involuntary transitional events
Voluntary transitional events
End of continuity with middle age

Category III: Revised Lifestyle

Characteristics: Adaptation to changes of early transition
Stable lifestyle appropriate to older adulthood
Socialization realized through age-group
affiliation

Category IV: Later Transition

Characteristics: Loss of health and mobility
Need for assistance and/or care
Loss of autonomy

Category V: Final Period

Characteristics: Adaptation to changes of later transition
Stable lifestyle appropriate to level of
dependency
Sense of finitude, mortality

Source: Adapted from Fisher, J. C. (1993). A framework for describing developmental change among older adults. *Adult Education Quarterly 43*(2), 81.

An easily understood example of a diagram showing a complex process appears in Figure 12.2 (page 385). This diagram depicts a grounded theory about how departmental chairpersons at universities facilitate the growth and development of their faculty members. The diagram shows that the career stage of the faculty member determines the type of faculty issue chairpersons are concerned with, and the faculty issue determines the specific strategy a chairperson uses in working with a faculty member. The diagram also lists the outcomes resulting from applying the strategies.

A similar type of diagram is called a network diagram. A **network diagram** shows the direct links between variables or events over time (Miles & Huberman, 1994). An example of a network diagram is the path analysis diagram that appears in Figure 11.5 (page 352). The path analysis diagram was based on quantitative research. However, network diagrams can also be based on qualitative data. Qualitative researchers often use these diagrams to depict

■ **Network diagram**
A diagram showing the direct links between variables or events over time

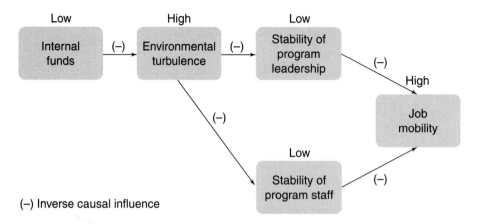

(−) Inverse causal influence

■ **FIGURE 17.4**   Network diagram for job mobility

Reprinted from M. B. Miles and A. M. Huberman, *Qualitative Data Analysis: An Expanded Source Book,* p. 231, copyright © 1994 by Sage Publications, Inc. Reprinted by Permission of Sage Publications, Inc.

their thinking about potential causal relationships. We have included an example of a part of a network diagram based on qualitative data in Figure 17.4. This diagram is based on a school innovation and improvement study by Miles and Huberman (1994). According to the diagram, low internal funds in school districts resulted in high environmental turbulence in those districts (e.g., a shortage of money resulted in uncertain operating conditions for principals). This resulted in low stability for the leaders of the various school improvement programs and in low stability for the program staff. As a result of this instability, job mobility was high.

To learn more about causal network diagrams, you should take a look at the work of Miles and Huberman (1994). They provide an extensive discussion of the issues surrounding causal analysis in qualitative research, and they discuss how to develop causal networks based on a single case or on multiple cases. If you are interested in cause-and-effect relationships with qualitative data, you should also review Chapter 8 on research validity in this book, especially the sections on internal validity. Miles and Huberman (1994) also discuss how to construct many different kinds of interesting matrices (i.e., classifications of two or more dimensions) to aid in the analysis and presentation of qualitative research data.

REVIEW   **17.9** How do qualitative researchers show relationships among categories?

QUESTIONS   **17.10** How are network diagrams used in qualitative research?

CORROBORATING AND VALIDATING RESULTS

In Chapter 8, we discussed how to assess and promote the validity or trustworthiness of your qualitative research data (in the last section of the chapter). We recommend that you take a moment right now and review the five types of validity and the strategies that are used to promote qualitative research validity (they are shown in Table 8.2 on page 250). The point is that it is essential that you think about validity and utilize the strategies throughout the qualitative data collection, analysis, and write-up process whenever possible.

17.11 What are the five types of validity that are of potential importance in qualitative research, and what are their definitions?

17.12 What are the thirteen strategies that are used to promote validity in qualitative research, and what are their definitions?

REVIEW
QUESTIONS

COMPUTER PROGRAMS FOR QUALITATIVE DATA ANALYSIS

Qualitative researchers are just beginning to capitalize on the possibilities for computer use in the analysis of qualitative data. Although qualitative researchers have been using word processors for transcribing and editing their data for quite some time, it has been only during the last decade that a number of qualitative data analysis computer programs have readily become available. The developers of these programs examined the procedures that qualitative researchers follow when making sense of their data and then developed programs that help to automate these procedures. Before we examine the potential of using qualitative data analysis programs, we will look at how qualitative researchers have traditionally made sense of their data without these programs.

Qualitative researchers traditionally use a filing system approach to data analysis. They begin their data analysis by transcribing their data and making copies of the various data documents. Then they hand code the data in the left margin of these copies. After this, researchers make copies of the coded data and cut the data into segments of text with the marked codes. Then a filing system is created and used, one folder being reserved for each code. The segments of text are placed into their appropriate folder. If a segment of text has more than one code, then more than one copy of the segment is made, and a copy of the segment is placed in all the relevant folders. This way, all the folders contain all the appropriate data segments. At this point, researchers can reread the segments of text in each folder, looking for themes occurring in the data.

More complex analyses require even more work when done by hand. For example, searching for two co-occurring codes typically requires making a folder with the two codes as its title, locating the two individual code folders, and then checking the text segments in those folders to see whether they include both codes in the left margin. If both codes are present, the segment of text is copied and placed into the new two-code folder. As you can see, doing complex data analysis by hand can be time consuming and quite difficult. Perhaps this is one reason why qualitative data analysis has not advanced as rapidly as has quantitative data analysis. Because of the increasing use of computer programs, however, we predict that the analysis of qualitative data will take a giant step forward during the next decade. One reason for our prediction is that procedures that are highly time consuming when done by hand are available with just a few keystrokes on the computer. So that you have a basic idea about the potential of computer data analysis, we list a few of the capabilities of qualitative data analysis computer programs.

Qualitative data analysis programs can be used to do virtually everything we have discussed in this chapter. They can, for example, be used to store and code your data. During coding, most programs allow complex hierarchical classification systems such as the one shown in Figure 17.2 to be developed. Most programs allow the use of many different kinds of codes, including co-occurring and facesheet codes. Enumeration is easily done with just a few clicks of the computer mouse. Many programs allow you to attach memos or annotations to the codes or data documents so that you can record the important thoughts you have during analysis. Some programs will produce graphics that can be used in presenting the data. Finally, the heart and soul of most qualitative data analysis programs are their searching capabilities, the topic to which we now turn.

■ **Boolean operators**
Words used to create logical combinations

You can perform simple or complex searches using computer packages that use Boolean operators. **Boolean operators** are words used to create logical combinations based on basic laws of thought. We all use Boolean operators every day when we think and talk about things. Some common Boolean operators we all use are AND, OR, NOT, IF, THEN, and EXCEPT. Qualitative data analysis computer programs are written so that you can search your data or a set of codes using these and many other operators.

You might, for example, search the codes or text in a set of interview transcripts concerning teacher satisfaction using the following string of words: "male AND satisfied AND first grade." The Boolean operator AND is called the intersection operator because it finds all intersections of the words or codes. This search would locate all instances of male, first-grade teachers, who were satisfied. Similarly, you could search for female teachers using this string of words: "female AND teacher." You can find disconfirming cases (instances that do not have any of the characteristics) by adding the word NOT to the search command (e.g., NOT teacher will find all nonteacher instances).

Another operator is the OR, or union, operator. This operator finds all instances that take on any one of the provided words or codes. For example, if you searched a document with the command "female OR first grade" you would come up with instances that are either "female" or "first grade" or both. Another kind of search command is called FOLLOWED-BY in one popular program. Using this you can find instances in which two codes occur in a specific order in the data (e.g., punishment FOLLOWED-BY quiet behavior). As you can see, you can do a lot of different kinds of searches using Boolean operators.

There are many qualitative data analysis computer programs currently available. The three most popular programs are NUD*IST (this stands for **N**onnumerical, **U**nstructured **D**ata **I**ndexing, **S**earching, and **T**heorizing, not what you were thinking about!), the Ethnograph, and ATLAS. There are many others. We have included under bonus materials on the book's companion website a list of websites for the different qualitative data analysis programs. Most of the companies will also send you a demonstration copy or allow you to download one from their Internet site free of charge. If you decide that you are interested in a qualitative data analysis program, testing out a demonstration copy is an excellent way to find out which program best suits your particular needs.

We conclude by listing some of the advantages and disadvantages of using computer programs for the analysis of qualitative data. The advantages are that qualitative data analysis computer programs can help in storing and organizing data, they can be used for all of the analyses discussed in this chapter plus many more, they can reduce the time required to analyze data (e.g., an analysis procedure that takes a lot of time by hand may take virtually no time with a computer program), and they can make procedures available to you that are rarely done by hand because they are either too time consuming or too complex. Some disadvantages are that computer programs can take time to learn, they cost money and require computer availability, and they can become dated. The biggest disadvantage is startup time. Nonetheless, if you are planning on doing a lot of qualitative data analysis for an extended period of time, we recommend the use of computer programs.

17.13 What are some of the capabilities of computer programs for data analysis?

17.14 What are some of the leading qualitative data analysis computer programs?

SUMMARY

Qualitative data analysis typically involves the analysis of text from interview or field note transcripts. Some basic procedures in qualitative data analysis are transcribing data, reading and rereading transcripts (i.e., immersing yourself in your data to understand what is going on), segmenting and coding the data, counting words and coded categories (enumeration), searching for relationships and themes in the data, and generating diagrams to help in interpreting the data. The goal of data analysis is to be able to clearly summarize your data and generate inductive theories based on the data. Some questions you might ask of your data are, What themes occurred in your interviews or field notes? What topics were mentioned most often? What issues were most important to the people in your study? What are the cultural characteristics of the people in your research study? How do your participants view the topic of your research? What kinds of relationships (e.g., strict inclusion, cause-effect, function, sequence) are apparent in your data? How can the categories you have identified in the data be ordered into meaningful grounded theories? The questions you can ask are virtually unlimited, and they will vary depending on your research problem, the type of qualitative research you are conducting (e.g., phenomenology, ethnography, case study, grounded theory, historical), and your own theoretical perspective based on your disciplinary training. Qualitative data analysis computer programs can aid in the analysis of qualitative data, but they do take quite a bit of time to learn.

KEY TERMS

a priori codes (p. 508)
Boolean operators (p. 521)
coding (p. 502)
co-occurring codes (p. 508)
diagramming (p. 516)
enumeration (p. 510)
exhaustive categories (p. 515)

facesheet codes (p. 510)
inductive codes (p. 508)
intercoder reliability (p. 504)
interim analysis (p. 500)
intracoder reliability (p. 504)
master list (p. 504)
memoing (p. 501)

mutually exclusive
   categories (p. 515)
network diagram (p. 517)
segmenting (p. 502)
transcription (p. 502)
typology (p. 514)

DISCUSSION QUESTIONS

1. In quantitative research, data analysis provides information on statistical significance and size of effects. How would you determine whether something was important or practically significant in qualitative research?

2. Table 17.6 lists nine kinds of relationships. Think of an example of one of these, and share it with the class.

3. What are the advantages and disadvantages of having more than one data analyst in a qualitative study?

4. Why is traditional qualitative data analysis said to be inductive? How might you also make it more deductive in your approach?

RESEARCH EXERCISES

1. Analyze the following data. The data are transcribed field notes from a classroom observation done in Mexico City by Robert Stake. As you code the data, be on the lookout for answers to the following questions: What topics appeared in the text? What was the context of the classroom like? What teaching style did the instructor use? Explain this teaching style. What were some of the norms of the classroom (e.g., arrival to class, speaking out in class)? What was the content of the lesson? What was the political persuasion of the students and/or teacher? What kinds of instructional materials were used in the classroom? After you finish coding the text, write a brief summary report on the observation, answering the questions just posed and adding any additional insights that emerge as you code the data.

Class Notes, October 23[1]

The temperature will climb into the 70's today, but now it is chilly in this white tile and terrazzo classroom. Eleven students (of 29 still on the roster) are here, each in a jacket or sweater. No doubt it was cooler still when they left home. The instructor, Senor Pretelin, reminds them of the topic, the Origins of Capitalism, and selects a question for which they have prepared answers. An answer from the back row is ventured. Two more students arrive—it is ten past the hour—now four more.—Senor Pretelin undertakes a correction of the answer, but asks for still more of an answer. His style is casual. He draws long on a cigarette. His audience is alert.—Marx is a presence, spoken in name, and looming from the cover of the textbook. Two books only are in sight. Several students have photocopies of the chapter assigned.—The chalkboard remains filled with last class's logic symbols, now unnoticed. Some students read through their answers, most concentrate on what Pretelin says about answers that are offered.—The first answers had been volunteered by males, now one from a female. The instructor draws her out, more of her idea, then improves upon the explanation himself.

—The coolness of the space is warmed by the exchanges.—Outside a power mower sputters, struggling with a thickness of grass for which it probably was not designed.—It is 20 past the hour. Another student arrives. Most are around 20, all have black hair. These are incoming freshmen in the social studies and humanities program, enrolled in a sociology course on political doctrines. Still another arrives. She pushes the door closed, and jams it with a chair, to thwart the breeze from the squared-out plaza.—Senor Pretelin is expanding an answer at length. He then turns to another question, lights another cigarette while awaiting a volunteer—again he asks for improvement, gets a couple of tries; then answers the question to his satisfaction. Another question. He patiently awaits student initiative. The students appear to think or read to themselves what they had written earlier.

—The haze of Mexico City shrouds the city-center several miles to the southeast. Yesterday's downpour did not long cleanse the sky.—Quiet again while awaiting a volunteer. The first young woman offers her answer. She is the only female of the seven or so students who have ventured forth. Heads nod to her reference to the camposinos, and to Pretelin's amplification. There seems to be an empathy for these abstract, at least distant, camposinos. If capitalistic advocacy exists in this classroom it does not speak out. A half hour has passed. The recital continues. Only a few students are correcting their notes (or creating them belatedly), most try to read or listen. Minds are mobilized, not idling. Finally a small wedge of humor.

—The air may relax a bit.—Four observers are dispersed about the room, little noticed even as they write. The instructor maintains his task, not ever stopping to take roll. Pretelin is a slight man, perhaps 40. He wears a smart jacket, a dark shirt buttoned high, a gold neckchain. His fingers are long and expressive.—For several minutes, the dragging of heavy objects outside the room interferes.—For a last time the students are sent to their answers, even asked to look further. Few have books. Then the students are invited to pose questions. The exchange becomes more good natured, but business-like still. The engagement goes on, minds "full on," provoked sociably, heads nodding agreement.—More immediate camposinos, now drawn 17 million strong to the streets below, make the noises of the city. A poster admonishes: "Admon. Vota. Platestda." Near the door the graffiti begins "La ignorancia mata. . . ." The hour draws to a close, a final cigarette, a summary, a warm smile.

Exercise Sheet

1. Are you going to collect qualitative data for any of your research questions? If yes, rewrite those questions here. If you are not proposing or conducting an actual research project, then write two hypothetical qualitative research questions here and use them for 2–5 below.)
2. For each question just listed, what kind of qualitative data you will collect?
3. What is your plan of qualitative analysis for each of the questions and data sources listed above?
4. How will you validate your findings? (*Hint:* see Table 8.2, and the surrounding material in Chapter 8.)
5. How will you decide if your qualitative findings are practically significant?

RELEVANT INTERNET SITES

www.ualberta.ca/~jrnorris/qda.html
Qualitative data analysis software links.

www.slais.ubc.ca/resources/research_methods/qualitat.htm
Lots of links to qualitative data analysis sites.

RECOMMENDED READING

Gahan, C., & Hannibal, M. (1998). *Doing qualitative research using QSR NUD-IST.* London: Sage.

Gibbs, G. R. (2002). *Qualitative data analysis: Explorations with Nvivo.* Buckingham, England: Open University Press.

Miles, M. B., & Huberman, A. M. (1994). *Qualitative data analysis: An expanded sourcebook.* Newbury Park, CA: Sage.

Patton, M. Q. (2002). *Qualitative research and evaluation methods.* Thousand Oaks, CA: Sage.

ENDNOTE

1. Reprinted from Robert E. Stake, "Class Notes, October 23," *The Art of Case Study Research,* pp. 88–90, copyright © 1995 by Sage Publications, Inc. Reprinted by Permission of Sage Publications, Inc., and the author.

18

Preparation of the Research Report

After you have conducted a research study, you should consider preparing a research report and submitting it to a journal for publication. Before preparing the research report, you should critically review it and ask yourself whether the study is free from flaws and important enough to justify publication. Would others be interested in the results, and would it influence their work or have some educational impact? As a general rule, you should never conduct a study that you do not think is publishable. If the study is important and free from flaws that would preclude drawing unambiguous conclusions, you should proceed with the preparation of a research report because this is the mechanism for communicating the results of research studies. Table 18.1 lists some of the journals in which educational researchers publish.

The preparation of research reports differs somewhat depending on whether you conducted a quantitative or a qualitative research study. Remember that quantitative studies focus on hypothesis testing and are epitomized by experimental research studies, whereas qualitative studies are more often exploratory and bridge a variety of approaches or methods from ethnography to historical research. Because of the different goals and approaches of quantitative and qualitative research, the approaches to writing quantitative and qualitative research reports differ. We focus first on quantitative research report writing and then on qualitative research report writing. However, before this discussion, we want to cover a number of general principles that must be adhered to in writing either type of research report.

■ **TABLE 18.1**   Journals That Publish the Results of Educational Research

American Educational Research Journal	Journal of Curriculum and Supervision
American Journal of Education	Journal of Curriculum Studies
Anthropology and Education Quarterly	Journal of Education
Applied Measurement in Education	Journal of Education for Students Placed at Risk
Art Education	Journal of Educational and Behavioral Statistics
Cambridge Journal of Education	Journal of Educational Research
Child Development	Journal of Information Technology for Teacher Education
Cognition and Instruction	Journal of In-service Education
Creativity Research Journal	Journal of Literacy Research
Cross Cultural Psychology	Journal of Negro Education
Curriculum Studies	The Journal of Research in Science Teaching
Curriculum/Technology Quarterly	Journal of Vocational Education and Training
Early Childhood Education Journal	Kappa Delta Pi Record
Education and Urban Society	New Teacher Advocate
Education Action Research	Oxford Studies in Comparative Education
Educational Assessment	Phi Delta Kappan
Educational Evaluation and Policy Analysis	PROSPERO
The Educational Forum	Reading Research Quarterly
Educational Policy	Research in Post-Compulsory Education
Educational Psychologist	Research in the Teaching of English
Educational Psychology Review	Review of Educational Research
Educational Research and Evaluation	School Leadership and Management
Educational Researcher	Teacher Development
Elementary School Journal	Teacher Education Quarterly
FORUM: for promoting 3–19 comprehensive education	Teachers and Teaching: theory and practice
	Teachers College Record
Harvard Educational Review	Teaching and Teacher Education
International Studies in Sociology of Education	Theory into Practice
Journal for Research in Mathematics Education	Urban Education
Journal of Classroom Interaction	The Urban Review

GENERAL PRINCIPLES RELATED TO WRITING THE RESEARCH REPORT

Perhaps the overriding general principle that must be followed in writing the research report is that it must be prepared in a manner that clearly communicates to the reader. Good writing is a craft that requires thoughtful concern for the presentation and language used. Good writing is usually a developmental process that is acquired over time. Instruction in developing good writing is obviously not the purpose of this textbook or the course you are taking.

We discuss some of the general principles to which you should adhere when preparing a research report, which are elaborated on in more detail in the APA publication manual

(2001). If you have difficulty with writing, there are several books that can be very helpful. W. Strunk, Jr., and E. B. White's *The Elements of Style* (1979) is a classic and has the virtue of being short. Gage's *The Shape of Reason* (1991) and Rosnow and Rosnow's *Writing Papers in Psychology* (1992) are excellent and can be of assistance in writing clearly, as can the APA publication manual. Hult's book *Researching and Writing in the Social Sciences* (1996) and Becker's book, *Writing for Social Scientists* (1986) are also excellent references.

Clear communication requires an orderly presentation of ideas. There must be a continuity of words, concepts, and thematic development from the beginning to the end of the report. This continuity can be achieved by the use of punctuation marks to show the relationship between ideas and by the use of transitional words, such as *then, next, therefore,* and *however.* Some transition words (for example, *while* and *since*) can create confusion and should be used cautiously. Because you are so familiar with the material you are reporting, objectivity is frequently lost, and problems in clarity of communication might not be immediately apparent. One good technique to use is to write the research report and then put it aside for several days before reading it again. A later reading of the report can uncover difficulties in clarity of communication.

Preparation of the research report requires a smoothness and economy of expression. Smoothness of expression is achieved by avoiding ambiguity, insertion of the unexpected, shifting topics, tense, or person, all of which add to the confusion of the reader. For example, an unnecessary shift in verb tense might create an abruptness that precludes smooth expression. By being consistent with verb tenses, clarity of expression is enhanced. Economy of expression is achieved by being frugal with words. This means eliminating redundancy, wordiness, jargon, evasiveness, overuse of the passive voice, circumlocution, and clumsy prose as well as overly detailed descriptions of any part of the research report such as participants or procedures. For example, rather than using *at the present time,* use *now.* The phrase *absolutely essential* is redundant and can be reduced to *essential.* These are only a few of the issues that need to be considered in preparing a clearly presented report. Other issues, such as the use of correct grammar, are addressed in the APA publication manual.

Language

The language that is used to communicate the results of research should be free of demeaning attitudes and biased assumptions. There are three guidelines that should be followed to achieve this goal: specificity, being sensitive to labels, and acknowledging participation.

Specificity   When referring to a person or persons, you should choose accurate and clear words that are free from bias. When in doubt, err in the direction of being more rather than less specific. For example, if you are describing age groups, it is better to provide a specific age range (for example, *ages eight to twelve*) instead of a broad category such as *under twelve. People at risk* is also too broad. Instead, identify the risk and the people involved (e.g., children at risk for sexual abuse). Similarly, *gender* is preferred in referring to men and women as a social group rather than *sex,* as *sex* can be confused with sexual behavior.

Labels   The preferences of the participants in any study must be respected, and participants should be called what they prefer to be called. This means avoiding labels when possible or as has been common in science, broadly categorizing participants as objects (e.g., the elderly), or equating participants with their conditions (e.g., depressives, stroke victims). An effective option is to place the person first, followed by a descriptive phrase (e.g., *children with a diagnosis of attention-deficit disorder*). Similarly, sensitivity should be given to any suggestion that one group is better than another or is the standard against which another is to be judged. For example, it would be inappropriate to contrast *abused children* with *normal children,* thus stigmatizing the abused children. A more appropriate contrast would be between *abused* and *nonabused* children.

Participation You should write about the participants in your study in a way that acknowledges their participation. In the past, research reports have used the term *subjects.* This impersonal term should be, and is being, replaced with more descriptive terms such as *research participants, children,* or *high school students,* as we have done in this book. You should also use the active voice when writing the research report (e.g., "the students completed"). In general, tell what the research participants did, and do so in a way that acknowledges this participation.

   These are the guidelines that need to be followed to avoid writing in a way that reflects demeaning attitudes and biased assumptions. Keeping these in mind, specific attention should be given to the following issues.

Gender Participants should be described in such a way that avoids ambiguity in sex identity or sex role. This means that you should avoid using *he* to refer to both sexes or *man* or *mankind* to refer to people in general. The words *people, individuals,* or *persons* can be substituted without losing meaning or clarity of expression

Sexual Orientation The term *sexual orientation* should be used unless there is some intentional indication of choice. Terms such as *homosexual* should be replaced with terms such as *gay men, lesbians,* and *bisexual women or men.* Terms such as *same gender, male-male, female-female,* and *male-female,* should be used to indicate specific instances of sexual behavior regardless of sexual orientation.

Racial and Ethnic Identity Researchers should ask participants about their preferred designations because nouns referring to racial and ethnic groups change and can become dated and, sometimes, negative. When referring to a specific racial or ethnic group, remember to make sure that the first letter of the noun, such as Black, is capitalized.

Disabilities When describing handicapped individuals, it is important to maintain their integrity as human beings. Language equating them with their condition, such as describing participants as *cancer victims,* should be avoided. Instead, describe a participant as *a person who has a cancer.*

Age The general rule to follow regarding age is to be specific in describing the age of participants and avoid open-ended definitions, such as *over 65.* People of high school age and younger can be referred to as *boys* and *girls.* Call people eighteen and older *men* and *women. Older person* is preferred to *elderly.*

Editorial Style

Editorial style refers to the rules or guidelines a publisher uses to ensure a clear, consistent presentation of published material. These rules specify the construction of many of the elements that are included in a research report, such as tables and figures, as well as the uniform use of punctuation and abbreviations. Below we list and discuss some of these rules. The APA publication manual (2001) lists many other rules and guidelines and should be consulted if you have questions about any other style issue that is not presented here.

Italics   As a general rule, use italics infrequently. Underline any words that are to appear in italics if you are using a typewriter; otherwise use the italics function of your word processor.

Abbreviations   Use abbreviations sparingly. In general, abbreviate only when the abbreviations are conventional and likely to be familiar to the reader (such as IQ) or when you can save considerable space and avoid cumbersome repetition. In all instances, the Latin abbreviations *cf.* (compare), *e.g.* (for example), *etc.* (and so forth), *i.e.* (that is), *viz.* (namely), and *vs.* (versus, against) are to be used only in parenthetical material. The exception to this rule is the Latin abbreviation *et al.,* which can be used in the text of the manuscript. The unit of time *second* is abbreviated *s* rather than *sec.* Periods are omitted with nonmetric measurements such as *ft* and *lb.* The only exception is inch, which is abbreviated *in.* with the period. Units of time such as *day, week, month,* and *year* are never abbreviated. There are many other abbreviations, identified in the APA publication manual, that can be used in a research report. Note that they should appear in Roman type in your report, not in italics or underlined.

Headings   The headings that are used in a manuscript serve to indicate the importance of each topic as well as the organization of the manuscript. There are five different levels of heading in a manuscript that have the following top-down progression: (level 1) centered main heading in uppercase letters, (level 2) centered main heading in upper- and lowercase letters, (level 3) centered main heading, italicized in upper- and lowercase letters, (level 4) flush side heading, italicized in upper- and lowercase letters, and (level 5) indented, italicized, lowercase paragraph heading ending with a period. However, all headings are not used in every manuscript. If only one level of heading is needed in an article, use level 2. If two levels are needed, use level 2 and 4 as follows:

Method

Procedure

If three levels of heading are needed, use levels 2, 4, and 5 as follows:

Method

Procedure

    Instruments.   (Text begins on this same line.)

If four levels of headings are needed, use levels 2, 3, 4, and 5 as follows:

Experiment 1
Method

Procedure

   Instruments.   (Text begins on this same line.)

If five levels of headings are needed, use all of the headings in the order specified earlier.

Quotation A quotation of fewer than 40 words should be inserted into the text and enclosed with double quotation marks. Quotations of 40 or more words should be displayed in a free-standing block of lines without quotation marks. The author, year, and specific page from which the quote is taken should always be included.

Numbers Use words to express numbers that begin a sentence as well as any number below 10. Use figures to express all other numbers. Exceptions to this rule are specified in the APA publication manual. When you express numbers, make sure that you use Arabic and not Roman numerals.

Physical Measurements State all physical measurements in metric units. If a measurement is expressed in nonmetric units, put its metric equivalent in parentheses.

Presentation of Statistical Results When presenting the results of statistical tests in the text, provide enough information to allow the reader to fully understand the analysis that was conducted. Although sufficient information depends on the statistical test and analysis selected, in general it means including information about the magnitude or value of the test, the degrees of freedom, the probability level, and the direction of the effect. For example, *t*- and *F*-tests could be reported as follows:

$t(28) = 4.67, p = .04$

$F(3,32) = 8.79, p = .02$

When reporting a chi-square value, you should report the degrees of freedom and the sample size in parentheses as follows:

$\chi^2(3, N = 52) = 8.72, p = .03$

After the results of a statistical test are reported, descriptive statistical data, such as means and standard deviations, must be included to clarify the meaning of a significant effect and to indicate the direction of the effect.

Reference Citations in the Text In the text of the research report, particularly in the introductory section, you must reference other works you have cited. The format is to use the author-date citation method, which involves inserting the author's surname and the publication date at the appropriate point, as follows:

> Smith (1999) found that . . .
> It has been demonstrated (Smith, 1999) . . .

With this information, the reader can turn to the reference list and locate complete information regarding the source. Multiple citations involving the same author are arranged in chronological order:

> Smith (1987, 1993, 1998, 1999)

Multiple citations involving different authors are arranged alphabetically, as follows:

> Several studies (Adams, 1997; Cox, 1994; Smith, 1998; Thomas, 1999) have revealed that the developmental changes . . .

If a citation includes more than two but fewer than six authors, all authors should be cited the first time the reference is used. Subsequent citations include only the name of the first author, followed by the abbreviation *et al.* and the year the article was published as follows:

> Smith et al. (1998)

If six or more authors are associated with a citation, only the surname of the first author followed by "et al." is used for all citations.

You should consult the APA publication manual if you encounter references from other sources such as works with no author, authors with the same surname, or personal communications.

Reference List

All citations in the text of the research report must be accurately and completely cited in the reference list so that it is possible for readers to locate the works. This means that each entry should include the name of the author, year of publication, title, publishing data, and any other information necessary to identify the reference. All references are to appear in alphabetical order and typed double-spaced with a hanging indent and on a separate page with the word *References* centered at the top of the page in uppercase and lowercase letters.

The general form of a reference is as follows for a periodical, book, and book chapter:

> Canned, I. B., & Had, U. B. (1999). Moderating violence in a violent society. *Journal of Violence and Peace Making, 32,* 231–243.
> Breeze, C. (1997). *Why children kill.* New York: Academic Publishers.
> Good, I. M. (1998). Moral development in violent children. In A. Writer & N. Author (Eds.), *The anatomy of violent children* (pp. 134–187). Washington, DC: Killer Books.

If you have cited information obtained from the Internet, you must cite the reference to this material in the reference list. In citing Internet sources, you should, when possible, reference specific documents and not home pages or menu pages and provide Internet addresses that work. An example follows of a reference for article published in a journal appearing only on the Internet, and for a document appearing on the Internet.

Van Camp, R. & Roth, C. (2002). Role of parental discipline on classroom behavior. *Journal of Child and Adolescent Behavior, 21,* 121–132. Retrieved September, 24, 2002, from *http://jcab.org/articles.html*

Task force on teen pregnancy in the Southeastern Region. *Methods for reducing teen pregnancy.* Retrieved November, 12, 2002, from *http:// www.reduceteenpregnancy.org*

Consult the APA publication manual to see how to present other items that could be included in a reference list.

Typing

In typing the manuscript, double-space all material and select a serif typeface. A preferred typeface is 12-point Times Roman. There should be 1 inch (2.54 centimeters) at the top, bottom, left, and right of every page. You should use the italic and bold functions on your word processor as well as other special fonts or styles of type as specified in the APA publication manual. Each page should contain no more than 27 lines of text.

WRITING QUANTITATIVE RESEARCH REPORTS USING THE APA STYLE

The style most journals of interest to educational researchers either recommend or specify that authors follow when preparing their research reports is the style specified in the *Publication Manual of the American Psychological Association* (American Psychological Association, 2001). We refer to this manual as the APA publication manual. It is the style we will discuss because it is so prevalent among the journals of interest to educational researchers.

There are seven major parts to the research report:

1. Title page
2. Abstract
3. Introduction
4. Method
5. Results
6. Discussion
7. References

We discuss each of these parts in some detail, explaining the content of each and the material that should be included. We have also included three published research articles on the companion website for this textbook at www.ablongman.com/johnsonchristensen2e to illustrate each part of the research report. As we discuss each part of the research report, you should read that section in one of the appended articles to make the material we are presenting more meaningful.

Title Page

The title page contains a running head, title, author(s) name, and institutional affiliation of the author(s). The running head, which is an abbreviated title, is typed flush left at the top of the page in uppercase letters. It should be a maximum of 50 characters, counting letters, punctuation, and spaces between words. The title is centered on the page and typed in uppercase and lowercase letters. It should summarize the main topic of the paper and concisely identify the variables or theoretical issues under investigation and the relationship between them. The title should be 10 to 12 words long and should inform the readers about the study. The names of authors who have made a substantial contribution to the study should appear immediately below the title typed in uppercase and lowercase letters and centered on the page. The preferred form is to use the author's first name, middle initial, and last name with titles and degrees omitted. The institutional affiliation where the author(s) conducted the study is centered under the author(s) name(s).

The title page and each subsequent page of the paper also have a header and page number appearing in the upper right-hand corner. The header consists of the first one to three words of the title placed above or five spaces to the left of the page number; these allow for identification of the page of the manuscript if the manuscript pages are separated during the review process. All pages should be numbered consecutively, beginning with the title page.

Abstract

The abstract is a comprehensive summary of the contents of the research report. It should not exceed 120 words and should be typed on a separate page with the word *Abstract* centered at the top of the page in uppercase and lowercase letters and no paragraph indentation. The abstract should be accurate, concise, specific, and self-contained. An abstract of an empirical study should include a brief statement of the problem, a description of the research participants, a summary of the method used, including a description of the instruments and the procedure used for data collection, the findings or results of the study, including statistical significance levels, and any conclusions and implications.

Introduction

The research report begins with the introduction, which is not labeled because of its position in the paper. Type the title of the paper centered at the top of the page. The introduction presents the specific problem being investigated in the context of prior research and describes the research strategy. The introduction usually begins with a general introduction to the problem area and perhaps a statement of the point of the study. The introduction continues with a review of prior studies that have been conducted in the area and relating to the specific issue being investigated. This review is not exhaustive but cites only studies that are directly pertinent to place the current study in the context of prior work and to give an appropriate history and recognition of the work of others. An exhaustive review of the literature would be more appropriate for a thesis or dissertation.

After introducing the research problem and reviewing prior literature, you should tell what you did in the study you are reporting. This might take the form of stating the purpose of the study and any hypotheses that would give clarity to the paper. Overall, the introduction should specify the purpose of the study, show how it relates to prior work in the area, and identify hypotheses to be tested.

Method

The method section follows the introduction. It does not start on a separate page. The purpose of the method section is to tell the reader exactly how the study was conducted. It permits the reader to evaluate the appropriateness of the design of the study and be able to make an assessment of the reliability and validity of the results. If the method is presented well, another researcher can replicate the study.

To facilitate communication of the method section, it is typically divided into subsections: participants, apparatus or materials, and procedure. Additional subsections may be included if the research design is complex to help communicate specific information.

Participants The participants subsection should identify the major demographic characteristics of the participants such as their age and gender as well as how they were selected. Any other pertinent information should also be included, such as how they were assigned to the experimental treatment conditions, the number of participants that were selected for the study but did not complete it (and why), and any inducements given to encourage participation.

Apparatus or Instruments This subsection describes the apparatus or instruments used and why they were used. Sufficient detail should be included to enable the reader to obtain comparable materials or equipment. Commercially marketed equipment should be accompanied by the supplier's name and location as well as the model number of the equipment or, in the case of a measuring instrument such as an achievement test, a reference that will enable the reader to obtain the same test. Custom-made equipment should be described and illustrated with a photograph.

Procedure The procedure subsection tells the reader exactly how the study was executed, from the moment the participant and the researcher came into contact to the time the participant left the study. This subsection represents a step-by-step account of what the experimenter and participant did during the study, including any instructions, stimulus conditions that were presented to the participants and the responses they were to make, and any control techniques that were used, such as randomization or counterbalancing. In other words, in the procedure subsection, you are to tell exactly what both you and the participants did and how you did it.

Results

The results section follows the method section. It does *not* start on a separate page. The purpose of the results section is to summarize the data that were collected and their statistical treatment. In making this presentation, remember that any discussion of the results takes place in the discussion section. This section is limited to presenting the data and the analysis of the data. It should tell the reader how the data were analyzed and the results of this analysis. In presenting the results of statistical analysis, always state the alpha level used because the alpha level determines whether the results are statistically significant. This can be accomplished by stating the alpha level selected for all statistical tests conducted. For example, you could state that

> The .05 alpha level was used for all statistical tests.

Then, when reporting the results of each statistical test, you should report the actual probability value of the computed statistic, which might be .006. If you do not make a general statement of the alpha level used for your statistical tests, you should specify this alpha level when reporting the results of each statistical test along with the probability value.

Results of any inferential tests (e.g., t-tests, F-tests, and chi-square) should be accompanied by the magnitude of the obtained value of the test, along with the accompanying degrees of freedom, probability level, and direction of the effect. Be sure to include sufficient descriptive statistics, such as cell sample size, means, correlations, and standard deviations, so that the nature of the effect can be understood and a future meta-analysis can be performed. You should also provide evidence that your study has sufficient power to detect an effect, particularly if you do not want to reject the null hypothesis. It is also strongly recommended that you provide some index of effect size or strength of relationship. Many journals are now requiring that effect size indicators be provided when the results of inferential statistical tests are reported.

In reporting and illustrating the direction of a significant effect (nonsignificant effects are not elaborated on for obvious reasons), you should decide on the medium that will most clearly and economically serve your purpose. Generally, tables are preferred for presenting quantitative data and illustrate main effects most efficiently. Figures illustrate interactions most effectively. If you use a figure or table, make sure that you tell the reader, in the text of the report, what data it depicts. Then give a sufficient explanation of the presented data to make sure that the reader interprets them correctly. When means are reported always include an associated measure of variability, such as standard deviation or mean square error.

Discussion

The discussion section has the purpose of interpreting and evaluating the results obtained, giving primary emphasis to the relationships between the results and the hypotheses of the study. Begin the discussion by stating whether the hypotheses of the study were or were not supported. Follow this statement with an interpretation of the results, telling the reader what you think they mean. In doing so, you should attempt to integrate your research findings with the results of prior research. Note that this is the only place in the research report where you are given any latitude for stating your own opinion; even there, you are limited to stating your interpretation of the results and what you think the major shortcomings of the study are. In general, the discussion should answer the following questions:

1. What does the study contribute?
2. How has it helped solve the study problem?
3. What conclusions and theoretical implications can be drawn from the study?

When discussing the shortcomings of the study, you should mention only the flaws that might have had a significant influence on the results obtained. You should accept a negative finding as such rather than attempting to explain it as being due to some methodological flaw, unless, as may occur, there is a good reason why a flaw did cause the negative findings.

References

The reference section provides a list of all citations in the text of the research report. In preparing the list of references, you should begin on a new page with the word *References* typed in the top center of the page. All entries are double-spaced, although some theses and dissertations specify that the reference list be single-spaced. Type references using a hanging indent format; set the first line of each reference flush left and subsequent lines are indented.

Author Notes

Author identification notes appear with each printed article and are for the purpose of identifying the departmental affiliation of each author, acknowledging the basis of a study (such as a grant or a dissertation), acknowledging colleagues' contributions to the conduct or assistance in preparation of the manuscript, and designating the address of the author to whom reprint requests are to be sent. These notes are typed on a separate page, with the words *Author Note* at the top center of the page in uppercase and lowercase letters. Each note should start with a paragraph indentation and should be arranged as follows.

First paragraph: Complete departmental affiliations at the time of the study for all authors, including the name of the author followed by the departmental affiliation and university name followed by the subsequent author name and departmental and university affiliations.

Second paragraph: Any changes in author affiliation should be stated here.

Third paragraph: Grants or any other financial support for the study is stated here in addition to acknowledgment for assistance from colleagues in conducting the study or critiquing the manuscript. This paragraph would also provide disclosure if the paper was based on a thesis or dissertation or a paper presented at a meeting.

Fourth paragraph: A complete mailing address for correspondence, which may include an email address

Footnotes

Footnotes are numbered consecutively, with a superscript Arabic numeral, in the order in which they appear in the text of the report. Most footnotes are content footnotes, containing material needed to supplement or amplify the information provided in the text. Such footnotes are typed on a separate page, with the word *Footnotes* centered in uppercase and lowercase letters. The first line of each footnote is indented five to seven spaces or one half inch, and the superscript numeral of the footnote should appear in the space just preceding the beginning of the footnote. Footnotes are typed in the order in which they are mentioned in the text.

Tables

Tables are expensive to publish and therefore should be reserved for use only when they can convey and summarize data more economically and clearly than can a lengthy discussion. Tables should be viewed as informative supplements to the text. Although each table should be intelligible by itself, it should also be an integral part of the text. As a supplement, only the table's highlights should be discussed. If you decide to use tables, number them with Arabic numerals in the order in which they are mentioned in the text.

Each table should have a brief title that clearly explains the data it contains. This title and the word *Table* and its number are typed flush with the left margin and at the top of the table. Each column and row of data within the table should be given a label that identifies, as briefly as possible, the data contained in that row or column. Columns within the table should be at least three spaces apart. The APA publication manual should be consulted for a list of the various types of headings that can be used in tables. When placing data in the rows and columns, carry each data point out to the same number of decimal places, and place a dash to indicate an absence of data.

If you report the results of ANOVA statistics in a table, make sure that you include degrees of freedom and *F*-ratios for each source and mean square errors. Mean square errors are enclosed in parentheses and explained in a general note to the table. The APA publication manual should be consulted for the specifics of other tables such as regression tables and path and LISREL tables.

When writing the manuscript, you should refer to the table somewhere in the text. This reference should tell what data are presented in the table and briefly discuss the data. When referring to a table, identify it by name, as in "the data in Table 2." Do not use a reference such as "the above table" or "the table on page 12."

Figure Captions

Each figure has a caption that not only provides a brief description of the contents but also serves as a title. These captions are typed on a separate page that precedes the figures with the words *Figure Captions* centered and typed in uppercase and lowercase letters at the top of the page. Flush with the left margin of the page, each caption should begin with the word *Figure* and the number of the figure, followed by a period all in italics. The caption, which is not italicized, is typed on the remainder of the line. If more than one line is needed, each subsequent line also begins flush left.

Figures

Figures are very time consuming and expensive to produce and should be used only when they complement the text or eliminate a lengthy discussion of the data. Figures may consist of charts, graphs, photographs, drawings, or other similar means of representing data or pictorial concepts. Figures can be mechanically produced, but most are computer generated. Computer-generated figures should be on high-quality paper and produced by software and hardware that produces smooth curves and crisp lines showing no jagged areas. The output should have a minimum resolution of 300 dots per inch.

Once the figures have been prepared, number them consecutively with Arabic numerals in the order in which they are used in the manuscript and write this number with a pen or pencil as close to the top right edge as possible. On the back of the figure, write a short title. Also write the word *top* on the back to designate the top of the figure.

WRITING QUALITATIVE RESEARCH REPORTS

We agree with Sharon Merriam (1998) that "There is no standard format for reporting qualitative research" (p. 227). Lofland (1971) stated three decades ago that diversity in style was rampant in qualitative research. Diversity is still somewhat common today. For example, there are many nontraditional and creative styles that are sometimes used by qualitative researchers (e.g., such as incorporating stories, poems, essays, drawings, and photographs in qualitative reports). At the same time, we and a growing number of scholars (e.g., Berg, 1998; Merriam, 1998) also believe that some structure to qualitative journal articles is helpful because readers will know what information to expect and where that information will be located, and some structure can aid in the comparison of separate qualitative research reports. In short, when you write a qualitative research article, you need to find a balance between the creative end of writing and the structured end of writing that works best for you and for the outlet in which you plan to disseminate your qualitative research (a journal, dissertation, thesis, evaluation report).

A good way to learn how to write the qualitative research report is to examine published examples and to use ideas learned there to aid you in writing your own article. We have included an ethnographic study on the companion website for this textbook at www.ablongman.com/johnnsonchristensen2e to illustrate a qualitative research report.

Earlier in this chapter, we discussed some general principles related to writing the research report. These principles apply to quantitative research, qualitative research, and mixed research. We would like to add to that discussion two points that are especially relevant in qualitative research. First, qualitative researchers tend to view the use of the first person (i.e., *I* rather than *the researcher*) and the active voice ("I interviewed the teachers" rather than "the teachers were interviewed by the researcher") very positively. (The APA publication manual also now recommends these practices for quantitative research.) They believe that this helps to situate the qualitative researcher in his or her research and encourages qualitative researchers to take responsibility for their active role in their research. This makes sense because of the central role that the qualitative researcher must play in virtually every step during the conduct of a qualitative research study (e.g., the researcher is the "data collection instrument" because the researcher must make on-the-spot decisions about what is important and what should be noted and recorded, the researcher must manually code transcripts rather than using a statistical analysis program to provide an output of standard statistical results, the researcher must make interpretations throughout the research study, and so on).

Second, pseudonyms (i.e., fictitious names) are commonly used in qualitative research. Because of the small number of participants common to qualitative research and the in-depth information obtained about these individuals, qualitative researchers must be cautious to ensure that the identities of their research participants are adequately concealed. The guarantee of confidentiality may not be sufficient if the readers of a report are able to identify individuals based on descriptive information given about them in the report. For example, if you are conducting an ethnography of an elementary school, everyone in the school will know the principal, the librarian, and so forth. It might not be enough to use pseudonyms just for the individuals. You might also need to give a pseudonym to the school or city in the published version of the report. A last resort strategy is to withhold certain revealing information about an individual to make him or her less identifiable. In most cases, you will be able to obtain written permission from the participants in your study to use pseudonyms without any additional effort to conceal their identities. These ethical issues are especially critical in qualitative research.

Earlier in this chapter, we discussed the seven major parts to the quantitative research report as recommended in the APA publication manual (the title page, abstract, introduction, method, results, discussion, and references). These seven sections can also be used quite effectively with qualitative research reports. Most of the earlier comments about these seven sections also apply to the qualitative research report. We do not repeat those ideas here; however, we highlight several important issues surrounding these seven sections in relation to writing a qualitative research report.

The title page is essentially the same for quantitative and qualitative research reports. You should always try to write a title that is clear and descriptive, regardless of the type of report. The abstract is also very similar for quantitative and qualitative research reports. When writing an abstract, your goal is always to succinctly describe the key focus of the article, its key methodological features, and the most important findings.

In the introduction, you should clearly explain the purpose of your research and then report any research literature that is relevant to your study. (Deering (1996) used the term *background* rather than *introduction*.) For example, if you are hoping to fit your study into a larger body of research, much of this material will be placed in the introduction. The qualitative research introduction section does, however, differ somewhat from the quantitative research introduction. For example, the qualitative report will usually not include any deductive hypotheses (tentative predictions about the relationships between variables based on prior literature and theory) because qualitative research is usually done more for exploratory than confirmatory reasons. Research questions and issues are often reported in the qualitative report introduction. However, they are usually stated in open-ended and general forms (e.g., the researcher hopes to: "discover," "explore a process," "explain or to understand," or "describe the experiences") rather than in the form of highly specific questions, which is more common in quantitative research (Creswell, 1994, p. 71).

The methods section is sometimes incorporated into the introduction of the qualitative research report. However, it is becoming more common for qualitative research authors to include a separate section on methods. We believe that a separate methods section should be included in all qualitative journal articles. The author might wish to relegate the methods to an appendix in a more popularized version of a report, but even here it is essential that the researcher describes the methods that were used to carry out the research study. Otherwise, the reader is left hanging, without sufficient information to evaluate the quality of the research study.

The methods section needs to include information telling how the study was done, where it was done, with whom it was done, why the study was designed as it was, how the data were collected and analyzed, and, importantly, what procedures were carried out to ensure the validity of the arguments and conclusions. It is becoming common today for qualitative researchers also to include a section in the report in which they reflect on their personal biases and their disciplinary backgrounds and how this may affect the validity of their research. Researchers should also discuss what strategies they used to ensure qualitative research validity (e.g., see our discussion of triangulation, low-inference descriptors, extended fieldwork, and reflexivity in Chapter 8). When you read the methods section of a qualitative research report, a key question will be, Did the authors convince you that they conducted their study effectively and appropriately?

Perhaps the most important section in a qualitative research report is the results section (sometimes called the findings section in qualitative research reports). This is where the researcher provides the bulk of the evidence supporting his or her arguments. The overriding concern when writing a results section is to provide sufficient and convincing evidence. Assertions made by the researcher must be backed up with empirical data. You do not want the reader to go away saying, "I'm not sure that I agree with this writer's contentions." Qualitative researchers should try to minimize the situation in which their readers must take the researchers' word for their arguments. We should all keep in mind the following point when working on our results sections: "It's about evidence." As Bogdan and Biklen (1998) point out: "The qualitative researcher, in effect, says to the reader, 'Here is what I found and here are the details to support that view' " (p. 195). If we follow this advice, we are likely to produce a results section that is convincing and defensible.

The qualitative researcher needs to find an appropriate balance between description and interpretation to write a convincing results section. On the one hand, you don't need to overkill with extensive descriptive detail and little interpretative commentary. For example, you don't want to provide pages and pages of interviews and fieldnotes with no interpretation. Keep in mind that such information might very well seem important to you because you are immersed in your research data; however, such detailed information is probably not important to your reader, and in journal articles, space is always limited. On the other hand, you do need to provide sufficient descriptive detail to support your conclusions and interpretative commentary. If you don't provide sufficient descriptive detail, the reader will be forced to rely too heavily on your word without supportive evidence, and if you don't provide enough interpretative commentary, your reader will end up lost in the details. Finding the best balance between description and interpretative commentary takes time and practice in writing qualitative research reports. It also depends on the audience and the outlet for your report. For example, space will be more plentiful in a book or a dissertation than in a journal. Also, the readers of journal articles are usually less willing to take your word for your interpretations than are readers of a best-selling nonfiction book version of your qualitative research.

One effective strategy for writing a results section is to provide quotes from your research participants and to include short sections from your field notes and your other data to get your reader close to your research participants and to the real-world situations described in your report. You should provide some rich and vivid description of the context, setting, participants, cultural scenes, and interactions among the participants. This way, the reader can vicariously experience what it is like to be in the same situation as the research participants. The use of vignettes (e.g., detailed examples) and low-inference descriptors (e.g., quotes from the participants) are helpful for this purpose. Another way to present your data is to make interpretative statements and follow each statement with one or more illustrative examples. Intermixing your descriptive data with interpretative commentary throughout your results section helps your reader to follow your line of reasoning. Regardless of the specific format of your results section, remember that *you must always provide data (descriptions, quotes, data from multiple sources, and so forth) that back up your assertions.*

The results section of a qualitative report will usually include more subheadings than the results section of a quantitative report. The particular organization identified by the subheadings will vary depending on the type of qualitative research conducted and the results of the data analysis. For example, the qualitative research results may be organized around the research questions or research issues examined in the research, they may be organized around an a priori literature-based conceptual scheme applied to the research data, they may be organized around a typology that is developed during data analysis, they may be organized according to the key themes found in the data, or they may be organized around a conceptual scheme based on a grounded theory generated from the research data. Regardless of the exact format, remember that you must convince your reader of your arguments. That is the key for effective report writing.

In the discussion section (sometimes called the conclusion), the qualitative researcher should state the overall conclusions and offer additional interpretation of the findings. The researcher should also determine whether the results are consistent with other results published in the research literature. Even if the research is exploratory, it is important to fit your findings back into the relevant research literature in your discussion section. It is also helpful to provide suggestions for further research, because research is rarely done in a vacuum. Virtually all research can and should be related to the big picture of where we have been and where we are going in our efforts to increase research-based knowledge.

The references section is the same in a quantitative and qualitative report. If the APA referencing style is used, the references will follow the APA format described earlier in this chapter. Finally, the ancillary components discussed earlier (charts, tables, figures, and so forth) also have an important place in qualitative research reports. For example, a data chart or matrix is very helpful when it would take a great deal of narrative text to convey the same information. An excellent source for learning more about displaying qualitative research data is Miles and Huberman's (1994) book entitled *Qualitative Data Analysis: An Expanded Source Book.*

WRITING MIXED RESEARCH REPORTS

We have explained in some depth how to write a quantitative research report and how to write a qualitative research report. When the report is based on both quantitative and qualitative research, however, what should one do? Our advice is, first and foremost, to know your audience and write in a manner that clearly communicates to that audience. Second, the suggestions provided throughout this chapter apply equally to mixed research.

We believe that in most cases, you should try to use the same seven major parts of an APA report discussed earlier in this chapter (i.e., title page, abstract, introduction, method, results, discussion, and references). The primary modification for mixed reports is that you will need to organize the qualitative and quantitative parts in a way that works for your reader. For example, one effective organization style is to organize the introduction, method, and results by research question. Another style is to organize some sections (e.g., method and results) by research paradigm (quantitative and qualitative). Yet another style is to write two essentially separate subreports (one for the qualitative part, one for the quantitative part); but remember that if you use this style, at some point you need to relate the qualitative and quantitative findings (e.g., in the discussion section). As in all empirical research reports, the key is to clearly address each of your research questions, to make your report highly readable, and to provide your reader with sufficient, convincing, and defensible evidence for each of your research findings and recommendations.

DISCUSSION QUESTIONS

1. What writing errors or writing problems do you think are most common among beginning research methods students?

2. What section of a research report do you believe is the most difficult to write?

3. What type of research do you think is the most demanding of a writer: quantitative research, qualitative research, or mixed research?

RESEARCH EXERCISES

1. Take one of the article reviews you conducted this semester and critique your writing.
2. Using Research Navigator, find a qualitative research article, read this article, and then answer the following questions.
   a. What are the various sections of the article?
   b. What did the author(s) attempt to accomplish in each section?
   c. What evidence did the author(s) use to support the conclusions or interpretations?
   d. How do the format and style of this report differ from the way in which quantitative study would be reported?

RELEVANT INTERNET SITES

http://sut1.sut.ac.th/strunk
William Strunk's famous and very useful *Elements of Style.*

www.gse.harvard.edu/~writing/links.html
Harvard's page on writing research papers.

www.indiana.edu/~wts/wts/plagiarism.html
Plagiarism.

www.apastyle.org/faqs.html and
http://owl.english.purdue.edu/handouts/research/r_apa.html
Several useful links for APA writing style.

RECOMMENDED READING

American Psychological Association. (2001). *Publication manual of the American Psychological Association* (5th ed.). Washington, DC: Authors.

Becker, H. S. (1986). *Writing for social scientists.* Chicago: University of Chicago Press.

Manhard, S. J. (1998). *The goof-proofer: How to avoid the 41 most embarrassing errors in your speaking and writing.* New York: Fireside.

Rosnow, R. L., & Rosnow, M. (1992). *Writing papers in psychology.* New York: Wiley.

Rudestam, K. E., & Newton, R. R. (2001). *Surviving your dissertation: A comprehensive guide to content and process.* Thousand Oaks, CA: Sage.

Strunk, W., & White, E. B. (2000). *The elements of style.* Boston: Allyn and Bacon.

APPENDIX A

Quantitative Research Article
Abstract and Link to Full Text

THE LONG-TERM EFFECTS OF SMALL CLASSES IN EARLY GRADES: LASTING BENEFITS IN MATHEMATICS ACHIEVEMENT AT GRADE 9

The full text of the following journal article is available on the *Educational Research* companion website at www.ablongman.com/johnsonchristensen2e.

Nye, B., Hedges, L. V., & Konstantopoulos, S. (2001). The long-term effects of small classes in early grades: Lasting benefits in mathematics achievement at grade 9. *The Journal of Experimental Education, 69*(3), 245–257.

Abstract

Reducing class size to increase academic achievement is a policy option currently of great interest. Although the results of small-scale randomized experiments and some interpretations of large-scale econometric studies point to positive short-term effects of small classes, some scholars view the evidence as ambiguous. Project STAR in Tennessee—a four-year, large-scale randomized experiment on the effects of class size—provided persuasive evidence that small classes have immediate positive effects on academic achievement. Unlike most other early education interventions, these effects persisted for several years after the children returned to regular-sized classes. The authors of the present article report analyses of a six-year follow-up of the students in that experiment. Class-size effects persisted for at least six years and remained large enough to be important for educational policy. The results suggest that small classes in early grades have lasting benefits and that those benefits are greater for minority students than for white students.

Qualitative Research Article
Abstract and Link to Full Text

"YOU DON'T HAVE TO BE SIGHTED TO BE A SCIENTIST, DO YOU?" ISSUES AND OUTCOMES IN SCIENCE EDUCATION

The full text of the following journal article is available on the *Educational Research* companion website at www.ablongman.com/johnsonchristensen2e.

Erwin, E. J., Perkins, T. S., Ayala, J., Fine, M., & Rubin, E. (2001). *Journal of Visual Impairment & Blindness, 95*(6), 338–352.

Abstract

This qualitative study explored the issues and outcomes associated with implementing Playtime Is Science for Students with Disabilities, a curriculum and set of materials that were modified for students who were visually impaired. It found several student-related outcomes, such as persistence, positive peer-related skills, risk taking, and making meaningful connections about the world, and themes regarding implementation of the curriculum, such as teachers' interest level, issues associated with power, and how teachers supported students' learning.

Mixed Research Article
Abstract and Link to Full Text

THE ROLE OF COOPERATIVE LEARNING IN RESEARCH METHODOLOGY COURSES: A MIXED-METHODS ANALYSIS.

The full text of the following journal article is available on the *Educational Research* companion website at www.ablongman.com/johnsonchristensen2e.

Onwuegbuzie, A. J., & DaRos-Voseles, D. A. (2001). The role of cooperative learning in research methodology courses: A mixed-methods analysis. *Research in the Schools, 8*(1), 61–75.

Abstract

This study investigated the effectiveness of cooperative learning (CL) in a graduate-level research methodology course. Participants comprised 193 graduate students enrolled in several sections of this course. Eighty-one students were in sections wherein CL groups were formed to undertake the major course requirements; 112 were in sections wherein all assignments were undertaken individually (IL). Students' conceptual knowledge of research concepts, methodologies, and applications was measured individually in both groups via midterm and final examinations. A split-plot analysis of variance revealed a group by examination time interaction, whereby CL students had statistically significantly lower performance levels on the midterm examination than did IL students (effect size = 0.48). However, no statistically significant difference in achievement was found with respect to the final examination. Analysis of reflexive journals indicated that most students (70.4%) tended to have positive overall attitudes towards their cooperative learning experiences. Implications are discussed.

References

Alkin, M. (1979). *Using evaluations: Does evaluation make a difference?* Beverly Hills, CA: Sage.

American Association for the Advancement of Science. (1990). *Science for all Americans: Project 2061.* New York: Oxford University Press.

American Educational Research Association (AERA). (1992). Ethical standards of the American Educational Research Association. *Educational Researcher, 21,* 23–26.

American Educational Research Association, American Psychological Association, National Council on Measurement in Education. (1999). *Standards for educational and psychological testing.* Washington, DC: APA.

American Psychological Association. (1954). Technical recommendations for psychological tests and diagnosis techniques. *Psychological Bulletin, 51,* 201–238.

American Psychological Association (APA). (2001). *Publication manual of the American Psychological Association* (5th ed.). Washington, DC: Author.

Anderson, D. B., & McGraw, K. M. (1979). Don't the girls get prettier at closing time: A country and western application to psychology. *Personality and Social Psychology Bulletin, 5,* 122–125.

Anderson, J. R. (1995). *Cognitive psychology and its implications.* New York: W. H. Freeman.

Angeles, P. A. (1992). *Philosophy.* New York: HarperCollins.

Asher, H. B. (1983). *Causal modeling.* Beverly Hills, CA: Sage.

Babbie, E. (1998). *The practice of social research* (8th ed.). Belmont, CA: Wadsworth.

Babbie, E. R. (1990). *Survey research methods.* Belmont, CA: Wadsworth.

Baer, R. A., Tishelman, A. C., Degler, J. D., Osnes, P. G., & Stokes, T. F. (1992). Effects of self- vs. experimenter-selection of rewards on classroom behavior in young children. *Education and Treatment of Children, 15,* 1–14.

Bailey, K. D. (1994). *Typologies and taxonomies: An introduction to classification techniques.* Thousand Oaks, CA: Sage.

Bakeman, R. (2000). Behavioral observation and coding. In H. T. Reis & C. M. Judd (Eds.) *Handbook of research methods in social and personality psychology* (pp. 138–159). Cambridge, UK: Cambridge University Press.

Baloche, L. (1994). Creativity and cooperation in the elementary music classroom. *The Journal of Creative Behavior, 28*(4), 255–265.

Bandalos, D. L., Yates, K., & Thorndike-Christ, T. (1995). Effects of math self-concept, perceived self-efficacy, and attributions for failure and success on test anxiety. *Journal of Educational Psychology, 87,* 611–623.

Barlow, D. H., & Hersen, M. (1992). *Single-case experimental designs. Strategies for studying behavior change* (Rev. 2nd ed.). Boston: Allyn & Bacon.

Barnette, J. J. (1999). *Likert response alternative direction: SA to SD or SD to SA: Does it make a difference?* Paper presented at the annual meeting of the American Educational Research Association (Montreal, Canada).

Barnette, J. J. (2000). Effects of stem and Likert response option reversals on survey internal consistency: If you feel the need, there is a better alternative to using those negatively worded stems. *Educational and Psychological Measurement, 60*(3), 361–370.

Baron, D. (2002, February). Will anyone accept the good news on literacy? *The Chronicle Review: The Chronicle of Higher Education* (Section 2), p. 10.

Baron, R. M., & Kenny, D. A. (1986). The moderator-mediator variable distinction in social psychological research: Conceptual, strategic, and statistical considerations. *Journal of Personality and Social Psychology, 51*(6), 1173–1182.

Bartlett, T. (2002, May 10). Students become curricular guinea pigs. *The Chronicle of Higher Education,* A12–A14.

Bass, R. R. (1997). Development of a pseudo aggression device. *Journal of Fictitious and Nonexistent Devices, 99,* 1–2.

Bastick, T. (2002). Materialist culture and teacher attrition in the Caribbean: Motivational differences between novice and experienced Jamaican teacher trainees. Retrieved August 28, 2002, from the ERIC database.

Baumrind, D. (1985). Research using intentional deception: Ethical issues revisited. *American Psychologist, 40,* 165–174.

Becker, H. S. (1986). *Writing for social scientists.* Chicago: University of Chicago Press.

Benson, J., & Hocevar, D. (1985). The impact of item phrasing on the validity of attitude for elementary school children. *Journal of Educational Measurement 22,* 231–240.

Berg, B. L. (1998). *Qualitative research methods for the social sciences.* Boston: Allyn & Bacon.

Berge, B. M. (2000). *Action research for gender equity.* Philadelphia: Open University Press.

Bickel, J. (1975). Sex bias in graduate admissions: Data from Berkeley. *Science, 187,* 398–404.

Biehl, J. K. (2002, April 27). 18 die in german high school shooting. Ex-student targets teachers, kills self. *The Boston Globe,* p. A1.

Bijou, S. W., Peterson, R. F., Harris, F. R., Allen, K. E., & Johnston, M. S. (1969). Methodology for experimental studies of young children in natural settings. *Psychological Record, 19,* 177–210.

Blackburn, S. (1994). *The Oxford dictionary of philosophy.* Oxford, England: Oxford University Press.

Bodycott, P., Walker, A., & Kin, J. L. C. (2001). More than heroes and villains; Pre-service teacher beliefs about principals. *Educational Research, 43,* 15–31.

Bogdan, R. C., & Biklen, S. K. (1998). *Qualitative research education: An introduction to theory and methods.* Boston, MA: Allyn & Bacon.

Bollen, K. A., & Lennox, R. (1991). Conventional wisdom on measurement: A structural equation perspective. *Psychological Bulletin, 110*(2), 305–314.

Borden, M., Bruce, C., Mitchell, M. A., Carter, V., & Hall, R. V. (1970). Effects of teacher attention on attending behavior of two boys at adjacent desks. *Journal of Applied Behavior Analysis, 3,* 199–203.

Bos, J., Huston, A. C., Granger, R., Duncan, G., Brock, T., & McLoyd, W. C. (1999). *New Hope for people with low incomes: Two-year results of a program to reduce poverty and reform welfare.* New York, NY: Manpower Research Demonstration Corporation.

Box, G. E. P., & Jenkins, G. M. (1970). *Time-series analysis: Forecasting and control.* San Francisco: Holden-Day.

Box, G. E. P., Hunter, W. G., & Hunter, J. S. (1978). *Statistics for experimenters.* New York: Wiley.

Bracht, G. H., & Glass, G. V. (1968). The external validity of experiments. *American Educational Research Journal, 5,* 437–474.

Brewer, J., & Hunter, A. (1989). *Multimethod research: A synthesis of styles.* Newbury Park, CA: Sage.

Breznitz, Z. (1997). Effects of accelerated reading rate on memory for text among dyslexic readers. *Journal of Educational Psychology, 89,* 289–297.

Bro, R. T., Shank, L. L., McLaughlin, T. F., & Williams, R. L. (1996). Effects of a breakfast program on on-task behaviors of vocational high school students. *The Journal of Educational Research, 90,* 112–115.

Brody, J. E. (1973, October 29). New heart study absolves coffee. *New York Times,* p. 6.

Brown, R., Pressley, M., Van Meter, P., & Schuder, T. (1996). A quasi-experimental validation of transactional strategies instruction with low-achieving second-grade readers. *Journal of Educational Psychology, 88,* 18–37.

Brown, T. (1996). The phenomenology of the mathematics classroom. *Educational Studies in Mathematics, 31,* 115–150.

Bryman, A., & Burgess, R. G. (1994). *Analyzing qualitative data.* (Edited). London: Routledge.

Burnam, B., & Kafai, Y. B. (2001). Ethics and the computer: Children's development of moral reasoning about computer and Internet use. *Journal of Educational Computing Research, 25,* 111–127.

Butler, R., & Neuman, O. (1995). Effects of task and ego achievement goals on help-seeking behaviors. *Journal of Educational Psychology, 87,* 261–271.

Campbell, D. T. (1969). Reforms as experiments. *American Psychologist, 24,* 409–429.

Campbell, D. T. (1979). Degrees of freedom and the case study. In T. D. Cook & C. S. Reichardt (Eds.), *Qualitative and quantitative methods in evaluation research* (pp. 49–67). Beverly Hills, CA: Sage.

Campbell, D. T. (1986). Relabeling internal and external validity for applied social scientists. In W. M. K. Trochim (Ed.), *Advances in quasi-experimental design and analysis: New directions for program evaluation.* San Francisco: Jossey-Bass.

Campbell, D. T. (1988). Definitional versus multiple operationism. In E. S. Overman (Ed.), *Methodology and epistemology for social science: Selected papers,* (pp. 31–36). Chicago: University of Chicago Press.

Campbell, D. T., & Boruch, R. F. (1975). Making the case for randomized assignments to treatments by considering the alternatives: Six ways in which quasi-experimental evaluations in compensatory education tend to underestimate effects. In C. A. Bennett & A. A. Lunsdaine (Eds.), *Evaluation and experiment: Some critical issues in assessing social programs.* New York: Academic Press.

Campbell, D. T., & Fiske, D. W. (1959). Convergent and discriminant validation by the multitrait-multimethod matrix. *Psychological Bulletin, 56,* 81–105.

Campbell, D. T., & Stanley, J. C. (1963). *Experimental and quasi-experimental designs for research.* Chicago: Rand McNally.

Carr, E. H. (1963). *What is history?* New York: Knopf.

Carr, M., & Jessup, D. L. (1997). Gender differences in first-grade mathematics strategy use: Social and metacognitive influences. *Journal of Educational Psychology, 89,* 318–328.

Chamberlin, T. (1965). The method of multiple working hypotheses. *Science, 147,* 754–759.

Chaplin, W. F., John, O. P., & Goldberg, L. R. (1988). Conceptions of state and traits: Dimensional attributes with ideals as prototypes. *Journal of Personality and Social Psychology, 54,* 541–557.

Christensen, L. (1991). Issues in the design of studies investigating the behavioral concomitants of foods. *Journal of Consulting and Clinical Psychology, 59,* 874–882.

Christensen, L. (1993). Effects of eating behavior on mood: A review of the literature. *International Journal of Eating Disorders, 14,* 173–183.

Christensen, L. (1997). *Experimental methodology.* Boston: Allyn & Bacon.

Christensen, L. (2001). *Experimental methodology.* Boston: Allyn & Bacon.

Christy, T. E. (1975). The methodology of historical research: A brief introduction. *Nursing Research, 24,* 189–192.

Cliff, N. (1984). An improved internal consistency reliability estimate. *Journal of Educational Statistics, 9,* 151–161.

Cochran, W. G. (1977). *Sampling techniques.* New York: Wiley.

Cohen, J. (1968). Multiple regression as a general data-analytic system. *Psychological Bulletin, 70,* 426–443.

Cohen, J., & Cohen, P. (1983). *Applied multiple regression/correlation analysis for the behavioral sciences.* Hillsdale, NJ: Lawrence Erlbaum.

Cohen, R. J., Swerdlik, M. E., & Phillips, S. M. (1996). *Psychological testing and assessment: An introduction to tests and measurements* (3rd ed.). Mountain View, CA: Mayfield.

Coles, A. P. (2002). How the Mayor should fix the schools. *City Journal, 12*(3), 44–51. Retrieved August 29, 2002, from the ERIC database.

Collingwood, R. G. (1940). *An essay on metaphysics.* Oxford, England: Clarendon.

Converse, J. M., & Presser, S. (1986). *Survey questions: Handcrafting the standardized questionnaire.* Newbury Park, CA: Sage.

Cook, T. D. & Shadish, W. R. (1994). Social experiments: Some developments over the past fifteen years. *Annual Review of Psychology, 45,* 545–580.

Cook, T. D., & Campbell, D. T. (1979). *Quasi-experimentation. Design and analysis issues for field settings.* Chicago: Rand McNally.

Cosbie, J. (1993). Interrupted time-series analysis with brief single-subject data. *Journal of Consulting and Clinical Psychology, 61,* 966–974.

Creswell, J. W. (1994). *Research design: Qualitative and quantitative Approaches.* Thousand Oaks, CA: Sage.

Creswell, J. W. (2002). *Educational research: planning, conducting, and evaluating qualitative and quantitative research.* Upper Saddle River, New Jersey: Pearson Education.

Creswell, J. W., & Brown, M. L. (1992). How chairpersons enhance faculty research: A grounded theory study. *The Review of Higher Education, 16*(1), 41–62.

Crocker, L., & Algina, J. (1986). *Introduction to classical and modern test theory.* Fort Worth, TX: Holt, Rinehart, and Winston.

Cronbach, L. J. (1951). Coefficient alpha and the internal structure of tests. *Psychometrika, 16,* 297–334.

Cronbach, L. J. (1982). *Designing evaluations of educational and social programs.* San Francisco: Jossey-Bass.

Cronbach, L. J. (1984). *Essentials of psychological testing* (4th ed.). New York: Harper & Row.

Cronbach, L. J. (1991). *Essentials of psychological testing.* New York: Harper & Row.

Cronbach, L. J., & Furby, L. (1970). "How should we measure change"—Or should we? *Psychological Bulletin, 74,* 68–80.

Cronbach, L. J., & Meehl, P. E. (1955). Construct validity in psychological tests. *Psychological Bulletin, 52,* 281–302.

Cross, T. L., & Stewart, R. A. (1995). A phenomenological investigation of the Lebenswelt of gifted students in rural high schools. *The Journal of Secondary Gifted Education, 6*(4), 273–280.

Daley, C. E., & Onwuegbuzie, A. J. (in press). Attributions toward violence of male juvenile delinquents: A concurrent mixed methods analysis. *Journal of Social Psychology.*

Dane, F. C. (1990). *Research methods.* Pacific Grove, CA: Brooks/Cole.

Davis, J. A. (1985). *The logic of causal order.* Beverly Hills, CA: Sage.

Davis, J. A., & Smith, T. W. (1992). *The NORC General Social Survey: A user's guide.* Newbury Park, CA: Sage.

Deemer, S. A., & Minke, K. M. (1999). An investigation of the factor structure of the Teacher Efficacy Scale. *Journal of Educational Research, 93,* 3–10.

Deering, P. D. (1996). An ethnographic study of norms of inclusion and cooperation in a multiethnic middle school. *The Urban Review, 28*(1), 21–39.

DeLaPaz, S. (2001). Teaching writing to students with attention deficit disorders and specific language impairment. *The Journal of Educational Research, 95*(1), 37–47.

Denzin, N. K. (1978). *The research act: A theoretical introduction to sociological methods.* Englewood Cliffs, NJ: Prentice Hall.

Dever, M. (1997). *Exploring feminist research: A student-centered model.* Feminist teacher, 11(2), 91–103.

Dey, I. (1993). *Qualitative data analysis: A user-friendly guide for social scientists.* London: Routledge.

Deyhle, D. M. (1992, January). Constructing failure and maintaining cultural identity: Navajo and Ute school leavers. *Journal of American Indian Education,* 24–47.

Diener, E., & Crandall, R. (1978). *Ethics in social and behavioral research.* Chicago: The University of Chicago Press.

Drew, N. (1986). Exclusion and confirmation: A phenomenology of patients' experiences with caregivers. *IMAGE: Journal of Nursing Scholarship, 18,* 39–43.

Dykeman, C., Daehlin, W., Doyle, S., & Flamer, H. S. (1996). Psychological predictors of school-based violence: Implications for school counselors. *The School Counselor, 44,* 35–44.

Educational Testing Service. (2002). *GRE 2002–03 Guide to the Use of Scores.* Princeton, NJ: Author.

Ellickson, P. L. (1989). *Limiting nonresponse in longitudinal research: Three strategies for school-based studies* (Rand Note N-2912-CHF). Santa Monica, CA: Rand Corporation.

Ellickson, P. L. and Hawes, J. A. (1989). An assessment of active versus passive methods for obtaining parental consent. *Evaluation Review, 13,* 45–55.

Farreil, E., Peguero, G., Lindsey, R., & White, R. (1988). Giving voice to high school students: Pressure and boredom, ya know what I'm sayin'? *American Education Research Journal, 25*(4), 489–502.

Feist, J. (1990). *Theories of personality.* Fort Worth, TX: Holt, Rinehart, and Winston.

Festinger, I. (1957). *A theory of cognitive dissonance.* New York: Harper & Row.

Fetterman, D. M. (1998). Ethnography. In L. Bickman, & D. J. Rog (Eds.), *Handbook of applied social research methods.* Thousand Oaks, CA: Sage.

Finkel, S. E. (1995). *Causal analysis with panel data.* Thousand Oaks, CA: Sage.

Fisher, J. C. (1993). A framework for describing developmental change among older adults. *Adult Education Quarterly, 43*(2), 76–89.

Flannery, D. D. (1991). Adults' expectations of instructors: Criteria for hiring and evaluating instructors. *Continuing Higher Education Review, 55.*

Flynn, J. R. (1987). Massive IQ gains in 14 nations: What IQ tests really measure. *Psychological Bulletin, 101,* 171–191.

Forbes Family. (2002, September 9). The Forbes family (and "Forbes") continues to ride Harleys. *Min Media Newsletter.* Available online: Retrieved October 2002 from Lexis-Nexis.

Forness, S. R., & Kavale, K. A. (1996). Treating social skill deficits in children with learning disabilities: A meta-analysis of the research. *Learning Disability Quarterly, 19,* 2–9.

Fournier, R. (2002, January 9). Bush signs education bill worth 26 billion. *Mobile Register,* p. 2A.

Fraenkel, J. R., & Wallen, N. E. (1996). *How to design and evaluate research in education.* New York: McGraw-Hill.

Frankfort-Nachmias, C., & Nachmias, D. (1992). *Research methods in the social sciences* (4th ed.). New York: St Martin's Press.

Fritze, R. H., Coutts, B. E., & Vyhnanek, L. A. (1990). *Reference sources in history: An introductory guide.* Santa Barbara, CA: ABC-CLIO.

Frontman, K. C., & Kunkel, M. A. (1994). A grounded theory of counselors' construal of success in the initial session. *Journal of Counseling Psychology, 41*(4), 492–499.

Fuertes, J. N., Sedlacek, W. E., & Liu, W. M. (1994). Using the SAT and noncognitive variables to predict the grades and retention of Asian American university students. *Measurement and Evaluation in Counseling and Development, 27,* 74–84.

Fultz, M. (1995). African American teachers in the South, 1890–1940: Powerlessness and the ironies of expectation and protest. *History of Education Quarterly, 35,* 401–422.

Gage, J. T. (1991). *The shape of reason* (2nd ed.). New York: Macmillan.

Gahan, C., & Hannibal, M. (1998). *Doing qualitative research using QSR NUD-IST.* London: Sage.

Gail, M. H. (1996). Statistics in action. *Journal of the American Statistical Association, 91*(433), 1–13.

Galenson, D. W. (1998). Ethnic differences in neighborhood effects on the school attendance of boys in early Chicago. *History of Education Quarterly, 38,* 17–35.

Gallo, M. A., & Horton, P. B. (1994). Assessing the effect on high school teachers of direct and unrestricted access to the Internet: A case study of an East Central Florida high school. *ETR&D, 42*(4), 17–39.

Gentile, J. R., Voelkl, K. E., Mt. Pleasant, J., & Monaco, N. I. (1995). Recall after relearning by fast and slow learners. *The Journal of Experimental Education, 63*(3), 185–197.

Gibbs, G. R. (2002). *Qualitative data analysis: Explorations with Nvivo.* Buckingham, UK: Open University Press.

Gilbert, L. M., Williams, R. L., & McLaughlin, T. F. (1996). Use of assisted reading to increase correct reading rates and decrease error rates of students with learning disabilities. *Journal of Applied Behavior Analysis, 29,* 255–257.

Glaser, B. G. (1978). *Theoretical sensitivity.* Mill Valley, CA: Sociology Press.

Glaser, B. G., & Strauss, A. L. (1967). *The discovery of grounded theory: Strategies for qualitative research.* New York: Aldine De Gruyter.

Glass, G. (1976). Primary, secondary, and meta-analysis of research. *Educational Research, 5,* 3–8.

Glass, G. V. & Hopkins, K. D. (1984). *Statistical methods in education and psychology* (2nd ed.). Englewood Cliffs, NJ: Prentice-Hall.

Glass, G. V., & Hopkins, K. D. (1996). *Statistical methods in education and psychology* (3rd ed.). Boston: Allyn & Bacon.

Glass, G. V., Willson, V. L., & Gottman, J. M. (1975). *Design and analysis of time series.* Boulder, CO: Laboratory of Educational Research Press.

Goffman, E. (1959). *The presentation of self in everyday life.* Garden City, NY: Anchor Books.

Gold, R. (1958). Roles in sociological field observations. *Social Forces, 36,* 217–223.

Goldenberg, C. (1992). The limits of expectations: A case for case knowledge about teacher expectancy effects. *American Educational Research Journal, 29,* 517–544.

Gray, W. (1991). *Historian's handbook: A key to the study and writing of history.* Prospect Heights, IL: Waveland.

Green, A. J. (1995). Experiential learning and teaching: A critical evaluation of an enquiry which used phenomenological method. *Nurse Education Today, 15,* 420–426.

Greene, J. C., Caracelli, V. J. (Eds.) (1997). *Advances in mixed-method evaluation: The challenges and benefits of integrating diverse paradigms.* New Directions for Evaluation, 74. San Francisco: Jossey-Bass.

Greene, J. C., Caracelli, V. J., & Graham, W. F. (1989). Toward a conceptual framework for mixed-method evaluation designs. *Educational Evaluation and Policy Analysis, 11,* 255–274.

Grimm, L. G., & Yarnold, P. R. (1995). *Reading and understanding statistics.* Washington, D.C.: American Psychological Association.

Grisso, T., Baldwin, E., Blanck, P. D., Rotheram-Borus, M. J., Schooler, N. R., & Thompson, T. (1991). Standards in research: APA's mechanism for monitoring challenges. *American Psychologist, 46,* 758–766.

Guba, E. G., & Lincoln, Y. S. (1981). *Effective evaluation.* San Francisco: Jossey-Bass.

Guba, E. G., & Lincoln, Y. S. (1989). *Fourth generation evaluation.* Newbury Park, CA: Sage.

Guba, E. G. (1990). *The paradigm dialog.* Newbury Park, CA: Sage.

Guerrero, S. H. (1999). (Edited). *Gender-sensitive and feminist methodologies: A handbook for health and social researchers.* Quezon City: University of the Philippines Center for Women's Studies.

Guilford, J. P. (1936). *Psychometric methods.* New York: McGraw-Hill.

Guilford, J. P. (1959). *Personality.* New York: McGraw-Hill.

Gunter, P. L., Shores, R. E., Jack, S. L., Denny, R. K., & DePaepe, P. A. (1994). A case study of the effects of altering instructional interactions on the disruptive behavior of a child identified with severe behavior disorders. *Education and Treatment of Children, 17,* 435–444.

Hall, C. S., & Lindzey, G. (1970). *Theories of personality.* New York: Wiley.

Hall, R. V., & Fox, R. W. (1977). Changing-criterion designs: An alternative applied behavior analysis procedure. In C. C. Etzel, G. M. LeBlanc, & D. M. Baer (Eds.), *New developments in behavioral research: Theory, method, and application* (in honor of Sidney W. Bijou). Hillsdale, NJ: Lawrence Erlbaum.

Harchar, R. L., & Hyle, A. E. (1996). Collaborative power: A grounded theory of administrative instructional leadership in the elementary school. *Journal of Educational Administration, 34*(3), 15–29.

Harlow, L. L., Mulaik, S. A., & Steiger, J. H. (Eds.). (1997). *What if there were no significance tests?* Mahwah, NJ: Lawrence Erlbaum.

Harnett, D. L. (1982). *Statistical methods* (3rd ed.). Reading, MA: Addison Wesley.

Harry, B. (1992). An ethnographic study of cross-cultural communication with Puerto Rican-American families in the special education system. *American Educational Research Journal, 29*(3), 471–494.

Hays, W. L. (1994). *Statistics.* New York: Holt, Rinehart, and Winston.

Heinsman, D. T. and Shadish, W. R. (1996). Assignment methods in experimentation: When do nonrandomized experiments approximate answers from randomized experiments. *Psychological Methods, 1,* 154–169.

Henry, G. T. (1990). *Graphing data: Techniques for display and analysis.* Thousand Oaks, CA: Sage.

Hersen, M., & Barlow, D. H. (1976). *Single case experimental designs: Strategies for studying behavioral change.* New York: Pergamon.

Hersen, M., & Bellack, A. S. (1988). *Dictionary of behavioral assessment techniques.* New York: Pergamon.

Hilgartner, S. (1990). Research fraud, misconduct, and the IRB. *IRB: A Review of Human Subjects Research, 12,* 1–4.

Hill, B. A. (1956). The environment and disease: Association or causation? *Proceedings of the Royal Society of Medicine, 58,* 295–300.

Hitler diaries trial stirs judge to disbelief and ire. (1985, January 6). *New York Times,* p. A14.

Holden, C. (1987). NIMH finds a case of "serious misconduct." *Science, 235,* 1566–1567.

Holland, D. C., & Eisenhart, M. A. (1990). *Educated in romance: Women, achievement, and college culture.* Chicago: University of Chicago Press.

Holmes, D. S. (1976a). Debriefing after psychological experiments: I. Effectiveness of postdeception dehoxing. *American Psychologist, 31,* 858–867.

Holmes, D. S. (1976b). Debriefing after psychological experiments: I. Effectiveness of postexperimental desensitizing. *American Psychologist, 31,* 868–875.

Holy Horatio. (1974, June 10). *Time, 103,* 18.

Howe, K. R., & Dougherty, K. C. (1993). Ethics, institutional review boards, and the changing face of educational research. *Educational Researcher, 22,* 16–21.

Howell, D. C. (1997). *Statistical methods for psychology.* Belmont, CA: Duxbury Press.

Huber, G. P., & Van de Van, A. H. (1995). *Longitudinal field research methods: Studying processes of organizational change.* Thousand Oaks, CA: Sage.

Huberman, A. M., & Miles, M. B. (1994). Data management and analysis methods. In N. K. Denzin & Y. S. Lincoln (Eds.), *Handbook of qualitative research.* Newbury Park, CA: Sage.

Huck, S. W. (2004). *Reading statistics and research.* Boston: Allyn and Bacon.

Huff, D. (1993, originally published in 1954). *How to lie with statistics.* New York: Norton.

Hult, C. A. (1996). *Researching and writing in the social sciences.* Boston: Allyn & Bacon.

Humphreys, P. (1989). *The chances of explanation: Causal explanation in the social, medical, and physical sciences.* Princeton, NJ: Princeton University Press.

Hyde, J. S., Fennema, E., & Lamon, S. J. (1990). Gender differences in mathematics performance: A meta-analysis. *Psychological Bulletin, 107*(2), 139–155.

Iggers, G. (1997). *Historiography in the twentieth century: From scientific objectivity to the postmodern challenge.* Middletown, CT: Wesleyan.

Imich, A. J. (1994). Exclusions from school: Current trends and issues. *Educational Researcher, 36,* 3–11.

Isaac, S., & Michael, W. B. (1995). *Handbook in research and evaluation: For education and the behavioral sciences.* San Diego, CA: Educational and Industrial Testing Services.

Jenkins, J. J., Russell, W. A., & Suci, G. J. (1958). An atlas of semantic profiles for 360 words. *American Journal of Psychology, 71,* 688–699.

Jimerson, S., Carlson, E., Rotert, M., Egeland, B., & Sroufe, L. A. (1997). A prospective, longitudinal study of the correlates and consequences of early grade retention. *Journal of School Psychology, 35*(1), 3–25.

John, O. P., & Benet-Martinez, V. (2000). Measurement: Reliability, construct validation, and scale construction. In H. T. Reis & C. M. Judd (Eds.), *Handbook of research methods in social and personality psychology* (pp. 339–369). Cambridge, UK: Cambridge University.

Johnson, D. (2002, January 21). High school at attention. *Newsweek,* pp. 42–44.

Johnson, R. B. (1994). Qualitative research in education. *SRATE Journal, 4*(1), 3–7.

Johnson, R. B. (1995). Estimating an evaluation utilization model using conjoint measurement and analysis. *Evaluation Review, 19*(3), 313–338.

Johnson, R. B. (1997). Examining the validity structure of qualitative research. *Education, 118*(2), 282–292.

Johnson, R. B. (2001). Toward a new classification of nonexperimental quantitative research. *Educational Researcher, 30*(2), 3–13.

Johnson, R. B., & Turner, L. A. (2002). Data collection strategies in mixed methods research. In A. Tashakkori & C. Teddlie (Eds.), *Handbook of mixed methods in social and behavioral research* (pp. 297–319). Thousand Oaks, CA: Sage.

Jonassen, D. H., & Grabowski, B. L. (1993). *Handbook of individual differences, learning, and instruction.* Hillsdale, NJ: Lawrence Erlbaum.

Jones, J. H. (1981). *Bad blood: The Tuskegee syphilis experiment.* New York: Free Press.

Jones, P. M. (1997, January 8). Results mixed in cities where mayors took over schools. *Mobile Press Register,* p. 1D (Newhouse News Service).

Judd, C. M., Smith, E. R., & Kidder, L. H. (1991). *Research methods in social relations.* Fort Worth, TX: Harcourt Brace Jovanovich.

Kaestle, C. F. (1992). Standards of evidence in historical research. *History of Education Quarterly, 32,* 361–366.

Kaestle, C. F. (1997). Recent methodological developments in the history of American education. In R. M. Jaeger (Ed.), *Complementary methods for research in education* (pp. 119–132). Washington, DC: American Educational Research Association.

Kalton, G. (1983). *Introduction to survey sampling.* Newbury Park, CA: Sage.

Karabenick, S. A., & Sharma, R. (1994). Perceived teacher support of student questioning in the college classroom: Its relation to student characteristics and role in the classroom questioning process. *Journal of Educational Psychology, 86*(1), 90–103.

Kaufman, J. S., & Poole, C. (2000). Looking back on "causal thinking in the health sciences." *Annual Review of Public Health, 21,* 101–119.

Kazdin, A. E. (1973). The role of instructions and reinforcement in behavior changes in token reinforcement programs. *Journal of Educational Psychology, 64,* 63–71.

Kazdin, A. E. (1978). Methodological and interpretive problems of single-case experimental designs. *Journal of Consulting and Clinical Psychology, 46,* 629–642.

Keith, T. Z., & Reynolds, C. R. (1990). Measurement and design issues in child assessment research. In C. R. Reynolds & R. W. Kamphaus (Eds.), *Handbook of psychological and educational assessment of children: Intelligence & achievement* (pp. 29–61). New York: Guilford Press.

Kendall, M. G., and Smith, B. (1954). *Tables of random sampling numbers, tracts for computers No. 27.* Cambridge, England: Cambridge University Press.

Kenny, D. A., Kashy, D. A., & Bolger, N. (1998). Data analysis in social psychology. In D. Gilbert, S. Fiske, & G. Lindzey

(Eds.), *The handbook of social psychology* (Vol. 1, 4th ed., pp. 233–265). Boston, MA: McGraw-Hill.

Keyser, D. J., & Sweetland, R. C. (1984–1994). *Test Critiques* (Vols. I–X). Austin: Pro-Ed.

Kiecolt, K. J., & Nathan, L. E. (1985). *Secondary analysis of survey data.* Newbury Park, CA: Sage.

Kirk, R. E. (2001). Promoting good statistical practices: Some suggestions. *Educational and Psychological Measurement, 61*(2), 213–218.

Kish, L. (1965). *Survey sampling.* New York: Wiley.

Knapp, T. R. (1978). Canonical correlation analysis: A general parametric significance testing system. *Psychological Bulletin, 85,* 410–416.

Knight, J. A. (1984). Exploring the compromise of ethical principles in science. *Perspectives in Biology and Medicine, 27,* 432–441.

Knoke, D., & Bohrnstedt, G. W. (1994). *Statistics for social data analysis.* Itasca, IL: F. E. Peacock.

Koomey, J. G. (2001). *Turning numbers into knowledge: Mastering the art of problem solving.* Oakland, CA: Analytics Press.

Krueger, R. A. (1998). *Moderating focus groups.* Thousand Oaks, CA: Sage.

Kuder, G. F., & Richardson, M. W. (1937). The theory of the estimation of reliability. *Psychometrika, 2,* 151–160.

Kuhn, T. S. (1962). *The structure of scientific revolutions.* Chicago: University of Chicago Press.

Kusche, C. A., & Greenberg, M. T. (1983). Evaluative understanding and role taking ability: A comparison of deaf and hearing children. *Child Development, 54,* 141–147.

Lance, G. D. (1996). Computer access in higher education: A national survey of service providers for students with disabilities. *Journal of College Student Development, 37*(3), 279–288.

LaPiere, R. T. (1934). Attitudes vs. Actions. *Social Forces, 13,* 230–237.

Lasee, M. J., & Smith, D. K. (1991). *Relationships between the K-ABC and the Early Screening Profiles.* Paper presented at the Annual Meeting of the National Association of School Psychologists, Dallas, TX.

Lawrence, S., and Giles, C. L. (1999). Accessibility of information on the Web. *Nature, 400,* 107–109.

LeCompte, M. D., & Preissle, J. (1992). Toward an ethnology of student life in schools and classrooms: Synthesizing the qualitative research tradition. In M. D. LeCompte, W. L. Millroy, & J. Preissle (Eds.), *The handbook of qualitative research in education* (pp. 815–859). San Diego, CA: Academic Press.

LeCompte, M. D., & Preissle, J. (1993). *Ethnography and qualitative design in educational research.* San Diego, CA: Academic.

LeCompte, M. D., Preissle, J., & Tesch, R. (1993). *Ethnography and qualitative design in educational research* (2nd ed.). San Diego, CA: Academic Press.

Leikin, S. (1993). Minors' assent, consent, or dissent to medical research. *IRB: A review of human subjects research, 15,* 1–7.

Leland, J. & Joseph, N. (1997, January 13). Hooked on ebonics. *Newsweek,* pp. 78–79.

Lewin, K. (1946). Action research and minority problems. *Journal of Social Issues, 2,* 34–46.

Likert, R. (1932). A technique for the measurement of attitudes. *Archives of Psychology, 140,* 5–53.

Lincoln, Y. S., & Guba, E. G. (1985). *Naturalistic inquiry.* Newbury Park, CA: Sage.

Lincoln, Y. S., & Guba, E. G. (2000). Paradigmatic controversies, contradictions, and emerging confluences. In N. K. Denzin and Y. S. Lincoln (Eds.), *Handbook of qualitative research* (pp. 163–188). Thousand Oaks, CA: Sage.

Linder, D. E., Cooper, J., & Jones, E. E. (1967). Decision freedom as a determinant of the role of incentive magnitude in attitude change. *Journal of Personality and Social Psychology, 6,* 245–254.

Lofland, J., & Lofland, L. H. (1995). *Analyzing social settings: A guide to qualitative observation and analysis* (2nd edition). Belmont, CA: Wadsworth.

Lofland, J. (1971). *Analyzing social settings: A guide to qualitative observation and analysis.* Belmont, CA: Wadsworth.

Lonborg, S. D., & Phillips, J. M. (1996). Investigating the career development of gay, lesbian, and bisexual people: Methodological considerations and recommendations. *Journal of Vocational Behavior, 48*(2), 176–194.

Maddox, T. (Ed.). (1997). *A comprehensive reference for assessment in psychology, education, and business.* Austin, TX: Pro Ed.

Manhard, S. J. (1998). *The goof-proofer: How to avoid the 41 most embarrassing errors in your speaking and writing.* New York: Fireside.

Manthei, R. and Gilmore, A. (1996). Teacher stress in intermediate schools. *Educational Research, 38,* 3–18.

Mantzicopoulos, P., & Knutson, D. J. (2000). Head Start children: School mobility and achievement in the early grades. *Journal of Educational Resaerch, 93*(5), 305–311.

Martinez-Pons, M. (1996). Test of a model of parental inducement of academic self-regulation. *Journal of Experimental Education, 64*(3), 213–227.

Maruyama, G. M. (1998). *Basics of structural equation modeling.* Thousand Oaks, CA: Sage.

Max, J. (2002, October 28). V-room, vroom. *Newsweek,* p. 79.

Maxwell, J. A. (1992). Understanding and validity in qualitative research. *Harvard Educational Review, 62*(3), 279–299.

Maxwell, J. A. (1996). *Qualitative research design.* Newbury Park, CA: Sage.

Mayer, G. R., Mitchell, L. K., Clementi, T., Clement-Robertson, E., & Myatt, R. (1993). A dropout prevention program for at-risk high school students: Emphasizing consulting to promote positive classroom climates. *Education and Treatment of Children, 16,* 135–146.

McCullough, J. P., Cornell, J. E., McDaniel, M. H., & Mueller, R. K. (1974). Utilization of the simultaneous treatment design to improve student behavior in a first-grade classroom. *Journal of Consulting and Clinical Psychology, 42,* 288–292.

McGuigan, F. J. (1963). The experimenter: A neglected stimulus object. *Psychological Bulletin, 60,* 421–428.

McKelvie, S. (1978). Graphic rating scales: How many categories? *British Journal of Psychology, 69,* 185–202.

McMenamin, J. (2002, September 20). Schools step up anti-drug efforts with crisis hot line, skits in Carroll; Principal leads campaign after son's fatal overdose. *The Baltimore Sun,* p. 6B.

Menard, S. (1991). *Longitudinal research.* Newbury Park, CA: Sage.

Menninger, K. A. (1953). *The human mind* (3rd ed.). New York: Knopf.

Merriam, S. B. (1988). *Case study research in education: A qualitative approach.* San Francisco: Jossey-Bass.

Merton, R. K. (1948). The self-fulfilling prophecy. *Antioch Review, 8,* 193–210.

Merton, R. K., & Kendall, P. L. (1946). The focused interview. *American Journal of Sociology, 51,* 541–557.

Merton, R. K., Fiske, M., & Kendall, P. L. (1956). *The focused interview.* New York: Free Press.

Messerli, J. (1972). *Horace Mann.* New York: Knopf.

Messick, S. (1989). Validity. In R. L. Linn (Ed.), *Educational measurement* (3rd ed., pp. 13–103). New York: Macmillan.

Messick, S. (1995). Validity of psychological assessment: Validation of inferences from persons' responses and performances as scientific inquiry into score meaning. *American Psychologist, 50,* 741–749.

Miles, M. B., & Huberman, A. M. (1994). *Qualitative data analysis: An expanded source book.* Thousand Oaks, CA: Sage.

Miller, D. C. (1991). *Handbook of research design and social measurement.* Newbury Park, CA: Sage.

Mischel, W. (1999). *Introduction to personality.* New York: Holt, Rinehart, and Winston.

Moore, D. S. (1993). *Telecourse study guide for against all odds: Inside statistics and introduction to the practice of statistics.* New York: W. H. Freeman.

Moore, D. S., & McCabe, G. P. (1993). *Introduction to the practice of statistics.* New York: W. H. Freeman.

Morgan, D. L. (1998). Practical strategies for combining qualitative and quantitative methods: Applications to health research. *Qualitative Health Research, 3,* 362–376.

Morgan, D. L., & Krueger, R. A. (1998). *The focus group kit.* Newbury Park, CA: Sage.

Morse, J. M. (1991). Approaches to qualitative-quantitative methodological triangulation. *Nursing Research, 40,* 120–123.

Moustakas, C. (1990). *Heuristic research: Design, methodology, and applications.* Newbury Park, CA: Sage.

Moustakas, C. (1994). *Phenomenological research methods.* Thousand Oaks, CA: Sage.

Muller, L. E. (1994). Toward an understanding of empowerment: A study of six women leaders. *Journal of Humanistic Education and Development, 33,* 75–82.

Murphy, L. L., Conoley, J. C., & Impara, J. C. (1994). *Tests in print IV.* Lincoln: University of Nebraska Press.

Myers, D. G. (2001). Do we fear the right things? *American Psychological Society Observer, 14*(10). Retrieved August 30, 2002, from http://www.psychologicalscience.org/observer/1201/prescol.html.

Neisser, U. (1979). The concept of intelligence. *Intelligence, 3,* 217–227.

Neufeldt, S. A., Karno, M. P., & Nelson, M. L. (1996). A qualitative study of experts' conceptualization of supervisee reflectivity. *Journal of Counseling Psychology, 43*(1), 3–9.

Newman, I., & Benz, C. R. (1998). *Qualitative-quantitative research methodology: Exploring the interactive continuum.* Carbondale: Southern Illinois University Press.

Norton, M. B. (1995). *Guide to historical literature* (3rd ed.). New York: Oxford University Press.

Nunally, J. (1978). *Psychometric theory.* New York: McGraw-Hill.

Nunnally, J. C., & Bernstein, I. H. (1994). *Psychometric theory.* New York: McGraw-Hill.

Nye, B., Hedges, L. V., & Konstantopoulos, S. (2001). Are effects of small classes cumulative? Evidence from a Tennessee experiment. *The Journal of Educational Research, 94*(6), 336–345.

O'Brien, D. (2002, July 11). Boy, 16, gets 25 years in killing: Ex-high school wrestler fatally shot on mall lot. *The Baltimore Sun,* p. 3B.

Ohles, J. F. (Ed.). (1978). *Biographical dictionary of American educators.* Westport, CT: Greenwood.

Okey, T. N., & Cusick, P. A. (1995). Dropping out: Another side of the story. *Educational Administration Quarterly, 31*(2), 244–267.

Onwuegbuzie, A. J., & DaRos-Voseles, D. A. (2001). The role of cooperative learning in research methodology courses: A mixed-methods analysis. *Research in the Schools, 8,* 61–75.

Onwuegbuzie, A. J., & Teddlie, C. (2002). A framework for analyzing data in mixed methods research. In A. Tashakkori & C. Teddlie (Eds.), *Handbook of mixed methods in social and behavioral research* (pp. 351–383). Thousand Oaks, CA: Sage.

Onwuegbuzie, A. J. (in press). Expanding the framework of internal and external validity in quantitative research. *Research in the Schools.*

OPRR Reports. (1991). *Code of federal regulations 45* (Part 46, p. 5). Washington, DC: U.S. Government Printing Office.

Osgood, C. E., Suci, G. J., & Tannenbaum, P. H. (1957). *The measurement of meaning.* Urbana: University of Illinois Press.

Otiene, T. N. (2001). Higher education: A quantitative inquiry into the educational experiences of seven African women. Retrieved April 25, 2003, from http://libproxy.usouthal.edu:2140/webstore/download.cfm?ID=634874&CFID=3211423&CFTOKEN=63588799.

Patton, M. Q. (1987). *How to use qualitative methods in evaluation.* Newbury Park, CA: Sage.

Patton, M. Q. (1990). *Qualitative evaluation and research methods.* Newbury Park, CA: Sage.

Patton, M. Q. (2002). *Qualitative research and evaluation methods.* Thousand Oaks, CA: Sage.

Pedhazur, E. J. (1997). *Multiple regression in behavioral research: Explanation and prediction.* Fort Worth, TX: Harcourt Brace.

Pedhazur, E. J., & Schmelkin, L. P. (1991). *Measurement, design, and analysis: An integrated approach.* Hillsdale, NJ: Lawrence Erlbaum.

Pence, G. E. (1980). Children's dissent to research—A minor matter? *IRB: A Review of Human Subjects Research, 2,* 1–4.

Pennebaker, J. W., Dyer, M. A., Caulkins, R. S., Litowitz, D. L., Ackreman, P. L., Gladue, B. A., & Delaney, H. J. (1990). Gender differences in perception of attractiveness of men and women in bars. *Personality and Social Psychology Bulletin, 16,* 378–391.

Phi Delta Kappa. (1996, September). The 28th annual Phi Delta Kappa/Gallup poll. *Phi Delta Kappan.*

Phillips, D. C., & Burbules, N. C. (2000). *Postpositivism and educational research.* New York: Rowman & Littlefield.

Phillips, S. R. (1994). Asking the sensitive question: The ethics of survey research and teen sex. *IRB: A Review of Human Subjects Research, 16,* 1–6.

Pillemer, D. B. (1991). One- versus Two-Tailed Hypothesis Tests in Contemporary Educational Research. *Educational Researcher, 20*(9), 13–17.

Popper, K. R. (1965). *Conjectures and refutations.* 2nd ed. New York: Basic Books.

Popper, K. R. (1974). Replies to my critics. In P. A. Schilpp (Ed.), *The Philosophy of Karl Popper* (pp. 963–1197). La Salle, IL: Open Court.

Popper, K. R. (1985). Falsificationism versus conventionalism. In D. Miller (Ed.), *Popper Selections.* Princeton, NJ: Princeton University Press. (Originally published in 1938)

Prevenier, W., & Howell, M. C. (2001). *From reliable sources: An historical methods.* Cornell, NY: Cornell University Press.

Pring, R. (2000). The 'false dualism' of educational research. *Journal of Philosophy of Education, 34*(2), 247–260.

Rech, J. F. (1996, winter). Gender differences in mathematics achievement and other variables among university students. *Journal of Research and Development in Education, 29*(2), 73–76.

Reichardt, C. S., & Cook, T. D. (1979). Beyond qualitative versus quantitative methods. In Cook, T. D., & Reichardt, C. S. (Eds.), *Qualitative and quantitative methods in evaluation research.* Newbury Park, CA: Sage.

Reichardt, S. S., & Rallis, S. F. (1994). Qualitative and quantitative inquiries are not incompatible: A call for a new partnership. In C. S. Reichardt, & S. F. Rallis (Eds.), *The qualitative-quantitative debate: New perspectives.* (pp. 85–91). San Francisco, CA: Jossey-Bass.

Resnick, J. H., & Schwartz, T. (1973). Ethical standards as an independent variable in psychological research. *American Psychologist, 28,* 134–139.

Reynolds, A. J. (1998). Confirmatory program evaluation: A method for strengthening causal inference. *American Journal of Evaluation, 19*(2), 203–221.

Richardson, M. W., & Kuder, G. F. (1939). The calculation of test reliability based upon the method of rational equivalence. *Journal of Educational Psychology, 30,* 681–687.

Rieman, D. J. (1986). The essential structure of a caring interaction: Doing phenomenology. In P. M. Munhall & C. J. Oiler (Eds.), *Nursing research: A qualitative perspective* (pp. 85–105). Norwalk, CT: Appleton-Century-Crofts.

Roberson, M. T., & Sundstrom, E. (1990). Questionnaire design, return rates, and response favorableness in an employee attitude questionnaire. *Journal of Applied Psychology, 75,* 354–357.

Roberts, P., & Le-Dorze, G. (1994). Semantic verbal fluency in aphasia: A quantitative and qualitative study in test-retest conditions. *Aphasiology, 8*(6), 569–582.

Robinson, J. P., Shaver, P. R., & Wrightsman, L. S. (1991). *Measures of personality and social psychological attitudes.* New York: Academic.

Rogosa, D. (1988). Myths about longitudinal research. In K. W. Schaie, R. T. Campbell, W. Meridith, & S. C. Rawlings (Eds.), *Methodological issues in aging research* (pp. 171–210). New York: Springer.

Rosenberg, D. (2002, June 10). Fighting G-force. *Newsweek,* p. 49.

Rosenberg, M. (1968). *The logic of survey analysis* (with forward by Paul F. Lazarsfeld). New York: Basic Books.

Rosenthal, R. (1991). Teacher expectancy effects: A brief update 25 years after the Pygmalion experiment. *Journal of Research in Education, 1,* 3–12.

Rosenthal, R., & Jacobson, L. (1968). *Pygmalion in the classroom.* New York: Holt, Rinehart & Winston.

Rosnow, R. L., & Rosnow, M. (1992). *Writing papers in psychology* (2nd ed.). New York: Wiley.

Rossman, G. B., & Wilson, B. L. (1994). Numbers and words revisited: Being "shamelessly eclectic." *Quality and Quantity, 28,* 315–327.

Rudestam, K. E., & Newton, R. R. (2001). *Surviving your dissertation: A comprehensive guide to content and process.* Thousand Oaks, CA: Sage.

Russell, William (personal communication).

Salmon, M. H. (1984). *Logic and critical thinking.* San Diego, CA: Harcourt Brace Jovanovich.

Savoye, C. (2001, November 13). First stop for urban teachers-in-training. *Christian Science Monitor, 93*(245), p. 14.

Schachter, S. (1959). *The psychology of affiliation.* Stanford, CA: Stanford University Press.

Schafer, M. & Smith, P. K. (1996). Teachers' perceptions of play fighting and real fighting in primary school. *Educational Research, 38,* 173–180.

Scheaffer, R. L., Mendenhall, W., & Ott, R. L. (1996). *Elementary survey sampling* (5th ed.). Belmont, CA: Duxbury Press.

Schlenker, B. R., & Forsyth, D. R. (1977). On the ethics of psychological research. *Journal of Experimental Social Psychology, 13,* 369–396.

Schouten, J. W., & McAlexander, J. H. (1995). Subcultures of consumption: An ethnography of the new bikers. *Journal of Consumer Research, 22,* 43–60.

Schouten, P. G. W., & Kirkpatrick, L. A. (1993). Questions and concerns about the Miller Assessment for Preschoolers. *The Occupational Therapy Journal of Research, 13,* 7–28.

Schumacker, R. E., & Lomax, R. G. (1996). *A beginner's guide to structural equation modeling.* Mahwah, NJ: Lawrence Erlbaum.

Schuman, H., & Presser, S. (1981). *Questions and answers in attitude surveys: Experiments on question form, wording, and content.* New York: Academic.

Schwandt, T. A. (1997). *Qualitative inquiry: A dictionary of terms.* Thousand Oaks, CA: Sage.

Scriven, M. (1967). The methodology of evaluation. In R. E. Stake (Ed.), *Curriculum evaluation.* Chicago: Rand McNally.

Scriven, M. (1993). Evaluation Thesaurus. Newbury Park, CA: Sage.

Sears, S. J., Kennedy, J. J., & Kaye, G. L. (1997). Myers-Briggs personality profiles of prospective educators. *The Journal of Education Research, 90*(4), 195–202.

Senne, T. A., & Rikard, G. L. (2002). Experiencing the portfolio process during the internship: A comparative analysis of two PETE portfolio models. *Journal of Teaching in Physical Education, 21,* 309–336.

Severson, H. H., and Ary, D. V. (1983). Sampling bias due to consent procedures with adolescents. *Addictive Behaviors, 8,* 433–437.

Shadish, W. R., Cook, T. D., & Campbell, D. T. (2001). *Experimental and quasi-experimental designs for generalized causal inference.* Boston: Houghton Mifflin.

Shaffir, W. B., & Stebbins, R. A. (Ed.). (1991). *Experiencing fieldwork: An inside view of qualitative research.* Newbury Park, CA: Sage.

Shank, G. D. (2002). *Qualitative research.* Columbus, Ohio: Merrill, Prentice Hall.

Sidman, M. (1960). *Tactics of scientific research.* New York: Basic Books.

Silverman, D. (1993). *Interpreting qualitative data: Methods for analyzing talk, text and interaction.* London: Sage.

Smith, H. J. (1997). *The role of symbolism in the structure, maintenance, and interactions of high school groupings.* Unpublished masters thesis, University of South Alabama, Mobile, Alabama.

Smith, J. K. (1984). The problem of criteria for judging interpretive inquiry. *Educational Evaluation and Policy Analysis, 6,* 379–391.

Smith, L. M. (1978). An evolving logic of participant observation, educational ethnography, and other case studies. In L. Shuman (Ed.), *Review of research in education* (Vol. 6, pp. 316–377). Itasca, IL: Peacock.

Snowling, M. J., Goulandris, N., & Defty, N. (1996). A longitudinal study of reading development in dyslexic children. *Journal of Educational Psychology, 88,* 653–669.

Society for Research in Child Development. (1993). *Ethical standards for research with children.* Directory of Members.

Spradley, J. P. (1979). *The ethnographic interview.* Fort Worth, TX: Holt, Rinehart and Winston.

Stake, R. E. (1978). The case study method in social inquiry. *Educational Researcher, 7*(2), 5–9.

Stake, R. E. (1995). *The art of case study research.* Thousand Oaks, CA: Sage.

Stake, R. E. (1997). Case study methods in educational research. In R. M. Jaeger (Ed.), *Complementary methods for research in education* (2nd ed.). Washington, DC: American Educational Research Association.

Stanfield, J. H., & Rutledge, M. (Eds.) (1993). *Race and ethnicity in research methods.* Newbury Park, CA: Sage.

Starch, D., & Elliot, E. C. (1912). Reliability of grading of high school work in English. *School Review, 20,* 442–457.

Sternberg, R. J., Conway, B. E., Ketron, J. L., & Bernstein, M. (1981). People's conception of intelligence. *Journal of Personality and Social Psychology, 41,* 37–55.

Stevens, S. S. (1946). On the theory of scales of measurement. *Science, 103,* 677–680.

Stevens, S. S. (1951). Mathematics, measurement, and psychophysics. In S. S. Stevens (Ed.), *Handbook of experimental psychology* (pp. 1–49). New York: Wiley.

Stewart, D. W., & Shamdasani, P. N. (1998). Focus group research. In L. Bickman & D. J. Rog (Eds.), *Handbook of applied social research methods.* Thousand Oaks, CA: Sage.

Stolzenberg, R. M., & Land, K. C. (1983). Causal modeling and survey research. In P. H. Rossi, J. D. Wright, & A. B. Anderson (Eds.), *Handbook of survey research.* Orlando, FL: Academic.

Strauss, A. (1995). Notes on the nature and development of general theories. *Qualitative Inquiry, 1*(1), 7–18.

Strauss, A., & Corbin, J. (1990). *Basics of qualitative research: Grounded theory procedures and techniques.* Newbury Park, CA: Sage.

Strauss, A., & Corbin, J. (1994). Grounded theory methodology: An overview. In N. K. Denzin & Y. S. Lincoln (Eds.), *Handbook of qualitative research.* Thousand Oaks, CA: Sage.

Stringer, E. T. (1996). *Action research.* Newbury Park: Sage.

Sudman, S. (1976). *Applied sampling.* New York: Academic.

Suen, H. K., & Ary, D. (1989). *Analyzing quantitative behavioral observation data.* Hillsdale, NJ: Lawrence Erlbaum.

Susser, M. (1977). Judgement and causal inference: Criteria in epidemiologic studies. *American Journal of Epidemiology, 105,* 1–15.

Susser, M. (1991). What is a cause and how do we know one? A grammar for pragmatic epidemiology. *American Journal of Epidemiology, 133,* 635–648.

Tabachnick, B. G., & Fidell, L. S. (1996). *Using multivariate statistics.* New York: HarperCollins.

Tallerico, M. (1993). *Gender and politics at work: Why women exit the superintendency.* Fairfax, VA: National Policy Board for Educational Administration.

Tashakkori, A., & Teddlie, C. (1998). *Mixed methodology: Combining qualitative and quantitative approaches.* Thousand Oaks, CA: Sage.

Tashakkori, A., & Teddlie, C. (Eds.) (2002), *Handbook of mixed methods in social and behavioral research.* Thousand Oaks, CA: Sage.

Taylor, S. J., & Bogdan, R. (1984). *Introduction to qualitative research methods.* New York: Wiley.

The Atlanta Journal and Constitution. (2002, May 8). Without excuses, schools succeed. *The Atlanta Constitution,* p. 15A.

Thompson, B. (1998, April 15). *Five methodology errors in educational research: The pantheon of statistical significance and other faux pas.* Invited address presented at the annual meeting of the American Educational Research Association, San Diego.

Thorkildsen, T. A., Nolen, S. B., & Fournier, J. (1994). What is fair? Children's critiques of practices that influence motivation. *Journal of Educational Psychology, 86,* 475–486.

Tryfos, P. (1996). *Sampling methods for applied research: Text and cases.* New York: Wiley.

Tryon, W. W. (1982). A simplified time-series analysis for evaluating treatment interventions. *Journal of Applied Behavior Analysis, 15,* 423–429.

Tunnicliffe, S. D. (1995). The content of conversations about the body parts and behaviors of animals during elementary school visits to a zoo and the implications for teachers organizing field trips. *Journal of Elementary Science Education, 7*(1), 29–46.

Turner, L. A., & Johnson, R. B. (2003). A model of mastery motivation for at-risk preschoolers. *Journal of Educational Psychology, 45*(3).

Turner, L. A., Johnson, R. B., & Pickering, S. (1996). Effect of ego and task instructions on cognitive performance. *Psychological Reports, 78,* 1051–1058.

U.S. Office of the Surgeon General. (1964). Smoking and health: Report of the advisory committee to the surgeon general of the public health service. Washington, D.C.: Public Health Service, Office of the Surgeon General. Available online at http://sgreports.nlm.hih.gov/NN/Views/AlphaChron/date/10006.

University of Chicago Press. (1993). *The Chicago Manual of Style* (14th ed.). Chicago: Author.

University of Michigan, Survey Research Center. (1976). *Interviewer's manual* (Rev. ed.). Ann Arbor, MI: Institute for Social Research.

Valentine, P., & McIntosh, G. (1990). Food for thought: Realities of a women-dominated organization. *The Alberta Journal of Educational Research, 36*(4), 353–369.

Van Haneghan, J. P., & Stofflett, R. T. (1995). Implementing problem solving technology into classrooms: Four case studies of teachers. *Journal of Technology and Teacher Education, 3*(1), 57–80.

van Manen, M. (1990). *Researching lived experience: Human science for an action sensitive pedagogy.* London, Ontario: State University of New York Press.

Vecchiotti, S. (2001). Kindergarten: The overlooked school year. Working paper series. Foundation for Child Development, New York. *http://www.ffcc.org.*

Velleman, P. F., & Wilkinson, L. (1993). Nominal, ordinal, interval, and ratio typologies are misleading. *The American Statistician, 47*(1), 65–72.

Viadero, D. (2001, November 28). Research: Smaller is better. *Education Week.* Available online: Retrieved October 30, 2002). http://www.edweek.org/.

Vogt, W. P. (1999). *Dictionary of statistics and methodology: A nontechnical guide for the social sciences.* Thousand Oaks, CA: Sage.

Wade, E. A., & Blier, M. J. (1974). Learning and retention of verbal lists: Serial anticipation and serial discrimination. *Journal of Experimental Psychology, 103,* 732–739.

Wang, J., & Staver, J. R. (1997). An empirical study of gender differences in Chinese students' science achievement. *The Journal of Educational Research, 90,* 252–255.

Wasley, P. A., Fine, M., King, S. P., Powell, L. C., Holland, N. E., Gladden, R. M., & Mosak, E. (2000). *Small schools: Great strides.* New York: Bank Street College of Education.

Way, N., Stauber, H. Y., Nakkula, M. J., & London, P. (1994). Depression and substance use in two divergent high school cultures: A quantitative and qualitative analysis. *Journal of Youth and Adolescence, 23,* 331–357.

Webb, E. J., Campbell, D. T., Schwartz, R. D., Sechrest, L., & Grove, J. B. (1981). *Nonreactive measures in the social sciences* (2nd ed.). Boston: Houghton Mifflin.

Webb, E. J., Campbell, D. T., Schwartz, R. D., & Sechrest, L. (2000). *Unobtrusive measures.* Thousand Oaks, CA: Sage.

Weber, M. (1968). *Economy and society.* New York: Bedminster.

Weber, R. P. (1990). *Basic content analysis.* (2nd ed.). Newbury Park, CA: Sage.

Wechsler, D. (1989). *Wechsler preschool and primary scale of intelligence—Revised.* San Antonio, TX: Psychological Corporation.

Weems, G. H., & Onwuegbuzie, A. J. (2001). The impact of midpoint responses and reverse coding on survey data. *Measurement and Evaluation in Counseling and Development, 34*(3).

Weick, K. E. (1968). Systematic observational methods. In Lindzey, G., & Aronson, E. (Eds.), *The handbook of social psychology* (Vol. 2). Reading, MA: Addison Wesley.

Weiner, B. (Ed.). (1974). *Achievement motivation and attribution theory.* Morristown, NJ: General Learning Press.

Weisner, T. (2000). Understanding better the lives of poor families: Ethnographic and survey studies in the New Hope experiment. *Poverty Research News, 4*(1), 10–12.

Weitzman, E. A., & Miles, M. B. (1995). *Computer programs for qualitative data analysis.* Thousand Oaks, CA: Sage.

Weng, L., & Cheng, C. (2000). Effects of response order on Likert-type scales. *Educational and Psychological Measurement, 60*(6), 908–924.

Wilson, S. L., Thompson, J. A., & Wylie, G. (1982). Automated psychological testing for the severely physically handicapped. *International Journal of Man-Machine Studies, 17,* 291–296.

Wilson, V. L. (1981). Time and the external validity of experiments. *Evaluation and Program Planning, 4,* 229–238.

Wineburg, S. S. (1991). Historical problem solving: A study of the cognitive processes used in the evaluation of documentary and pictorial evidence. *Journal of Educational Psychology, 33,* 73–87.

Witcher, A. E., Onwuegbuzie, A. J., & Minor, L. C. (2001). Characteristics of effective teachers: Perceptions of preservice teachers. *Research in the Schools, 8,* 45–57.

Wolcott, H. F. (1994). The elementary school principal: Notes from a field study. In H. F. Wolcott, *Transforming qualitative data: Description, analysis, and interpretation* (pp. 115–148). Thousand Oaks, CA: Sage.

Woolf, P. K. (1988). Deception in science. In American Association for the Advancement of Science and American Bar Association Conference of Lawyers and Scientists, *Project of Scientific Fraud and Misconduct: Report on Workshop Number One.* Washington, DC: AAAS.

Worthen, B. R., Sanders, J. R., & Fitzpatrick, J. L. (1997). *Program evaluation.* New York: Longman.

Wright, B. E., & Masters, G. N. (1982). *Rating scale analysis.* Chicago: Mesa Press.

Wurtman, R. J., & Wurtman, J. J. (1989, January). Carbohydrates and depression. *Scientific American,* 68–75.

Wynder, E. L., & Graham, E. A. (1950). Tobacco smoking as a possible etiologic factor in bronchogenic carcinoma. *Journal of the American Medical Association, 143,* 329–336.

Yin, R. K. (1981). The case study as a serious research strategy. *Knowledge: Creation, Diffusion, Utilization, 3,* 84–100.

Yin, R. K. (1994). *Case study research: Design and methods.* Thousand Oaks, CA: Sage.

Yin, R. K. (1998). The abridged version of case study research: Design and method. In L. Bickman & D. J. Rog (Eds.), *Handbook of applied social research methods* (pp. 229–259). Thousand Oaks, CA: Sage.

Yoder, P. (1990). Guilt, the feeling and the force: A phenomenological study of the experience of feeling guilty. (Doctoral dissertation, The Union Institute, 1990). *Dissertation Abstracts International, 50,* 5341B.

Young, C. H., Savola, K. L., & Phelps, E. (1991). *Inventory of longitudinal studies in the social sciences.* Newbury Park, CA: Sage.

Yow, V. (1994). *Recording oral history: A practical guide for social scientists.* Thousand Oaks, CA: Sage.

Zimney, G. H. (1961). *Method in experimental psychology.* New York: Ronald Press.

Index

Test-retest reliability, 134, 135–136
Test Review Locator, 154
Tests. *See also* Hypothesis testing; Testing
  anxiety about, 58–59
  in data collection, 162, 163
  educational and psychological, 147–152
  homogeneous and heterogeneous,
    136–137
  information sources on, 153–154
  measuring intelligence, 148
  unidimensional and multidimensional,
    143–144
Tests: A Comprehensive Reference for
  Assessment in Psychology, Education,
  and Business (Maddox), 153
Tests in Print (TIP), 155
Theoretical modeling. *See* Causal modeling
Theoretical saturation, 384, 500
Theoretical sensitivity, 383
Theoretical validity, 252–253
Theories. *See also* Grounded theory
  activity theory of causation, 39
  defined, 17, 19, 58
  examples of, 20
  as idea source, 58–59
  judging quality of, 19
Theory assessments, 10
Theory confirmation, 381
Theory generation, 381
Theory into Practice, 525
Theory triangulation, 250, 253
Think-aloud technique, 177
Third-variable problem. *See also*
  Confounding variables
  defined, 333–334
  examples of, 335–338
Third variables, 232. *See also* Confounding
  variables
Three necessary conditions
  applying, 335–338
  defined, 333–335
Time, 401
Time dimension
  classifying research by, 353–354
  in cross-sectional research, 343–344
  in longitudinal research, 343, 344–346
  in mixed method research, 418–421
  reasons for, 342
  in retrospective research, 343, 346–347
Time-interval sampling, 187–188
TIP (Tests in Print), 155
Titchener, E. B., 397
Title pages in research reports, 532, 538
Tomiak, J., 396
Tool function of theory, 58
Top-down approach, 18
Topics for research, 60, 82, 83, 395–396

Traits, versus states, 130
Transactional strategies, 301–303
Transcription, 502
Treatment variation validity, 245–246
Trend studies, 344
Triangulation strategy
  in mixed research, 423, 424, 426
  types of, 250, 251, 253, 254–255
t-test
  for correlation coefficients, 489–490
  for independent samples, 486–487
  in nonexperimental research, 331
  for regression coefficients, 490–491
Tukey Test, 488
Tuskegee syphilis experiment, 99, 114–115
Twenty-twenty hindsight, 329
Two-stage cluster sampling, 212
Type I errors, 482–483
Type II errors, 483
Type technique, 266
Typical-case sampling, 221
Typing style, 531. *See also* Editorial style
Typologies, 514–516

UMI Dissertation Abstracts International
  database, 66
Unidimensional tests, 143–144. *See also*
  Homogeneous tests
Unique case orientation strategy, 362
Universal laws, 255–256
Upper limits in interval estimation, 469
Urban Education, 525
The Urban Review, 525
Utilitarianism, 95–96

Vagueness, 401
Validation, 140
Validity. *See also* Evaluations; Internal
  validity; Measurement; Reliability
  based on internal structure, 143–144
  based on relation to other variables,
    144–146
  construct, 246–249
  content-related evidence in, 142–143
  defined, 140
  descriptive, 251
  in ethnographic research, 375
  external, 59, 242–246, 255–256
  of historical sources, 399–403
  interpretive, 251–252
  introduction to, 132–133, 140–142
  issues in quantitative research, 228–229
  in mixed research, 426
  participant similarity and, 146–147
  in qualitative research (*see* Qualitative
    research)
  researcher bias in, 249, 251

  statistical conclusion, 229–230
  testing and improving, 59
  theoretical, 252–253
Validity coefficients, 145
Validity evidence, 140
Variables. *See also* Extraneous variables;
  Independent variables
  categories of, 35–38
  confounding, 39–40, 228, 266–267
  contingency tables in analyzing,
    453–455
  inferring causation, 231–232
  intervening, 36, 38, 351
  manipulating, 265–266 (*see also*
    Experimental research)
  matching, 339–340
  regression analysis of, 455–459
  stratification, 207
  third, 232, 333–338
Variances
  ANCOVA, 274–275, 341–342
  ANOVA, 331, 487–489, 536
  in descriptive statistics, 447–448
  in inferential statistics, 464
Verbal conditioning study, 103, 105
Verbatims, 252
Verstehen. See Empathetic understanding
Violence of teenagers, 93, 359
Vivisimo meta-search engine, 70
Voice in qualitative research, 362
Voice recognition software, 502
Vyhnanek, L. A., 398

Weber, Max, 33
Web surveys, 176
White, E. B., 525
White, Ronald, 8
White, Victoria E., 7
Within-stage mixed model research,
  416–417
Women, education of, 74
Woodcock Reading Mastery Test, 152
Wrightsman, L. S., 153
Writing for Social Scientists (Becker), 526
Writing Papers in Psychology (Rosnow and
  Rosnow), 526
WWW Virtual Library, 70

X-axis, 437. *See also* Graphs; Regression
  analysis

Yahoo!, 69, 70
Y-axis, 437. *See also* Graphs; Regression
  analysis
Y-intercepts, 457

z-scores, 450, 452–453